Ariel and Prospero.
Double self-portrait.
Pastel on paper, 2002.

SLIM CHANCES

and unscheduled appearances

Edward Petherbridge

Indepenpress Publishing Ltd

First published in Great Britain by Indepenpress

ISBN: 978-1-78003-125-5

Printed and bound in the UK
Indepenpress Publishing Limited
25 Eastern Place
Brighton
BN2 1GJ

A catalogue record of this book is available from
the British Library

Cover design by Kathleen Riley

Contents

Illustrations

Front cover:
Edward Petherbridge as (clockwise from top left):
    Guildenstern in *Rosencrantz and Guildenstern Are Dead*
    Krapp in *Krapp's Last Tape*
    Cyrano in *Cyrano de Bergerac* (Photo: © Dee Conway)
    Malvolio in *Twelfth Night* (Photo: © Shakespeare Birthplace Trust)
    Lord Peter Wimsey in *Busman's Honeymoon* (Photo: © Dee Conway)
    Newman Noggs in *Nicholas Nickleby*

*   *   *

*   *   *

Colour Plates:

*   *   *

*   *   *

Back cover:
Edward Petherbridge (clockwise from top left) as:
    Algernon Moncrieff in *The Importance of Being Earnest*
    The Old Actor in *The Fantasticks* (Photo: © Geraint Lewis)
    The Hotel Manager in *Ruling the Roost* (Photo: © Nigel Luckhurst)
    Don Armado in *Love's Labour's Lost*
    Pierrot in *Knots*
    Atahualpa in *The Royal Hunt of the Sun* (Photo: © Chris Arthur)

Author's Preface

Letter to the Editor

> *All autobiographies are alibi-ographies*
> Clare Boothe Luce (1903–87)

Dear Kathleen,

I am about to confess to the crime and so need no alibi.

My confession, in the form of this letter to you, my editor, automatically gives you rightful pride of place amongst the acknowledgements.

I take full responsibility and claim, nay hope, that I was implicated, really there on every first night and, more to the point, committedly present on all the other 14,001 nights (at a conservative estimate), including that thin matinée day or for that sluggish Saturday night house well into a long run. What then was my crime?

This little trial and confession will be short, but bear with me whilst I present a touch of mitigating evidence. Someone sent it out of the blue the other day, a yellowing newspaper cutting from *The Sunday Times*, Harold Hobson's review on 16 April 1967 of *Rosencrantz and Guildenstern Are Dead*: 'It is a long play, but there is not a sentence, a look of any of the players, an intonation of any of their voices, any note of the music, any square inch of Desmond Heeley's set, or any gradation of Richard Pilbrow's lighting which did not give me intense pleasure.'

Cut to a night in September 2008, forty-one years on, and a hotel in a small German town an hour's drive from Cologne. Here I spent a lot of time alone between filming on *Pope Joan* until one night when five British actors descended convivially upon the dinner table. They included Oliver Cotton with whom I had not worked since he had helped to populate those square inches of set and to give Harold Hobson, amongst many others, such intense pleasure as we met regularly on Tom Stoppard's road to Elsinore. There was still more than a touch of the gypsy strolling player about him; in fact, he told me that he felt he could go back to the Old Vic of those days '*tonight* – find my dressing room, my costume and go on.' I admitted to the same fantasy, so vividly present had we been at that time.

Sitting to my left at that dinner was Suzanne Bertish, full of gossip fresh from London. A Mermaid Tavern atmosphere instantly pervaded our corner of that German town. Suzanne was fulminating against 'museum theatre', a certain kind of production she deplored for failing to 'de-fossilize' old plays. Meanwhile, I was remembering the two of us, not fossilized but alive and making illicit, candlelit Chekhovian love in Trevor Nunn's *Three Sisters* at

Stratford-upon-Avon's Other Place, when it was still the tin hut of blessed memory, and spending our days across the road in the large magic circle of the rehearsal room exploring the glories of *Nicholas Nickleby* and improvising chunks of the novel in dramatic action, mime and music.

Not all the experiences of life remain so vivid, of course. Some are best forgotten. Even so, one might make a special plea for forgotten or ignored evidence. I can't resist another quotation:

> Sooner or later we all discover that the important moments in life are not the advertised ones, not the birthdays, the graduations, the weddings, not the great goals achieved. The real milestones are less prepossessing. They come to the door of memory unannounced, stray dogs that amble in, sniff around a bit, and simply never leave. Our lives are measured by these.
> (Susan Brownell Anthony, 1820–1906)

I'd hate to think that I was about to give you or the reader the measure of me, whether by stray dogs or great goals missed or achieved! Olivier once said, to me I think, never go full out, never let the audience see your top, always keep a bit in reserve and they will not be able to see how much more there might be.

In any case I have found in writing this book that one's experience isn't there, waiting to be portrayed: it shifts like a restless life model and, when it does settle, that is when one feels it necessary to move the easel and change one's viewpoint.

*   *   *

In the cold, well actually the lovely bright dawn of a new day, I realize that I have left out the most crucial thing in this letter (apart from the question of my guilt which I will come to), and that is my relationship with the editor.

Jeffrey Archer once said to me of one of his editors, 'He was a brilliant man,' and then darkly, 'but you had to do all the work before lunchtime.' Archer apparently asked him why, since he was obviously so good, he wasn't a best-selling author himself. The man replied, 'There is a big difference between you and me – the first draft.'

You, however, are the author of more than one successful book, and in working order at all times of day. It has been very good to write some fresh pieces lately with you, as well as 'the audience', in mind. I remember once hearing the great Polish-American pianist Arthur Rubinstein say in a radio interview that concerts were unpredictable. One might get to the hall early, prepare thoroughly and be very happy with the acoustics, but then find there was something grey about the event. Conversely, one might have a bad journey, feel somewhat out of joint and then have THE miraculous happen and the concert take fire – perhaps from the idea of there being a single person one senses to be present, who is somehow the ideal special audience.

I have experience of ideal audiences, real as well as imagined.

But to come to the crunch: I call the next witness, one Roisin Gadelrab, an Irish- Egyptian journalist whose testimony appeared in the *Islington Tribune*, which I understand, my lord, to be a local paper of the type known as a 'freebie'. In presenting her evidence and confessing my culpability, I must first define the crime; it is that of hiding my light under a bushel or rather that of not fighting to claim the best possible light stand. I blame myself for depriving the world, or at least New Zealand, of my Lear by having a stroke after the second day of rehearsal (though Boots the Chemist might have advised me better than my local doctor about protecting myself against the stress of a long-haul flight). I blame myself entirely that it does not occur to our national companies to cast me in the role. I have no doubt that the Wellington and Dunedin dailies would have done for my reputation in tragedy what Ms Gadelrab in Islington did for my reputation in comedy, thereby giving my old friend Ian McKellen and the RSC, who happened by curious coincidence to be scheduled to play *Lear* in Wellington at the same time, a run for their money.

Ms Gadelrab wrote of my Old Actor in *The Fantasticks*: 'A genius turn from Edward Petherbridge as the crumpled, ageing Shakespearean luvvie whose every gesture, word or weary sigh was pure comedic gold' (17 June 2010). The genuine glitter of my duo with Paul Hunter shone through most of the crop of appalling reviews that prematurely closed the show. But what next? A substantial part of the actor's job lies in getting the part, and in knowing how to fight for position and chances in the here and now.

I have tried to make up in some measure by writing the book I was searching for as a boy on the two or three shelves of my local branch library that were devoted to the theatre. I was so curious to experience something of the authentic smell backstage, and if this book provides a whiff of that I will be pleased. The smell of success, relative success, is heady, although sometimes one breathes it without noticing, as if it were just God's fresh air. But the smell of failure is relative too, and similarly fresh and God-given it seems to me; and there is always a chance that the wind might change.

Dear Kathleen, I hope this letter will do and not need too much editing.

Love, Edward

Acknowledgements

In the mad dash to meet publishing deadlines, just when one has realized that one must cut the cable – the grey and purple passages will have to stand as they are – somebody says, 'You must do the Acknowledgements.' 'Heavens,' I cry, 'the book has too many beginnings as it is.' So, with the clock ticking…

This book would not have 'happened' as it has without the hard graft, loving care and creative research of Kathleen Riley, undertaken whilst writing, with a historian's flair and her love of the Theatre, her own book on Fred and Adele Astaire at the same time. Constantly available in cyberspace at my elbow, ours has been the most intimate of collaborations and yet her supreme tact has always assisted without ever once invading.

My debt to hordes of others, named and unnamed, is implicit in every page, even on the pages where I have allowed myself to be harsh.

Kathy Elgin gave me early editorial assistance. I should mention especially my old friends Caroline Blakiston and Sir Ian McKellen who read early draft chunks and more recent pieces and gave me much courage as well as gentle, subtle advice.

Perhaps I slipped the odd page or two to many others.

And, of course, my family. Emily, my wife, who has laughed and wept over the chapters, and gently shaken her head in certain places. Our son Arthur; it seems no time since I taught him to become a dab hand with an SLR camera, as his photos in this book testify. Now he bales me out on my digital camera to say nothing of my laptop. Our daughter Dora, whose scores of Edinburgh Festival Fringe criticisms for *Three Weeks*, in exactly 120 words, have been models of Brevity being the soul of wit – our phone discussions of them in the mornings of the summer of 2007 were the mainstay of my post-stroke recovery. And my son David, Dora and Arthur's half-brother (the three of them do not love one another by halves). David had been first at my side after the debacle in New Zealand, as was his mother Louise. Solitary as the act of authorship is, it is impossible to overestimate the importance of my family.

My elder brother Bill, who studied for a BA in English literature from the Open University whilst working as a police superintendent and bringing up three boys with his wife Doreen, thereby putting my subsequent Hon. D.Litt. from Bradford University into proper perspective. In which context I mention John Horton, sometime Chief Librarian of that university and member, with his wife, of the old Bradford Civic Playhouse – let them be representative of the members of that kind cradle of my teenage aspirations.

More recently, whilst the admirable John Peter of *The Sunday Times* was 'eating his kneecaps' in despair at *The Fantasticks*, I was being buoyed up by delight in the spirit and talent of the cast and by their expressions of affection; in failure, these things count.

The necessarily relentless upbeat tone of this piece will end soon, though I fear the list has omissions, but it has to contain the names of my friend Sara Kestelman and of Penelope Keith for reasons they will appreciate. Oh and, though he won't thank me for the exposure, my mostly laptop friend Alec Hamilton, if you take my meaning, my sternest critic, so he's not read too much of the text as yet, but as a student of life, poet and spasmodic email correspondent, he has given me pause, sharpened my wits and made me laugh out loud.

My parents lived long enough to see me just beginning to find my footing. In fact writing about Mother and Dad has made me realize the strength of their unspoken love for me, their suffering and quiet heroism. This book is dedicated to them: Willie and Hannah Petherbridge.

Edward Petherbridge
London, January 2011

Editor's Preface

Yes there are moments
Sometimes there is magic
Tenderness too is possible
Ah tenderness
Entices an uncertain gesture of delight
To adventure into being.

(R. D. Laing, *Knots*)

Perhaps the quality above all that distinguishes this autobiographical anthology is delight, but that of the most profound and elevated kind. The book begins and ends in thoughtful celebration of this vital state of being: the author's seven-year-old and seventy-three-year-old selves united across time and space in a sense of wonder, of reverential awe at the redemptive potency of an enchanted stage.

The small boy, seated in the gallery of the Bradford Alhambra at his first pantomime, discovers the best view of the city and of life he has ever had, a purely fantastic landscape but peopled with real and recognizable beings. This education, this epiphany of delight is recalled with the adult's sophisticated analytical might, whilst losing nothing of the immediacy of the child's experience – the wondrous sights, sounds and smells deeply nourishing his senses and drawing him towards some spiritual home.

As I write, Edward is on stage at London's Duchess Theatre in a brand new production of Tom Jones and Harvey Schmidt's minimalist musical, *The Fantasticks*. The show is boldly theatrical, a delicately woven fable, and absurdly, tenderly magical, dealing as it does in the peculiar alchemy of young love and old theatrical effects and relying on that tacit ancient covenant between actors and audience to 'make imaginary puissance'. Edward's character, The Old Actor (Henry Albertson), a tatterdemalion strolling player hired with his clown companion to help stage a spurious abduction, is on the surface a ridiculous, even pathetic figure, a failed and forgetful Thespic alchemist clinging to dubious past glories. Yet there is something magnificent about him too and something intensely moving about his unabashed joy, his resilient faith in the transformative power of theatre ('That's the whole trick: try to see me under light!'). At one point the narrator, El Gallo, shows Henry the 'set' for the young lovers' nocturnal tryst and the ensuing abduction – a plastic moon suspended from a pole and brought bewitchingly to life by subtle stage lighting. Gazing up at the pale blue moonlight, Henry suppresses a sob and says softly, 'Amazing.' It is one of the most affecting moments in the show.

The Fantasticks was conceived, in Tom Jones's words, as 'an attempt to celebrate romanticism'; appropriately there is an essential nobility that Henry, and indeed Edward, manifests, an immutable state of grace, if you like, which transcends the mutable, more worldly measures of success. That is what made Edward's portrayal of Newman Noggs, another character who recollects more prosperous times, so memorable. Apart from perfectly capturing Noggs's physical eccentricities (the cracking finger-joints and twitching limbs), Edward revealed his innate gentleness and gentility, the decency and sense of right that ultimately triumph against a villainous master and an unjust world. As Frank Rich wrote in the *New York Times*, he succeeded in elevating 'a comic type with rending poetry.' His empathetic embodiment of this funny, fallen gentleman was, in fact, the tender soul of an epic production, its humane core.

As I'm sure will be evident to the reader, this volume is a true labour of love. Although it is candid and insightful about the low ebbs and inescapable cruelties of the acting profession, what prevails is a deep love for the mystery and magic of the actor's craft in its most hallowed splendour and its most Crummlesian tawdriness alike. What is more, as I can avow, the writing of this book has been approached with the same sincerity and resolve, the same intrepid romanticism and loving diligence with which Edward invests all his creative endeavours – from a homemade five-minute webcam film to a West End performance.

The editing of the book has also been a labour of love; it is a wonderful privilege to share, as a first audience, in Edward's literary life, and to have revisited with him a remarkable career, one richly touched by history and still a 'going concern'. The cornucopia of prose, verse and art, which follows, reveals a man of many talents, of penetrative intelligence and infinite imagination, of wit, humanity and principle, whom I'm proud to call my friend.

Kathleen Riley
London, June 2010

Foreword

by Ian McKellen

New Year's Day, 1994: the leader of the walking tour arrived five minutes after the advertized time. His audience of fifty fans and tourists, already gathered outside the Embankment Tube station, were excited. Just as onstage, his eventual appearance didn't disappoint us – he half-swaggered down the station steps, arms outstretched, charming as Wimsey, alert as Guildenstern, attentive as Newman Noggs. As always onstage, he struck a characterful silhouette, with a fedora and a voluminous brown coat to his heels, with deep pockets, not just for swank but for all our £2 cash contributions.

Weighed down with clanking coins, he strode along the Strand, pleased as a theatre manager who has just emptied the box-office till. Stopping at some landmark, he lectured us like Gayev, then, with a matinée-idol smile, charmed and left us laughing and a bit in awe of his scholarship and his humour and his stylishness. His theatre stories were mostly new to me: one was unlikely, revealing the little known fact that the gas lamps outside the Savoy Hotel were fuelled by the waste from the hotel's loos. 'So you see, the farts of Noël Coward and Winston Churchill have lit up London.'

The ninety-minute promenade show, one of the finest even this Petherbridge aficionado has enjoyed, ended with Edward swinging round a lamp-post serenading the window of his old dressing room in the Fortune Theatre. It was an ode he'd penned during intervals and between shows, about the travails of a long run for the actor.

As the verses here show, his poetry is artful, intelligent and often very movingly personal as well as quirky. And he writes long letters, if you're lucky.

He paints and draws with glee: after his double stroke, through will and exercise and practice, he forced his fingers to work again. Had he not discovered the theatre, and seen only with his painterly eye, might he have followed the example of his Bradford contemporary David Hockney?

Had he gone to university rather than the local drama academy, he might have become lost to academia; playing the part of that part of himself, who is aware of his times and honours its traditions.

It's a life with a purpose and we are all lucky to be able now to read his recollections, his confessions, his opinions.

For theatre historians, Edward's witness of theatre icons (Norman Evans, Laurence Olivier) is invaluable. Social historians too are in luck. I doubt he has confided before so much detail of his upbringing in Bradford and his post-war earliest intimations about theatre, sex and a life beyond Bradford.

Those who haven't met Petherbridge or seen his work will sense, in his words here, what they are missing.

*   *   *

Edward and I worked together early in our careers in Laurence Olivier's National Theatre at the Old Vic and Chichester (1965/66) and a number of unforgettable times since. Some of our adventures in theatre are now recorded in this glorious book of memories.

In 1969 he came to see me as Hamlet on the defunct Prospect Theatre's tour, which ended at the Cambridge Theatre in London. He rang up when we were both home that evening and said he would like to work with me again, soon. I was about to do Chekhov's *Swan Song*, to open the new Crucible Theatre in Sheffield, playing the bombastic old actor. Edward agreed to play the supporting role of an ancient dresser, one of the Petherbridge collection of decrepitude.

His generosity in taking the supporting part had been learned under Olivier. During rehearsals, with David William our director, we complained that our inborn sense of 'company', believing that the player also serves who only stands and carries a spear, was out of fashion. Up and down the country, the local repertory theatres were losing their grants, actors losing their jobs and there was no longer any theatre being run by an actor. The directors were in charge.

We imagined a company of actors, of equals, paid the same, sharing out the parts large and small. David said we should stop complaining and start such a group ourselves. And we did. Over three years, Edward acted, wrote, adapted and directed for the Actors' Company. During our first tour, Trevor Nunn saw us in *'Tis Pity She's a Whore* (Edward a passionate Soranzo) and asked us how we'd formed a company in just six months, when he had failed to do anything like it at the Royal Shakespeare Company over as many years. The answer was because every major artistic decision, even casting, was taken by us all at our interminable meetings. The stakes for all of us in the Company were high.

During these meetings each of us grew in confidence and Edward emerged as our conscience and often as the arbiter of good taste and high standards in our work. Without his commitment, our experiment in democracy could not have happened.

*   *   *

Edward is a raconteur without equal, although the tagline can be a long time coming, thank goodness. One on one, or round the dinner table, he improvises, cracks a brand new gag, remembers another related story, all the time laughing and being deadly serious. He's managed the same sort of flow and eddy in this book.

As in his conversation, so on the page, he can suddenly veer from the main progression of a chapter's subject down enchanting, illuminating byways which may reach over the hills and far away, as some anecdote is recalled; and then back. This meandering, wittingly or not but certainly wittily, makes the point that all places, all events, all chances have informed the main intent of Edward's life. It seems, he seems to be saying, he was born to entertain, an actor through and through, from his fingertips to the pointed toe and tilted head of his Pierrot.

Ian McKellen
London, January 2011

Introduction

Theatre in My Lifetime

> *Let them be well used; for*
> *they are the abstract and brief chronicles of the*
> *time.*
>
> (*Hamlet*, Act II, sc.ii)

Albert Einstein, we're told, observed ruefully that he was alone amongst his friends in not entering a competition set in 1920 by the journal *Scientific American*, which offered a cash prize of $5,000 for the most cogent summary of his Special Theory of Relativity in no more than 3,000 words – 'so that a person with no special mathematical training may read it profitably.' 'Do you know,' said Einstein, 'I don't believe I could do it.'

Of the winning entry by L. Bolton of London, the 'Einstein Editor' declared: 'The real reason why his essay was ultimately chosen over its most pressing rivals was the extraordinarily fine judgment which he used in deciding just what he would say and what he would leave unsaid.'

I have set myself the task of writing this introduction in as near 2,000 words as possible. An attempt at a cogent summary of the theatre as I have known it. 'Theatre in My Lifetime' sounds pompous I know, but one peg on which to hang things is what the critic Harold Hobson wrote in 1950, lamenting the dearth of new playwrights:

> Our present school of drama, based on realism and social conscience, has flourished for more than fifty years. The span of time between *The Second Mrs Tanqueray* and *The Winslow Boy* is theatrically speaking enormous. Our characteristic contemporary drama is in its extreme old age. In its prime its vitality depended on the excitement caused by the new method of realism, which for the first time in many decades made stage characters talk, walk, speak, dress, behave and think like ordinary human beings.

When Beckett's tramps waited for Godot in the London of 1955, Hobson welcomed them with open arms and wrote about them for seven successive Sundays; was it because the revolution in playwriting had been accomplished in the old 'method of realism' by characters who talked, walked, spoke, dressed, behaved and thought like ordinary human beings? I would argue yes – except we had not seen this particular class of ordinary human being behaving anything like this *on the stage* before.

1

From 1964 I remember that first line 'What a dump!' in Edward Albee's *Who's Afraid of Virginia Woolf?* We of course knew, either from observation or personal experience, that marriage could be corrosive (Strindberg had written of a corrosive marriage in his play *The Dance of Death* in 1900), but somehow we had not been permitted to witness it so idiomatically as this, in the very vernacular of our own lives, and in a dramatic entertainment in public. We were learning, publicly, just how extraordinary our ordinary lives were.

To parody Hobson, the span of time between *Who's Afraid of Virginia Woolf?* and Albee's 2002 play *The Goat, or Who is Sylvia?* is enormous, but it is not a span that suggests our school of drama is in its extreme old age – unless with age has come wisdom. The play reads, even on a bus, like music and one can 'see' the action. It deals with a taboo subject with a light comic touch of breathtaking realism and segues effortlessly from domestic comedy to tragedy of Greek dimensions.

You may wonder how one gets back to Einstein from here. Well last week I saw a play about mathematics, Complicite's *A Disappearing Number*. It features an Indian genius of maths, Srinivasa Ramanujan, and his close collaboration with Cambridge don G. H. Hardy around the time of the First World War. On one, if not most levels, I am no wiser. I still have to face the fact that the little we know about our physical universe is a closed book to me since it can only be understood in terms of mathematics. And yet the play fascinates, partly because of cunning, fluid and imaginative staging, and partly because mathematical geniuses sometimes think, and occasionally talk, but certainly walk, dress and behave like ordinary human beings.

Taking the play to Hyderabad for the 2010 International Congress of Mathematics was perhaps not quite the coup that luring our military top brass to Kilburn to see twelve plays about Afghanistan in one day was, but the span of time and space covered by these two events, let alone by the total of seven plays I have mentioned so far, is – as Hobson might put it – 'theatrically speaking enormous', and might go on, who knows, like a run of numbers to infinity. But that is already 720 words and I have said little about the experience of a theatrical lifetime; have only touched the tip of the theatrical iceberg … No, that's the wrong metaphor: I need an elegant solution, a 'magic number', like the number 24, which repeatedly appears in the work of Ramanjuan. (These magic numbers, we're told, continually appear where we least expect them and for reasons that no one understands.) Three eights are twenty-four – I toss this in because of the 'rule of three' well known by comedians, and of course we do eight performances a week in the theatre. And forgive me for mentioning it – there being something magical about every birth – but I was born on the third day of the eighth month; this last little mathematical riff is the sum total of my understanding of the mystery of numbers.

But it is there, waiting to be written I'm sure, the pithy essay worthy of this grandiose title. I feel I could act the character of one who might write it with spare, questing freshness, intriguing close-up detail set against historical sweep, smashing the edifices of stale received opinion with evidence brought hot from the rehearsal rooms of Europe. It would have something of the heady, urgent inspiration of actors' after-supper shop talk – at its best, you understand – a sense of jostling exhilaration and mischief, the chance of pyrotechnic displays, fireworks lit under venerable principles, sacred cows served up as piquant cocktail sausages, the high priest and guru caught out as showbiz charlatan, the successful conventional hack exposed as self-appointed guardian of artistic standards.

Then there is the moment which does not set the table on a roar, rather the company falls silent. I'm going to catch myself plagiarizing Tom Stoppard in a minute, but why not quote his Player from *Rosencrantz and Guildenstern Are Dead* and say: 'Occasionally, from out of this matter, there escapes a thin beam of light that, seen at the right angle, can crack the shell of mortality.'

Arthur Koestler anatomized the joke, likening its structure to the creative process in science. The joke is a story, which leads off across a plane of existence where the landscape is familiar and the rules, assumptions and conditions are generally understood by the listeners. Suddenly there is a collision with another plane of existence wherein different conditions apply and a spark occurs as one set of perfectly viable, acceptable ideas or values is rendered redundant or absurd by another.

The connection with quantum leaps or the insights of lateral thinking doesn't have to be laboured, and I hope it won't be undermined when I tell you a minor, real-life example, told to me by Joanna McCallum, the daughter of Googie Withers. Googie Withers was sitting next to Sir Donald Wolfit at a theatrical lunch, and he said to her, 'I was interested to hear you are taking over from Peggy Ashcroft in *The Deep Blue Sea*?'

'Yes, I've already taken over, I've already opened.'

'Oh have you? What day is your matinée?'

'Oh, Wednesday,' she said.

'Good. Mine's Thursday, you can come and see my Lear.'

Looking back one is almost abashed at the quiet life one has led since first smelling the air and making one's wauling and crying entrance into this period of unprecedented, ever-accelerating radical change; a lifetime in which humanity's achievements have seemed to put us frighteningly lower than the beasts and headily higher than the angels. Do we dare ask 'What is this quintessence of dust?'

Between the upheavals, when those of us of the fortunate minority who are fed and warm and out of immediate danger, and not too thwarted in our daily existence by incompetent or corrupt government, do we regain much of our confidence, even complacency? Complacency – a dangerous though necessary default position. Actors slipping into it are fuelled by the reassuring idea that, in a world increasingly dominated by technology, they are amongst the few who, when employed, seem to be producing the unique handmade article. Manifesting the playwright's vision, the actor works his materials of body, mind and spirit. He shares with the creative artist the sense that, essentially, in no part of his 'process' is *he* replaceable.

It's always handy to be able to throw in a contradiction. Beckett, in his late period of reductive minimalism, when he was rehearsing his play *Play* at the National Theatre in 1964, demanded an ever more restricted utterance, less inflected, less expressive. One member of the cast remembered him saying, 'If there were machines who could play these parts, I wouldn't use actors.' In the same theatre on other nights, actors were being let loose on a vast repertoire and, consequently, the widest possible range of acting styles. As time has gone on, the plundering of the past has continued in a way unparalleled before our era, bringing period pieces blinking from the library into the limelight.

At the same time, despite the wholesale smashing of moulds in music, painting and sculpture, has acting remained essentially unchanged – a craft, or art if you insist, for which Hamlet's 400-year-old advice to the players remains relevant: 'Show virtue her own feature, scorn her own image, and the very age and body of the time his form and pressure'?

As we all know, in all but the rarest performances of *Hamlet*, we see the players blithely disregarding Hamlet's advice, plunging into the dumb show at pains to demonstrate how different the behaviour of itinerant mime artists is from that of Danish courtiers. 'Leave off thy damnable faces, and begin', shouts the frustrated Hamlet. One remembers Chekhov's remark when he saw a rehearsal of his *Seagull* at its very first production in St Petersburg in 1896: 'They act a lot, I wish there wasn't so much acting.'

Here is the problem. The great stumbling block of Style. We know, though, that if the curtain were ever to go up on real life the audience would realize the mistake immediately. Nevertheless, the painter J. B. Yeats compared Isadora Duncan dancing on stage to 'a kitten playing for itself.' Doesn't that chime perfectly with Henry Irving's advice to the actor: 'You must be moved by the impulse of being'?

It might help if we were able to think of acting as our natural state, as natural as the kitten's play. Through the imaginative game of Let's Pretend we extend the boundaries of our childhood experience. Parental, directorial intervention if you like, in the way we act, ensures that pretence creeps in. This is different, being the social modification of our most primal needs and attitudes, so that we may conform to what parents, relations, teachers and friends expect from us and find acceptable. Freud has taught us that becoming too skilled at these good-mannered pretences can make us strangers to our vital inner selves. Modern therapy has brought the primal scream into the clinic, the scream that was once heard with pity and terror by the audiences of Greek tragedy. Our complex and sophisticated adult games, developed to great peaks of Olympian skill, performed within the strictest rules, are the safe ritualization of the competitive struggles, stratagems, bluffs and deceptions of the elemental real-life struggle for the survival of the fittest.

4

But is playacting the most sophisticated variant of all in our human playfulness, the most vital, the most necessary? Taking us back to the heart of the game of Let's Pretend, the game not of disguise but of revelation. Tragedy, in the safety of play and understood convention, reveals the most dangerous elements of our human nature and dilemma. Comedy jokes about serious things, humiliations, deceptions, pain, danger, surprise, hubris and nemesis its poles, whether in the clown's routine or in the clash of attitudes in the most elegant comedy of manners.

I was amused to see a credit for 'Movement Director' in the programme of *Wanderlust* at the Royal Court's Theatre Upstairs the other night. It is an ultra-naturalistic play, done in an ultra-realistic style – lots of talking, moving, dressing *and undressing* like ordinary human beings – so one is forced to conclude that the movement director was brought in to stage the scenes of sexual intercourse, at least five of them, which are nothing if not realistic. Forty-six years ago the movement director Claude Chagrin employed French mime techniques to re-create the lost culture of the Incas for the National Theatre premiere of *The Royal Hunt of the Sun*. The span of time between that and the other night's choreographed spectacle of human beings doing that which, I imagine, has not fundamentally changed since well before the ancient Greeks is, by anyone's standards, enormous.

In my young day, we used to joke about the actor who was offered a tour of a play by a manager: 'I can only offer Equity minimum, but there's a practical cake in the last act.' Now … need I say more?

Transformation Scenes

Chapter 1

My First Acting Lesson from Norman Evans

Whether I was, despite all evidence to the contrary, born to play Lord Peter Wimsey and all the other aristocrats I've played – one of Stoppard's minor attendant lords; the Count Orsino; the exiled Duke of Milan, Prospero – whether I was born to play any of them, my first acting lesson was far from aristocratic. But we must remember that it was not uncommon in the late nineteenth century for the aristocracy themselves to take elocution lessons from mere actors, just as they'd learnt their deportment for centuries from mere dancing masters. In fact, Dr Johnson wrote that Lord Chesterfield's *Letters to His Son* taught 'the morals of a whore and the manners of a dancing master.' There's the class tension between the patron and the patronized for you! Conversely, one of Chesterfield's letters warned his son of the danger of being mistaken for a member of the literati. In the field of mistaken identity, which I know so well from the plays of Shakespeare and Feydeau, few things could please me more than that you should mistake these memoirs for literature and lump me in with the literati – but I shall have to do better than mere alliteration.

My first theatrical experience was an excellently vulgar affair. I can't exactly put my finger on what it was I learnt from the North Country comedian Norman Evans, whom, of course, I never met. He so precisely held the mirror up to the manners and essential nature of the majority of the people in his audience, they recognized themselves and laughed. So, life was a comedy after all! Maybe that's what I learnt – not just the distant life of fairy tale and fable, of lords and ladies, princes and princesses, but the life of the streets I lived in. There might even be a happy ending.

I was seven when my parents took me up the long, echoing, gaslit flight of stone steps, which led to the balcony of the Bradford Alhambra, where we found places just behind the limelight man, who operated from the aisle in the middle of the front row. I was soon aware that there were more privileged positions. The two ladies of Kirby's Flying Ballet, who were picked to fly out into the auditorium, only tossed their bunches of violets into the orchestra stalls, and, of course, the pantomime dog couldn't be expected to climb our stone steps and cavort on our perilous heights as he did on the broad, royal-blue upholstered ledge of the dress circle below. I imagined that the families who sat on gilt chairs in the eight stage boxes, four boxes on either side, were the owners of 'Brown Muffs' or Busby's, Bradford's two department stores. Or maybe they were happy, well-off families such as the one featured in the Peek Frean's Biscuits poster, enjoying tea (and biscuits, of course), the boy and girl sitting on the carpet before the fire, which blazed in a modern tiled fireplace, always an icon of prosperity and elegance in my mind. They owned a parrot, which sat on a perch in the corner behind an armchair, eyeing the biscuits.

Nevertheless, my gallery seat afforded me the best view of Bradford, and indeed of life, I'd ever had – not counting a magnificent range of hills and mountains bathed in pink and golden light, which had revealed itself one evening a year or two earlier, down the cobbled road at the corner of our street of back-to-backs, soaring up on the other side of the railway lines and beyond Bowling Park. I fully expected to be reaching the foothills next morning and exploring the streets and lanes, where, I imagined, donkeys pulled carts up through quaint mountain villages. I was thrilled that, after all, the great and beautiful world I'd become aware of by repute had turned out to be only a tram ride away. But no; the journey was impossible, as my mother explained when I persuaded her to come out to the corner and look: 'It's only made of clouds and sunset, Edward.'

There was no mistaking the landscapes of the pantomime for reality. Obviously the hills and villages were painted wood and canvas, and so much more magical for that. However, the inhabitants, who talked and danced and sang for us down there in theatrical sunshine, were real enough, and from then on, apart from a day when I wanted to be a plumber, I never wavered in my determination to become one of them.

The plumber's visit deserves a mention, if only because of the potent urban myth that the plumbing profession leads to happy-ever-after prosperity as surely as the plot of a pantomime. When the plumber came, my head and the kitchen sink were on a level; one of those large, shallow glazed-stone troughs it was. Our sole plumbing arrangements were a small, very modern I thought (until it started to leak), chromium gas geyser and a brass cold tap. It was the lead pipe, rising to this tap, that the plumber came to repair, spreading his tool bag open on the oilcloth covering the stone flagged floor. Watching him use the blow lamp, as he smoothed the new bulbous silvery joint, I thought that maybe I could do such a job one day. This role, for a few days, seemed possible, even desirable. Perhaps there was something *dramatic* in his visit; certainly it had a beginning, a middle and an end, and good effects – fire and noise and smells – and he left our kitchen changed, a transformation scene, if you like.

I think I must have accepted the curious conventions of pantomime as ordained by God, and still do; failures to honour them disappoint me as much as substitutes for the Authorized King James Version of the Bible and the Book of Common Prayer, or guitars and tambourines in place of *Hymns Ancient and Modern*. I could never understand why an appropriately reverent hush failed to descend for the rhyming prologue spoken by the Good Fairy in front of the blue velvet curtain with its elaborate fringe of heavy gold tassels – what a curtain that was! It was in the civic colours like the buses, but such swank, and in the era of the 'Utility Mark'. It was pre-war, of course; to buy

10

such a curtain new would have taken the entire town's clothing coupons. What, I wondered, could the other children have to chatter about now that the violins were atremble in the dark and this shining creature in white sequined tulle, diamond tiara and ballet shoes, silver wand held aloft, was speaking to us.

The pantomime dog must have been played by an amazingly agile dwarf with excellent timing, but neither he nor any pantomime cow I ever saw was so crass as to unmask and step out of character for the walk-down at the finale – no mere curtain call, but rather a ritual procession ending with the good arrayed in splendour and receiving their reward here on earth. Clad in his tin hat and carrying his rifle, and with his gas mask in a cardboard box slung over his shoulder on a piece of string, the dog practised his Home Guard drill under the supervision of the Dame (played by a man, of course). When he bumped into the gilded proscenium arch and fell back on his bottom with the tin hat over his eyes, naturally the dinner-jacketed man on the percussion, in the right-hand corner of the orchestra pit, accentuated the mishap.

It was Norman Evans as the Dame who unified all the elements – the transformation scenes and Tiller Girls, the Twelve Little Sunbeams, the glamour and dash (and legs!) of Marjorie Manners's Principal Boy. Evans's Dame Trot took them all – and us, stacked in reflected glory from stalls to balcony – as part of the same bothersome motley collection that made up her workaday world. I can see her now, far below in a circle of white light (our man adjusting the hissing limes saw to that), leaning over a bit of painted wall and looking out towards us, talking to an imaginary neighbour.

An exaggerated figure from a child's picture book, larger, more highly coloured than our local life but recognizable as the very stuff of it. Many a time her sisters and cousins had dropped their so similar voices to protect my young years when I passed them, as they gossiped on the corner – ''As she ... did she?' I'd seen them calling to one another as they pegged out their washing across the width of the cobbled street. Like her, they talked about cats and custard and Yorkshire pudding, and the price of things. Evans's lines were hardly immortal prose; often they mentioned food and ration books – we only laugh about important things – 'Oo, these grapes are sour, I'll be glad when I've 'ad enough' (I had never seen a grape). And there was always the moment when he slipped and caught his bosom on the top of the wall. 'Oo', he would say, rubbing it, 'that's twice in one week on the same brick!' But how to describe what it is that makes a great clown's slapstick seemingly portray something profound about the human condition. His act must have had something universal as well as parochial about it, or else how could he have got three rave reviews on Broadway in 1949.

Evans linked the fairy-tale world of the pantomime to the realities of back-to-back houses, washing day, coal-fired coppers and cold taps, and the join was as seamless and smooth as the well-crafted repair the plumber gave to our rising main. Come to think of it, Norman Evans's work was the

11

genuine popular drama of the kitchen sink, before it achieved 'higher' intellectual status at the Royal Court in Sloane Square a decade later. And why should bags of beans and beanstalks, Aladdin's caves and coaches made from pumpkin seem an incongruous background? The whole centre of Bradford was a cultural architectural fantasy in itself. The Alhambra Theatre may have borne no resemblance to the famous Moorish Palace at Granada, but it had three domes and was entirely faced, top to bottom on its three exposed sides, with washable white terracotta tiles, so as to glow in the soot-black town. In fact it had to be painted mud-colour in the war for that very reason. The mayor, the town clerk and all the humbler clerks worked in a Victorian town hall with a two-hundred-and-twenty-foot clock tower, based on the Campanile of the Palazzo Vecchio in Florence. The Florentine palace, begun in 1299, had bells in its tower that were rung in differing ways, whether to signify a citizens' call to arms, to make pubic announcements or to summon councillors to meetings. After World War II, Bradford's clock tower had a set of bells less prosaically functional. I used to hear them on my

Exchange & Market Street.   Bradford.

Wool Exchange and Market Street PC.

way home across town from grammar school, from one tram stop to another, playing a wide repertoire of tunes, including 'On Ilkla Moor Baht 'at' (something never attempted in Florence). Mind you, they had to stop these musical interludes as the vibrations were endangering the structure, which had been lit by limelight in the week it was officially opened in 1873. Our Wool Exchange was a Venetian Gothic palace, and I'd taken it for granted that my elementary school had medieval motifs in its stonework. Some of the teachers certainly had medieval methods; torture, mental and physical, was part of the syllabus.

In contrast, the Bradford panto was entirely benign; it was all for our delight, which is what education, in an ideal world, should be. I suppose I had discovered an ideal world, and wonder now how I got through the long year before our next visit to hear those jokes featuring local street names, cracked against fabulous backdrops. Amongst the microscopic patterns in my grey matter, there's one particular trace left by vivid colours. I look down from that gallery seat again and see yellow snakes emerging from a basket, and hear, is it an oboe in the pit? I still don't know how it was done and I've forgotten why, but I see my mother and father looking down and smiling, and feel the whole audience suffused in the absurd magic of the moment. We were held in the crucible in which the odd elements of our workaday lives were tested and synthesized. The rags-to-riches redemption, symbolized in the glittering costumes worn by our heroes and heroines, our representatives, in their finale walk-down, was the necessary catharsis of comedy.

The price and position of our seats became irrelevant and I still remember the fun and glow of it all, and Evans, as vividly and intimately as any child who might have watched from a gilt chair in a stage box. I wouldn't be surprised to find, on meeting such a child now, nearly seventy years on, vestiges of the sense of kinship and belonging that Evans conjured up between us all so long ago, with the whiff of carbolic and back-street credibility he brought onto that enchanted stage, from which Kirby's Flying Ballet fairies rose in flight and swung towards us, dropping their bunches of violets into the orchestra stalls far below.

Bishop Blaize, patron saint of woolcombers, on the cleaned stone edifice of Bradford's Wool Exchange.

Chapter 2

Toy Theatres and the Real Thing

In the kitchen a couple of days ago, I began to describe a particular scenic effect I'd created at a birthday party for my son David, about forty years ago. Hearing the washing machine had triggered my memory, because the sound effects necessary to enhance the illusion (the inside of a spaceship) had meant recording a washing machine's accelerations and decelerations, to be used in conjunction with a live vacuum cleaner. This sort of thing for me has been, through the years, a way of going on playing toy theatres, which I began to do at the age of seven.

Of course, I hear the sound of a washing machine most days, and I really can't remember the last time it reminded me of the engine of a spaceship, unless it was forty years ago, when I conceived the original idea. Perhaps it was also to do with reading the reminiscences of Sam Wild and his nineteenth-century fit-up fairground theatre, 'Old Wild's', and imagining so many peep shows and sideshows that stirred a lot of sedimentary nostalgia for a long-vanished kind of theatre, which I almost believe I actually saw.

Anyway, as I say, two days ago I was describing this birthday party of 1970 or so.

Then this morning, out of the blue, I received a letter from a paediatric neurosurgeon in Canada, who wanted to get back in touch with my son. He wrote:

> *Dear Edward,*
>
> *Many years ago, when I lived in London, I attended Bessemer Grange Primary School. I became firm friends with your son, David.*
>
> *We must have been five or six years of age. I remember well the party you staged for his birthday – complete with fireworks display to Tchaikovsky – and each room in the house made up to look like some mythical scene or other. I remember there being a Rocket Ship Room, complete with stars projected on the wall and, best of all, a wonderful shadow puppet show you put on for us all, including such wild characters as the space witch and the star dragon. I've never forgotten that party – in fact I think I remember it more clearly than some of the events that happened last week! Such is the ageing brain.*

I was delighted of course, but you have to admit it's an extraordinary coincidence, his letter arriving when it did.

In fact, my correspondent is conflating two parties, and the music was Handel's Music for the Royal Fireworks. Nevertheless, the coincidences don't stop there. Yesterday we had a friend round, and I told him about some play-acting I did in a backyard in Bradford as a young boy. This backyard story was by way of a companion piece to the spaceship story. Then, lo and behold, today I received a letter from my brother Bill in which he said:

> *Your fan club is extensive. Anne was shopping in Halifax[1] and was called upon to mention her name and was immediately asked if she and you were related. The query came from one Maureen Verity who claimed childhood acquaintance with you and Rita Wilkinson. She went on to describe attending your theatre performances, the ones you played for them behind the house in Pembroke Street.*

When I was about ten years old, I constructed a kind of miniature fairground booth out of a clotheshorse covered by a blanket. This arrangement, at a sideways right angle, was leant against the exterior wall in the passage, which led through our terrace of back-to-backs to the backyard with its middens and outside lavatories. It housed the stage on which the jointed cut-out figure of a clown danced magically, apparently without support. I'd just returned from a week's holiday in Bridlington where I'd seen this wonder demonstrated to a little crowd down by the harbour. I might have been somewhat disappointed on opening the package, which I think cost as much as two and sixpence, to find that the 'magic' device was obvious and simple once you knew how, but at least I was now in a position to mystify my friends, and perhaps the wonder lives on in the memory of its tiny public, once assembled in our passage in Pembroke Street.

However, it may be that Maureen Verity is remembering not that little peep show, made out of a cardboard box, which you had to crawl under the clotheshorse framework to see, but rather the more knockabout, life-size event staged behind John Lund's end-of-terrace house in the next street, Ackworth Street, when I might have been a touch older. John was the rival boy soprano soloist at Rehoboth Chapel just at the end of Ackworth Street (at the junction of Baird Street and Bowling Old Lane), but there was no singing in the decidedly secular shows we staged together in his yard, which contained, of course, the middens where the dustbins were kept and two outside lavatories – one for the Lunds and one for the lady who lived in the front house. The most effective place for the stage, avoiding the uneven patch of grass in the yard's centre, was, paradoxically, not the most practical. But it was demarcated in stone in a natural recess between the lavatory door of the lady in the front house, and the wall separating the yard from the Bowbridge Road pavement.

---

[1] It so happens that Sam Wild's reminiscences of the days of his touring fit-up theatre were dictated in Halifax, where he lived during his retirement.

What we were attempting in John Lund's yard was a dramatic variety sketch format, anarchic in spirit but always working towards a sense of structure and, of course, some 'payoff' or other, in the best vaudevillian tradition. There was a modicum of dressing-up, and I recall brazening these performances out with a slightly heady insecurity – improvisation based on the hastiest of rehearsals. What were these performances about other than my need to be up there holding forth in front of an audience? True rapport, real collaborative creativity we missed, but were, nonetheless, what we aimed at. Eventually, inevitably, a most curious atmosphere would descend on the proceedings when Mrs – I can't remember her name, but she lived in the front house – would come into the yard with the clear intention of going to her lavatory. The entire cast, sometimes three or four of us, and the audience, five or six of them, would immediately adopt a casual naturalism, as if we just happened to be standing or sitting in the yard, wondering what we might do next. And Mrs Thingumybob, looking neither right nor left, would disappear inside her lavatory and close the door. The action was suspended, disbelief was not: not exactly, but there was a tension in the air, as if disbelief were swinging out of kilter, like the pendulum of a grandfather clock in an earth tremor. In time the sound of the flush would be heard, like a bar bell at the end of an interval, and Mrs Whatsit would re-enter stage left. Without a word or a look, she would close the lavatory door, leave the prompt-side proscenium, cross the auditorium, exit at the gate and proceed down the Bowbridge Road pavement to the door of her front-end house, and our stage would become a stage again and the entertainment would be resumed.

Bertolt Brecht founded the Berliner Ensemble in 1949, some two years after our Ackworth Street performances, so the 'strange interludes' I have described, whilst unconsciously owing a little to Eugene O'Neill's play of that name (except that we could not have spoken our innermost thoughts aloud in soliloquy as O'Neill's characters do), predated, in their obstruction of the continuous flow of audience empathy, the famous Brechtian 'Alienation Effect', the conceptual device which was to dog so much of our work in the English theatre, especially in the classics, from the late 1950s well into the 60s.

It occurs to me that one piece of solo patter I might have used in these shows could have been learnt from my Uncle Harry, who was a tinsmith in his own workshop in Manchester Road, as my paternal grandfather had been. Not that my uncle taught it to me; he'd simply utter it rapidly occasionally and I, laboriously over a long time, caught it and could reproduce it at impressive speed:

This chap comes up to me an' 'e says, 'Can you dance?'
I said, 'Dance?'
'E says, 'Aye.'
I says, 'Who?'
'E says, 'You.'
I says, 'Me?'

16

'E says, 'Yes.'
I says, 'No.'
'E says, 'Aw.'

Uncle Harry would sometimes break into this routine on a Sunday evening when we had gone to sit in the front room of his and Auntie Edith's pebble-dashed house to watch *What's My Line?* on their television set, an amazing treat. Whilst *The Swans* or *The Potter's Wheel* was on the screen, during the intermission he felt he could liven things up with his only bit of patter, or he'd put the copper lid of the coal skuttle on his head and sing a song about a Chinaman. My father remained silent during these displays; little did I know then that Dad had a reputation amongst his workmates as a comic and a wit.

I suspect that John Lund was a better boy soprano than I was, had the better voice, but I believed at the time that I had superior interpretive powers. The only time I really envied him was when he coolly informed me one day that his mother had got him backstage at the Alhambra during a performance of the pantomime, so that he looked up into the height of the flies and watched the backcloths and front cloths going up and down, saw the scene shifters at work and the artists waiting to go on in the wings. He'd never divulged to me his mother's connection to the theatre. The thing that made it so difficult to bear was that I knew John was only a dabbler in theatre, whereas I had been quite serious about it since the age of seven when my mother and father had taken me up the Alhambra's long gaslit flight of stone steps and into the third row of the gallery, just behind the limelight man, to see my first pantomime, *Humpty Dumpty*. Of course I have seen all these things thousands of times by now, from Peterborough to Penang, indeed from Bradford to Broadway, Barnstable to Beijing, the Arcadia, Lowestoft to the Theatre Royal, Haymarket, but it would have meant so much to me *then*. It's as if a vital piece of my boyhood education was missed out. John Lund has not trod the boards in those places, playing kings and clowns, counts and commoners, though the last I heard of him, thirty years ago, was that he played the banjo as a hobby, and today I find I have a sneaking envy of him still, just for that!

When I was about nine, and had seen two or three pantomimes, I made my first model theatre, a cardboard box with a stage opening cut out of one side. It had lighting: I got hold of a torch bulb and fixed it inside the proscenium. I asked my brother Billy, who would just have been demobbed from the RAF in Ceylon, to wire it up to an Eveready battery. I'd cut out my first piece of scenery, a house with a door that could open, and possibly a tree. The whole thing stood on the little table by my bed. Any lighting effect worked in that little room, simply because there was no light. There was a gas bracket on the wall, but it was non-operational. I had a candle and, before I went to sleep, I would fix the loose wire to the terminal to complete the circuit, blow my candle out and stare at the stage, dimly aware of the inadequacy of my work as a scenic artist but mesmerized by the glow of light and the tantalizing potential of this magic box. By the time I was eleven and at grammar school with homework to do, I would sometimes arrange jam jars full of water around a couple of candles so that their light would be magnified and intensified – my own invention; I'd never seen those globes of water lacemakers used to use for the same purpose.

In our early teens, John and I went for joint weekly singing lessons with a bass from the chapel choir, Mr Farrar, a big man in a brown three-piece suit in a small front room with a maroon three-piece suite, a tiled fireplace and an upright piano. John and I were both strictly back-to-back. That meant we had no such thing as a front room, or a tiled fireplace for that matter. Mr Farrar used to talk a lot about bel canto, and I got the impression there was a genuine Italian influence somewhere. Our breathing exercises consisted of filling the lungs deep down and letting a tiny escape of air out through an 'S' sound, which had to be sustained evenly for fifty seconds if possible. My reward came in 1989 when a critic called me 'the long-breathed Petherbridge'. Mrs Farrar, who sang soprano in the chapel choir, played the piano. Our chapel choir's idea of the line between sacred and secular was fuzzy. I recall an 'anthem' which recurred in the evening service, the famous 'Just a Song at Twilight', which began, pianissimo, with the verse:

Once in the dear, dead days beyond recall,
When on the world the mists began to fall.

I remember the tune perfectly and its music-hall ballad trick of staying in four-four time and saving itself up for the real melody, which comes as the chorus breaks into slow-waltz time for:

Just a song at twilight, when the lights are low;
And the flick'ring shadows softly come and go.
Tho' the heart be weary, sad the day and long
Still to us at twilight comes love's old song,
Comes lo-oves old swee-eet song.

I knew that this sort of thing belonged on the Light Programme on the wireless, where I'd heard Anne Ziegler and Webster Booth sing it. Actually, I'd heard and seen them in person, topping the bill at Bradford Alhambra against looped pink satin drapes, lit dramatically in different colours, depending on the mood of each song – the drapes that is; Anne and Webster were in limelight.

Mrs Lund hinted darkly of backstage gossip, suggesting that the raised voices and language emanating from their dressing room told a different story – still, perhaps, part of love's old sweet song. I possess an old 78 rpm of Webster singing in that beautiful, noble tenor voice 'Pale Hands I Loved'. The last I heard of them, years ago, was that they were living in their retirement somewhere on the north coast of Wales and signing up as local extras on a BBC TV film, happily queuing up at the mobile canteen.

Maybe it was Webster Booth's dual fame – he was magnificent in oratorio – which confused Mr Farrar when choosing the anthems. Our Methodist chapel choir was an adult, middle-aged affair. It seemed exceptional to have a couple of boy sopranos. Somehow, John got himself into the Church of England choir at St Stephen's. So I defected, too. They had choir practice each week, something Rehoboth held only rarely. Sight-reading was never my strong point. I found the Psalms particularly foreign, but their chanting intonations and rhythms were second nature to the regulars I met at my first midweek evening rehearsal in the choir vestry, rough, potentially unruly lads with angelic voices. When Sunday came, and I had to dress up in a black surplice, impregnated around the armpits with the pungent evidence of former choristers, faith and musical ability were sorely tried, and I found the experience of being in the choir stalls well behind the pulpit during the sermon, having been issued with pencil and paper to draw, positively irreligious.

I was soon back in the chapel (loyalty may have had something to do with it) where we were up on the balcony behind the minister during the prayers and hymns, and then sidled round the horseshoe so that we could see him for the sermon. Mrs Farrar and her contralto counterpart would invariably fish boiled sweets out of their handbags, unwrap them from their cellophane paper and pop them into their mouths to see them through the eccentric, mannered oratory of Mr Coggle, whose socialist interpretation of the Gospels was not always to the taste of the chapel trustees. After all, one of them, the leading tenor, owned a greengrocery.

But Mr Coggle was the real thing: short and stocky in profound black, with black hair, an emphatic, serious face and a glint in his eye. His sermons and prayers seemed to come from deep inside and literally knocked him into a series of odd involuntary attitudes. When he clasped his hands and bowed his head, sitting in prayer always during the last verse of the hymn preceding his sermon, it was not pious convention; you simply knew that, with quiet fervour, he was asking God to guide him for the sake of the thirty or so people present, and that God was listening.

John Lund's most notable solo in chapel was 'How beautiful are the feet of them that preach the gospel of peace'. Although I questioned the 'depth' of his interpretation, my mind was taken off my own workaday knowledge of feet – chilblains, bunions, ill-fitting shoes and chiropodists, and the sound of clogs, by the pure, clear security of his high notes.

My friend Alwyn Sunderland had a deluxe Pollock's Toy Theatre given him by his parents, who had, and indeed lived above, the confectioner's shop on Gaythorne Road, a rock cake's throw from John Lund's backyard and opposite the splendid fish and chip shop. I knew he'd caught the theatre bug from me, but I knew his condition wasn't chronic. I didn't really envy him his expensive toy or, if I did, it doesn't still rankle the way John Lund's backstage visit does. I must have felt a bit like the RSC director (I really don't know which one it was, or I'd expose him), who, when first shown the

Globe on Bankside, said, 'It's wonderfully impressive – but terribly limiting.' He was quite wrong, of course, but only because he wouldn't know what to do without a concept, a set designer, dry ice, recorded effects, cunning lighting, etc, etc. The sort who, deep down, can't help thinking of the works of Shakespeare as a dodgy dossier that needs sexing up. This attitude leads to 'interesting' but, very often, dodgy productions. (One day I must write up my experiences in 'Designer Shakespeare'.)

Alwyn's top-of-the-range Pollock's was so well made and its scenery and figures, in all their mid-nineteenth-century quaintness, so definitive in their storybook style, that they left one nothing much to do. And even if I'd cleared the stage, the neat diminutive proscenium arch was something I couldn't negotiate. I didn't have the technique at the age of ten or eleven. I needed a more shambolic improvisatory arena.

During the school summer holidays, we saw what West Bowling had to offer in the theatrical line, but long days of leisure, messing about in the streets and parks, were the chief pleasure. I would often call for Alwyn at the shop and his mother would invariably open the till and hand him some coppers. We'd stroll through the cobbled streets and across the old field to Bowling Park. Sometimes we wouldn't walk up the long, tree-lined avenue, but struggle along the steeply sloping bank that fell away from the avenue behind a privet hedge down to the allotments. The grass and weeds were thick and tall and the route was hilariously laborious. One afternoon in the six-week summer holiday, which used to seem so deliciously long then, I remember three or four of us – the Mann brothers and their dog Lassie – making our riotous way along this bank when, for a moment, I was conscious of being happy. It had to do with fresh air and companionship and holiday time and, though it seems ludicrous to say it, because we were, after all, in an urban park with the Bradford dye works and the railway and miles of back-to-back houses and woollen mills all around us, but for a few seconds it might have been Merrie England. The memory of this transient feeling comes back from time to time. It is faint but indelible, and burnt into the neurons or whatever happens inside the cortex, but it resists being transcribed into words.

On days when just the two of us were together and his mother had given him coppers from the till, the magic ice cream moment would come when we went out of the sunlight into the quiet, cool, dark wooden café by the drinking fountain. The café smelt of tea and teacakes and vanilla. Alwyn would buy two cornets of ice cream, one of them for me. Not far away there was a weeping willow tree. It's still there, and the bank it overhangs, but the tree has grown and the bank seems entirely to have lost its deep dramatic curve. You can't stand at the top in the same way and grab hold of two fistfuls of sinewy hanging branches and swing out and return, until the park ranger in his brown uniform creeps up, as he did on one occasion, when we made a thrillingly successful retreat. But, for all that, we'd never have dreamt of spoiling a flowerbed or smashing a bottle on a path and, of course, 'tagging' hadn't even been thought of. Chalked cricket wickets on gable ends and the odd target in the shape of Hitler's face (the bull's-eye his moustache) – these were the extent of urban graffiti.

Before the long-awaited day when ice cream was reintroduced after the war,[2] we would go to watch the 'Holidays at Home' entertainments in Bowling Park. A big covered stage was erected in front of a large, sloping fenced-off area. You had to pay to go in. We never did, but nobody minded if you stood outside and looked through the open fence. I thought there was a terrible shortage of comedians, and no jugglers, acrobats or conjurors – just a lot of not very good singing and crooning into a microphone, but we quite liked an Indian accordionist in gaudy silk, who seemed to get very carried away. We could hear his peculiar, deep, passionate grunts during the more elaborate runs of notes.

In the children's playground, where the swings and roundabouts were, we arrived one day to discover that a simple wooden platform had been built, no more than eight feet across. An old black car drove into the playground and out of it got a small man in a black suit, carrying a very large suitcase. He mounted the platform, taking no notice of us and, in an absorbed sort of way, began to take various objects out of the suitcase, including a stool and a set of coloured wooden bricks; the bricks he tried to hold in his arms. I realized his show had started, and that it was a show, as soon as he dropped one brick and, in picking it up and attempting to include it in his armful, he dropped another; and so the process was patiently repeated until he suddenly kicked open the suitcase and threw all the bricks back inside and slammed the lid.

It was then that we heard a voice coming from inside the suitcase. He opened the lid and from somewhere inside brought out a little man in a dark suit, looking like a slightly grotesque, red-nosed miniature version of himself. He sat on the stool with the character on his knee. One began to notice the telltale ventriloquist's Adam's apple working overtime, but he had an old pro's authority and I willingly suspended my disbelief. I don't remember the dialogue. I expect it was sufficiently classic to justify his special travelling entertainer's wartime petrol allowance. But it is the unostentatious way in which he drew us in at the beginning that I remember, and the creepingly gradual way he adopted his comic persona, shedding it again after he'd finally closed the suitcase, from which a protesting voice still emanated. He dismounted the platform and, as his everyday self (who was equally, if not more, fascinating than the person he'd been a moment ago) got into his car as if nothing unusual had taken place and, with the ghost of a smile, drove away.

---

[2] Oh, how I remember repeated visits to Laverack's in a little yard off Bowling Old Lane just after the war, on the strength of a rumour that he would be selling ice cream. 'Not today, not yet,' he'd say and we'd leave with the sweet smell of vanilla in our nostrils and try again next day.

Chapter 3

Early Doors and Scenic Effects

It is 1941 or 42 at St Stephen's Church of England Primary. As usual I have brought my gas mask to school. I am too old to have the Mickey Mouse variety and young enough to envy the smaller children who still qualify. I enjoy the occasional sessions we have in the school's brick-built air raid shelter, and I dimly comprehend they are to acclimatize us to the dark, echoing place, hence the loud clapping and singing games which will drown out the sound of the bombs, when and if they fall.

The big central classroom in the junior department is quiet and I am in a queue to hand in my small individual blackboard and chalk at the end of what has seemed an interminable period spent copying some writing from the big board. I reach the tall, thin figure of Miss Hanley, the headmistress, but before I can put my board on the pile, she says sternly, 'What's this – writing uphill?' I realize, for the first time, that my writing is all on a slant across the board and feel defeated.

I was surprised to find, in an edition of the *West Bowling Local History Journal*, that my classmate Pamela Oglesby, née Craven, used the word 'kindly' to describe Miss Hanley. That is not the word I would use, but I'm sure boys were treated differently, there being a general belief that a kind hand would turn them soft. One of Miss Hanley's favourite threats to little boys was a sharp 'Do you want to have your pants taken down?'

Pamela Craven, sunny and apple-cheeked, was my first leading lady. Craven's was her father's butcher's shop on Gaythorne Road. In my 11 Plus year in the big school, she sat over on my right amongst the other girls, further away from the stone-mullioned windows that faced out onto Bowling Old Lane, though the windowsills were too high for us to be distracted by any activity in the street. I played the part of Barney Blue-Eyes to Pamela's Mrs Lollipop in what I think of as my acting debut on the English-speaking stage.

This inaugural stage, at the end of the hall, was quite high, had footlights and huge drapes of blackout curtaining reaching right up to the lofty ceiling. I always thought it superior to the stage of my Methodist Sunday school hall at Rehoboth. For a start, the bulbs for the footlights were fixed, not vertically, but horizontally behind the curved length of metal that masked them, so that the audiences at the St Stephen's Sunday school concerts could almost see the footwork in the song and dance numbers. This arrangement at least approximated the real thing I eventually observed at the Alhambra and the Prince's Theatre in town, where the footlights were cunningly positioned so that the entire surface of the raked stage and every artiste, the very last sylph *en pointe* could be seen head to toe from any seat in the stalls.

These days, although the term 'footlights' is still in use, they are a feature which has vanished from real theatres and I suppose from school halls, too, for health and safety reasons. However, designers who devise special floors to sit on top of the original boards of our Victorian theatres, sometimes quite substantial false floors to accommodate wiring and mechanical equipment for their computerized effects, as often as not ruin the sightlines from the stalls, so carefully arranged by Victorian theatre architects.[1] I confess that I never sat in the stalls of a real theatre until, at the age of fourteen, I discovered that Harry Hanson's Court Players at the Prince's Theatre sold two seats for the price of one on Monday nights. Normally I went to the gloomy doorway down the side street to offer my money at the little hatch protected by a sturdy criss-cross wire guard and with just enough room to slip your tenpence or shilling through and take your ticket from the lady in the tiny alcove, lit by a single gas mantle, before the climb up the stone steps to the balcony.

On this particular night, in some excitement, I braved the main foyer of the Prince's for the first time. A brightly, electrically lit lady behind a grand, gleaming brass grill greeted me as I made my way through the throng of middle-aged couples and asked shyly if 'two for the price of one' also meant I could buy one seat in the orchestra stalls at half price, as I was by myself. I never quite understood why grown-ups found me amusing when I was being earnest. But it was a kind little laugh the lady gave as she said, 'Ee lad, of course you can.' I handed over the still rather princely sum of one and ninepence and went along a curving corridor and *down* the carpeted stairs, emerging, as I'd often observed fortunate patrons do from my balcony seat aloft, from one of the arched entrances on either side of the stage, just past the end of the orchestra pit. There, under my nose, two spotlit pianists were playing the two grand pianos. It was like making a theatrical entrance because one came out facing the whole house. The balcony looked audaciously high and distant, seen at an acute angle up above the dress circle and the circle, whilst the orchestra stalls felt cosy and intimate. At last the house lights dimmed and the footlights glowed on the brown velvet curtain. It would be remembering it through rose, or at least autumnal-tinted, spectacles to describe the Prince's curtain as anything other than a disappointing dingy brown, but I suppose it had, in the days of Lillie Langtry's flying matinée visit of 1903 in *The Second Mrs Tanqueray*, gone better with the green and now faded gilt of the ornate auditorium.

I don't remember the play, but of course I expected, and got, a variation on the usual drawing room in the better postal districts of London or in the

---

[1] Cameron Mackintosh insists that the floor of the stalls at Drury Lane is always built up and realigned so that the sightlines are correct. On the other hand, Elaine Stritch refused to work on the Old Vic rake; the stage was made level and her long and eloquent legs were completely cut off from the view of the expensive seats when she moved 'up stage' in her one-woman show there.

Home Counties, except that it too was high. No real room in a house, even in the Home Counties, could be as tall as the Prince's Theatre's stock of flats, but to my astonishment the room had a ceiling. That *was* sophisticated; from the balcony I had been mostly aware of the carpet. How loud the actors' voices were down here, and how blue the eye shadow was, even on some of the men. It was like seeing and hearing the sea from the beach for the first time instead of from the cliff top.

Only once did I see the Court Players attempt an outdoor scene. It was in *Autumn Crocus*, a popular romance by Dodie Smith, which had a scene on a mountainside in Switzerland. I was back in the gallery again and despite the management's penchant for height in 'West End' drawing rooms, it struck me that they were out of their depth with the Swiss Alps. The first time I caught the peculiar smell of scenic size was at the Prince's. It is a type of glue I could wax lyrical about if I chose because I sometimes think that my lost spiritual home is in an old scene-painting shop.

Pat Phoenix was the leading lady with Harry Hanson's Court Players and was eventually to gain fame on television as *Coronation Street*'s Elsie Tanner in the 60s. She always struck me as a touch brash, not to say common, for the parts she played in Harry Hanson's 'Season of West End Successes', each rehearsed by the actors in a week whilst they were playing the current show twice nightly at 6.15 and 8.45. The part of Sadie Thompson in the adaptation of Somerset Maugham's *Rain* was more appropriate to her gifts, although her ever-present hint of the northern accent, so vital in its full-blown glory to *Coronation Street*, was out of place in Maugham's jungle. I was at her first night when she played Sadie Thompson, having once more invested in an orchestra stall.

It was an ambitious production; I have since learnt that rice is very effective as stage rain if lit properly (uncooked of course), or even half-inch nails, which can glint very nicely, but the Court Players had had the plumbers in and hired a number of real palms, such as you might see surrounding a café trio in those days, or glimpse through the windows of the glasshouse in Bowling Park. The palms lined the area upstage of the veranda at the back of the set and were the jungle. The company had had one dress rehearsal, of course, which by Equity rules should have finished at 4.15; no chance, I shouldn't think. As the curtain rose, two barefoot native girls in sarongs, carrying pots on their heads (I recognized them under their brown make-up and black wigs as the acting assistant stage managers), self-consciously set the scene by walking across the stage in an evocative manner, just as the smell of recently applied size wafted from the scenery across the footlights. It was either the jungle or their feet we thought we could smell. But it was the rain when it came, twice I think, that really broke the spell for the audience. It seemed to be preceded by a strange thudding and clunking noise and arrived, before it got into its stride, in a series of hesitant squirts and splutters, as in football changing-room showers. When the true downpour came, the noise as it splattered onto the palm leaves made the dialogue, already difficult to concentrate on – so unused were we to such heavy-duty realism – very difficult to hear.

The luxury of a fish-and-chip walk home was out of the question, but occasionally I managed chips and, on the way up Manchester Road, I would ruminate on the dramatic human dilemmas I'd seen enacted. If they'd had an unhappy ending, I'd try to apply my Rehoboth Methodist Sunday school morality to work out in what way the characters could have behaved differently to achieve a happier end. By the turn-off to Bowling Old Lane I had usually given up the struggle. Holding a bag of chips in my hands and all the intricacies of the plot in my head, whilst passing moral judgments on the characters' motives and inventing more wholesome strategies for them, was hard to sustain. I had yet to understand that 'terror and pity' were a sufficient response to tragedy and even to the dramas at the Prince's, and that the catharsis of a good laugh at human frailty might be an end in itself.

Bowling Old Lane, ca 1946. The poster on the right is advertising the Harvest Festival: I almost certainly sang solo in that year's Festival, although I have no billing on the poster.

As I walked the deserted pavements up the winding hill between the silent woollen mills, my thoughts might turn to the real problems of unfinished homework awaiting my return to Pembroke Street.

But to return to my acting debut in my eleventh year and the modest innocence of Barney Blue-Eyes and Mrs Lollipop, we gave just the one afternoon performance to an audience of our mothers. I entered from stage right and Pamela was on the left. 'Good morning, Mrs Lollipop. I've brought the eggs you wanted; six, I think, you ordered.' This is all the dialogue I remember. My eyes were not blue, so I think I must have been cast on the strength of talent, rather than type. The highlight of the performance, however, was nothing to do with acting, mine or anyone else's. It was the surprise appearance of real life on the stage, as opposed to the overwrought attempt at tropical realism I've been describing.

There was a crowd scene, centred on a picnic, in which we were all supposed to be having strawberries (just as unlikely as being able to order six eggs in 1947). I don't know how they kept it a secret from us, but, to our surprise, we were suddenly served with saucers of red jelly, and the way we must have fallen delightedly upon this feast raised the performance to a completely different level of commitment. The layman's first question to the professional actor, after 'How do you learn your lines?', is 'Do you ever lose yourself in your part?' Luckily there are enough un-strangled Desdemonas, unstabbed Poloniuses, sane Ophelias and promiscuous Saint Joans to prove that it is *finding* oneself in the part that is the important thing – that, and knowing the lines so deeply that they are rooted in the automatic memory like one's knowledge of the controls of a car. Only then can one be free to play at saying them spontaneously as if they have just occurred. These are perhaps the two first and most important lessons in acting. My young mind must have found little labour in learning Barney Blue-Eyes. We learnt hymns by osmosis and our times tables by chanting.

As the red jelly appeared, art and artifice went out of the window. I suddenly became conscious of the fact that the afternoon audience of mothers was laughing. It was for me a curious kind of acting lesson as well as a treat.

Actually I think my performance as Barney Blue-Eyes saved me from a painful encounter with Mr Coverdale, our headmaster by this time. There was usually only one reason a boy would be sent to see the headmaster and I forget the transgression that caused Miss Dyer to send me. One didn't *always* know what one had done. During one of Mrs Charlesworth's history classes, as she paced up and down the side of the classroom between us and the mullioned windows, her monotonous, metallic voice making it impossible for me to think of dates and kings and battles as being anything but deadly dull, she left one single lasting impression upon me; the hard-backed book she was carrying came into percussive collision with the back of my cranium. I can only assume that, even then, my bodily eloquence was such that she read my dreamy, inattentive expression on the back of my head, and it was too much for her.

Anyway, for whatever reason, I reached the headmaster's room. Mr Coverdale looked down at me with a puzzling mixture of derision and amused admiration. He said, 'Barney Blue-Eyes, *that's* you, isn't it?' I did not at all expect that my temporary alter ego from the performance of some days before would enter the equation. 'Barney Blue-Eyes', he repeated. Clearly I had attained a status akin to that of licensed fool. Perhaps for a moment he was incapable of subjecting a character, who had walked out of the magic pages of a child's storybook, to something so arbitrary, banal and savage as a ritual which involved reaching behind the cupboard by the door and assaulting this small, thin schoolboy with a cane. It was a sinister instrument, and God only knows where it had been *procured*. I use the word with its darker connotations advisedly, because it had a black rubber skin, that is to say, it had been inserted into a close-fitting black rubber tube. What firm of 'educational' suppliers had issued the catalogue describing it? To give Coverdale his due, he had inherited the apparatus from his unpopular predecessor Mr Baines.

I was in the room again one day in 1989 when I was appearing on tour in *The Misanthrope* at the Alhambra. The slight, friendly young headmaster asked exactly when I'd been at the school, in case there was a record; what he meant was that I might appear in Mr Baines's punishment book, the only trace my years there would have left, though I thought of suggesting a plaque on the prompt-side wing of the stage. He got the book out and referred to it, although I assured him my name would not appear; my memory would have recorded it far more poignantly than any record book. He looked, nevertheless, and I was appalled to glimpse the number of times the words 'six strokes' appeared, written in Mr Baines's neat hand.

From that room forty-two years earlier, Mr Coverdale had dismissed me unscathed, following at some distance. Suddenly he caught me up and began to spank my behind, driving me towards the classroom door and intending, I sensed, that I should make an undignified re-entrance into Miss Dyer's class. I intended to walk in unperturbed with my dignity intact, which I managed to my own satisfaction and relief, but how I despised him.

The extent of Mr Coverdale's pastoral interest in me only manifested itself once more when he entered our class on our very last Friday afternoon before the summer holiday, after which we would all go to our next schools. He carried a little pile of manila envelopes, one for each child who had passed 'the scholarship', as we used to say of passing the 11 Plus, which meant, of course, that most children 'failed the scholarship', rather than being positively selected to go on to an education more suited to their perceived abilities. Coverdale got right to the last envelope, which turned out to be for me, and scoffed, 'You didn't think you were going to get one did you?' And what was so amusing about that, especially for the children who hadn't got one?

The only other impression I have of him was an arbitrary and grotesque piece of acting, or rather mimicry, he 'treated' us to at the front of the class one day, demonstrating, he explained, the way Indians walked. I don't recall there being many people from the subcontinent in Bradford in those days, but, whilst I strove to find anything recognizable in his demonstration, I was completely unconvinced by the supposedly comic gait he adopted to show that they were only used to walking in mud in their villages, and not on our York stone paving slabs.

The headmaster's knowledge of the children, such as it was, derived from the morning assemblies where he would stand on a chair, make announcements and lead the hymns and prayers. He could see us more plainly than we could see him, having his back to the windows onto Birch Lane. The stage was not used, it was behind us, and the teachers flanked the hall, facing vigilantly inwards. I can see now our 11 Plus teacher, Miss Dyer, standing to the side of us by our classroom doorway. She was no longer in the first flush, but she had a head of black hair, a red woolly jumper showing her bosom to pronounced advantage, and red lipstick. Her method during the hymns was not to sing but to adopt a faraway look and a faint knowing smile, like some seasoned pedagogic saint or martyr even. She always kept a ruler handy and used it regularly for purposes she considered to be educational, but I forgive her a lot for the way she led the class in the choral speaking of John

Masefield's poems 'Cargoes' and 'Sea-Fever', teasing out every atom of committed expression from us by zealous example, enabling us to realize, there in the West Bowling classroom, how we could be transported by words, and such words!

I don't recall knowing what kind of ship was 'Quinquireme of Nineveh from distant Ophir' or where exactly on a map it was sailing, but it conjured up the most glowingly beautiful backcloths. It sounded beautiful, too, and we loved the chance for the rapid chant of 'Dirty British coaster with a salt-caked smoke stack'.

I have been thinking about it and am forced to concede that Miss Hanley was responsible for at least two joyous moments in my early schooling, still vivid to me all these decades on. Now in my seventy-third year and a D.Litt. (Honorary) of Bradford University, I write to her:

Dear Miss Hanley,

I often think of you at Harvest and Christmas time. The harvest was not particularly visible from West Bowling, but you used to get down the stuffed blackbird from the top shelf of the big glass-paned cupboard and place it on your desk and tell us about ploughs and worms and such like, and then, when we sang 'We plough the fields and scatter', I can still remember my sense of the rhythm of the seasons and the rolling years.

At Christmas we made paper lanterns under our teachers' instructions and coloured them with crayons. They were hung in festoons above us in all the classrooms, but I suppose it was you who decreed that the partitions between the classrooms should be opened and folded back so that we could all of us process and sing through and around the length and breadth of the place in which so much sober work was done. I can still feel what it was like; my young self, tossing my head back to see all those lanterns passing above – could I see which was mine? Then, later, the sense of expectation as we waited – for what we wondered? – in a darkish room by the arched Gothic door leading into an even darker vestibule. Then the heavy knock. Was there even a sense of reindeer outside; he couldn't have come on the tram, surely? In he came; if there was a sack and presents I don't remember, only that someone played the piano and he snatched you up into a dance for a moment or two. Magic, magic. None the less magic because now I know it was Mr Hoole, throwing off his workaday persona as our school caretaker, you entering into the novel fantasy of it and proving that transformation scenes don't only happen in elaborate pantomimes with machinery and fly towers and false floors, but everywhere where a simple sense of delight can be created.

Edward Petherbridge (typed horizontally)

Chapter 4

Fairy Tales, Lords and Commoners

I got quite excited when I read that the great critic and artist John Ruskin had lectured in the Bradford Mechanics' Institute in 1864, excited because I had sung on the selfsame stage with my grammar school choir at a lunch-hour concert in 1950. I remember the austere, untheatrical hall with the woodwork an institutional brown, the stage reached by two doors, one on either side, each leading to a little ante-room; the girls' school occupied the one on stage left.

I have found Ruskin's lecture of 1864 and read it; even on the page it makes all the BBC Reith Lectures I can remember hearing seem pallid indeed. I've sung through the two songs we sang in 1950, in so far as I remember them, and what can I say? My boy soprano is not what it was; and yet it would be neat if I could see a parallel, something complementary between it and my imaginings of the great Victorian sage and prophet, for so he seems to me, even in this one lecture, which must have assaulted the sensibilities of his assembled great and good industrialists like a fascinatingly discursive, vividly illustrated version of the Ten Commandments combined with the Sermon on the Mount, lightened with not a few shafts of wit. Yes, it would be nice to see some chimings between Ruskin's awesome rhetoric and the piping treble of the Grange Boys Grammar School choir singing 'How sweet is the Shepherd's sweet lot!' and then, augmented by the Grange Girls School – a rare, in my experience unique, circumstance – 'Nymphs and shepherds, come away!'

Well, of course, there *are* chimings. Ruskin and our choir expressed a yearning for the pastoral; Ruskin by describing the antithetical Bradfordian reality: 'This idol of yours, this golden image, high by measureless cubits, set up where your green fields of England are furnace-burnt into the likeness of the plain of Dura,' he thunders. Eighty-six years later we schoolboys piped Blake's song of innocence:

> How sweet is the shepherd's sweet lot!
> From the morn to the evening he strays;
> He shall follow his sheep all the day,
> And his tongue shall be fillèd with praise.

And the vision was compounded; we didn't sing 'Drake he's in his hammock' – that was saved for speech day – no, we continued our pastorally biased programme. After we had skulked offstage during some songs by the girls, we re-entered as if butter wouldn't have melted in our mouths (although we all still had our ration books, so butter was almost as rare as contact with the girls), and – girls on stage left, boys on the right – we sang: 'Nymphs and shepherds, come away. / In this grove let's sport and play.' Before you run away with the idea that our conductor and head of music, Mr Cliff, was a gentle, sylvan soul, I should tell you that the pep talk he gave us boys before the concert was to warn us that if we didn't sing well, 'the name of Grange will be mud throughout Bradford.' Each year he held a caning session for the boys who achieved low marks in his music exams. I despised him.

But I'd better come clean straight away. I find that the platform on which we sang with enforced sweetness was part of the improved, imposing Mechanics' Institute (opposite the Town Hall), not opened until 1871, seven years too late for Ruskin. But I can bring the chimings much nearer home – literally. Ruskin gives a picture of the mid-nineteenth-century Bradford my paternal grandfather was born into, a Bradford Engles described as a 'filthy hole'. Ruskin is subtler. He told his audience of Bradford worthies that they seemed to have realized their ideal in their worship of the 'Goddess of Getting-on':

> Your ideal human life then is, I think, that it should be passed in a pleasant undulating world, with iron and coal everywhere underneath it. On each pleasant bank of this world is to be a beautiful mansion, with two wings; and stables, and coach houses; a moderately sized park; a large garden and hot-houses; and pleasant carriage drives through the shrubberies. In this mansion are to live the favoured votaries of the Goddess; the English gentleman, with his gracious wife, and his beautiful family; he always able to have the boudoir and the jewels for his wife, and the beautiful ball dresses for the daughters, and hunters for the sons, and a shooting in the Highlands for himself. At the bottom of the bank is to be the mill; not less than a quarter of a mile long, with one steam engine at each end, and two in the middle, and a chimney three hundred feet high. In this mill are to be in constant employment from eight hundred to a thousand workers, who never drink, never strike, always go to church on Sunday, and always express themselves in respectful language.

My grandfather was thirteen when those words were spoken, and living some ten minutes' walk away up a low hill just out of the centre of the small town, but very much 'at the bottom of the bank'. His father was, according to the census of 1851, a 'woolcomber and ginger-beer seller'; his son, young James Petherbridge, was a beneficiary of the Factory Act of 1847, which had limited the number of hours women and children could work in textile mills to ten every weekday and eight on Saturdays, improvements that had been bitterly opposed for at least seventeen years. 'Better the children should work in the mill for twelve hours on a full stomach than run in the fields and lanes on an empty one,' said one mill owner.

It is so much easier to imagine almost anything Ruskin did than what the life of my own flesh-and-blood ancestors was like. Ruskin's whiskered patrician face beams out at us from drawings, paintings and photographs; not so long ago I saw an exhibition partly dedicated to his own art at Tate Britain, and his charming personality was extolled, even some of his detractors doing him proud. In 1869, five years after the Bradford lecture, Henry James wrote of Ruskin: 'He has been scared back by the grim face of reality into the world of unreason and illusion, and … wanders there without a compass and a guide – or any light save the fitful flashes of his own beautiful genius.'

Yet I have only vague ideas of the grim face of the realities my great-grandfather saw. The Bradford Woolcombers' Report of 1845 puts it at its extreme: 'We are men born for nobler purposes than to live like slaves and submit through destitution to be hurried to premature graves. All we ask is a fair day's wages for a fair day's work.' I like to think of my great-grandfather, James Petherbridge, being something of an entrepreneur, branching out into ginger beer when the wool-combing machine unveiled at the Great Exhibition of 1851 threatened the home-based craft of hand combing. How long before their little house in Lincoln Street, so insignificant a street that it was left off the map, ceased to be Great-Granddad's workplace, before the heat and fumes of the charcoal stove and the smell of the greasy raw wool in the hot combs were banished from their upper room. Did his son, my grandfather, receive an education beyond the age of eleven? The woolcombers were the lowest-paid textile workers in the country, and even the title of the report into their living conditions in 1845 was 'Mechanization and Misery'.

My mother's family lived in nearby Bingley – also part of the wool industry but smaller and, even in my day, relatively countrified. Mother's father was a drayman. Before I was old enough to sing of nymphs and shepherds, she told me, when the subject of fairies came up, that as a girl she had seen one in the woods near the River Aire in Bingley. I calculate that this must have been between 1908 and 1910, when she was at the fairy-seeing age. In answer to my close questioning she spoke hesitantly, as she always did, and gave scant detail; I gathered it was a fleeting glimpse, not much more material than the Bingley Woods fairy I see in my mind's eye now, and have done spasmodically over the decades, whenever I remember my urgent childish questionings and my mother's vague answers, trailing off into silence. It has a secure place in my grey matter – the evanescent vision of sunlight through green leaves, grass and bluebells and a small, delicate, winged feminine presence.

I have no reason to disbelieve my mother. Her sighting would pre-date by some seven or perhaps nine years the famous sighting by two girls in Cottingley, not far away from Bingley on the way to Bradford, in the last month of the First World War, with photographs to prove it. (This was at a time when my father to be, still in his teens, was in Egypt as a private soldier, unloading cavalry horses from ships, and his brother Jim was serving as a gunner in France where he was wounded.) After some time, Sir Arthur Conan Doyle, interested in spiritualism, got to hear of the Cottingley fairy phenomenon and had the photographs analysed. He was convinced of their authenticity and in 1922 published a book called *The Coming of the Fairies*; his correspondence had references to ectoplasm. I prefer my mother's pre-war story and the precious, nebulous glimpse of magic that I can 'see' whenever I choose; much prefer it to the photographic 'evidence' from Cottingley, which the girls finally confessed in their old age was contrived with cut-outs secured by hat pins.

In fact, Auntie Ethel, Mother's sister, and Uncle Bob lived in Cottingley, and during the 40s and early 50s we would often go to see them for Sunday tea; the trolley journey was through the salubrious, tree-lined suburbs of Bradford and a treat in itself. They lived on an estate of modern pebble-dashed houses and I admired theirs, neat with its back and front gardens and its modern tiled fireplace, always symbolic to me of the domestically desirable, in contrast to the old black-leaded iron range at home. We would have our tea and there was talk and the longish walk back to catch the trolley, but we never went near the beck and the woods to see where the famous Cottingley cousins had taken their photographs (oaks and thorns are reputed to attract fairies). Indeed I never heard anything about them. Uncle Bob was a gardener and gravedigger and, I suppose, a materialist where nature and spirits were concerned.

Whilst we're on the subject of photographic evidence, you can just pick out, in an aerial photograph of West Bowling, the house where my mother told me of the fairy.

West Bowling was the inner suburb of Bradford, not far from long, slum-cleared Lincoln Street, which we had to return to after our visits to my mother's sisters in 'nicer' areas. The photo is from 1961, and the first thing to strike me, seeing this aeroplane's-eye view of the serried ranks of blackened back-to-back stone houses, is the absence of trees, to say nothing of bluebells and fairies.

I recall going back to West Bowling late one Saturday night in January 1961. I had been playing Frank Chesney in *Charley's Aunt* on tour in Stockton-on-Tees, and after the show my wife had telephoned me at Stockton's Theatre Royal stage door from London, where she had received the news that Mother had died. One of the actresses in the cast had her parents visiting. They possessed a car and sweetly offered to take me the sixty-odd miles home – I forget where they had to get to. I found my father alone in the house, sitting opposite the empty chair. There was a fire burning in the tiled fireplace and electric light at last! Not gaslight – it was the 60s after all. My parents just survived into this era and had astonished me, when, returning from eighteen months in New Zealand in 1960 to visit them, they took me into town for a meal at a Chinese restaurant.

'She slipped through mi fingers,' Dad kept saying. There wasn't much else to say – well, now I can think of lots; lots I should have said, wish I had said. Mother had been waiting for the post all week and a letter from me, and indeed I had written one the day before but failed to post it. I hadn't even known that she was ill, with acute bronchitis. The next week I arrived back in Stockton and was horrified to see a station advertisement for a Tuesday matinée, Dad having fixed Tuesday for the funeral, thinking that would be safe. No understudy of course. I actually allowed myself to be persuaded by Carl Clopet that I must fulfil my contract. I spent the Tuesday morning in church. An Actors' Church Union priest held mass for me. My father said my mother wouldn't have wanted me to miss a performance. It was a small matinée, to which I should have conscientiously objected.

At Bradford's Theatre School I had been taught to speak in a way I think of now, and honour still, as 'Theatrical Aristocratic'. One wouldn't have dreamt of using the speech of a member of the current Royal Family as a model for Shakespeare's royalty. We were taught to speak an adaptive Standard English, which could encompass everything from the Bard's blank verse to the young man entering through French windows with 'Who's for tennis?'.

The chance of hearing actual live aristocratic English in West Bowling (which might have involved a Yorkshire accent for all I know) disappeared, along with trees, the chance of fairies and 'Merrie England' itself, when the people up at the stately home of Bolling Hall – three fields and a little wood and fifteen minutes' walk away from where our street would be built – sold their coal and mineral rights to the Bowling Ironworks.

Bolling Hall in the distance.

Although there is a fine patriotic ring to the idea that the cannon used at the Battle of Waterloo were manufactured in Bowling, it was not long before the 'Quality' decamped to escape the noxious fumes, over the hills and far away to somewhere still green and pleasant.

Attempts to see 'Jerusalem builded here' did frequently cease from mental fight, and the arrows of desire struck some odd targets, but my dad, thanks to Methodism, had abstained from alcohol all his life (I wish the Methodists had taken the same line on Woodbines) and I sang 'Oh! For the wings of a dove' and 'Where the bee sucks' at the chapel a street away. We had public baths and a library. As early as 1892 Keir Hardie had created a sensation by entering Parliament in a cloth cap and tweed suit and wearing a red tie, and the next year the Independent Labour Party was founded in Bradford in the name of equality. As for Merrie England, well, on May Day the great dray horses that pulled coal delivery carts were arrayed with shining horse brasses and coloured ribands plaited into their manes. My Church of England elementary school held an annual garden party in the grounds of St Stephen's vicarage, at which some of the girls did a maypole dance and some boys a sword dance with an impressive end which, like the maypole, depended on interlacing, in this instance the interlacing of the 'swords' (wooden batons) in a rosette carried aloft by the leading boy. I envied him, all of them, but perhaps I was passed over when it came to these performances because I was a Methodist Sunday school boy.

From my aerial view of history I swoop down to the detail of my boyhood's West Bowling and pick out, two minutes away from our house, the cinema hoarding next to the public urinal on Gaythorne Road. Incidentally, the year of the Cottingley Fairies, 1917, was also the year of Marcel Duchamp's artwork urinal or *Fountain*, a mere seventeen years after Ruskin's death, but let that pass. What I am chiefly remembering, from when I was nine in 1945, is the huge poster of the film *The Dolly Sisters* with its alluring full-length portrait in full colour of Betty Grable (whose legs were insured for a million dollars) and June Haver. Even more vividly I remember the poster of Jane Russell looking sultry in the straw in *The Outlaw*; I was six when that film was produced, but, owing to lengthy wrangling with the censorship office, it was not generally released until 1946. The posters and their stars stared boldly at the trams going past and into the windows of the houses opposite. Parallel with the tram route and behind the hoarding, sunken below the level of the road, was a terrace of low-built cottages called Long Row, which was part of old West Bowling, old enough to have been mentioned in the Woolcombers' Report of 1845 as an example of terrible overcrowding. The film itself I saw on our local screen round the corner at the Birch Lane Cinema, near Oaks Fold where there survived, despite the best Hollywood could do, a blackened stone house or two from the early eighteenth century.

Birch Lane Cinema from Cranbrook Street, ca 1915.
From the collection of Graham Hall

Note all these arboreal street names, though there was not a thorn, birch or oak in sight unless you walked to the municipal park, once the grounds of Bolling Hall, its magic casements rescued from tenement status to attain that of municipal museum by 1915. Magic was now a modern phenomenon and the province of the silver screen.

Homing in on the receiver on our windowsill, BBC Radio had a more utopian influence; certainly Lord Reith sought to emphasize the pastoral – restoring a healthy balance, he perhaps thought, for our predominantly urban nation, and he insisted on the highest standards of 'Standard English' in the speech of the announcers. What of the theatre? There *was* magic.

Today I have it from the horse's mouth; more precisely I have the word of a fairy, a pantomime fairy – I saw her with my own eyes when I was seven, and read her evidence today on her website. What could be more magical than this encounter in cyberspace? Yvonne Sellers (née Woodroffe) takes me backstage at the pantomime and into the girls' dressing room no less. 'Pantomime was a fairy-tale time', she writes, authoritative words coming from an ex-Tiller Girl and Kirby's Flying Ballet veteran, who'd earned an extra ten shillings a week at the Bradford Alhambra in 1943 for applying make-up to the faces of the Twelve Little Sunbeams, and, because the 'King of Pantomime', Francis Laidler, was by then seventy-four or so, he insisted on the bygone style of cupid's-bow lips and well-rouged cheeks for the dozen twelve-year-old girls. They were local girls, of course, and sat in a row on the ledge of the dressing table whilst Yvonne, assisted by another Tiller Girl, got to work and made a production line of the lined-up juveniles. These two Tiller Girls, their ears attuned to London, remarked what broad Yorkshire accents Sunbeams had! I wonder what accents the Cottingley Fairies were supposed to have spoken in?

Kirby's Flying Ballet, ca 1944 at the Alhambra.

It is reassuring that Yvonne thinks, thought then, of the pantomime season as 'a fairy-tale time'. The pantomime people were in the business of transformation and redemption; true it was nigh impossible to get tights at the time and the Tiller Girls had to make up their legs with 'glycerine, ochre and something else' whilst standing on sheets of newspaper, and there was no question of having baths after the show at their digs (but they could and did go to the municipal Turkish baths, right next door to the theatre, *before* the show). She claims that they enjoyed the audiences 'as much as they enjoyed us' – it was redemption and transformation in a gloriously pagan way, of course: the good getting their reward here on earth.

It's a wonder my seven-year-old mind wasn't seriously sexually confused, what with the Dame being played by a middle-aged man and the Principal Boy by a young woman, and the cow, if the panto was *Jack and the Beanstalk*, by two young men, but the elegant high point of gender transformation for me definitely belonged to the Twelve Little Sunbeams. They had a number, a Victorian chocolate-box affair, in which half of them dressed in crinolines and half in top hats, white tie and tails. The climax came when the 'girls' curtseyed and the 'boys' raised their top hats to reveal what appeared to me from the gods to be perfect brilliantined short back and sides haircuts – wigs of course – but what immaculate artful artifice!

I made the mistake of going to a Bradford Alhambra pantomime in the 1974/5 season, by which time I had become, I thought, a seasoned London sophisticate, though the lure of the posters for *Jack and the Beanstalk*, which I saw on my visit 'home' that year, were too much for me. I discovered that the best blue and gold curtain in the world (the civic colours after all) with the finest heavy gold tassels, had been replaced by an impostor in red, and the orchestra pit only accommodated a Hammond organ, a trumpeter and a drummer. The star, the famous Charlie Drake, sulked his way through the show because a girl he had introduced into the chorus was banned by Equity. It was a low ebb in fairyland, and all I could wonder at when the Twelve Little Sunbeams came on was what broad Bradford accents Sunbeams had.

The meteoric rise of one of the Sunbeams is the stuff almost of fairy tale. Pat Paterson was born in Round Street, West Bowling in 1910. I can see her part of the very straight street of back-to-backs now, with its doors opening directly onto the pavement. Her house, number 15, was just opposite the entrance of my infant and junior school, St Stephen's. More to the point, that large hoarding for the cinema posters overlooked it, tangentially.

By the turn of 1920, long before I was thought of, Pat Paterson was more or less ten and appearing as a Sunbeam in Francis Laidler's *Babes in the Wood* at the Prince's Theatre. At fifteen or thereabouts, removed by her father from a subsequent pantomime, she ran away from home to London with a boy in the show, and by seventeen was in a West End revue, *Stop Flirting* – which is just what her father had wanted her to do when he took her out of the Bradford pantomime. It can't have been long before her name appeared on the Gaythorne Road hoarding, if not in the first minor British films in which she danced and sang, then at least in small print below the name of Anna Neagle in the film of Noël Coward's *Bitter Sweet*, when Pat was only twenty-three.

Definitely by the next year, 1934, her name would appear for West Bowlingites to gawp at, next to Spencer Tracy's in the Hollywood film *Bottoms Up*. Now I have procured a bad copy of this film on DVD, but I can say that I have looked into the pretty face of Pat Paterson of Round Street, seen her graceful movement and heard her English voice. She was playing an English girl in a way Lord Reith could not have faulted and, what's more, her character was having to pass herself off as the daughter of a hereditary lord (not a mere created Presbyterian Scottish one like Reith). George Bernard Shaw's Professor Higgins himself could not have complained, and you will remember that Shaw was present in Bradford at the birth of the Labour Party.

So I have discovered that I am not the first West Bowlingite to pass himself off as a member of the aristocracy since the genuine articles of Bolling Hall fled all those years ago.

View over West Bowling, from Bowling Park drive, during the National Coal Strike, March 1912. The people are scavenging for coal.

From the collection of Graham Hall

View over West Bowling, 1990.

Chapter 5

Chapel Street

This image from Chapel Street's Civic Playhouse is not only redolent of Bradford Bohemia (Harry Hanson did not produce Sartre; Kenneth Mellor and David Giles remained life-long partners), but also of the wider cultural landscape of the country. Thelma Piggot (opposite Kenneth's Romeo) was my first sight of Juliet, indeed live Shakespeare – I can still see and hear her doing the poison speech from a circular bed in 1952. As Thelma Barlow, however, she played in over 2,000 episodes of *Coronation Street*, whilst Kenneth designed the colour schemes for all the London Thames bridges throughout the 1970s and 80s. David Giles directed two of the Actors' Company's biggest successes, *The Wood Demon* and *'Tis Pity She's a Whore* (both designed by Kenneth Mellor), and his TV credits include *The Mayor of Casterbridge* and *The Barchester Chronicles*.

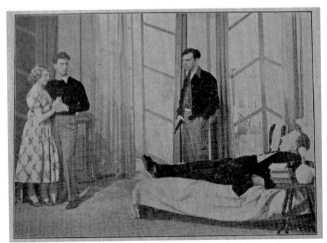

**Thelma Piggott, Kenneth Mellor, David Giles and
Tom H. Walton in *Crime Passionel* (Sartre).**

Sloping, cobbled Chapel Street, with its crazed lamp-posts, was an apparently unloved backwater of the old warehouse district known as Little Germany,[1] and home not only to the Civic, Priestley's plain-fronted gem of a miniature theatre, but also, tucked away in two disused wool warehouses, the Northern Theatre School.

---

[1] Little Germany derived its name from the mostly German merchants who established the area in the nineteenth century.

One of Chapel Street's
crazed lamp-posts.
Photo: © EP

Snapshot of Little Germany in 2009,
showing how grand we didn't realize
it was under all the soot.
Photo: © EP

As such, the street nursed the talents of – as well as those mentioned above – Billie Whitelaw, William Gaskill, Robert Stephens, Brian Bedford, Christine Howarth, Tom Bell, Bernard Hepton, Robert Fyfe, Barbara Young (who played the theatrical landlady in *Have His Carcase* and was also to find fame in *Coronation Street*), George Leyton, Peter Firth, Duncan Preston – and me.

I had wanted to go to RADA, but in 1953, as a suppliant for a local-authority grant at a pigeonhole in the Town Hall (for all the world like a gallery box office), I was told, arbitrarily and disdainfully, by an official: 'You want us to send you down to London and you've got nothing but Art and English Language at O Level! You'll stay i' Bradford.' There was, nonetheless, a certain charm in being a drama student in Bradford, carrying a bag containing ballet shoes, the Complete Works and the Oxford Book of English Verse uphill in the narrow workaday canyons of Little Germany, underneath the bales of wool swinging out from the grim, velvet-black warehouses; the soot in the air and on the masonry created the unlovable, archetypal 'dark satanic' – inconceivable that the area would ever be scoured honey-coloured and developed as luxury apartments.

Esmé Church, the School's founding principal, had the status of a minor goddess in Chapel Street, and no wonder: she had been a West End and classical actress for years – not a star, but she had directed the famous Edith Evans-Michael Redgrave *As You Like It*; acted with and directed Laurence Olivier; and run the Old Vic School of Acting. And in 1934 she appeared alongside Ivor Novello and Fay Compton in Basil Dean's film version of *Autumn Crocus*. She'd toured the North during the war when the Old Vic Company was avoiding the bombs and taking the classics to remote industrial and mining towns. Peace came, she arrived at a certain age and, with her designer Molly McArthur, bought a part-Elizabethan, part-Georgian farmhouse in the dales outside Bradford on an old Roman road (they had been delighted to find Roman coins in their garden).

Esmé Church in the 1930s.

Amazingly Esmé assumed the professional directorship of the amateur Civic, and from this connection developed the Theatre School, partly funded, it was thought, by friends such as Edith Evans and Lewis Casson, and reliant too on new grants available to full-time students wanting to be professional. Eventually the joint operation of separate interests foundered and Esmé and Molly broke with the amateurs, sacrificing the use of their theatre to set up shop in a tiny terrace cottage, number 26 Chapel Street.

Esmé Church and John Laurie in Ibsen's *The Vikings at Helgeland*, Old Vic, 1928.

At the Northern Theatre School, within the limitations set by the willowy frame of a boy still in his late teens, I had aspired not merely to play kings and princes but to the protean, to transformation. I learnt a fresh Shakespeare speech and a poem every week to recite from the far end of the upper ex-wool-sorting room, and we did sight-reading sessions from the Oxford Book of English Verse. We did choral singing and I even got free extra tuition singing Lieder. The famous movement guru Rudolf Laban taught at the Theatre School; I missed him by a term, but studied with his young assistant Geraldine Stephenson.

41

I worked enthusiastically in the free-movement classes in adjacent Cater Street where we were encouraged to embody everything – earth, fire, air and water, a moment in the life of a gnat, an autumn leaf in the wind, the beginning of Time – all to the accompaniment of evocative études on the piano by a good pianist who impressed us one morning by doing a solo concert live from Leeds on the BBC Home Service. My leviathan won special praise: I came round a corner, as from behind a boulder. Our teacher, Doris McBride, had been with the Ballet Rambert corps de ballet. She was now in her fifties, verging on the portly and had iron-grey hair swept into a bun. I will never forget her first words to us on our first Monday morning as we gathered around the upright piano in that disused wool warehouse. Precisely, quietly and persuasively, she said just three words: 'Economy and selection.' This was paradoxically good advice before being asked to move freely.

I wonder if, the year before, I heard Edward Gordon Craig's radio talk on Isadora Duncan. He was eighty-one at the time and he was remembering her from almost fifty years before:

> She was speaking in her own language, not echoing any ballet master, and so she came to move as no one had ever seen anyone move before. ... Then again the music is off, and she runs from it – it runs after her then – for she has gone ahead of it. How is it we know she is speaking her own language? We know it, for we see her head, her hands, gently active, as are her feet, her whole person. ... She was telling to the air the very things we long to hear; and now we heard them, and this sent us all into an unusual state of joy, and I sat still and speechless.

I remember Doris McBride attempting, once and only once, to get us to do something that was undoubtedly inspired by Isadora Duncan – a kind of Bacchanalian procession, or progression rather; a frieze, that's how I thought of it, for that was the visual reference I'm certain she gave us, otherwise why would I still recall, from a morning fifty-six years ago in Cater Street, a vision of robed figures in marble bas-relief? I had already played Talthybius in a Sunday-night staging of Euripides' *The Trojan Women* at the Civic, but this was going to be much more challenging.

Miss McBride demonstrated a little and I formulated another impression to add to attic shapes in fixed stone and fair attitudes, that of the girls of her Greek dance class in Leeds, rather practised, I fancied, at the sort of thing she tried to elicit from us, as she evoked something of the asexual ecstasy in movement. Perhaps she was remembering the notices of the special dance performance given at the Scala in 1927 by the Ginner-Mawer School, from which she had graduated:

> The various Greek dances called 'To Persephone,' 'Nike,' 'Menades' (arranged by Miss Doris McBride) ... attained a rare poetic beauty ... a most artistic performance, several of the

items of which should not be out of place in the better-class variety theatres.[2]

One of Miss McBride's young pupils in 1927 was ten-year-old Wendy Toye, who, the year before, had danced before Diaghilev at the Palladium in a ballet she herself had choreographed to the music of Scarlatti, and won a Charleston competition at the Albert Hall, judged by Fred Astaire. The year before that, she had led the almost blind and deaf Ellen Terry onto the stage in Walter de la Mare's *Crossings*, Terry's very last play, squeezing the old lady's hand when it was time for her to speak.

On this particular Monday morning in 1953, something seemed to demand us going round in a large circle, or we wouldn't have far enough to go. But where were we going and what were we going to do when we got there? I knew that these were not questions to be voiced, and that alcohol and fertility were best kept out of the equation. So there I was, probably the sole male in the class, in my ballet shoes and white shorts, trying to concentrate not on the where or the why, but the magic Bacchanalian *how*, sensing that what was needed was a graceful organized chaos, and that, if we could have done it in slow motion (and long robes), it would have been more like the museum frieze in action we all envisaged – or Isadora's classical frieze come to life. As it was, the tumbling speed and the sound of our feet on the floor unavoidably created the general effect of a mad dash – like a sales queue let loose.

I suppose it did at least set my mind going. When I came to direct the chorus in Euripides' *Bacchae* in 1974, I already knew at first hand some of the difficulties involved. In fact, I had two stabs at it, demanding a completely new design and designer for our Wimbledon season. Harold Hobson's first review was derisory (all the sensuality of a bra advert, I think he pronounced), but his second review seemed to suggest I had triumphantly cracked the most difficult of Greek tragedies! In a sudden connective afterthought, I realize that, in my revised production, when Pentheus, dressed in feminine garb, began his fateful pilgrimage to Mount Cithaeron to the music of Pink Floyd, all the movement was in slow motion. Second time lucky with the spirit of ancient Greece. But I feel sure Miss McBride essayed the Bacchanal with us but once.

On Friday mornings we attempted ballet. We had no barre, only a chair back each to hold onto. I had been hopeless at French at school and the ballet terms were more challenging than the positions and the sequences themselves. The idea was that, however unsuited to ballet we were, we would develop strength and dexterity, poise and style. To the same end we had tumbling and fencing on Wednesday nights. Lectures in the history of drama from Leeds University's Department of Extra-Mural Studies were held on Thursday evenings in the tiny front room of the School's headquarters, a little terrace cottage, cowering in the shadow of the warehouse opposite. The room

---

[2] *The Stage*, 7 July 1927.

had only two features, a sombre hand-painted oriental screen fixed to one wall, and a two-bar electric heater built into the chimney piece opposite. Over the period of three years, a series of lecturers spoke to us on everything from the Greeks to the plays of Sartre and T. S. Eliot, and I even managed to read a few of them.

I had grown away from my school friends, but had made no new male friends. In fact, for two whole terms, I was the only boy in my class. Gradually I came to spend a lot of time with one of my classmates, a New Zealander, in her bedsit, just up the hill from where Delius was born; she was

Louise and I in Chapel Street.

the girl I would subsequently marry. Louise Harris was twenty-two, gamine, lithesome, and somehow contrived to have a suntan most of the year – in Bradford! She was the recipient of an arts bursary granted her by the New Zealand government and had an English degree from the University of Otago, so she might be said to have had an academic influence on me, as well as awakening me in other, less cerebral ways.

At the weekends Louise regularly escaped Bradford by train to meet friends in London and to visit a voice teacher in Kensington with the aim of eradicating her antipodean accent. The eradication of my northern accent was almost entirely in the hands of the BBC and my own determination. On Saturdays I went alone to the Leeds Grand to see the matinée of whatever West End play was on its pre-London tour. I was deeply impressed by Terence Rattigan's *Separate Tables* and realized, at a post-West End tour matinée of *An Evening with Beatrice Lillie*, the limitations of a thin Leeds matinée audience, as I am sure she did. Sundays I had my poem and Shakespeare soliloquy to polish ready for Monday morning. I still went to Chapel occasionally, though I was already, at seventeen, harbouring Anglican leanings. At home afterwards in the evening I listened to the Palm Court Orchestra in the 'Grand Hotel' programmes on the wireless.

When I was still seventeen, one of the older students took me to Leeds City Varieties, down the cobbled back street of Swan Street, to see the first house, shabby and very sparse. Like Wilton's Music Hall in London, the City Varieties, built in 1865, is a rare surviving example of a Victorian music hall; it is currently 'being restored to its former glory'. The show may have been *We Couldn't Wear Less*, or possibly *A Look at Bedtime*. On stage, a rather stout middle-aged woman, wearing an exaggerated pinstripe suit and trilby, and smoking a cigar, announced a series of tableaux, 'Little Miss Muffet'.

The pink curtains parted to reveal an unclothed young lady sitting on a stool, frozen in an attitude of eating her curds and whey; when a spider jerked down beside her from the flies, she moved not a muscle, being constrained by the Lord Chamberlain. It was a thin house, as I say, and behind us in the stalls were two women who had come in from shopping, nursing bulging brown paper bags on their knees.

The act continued; I was rather transfixed to see my first naked lady, especially as she was lit in pink light and might have had on pink body make-up. She was called Peaches Page. The climax came as our compère announced, after a particularly meaningful draw on her cigar, 'Submission': the pink curtains swept open to reveal a flight of steps down which Miss Page was beautifully draped in a decidedly classical position, head nearest the footlights, her hair trailing towards us and her legs discreetly soaring away upstairs. The carrier bags behind us crinkled agitatedly, and one woman said, quite clearly to the other, 'Ooh, if I 'ad a gun I'd shoot 'er.'

Our drama tutors were an odd assortment of failed performers, but none the worse for that. Charlie or, as he preferred, Charles Gordon was a good-natured, heavily built and ungainly baritone who had had a concert career in Australia and a nebulous period on the British stage. He taught voice by the effective mumbo-jumbo method; we each had to imagine a metal

Our Theatre School class.

bow of steel coming out of our foreheads, holding its tension as it curved down to attach to our diaphragms. The sound, originating from the forehead, travelled down this bow to resonate and be supported by the diaphragm. The vocal chords and the throat were never mentioned: a dangerous source of the wrong kind of tension, we gathered. The idea was to train us up to be effortlessly audible in the large theatres we would be touring to in our third year and we started most days with half an hour of his breathing and vocal exercises. It was left up to us to discover how this vocal technique was to be adapted to the drawing-room naturalism we were destined to attempt in weekly rep.

Nor was Charlie in his element advising on the interpretation of our Shakespearean speeches. One sensed that he quickly ran out of ideas and would fall back on jokes and stories about Eleanora Duse, Sarah Bernhardt and Henry Irving, usually variants of the mystic hold they had over their audiences, emanating from their diaphragms; I used to find these accounts strangely compelling. Once a week we had field trips to read one-act plays or single acts from full-length plays to the Shipley Blind Institute. I read Ivor Novello's part in *Autumn Crocus* and stuck to what I believed was my subtly erotic Novello allure, whilst Charlie tried to make it all upward inflections and ebullience.

Each week he invited Louise and me to the front room of his terrace residence in Manningham, where he eked out his income by having two or three students as lodgers. Here we had free singing lessons. Schubert songs on the radio transport me back to these evenings and I realize how many of these beautiful love songs I sang – in English, of course – to his accompaniment, my voice not long recovered from the loss of its 'Oh! For the wings of a dove' status. After the heartache of *Winterreise*, I always sang that famous drinking song based on Ludwig Fischer's 'Im tiefen Keller sitz' ich hier':

> My lodging is a cellar here
> Upon a cask I am seated
> The choicest wines my heart can cheer
> To me is freely meted
> The cellar man deserves my praise
> From duty never shrinking
> He deftly fills the glass I raise
> When drinking, drinking, drinking.

Its final descending 'drinkings' and 'D, R, I, N, K, I, N – Geee' quite made me forget my seventeen-year-old freshness and twenty-nine-inch waist; I became a portly bass on a European concert platform.

The climax of these evenings was the tea and homemade cake as we listened to the intimate, sophisticated satire of Peter Ustinov and Peter Jones in their BBC Home Service programme *In All Directions*. Not long ago I happened to tune in to BBC Radio 7 and instantly recognized that I was listening to one of these fifty-five-year-old programmes for the first time since Charlie Gordon's front room. One item was a surreal trip around various departments of Broadcasting House. In another, Ustinov and Jones played elderly women, Bloomsbury types, as I recall, and there was the usual rambling conversation between the two East End spivs, Morris and Dudley Grosvenor. There were also the witty and elegant musical interludes provided by a live quartet. Sometimes we would listen to another classic of the period, the Third Programme's Hilda Tablet sagas, whose principal satirical targets were the composers Dame Ethel Smyth and Elisabeth Lutyens. This programme made us feel completely cosmopolitan and in the know in that forgotten corner of Bradford's suburbia.

Charlie's piano was in the recess to the left of his fireplace, and to the left of the piano was a chest of drawers, the bottom one stuffed with his newspaper cuttings; I recall him opening it but once to show us an Australian review, with photograph, of a Lieder recital he had given. He kept mum about his career in light music, apart from a hint that he had appeared in the musical comedy *1066 and All That*. Charlie wasn't to know that, one day, there would be a virtual bottom drawer in which, out of curiosity, it would be possible to rummage at will without moving from one's own fireside, and to learn for exactly how long he had hung onto his supporting chorus parts in *1066 and All That*, and how uneasy, sometimes, might have lain the head that wore his particular crown. In January 1938, he announced in *The Stage* that he had just completed 1,066 performances in *1066*, having been in the piece since its premiere in 1935, and being the sole survivor of the original cast – thus demonstrating his need to hang onto secure employment whilst he got it. The cyberspace bottom drawer also reveals Charlie's career in campanology; in *Stage* adverts of the 1920s and 30s, he is billed as 'The Only Baritone with a Handbell and Chime Musical Specialty' or simply 'Monarch of the Bells', proclamations followed with poignant frequency by 'Vacant for Summer'.

Some time in the mid-60s, I asked Charlie to give me a lesson before a musical audition for *The Pajama Game*. Louise and I took our son David, when he was just walking, to see Charlie in a little flat he had somewhere in West London. Charlie, a lifelong bachelor, had no experience of children and couldn't understand why we weren't able to stop David from wanting to play with the knick-knacks on his coffee table.

Charlie must have been at least sixty when he taught me at the Northern Theatre School. I don't know how you spin out speech-teaching over a two-year course, unless you are a sophisticate and teach 'interpretation'; no wonder Charlie struggled a bit and took to rehearsing us in opera, namely *The Marriage of Figaro*. I did the famous drill aria with Cherubino (Juliet Cooke, our only decent female singing voice). Esmé's set and costume designer, Molly MacArthur, astonished me by saying that I had captured the right style. We had never considered the performance style, and if I had sung stylishly it was as much to do with untutored instinct and the rigours of Miss MacBride's ballet classes as anything, but I was surprised, too, by the applause the number drew from the watching second-year students.

With Juliet Cooke in a one-act play we did in our second year.

I have met some brilliant speech teachers since those days, particularly those who teach accents and dialect. I have also, of course, met some less than brilliant ones. The man who coached Olivier, helping him to lower his speech for Othello, reputedly by an octave, never impressed me, especially when we had to find a piece of wall to press our lower backs against by bending our knees slightly and then do HAs and Hummms. Another time I woke up to hear a chain-smoking speech specialist, addressing the entire National Theatre Company in the stalls, say in her quiet, deep, rounded tones, 'Remember that an excess of chest

47

tone creates a soporific effect.' Much later I had to ask, on the stage of the Royal Shakespeare Theatre, 'I'm sorry, but I am pushing sixty – what ARE we doing on our hands and knees chanting in chorus, exaggeratedly emphasizing the consonants of "Ye elves of hills, brooks, standing lakes, and groves"?'

Margaret, Mrs Jowett, also taught voice and was the antidote to Charlie. Her best phrase was 'Do it on a quiet think' and her physical credo was that we should all 'lift the egg out of the egg cup', meaning that the upper part of the body should sit very lightly on the hips. She was plain, bespectacled and slightly stout, completely untheatrical and suburban, but she combined the parochial with the mystical. She had what I would call a Zen attitude to performance. I used to enjoy her Friday mornings after ballet when we read in turn at sight, from the Oxford Book of English Verse, Edmund Spencer's *Prothalamion* and *Epithalamion*, but I don't recall being challenged by the moderns. On Sundays she held musical evenings for the students in her home, very near the town centre.

We have it from a Bradfordian, J. B. Priestley, writing in his classic travelogue *English Journey*, that there was nothing to do in Bradford on a Sunday evening apart from 'monkey-parading' and listening to the Salvation Army Band, whilst waiting for the pubs to open. That was in 1934; in the early 50s it was no different, despite Priestley's plea, in his immediately influential book, for a non-Sabbatarian town fit for a son or daughter to work in away from home: 'Please give me … a wicked wide-open city, busy dishonouring its Sabbath, blazing with lights on Sunday evening, with concerts, theatre, cinemas, dance halls, restaurants, in full naughty swing. There I could trust my innocent child. But not – oh, never – in this barbaric gloom and boredom.'

Somehow my innocence stayed intact. At least once I remember wandering into town and listening to the Salvation Army Band. There was a big, spare, cinder-covered piece of waste in the centre of Bradford; who knows what decent Victorian buildings had been demolished to create it, or why? There were one or two cars parked in it, but it served as a sort of desultory speaker's corner. Faced with such limited cultural offerings, you'd have thought that I would have jumped at the chance of musical evenings at the home of Mrs Jowett, but they were oddly constrained occasions with a handful of second- and sometimes even third-year students escaping from their digs for tea and sandwiches and choral singing of pieces they knew and I didn't. I attended no more than twice.

Alone amongst our teachers, Mrs Jowett brought no whiff of the professional theatre. Her elderly husband was the organist at a local church. Now I think of it, I don't believe I ever saw her laugh, but a sense of clubby irony amongst the students, or even suppressed laughter, seemed not far away. There was a baby grand in the window bay of her austere, quite expansive but cheerless front room, a room I had passed many times without realizing on the top of a tram on the way to school along Easby Road – it was near her house, three years earlier, that I had taken the tram-top decision to be intelligent. Frail Mr Jowett was prevailed upon by his wife to play Beethoven's *Moonlight Sonata*. 'You've done it again, Freddie,' she said afterwards, but one felt that we might have heard his last faltering attempt. In fact, he died soon afterwards.

At the first class she took, following his demise, she wore a black skirt and a purple jumper. She had brought a pianist with her. Freddie's death was not referred to, but she addressed us on the subject of the voice as an instrument having sometimes to rise above … how she put it I can't recall; it was her high Zen style we witnessed that morning and, no doubt, she was mindfully living in the moment as she warned us of our spirit sometimes causing us to sing flat. Then she sang to us, in a firm voice, a defiant avowal of faith, 'I know that my Redeemer liveth' from the *Messiah*. She sang it slightly sharp.

Miss Sugden, of Sugden's Flour (a local firm), had a cosmopolitan air and a theatrical upper-class manner, was always well turned out and, at fifty, proud of her good legs and slim figure. She was not averse to demonstrating how West End acting should go, though her credentials, apart from a good finishing school and service as an officer in the WAAFS, were doubtful. She taught us at least once a week and was also the tour manager of the Northern Children's Theatre, Esmé Church's pride and joy, which she founded in 1946 using her final-year students. One day, after a Children's Theatre performance, Miss Sugden came into the dressing room and told me, 'People are noticing a quality.' The following year, having become a conscientious objector during my period of National Service, I received a searing letter of disapproval from her when I was confined to the guardroom and refusing to wear uniform.

The only genuine West End visitor to Chapel Street in my student days was the desiccated Anglican E. Martin Browne, director of T. S. Eliot's plays and the revived York Mystery Cycle. The whole school participated in his first two revivals of the Mystery Plays at the 1951 and 1954 York Festivals, Esmé herself playing Mary Cleophas. On the latter occasion, I played the part of a Jewish soldier. I think I may have mocked the professional Jesus of Joseph O'Connor, and possibly had a line; I certainly remember carrying a banner and Martin Browne's repeated rehearsal cry, 'Back on the banners.'

The second-year boys were all soldiers and palm-bearers. We were arranged by Geraldine Stephenson as group leaders in amongst the amateur crowd. The boys were bad souls, too, or rather they were demons choreographed to carry screaming bad souls into the jaws of Hell stage left. I was a good soul, so no athletic carrying on, or carrying off, in black tights; instead I made a smooth ascent up the uneven wooden staircase to the top of the ruins of St Mary's Abbey, white-robed and with my arms fixed in an aspirational, asymmetric, reaching adoration gesture. This was somewhat tricky with John Westbrook, in golden chainmail (knitted string) as

Archangel Michael, appearing in a spotlight on the topmost crag of the ruins stage right, as O'Connor declaimed:

> Michael, my angel, here with speed and guard this fiend that he not flit
> And, Devil, I command thee go down into thy cell where thou shalt sit.

John van Eyssen was the rather dashing professional Lucifer, with a beautiful lady friend in evidence (Joseph, by contrast, seemed restrained and celibate). Then the recoding of a heavenly piece of choral music helped us to negotiate our smooth, spiritual ascent into Heaven.

A nineteen-year-old local actress, by the name of Judith Dench, played the Angel at the tomb of the Resurrection. I saw the next cycle in 1957 when Judi had graduated to playing a gracefully refined, almost Pre-Raphaelite Virgin Mary, and her father, Dr Reginald Dench, was very convincing on the aforementioned steps in the Abraham and Isaac scene, which made sense and was mythically moving in a way I had never found before, nor since.

Back in Bradford, Browne watched some of our class work and complimented us on our movement, but said our use of the spoken word needed more thought. He then proceeded to read us a bit of dialogue from Eliot's *The Cocktail Party*, including the lines: 'And this is the first time I've ever seen you without Lavinia / Except for the time she got locked in the lavatory / And couldn't get out.' I remember Louise being very scornful afterwards, deriding the reading and the writing itself as precious and bloodless. There was no hope of seeing *The Cocktail Party* at Bradford's Prince's Theatre performed by Harry Hanson's Famous Court Players, even though it was a 'West End Success', but, of course, the amateurs at the Civic did it.

When the weekly rep at Halifax needed to swell their ranks to stage Daphne du Maurier's *Rebecca*, I was one of Esmé's students to leave the rigours of Chapel Street at the tender age of seventeen and enter a professional theatre's stage door for the first time, my task to convince, in the smallest part, that I was Frith, the white-haired butler of Manderley. The first morning's rehearsal was a question of getting through the play, no questions asked, as an act not of investigation but familiarization, following the West End moves as marked, because, of course, one was going to discard the book the next morning and 'act' the first act, not touching it again until the run-through of the whole play on Saturday morning.

My first real shock that morning was seeing the actress playing the second Mrs de Winter holding the French's Acting Edition in one hand, giving very little expression to the lines, and perfunctorily marking putting flowers in a vase with the other.

The following Monday morning there arrived by train a stiff white shirt and one wing collar, and a wig in a box from London's 'Wigs by "Bert"', or possibly Madame Gustave of Long Acre, in time for the afternoon dress rehearsal. Nobody advised or assisted me with my make-up, which came out of my own cigar boxful of Leichner that had made me feel so professional when I played my first parts at the Civic as an amateur. Wigs in those day, hired rep wigs, had the old-fashioned 'skin piece' that came halfway down the forehead and had to be made up to match, no doubt with wrinkles in Frith's case.

I also did a play at York, while still at theatre school, rehearsing a small part in a nautical light comedy and going round with the young ASM, borrowing furniture from shops for the set. That was the usual practice in rep; the shop got a credit in the programme, nothing more. I used to break off from dressing and making up to go round and do the calls: 'A quarter of an hour please!' Sometimes I added: 'Five minutes late!' I was hopeless at, and mystified by, the duties that the real ASM performed, though he seemed to have ample time to walk about the town and chat animatedly to me. In the wings one night, I made some mock-innocent remark, purporting not to understand a particular double entendre. The rather raddled actor in his late thirties, standing nearby, said, 'You've lived – I can tell by your eyes.'

Esmé and Molly rarely taught. The third-year touring company absorbed most of their time, though Esmé landed a part in Tyrone Guthrie's West End production of Thornton Wilder's *The Matchmaker*, which went to Broadway and she with it. One idiosyncrasy Esmé shared with Guthrie was a protracted and pregnant sniff, an impressive inhalation of breath by way of an overture to her pronouncements. The moment when I really felt I had missed the best was when I met Ruth Gordon in New York in 1982 during the run of *Nicholas Nickleby*. She said that everybody in *The Matchmaker* enjoyed Esmé's classes in Shakespeare, including some of the stagehands; they called it 'the University of Broadway'.

Esmé only gave us post-mortems after our end-of-term shows: we hung on every word. Once we spent two mornings working through *The Merchant of Venice*, as if she were mapping out a production; it came alive instantly. I watched her suggest the moves, moods and inflections to not specially promising students, but the ghost of an old, real Old Vic production seemed to hover over the Cater Street rehearsal-room floor. I recall a similar experience during the one make-up class Molly gave in the dingy front 'parlour' of number 26. She demonstrated on Louise, transforming her into an elfin Titania with the smell of the wood outside a Warwickshire Athens about her and a whiff of the Waterloo Road. One day Esmé took me aside gently to admonish me for yawning. I began to apologize, but she said, 'No, no, it is the lack of sleep I'm concerned about' (I was spending a lot of time with Titania). 'You must take care and not jeopardize your work. You see, you are one of those students who is going places.' I was thrilled by her use of the Americanism: its incongruity within the setting of her magisterial Edwardian English lent the romantic yet hard ring of show-business currency.

I discovered Molly's attitude to Bradford was romantic. One day she was working on one of my costumes at a fitting in her workshop, a brick extension at the back of number 26, in which even the scenery for the plays, two each year, was made. Back in her Old Vic days, she had created the Watteau-inspired costumes and settings for the Evans-Redgrave *As You Like It*. Molly was diminutive with almost white hair and black eyebrows. She always wore a sort of artist's felt hat, topcoat and longish skirt. As usual, she had a cigarette constantly in her mouth and, as she looked up at me, the smoke curled into her eyes from a long column of ash, always threatening to break off and spoil the costume, though it never did. Someone made a disparaging remark about Bradford. Probably me. 'I love it', I was astonished to hear her say. 'It's like Brussels.' The 60s mania for demolition and disastrous redevelopment had not yet struck.

The romance of the plays we did on tour for Moss Empires Theatres, which were full of excited schoolchildren, was not diminished by the fact that we hauled the scenery in and out of railway trucks on sidings, in and out of lorries, and in and out of numerous dock doors. We learnt the ropes, literally, in countless fly galleries. Nostalgia being what it is, I long to be in the thick of it all again – perhaps just for a day. 'Ee lad,' my Auntie Ethel used to say, 'if only I was your age, knowing what I know now.' Ee lad, if only I was the age I was, knowing and believing what I knew and believed then. In our second show, *The Dancing Master's Kit*, which Molly had written under her married name, I played an old dancing master at the time of the French Revolution, a young man at a ball, and a gardener's boy who became a harlequin in a pantomime. With the aid of coconut shells against the brick wall in the wings, I made the sound of horses' hooves to accompany my own elopement during the ball, whilst starting my quick change from the Byronic white breeches and blue tailcoat Molly had moulded on me into my harlequin costume. A true marriage of industry and art.

The cast of our second play for the Northern Children's Theatre, *The Dancing Master's Kit*. Louise and I are in the foreground; I am dressed as Harlequin. John Pickles is on the left in evening dress; he was to get me my first West End part in Bill Naughton's *All in Good Time*.

I can't imagine what my life would have been like if I had gone to a London drama school. Had I gone to RADA and flourished, I might have won a medal, got a posh rep contract or at least picked up sufficient savvy and a good agent. Instead, I found a dear friend and honorary 'aunt' in Winnie Hodgkinson. She and her husband Joe, who was to become the Arts Council's Director of Drama, were Louise and my patrons. Winnie was our enthusiastic, eccentric first-year acting tutor, and didn't let us touch a script until the third term. We improvised our own playlets or did stylized mimes to border ballads like 'The Twa Sisters', taking turns at action and recited narration. Amongst the many improvisations I remember from these classes was one about a shipwreck we called 'The Open Boat', the whole thing taking place in a huddle on the grimy floor cloth.

A lesson in mime.

The only other boy having dropped out, I was all the noble wooers for a time. Winnie was keen to stretch me beyond the Ariels and Marchbanks, as it were, and I think was concerned that I was on the cusp of effeminacy. When we finally got onto doing plays, she cast me as the heavy husband, Sir Harry Sim ('of a pleasant rotundity with a thick red neck'), in J. M. Barrie's *The Twelve-Pound Look*. In this one-act curtain-raiser, I had the unnerving experience of discovering that the typist (or typewriter, as they were then called), sent by an agency to assist me with my correspondence, was none other than the first wife who deserted me for the independence I was too possessive and pompous to allow her. The twelve pounds is what she saved to buy the typewriter and thus her emancipation.

Winnie had wanted to be an actress herself, but said her voice – thin and slightly high – was against it. She had worked at the Old Vic School, but I recall her saying that she had to carry the Vic-Wells Ballet wages from the bank across London to Sadler's Wells Theatre. She knew Ninette de Valois;

in fact, she and Joe knew everybody, even if there was something scatty and amateur about her (though her most damning word was 'amateur'), even as she was setting the highest standards. Winnie was incapable of giving one the kind of practical acting tips some teachers insisted on dispensing, which depended on one's own taste and emotional wisdom as much as theirs. However, she did give us a prophetic piece of advice one day, telling us that the theatre was changing and that actors were going to have to be able to be acrobatic, to sing, dance, mime and play instruments.

In my case, it took about eight years for Winnie's prophecy to be fulfilled. For the most part, in my first jobs I disported myself in tatty provincial copies of West End drawing-room settings, with an occasional 'hall in the castle' or battlefield in Shakespeare. But even in such uninspiring theatrical circumstances, I came to appreciate the benefits of my early training in free movement. In weekly rep I was to discover the surprising physicality involved in obeying 'simple' stage directions, such as *Enter* or *moves down R.*, and in handling the standard drawing-room props of cigarette cases and soda siphons. I also realized that to find oneself effortlessly with one's weight on the correct foot, to be able instinctively to know what to do – and more importantly what not to do – with one's hands, to act with one's whole body and soul within the elegant confines of high comedy, such as Wilde's, was to be 'bounded in a nutshell and count oneself a king of infinite space'.

Chapel Street

A Charlie Chaplin corner, Chapel Street
Where yarns theatrical and woollen meet
An upper room where once raw wool was sorted
Raw actors such as I was there cavorted.
(The building's number and my age seventeen
Oh to be so innocent and green)
An ill assorted batch, uneven blend
In turn soliloquizing from the end
The draughty end without the small gas fire
Or singing as an undistinguished choir
Descanting so plangently upon
The river with Orlando Gibbons' swan
Flicking gliding punching slashing floating
À la Laban; then for feelings groping
Improvising turbulent emotion
In an open boat upon an ocean
Drifting on the dusty floor's stage cloth
Imitate the tiger and the moth
Spout at sight the Oxford Book of Verse
Fear and love the magic word 'rehearse'
Adolescence striving to evince
Commoner and clown and tragic prince
Discovering the mystery I AM
In silent streets long after the last tram
Hours of youth to squander while you sleep
Life to learn that time's not yours to keep.

Chapter 6

Keeping it West End

*The English theatre has a wonderful ability to
encourage you to collude with your own disappearance.*

Peter Gill

*I wanted to change the attitude of the public towards the
theatre. All I did was to change the attitude of the
theatre towards the public.*

George Devine

Even when I took the decision to risk the weekly outlay involved in renting a
TV set, which was not until 1963 – that momentous year for Philip Larkin – I
can remember the man who installed it brushing aside my qualms at the
financial liability, 'You may as well give up altogether if you're worried,' he
said.

I am sure I never watched *Top of the Pops* for more than the number of
seconds it took to turn it off. And it was not until 1966 that I bought *my* first
Beatles LP, *Revolver*, on the strength of the novel 'classical' use of a violin in
'Eleanor Rigby' and a trumpet in 'Penny Lane'. All the more remarkable
then that, without a Beatles number to be heard and nothing but electric
guitars, saxophones, keyboard and drum kit blasting out an evening of 50s
and 60s Rock and Roll, I was to be found on my feet, swaying and clapping,
only a week ago at the Playhouse.

The hero of *Dreamboats and Petticoats* is a shy schoolboy dealing with
O-Levels and acne (we have to imagine the latter! In fact he is fresh-faced as
well as very good looking). He has an Estuary accent, complete with Fs for
Ths, but when he bursts into song he enters another language entirely,
another state of being in fact – confident, passionate (even in his laments
about being unloved), from the heart and, of course, American. The audience
almost takes the transformation of his personality for granted – after all, how
else would you sing 'Do You Wanna Dance?' or 'Dream Baby Dream'?

People still express surprise that I ever had a broad, working-class
Bradford accent, but, as a teenager myself, I simply acquired another voice to
'sing' with, and since it was a speaking voice, I spoke with it in life as well as
on the stage. The great teenage liberation of the 50s and 60s was all about
utterance as working-class boys and girls were released into song and the
romance of the classless American idiom and, on a less noticeable scale,
countless provincial working-class acting students learnt the West End Drawl

56

and the heroic, noble way of handling verse – their passport into 'The Profession' and, in all but exceptional cases, insecurity and unemployment.

Drawing another arc between the early 50s and the present, two days ago I sat in an orchestra stall at the National Theatre, watching entranced Terence Rattigan's *After the Dance* and, if it was not an utterly perfect performance, it seemed to have all the verities on so many levels – in the writing, staging and acting – the sort of spellbinding theatrical quality I began to imagine I had not witnessed, and had been missing, since I saw the pre-West End tour of Rattigan's *Separate Tables* in Leeds in 1954 – with Margaret Leighton and Eric Portman in the leading roles. Almost straightaway I was running into other veteran theatre people who had not felt spellbound and were indeed quite angry at the failure they perceived – a failure of style. This has made me wonder what we mean, or ever meant, by 'West End', a phenomenon of which Rattigan was for so long the apotheosis. An impossible thing to define: 'Oh, Noël, the West End isn't what it was,' declared a party guest to Coward in the early 60s. 'It isn't,' The Master replied, 'but then – it never was.'

My third instance is taken from what we call 'real life'. I dropped in at a lunchtime flat-warming party before I went to the Rattigan matinée. My hostess had finally got her divorce, was looking a little older than when I had last seen her, but well, slimmer, beautifully dressed. The immaculate flat was charming and through French windows a string trio was playing in the garden 'Ain't misbehavin' … all by myself'. I had heard tell of some of the history, the pain that was nowhere in evidence in this delightful setting and the party chitchat – a perfect starting point, or final tableau, for a play by Rattigan.

As I set off for the South Bank, I mused on the words of General Sir David Richards after seeing, less than a mile away in Kilburn, *Afghanistan: The Great Game*, which he described as 'fascinating, entertaining and historically accurate of Britain's involvement in Afghanistan since 1840. … Nothing learnt in the classroom will have the same subliminal effect as this. It is crucial that all of us out there have a more nuanced understanding of the historical background that got us to this point.' (*The Times*, 3 August 2010)

Certainly the West End, and the theatre beyond, is as broad if not broader a church than it was in my young day.

*   *   *

We London actors take it for granted now, but in the late 1950s and early 60s we were aware of there being a great breakthrough, of being increasingly let loose on a cornucopia of diverse styles such as no other age of actors in the long history of theatre had attempted. The world repertoire was fairly ransacked. An extraordinary development, in view of the miniature scale of what history claims to be *the* two seminal dramas of mid-twentieth-century London theatre: Samuel Beckett's famous tramps, at last imported from the theatres of Europe, and John Osborne's storm in a provincial attic flat. On one level, that of Samuel French's *Guide to Selecting Plays for Performance*, both were 'five actors, one set'.

A previous fellow drama student of mine, Ralph Broome, with whom I had acted in my professional debut at the first Ludlow Festival in 1956, performing Marlowe's *Edward II* in the castle keep, gave Osborne sanctuary in a Derby bedsit in the mid-50s, whilst they were working in weekly rep there. A year or so later, Ralph took himself to the Royal Court to see *Look Back in Anger* and was amazed to recognize every detail of his attic room in Derby – the water tank, the ironing board, the sound of church bells outside. Others no doubt recognized the dialogue. There was a story that one female audience member involuntarily said aloud, 'I never said that!'

All over the country underpaid, overworked actors were living in such rooms, trained to simulate quite another life in their evenings: tennis on green lawns, cocktails and witty repartee before dinner, for which, of course, you would dress. The possession of a dinner jacket for the rep actor of the 50s and early 60s was as staple a part of his equipment as his own tights, wig and spirit gum had been for the lowly touring Shakespearean at the turn of the century. One can imagine the young John Osborne in the wings of the old Derby Playhouse (a splendid Victorian house, designed by Frank Matcham and demolished in the 60s!), waiting to go on, poised by the fire bucket and the lighting stands outside the French window upright, trying to imagine a formal garden and a private income whilst nursing a burning desire to tell it as it really was, to launch into something shocking from one of his tirades back in the attic digs. Effectively he did. Jimmy Porter has his place in history.

The realities of 'let's pretend' in weekly rep were harsh, tawdry and hilarious by turns, with just enough residual 'theatre magic', enough absorption in the personal responsibility of keeping the ball in the air and the show on the road to make one feel alive. What one was doing mattered and might even have sometimes the faint but unmistakable sweet smell of success about it.

From a twentieth-first-century perspective, the rigours of weekly rep are tinged with a roseate nostalgia and denote a healthy, even halcyon theatrical climate. Allow me to quote you some statistics that are both pertinent and staggering. According to *The Stage Year Book* for 1953 – the year I entered drama school *and* made my weekly rep debut at Halifax on temporary loan from Esmé Church – no fewer than 124 theatres in Britain had permanent repertory companies. In addition, 66 travelling or seasonal companies presented summer rep at over 100 further venues – 224 repertory seasons – most of them operating for 52 weeks a year. As these figures illustrate, weekly rep, like the Northern Children's Theatre, is now, essentially, a vanished world.

In 1957, in search of an agent, I found myself with my back to the window in a tiny first-floor office in Rupert Street, Soho, only a few yards from the south side of Shaftesbury Avenue. Pressed against a radiator that was painted red, I was wedged in place by the end of the secretary's desk. She stopped typing and leant back as I auditioned for Vincent Shaw, whose desk I faced. It was an intimate space for Shakespeare, but I gave them my 'What must the king do now?' from *Richard II*, following it up with a speech from T. S. Eliot's *The Confidential Clerk*. No doubt I had bought a copy of Eliot's 1953 play because it had at least one long speech for Colby, the young clerk, that would make a good audition piece; modern plays seldom furnished one with such pieces. Straightaway Shaw said, 'Well you're obviously West End material and I'd like to represent you.' He kept me moderately busy in tatty weekly rep for some months.

First he got me a 'special week' playing a small part in Edgar Wallace's *The Case of the Frightened Lady* at the Connaught Theatre, Worthing, where the waspish director, Guy Vaesen, castigated me for playing a scene in profile, looking at the person I was speaking to. Clearly, he implied, I had no idea of strategies to share my performance full face with the audience, and I really think I might not have had, except I had done Esmé Church's costume plays to those vast audiences in the Moss Empires variety theatres and played Gaveston in *Edward II* in the open air at Ludlow Castle.

Over a drink in the bar of the Connaught, after the Monday opening night, the company manager, Melville Gillam, issued what I had been warned was his habitual injunction: 'Keep it West End.' I thought I knew what he meant, in terms of what we were to avoid; even at theatre school we had an expression to encapsulate a certain kind of acting, the antithesis of West End – 'reppy'. But I also knew just how far away we were from *getting* it West End – let alone keeping it there! Maintaining the West End Style was the fantasy of such companies, perhaps best epitomized by 'Harry Hanson's Famous Court Players'. The self-styled 'Woolworth of the profession', unapologetic purveyor of popular plays at popular prices, Hanson had companies up and down the country, playing twice nightly like the one at Bradford's Prince's Theatre, and they were always billed 'in a season of West End Successes'. Sets of French's Acting Editions of those plays were hired, with original moves noted and always a photograph of the set.

When I was in my early teens, Sylvia Melville was the leading lady in Bradford's weekly rep and I used to see her doing long seasons, practically year round at the Prince's. Her father, Fred D'Albert, had run a fit-up theatre in Selby. She and her husband, Martin Carroll, also in the company, were on a joint salary, less than they would have earned if they had been employed singly. They lived in a flat with their school-age daughter and had to go down to the landlady for hot water, which they carried back upstairs. When I later worked with Sylvia, she told me that, when she felt low, she would withdraw most of her savings from her Post Office book and walk round the town in her best coat. Then, at the end of the day, she would put all her savings back in the Post Office. She was a very sweet woman and Louise, my wife, became fond of her when they were in a company together.

I worked with her husband, too, in a dreadful Carl Clopet tour of *Charley's Aunt*, in which I played Jack Chesney. It was rumoured that Clopet sometimes helped out even with modern-dress wardrobe, which one provided oneself in rep and on his sort of tour. He had recently done a production of *The Grass is Greener* and said to his stage manager, 'Look, when that girl comes on in Act Two she's got to look like a million dollars; even if you have to go out and spend fifteen pounds.' Incidentally, I also played Jack Chesney for the Arthur Brough Players at the Leas Pavilion, Folkestone, which had institutionalized the Tea Matinée: the rows were thinned out and tables set with white cloths, and waitresses moved about serving tea during the action!

A decade or so later, when I was in *Rosencrantz and Guildenstern Are Dead* at the National Theatre, I was dressing for a performance one night and Graham Crowden read out to me an obituary from *The Stage* because he thought the career of the actress sounded so funny – the epitome of 'tat', as we used to call it:

> She made her debut at the age of one month, when she was tipped out of a basket in a farce entitled *Muldoon's Picnic*. She had her first speaking part at the age of five and continued to play in her father's company until she reached her early twenties, at Blackpool and St Anne's. ... For the past ten years she had spent her time in summer repertory seasons and should have appeared once again this year as Frank Marlborough's leading lady at the Spa Theatre, Bridlington.

When I looked, it was Sylvia's obituary.

My sister-in-law's grandmother would work all day at a mill and, once a week, washed the stone steps up to the gallery of the Prince's Theatre. Her husband had died when she was six months pregnant with Doreen's mother, and her widow's pension was ten shillings. For washing the gallery steps she was paid 1/6d. Decades later, from 1948, Doreen and my brother Bill would sit in the splendour of the Prince's dress circle every Saturday night to watch the first house of Harry Hanson's Court Players. The audience enjoyed watching their favourites every week in a reliable if unchallenging programme of domestic comedies and thrillers, but how they thought about the theatre was soon to change. Despite Hollywood's glamorous pervasiveness, and even the new realism of, for example, *On the Waterfront*, these spirited but inferior copies of West End plays presented by impecunious actors had held their own. By 1960, however, the elegant Prince's was scheduled for demolition. It had taken television to do it.

1957 was an eventful year, and included my marriage to Louise, a brief stint in National Service and a slightly longer stint in Wormwood Scrubs as a conscientious objector, followed by my first professional rep engagement at the Opera House in Scarborough. Scarborough's now famous theatre in the round had been founded in 1955 in the concert room of the public library. Alan Ayckbourn, three years my junior, was yet to emerge and make the seaside town the powerhouse, for forty years, of his plays which were to become West End, National Theatre or RSC hits. Fresh out of prison, and months away from my majority, I needed a rest cure combined with a job, and the seaside rep at Scarborough seemed a fair prescription. True, all the plays were rehearsed in a week, but the core programme of three plays was presented in rotation, so once the plays were on, one was free of the grind of rehearsal every morning on a darkened stage with the curtain down, and learning lines into the small hours. The play we started with, *Tell-Tale Murder*, lasted only a week, being deemed 'unsuitable for children'. The plot involved two old women, a house troubled with flies, and the presence of a body under the flagstones in an off-stage room. I only recall that there was a choice of two endings:

'We will have to spend the rest of our lives here … with him.'
or
'Only the flies know, and they won't tell.'

Come the dress rehearsal, I was faced with the mandatory drinks table for the first time in my career (and life), with its authentic assortment of glasses and decanters. Wearing my equally mandatory dinner jacket, I said to Jeffrey Dench, eight years my senior and similarly dressed, but wearing white grease paint in the hair on his temples, 'What'll you have, Father-in-Law?' 'Sherry' came the reply, and to his credit, he lifted his eyebrows only momentarily as I handed him a full brandy glass.

The director, Geoffrey Staines, shamed me at the note session, having already shown his impatience during the week with my wilder paraphrasings of the script. When it came to us doing the rather charming replacement play, *The Magic Cupboard*, Staines tried to give me a kind of halfwit characterization, which he illustrated by demonstrating how the character might go about sawing a piece of wood. I thought it wildly inappropriate and ignored it. At the dress rehearsal, I saw him trying to palm off the same piece of characterization, identically illustrated, on one of the stage-management boys who was playing a walk-on removal man. This was my introduction to the lowest common denominator in the hack rep director; I didn't know it, but there was even lower to come, especially in another seaside company.

I had been spoiled in Scarborough a couple of years earlier at a rather stimulating summer school I attended. The drama course was full of talentless amateurs, but Geraldine Stephenson, who had left Bradford to join Laban in the South West, was teaching, so I was happy to work with her again. The pioneering Stephen Joseph gave talks and demonstrations of his beloved Theatre-in-the-Round approach, and Robert Lang was amongst some students from Bristol Old Vic Theatre School whom we watched rehearse with their tutor. The artist in residence was the illustrious Victor Pasmore; L. A. G. Strong, the famous poet, essayist and novelist of the time, gave some witty and insightful talks about the creative process; and the course had a string orchestra, which was my introduction to the Brandenburg Concertos.

I remember Pasmore as a bearded presence accompanied by his comely wife of whom I had seen a nude study in pinks with yellow hair. He always looked serious, and now that I have discovered and read an interview he gave in 1960, chiefly about abstraction, I realize that if he had given us a talk, I wouldn't have understood a word of it – and am not sure that I would now. However, had I encountered him properly he would have been the first conscientious objector I had ever met. By contrast, I remember Strong as a smiling presence who gave us a charming talk about his writing and the mysterious sources of inspiration.

All this was far cry from the so-called Opera House. I knew all too well that to serve one's apprenticeship in most rep companies was to be in the Cinderella of the art of theatre, where you stayed amongst the ashes with no chance of the mice becoming white horses – unless you escaped.

During my imprisonment and while I was at Scarborough, Louise was with Lincoln rep. On 28 October 1957, Kenneth Tynan, then theatre critic of the *Observer*, turned up to see the rep at Lincoln's Theatre Royal. He wore a red velvet jacket. The play he had come to see was the premiere of Keith Gardner's *The Liberators*, a topical piece about the Hungarian Revolution. In the following Sunday's *Observer* Tynan singled out Lincoln, under its young director John Hale, as part of a mini-renaissance in provincial theatre. Hale had been a naval officer and, Louise told me, was prone to refer to the stage as 'on deck' and to be over keen on pace.

This evening I rang Louise in New Zealand to see if she remembered Tynan's visit. To my amazement, she had no recollection of the event at all, and found the idea bizarre, but we reminisced about our rep days, concurring, then selectively remembering often rather different things. We certainly remembered that we had spent a lot of time dashing about the country on Sunday trains to see each other and actually made love in the lavatory of a York to London express; although it may be ungallant to say it, I only remembered this occurrence on being reminded of it, but, I hasten to add, I do recall other trysts in similarly unorthodox circumstances.

Louise was rescued from Lincoln's weekly treadmill by the guest director Peter Coe, who introduced her to the comparative luxury of fortnightly rep at Ipswich. For a time, she was his favourite juvenile. Although, I blush to say, I never saw *Look Back in Anger* at the Royal Court, where it was frequently revived, I did see Louise in her slip at the ironing board as Alison at Ipswich. The male juvenile lead, Clinton Greyn, played Jimmy, and the audiences never quite trusted him again. Louise remembers the tut-tuts from the stalls at the sight of her in her slip, but in *Doctor in the House*, when one of the nurses crossed the room to comic effect in her skirt and bra, the audience roared with indulgent laughter.

Coe was a gentle, sensitive soul and a dab hand at Brechtianizing the superstructure. I was in his rather thrilling Ipswich *Moby Dick*, based on Orson Welles's London version. The proscenium curtain and pelmet were torn away, the footlights were removed and, in true Brechtian style, the lighting rig was completely exposed. This is commonplace now but was revolutionary then.[1] The imaginary ship and the whale appeared on a stark stage, bare to the back wall. We knew from Tynan's reviews that real Brechtian actors looked like people you saw at bus stops (or on whaling ships) and had faces like potatoes. Louise played the cabin boy and I was a non-speaking deckhand, praised by the manager for my mime of salt spray in the face when he was trying to soften the blow that there were no more parts for me. I stayed at Ipswich only for one more play that required extra numbers, *Henry IV, Part 1*, in which I took the part of Prince John. Coe attempted the battle scenes in Peking Opera style, having us trot about with flags to farcical effect.

To direct their production of *Rookery Nook*, Ipswich engaged David Stoll. He began by moving the furniture to create more acting space and giving the actors timing demonstrations, but most of all what struck me, having heard Louise's description of rehearsals, was how in performance he was of a different element from the other actors. I had already seen the famous Aldwych farceur, Ralph Lynn, in the pre-West End tour of his last West End appearance. He was like a feverish stick insect, and Stoll, who had understudied him for so long, was relatively calm, beatifically so, although the character is *in extremis* much of the time. He had a wonderful way, whilst somehow suggesting the *extremis*, of attending to the other performers when they spoke to him, and a deep charm and confidence as an actor, such as rep performers rarely ever had the time or space to achieve. He knew the play backwards, of course, but, with him, it was the familiarity that bred freshness.

We spent Christmas Day 1957 in the company of young Mary Miller, who had joined Ipswich rep, and her husband, a local doctor. They had taken under their wing three refugees from the Soviet clampdown on the Hungarian

---

[1] The elimination of footlights in favour of exposed overhead lighting did, however, have notable antecedents. In 1910, William Poel had installed front lighting in the balcony of His Majesty's Theatre for *The Two Gentlemen of Verona*, and Harley Granville-Barker, in his three Shakespearean productions at the Savoy Theatre between 1912 and 1914, replaced the footlights with a batten of 'torpedo' lamps mounted in view of the audience across the front of the dress circle. In the American theatre, experiments in front-of-house lighting occurred as early as 1879, the year Edison demonstrated his new incandescent light bulb. These were conducted by David Belasco at the San Francisco Grand Opera, using an old bulls-eye lantern from a locomotive to light the action of *The Passion Play*. With his electrician Louis Hartmann, he eventually developed the first incandescent spotlights. But one of the earliest and canniest uses of a spotlight was by Henry Irving at London's Lyceum; Percy Nash, Irving's stage manager from the time of *Robespierre*, recalled: 'A special operator always followed the chief's face with a small "pin" light of steel-blue; however dark the scene was you always saw Irving's face.' The now standardized FOH lighting rig can have its drawbacks: at the recent excellent production of *All My Sons* at the Apollo (I had purchased the last seat in the house on the last night), my view of the stage from the front row of the third gallery was dissected by a completely unused lighting bar left hanging at least a foot proud of the plasterwork.

revolution. The atmosphere was happy, but I was incredibly naïve or insensitive and talked about how impressed we had been by the Bolshoi Ballet's first visit to Covent Garden the year before. We'd not seen them in the flesh – it was the hottest ticket imaginable, the visit signifying a remarkable thawing of the Cold War – but we had managed to see the colour film shot during a performance, including various show pieces and the legendary Galina Ulanova as Giselle.

On a YouTube screen, I have just seen the scarlet curtain at Covent Garden, with its golden ERII, part and close on that Soviet visit of fifty-three years ago, and sat entranced, as I remember being entranced as a young man, by the unashamed high-nineteenth-century hokum of *Giselle*, pulling all the right sentimental strings, and dominated by the apparently frail figure of Ulanova of whom Margot Fonteyn declared, 'I have never seen another dancer with her liquid quality of movement, each step melting into the next with an inevitability that built its own tension. She symbolizes the triumph of Soviet ballet.' Ulanova was forty-six at the time and I noticed again how, on two occasions, she seems almost to fall into the wings down right with exhaustion, yet she is a completely credible young country girl. Compromised somewhat by my laptop, the music sounds sometimes gorgeously, jauntily vulgar as well as having a limped pathos. One marvels now at the monstrous artistic traditionalism, nay conservatism that Stalin had imposed, and that Khrushchev, who had denounced Stalin, subsequently presided over.

But I can still see a shadow over the Christmas table; it was just not possible to praise anything Soviet, even the delicate Ulanova, in the presence of these boys after what they had been through, though we only knew that they had left Hungary, nothing more. A dock strike had delayed the arrival of the Soviets' scenery, and redirected the plane conveying the dancers from Heathrow to a RAF Station at Marton. Ulanova refused to disembark from the plane until the Soviet authorities had given the all-clear, which shows what a perception of the Wicked West the sweet Giselle had.

Early in the New Year, somehow I landed a job in the West End, that is to say, I rehearsed for a week and played seven performances at the Hovenden Theatre Club, a dingy garret in Garrick Yard off St Martin's Lane, the same forgotten nook, had I but known, that had once housed Thomas Chippendale's furniture workshop; in the 1920s Douglas Byng, famous for cabaret drag, ran the place as a nightclub called the Kinde Dragon, and Gracie Fields had been amongst the guest turns. It lay derelict until the Motleys took it over as their workshop and scenic studio, where West End luminaries including Gielgud, Ashcroft, Olivier and George Devine dropped in for tea, crossing the last kidney-cobbled yard in London. I detected no hints of this former romance in 1958. Now the members paid an annual subscription of 7/6 to drink at the bar and see plays and even rehearsals, and as an actor one had a reduced membership fee of half a crown.

Banana Republic by Kenneth McClellan was the play, concerning the president of a South American republic who is deposed by a younger man. Stripling that I was, I played a colonel, which might have suggested that the army was hard pressed. I had one cell scene, but more vividly I remember my own incarceration in the cramped communal dressing room from which one could hear little and see nothing, before issuing through a curtain onto the postage-stamp performance space and finding the tiny audience almost on top of the action.

It is only subsequent research that has evoked Garrick Yard's picturesque past; Valerie Hovenden had created the Club as a haven and studio for London's struggling acting fraternity, to give young actors experience of classical and new drama. But, in spite of this altruism and the sprite-like quality praised in her obituaries, she seemed to me to have that touch of workaday gloom that afflicted so many who worked on the tatty fringes. I remember sitting up at the bar with her, and her saying lugubriously, 'I suppose we will be praised with faint damns.' Now I have learnt that her first husband, an Irish engineer named John Henry Woullfe Flanagan (nicknamed 'Feathers'), adopted the glorious pseudonym of Dionysius MacDuffy, under which he translated Aristophanic comedies and other Greek plays for the Club, even on occasion performing in them.

In her biography of Angus Wilson, Margaret Drabble lists my name among 'some interesting talent' Valery managed to attract to the Club. The other names listed are Lindsay Kemp, Bernard Kops, Margaretta D'Arcy, Ann Jellico, Charles Osborne, James Kirkup, Ian Calder and Patricia Taylor. Of course, I was unheard of and desperate to do anything. The old inn, like the workshop building in the yard, has been demolished, as has Chippendale's house in St Martin's Lane; there is now an unlovely 1960s frontage with blue and cream tiles.

McClellan later became a devoted member of the Equity Council. When Equity was debating control of entry, Dame Sybil Thorndike argued that members should not refuse to work with amateurs, reminding the Council that 'amateur' meant 'lover'. In response, McClellan remarked, 'We've been told that the word "amateur" means "lover". But who wants a lover without technique?'

Shortly after *Banana Republic*, I went into Michael Boys's studio in a house on Sackville Street, off Piccadilly, now blandly immaculate corporate headquarters, then a bohemian setting of eighteenth-century panelling. Boys produced one image designed to fit me for nearby Shaftesbury Avenue, and another, besweatered, for Sloane Square – emblematic of my being prepared to jump either way! As it was, I was soon clearing tables and serving coffee at Lyons Corner House in the Strand and, in the afternoons, emergency-caretaking at the restored Chelsea Old Church, which had suffered severe bomb damage during the Blitz, to prepare it for its ceremonial reopening by the Queen Mother in May 1958. Afterwards, I got a letter from the vicar:

When the Queen Mother came in and looked up at the sparkling glass shades on all the lamps, I felt so thankful for your hard work.

One of my regular customers at Lyons was a middle-aged lady who appreciated my care in making sure that her coffee was hot and always left a threepenny bit for me under the edge of her saucer. She asked me one day, 'What is it you do, really?'

'I'm an actor.'

'Ah,' she replied, 'I knew you were something.'

I'm still grateful for that compliment.

Michael Boys's 1958 studio portraits of me.

**Shaftesbury Avenue version (above)
and
Sloane Square version (right).**

Photos: © Michael Boys

I was rescued from table-clearing by the opportunity to make my professional Shakespearean debut at Northampton's Royal, an intimate gem of a 600-seater Victorian horseshoe theatre. In Lionel Hamilton's production of *Hamlet* I doubled as poisoner and priest – the player who acts the part of Lucianus in 'The Murder of Gonzago' and the priest who presides at Ophelia's funeral. A member of the Old Vic Company came up to see our effort; they had Michael Benthall's production, with John Neville and Coral Browne, in their current repertoire, and he was astonished to see so many identical moves and pieces of business. It transpired that Lionel Hamilton had persuaded somebody in the Old Vic stage management to procure him the *Hamlet* prompt script for long enough to copy out the moves!

My all-time nadir in the weekly rep system was reached on Saturday the 5th of April 1958, when I realized in the Arcadia Theatre, Lowestoft just what I had got myself into in joining Earl Armstrong's touring repertory company. Approaching the theatre's front-of-house display, I noticed in pride of place the oil-on-canvas portraits of the Armstrongs in their prime, surrounded by the usual 8 x 10 photographs of the supporting cast. I crept into the stalls and watched appalled as the most incompetent, lifeless performance of Somerset Maugham's *The Circle* was in progress. The set was predominantly pink, the acting ill-graced, especially when the leading man tried to exit up centre through double doors and the doorknob came off in his hand.

I was amazed to see that the heavy leading lady was none other than the woman to whom I had not been introduced in Armstrong's basement flat at 53 Belsize Park Gardens where I had been taken on; I'd assumed she was his cleaning lady. I had responded to an advert in *The Stage* on 27 March: 'Open at once, Artists for first-class rep. company. Barbara May contact, also opening for good lady student. – Phone Armstrong, Primrose 1645.'

The day after my arrival, I was rehearsing the part of Frankie, the simple farmer's boy in *Gathering Storm*, and by the Friday I had already opened as Colonel Howard Barnes-Bradley ('good-looking jolly type of forty-five with a military moustache') in Basil Thomas's *Book of the Month*, and all for £6 a week when the Equity minimum was £7.10. During my interview in Belsize Park Gardens I had not been told that everybody in the company was expected to put up the sets, and, on that first day, in my dismay at the standards, I held aloof, preserving my own. I waited alone beneath the stage in the dressing room until the hammering stopped. When I emerged, nothing was said about my failure to 'muck in', but I was informed that there was no time left for a dress rehearsal. Armstrong actually said, 'We'll just have to trust to luck. We're papering the house.' Never having heard the expression before I thought, for a moment, we were expected to redecorate the auditorium.

I had no idea what a 'front-of-house return slip' was either, but I learnt one night when Armstrong, in full slap, came through the pass door from front of house into the gloom of the wings, and came up to me even more gloomily. Thrusting a piece of paper at me, he asked, 'Have you ever seen a return slip like that?' I peered at the scribbled figures and read the total at the bottom.

'Two and two?' I queried in some surprise.

He snatched the return slip back and, sounding wounded, said, 'Two guineas! I know the house is papered!'

Nearly twenty years later, in a letter to *The Stage* on the issue of Arts Council grants, Armstrong boasted proudly: 'I had plays and comedies produced that brought the public in, and they went away satisfied. I have known them to come two and three times to the same production. If the public is given what they want to see, they will return for more, that is my firm belief.' Be that as it may, *Theatre World* of 1958 reports 'that lack of public support compelled Earl Armstrong's Company to close a week early at the Arcadia, Lowestoft.'

Frankie in *Gathering Storm* was a good part. I imagine the Armstrongs had done the play often with many different actors – they paid so little that nobody stayed long. My first stage direction read: 'He is still in his teens. Only after a time does one notice the slightly bewildered look in his eyes.' Frankie is duped by the villain in the last act into thinking he has killed his beloved grannie.

We rehearsed on stage on the current set, furniture rearranged as appropriate, with Catherine Armstrong directing from the most comfortable chair, stage left facing front, nose in the book, only moving if the chair was needed or if it was her turn to get up and act. I can hear her now, as my grannie (she was hard to love), making an exit upstairs accompanying me, while chanting in a deep, resonant voice, reminiscent of Sybil Thorndike, whom she professed to know: '"Come, let's to bed," says Sleepy head; "Tarry awhile," says Slow; "Put on the pan," says Greedy Nan, "Let's sup before we go."'

In *Book of the Month* she had a more glamorous part. There was an act drop during which the house lights stayed down and she had a 'quick' change into an evening gown – again no dress rehearsal. We waited and waited and eventually she laboured up the steps from the under-stage dressing rooms in a white full-length gown in which, I have to say, I did not think her appearance worth the wait!

Catherine and Earl were each of them born in the proverbial trunk to old theatrical families, very much in the manner of the Dickensian Crummleses. Her obituary can only boast that her grandfather, Henry Loydall, is mentioned in *The Era Almanac* for 1864 as playing Macbeth at the Effingham Theatre. Effingham is near Hampton Court and was at the time a village with some 122 houses. Earl (born Jack Preece) was carried on stage at the age of two weeks in the company run by his mother under the name Madame Ada Lauderdale. His company was a continuation of Ada's. Despite their 'romantic' pedigrees, the Armstrongs were a joyless couple; their business was to make fun, but they seemed not to derive any from the process.

I discovered that, although I was on less than the Equity minimum, I was being paid more than most of the other actors and, soon after the close of *Gathering Storm*, I was given a few days' notice. On the night of my final performance at the Arcadia, I was in the wings waiting to go on, standing near the fireman in his uniform who was half watching the show. 'I hear he's given you your notice,' he said in a low voice. 'Yes,' I replied, 'I finish after this performance.' After a slight pause, he looked at me and said, 'I'd have though you'd have been the only one he'd 'ave kept.'

I had a relatively easy time at Lowestoft. My friend Caroline Blakiston, I now learn, had worked a gruelling schedule with the Armstrongs a year or two before, for a summer season based at Prestwick on the south-west coast of Scotland. Having opened each week's play at Prestwick, they not only rehearsed for the next but took the current play to five other town halls for one-night stands, travelling, erecting the set, performing, packing up and taking the set and props and themselves back to Prestwick, to rehearse the next morning and travel on to the next town, and so on round the circuit every week for the whole summer.

Caro's first part with the Armstrongs was Louise, the French maid, in *Private Lives*. Being well educated, she was proficient at the French and went down very well indeed with the audiences. In the real West End, the French of a French maid would have been taken for granted, but, beside the West End simulacrum created by Earl and Catherine Armstrong, it must have shone like a good deed in a naughty world.

They also did Noël Coward's 1927 comedy *The Marquise*, which requires an aristocratic setting of some grandeur, transportable in a horse box. Every Saturday night after the show, Caro was dropped off with her suitcase at a particular 'road end', as they say in Scotland, where lived old friends of her family. She would walk up the long drive to the Georgian mansion at the top and stay the weekend with the principal aristocratic family in that part of Scotland, whilst the Armstrongs and their company went back to their digs. But, although she weekended in a baronial hall, Caro was short of money (her parents not being well off despite their aristocratic connections). She was grateful to her kind Scottish landlady, who used to make her Marmite and tomato sandwiches to take with her to each date.

My experience at Lowestoft seems to come from another world, a world that was to me passé or lifeless, even at its best. At the same time, it has to be said, I have memories of desultory plays with sauce bottles on the table at the Royal Court. The Court had set a new theatrical agenda. Peter Gill goes so far as to call the values of the West End circa 1957 'shoddy' when, in fact, it is on record that the Court had to bail itself out by casting West End stars in classic plays and transferring them to the West End to stay afloat. Only Olivier's talent and star status saved Osborne's *The Entertainer*.

From Lowestoft I was invited back to Northampton. I suppose my character work as the elderly Priest in *Hamlet* led to my playing the cameo of Pepys, a grey-haired solicitor in the farce *One Wild Oat*. I think my first line was: 'I'm from Featherstone and Featherstone, Solicitors of Locksbottom.'

'Locks what?'

'Bottom, sir; it's near Orpington in Kent.'

I had light stage-management duties only in *The Diary of Anne Frank* – so light that I read in the little Boots diary I kept at the time: '24 May – Night off for *Cherry Orchard* Moscow Arts Sadler's Wells.' It must have been a close-run thing, for, in that week, I was rehearsing for Walter Greenwood's comedy *Saturday Night at the Crown*. One always did one's best in the rushed rehearsals and short runs of these West End plays, only too well aware how far from the 'real thing' our weekly-rep replicas were. I had seen the marvellous actress and comedienne Thora Hird play the lead in *Saturday Night at the Crown* at the Garrick, a wonderfully vibrant performance, but I recollect virtually nothing of our Northampton attempt.

I did my own cooking at my digs and my most vivid recollections from my stay in Northampton are to do with my accommodation rather than the theatre: the night when the landlady's cat ate the steak I had bought to make a stew, and the way the house came alive at weekends when the landlady's husband came home, in spite of the fact that they never spoke to each other. He lit fires in the kitchen and sitting room and always wore the same thing around the house on these Saturday mornings, this Pinteresque Prometheus – trousers with braces, a woolly vest and invariably his trilby hat.

Another piece of sartorial eccentricity occurs to me from one weeknight before I went in for the performance. We were very near the Royal, but also near the variety theatre, which in common with many minor variety dates struggling to survive, was taking tours of such shows as *Strip, Strip, Hooray!* One weeknight before I went in for the performance, I was looking out of the window when I saw what could only have been the nude show's comedian strolling down the deserted street; it was still daylight and he must have been going in to do the first house which might have begun at 6 p.m. It was his loose and rather louche light-coloured suit, with its pronounced check pattern, and his already made-up face that made it impossible for him be an ordinary citizen of the town. He looked strangely content, whilst I thought how illegitimate it was of him not to be more discreet by dressing and making up when he got to his dressing room at the theatre. Osborne had written *The Entertainer* the year before, dramatizing the death of the music hall, but this comic seemed to have no qualms. He would certainly have been earning more money than we at the rep, and not under the constant pressure to learn a new part every week. I often wonder for how long he went through life with that confident stroll, that insouciant manner – and how long he remained a comedian.

In mid-June Louise and I set sail for New Zealand on the Good Ship Rangitoto. I suppose we weren't so far away from having our meals served to us by the future Deputy Prime Minister John Prescott, who was a steward with the New Zealand Shipping Company; he waited on the Captain's table on the Rangitata, where he served an exhausted and lately resigned Sir Anthony Eden in the wake of the Suez Crisis. On the sister ship, we were seated lower down at the Purser's table, but it was good training, in that my dinner jacket was in regular use in the evenings at the dining table and the occasional cocktail party. Up until then, I had only ever worn it in plays. There was a couple on the table who were emigrating on an assisted passage, and the husband didn't have a dinner jacket in his luggage. My rather fatuous idea of keeping the whole table happy was to wear my dinner jacket on alternate evenings. I was soon wearing a tan for the first time in my life – there was a modest swimming pool – and using the other important item in my luggage, my Bullworker chest developer. My golden youth status was initially wasted in the New Zealand Players. Wary of giving an English actor the juvenile lead, the director cast me as Elgin, the elderly butler, in Agatha Christie's *Spider's Web*, which we toured in for three months, whilst Louise, a Kiwi, was leading lady in the Margaret Lockwood part.

Notwithstanding my subservient creaking from Invercargill, the southern most English-speaking city on the planet, to Whangarei in the subtropical north of the North Island, I continued to make the most of the sun and the constant proximity of the sea, and I still have an affection for asparagus rolls and Pavlova Cake, invariably served at after-the-show hospitality events.

I believed I was the only actor in New Zealand at that time (there were not very many anyway) who could do justice to Algy in *The Importance of Being Earnest*, which was to be our next production, destined for the same three-month tour, and I threatened to leave to join a company in Auckland called C. A. S; the director, who wore one red sock and one blue, offered me Da in *The Playboy of the Western World*, so I'd obviously convinced as the elderly Elgin, and professionals of advanced years were practically nonexistent then.

Studio portraits of myself as Algernon Moncrieff, and Louise as Gwendoline in *The Importance of Being Earnest*.

The population of New Zealand was then about the same as Greater Birmingham and yet, in the South Island alone, Invercargill, Dunedin, Omaru, Timaru and Christchurch had Victorian or Edwardian theatres. We played for a week in Wellington, over a week in Auckland, and even in the smallest towns there was somewhere to play and an audience to play to. I am remembering a white, sunlit school hall, rather hot, somewhere in the North with a full house of the whole school for a special matinée: young children with bare feet on the front row and us on stage in David de Bethel's authentically designed clothes, those high starched collars, the corsets on the women. I can still hear the delighted laughter of those children who seemed to take to Wilde's style and identify with our vanities and the problems they got us into.

Amongst my mental luggage were the impressions brought from home of tatty and not so tatty rep, the *real* West End and those made by the Berliner Ensemble and the Moscow Arts Theatre. My father-in-law was a little alarmed at the way I went on about them in NZ Radio interviews, but the Soviets clearly wanted to soften up New Zealand attitudes too and I can even now visualize *The Dying Swan* being danced exquisitely in a 'Stars of the Bolshoi' tour of the main cities we managed to see.

Wilde was an English export to Russia, of course. I quote from the first *International Theatre Annual* of 1956 an article by Cecil Wilson, who was impressed by how the Moscow actors wore their full evening dress 'with an elegance and ease quite surprising in a city that hardly dresses up for anything':

> Moscow's partiality for Wilde, shared with the plays of Shakespeare, Sheridan and Shaw has an obvious explanation in the artificiality and the overbearing vanity of his aristocrats; it might well serve the Soviet sociological book to accept these pampered puppets as direct reflections rather than caricatures of the English ruling class. But what impressed me at a matinée of *An Ideal Husband* was the Russian respect for these people. They laughed *with* them, and not at them; their laughter echoed genuine mirth, not scorn.

Should anyone need to be reassured of Wilde's understanding of the world beyond the Café Royal, they ought to read, not 'The Soul of Man Under Socialism', but the two long letters he wrote to the *Daily Chronicle* after his release from Reading Gaol, in which he fulminates against the systemic cruelty practised in English prisons and pleads for humane treatment of the men and boys he had met during his incarceration, who had never uttered an elegantly turned phrase or had a decent shirt to their backs. Remembering the faces and the laughter of the children at our schools matinée in New Zealand, it is hard not to think also of the child prisoners whose terror Wilde graphically describes in the first of his letters. In the cell opposite his own he caught sight of a small boy:

> The child's face was like a white wedge of sheer terror. There was in his eyes the terror of a hunted animal. The next morning I heard him at breakfast time crying, and calling to be let out. His cry was for his parents. From time to time I could hear the deep voice of the warder on duty telling him to keep quiet. Yet he was not even convicted of whatever little offence he had been charged with. He was simply on remand. ... This terror that seizes and dominates the child, as it seizes the grown man also, is of course intensified beyond power of expression by the solitary cellular system of our prisons. Every child is

confined to its cell for twenty-three hours out of twenty-four. (27 May 1897)

I have no doubt that, in bringing to public attention some of the dehumanizing punitive measures he had witnessed, whilst residing at Her Majesty's pleasure, he made a material difference and furthered the cause of prison reform. Theatre too can effect social change. It was, after all, a West End play that, not many years later, led to the ending of the 'silent system' in prisons under which inmates were forbidden to speak to one another, the purpose being to break their wills. The play was John Galsworthy's *Justice*, directed by Harley Granville-Barker at the Duke of York's in 1910.

I feel doubly close to Wilde; to speak Algy's lines for four months and identify with him night after night is one thing, but I don't think it either fanciful or sentimental to see myself as a beneficiary of Wilde's concern for prisoners and his benign influence, ruined and disgraced though he was. At least I was allowed the companionship of books in my long, silent nights in Wormwood Scrubs. Wilde had argued:

Deprived of books, of all human intercourse, isolated from every human and humanising influence, condemned to eternal silence, robbed of all intercourse with the external world, treated like an unintelligent animal, brutalised below the level of any of the brute creation, the wretched man who is confined in an English prison can hardly escape becoming insane. (23 March 1898)

However many degrees of separation you allow lay between Wilde and me, just prior to our departure for New Zealand and on our return to London, we lived in Tite Street, Chelsea, a few doors from the 'house beautiful' Wilde had occupied with his family from 1884 until his trial in 1895.

In 'The Soul of Man under Socialism', Wilde says, 'Man is made for something better than disturbing dirt. All work of that kind should be done by a machine.' He was quite certain that, eventually, the machine would leave people free to be poets, artists and philosophers. When, rather more recently, I had just read the essay, I looked out of the window, digesting this prophecy, to see men shifting dirt with spades, much as they had done at least a century and a half before, not a mile up the hill in Hampstead, and been immortalized in their toil by Ford Madox Brown in his painting 'Work' (finished in 1863). The main difference was that my workmen were not laying drains but fibre-optic cable. Nevertheless, here I draw close to Wilde again. From Tite Street I went to Sloane Square one day, not to the Royal Court, but to Peter Jones department store on the opposite corner. The vicar of Chelsea Old Church, my employer at the time, got me to select the vacuum cleaner I thought most efficient to help 'disturb the dirt'.

I understand now why I was so nervous when I elected to appear to defend a parking fine about the same time as the laying of the fibre-optic cable. Why? I had after all been cool at my court martial and throughout my tribunal hearing when I was a mere stripling. Much later I had appeared at a police disciplinary hearing as a witness for a boy I'd seen attacked by the police, and found that rather more exacting, but why should I have been so very nervous on this trivial parking penalty occasion? Answer: it was at Bow Street Magistrates' Court where Wilde was first charged, though I didn't realize it at the time; I might have been standing in the selfsame dock.

In Tite Street Louise and I lived in a terrace house owned by Winnie and Joe Hodgkinson, exactly like the one Wilde had lived in at number 34. We had a bedsit in the house for £2 rent a week, and we occupied what would have been the main reception room on the first floor, with French windows onto a balcony, and shared use of a kitchen with a single actress a few flights up, Anthea Boyle, who had been with us at the Northern Theatre School. The Royal Court was a twelve-minute walk away. Less than five minutes away, on the King's Road, Mary Quant had opened her shop, Bazaar, in 1955, though it surprises me to realize that the miniskirt did not come in until a decade later and wasn't worn nationwide until I was playing Stoppard's Guildenstern in 1967. I remembered the sensation in Bradford when skirts went *down* to calf-length with Dior's 'New Look' of 1947, though, with money and clothing coupons tight, many ladies extended their coat skirts by letting in a band of a different material about eight inches wide several inches above the hemline.

Joe and Winnie had not long come down from the North themselves, from Manchester where he had been Regional Director of the Arts Council, and seems not to have endeared himself to Joan Littlewood. Their five-storey house in Tite Street was paid for, I'm sure, by their tenants, who were treated as friends, housed in the basement, ground floor, first floor and attic. Our big room had once, by way of a recess, gone right through to a back window, but a temporary wall now formed a small box room with ladders and paint, and I think this is where a very large framed dun and black poster of *Mutter Courage und ihre Kinder*, given to Joe by Helene Weigel but not signed, ended up. Joe and Winnie would ask us up to dinner now and then, and we once had coffee with Dame Sybil Thorndike and Sir Lewis Casson, after Winnie had invited Sybil up to see our little kitchen.

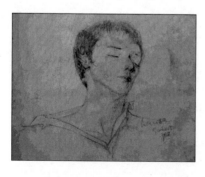

My drawing of Louise, 1962.

Louise and I both landed acting jobs at the subsidized Hornchurch rep, I suspect through Joe's influence in his new capacity as the Arts Council's Director of Drama, but this was never acknowledged. Hornchurch was an hour's daily commute on the District line Tube to rehearse and perform and an hour back at night; it would have been so much easier to sleep in the dressing rooms of the Queen's Theatre. Agatha Christie's *The Unexpected Guest* was welcomed with open hearts and full houses by our public. It had followed the fortnight of *The Merchant of Venice* in which we played Lorenzo and Jessica, and which got only a very moderate box office. There were also the comedies *Not in the Book* and *You Can't Take it with You*, and the grit and sweat of Willis Hall's recent play, *The Long and the Short and the Tall*, set in the Malayan jungle in 1942.

At Hornchurch I learnt one useful lesson from a not very able, rather plain and, therefore, 'character' actor. We used to discuss the work seriously in the dressing room, and one night I was bemoaning the fact that I wasn't getting a laugh on a very good line. Without turning from the mirror, this actor said, 'Well you won't get it; you're not doing your preparatory movement.' I was astounded. What did he mean? I had played Algernon Moncrieff, unerringly getting my laughs all over New Zealand with no thought of anything so calculated as a preparatory movement. He was quite right, of course. I was at the side of the stage at that point in the play, out of immediate focus, and needed to make a move to draw the eye before I spoke the line. The character actor was a born teacher; he later ran the drama course at the Arts Educational School and became Head of Theatre at the Western Australian Academy of Performing Arts.

A few months later, I embarked on a No.1 post-West End tour of John Mortimer's *The Wrong Side of the Park*, which included my debut at Bradford's Alhambra. The central character in the play was a house based on Mortimer's own home at 23 Harben Road, NW6, in 'the remote upland of Swiss Cottage', where he felt 'constantly menaced by the march of civilization in the shape of great red flats full of Formica kitchen equipment and well-planned lives.' Margaret Leighton had been the original star and there was a showy part of a young lodger, called Miller, that had been played by Robert Stephens, who had already had success as Osborne's George Dillon. Jean Kent, the 'screen siren of the 40s', as she was called by one journalist, played the Leighton part, and Vincent Shaw, who I later realized represented her by then, secured me the part Robert had played. My father thought I was made.

The 'director' had been the stage manager and kept trying to get me to do Robert Stephens's inflections, which I sort of remembered from seeing the original production, but Robert's vocal technique was idiosyncratic even then. At one point Miller says:

Those flats have done something to this neighbourhood! There's call for a new garage and the fish and chip shop on the corner is now called 'Sea Food Caterers. Take-away Service'. On Sundays the place used to be full of torn-up newspaper and children in mobile packing-cases asking for a penny for the guy at the end of June! What've we got now? Dentists Simonizing their Consuls, young men in television wearing hacking jackets to polish up the Jag. Civilization is slowly moving down towards Kilburn.

I was quite stubborn about not giving 'Kilburn' an upward inflection, and much else. When my father saw the play, all he said about me was, 'Did the director tell you to do it like that?' I couldn't lay what I presumed might be the blame at his door.

My dad was very keen on the veteran actor who played the old father; he liked the comedy in his part ('What've we got here now? Flats. Bloody little beehives with nowhere to put the pram') and slipped into the gallery to see the play a second time, I think on the strength of his performance. This actor had a very characteristic, almost character walk on and off the stage. At the curtain call one night, glancing down as we bowed, I saw that he had little square holes cut out of each of his black shoes to allow his bunions to protrude – he wore black socks, of course. What would Melville Gillam of Worthing have said? This was hardly keeping it West End, but it was the nearest I had got to it thus far.

As Simon Sparrow in *Doctor at Sea* (1962)
with Pat Cawfield and Ronald Shiner.

One of my last rep engagements was at Palmers Green, an outer suburb of North London, in the borough of Enfield. The Intimate Theatre had been founded in 1935 by the young John Clements, a graduate of St John's College, Cambridge, who ran the weekly rep there until 1941. He was to have a distinguished career as an actor-manager and film director, and his production of *The Rivals* in the West End enjoyed a record commercial run. He seems wildly atypical, even inexplicable as a weekly-rep merchant. When I did two special weeks there, twenty years after Clements's tenure, it had become a joke: 'What I say about Palmers Green, darling,' said the actress playing the lead in *Watch it, Sailor!*, as we began the long journey home after rehearsals on day one, 'is that it pays the stamp.'

The Intimate was so far out of Central London that Equity rules stipulated more rehearsal money, so to avoid the extra payment we rehearsed in a North London pub *just* inside the designated line. I rehearsed first the Brian Rix lead in *Simple Spymen*, the farce scheduled to open as a Boxing Day matinée; there was a tiny fireplace in the upper room of the cheerless pub, and on Friday of rehearsal week, the stage manager came round for the coffee money.

'That's a bit steep for coffee,' I said.

'It includes coal money,' he replied.

Wrathfully I invoked Equity and paid half.

The management obviously had a thing about heating expenses, because, having had Christmas Day off, we arrived early on the 26th to dress-rehearse in freezing conditions, and the theatre was clearly not going to warm up in time for the matinée – nor were we, unless it was with anxiety. There were two sets, but we were so behind that we had to rehearse the last act in the first-act set with the iron in (i.e. the fire curtain down) and whispering because the house was coming in. They didn't warm up in any sense.

It was the first time in rep that it fell to me to make the curtain speech announcing the next week's play, and having ended up in some ludicrous predicament involving gun powder, soot and a lavatory seat around my neck, I stepped forward from the centre of the bowing line and, as the applause, such as it was, faded, I tossed in the throwaway line, 'What a way to earn a living!' The character man on the end of the line-up said darkly and just audibly, 'Who said it was a living?'

No account of an actor's life in the 50s and 60s would be complete without a mention of Chadwick Street in Westminster; it was, and still is, surrounded by streets with grander or quainter names: Old Pye Street, Greycoat Place, where the Grey Coat School was, complete with its two statues of scholars in their long grey coats at the gate. The elegant eighteenth-century Lord North Street, where John Gielgud lived, was not far away, and Smith Square, where 'Binkie' Beaumont lived, with its imposing church in the centre and the Labour Party Headquarters oddly placed in one corner. There was Perkin's Rents and Little Dean's Yard, Abbey Orchard Street. But prosaic Chadwick Street had a Labour Exchange built in the uniform, nationwide style of the time, where unemployed actors from any part of London could turn up to sign on for benefits, rather more regularly than most casual freelancers. Amongst members of the profession, this was referred to, with jovial familiarity, as 'The Club'. One always thought the sympathetic regime there was too good to last.

There was a story that Eric Portman turned up from time to time, collected his dole money, and went straight into the corner shop and bought several packets of expensive cigarettes with it, but I never saw anyone so illustrious. I always had a touch of guilt about signing on, but it was important to do so; otherwise you would end up owing National Insurance payments for your weeks out of work.

One day I saw Lionel Hamilton, for so many years the director of Northampton rep, standing irresolute near one of the queues. I said hello awkwardly; it seemed so strange to see someone I'd thought of as a permanent fixture, an authority figure, in the same boat.

The intricate narrative of my 'interim' years, between drama school and the West End proper, includes my first appearances on television and on the London stage, the two events being connected. My first taste of TV naturalism at 'the coal face' was a rehearsal I witnessed of *Richard II* for a groundbreaking cycle of Shakespeare's history plays entitled *An Age of Kings*. The director, Peter Dews, had been a schoolmaster in Bradford when he played Falstaff to my Slender in Coronation Year at the Civic. By 1960 he had risen in TV. In the large rehearsal room I saw the antithesis of the Shakespeare I had come to expect, but, now I come to think of it, even the great epic histories often boil down to intimate scenes between two or three characters. But then, as the little knots and huddles of actors whispered and muttered to each other in various locations about the room, on patches of floor marked out with gaffer tape to delineate the different studio sets, I could make nothing of it all, being too shy to follow the action as the director did, close up.

I learned fast, however, when Dews cast me as Dapper in *The Alchemist*, televised live from Birmingham. Just once I was reprimanded in the studio by a floor manager: 'Do the cross as rehearsed, you're out of shot.' It was a polite reprimand, but I could hear Peter cursing over the floor manager's 'cans'. He also cast me in a TV play by John Arden. The script arrived at the stage door of the Lyceum in Edinburgh where I had done ten plays in eleven weeks for Whatmore Productions, and might have done another ten, but the envelope with 'BBC TV' emblazoned on it was my rescue package, causing a sensation in the company, a frisson of envy.

My first television role – Dapper in *The Alchemist*,
BBC, 1961. Alan Dobie as Face.

Louise, meanwhile, was at Nottingham's fortnightly rep, where she did Rattigan's *The Winslow Boy*, feeling the play had the reliability and smoothness of a Rolls-Royce engine. When I was offered a smallish part in Arden's TV play *Wet Fish*, Louise was offered the leading part of the girl. However, the director at Nottingham, Val May, had cast her in some paltry parts in a revue and stuck by the letter of the contract, refusing to allow her to fulfil this golden opportunity of her first TV appearance.

Wet Fish was a play about small-town politics and very ordinary I thought. Arden and his wife, Margaretta D'Arcy, were difficult, and afterwards, in a letter to *The Listener*, he complained bitterly about 'the basic refusal of the producer concerned to consult me over the production.' 'I was appalled,' he protested, 'to discover that *Wet Fish* was cast and put into rehearsal entirely uncritically, my notions as to the relative importance, rhythms and meanings of episodes and characters being ignored, or rather never sought.'

Over forty years later, while working on Arden's radio play *Wild Ride to Dublin*, I found myself driving along the North Circular with him – we'd had to migrate to another studio because we had run out of time. We passed a giant IKEA store. He enquired what it was and, on being told, said very mildly, 'I suppose it fulfils a need.' It seemed a strange comment from this notorious Marxist firebrand and one-time member of Sinn Féin, who trampled the US flag, picketed the RSC premiere of his own play, *The Island of the Mighty*, at the Aldwych, accusing the director of having an 'imperialist' attitude, and continually complained about how his plays were misinterpreted or politically censored.

David William, who had been a much-praised Richard II in *An Age of Kings*, played Ananias in *The Alchemist*. I asked him if he thought my part would lead to anything and he replied cryptically in the affirmative. As it turned out, he directed my London debut, casting me as Demetrius in *A Midsummer Night's Dream* and Dumain in *Love's Labour's Lost* in the New Shakespeare Company's season at the Open Air Theatre in Regent's Park.

David could easily be cast as my elder brother. In fact, I once had a conversation with an actress who knew us both and clearly thought she was talking to him! As a director, he was exacting and sometimes inspiring, a sort of zealot. In the *Dream*, he insisted doggedly on squeezing from the scene where the lovers wake from their dream, just after Theseus's exit, something I thought wasn't there, a sense of mystery and discovery. Peter Dews said to me once, 'Seeing a production of David's is like going to church, except there is always one touch of vulgarity that would make Bernard Delfont blush.'

After the tired, reach-me-down revivals of the last days of the old Park, his productions set a fresh standard and really thrilled the critics. Of David's *Love's Labour's Lost* Bernard Levin wrote:

> The wit and imagination of his reading is above all praise. He builds
> stage pictures of delicate loveliness, grouping and regrouping his

players in an effortless endless flow. He creates moods and changes them as an opal changes colours. ... In the whole cast there is not one player who is not perfectly chosen. ... I could list them all; everyone plays up to astonishing heights; they listen to each other; they look at each other; they fit as if they had been playing together for twenty years. A miracle in Regent's Park with mulled claret to wash it down in the interval. (*Daily Mail*, 22 August 1962)

The lovers in the *Dream* were found particularly convincing:

The rude fun is balanced by better than average lovers. (*Mail*)

The sweet and melting Heather Chasen stood out among the quartet of lovers, who staged with full gusto an excellent derisory quarrel in the magic wood. (*Daily Tel.*)

The big scene between the lovers in the forest, ending in their realisation of love and happiness, is brilliantly done, the sexual impulse in the wooing being aptly brought out. (*The Stage*)

It makes for heady reading now, but somehow, at the time, I took with a pinch of salt the rapturous metropolitan critical attention that was at last trained on work in which I was involved. For one thing Demetrius and Dumain are not parts to quicken the pulse.

A rehearsal for *A Midsummer Night's Dream*, Regent's Park, May 1962.
I am seated far right next to Heather Chasen (Helena).
Bottom is being played by Patrick Wymark, far left in the dark jacket.
Photo: © Topfoto / ArenaPAL

David had worked at the Park with Robert Atkins, the founder of the Open Air, and remembered the trunk coming out with *The Tempest* costumes and the young actress, cast as Miranda, saying, 'Oh dear, this doesn't fit.' 'Strange, it always does,' Atkins replied. But Atkins's company had had their glory days, too – I have a marvellous picture of Robert Eddison as an art-deco Oberon. For our *Dream*, we had Watteau-esque costumes specially designed by Dawn Pavitt. We still played in the same sloping field of old, not the impressive amphitheatre that now graces the Park; there were deck chairs at the front and benches to infinity at the back and, when the breeze caught the leaves, the mike system was inadequate. A lugubrious Clement Freud did the catering and, as Levin's review indicates, there was a licence – wine rather than cocoa.

In this age of e-mail and mobile phones, I wonder how, in early 1963, I happened to be in the right place at the right time, namely by the black dial phone on the mantlepiece in our little kitchen in Tite Street, SW3, instead of 'keeping it West End' on tour at one of the Theatre Royals in our provincial cities or doing a 'special week' nowhere special in tatty rep. John Pickles, who, as far as I knew, had been rather solidly at the fortnightly rep in Sheffield, was ringing me out of the blue, telling me that he was to play the leading young man in a North Country working-class domestic comedy at the Mermaid Theatre in London.[2] Bernard Miles was to play the star part of his father and there was a little part of a younger brother up for grabs.

Nowadays the Mermaid, the crowning achievement of Bernard Miles, counts for nothing; the City of London Planning Committee even stripped the building of its status as a theatre in 2008. In any case, it has been smothered for years, wrapped in a plastic-clad office development and circumnavigated by a major road that cuts it off from pedestrians and its old relationship with the Thames alike. In such obscurity it has languished as a conference centre, but in 1959 it opened glowing as a new dawn, the first theatre to be created in the City of London, as opposed to the West End, since Shakespeare's day, with a bold, iron-pillared, industrial/classical entrance. It was a perfect example of British post-war make-do-and-mend. Wrought by public subscription out of a thick stone-walled, bomb-damaged warehouse, its southerly foundations were set in the riverbed, its eastern flank lapped by the murky waters of Puddle Dock. Puddle Dock, E1 was its romantic postal address. Its interior walls were russet-coloured bare old London brick, its 600 seats arranged in one steep slope up the oblong length of the warehouse shell. Tynan welcomed its broad 'Brechtian' end stage, sans proscenium, whilst deploring the 'Oops my dear' musical version of Fielding, entitled *Lock up*

---

[2] There is a good *Picture Post* photo of John Pickles, circa 1953, which wasn't published in their article about the Northern Theatre School; he stands in pride of place, a second-year student, holding a heroic position, being choreographed by Miss McBride and partnered by Anthea Boyle. I am to be glimpsed looking lank and callow on the sidelines in a pair of unbecoming shorts, which may be why the precious photograph does not survive in my collection.

Your Daughters, that ran twice nightly in the theatre for months before transferring to Her Majesty's Theatre.

I took a No. 22 bus from the King's Road, hopped off, as you could then, at Piccadilly Circus, walked down the Haymarket and entered the stage door of Her Majesty's in King Charles II Street and stood on the stage of Herbert Beerbohm Tree's theatre where Bernard, another begetter of a theatre, was starring in the musical and looking forward to starting rehearsals back at the Mermaid for *All in Good Time*. In the stalls were, as well as Miles, his wife Josephine Wilson, who was to direct, and Bill Naughton, the author of *All in Good Time*.

I had to convince as a young working-class lad from Barnsley. It was a cinch; I didn't have to think about it, the years of Southern upper-crust nurture fell away and I was the pre-Theatre School boy again. I landed the scrap of a part there and then. Bill Naughton was fifty-three at the time, and was Bolton through and through (he had been a weaver and coalbagger), although his best known work celebrated a London wide boy and sexual adventurer named Alfie, a part for which John Neville had cast off his princely Old Vic persona and drawn on his Wilsden vernacular, acquired as the son of a truck driver. Bill loved to play football before rehearsal and several of the cast joined him, but that was not the sort of networking I could rise to.

All in Good Time was another Mermaid success. Terrific reviews. I remember stealing glances at Olivier who came to see it one night. We even transferred to the West End, to the Phoenix Theatre (which had opened in 1930 with the premiere of *Private Lives*). However, the tedium of the part was as considerable as the dramatic impact was negligible. We were soon on half-salary with poor houses and closed prematurely, but not before Josephine Wilson had entered my dressing room one night to tell me, rather delicately, that Bill Naughton had written a radio script, *November Day*, and they wanted Lois Dane and me to do it. This meant an unavoidably pointed passing over of John Pickles, but, in spite of that and its cruel unfairness to John, I suppose I was grateful that, even within the confines of my contribution, they had recognized something they liked.

Ironic really that, after all my endeavours in the provinces at 'keeping it West End', and the part that BBC Radio had played in 'grooming' my voice, my first West End play and my first radio play should be in the North Country working-class vernacular. Some actors are not able to lose their native accent, feeling that to do so would be to betray their roots and put on artificial airs. I was one of the many working-class actors of the 1950s who had no such qualms. In any case, as a boy, as I never tire of acknowledging, the radio was my ear's window on the world; what a wide and infinitely coloured world it was and I wanted to be as multicoloured as I could. So I am not sentimentally attached to my native utterance; pragmatically, one searches for the appropriate voice wherever it might come from, but I found that I was especially moved listening again recently to Naughton's *November*

Day, a day in the life of a young married man in the Depression who lands a day's work as a coalbagger.

There is a purity about the script; it has something so honest and authentic, reminding me a little of the plays of D. H. Lawrence in its lack of political posturing and cultural self-consciousness. The spare language is a kind of poetry; one line in particular I remember and love: 'If I had a Clydesdale mare like that o' thine …'. The hero is so busy keeping up with his arduous work and absorbing the rich talk of his newfound workmates and bosses, he speaks little in the central part of the single November day, but all the time one has the sense of him striving and learning, leading to the transformation which happens between the intimacy of waking up to the alarm clock and wrenching himself out of the warm bed, away from his wife and bairn, for the routine of failing to get work and coming back home to breakfast, the shock of being taken on and having grit himself to survive the challenge.

But beyond authenticity, and far beyond sentiment, I found a kinship with the voice of the young character I played. It was as if he were someone I might have been. A hero, yes, perhaps an idealized one, finding, after his exhausting day's work, a moment of fulfilment, even redemption, with his wife and child as he sits naked before the kitchen fire with the baby on his knee. I knew that kitchen and that man, his life with his wife and baby, and felt proud to know them.

I got a new agent out of the job, whilst I was still at the Mermaid. The former popular singer turned agent, Joan Reddin, poached me from Vincent Shaw. At her written request, I went to see her at her office. After a few minutes she said, 'Why are you here?'

'Because you invited me to see you,' I replied.

It transpired that she hadn't connected me with Naughton's Lancashire lad – that was the type she was after. I darcsay I added, 'I'm an actor.'

The magic words 'Royal Court Actors' Studio' had caught my eye in an advertisement on the stage-door noticeboard at the Phoenix, as the short-lived run of *All in Good Time* was coming to an end. It was here that I first met Bill Gaskill, who had attended the teenagers' Saturday morning acting classes in Chapel Street a few years before I did. The Studio developed out of Bill's classes at City Lit and, through designer's Jocelyn Herbert's initiative, found a home at the newly built but not yet opened Jeanetta Cochrane Theatre in Kingsway. It was subsidized by a three-year grant from the Gulbenkian Foundation. The idea was to provide a joint training ground for the Court and NT, but anyone could go along. A small, slight Peter Gill was an occasional attendee and even offered a series of art classes, but actors fortunate enough to be in employment at the Court, or any other theatre, tended to stay away. There was improvisation with Bill or Keith Johnstone, comic mime with Claude Chagrin and movement with Yat Malmgren. For all the social commitment and gritty realism at the Court, much of the Studio's work centred around masks – the comic half-mask with Bill and the neutral tragic mask with George Devine.[3]

There was something highfalutin and mystical by turns in the sessions Bill ran, though I quite liked it when it was my turn. The method was a strict routine. You were to select a mask from a prop table of varyingly grotesque examples, put it on and go directly to a mirror to see yourself in it: in this crucial encounter you had intuitively to decide on the person, character, clown, creature you were. There was a strong element of mumbo-jumbo in the moment of transformation in the mirror; it was a sort of shaman moment, although Bill kept his cool cerebral analysis at the ready, mixed with amused approval when things went right and a dreamlike detachment akin to boredom when the sense of purpose evaporated. You then turned from the mirror, usually to face another actor who had completed the same process at the other side of the stage. Then you acted out this encounter, rather like two strange animals meeting in that grunts seemed to come out rather than words, though our mouths were free. There seemed to be no progression in the exercise, and I recall going back to a class after some months away and seeing remarkably similar crude encounters, though there was no reason why sophisticated, or at least coherent, dialogue could not have been encouraged, or less primeval movement achieved.

Much was made of the release an actor could gain through the mask. When Peggy Ashcroft had disastrously played Brecht's *Good Woman of Setzuan*, she had played the Chinese whore with a heart of gold in her customary Kensington. To make ends meet she pretended to be her ruthless brother and, in donning a mask for this 'role', she convinced not only the other characters but us, in a way that she might have done if she had worn a mask for the 'Good Woman'.

For all the good that these classes did me, they seemed hopelessly hothouse when I had to adapt to toeing the line and coming up with the goods in an episode of the TV crime series *Dixon of Dock Green*. And, by the winter of 1963-64, having failed to distinguish myself at an audition for walk-ons and bit parts in Olivier's first season at Chichester, I was working on the sock, tie and handkerchief counter at Jones & Higgins department store in Peckham, about 500 yards from where I lived. The tone of my 'Can I help you?' or 'We have some rather nice boxed ones, if you're looking for a present' must have been a bit startling in Rye Lane, SE15, too posh even for a Bond Street sales assistant, but it was unaffected and from the heart. I'd been encouraged to talk, and been determined to think, even dream, in Standard English at the Northern Theatre School.

---

[3] Recently I met Arnold Jarrow who told me he had in those days worked at the Court on and off for eight years as well as attending Studio classes. He was fortunate enough to experience Devine's comic mask classes: 'He was a mine of information – tips really about gags and timing – he would give you a piece of business and say, "I guarantee that will get a laugh".'

I had to curtail my Studio attendances, able only to go to the classes on Wednesday afternoons, half-day closing. Bill asked me what I was working on and I told him, the sock counter at Jones & Higgins. 'You oughtn't to be doing that,' he said gravely, and soon afterwards – for which he has my eternal gratitude – I was sitting in the tiny canteen in Aquinas Street waiting to 'go on' for my NT audition, and having a cup of tea with other candidates, Sheila Reid, Edward Hardwicke and Neil Fitzpatrick.

The audition was timely as I'd been summarily sacked from the sock counter. I was called into the office of the head of personnel, a retired army major by the look of him. 'This is the end of the line, Petherbridge,' he said. I thought he must be referring to some of the merchandise that had been selling rather well, until he explained that he knew I'd been fiddling the till. Maths was never my strong point, and I might have been a shilling out now and then, but I knew I was innocent. The head saleslady had occasionally relieved me of a customer's cash, saying, 'I'll put that through for you,' and I can only suppose that her little sideline ended with my exit. I'd given a good performance as an attentive and helpful sales assistant.

Cameo in *An Awfully Big Adventure*

When I was filming Dick St Ives
In some of Dublin's quainter dives
Interesting emanations
Issued from the film's locations
For instance – the Olympic Theatre
Where one quickly learnt to fear to
Loiter near the back stalls Gents
Because of certain pungent scents
Caused by clapped out ball and cock
Plaster work, bright pink Baroque
Swirled encircling circles, boxes
Such are Theatre's paradoxes
Rampant stucco celebration
Over rot and dank stagnation
Perfect! That's the film's main theme
Rotting fabric of a dream.

Where was I? Playing Dick St Ives
A thespian who *just* contrives
To hang on by a slender thread
To fading visions in his head
Of how it all was meant to be
A café scene – he's taking tea
(See it and you'll raise a 'but'.

Oh, the scene was very cut)
Dick hears whispers of *St Ives*
Maybe six or seven wives
Tighten grips on pastry knives
This actor of so many lives
Sits and breathes the selfsame air
Just across the tables – *there*
Adjusting furs they pass the butter
Glad his lovely name to utter
Richard, never Dick, St Ives
Breathe the quickened teatime wives
Nod and smile if they feel able
Blush and rearrange the table
Going out, contrive to sidle
Past their Repertory idol.

86

Velvet collar hints romance
Of kinds their husbands would not chance
Mowing lawns behind the privet
Dick is sure that he can rivet –
Hero, thespian and pet
Part high priest of smart box set –
Firmly rivet fond attention
Stirring yearnings wives don't mention.

Drinks table above the couch
Business with tobacco pouch
Throw away a line – so deft
Hesitate, then exit left
Better not to measure wages
Rather count the scripted pages
In Act Two his voice will harden
Gazing out across the garden
Seeing pleasant green Home Counties
Richard, when he cares to count his
Blessings, knows they've not included
Far green hills past bowers secluded
Viewed through open windows – French
No; he knows the subtle stench
Of someone's cooking down the hall
Life's domain is rather small.

Dickie's conflicts, were they staged
Would leave his audience enraged
Or at best, say, disappointed
Guardians of taste, appointed
By the Lord High Chamberlain
Edit language, skirt round sin
Though he has a certain pride
Narrow is the gap, not wide
Between his rather guarded hubris
And his tawdry nemesis
Unless his drama's sketched with tact
Punished or redeemed, he's lacked
In life a good plot line –
Missed he knows – something that's fine
What price The Theatre? Should he chuck it?
It's the fireman and his bucket
That he sees when gazing off
Shooting cuffs, just like a toff.

When I was filming Dick St Ives
In some of Dublin's quainter dives
Interesting emanations
Issued from the film's locations
Edits? Something to deplore –
Oblivion on the cutting room floor
Still, I saw the film – and winced
What was left, I fear, convinced.

Olivier's National Theatre

Chapter 7

The Triumphs of Repertoire, the Glories of Ensemble: *Othello*

In February 1964 I spoke my first lines as a National Theatre player. I had only two lines, but they were spoken to Laurence Olivier's Othello.

I'd first seen Olivier in his film of *Henry V* at our little local cinema when I was eight. It was all well above my head, but the year before, seated in the gallery of the Bradford Alhambra for a performance of *Humpty Dumpty*, I'd taken the decision to become an actor, and was consequently predisposed to respect any film that began and ended its action in a theatre. In any case, I believe I'd got wind even then of Olivier's reputation as a great actor. I know that if the building in Birch Lane were still a cinema, I would be able to take you now almost to the very seat I sat in, experiencing the mid-1940s equivalent of the feeling 'this is where it's at.'

You'll gather I wasn't one of those precocious children who devour the classics early and commit chunks of Shakespeare to memory; who have recourse to old chests and attics where the materials for fabulous costumes and props are to be found, alcoves in drawing rooms to serve as stages, and the flair of a young Diaghilev to make my version of *Henry V* the high point of a house party or an aunt's visit. But I was stagestruck. I had ambitions, though I sat there in the Birch Lane cinema 'little dreaming', as they say in theatrical memoirs.

At a much later, 'grown-up' viewing of *Henry V*, I was thrilled by a subtle moment in the opening scenes when the camera, moving to show us round the crowded activity backstage in the Globe Theatre's Tiring House, suddenly comes upon Olivier, attired as the King, standing still and quiet, waiting by the door which leads onto the stage. He's about to make his first entrance. Very, very gently he clears his throat. I hardly dare risk re-examining that moment. Film performances stay the same; we change. Perfectly, I thought, Olivier caught the moment just before an actor starts to act, before he steps from a private into a public reality. Typically imaginative and cunning of him to let us into that lone intimacy, to make it his star entrance into the film, and then to take us with him in his pocket onto the stage of the Globe.

This was the titan whom I found myself standing next to in a rehearsal room in 1964, and to whom I addressed the lines:

> 'Tis true, most worthy signor.
> The duke's in council, and your noble self
> I am sure is sent for.

91

while wishing there were not quite so many sibilants in them.

At one point in the routine of performance, I would stand with Olivier on the cusp between private and public reality. It was before one of his Act IV entrances: I was behind Sir, waiting in the Old Vic's OP Assembly in my parti-coloured tights for my third (non-speaking) characterization as a Venetian gentleman, along with Lodovico and other attendants. As always, he was utterly still and quiet and, in deference to him, so were we. The burden of Othello apart, he always felt that his deportment in the wings in every production must set an impeccable example. He'd been playing Othello at the rate of one mid-week matinée per week for a long time. Aside from other considerations, it was a way of ensuring a capacity matinée. He was beginning to have occasional tricky moments when he would have little dries, which he would cover by keeping going in the metre. I distinctly recall, in the arrival at Cyprus, 'I prattle out of fashion, and I dote / In mine own comforts' becoming one afternoon, 'I prattle out of fashion, and am botched / In mine own infancy.'

On another afternoon there was a certain subdued tension in the atmosphere in the OP Assembly: I forget what momentary loss of fluency had occurred. Unexpectedly, as we stood in the gloom, Olivier, still looking at the ground, broke the uneasy silence by murmuring, 'Anyway, I've fucked up better productions than this.'

But I also remember standing near him at our very first performance of *Othello*. It was in Birmingham at the Alexander Theatre. In the Senate scene, I was diagonally nine feet behind him to his left as he began:

Most potent, grave, and reverend signors,
My very noble and approved good masters.

It was like watching a Rolls-Royce on its maiden run. We know that you can stand a silver sixpence vertically on its rim on the bonnet of a Rolls, whilst the engine is idling, and there will be no vibration to disturb the balance of the coin. A Rolls doesn't have nerves. All I saw of Sir's that night was the slightest shift in some deep psychic gear, the faintest slowing in speed, masking the effort to shake off all possibility of superfluous vibration so that Othello's powerful engine could be seen, at this stage in the play, only to be proudly turning over in neutral.

*   *   *

Knowing as much as I do about the glories of ensemble work from mostly bitter experience, it was nevertheless a bit of a shock to read in Joan Plowright's memoirs, *And That's Not All*, how, quite early on in her career as part of the English Stage Company at the Royal Court in the mid-1950s, she came to think of herself no longer as merely a part of what she called 'the ensemble'. Clearly there was in her mind a tangible dividing line, and she'd crossed it for good. Just as there was a divide in Olivier's mind when some years later he got wind of the fact that the director John Dexter had seduced some young man auditioning for the National Theatre Company. Threatening Dexter with the sack and worse, Olivier said, 'We do not fuck the help!'

Unmolested, I joined the National in February 1964, four months after its inception, as part of the first fresh intake on a twelve-month contract in my eighth year as an actor at the age of twenty-six. I was to walk on with my two lines in *Othello* and take play-as-cast potluck as the season progressed, but I didn't quite see myself as the theatrical equivalent of below-stairs domestic help. For one thing the acting company, including Olivier himself, was listed alphabetically, so that one could be convinced of a new world order in which Clive Rust had equal billing with Lynn and Michael Redgrave and Joyce Redman. National Theatregoers knew the Prufrocks, Pembers, Petherbridges and Pickups from the Plowrights, of course, but not so securely as we do now in the knowledge of hindsight 'Kay Gallie, Michael Gambon, Reginald Green'. After all Stanislavski had said at the Moscow Art Theatre, 'There are no small parts, only small actors', and I didn't think I was a small actor – what actor does at twenty-six? I looked forward to the security of twelve months' work at eighteen pounds a week and an extra one-pound performance fee, so that I might eventually average twenty-one pounds a week. The year before £3,200, provided by my parents-in-law, had secured Louise and me outright a derelict house in Highshore Road, Peckham.

Early on during my time at the Old Vic of the 1960s, a coin-operated milk-dispensing machine was installed in the backstage canteen (no such thing as a green room). Battery eggs, poached, scrambled or fried, dubious 'pork' sausages (for which Olivier would occasionally queue with us), factory-sliced bread and pieces of cheese cut from large blocks, snug in polythene wrapping, and meat and two veg were available. It was a steamy basement, immediately beneath Sir Laurence's ground-floor dressing room, which had once been Lilian Baylis's office. Daylight crept down into this canteen from windows up at pavement level, while fluorescent tubes in the ceiling provided the most debilitating and least theatrical light source ever devised. Here was where the frustrations and gossip and jokes, the fury and excitement of the day were brought.

Long days sometimes, canteen coffee, then the ten o'clock rehearsal up in the lofty skylit room at the very top of the building, where in summer one wanted to throw open the side windows (bricked up now) looking down onto Waterloo Road, but couldn't because of the traffic noise, which would have disturbed the atmosphere and the process of pretending to be someone else, somewhere else and usually some*when* else. When I joined the company, National Theatre rehearsals confirmed what my previous eight years of professional experience, in less exalted circumstances, had taught me, that rehearsal wasn't a series of planning sessions to work out the strategy of an imminent campaign. It was the start of the battle, a series of skirmishes (one hoped for friendly matches) for which that cup of coffee or plastic cup of milk from the machine was the minimum requirement before one stepped, armed to the teeth, onto the rehearsal room floor; the charmed space where alliances and partnerships, and even marriages, are made and enmities and jealousies forged, to last a lifetime. As likely as not, any one of us would be on stage at night or at matinées in whatever alternative worlds the changing repertoire threw up: the vast Inca Kingdom, the rotten state of Denmark (Shakespeare's or Stoppard's as the case might be), the Home Counties house from whose French windows on a clear day you could see Marlow (or, irresistibly, as Noël Coward famously quipped, when trying to rid Edith Evans of the obtruding 'very': 'Edith, on a clear day you can see Marlow. On a very clear day you can see Marlowe and Beaumont and Fletcher.'). Whether we were intent on making our pretendings as real as our real selves, or vice versa, is uncertain. But reality came into it, I'm positive.

During some sort of lull one mid-morning, I was sitting alone in the Old Vic basement canteen. There was nobody about with whom to prattle or moan, when three men, unmistakably from the 'real' world, walked in. They were wearing raincoats over suits, and two of them were carrying clipboards. Solemnly they formed a semicircle round the large blue-and-white milk machine, which stood on the floor and was a standard leading man's height. Pause. Eventually what seemed to me to be the most senior member of the trio felt in his trouser pocket and produced a coin, stepped forward slightly and inserted it into the slot. It dropped deep inside the machine with a reassuringly technical clunkity-ping. Another pause. They all watched. A plastic cup dropped into position in the little recess just below waist height. A further slight pause, and then an eccentric triple jet of milk squirted down and knocked the lightweight plastic cup sideways. The milk splayed out towards the semicircle of men. Change of rhythm. For the first time they moved rather quickly, backwards. Unwittingly they obeyed the rules of comedy and did not themselves laugh. When the wayward jets ceased, one man made a note on his clipboard and the junior member of the inspectorate gazed at the machine more intently. Their boss looked in the direction of the counter, expecting someone to appear with a mop, which they did. There wasn't an artisan amongst them to investigate the machine's innards. Nobody spoke.

Around this time, in a completely separate operation I am sure, the National was experiencing another, more prying intrusion – more unmistakable men in suits from the real world. Actually, Olivier usually wore a suit and spectacles and, in his overcoat and trilby hat, gave a convincing impression of the Man from the Prudential. It was a protective mask, of course: he could not go naked about the world, or even the canteen, as the great, protean, tragicomic creature that he was. He only needed to take his spectacles off to create a poetic effect, which he couldn't help doing even playing the raincoat-wearing police inspector in the movie *Bunny Lake is Missing*. We National Theatre players looked askance at the men from the firm of consultants undertaking one of those studies to see what improvements in efficiency might be made. We assumed that behind their masks lurked nothing more creative than accountancy. I never saw them come into a rehearsal room, nor ask any actor, who had rehearsed all week

94

and played three or four nights in up to six productions at any one time, when exactly they thought about their roles, made time to learn lines, or whether the practice of confining less privileged actors to walk-on parts, or even on-stage furniture shifting, was an efficient use of university-degree material or made appropriate demands on the skills acquired in two or three years' training at drama school and several seasons in provincial rep and on tour.

They would have been impressed to learn that Noël Coward had written *Hay Fever* in three days, but what did they make of the hours spent by the stage staff shipping, amongst other odd items, Peruvian gold, Mother Courage's cart, bits of a Salem courthouse and Judith Bliss's French windows in and out of the doors of the small scene dock and across the pavement of Waterloo Road, into or out of a waiting scenery truck, to and from storage? Was this so that visitors to London could gorge themselves in one theatre on five or six National Theatre productions in any given week? Was it to keep the company tuned and busy? Or was the repertoire system, as I heard Kenneth Tynan declare, simply a means of enabling actors to become stale in five productions at once?

Sooner or later, one had one's glory nights, but the tedium of routine and the frustration at unharnessed ambition are feelings I can so easily conjure up when I think of egg and chips in the Old Vic canteen, constant Tannoy announcements over the loud chatter, the stone steps up to the minor dressing rooms (they made you hold onto your bit parts for YEARS). Yet it only took a trip 'out front' for the vivid, life-affirming purpose of it all to manifest itself. Then it was as if one had emerged from the dust, mouldering cassocks and battered hymnals in some dull old vestry to find the priests and congregation in a state of grace and the choir soaring. It was to find one's colleagues, by the force of ritual and routine, galvanized into a heightened existence. The disparate base elements of the Old Vic day – the fan mail picked up from Ernie at the stage door; the cast lists, the rehearsal calls posted on the noticeboard; the young would-be designer with his brush and pot of dark brown paint in his solitary work, making sure that the little dents and damage done to Sean Kenny's huge, plain-plaster proscenium would be perfectly disguised as dark wood once more before the house was opened; the usherette counting her change in the gallery and dreaming of life in Dressing Room No. 1; the thousand little tasks of the day to do with electric wires and curled wigs – all would be focused.

One afternoon I dropped in on a full dress rehearsal of *Juno and the Paycock*, well into its run (it must have been some sort of refresher rehearsal, maybe because it had been out of the repertoire). The sturdy Frank Finlay was a wonderful wisp of flotsam in an oversized overcoat as Joxer. Colin Blakely and Joyce Redmond played the title roles and I can still see them inhabiting that large, once elegant room in a Dublin terrace. I don't know who else was watching because I was utterly alone in the stalls of what seemed to be an empty theatre, and I still treasure the experience of looking into that room where the characters lived and the actors showed such effortless assurance, and without an audience – the nearest thing to 'art for art's sake' I've ever seen.

Did they know, the men in suits, that Sir Laurence Olivier, Artistic Director as well as leading actor in the company and occasional director of plays, had personally taken time to write to London Transport to request that the bus stop outside the scene dock doors be moved a little further down Waterloo Road because the ding-ding of the bell and the groan of the engine when the bus restarted could be heard on stage?[1] Did they know that Olivier had sent a personal reply to a lady who had written to complain that the draught on her feet in the stalls had marred her appreciation of a performance?

Did any of those consultants, or us for that matter, think of calling a halt to the 1960s mania for concrete Brutalism and conceive instead of preserving the beautiful Old Vic as the heart of the National Theatre? Did anyone think of acquiring the neighbouring plot to the south for modest expansion and maybe improving the Young Vic; or perhaps acquiring the splendid Hackney Empire as a second auditorium (a national asset if ever there was one, with its stage boxes housed in exotic Indian pepper pots) and taking the NT closer to 'the people'? We thought of none of these things. Rather, we now witness nightly the theatrical miracle of the National Theatre on the South Bank, rising above and being greater than the sum of architect Denys Ladun's decidedly dodgy pre-stressed concrete parts, his Brutalist Epidaurus with brutal acoustics to match. Ah well, the milk machines in the canteen have been perfected; unlike our National Theatre, they've become smaller. The handiwork, the craft of creating theatre, as opposed to theatres, survives and transcends.

I do not need to labour the connection between the longueurs in the lives of Stoppard's bemused and underused Elizabethan attendant lords and my fleeting involvement in Othello's tragedy: one of 'certain officers with torches', the one with two lines; a peaceable non-speaking Cypriot with a turban, beard, brown make-up and bare feet, playing a tin whistle in the 'And let me the cannikin clink' scene (I'd begun by thinking of this as very nearly a featured role on account of my musical contribution); and, moments later, one of about six rioting Cypriots in the gloom down R., struggling mimetically against two Venetian soldiers who were barring our entrance with a horizontal halberd. The soldiers were played by Peter John, now a club marvellous comedian specializing in drag, and Tom Kempinski, whose play *Duet for One* so impressed me at the Duke of York's in 1980. Peter would sometimes murmur subversively, sibilantly under his breath such remarks as 'Oh, settle down – you Cypriots are all the same!' Big as they both were, we had to struggle mimetically or we'd have won the day, but we knew our place and were instantly pacified by Sir Laurence's slow, well-lit entrance from up

---

[1] Confusingly, a second bus stop has appeared a few yards to the north, nearer to the front-of-house entrance, to spoil my story – have people no sense of history?

centre as Othello, dressed in his long white robe, casually cradling a gleaming scimitar on his right arm, and his 'What is the matter here?'

When calm was re-established and Cassio cashiered, I removed the beard, washed off the brown make-up and put on parti-coloured tights to walk across the stage in Othello's wake as a Venetian gentleman and witness him strike Desdemona's face – rather hard one night because she'd been difficult, as Robert Stephens maintained. According to his account, imparted on several occasions in later years, I was supposed to have inadvertently gasped and blurted out 'Maggie!' However, unlike Sir Robert, who'd terribly wanted to play Iago but never did, I was there, of course, and would have remembered.

My whole costume – cap, cape, voluminous shirt, doublet and sword – was carefully copied from an inch-high supernumerary in a large oil painting of Venice by Caravaggio. I remember looking closely at him, examining the few tiny, deft brushstrokes from which he'd been composed and wondering if he'd been 'made up' or if Caravaggio had actually seen him. Either way he still survives, his inch in history secure, whereas my life-size version of him does not. Who would remember it? Perhaps I *should* have called out 'Maggie!' The costume flits by still, digitally remastered on DVD, but worn by David Hargreaves because I had left the cast by the time they came to film the production. Even Sir's Othello does not really survive that film (or so I thought at the time and so, in fact, thought Sir Laurence who always watched the rushes and would say, apparently, 'I can't get the measure of it. Frank's got it, but I can't.'). If you did not see his Othello on the stage, you must take it on trust that those – and they were legion – who called it great might well have been right, unless you want to believe Sir Richard Eyre, who is on record, in his published diary *National Service*, as finding it 'almost risible.'[2]

I have recently seen the film version. The cover reminds me that Olivier, Smith, Finlay (as Iago) and Joyce Redman (as Emilia) gained Oscar nominations for their performances. Olivier uncompromisingly gives his theatre performance, with a vocal concession now and then to the intimate proximity of the microphone. One sees immediately why Eyre and others would label it 'almost risible', but I have met LA film actors who flew to London and somehow got tickets to see the stage production and were bowled over, as if there were not reams enough of critical praise to quote. Meanwhile, the only thing I can say, having had the whole shebang at finger-tip command on the screen of my laptop, is that it might have been more appropriate to install cameras in the Old Vic for a few live performances and film it in its proper context. Then we would have known what we were seeing. As it is, it's not a *film* film, but rather an uneasy hybrid: the set is Jocelyn Herbert-Sloane Square-Brechtian, expanded from the stage production to fill a big film studio. When it gets slightly decorative, as in

---

[2] The qualifying 'almost' has disappeared from Eyre's latest repetition of this opinion.

some of the Venice scenes, it looks lightweight – plywood and patches of metal foil, like something designed for a Selfridges shop window. You get your money's worth with Sir Laurence. The circus comes to town, you see the tent go up and the lions fed, but Olivier's every thought and expression is visible at the back of the gallery, so to speak. You can even hear the influence of Noël Coward, whom Olivier once understudied, in the artic-u-la-tion. *Othello* is not a film script and this is not film acting, though, needless to state, Olivier has given some great film performances. I begin to sympathize, I am shocked to admit, with those people who used to complain of Olivier on the stage that you could see the wheels going round.

I was understudy for Frank Finlay's Iago for some time. It is the longest part in Shakespeare and I watched as much of every performance as I could for the purpose of keeping the lines and moves in my head. In London, I would creep through a tiny door reached from the landing, one level up from my third-floor dressing room, and into the darkness of the Old Vic flies. There, out of bounds, I'd peep down between the close sets of tied-off ropes, squatting out of sight on top of the great heaps and coils of hemp that completely covered the fly gallery floor. Always I was somehow irrationally apprehensive in case I might accidentally unleash the great weight of something hanging up there over the action below, where Iago was sowing his poisonous seeds of jealousy and cleverly simulating concern:

IAGO	But I am much to blame;
	I humbly do beseech you of your pardon
	For too much loving you.
OTHELLO	I am bound to thee for ever.
IAGO	I see this hath a little dashed your spirits.
OTHELLO	Not a jot, not a jot.
IAGO	I'faith, I fear it has.
	I hope you will consider what is spoke
	Comes from my love. But I do see you're moved.
	I am to pray you not to strain my speech
	To grosser issues nor to larger reach
	Than to suspicion.
OTHELLO	I will not.
IAGO	Should you do so, my lord,
	My speech should fall into such vile success
	As my thoughts aimed not at. Cassio's my worthy friend –
	My lord, I see you're moved.
OTHELLO	No, not much moved.

By which point I could see Olivier below, standing like a bull that had received the blade of the picador's lance.

Reading again these lines, I am struck, shocked even, by the formal beauty of the writing – though it is not a 'beautiful' scene – as if I'm eavesdropping on the two actors saying the words all those years ago but absorbing, too, the words neat, direct from the page like some miraculous transcript of reality that goes straight for the heart and happens to be in blank verse, for God's sake! Olivier called Shakespeare 'the nearest thing in incarnation to the eye of God.'

I suppose I had Iago's lines perfectly memorized. I was never put to the acid test, except one morning during an understudy rehearsal of this very scene, when I sensed a subtle change of atmosphere in the rehearsal room. Then I noticed in my peripheral vision that Sir had slipped in and was sitting on a bench just inside the door. At the end of the sequence we behaved as if he hadn't been there. He'd often leave as quietly as he'd arrived – it was his modest fly-on-the-wall performance – but he made a moment to come up to me and whisper, 'It is perfectly possible to play Iago as a Renaissance villain, but not in this production. He's a non-commissioned officer.'

I thought of Frank's brilliantly funny, absolutely authentic performance as the corporal in Wesker's *Chips with Everything* at the Royal Court and knew that it was because of the barrack-room qualities he'd caught so perfectly there that he'd been cast as Iago. I'd also seen Tito Gobbi's Iago threatening to act and sing Mario del Monaco's Otello off the stage at La Scala, Milan in 1960, and knew Olivier was determined that even the foothills of the heights of his Othello would not be scaled by the actor playing Iago, nor would Iago be played 'entirely for laughs', as Olivier confesses he himself had played him against Ralph Richardson's 'boring' Othello. Frank's list of credits at the time contained just one Shakespearean character – the First Gravedigger in Olivier's inaugural NT production of *Hamlet* in 1963.

I do not subscribe to the dismal showbiz philosophy that *Othello* must be by its nature a competition, and the better the Othello, the worse will appear the Iago, or vice versa. Giant though Olivier was, he was not big enough to conceive of truly sharing the play with Iago, and his 'triumph' is, as I thought at the time, accordingly both inflated and diminished, and the great play suffers.

Astonishing that the wise and brilliant Trevor Nunn should cast the wonderful bass-baritone Willard White as Othello alongside McKellen's Iago. He might just as well have expected Ian to be able to sing Iago in Verdi's *Otello*. I recall a radio interview in which Willard White described his realization, as he observed Ian rehearse, of what an overwhelming multitude of choices there were in the interpretation of a line of Shakespeare, as opposed to a stave of music. Once again, however, I find myself revising my reaction. Sir Willard's performance seems much fuller and more at his command in the screened version of the production on DVD.

Thank God I never had to pit my Iago, straining for a touch of the barrack-room 'honest soldier', or, for that matter, my lightweight Renaissance villain against Sir's Othello, which I can still see vividly as if from behind my tin whistle (I did a little entr'acte link around 'These letters give, Iago, to the Pilot') or from down R. in the underlit OP Assembly. I was still in the cast when over one Sunday we made the LP, enacting the whole production in our rehearsal clothes on the vast floor of a recording studio in West Hampstead, now the ENO rehearsal rooms. Without me, the production went to Moscow and West Berlin, the film was made, and then it returned to the repertoire.

One afternoon before I rejoined its ranks (its other ranks), I stood at the back of the dress circle in the Old Vic, able to watch a matinée. Dexter's production was not good. Bewigged actors in scarlet damask stood about superfluously in the Venetian court; the supporting 'character acting' was both thin and coarse. The result was an unhappy amalgam of British reach-me-down Berliner Ensemble with echoes of the old Old Vic on a bad day. Only the stars acted with authority and managed to create and inhabit a world. I knew Sir Laurence's every smallest gesture, each note and inflection of his performance – he was nothing if not minutely consistent – and all I can say is that three times that afternoon I experienced the quite unexpected sensation of something very like what the Ghost describes might happen to 'each particular hair' on Hamlet's head, happening to those on mine.

Chapter 8

Masks and Faces: *The Royal Hunt of the Sun*

Few people could have predicted that, when we got our National Theatre Company, the first play it would produce by a living author on the stage of the Old Vic would be Noël Coward's 1925 drawing-room comedy *Hay Fever*. That was in October 1964. Strictly speaking, Peter Shaffer's historical epic *The Royal Hunt of the Sun* came first, but was put on in the National's 1964 summer season at Chichester and didn't hit the Old Vic stage until December.

I was lying on the grass in the Chichester sun, during a brief respite from John Dexter's rigorous, not to say tyrannical, rehearsals for *The Royal Hunt*, when I heard the news that Noël Coward himself was going to direct *Hay Fever*. After my walk-ons in *Othello*, I'd hoped for something better but I had little hope of being cast as Simon, the young son of Coward's Bliss family. In any case, I had already played him in weekly rep four years earlier and decided that a week's rehearsal had been quite enough to plumb that vapid young man's shallows. So the part was not one I was going to feel too regretful about, though I would have liked to notch up being directed by 'The Master', as Coward was still known throughout the profession, the term by then having acquired a slight pre-Royal Court Watershed quaintness.

Although Coward had written *Hay Fever* in just three days, I don't think I knew then that he had described it as 'far and away one of the most difficult plays to perform that I have ever encountered.' Be that as it may, a three-month rehearsal period was what the company had been allotted to deal with the difficulties of *The Royal Hunt*, Peter Shaffer having turned from his successful drawing-room mode to write a play that he intended would create 'magic' out of 'Total Theatre'. Shaffer wanted to show the Inca civilization and its conquest and destruction by the Spanish Conquistadors.

On that open-thrust stage at Chichester the Spaniards would have to climb the Andes and discover the Inca culture, a culture they would savagely destroy. There was the whole Spanish/Peruvian culture-clash dialectic, a massacre of Peruvian Indians to stage, the creation of an agricultural Inca 'Toil Song' with actions of sowing and reaping, as well as the chanting of laments and a suggestion of life in the Sun God's court. Was twelve weeks going to be enough? Would our imaginations and techniques be stretched sufficiently for such a Total Theatre task? There was much to do. My modest-sized speaking part looked good in the cast list, coming immediately after the Sun God himself, but I have to say that beside Shaffer's 'Villac Umu, High Priest of Peru', Coward's Simon Bliss seemed to have the multi-layered dynamic of an Ibsen character.

'Why did I write *The Royal Hunt*?', Peter Shaffer asked in a programme note. 'To make colour? Yes. To make spectacle? Yes. To make magic? Yes – if the word isn't too debased to convey the kind of excitement I believed could still be created out of "total" theatre. The "totality" of it was in my head for ages: not just the words, but jungle cries and ululations; metals and masks and the fantastic creations of the pre-Columbian world. It was not that I wanted to see the real horses of Ben Hur canter painfully around the stage again; but I did deeply want to create, by means both austere and rich – means always disciplined by a central aesthetic – an experience that was *entirely and only theatrical.*'

I can't resist some bizarre statistics now. When Noël Coward had written and directed his own total-theatre entertainment, *Cavalcade*, at Drury Lane Theatre in 1931, the *Ben Hur* tradition of real chariot races was not long dead in that theatre. Coward engaged no horses, only 400 human extras for the crowd scenes. In 1533 the vast Inca Kingdom was conquered and its culture destroyed by the Spanish invading army of less than 200 men. We, however, were sixteen actors playing the Peruvians and fifteen actors playing the Spaniards.

There was excitement about the Total Theatre aspect of the production, although you might say that your average young actor had already been through a training theatrically broad. Even in the two disused wool warehouses in Bradford's Chapel Street, where I had trained (and Robert Stephens before me), I had taken it for granted that one needed to stretch one's imagination and technique by pretending to be earth, air, fire and water. I expected to, and did, imitate anything from a tiger to a moth, boldly improvising études to the piano music. In other classes I tumbled, danced, worked at the barre and mimed, sang and fenced and spouted Shakespeare, the better to be able to pretend to be an 'ordinary' human being walking, probably through French windows, into an ordinary, if well-appointed, drawing room (such as the Bliss family's). This drawing room had three walls and a dark space beyond the footlights in which sat upwards of a thousand people, whom one would try to convince that the 'very torrent, tempest, and, as I may say, whirlwind' of passion, in the third act by the drinks table, 'o'er-stepped not the modesty of nature.'

Rivalling Hamlet's advice to the Players (which is not Shakespeare's advice, of course, not a pro's advice but a prince's) is that of Laurence Olivier (prince among players) to the students at the opening of the Old Vic Theatre School in 1947: 'The difference between the actual truth and the illusion of truth is what you are about to learn. You will not finish learning it until you are dead.' During that three-month rehearsal period for *The Royal Hunt*, the difference between the actual truth and the illusion of truth was very wide.

Since drama school, I had been subconsciously preparing myself for the dawn of that brave new theatrical world Winnie Hodgkinson had predicted; I was actually on the look-out for further training, though I don't think the phrase 'Total Theatre' had yet been coined. Meanwhile I managed to get to London to see what struck me as the apotheosis of drawing-room naturalism, with an outdoor scene thrown in. I saw the Moscow Art Theatre's *The Cherry Orchard* on their first astonishing visit, emerging from behind the Iron Curtain into London at Sadler's Wells in 1958. The cast bristled with veterans who had been directed by, and even acted with, Stanislavski himself. They had survived the Stalin years; many of them had been awarded Stalin Prizes. Stalin had died only five years earlier, having since the mid-1930s established and maintained Socialist Realism as the touchstone of Soviet culture. So it was amazing to see these actors who exuded a Chekhovian atmosphere so poignant that they seemed still to be related to the carefully posed figures in the famous 1898 photograph of Chekhov reading *The Seagull* to the original company of the Moscow Art Theatre. But they were vibrantly alive, and indeed they must have been as intrigued and excited to be playing in the West as we were at their arrival from the East.

It had never been made known to us, or indeed I suppose officially to them, that the young actor on the extreme right of that famous photograph, Meyerhold, the first Constantine, had been tortured and eventually executed by firing squad at the beginning of 1940, ostensibly on a charge of spying but really for his bold denunciation of Socialist Realism. Shortly after his arrest, his wife, actress Zinaida Raikh, was found murdered in their flat in Gorky Street. Meyerhold was praised in a Soviet book called *Moscow Theatres*, published in English in 1959, while at the same time castigated for his decadence and 'his grave and serious errors'. Is the following quote from the book, which is obviously a commissar-checked Soviet description of Meyerhold's theatre, and is it in fact a description of the *Total* Theatre that by then even the Soviets were beginning to embrace? 'In exaggerated symbolic images, unexpected mise-en-scènes, tense satiated rhythms, and a dynamic approach, Meyerhold's works render the great ideas of the contemporary world.' The book's chilling euphemistic final words on Meyerhold are: 'He left the stage at a time of great emotional strain, when the audience cooled to his theatre, and he himself sought new and, possibly, fruitful paths.' The Soviet actors I saw certainly spent their lives learning the difference between the actual truth and the illusion of truth.

The Moscow Art Theatre made a big impact here in 1958, despite the fact that already, two years earlier, we had seen Bertolt Brecht's own company, a company dedicated to transcending, if not exploding, the Stanislavski System. On 20 January 1953 Brecht wrote in his journal: 'In my view the elaborate exercises Stanislavsky prescribed for actors may have become necessary because only with extraordinary means, with almost yoga concentration, could they shore up figures from the private bourgeois sphere.'

The Berliner Ensemble's *Trumpets and Drums* was stunningly witty and stylish, even in impenetrable German. I found their grey *Mother Courage* a heady mixture – thrilling and boring by turns. There were its spare yet intriguingly arid scenic devices (we'd seen nothing like them) and its swift, fluid epic style, interspersed with long waits during which we stared at a white sheet of a traverse curtain and, having read the projected words on it, sank down onto the linoleum beneath our standing positions at the back of the second circle till the next scene, only to find that one flat had been moved three feet. This was the Alienation Effect, kicking in to leave us in possession of our objective moral and political judgment, so that we would not be swept up in waves of empathy for the characters. But, oh, how we were moved by the deaf-and-dumb daughter on the roof beating the drum, trying to save the children! I heard that Brecht rehearsed that scene endlessly in despair of his beloved 'A' Effect. The marvellous fat actress who played it got the lion's share of the cheers at the curtain calls.

That Palace Theatre production with Brecht's widow, Helene Weigel, pulling that never-to-be-forgotten cart against the revolving stage at the opening with her children, all of them singing a wonderful dissonant marching song, and at the end bent and alone, caused the British Theatre to remove wholesale the footlights and strip stages, in order to expose the lighting, and resulted in troupes of bewildered or infuriated actors being told by young ambitious directors that they must adopt the 'A' Effect – and not just in the plays of Brecht. It wouldn't surprise me to learn that some green director then, trying to make a splash in a provincial backwater, had invoked the 'A' Effect in Agatha Christie. They certainly tried it in Shakespeare.

During the lifetime of *The Royal Hunt* I was introduced to, and shook the hand of, Helene Weigel at a little reception up in the Old Vic rehearsal room, and was surprised to see her wearing a lovely cream-coloured silk blouse and a vivid shade of lipstick. The Berliner Ensemble did a special performance of *Mahogany*, which I saw. Robert Stephens got the opportunity to meet Weigel properly and asked her about the 'A' Effect. She said, 'Oh, don't worry about that; it's something Bertolt devised to stop our German actors being theatrical in the old-fashioned way.'

Still preparing myself, had I but known it, for Total Theatre, in 1962 I discovered a marvellous French teacher of mime, the Lecoq-trained Claude Chagrin, at London's City Lit, where Steven Berkoff was a fellow pupil. Later I worked with her at the Royal Court Actors' Studio. She taught comic mime and was rigorous in inducing us to be at once fluid and precise; I owe much to her and can still manage a quintessential impression of punting, though I'd need to rehearse before actually taking you on the river.

Claude's criticisms of the improvisations we created with our newly, shakily acquired pieces of formalized technique were delivered in attractive broken English, punctuated with abstract sounds and gestures, and were themselves poems of poised clowning and wordless eloquence. So, when the time came for me to become one of Shaffer's Incas, I had a head start because Claude turned up as the movement director, advising and devising everything from the Spaniard's climb up the Andes to the massacre of the Incas. She and the composer Marc Wilkinson invented an emblematic stage version of the lost Inca culture. Not many opportunities for clowning though.

George Devine, a famously avuncular, pipe-smoking figure, could create a rarefied atmosphere. I met him only once, in 1963, when I attended a mask class he gave at the Royal Court Actors' Studio. The ambience was almost religious. I'd had experience, through Bill Gaskill, of the comic half-mask in which one could speak. But it was the full, noble or neutral mask Devine was dealing with, and the convention was that you must not speak. Unlike the ancient Greek tragic masks, which were designed for speaking 'through', it was felt that these masks would be compromised by a voice coming muffled from behind a motionless mouth.

Devine didn't put on the mask himself. He held it reverently, as if reluctant to hand it over until he had taken us through his long list of dos and don'ts and suggested the short, simple solo 'études' we would improvise (e.g. 'receiving bad news in a letter', 'waiting', 'watching the sunrise' – poignant, classic 'dramaticules'). We were told that the mask would 'find us out' in anything that was not elementally pure and genuinely felt. The marvellous paradox I remember him uttering was: 'The mask will not hide you; it will reveal you.' The next year, my fellow Peruvian Indians and I were to spend all of our stage time behind masks – masks neither comic, tragic, noble nor neutral. The hitch was they hid us.

Those were the days when the word 'Peruvians' in a script had white actors reaching for their brown bole. We all used Max Factor Pan-Cake, a shade paler than Olivier's in *Othello*, and, following his example, washed it off in the showers with Fairy washing-up liquid.

Although it's a play about Christians invading another culture, a culture ruled over by a dictator/God, a play about Christians using evangelism and 'The Prince of Peace' to put a gloss on their slaughterous, conquering lust for empire and Peruvian gold, I should imagine that when Trevor Nunn revived the play forty-two years later in 2006, the rehearsal discussions about the Iraq War were over in no time. When I was in Syria in 2005, admiring a huge Crusaders' castle dominating a particularly fertile valley of olive groves, I wondered if there had appeared any anti-Crusade protest slogans daubed on medieval church walls at home: 'No War For Olive Oil'.

Having 'done my bit' in my bit part for so long (four years in the repertoire!) and played Atahualpa, the Sun God, at six performances, I still remember the sensations of being in the production, precisely what our bare feet on the boards felt and sounded like. As a rank-and-file Inca, I also recall my feathered and furred cloaks; the Velcro fixed to our horsehair wigs/headdresses to adhere to the complementary patches on our gold masks, clamping us into uniform anonymity; the sound of Colin Blakely's Northern Irish Pizarro and of Marc Wilkinson's music. Can I call up something essential about the play? Is it the now familiar variation on the Shafferean struggle – the emotional, spiritual, philosophical 'affair' between a raw, sometimes maladjusted hero who possesses something primitive, pure, elemental, and the civilized, conventional, 'conditioned' hero who has dried up, lost faith and belief? God is in the equation too, unquantifiable except possibly as a zero, or an absence amounting to less than nothing, making the equation insoluble and tragic, with no hope of balance or resolution of The Problem.

The Royal Hunt of the Sun was directed by John 'all problems are technical problems' Dexter and, allegedly, co-directed by Desmond 'all problems are probably spiritual' O'Donovan. The latter was tall with a beatific expression and, for one still young (he was thirty-one when I joined the company), a rather generous paunch. Bill Gaskill writes about him in his book, *A Sense of Direction*. He'd been educated at Stonyhurst and Oxford and had spent six years in a monastery, but suffered a nervous breakdown before his final vows. John Dexter was not tall and had left school in Derby at fourteen to work in a factory, struggled up from bit parts and became a self-styled rough (very rough) diamond, showman and, by turns, a charming magician and foul-mouthed martinet. Peter Cellier, son of the distinguished actor Frank Cellier, had some difficulty, during technical rehearsals of *The Royal Hunt*, with a heavy seven-foot crucifix he had to carry on in the first encounter with the Incas. Dexter's voice rang out from the auditorium: 'If I hear another murmur about that crucifix, Cellier, I'll smother it in KY and shove it up your arse!'

A year later, Albert Finney was to have a way of cutting Dexter down to size in rehearsals of *Armstrong's Last Goodnight*, by quietly singing *The Archers* signature tune – Dexter had appeared as a policeman in some episodes of the popular radio serial. I don't remember anyone else having the clout to risk that kind of strategy, apart from Colin Blakely. One Saturday afternoon, between the matinée and evening performances of *The Royal Hunt*, we were summoned up to the Vic rehearsal room, where Colin alone pierced the cowed silence as we were arraigned for supposedly allowing the production to go to the dogs. I remember Dexter saying to Robert Lang, 'You spoke every line as if the curtain was about to come down and I wish to Christ it had.' When Dexter began his list of caustic comments on Colin's performance, Colin quietly but firmly punctuated each criticism with the word 'bollocks'. It was like watching a war of nerves between two armadillos.

Dexter's rise at the Royal Court had been meteoric. Between 1957 and 1962, he'd successfully directed several Arnold Wesker premieres, most notably *Roots*, *The Kitchen* and *Chips with Everything*, and a commercial West End musical with Tommy Steele, *Half a Sixpence*. Dexter had none of the cold, puritanical theorizing and second-hand Brechtian approach which, for my money, dogged a lot of the work at the Royal Court and made it look in need of a blood transfusion. Olivier had invited him to the newly built Chichester Festival Theatre to direct *Saint Joan*, with Joan Plowright in the title role. Dexter's productions of *Othello* and *The Royal Hunt of the Sun* were the first two plays in which I appeared at the National.

The National's visiting movement teacher, Yat Malmgren, was originally a Swedish ballet dancer, a Rudolph Laban collaborator, and co-founder of

London's Drama Centre. Yat thought that the big theatrical set pieces of the Inca 'Toil Song' and 'The Massacre' looked like 'something you might see in a South American cabaret.' He was in the minority. As Total Theatre, it was an immensely popular and, for the most part, critical success. 'By means austere and rich' meant, in design terms, a raked wooden platform backed by a bare wooden wall, uncompromisingly non-representational and very much influenced by the stark, functional simplicity of the Berliner Ensemble's house style, but actually derived from an older, even simpler notion of essential theatre: 'two boards and a passion.' When the audience entered at the beginning of the play with the curtain up, they saw the uncompromising timber, the there's-nothing-up-our-sleeves 'unworthy scaffold'. This, by 1964, was just the right modish springboard for a great big historical epic.

The subject, such a broad canvas, was, as I have said, a new departure for Peter Shaffer whose track record to date was a series of small-cast, dare I say, domestic subjects, which had been hits on Shaftesbury Avenue. There's a story told about a weekend at legendary impresario Hugh 'Binkie' Beaumont's country house. Shaffer had been invited down by the powerful West End entrepreneur to discuss his new play about the Conquistadors' conquest of Peru. It was a distinguished house party, several Beaumont stars including Gielgud were there, but by Sunday dinner his play had still not been mentioned. At one point Shaffer left the dinner table to go to the bathroom and, as he quietly let himself back into the dining room, Beaumont was in full spate about the play. What Shaffer heard was: ' … and then she has them climbing the Andes.' At the time, this story, no doubt happily related by Peter Shaffer himself, epitomized the gulf between the old West End and the bold new subsidized sector under the theatrical influence of Europe and the wider world (on our doorstep at the Aldwych in Peter Daubney's annual World Theatre Seasons between 1964 and 1975). Subsequently, Shaffer's *Black Comedy* combined the influences of French farce and particularly Peking Opera's brilliantly skilled scene of a sword fight in the dark, performed in bright light.

At the beginning of *The Royal Hunt*, Michael Annals's timber wall was emblazoned with a segmented steel disc, about twelve feet in diameter, bearing the emblem of the cross. The play starts in Christian Spain, with Pizarro recruiting an army, through the lure of gold, to conquer the 'heathen' Inca Empire. The moment when the play and the production effected the transition from Christian steel to Inca gold must rate as one of the simplest and most brilliant *coups de théâtre* ever devised. Annals was doodling on a paper napkin in the dining car of the Brighton Belle, designing portable sun emblems, when he let out a Eureka cry. As he unfolded the napkin, there came to him the idea: the petals of the sun opening. It was part theatrical dissolve, part 'jump cut', transporting the audience from Christian Spain to the heart of the Inca civilization. Loud chants of 'Incah — ah!' I've still got the LP – proof of my own amazing, unrecognizable vocal contributions, particularly in my solo lines in the opening lament of Act Two. I truly wonder that my vocal chords have survived; I felt I was sacrificing something of them on the altar of theatrical effectiveness every time I climbed up into Sean Kenny's permanent proscenium to open the act unseen, my voice echoing in the stone stairwell behind me as I put my entire heart and guts into that gobbledygook cry from the Inca heart. A short version of that second-act lament – the Incas seemed to be lamenting even in triumphant mode – heralded the first-act sunburst of the Incas onto the amazed Conquistadors; drums and cymbals, xylophones and lion roars (achieved with string, French chalk and pigskin drums) as the stage filled with gold-masked, befeathered actors and the cold, silvery sheened segments of the great disc cracked open, transforming into jagged asymmetrical petals inlaid with gold, and revealing Robert Stephens as the Sun God, dressed in shimmering gold bottle tops and white feathers.

The production had been designed for Chichester's thrust stage, with an eye to transferring it into the Old Vic repertoire. It should be recorded, however, that, in its sell-out summer season at Chichester there were lots of seats round the side which afforded no view of this simple but spectacular transforming device, or of Robert. The occupants of these seats did get an extraordinarily tantalizing idea of *where* Robert was from the lights twinkling on the occasional spurts of saliva issuing from his curious vocal pyrotechnics.

I remember standing, masked, in one of the 'vomitories' on the first night at Chichester, fully Inca-d in, with a very large cymbal and something to bash it with, waiting to lead my contingent of Peruvians up onto the stage towards the slaughter and thinking, 'They're about to get their money's worth.' Big effects to befit big themes. It's very easy to be disaffected by a play's success when your own contribution to the big theme seems a mean thing. Swelling a progress in Shakespeare – being a completely replaceable blur of a Senate officer or rioting Cypriot in *Othello*, as I was – seemed par for the course, but *The Royal Hunt*, you understand, had been given a twelve-week rehearsal period to allow time for the creation of the Inca civilization (about which little is known, so thoroughly did the Spaniards do their job). 'Effective' as the results, our chants and feathers, gold masks and routines were, they were deadly to perform. The masks masked us efficiently without creating the fascination of a blankness onto which the audience could project their imagination.

Whenever one sees the corps de ballet in *Swan Lake* or *Les Sylphides*, one marvels at the accomplishment, the musicality, the grace, the discipline, the immensely rigorous and relentless training behind the perfection of the result; the entire point being that you succeed in the corps de ballet in exact proportion to the extent to which your individual personality is submerged within your consummate achievement of the traditional style. Uniformity was the touchstone for us Incas, *and* anonymity, stylized into a series of emblematic appearances. But the technique involved was not at all what could be called a life-enhancing extension of one's imaginative or technical abilities, and, in any case, the essence of the drama was elsewhere.[1]

'I suppose what is most distressing for me in reading history', wrote Peter Shaffer in his programme note, 'is the way man constantly trivializes the immensity of his experience: the way, for example, he canalizes the greatness of his spiritual awareness into the second-rate formula of a Church – any Church.' I'm no theologian, but leaving the Church Universal aside, as canals go, the Anglicans haven't done *too* badly with the King James translation of the Bible and the Prayer Book. Popes have banned many books and suppressed Galileo, yet patronized music, painting and sculpture effectively. More to the point, the immensity and greatness of my *talent* as Villac Umu were boiled down to a few statuesque appearances and my participating in various chants and laments, canalized into a narrow backwater indeed – what I knew was essentially a second-rate formula. South American cabaret would at least have been more fun.

'Ambition, avarice, the love of change, the morbid spirit of discontent, those passions which most agitate the minds of men, found no place in the bosom of the Peruvian.' (They were, however, rife in the ranks of the National Theatre's Peruvians in their feathers and brown body make-up.) So wrote William H. Prescott, the Massachusetts-born historian who wrote his *History of the Conquest of Peru* in 1847, though he never visited Peru and was almost blind. He continued:

> The very condition of his [the Peruvian's] being seemed to be at war with change. He moved on in the same unbroken circle in which his fathers had moved before him, and in which his children were to follow. It was the object of the Incas to infuse into their subjects a spirit of passive obedience and tranquillity – a perfect acquiescence in the established order of things. In this they fully succeeded ... and no people could have appeared more contented with their lot, or more devoted to their government.

Some Total Theatre attempts had been made to suggest Prescott's vision, and clearly Desmond O'Donovan was hopeful of enhancing them. He got his chance.

In London it was necessary to re-rehearse the production to adapt it to the Old Vic stage. It was at this point that Desmond O'Donovan, who was not taken seriously by the cast, obtained permission to re-rehearse the Peruvians all on his own. He was particularly keen to rearrange the 'Toil Song' in which, as things stood, two lines of Indians did a synchronized planting, sowing and gathering routine in strict 4/4 time, whilst singing an

---

[1] When I saw the recent production of Schaffer's *Equus*, I asked John Napier if I was right to find the horses so spectacularly superior to those in Dexter's original production, such a potent presence, leading characters. He told me that his designs for their heads and hooves were exactly as before but that he had insisted on the horses being played by dancers.

extraordinarily catchy number. I never did the agricultural stuff, being Chief Priest of the Sun, but I could recreate it for you now, the tune, the gobbledygook words and actions, without rehearsal – perfectly, right now! Wait for the radio serialization.

Desmond, clearly, had been reading the more rhapsodic accounts of the contented Peruvian peasantry and the idyllic descriptions of the landscape in which they worked. For example: 'An industrious population settled along the lofty regions of the plateaus, and towns and hamlets, clustering amidst orchards and wide-spreading gardens, seemed suspended in the air, far above the ordinary elevation of the clouds. ... They had been taught that work was gaiety. This amorphous and sad people worked with joy.'[2] Desmond wanted to get rid of the 4/4 time clockwork synchronicity of the figurative mimetic demonstration of planting, sowing and gathering and replace it with ... ah, here was the problem! His heart and imagination were in the right place, but he was like somebody who wants to paint a picture but has absolutely no idea how to handle a brush or paint (I'm not absolutely sure that that analogy entirely holds in this post-Jackson Pollock world). To my mind he was one of those university-educated candidates for the theatre who had little grasp of theatre as a *craft*. At any rate he was no choreographer. Nor could he convince us as a group that there was a new path to find or draw out of us collectively a sense of creative exploration, experiment and improvisation. After a couple of long rehearsal sessions, he attempted to put his version onto the Vic stage, under the merciless working lights, for John Dexter to see the 'amorphous and sad people working with joy.' It must have looked hilariously amorphous and extremely sad. 'It should be rather peaceful ... beautiful', Desmond kept saying. Dexter said briefly, not without an ironic twinkle: 'Yes, interesting. We'll go back to what we did before.' And the rehearsal continued under his not especially benign tyranny, in his very sure showman's hands. Business as usual.

I can't help wondering what the combined forces of Miss McBride, our pianist and the class of '53 in the warehouse in Little Germany, Bradford would have done with the 'Toil Song' after a couple of years struggling with the elemental and the abstract in our Monday morning 'free movement' sessions.

As mentioned, Noël Coward just pipped Shaffer to the post in becoming the first living playwright to be performed by the National Theatre at the Old Vic. The winter revival of his *Hay Fever* was a critical and box-office triumph. The French windows, sofa and drinks table had pride of place on the stage, but Sandy Tyrell (Robert Stephens) had already created Atahualpa, the Inca Sun God, in the summer season at Chichester, Simon and Sorrel Bliss (Derek Jacobi and Louise Purnell) had played Peruvian mortals, and Richard Greatham (Robert Lang), the house guest privileged to have the hilarious business with the barometer, had portrayed Shaffer's Old Martin.

---

[2] From *The Conquistadors* by Jean Descola (1957), as quoted in the programme.

Word got round backstage at our Old Vic dress rehearsal for *The Royal Hunt* that Noël Coward was out front. I discover now from his diary that, since his triumph a week or two earlier with *Hay Fever*, he'd had quite a time, seeing 'Rudi and Margot dance *Le Corsair* ... their dancing was exquisite', having supper with them afterwards, and then a few days later accompanying them to 'Marlene's opening night ... staggeringly good ... She has learnt so much, so much'. A night or two later he was sitting next to 'the darling QM' [Queen Mother], watching himself on TV narrating Terence Rattigan's tribute to Winston Churchill. And so down the Waterloo Road to see our dress rehearsal, which he 'thoroughly enjoyed. Bob Stephens and Colin Blakely are fine, the direction superb, and it is a beautifully written play.'

For three memorable nights I shared a cupboard of a dressing room with Anthony Hopkins when the production went on tour to Nottingham. On stage Tony was always disciplined, yet eclipsed like me; it was in his dressing-room performance on those nights that Tony was amazing and entrancing. We sat on tall stools, crammed into the tiny room, with a sort of bar counter serving as a dressing table. Perhaps I call it a bar counter because of the number of beer bottles it accrued from Monday to Wednesday. Tony was fuelled by alcohol in those days. He had taken over the part of Manco from Edward Hardwicke (the two of them eventually and famously played brothers in the 1993 film version of William Nicholson's *Shadowlands*). I recall the colours of those three Nottingham nights particularly vividly: the tiny room painted a shiny maroon and, hanging close behind us and threatening to envelop the space, our two bright yellow feathered cloaks. Our two blessedly unmasked brown faces in the mirror complete the picture. In our waits between scenes, to alleviate that deep Thespic melancholy that ambitious bit-part players feel in the best of circumstances – and these were the worst – Tony kept up a hilarious compulsive stream of improvisation, imitating members of the company and moving into inspired set pieces. One of these set pieces was a pastiche on the final duologue from *The Bridge on the River Kwai*, set on Waterloo Bridge and starring his uncanny realizations of Olivier and Paul Scofield as they philosophized about the National Theatre.

For one scene I had a rather special massive white fur cloak with a towering headdress, a white bear's head. Goodness knows how that headdress fitted into that room in Nottingham! It was in this get-up that I surprised the Spanish Army on their way across the Andes, appearing down at the front of the stage, back to the audience, with the army in a line facing me and looking downstage. I would open my cloak wide to reveal myself and the sun emblem on my chest. One night in the Old Vic dressing room, a kind of big chorus room, overcome with ennui, I decided to enhance my appearance before the army with a large flashing electric bicycle torch affixed to the sun on my chest. The most dramatic reaction came from the kneeling Derek Jacobi, dressed in a sort of Inca 1920s bathing suit made out of glittering 'gold' flattened bottle tops. He glittered and shimmered more than usual that night, but he went on interpreting everything I said as usual (though I was speaking English of course), eloquently turning my words into sign language as the tears ran down his cheeks, compromising his Inca tan.

Some weeks later, under my yellow feathers, I made up my bare legs with black eyeliner, simulating long net stockings, and affixed a large artificial rose to my crutch. This was chiefly for the benefit of Ron Pickup, upstage of me in the scene; he was providing meal-time music in an otherwise silent sequence during which Louise Purnell solemnly mimed feeding Robert Stephens's Sun God by hand, whilst the rest of the court stood emblematically around. The 'reward' was Ron, standing there trapped, continuing to play his curious hand-held keyboard instrument, striking the thin, twanging metal keys with a bamboo hammer, apparently moved to tears by the effect. Tony was able to bury the lower half of his face in his yellow feathers. From that night on I never risked such a coup again, but I could always get Tony to turn determinedly away from me by the merest twitch of my feathered cloak.

I have just re-read this passage unsmilingly, but only yesterday as I typed it I laughed uncontrollably, and afterwards spasmodically all the way down to the shops on an errand. It was cathartic and helped to make up for the memories I retain, not least of the walk home on *The Royal Hunt* nights from the bus up Bellenden Road in Peckham, feeling that my part in the show was the antithesis of acting.

At three o'clock one afternoon I had been telephoned and told I would be going on for Robert Stephens, who had injured his finger rehearsing a sword fight in John Osborne's adaptation of Lope de Vega's *A Bond Honoured* (did we call it *Lope Back in Anger*?). I am prisoner, holding onto one end of a long rope which the despairing Pizarro of Colin Blakely holds taut as he charges round me, wrenching me, spinning me about, shouting as I gyrate, 'Get up, get up, get up.' I was there when Dexter created the business, late one night at end of one of our endless 9 a.m.-to-10 p.m. Chichester technical days. Contrived but effective is what I remember thinking, but mostly contrived. Anyway, so much easier to perform than – to take a random moment of what Shaffer calls Total Theatre – Nijinsky leaping out of the window in *Le Spectre de la Rose*. There is a point at which sheer hokum, well enough conceived and executed, becomes profound. I know this: I have played Cyrano de Bergerac and heard the audience sobbing; I saw Alicia Markova dance *The Dying Swan*. And I remember the hushed, pin-drop attention in the theatre as, covered in chocolate-coloured Max Factor Pancake, I intoned with powerful magisterial calm, after Colin collapsed and recovered his breath: 'Pizarro! You will die soon, and you do not believe in your God. Believe in me. I will give you a word and fill you with joy.'

Amazing how Colin could come up with the controlled, vigorous performances he gave and yet down as much alcohol as I now know he did. In those days I had not much idea of what went on in the dressing rooms nearer the stage and had never so much as spoken to him in the pub. So, as we came off after our first scene that night when I first went on for Robert, I was hugely encouraged when he muttered to me, before rushing away to do a quick change, 'You're a very good actor.' It was so much more gratifying than if he'd said, 'Well done.' He wasn't telling me anything I didn't already know, but there are some well-known things one never tires of hearing, and that was the perfect moment for him to have said it.

**Atahualpa, the Sun God, which I played six times,
understudying Robert Stephens.**
Photo: © Chris Arthur

Chapter 9

Bringing the Lights Up: Gaskill and Zeffirelli

In 1965, William Gaskill, who was responsible for me being in the company, resigned from the National to take over the artistic direction of the Royal Court from George Devine. The advent of *A Flea in Her Ear* and *Hay Fever*, combined with Arthur Miller's *The Crucible*, which was designed, he thought, to look like 'a gnomes' tea party', had been too much for him. He realized that 'the socialist ensemble of my dreams' was not going to materialize. Thank God! I discovered him then to be, for my taste, the worst kind of theatrical puritan. It was as if he'd just descended, Moses-like, from a socialist Mount Sinai, armed with the Brechtian tablets, only to discover his actors dancing round the golden calf of intellectually bankrupt, right-wing theatrical fustian.

Bill's rehearsals were an education – that was the trouble. Occasionally, he would lurch out of a concern with the 'A' Effect into showbiz mode. After a rehearsal of John Arden's *Armstrong's Last Goodnight* at Chichester, he said, 'When Robert [Stephens] comes on, it's as if the lights come up. You should all of you create that effect when you come on.' Quite difficult, and I would say inappropriate, if you're playing the Scottish and English ambassadors in the opening. Be that as it may, as far as bringing the lights up is concerned, there is, after all, such a thing as light and *shade*. How about bringing on a bit of *shade*, or even gloom?

With Bill's instruction in mind, I read in the programme for *Armstrong's Last Goodnight*: 'The house lights up in the interval. Guinness is served in the bar.' The programme also contains full-page adverts for BP, Benson & Hedges, Nescafe, Yardley and *The Sunday Times*. In describing his two years at the NT, however, Gaskill boasts of 'the elegant and serious presentation of the theatre through its programmes, which at the time had no advertisements', and says he was determined that 'the same seriousness should inform our plans at the Court.' The theme of the lights coming up once more gleams at us from the programme for his *Three Sisters* at the Court: a full-page cartoon showing the beam of a spotlight illuminating the centre of a stage, where a hand is emerging from the prompter's box, pouring a glass of … well, the caption reads:

> A strong line is good for the curtain
> A prompter is good for the cue
> And applause for an actor it's certain
> Is as good as a Guinness for you.

There are a further six pages of advertisements.

A large proportion of Bill's notes were prefaced by the words 'You should', so much so that Ron Pickup and I developed a mutual language of reflex reaction, involving broad or subtle variants of a supporting elbow slipping off the arm of a chair, every time the phrase occurred. I think Ron was more successfully covert than I. But Bill had his revenge on me in his dismal production of the early-seventeenth-century comedy, *The Dutch Courtesan*, by Marston (who is not visible under any conditions from Judith Bliss's drawing room). In fact, Noël Coward, when he went to see it, fled so eagerly at the interval that he knocked a man down. In his diary he describes the experience as 'dirty, dull, badly directed, indifferently acted and largely – thank God – inaudible.'

When the production transferred from Chichester to the Old Vic, Bill deputed his co-director, Piers Haggard (son of actor Stephen), to tell me that he wanted me to join the cast and take over one of the parts. It was a small but rather effective comic part of a foppish lover, affording opportunities which I believed had not been exploited by the outgoing actor. But, just as my lights were coming up so to speak, and I was envisaging these possibilities, Haggard informed me that all the character's lines, and the entire subplot involving him, were to be cut. 'But Bill thinks you'll wear the costume well and be very good filling his place in the dance.'

There was even worse to come: the amended design for the proscenium stage at the Vic involved the moving of scenic units on trucks, as well as carpets, stools etc. Bill decided this would be done more deftly by costumed actors than by costumed stagehands, and we, unlike stagehands, didn't have to be paid extra for wearing costumes, or paid a small 'Pickfords' fee. So during each anonymous evening, as one of several very disgruntled actor/scene-shifters, I made an inexplicable appearance from nowhere in a foppish cloth-of-gold costume to join in a little pavane. We were all in the Englischer Ensemble of Bill's dreams, but some actors were more ensemble than others.

A further insult came on the day I was cornered in the yard at Aquinas Street by a grim-faced choreographer named Belinda Quirey. She'd got wind of the fact that her dance was to include a newcomer and, presuming at first sight that I was of the very lowest of the company, mere proscenium-arch fodder, she subjected me to a barre routine in a manner suggesting that my musculature was not up to the task of executing her utterly unspectacular apology of a pavane in the second act.

No job gave me a stronger sense of desolation, of being nothing, than standing in the plainest of seventeenth-century garb with Christopher Timothy, on *Dutch Courtesan* nights, waiting to lay a carpet to give Billie Whitelaw somewhere to lounge. The point was to lay it quick and get off, then, at the end of the scene, reappear to whisk it away – ad nauseam. I wasn't even playing the part of a servant. I could not, even though I was on a stage, say to myself – as I'd been able to at Lyons Corner House – 'I'm an actor.' The carpet or furniture removal department at Jones & Higgins would have utilized infinitely more of our skills.

By now the company included Albert Finney, who was to play Don Pedro in Franco Zeffirelli's production of *Much Ado About Nothing*. At the same time I noticed a small influx of other actors about my age. Ian Mckellen, who had had his first West End success in a play called *A Scent of Flowers*, arrived to play Claudio, and two striking young men, Ron Pickup and Michael York. Zeffirelli had wanted to hold auditions for the smaller parts since he didn't know the company. I remember him wearing dark glasses or, if he didn't, he gave that impression. I gleaned before I went in that he wouldn't say much and would ask me to read a speech of Benedick's – the part Robert Stephens was doing. The result was that, a few days later, the part of Conrade appeared opposite my name on the noticeboard.

Conrade in Zeffirelli's
Much Ado About Nothing.
Photo © Chris Arthur

Franco became subtly much livelier in rehearsal and amazingly inventive. At lunchtime one bitter cold day, Neil Fitzpatrick and I left the warmth of Franco's Messina for the South Bank, just in front of the Festival Hall where we found a silent crowd, already several deep, lining the riverside and waiting. The whole of Waterloo Bridge was lined with people, and the embankment on the north side; there were no sounds of traffic. After some time, the crowd around us stirred slightly and then, for a moment, we glimpsed the Union Jack draped over Churchill's coffin as the barge, which had carried him down the Thames to St Paul's, approached. We didn't know that Noël Coward and his party, shedding 'proud tears', had moved from the television set they had been watching since 9.30 a.m. to the window of his Savoy Hotel sitting room directly opposite us, to see this moment of the barge arriving on its progress to Waterloo Station. We were told later by the stage manager, who had accompanied Franco to the station to watch from there, that Franco had somehow managed to burst onto the platform and follow the train down the platform as it left. Rehearsal was late in re-starting. Years later Ian told me that he had had the morning off and watched the procession on its way to St Paul's and that, comparatively speaking, a holiday atmosphere prevailed.

Much Ado was exuberantly designed, and it gives me great and not at all perverse pleasure to recall it with admiration and affection. The statues were all life-sized and played by actors. I remember them wrenching off their baroque foam padding as they came back upstairs, cursing and sweating into the dressing rooms, but, when their 'carved' shepherd and nymph lamp-bearer momentarily joined in the dancing in the ball scene to Nino Rota's town-band carnival music, it was worth it, at least from out front. And who'll forget the town-square plinth with its statue of a soldier having its sword borrowed in exchange for an umbrella by a member of the watch, when the watch is apprehending Conrade and Borachio. All the obscure and seemingly corny puns of this scene were cut, and the pay-off at the end of the scene, with the baddies captured, came after the fracas as the square emptied to thunder and lightning; out came the statue's hand to test for rainfall, and the lights went down at the end of the first half on the solitary figure on the plinth (Christopher Timothy, still a world away from sick animals in Herriot country), putting up the umbrella against the downpour.

Then there was Roy Holder's St Sebastian statue, standing on the altar at Hero's wedding, being prudishly shocked out of his ecstatic martyred pose when Claudio said the line, 'There, Leonato, take her back again: / Give not this rotten orange to your friend.' But none of this undermined the passion of the characters and situation. The initially farcically ancient priest of Paul Curran (sans false teeth) silenced the house with his wise, fatherly advice to the family at the end of the scene, convincingly paving the way for the famous 'Kill Claudio' duologue that follows. So much did one care about them, this family in crisis.

There was a series of swiftly changing wings and backcloths, which Zeffirelli introduced us to at the read-through by showing us four little rectangles of hardboard he'd painted in a thick texture, each in one primary colour, to transport us, he said, from sunlight to red interior and shady gardens 'and there is a blacka one for night, thata I haven'ta bothered to deesigna.' I was told he would go and look at whichever primary-coloured backcloth was in progress, as they were being painted on the huge paint frame in the Old Vic Annexe, just across the street to the east, and say, 'It's not-a-like-a-the deesigna.' The booking leaflet didn't call him 'the audacious young Florentine' for nothing. The scenic staff would shake their heads and set to work again, mixing canteen eggs into the paint in a Florentine manner, sticking fishing net to the canvas with size, mixing and mottling and hoping to achieve the effect required by the maestro.

The Old Vic's proscenium, which Zeffirelli remembered affectionately from directing *Romeo and Juliet* at the Vic in 1960, had been replaced by Sean Kenny's permanent forestage and dark-brown 'wooden' structure, and the effect of Franco's designs didn't quite work, set behind this dark no man's land. So the weekend before we opened, an elaborate proscenium of fairy lights appeared which had been no part of the original design. It could be illuminated in single colours to match the backcloths, borders and wings or, for the finale, when the cast literally did a knees-up for the audience, all the colours at once.

Zeffirelli sat on the bare stage one day, all of us in the stalls, whilst very quietly and simply he turned over the pages of the script, making little points about the play and the run-through we'd just done, sometimes expanding on them slightly. There was something so charming and illuminating in what he was doing that I thought it would have been sufficient if the audience came to see him. Indeed, on the rehearsal-room floor he had a Pandora's box of ready-made characters and gags for all of us. I was appalled, at Stratford a few years ago, when I saw my little part of Conrade thrown away, played, it seemed, grudgingly.

Olivier saw the last Saturday morning run-through of the whole play in the Old Vic rehearsal room, before we broke for lunch (followed by two performances of *The Royal Hunt of the Sun*, I shouldn't wonder) and was so carried away by how Italian it all was in spirit that he said we must do the whole play in Italian accents or it would be incongruous – which, on the Sunday night dress rehearsal, we did. However, in the face of the grave misgivings voiced by some of the principals, Olivier modified this idea to include only those characters 'below the salt'. Amongst the beaming faces on the front rows during the finale knees-up, there were always one or two appalled purists with expressions of stone.

One of my vivid impressions is a lovely piece of Maggie Smith's business, which I saw for the first time on stage at a rehearsal. Shakespeare has Beatrice very self-absorbed and ill on the morning of Hero's wedding, and for Maggie's entry into this scene she was cloaked in an enormous duvet as if she had just got out of bed. Just at the right moment she produced, from inside the depths of this enormous duvet, coffee in a tiny cup and saucer. How passionately and delicately she and Robert Stephens played the church scene. I was not too captivated by Robert's Benedick; everything he did seemed to me to be a little touched by the Sun God, his Atahualpa. But when I left the production and saw it from out front, the sheer animal spirits of his performance were irresistible.

I did not know how exactly to find my territory, box my corner, in my little role of Conrade. He is inseparably part of the wicked Don John-Borachio-Conrade trio. Zeffirelli demonstrated a tortured, tortuous obsessive Don John for Derek Jacobi, reflecting his inner turmoil in an inability even to walk straight, being controlled by phobias about floor patterns and the freakish need to control us, and create havoc for his brother Don Pedro. He suggested that I should be a weedy and obsessive nibbler, with a little paper cone of nuts, a stammer and a slight tendency to trip, so I had a cartoon basis to go on. Tom Kempinski, who'd played Tybalt in Zeffirelli's *Romeo and Juliet*, was to be a simple, big, beefy, sweaty Italian who, when it came to it, wept freely with the shame and guilt of his part in Don John's wicked plot against Hero and Claudio. Tom found free, copious weeping very difficult, but that was nothing to Derek's difficulty in entering into the physical characteristics offered him by Zeffirelli. I was disheartened by what appeared to me to be Derek's instinctive ability, even whilst somewhat at sea in his part, to ensure that nothing I did would be allowed into the mix: it was either ignored or demolished by a savagely swift take-up of a cue. A comic, functioning, dysfunctional trio this was never going to be, and it wasn't until months later, when Finney left and Derek took over his part of Don Pedro, that Ron Pickup as Don John transformed things at a stroke. In a glorious first rehearsal upstairs at the Vic he improvised, in a single run at our first scene, a 'routine' in which instinctively we saw our places. We never looked back and, from then on, that scene invariably ended with an exit round.

According to the programme note, Arden's *Armstrong's Last Goodnight* dealt with 'the problems of the Congo (that's news to me) translated into terms of Scottish border conflicts of the early sixteenth century.' The Scottish element I do remember, of course, and the invented Scottish archaisms that made the dialogue rather opaque, and yet the credits for the play include, in addition to 'swords and saddlery by Reg Amos', 'Stockings by Kayser Bondor'. The kind co-operation of Tootal Broadhurst is also acknowledged!

The double-page panoramic view of the theatre in the lavish Chichester programme includes the familiar huge car park beyond, in which I can count only five cars! It was while crossing this near-deserted car park one lunchtime, chatting with Bill Gaskill, co-director of the play with John Dexter, that I made some remark about the enviable sense of belonging which must be felt by the permanent members of the Moscow Art Theatre Company. No doubt I was concerned and ambitious about the possibility of achieving 'tenure'. Bill said dryly that there were people in the MAT Company who hadn't spoken to each other for thirty years.

Then there was the morning when a few of us young actors, walking up to the theatre, saw a splendid chauffeur-driven black Rolls-Royce draw up and the relaxed, boyish figure of Albert Finney, our Armstrong, get out, dressed incongruously in jeans and sports shirt. He waved to us, looking only faintly abashed. In 1963 he had been Tom Jones in Tony Richardson's film and we gathered he had since taken months off to travel the world. He found at Chichester that, although he was perfectly fit, he was initially out of condition for that special brand of energy the theatre demands.

With hindsight you might think that the first short scene of the play, involving four commissioners at a peace conference, two English and two Scots, would have had every chance of getting things off to a fine start, since David Ryall and I played the English commissioners and the Scots commissioners were played by Derek Jacobi and Ian McKellen. We were all done up in heavy robes, caps and uncomfortable false beards and moustaches. Derek was the only one of us not to have another part later on in the play, and he was so detached from his involvement that he claimed never to have watched a moment of the play in rehearsal or performance beyond the end of our peace conference, which was probably no more than the first four minutes, if that. At a dress rehearsal Arden came up onto the stage and took the opportunity to give us some historical/political background, but it was to no avail; he hadn't *implied* it in the scene so we couldn't act it.

We sweated in our itchy beards and moustaches and our sixteenth-century robes. The only sensational effect I managed to create was in the business of handing a parchment scroll to Derek; one night in unrolling it, he found that I had pasted in a newspaper cutting of an advertisement that read: 'Banish facial hair forever!' This had a delightfully explosive effect. Let R. H. Bowden's programme note put this incident in context: 'Repeatedly Arden's central theme has been that chaotic energy that keeps man alive and, at the same time, threatens his social existence.' I rest my case.

They made an unlikely double act, Dexter and Gaskill; Dexter the cruel and ruthless galvanic ringmaster, Gaskill with his cool Chinese water torture, a relentless drip, drip of corrective Brechtian theory. Considering how intolerant they could both be, how withering their criticisms, it must have been quite a strain for them to exude harmony with each other and keep up a united front for the benefit of the actors.

The three stars – Stephens, Finney and Geraldine McEwan – were properly at the centre, and they all gave epic theatre grit and the 'real drive' of the kind that I have just read Jack Lambert admiring Brecht for, immediately after his death in 1956, 'his ability to drive actors to real attack.' There seemed to be an idea that in losing the 'ham' of the nineteenth century and embracing, if that is the word, the so-called 'throwaway' naturalism of the West End box-set play, English actors, with a few great exceptions, were in danger of being incapable of the kind of epic realism of the Berliner. But they didn't need to be driven – the vast reaches of the Chichester stage and the even vaster reaches of that splayed auditorium, demand real drive, and the curious archaisms of Arden's script begged to be spouted, not in poetic arches of theatrical rhetoric, but in direct hammer blows and with incisive scythe swipes and spitted out staccato, rapid-fire, accompanied often by physical swagger, or from Geraldine, diamond-sharp poise.

I don't think we had to learn any of that from Bertolt Brecht – just to be reminded.

Chapter 10

The Old Smell: *Trelawny of the 'Wells'*

> ROSE
>
> But you, dear Mrs Telfer –
> you weren't at the reading – what are *you* cast for?
>
> MRS TELFER
>
> I? [*Wiping away a tear.*] I am the Wardrobe-
> mistress of this theatre.
>
> ROSE
>
> You! [*Embracing her.*] Oh! oh!
>
> MRS TELFER
>
> [*Composing herself.*] Miss Trelawny – Rose – my
> child, if we are set to scrub a floor – and we may
> come to that yet – let us make up our minds to scrub
> it legitimately – with dignity.

A few days ago, Emily told me she had met an actor we know in the street – you might remember him for a moving small part in a very famous British film. I acted with him in the West End a few years ago, when he played an important part. He told Emily that he was hoping to get a job washing up at Pizza Hut.

In 1959 Dame Sybil Thorndike wrote a piece for a splendid booklet published to celebrate the opening of the new Mermaid Theatre at Puddle Dock in the City of London. Here is a short extract from 'The Lure of the Theatre':

> Going into the old theatre at Margate, the second oldest theatre of England still working ... here was the old smell again. What was it? Escaping gas? Smell of many people seeing many plays and general thrilling airlessness? Yes, a lure this, but we mustn't deceive ourselves that this is the theatre, for unless we have a life behind these smells and lures and lights and machineries, then it is only a dead thing. But I believe it's this curious lure that gets us in the beginning.

The most poignant example I know of this 'old smell' is as recent as the year 2000, when my two youngest children, not noticeably stagestruck and then aged sixteen and thirteen, came with me one afternoon to the stage door of the Theatre Royal, Haymarket, where I was appearing. I think I was just dropping in to pick something up from the stage door. Dora and Arthur asked where the stage was and I was able to point to the double doors near the stage doorkeeper's cubbyhole. They opened them to peep inside at the darkened stage and, like two children recognizing an old friend, they said as one, 'The smell!' I knew to my cost it was not necessarily the sweet smell of success. The play I was then appearing in at the Haymarket was Jeffrey Archer's *The Accused* and we had been savaged by the critics.

Arthur Wing Pinero's play *Trelawny of the 'Wells'* is entirely about the theatre and reeks of it. Pinero had been an actor in Henry Irving's company at the Lyceum in the late 1870s and early 1880s; what an aroma that theatre must have had in his day! One morning the young Pinero was sitting on stage at a rehearsal, perched on a slender piece of scenery, a ground row. Irving said to him, 'Don't sit there, Pinero, you'll cut yourself.' 'That's all right, Gov'ner,' Pinero replied, 'we're used to getting our parts cut at this theatre.'

Premiered in 1898 but set in the theatre of the 1860s, *Trelawny of the 'Wells'* was certainly going to be at home in the Old Vic of 1965. However, it was due to start its life in the National's summer season at the three-year-old Chichester Festival Theatre, where there could be no 'old smell'; its lure, its 'lights and machineries' were radically different from those of eighteenth- and nineteenth-, even twentieth-century theatres, inspired as it was by the open-stage theatre Tyrone Guthrie had founded in Stratford, Ontario, which had banished the picture-frame stage and created in its place a hybrid, part-wooden 'O', part permanent version of the tent Guthrie and his designer, Tanya Moiseiwitsch, conceived for his first Stratford Festival.

George Bernard Shaw was at the very first night of *Trelawny* in 1898 in his capacity as critic, and wrote: 'The delicacy of this mood (of thirty or forty years before) inspires the whole play, which has touched me more than anything else Mr Pinero has ever written.' This is surprising, coming from the critic who spent his time castigating London for being behind the times, for having no Ibsen of its own and a theatre that could only extract two weeks of business out of the Scandinavian Ibsen. He did carp, of course, finding the period atmosphere unconvincing: 'On the whole I doubt whether the Court company knows a scrap more about the professional atmosphere of the old "Wells" than the audience.' What chance did we National Theatre actors have sixty-seven years later?

Did you just spot the word 'Court'? Yes, it was no less than the Royal Court Theatre, Sloane Square in which Shaw sat watching *Trelawny*, the same theatre he was to influence so greatly as a playwright only six years later, together with Harley Granville-Barker, who, as well as his own plays, would produce eleven of Shaw's and, at last, some by 'the terrible Ibsen', as Shaw put it in salutary terms.

In the spring of 1965, when we met in the National's Aquinas Street rehearsal room to do our first reading of *Trelawny of the 'Wells'*, what was to be made of this quaint, well-constructed, sentimental backstage comedy? Since the *first* first night of *Trelawny* and the revolutionary collaboration of Shaw and Granville-Barker, the Royal Court had housed another theatrical 'revolution', that associated with the English Stage Company and the year

1956. Two of its directors, Dexter and Gaskill, had been lured to the National by Olivier (or 'expelled' by George Devine, depending on whose book you read), and The Theatre was moving on, as it always is.

True, Pinero's play was about a kind of revolution. I can still hear its downtrodden young actor, Tom Wrench, about to transform himself into 'new-wave' playwright hero – still hear him in the unmistakeable voice of Robert Stephens, fresh from the Royal Court himself, fulminating against 'vapid trash' and 'turgid rodomontade', and rhapsodizing about the possibilities of 'real locks, to work; and handles to turn.' Tom Wrench was a portrait of the failed actor turned successful playwright, T. W. Robertson, and sure enough, if you turn to the memoirs of the first producers and stars of Robertson's comedies, you will read: 'It was in *Caste* that we made a distinct stride towards realistic scenery. The rooms for the first time had ceilings, while such details as locks to doors, and similar matters, had never before been seen on the stage.'[1] Squire Bancroft tells us that several people thought he was mad when he played a comedy part in a subdued fashionable suit and with short dark hair.

Trelawny of the 'Wells' at Chichester.
L to R:
Billie Whitelaw (Avonia Bunn), Graham Crowden (Augustus Colpoys),
Michael York (Arthur Gower), Louise Purnell (Rose Trelawny),
Pauline Taylor (Imogen Parrott), myself (Ferdinand Gadd),
Wynne Clark (Mrs Telfer), Robert Stephens (Tom Wrench).
Photo: © Angus McBean

---

[1] Mr and Mrs Bancroft, *On and Off the Stage* (London, 1888).

'The drawing-room comedy of furniture and manners, with a tastefully conducted intrigue as a pretext, is as dead as Donizetti and deader.' Thus pronounced Shaw of the Robertson revolution of gentility and verisimilitude, three years before it was celebrated in *Trelawny*, putting the knife in with:

> The stockbrokerly young gentleman, standing on the stage with his manners carefully turned to the audience like the painted side of an old stage banner, has suddenly been taken by the scruff of the neck by the grim Norwegian giant, and, with one ruthless twist, whisked round with his seamy side to the footlights, to stare in helpless bewilderment at the atmosphere of poetry, imagination, tragedy, irony, pity, terror, and all the rest of it, suddenly rising in the theatre from which they had been swept, he had hoped, for ever, along with the 'stage lovers all sixty and dressed like waiters in a penny-ice shop.' And now he may shriek, with Judge Brack, that 'People don't do such things.'

The year before our first reading of *Trelawny*, the National had staged Ibsen's *The Master Builder* and George Devine, directing Beckett's *Play* for the Company and in dispute with Tynan about the style of the production, had written: 'You'll have to have a bit more guts if you really want to do experimental works.' But I remember no faint hearts nor any sense of futility or foreboding when we read Pinero's play, even though the production was not in the hands of a director used to the old smells, lure and machineries, but those of Desmond O'Donovan, suddenly promoted from assistant director, despite his flaccid attempts to inject the 'beautiful' into Peter Shaffer's Incas.

A saving grace was that Motley were doing the costumes and Alan Tagg the sets. Tagg had the double problem of adapting the scenery to Chichester and then to the Vic. The Motley ladies had started out in 1932 with the OUDS production of *Romeo and Juliet*, which had also marked John Gielgud's directing debut. What brings in the authentic smell of the theatre and its lure is that the following year they moved into cheap premises, lamentably long gone, in St Martin's Lane – into what had been an old coaching inn with the only remaining kidney-cobbled yard in London, Garrick Yard, just behind the famous Club. It had been Thomas Chippendale's furniture workshop where he entertained actors to tea, as indeed the Motleys did; in the whitewashed room where they cut cloth on the floor, they were regularly dropped in on by a host of them – Ashcroft, Olivier and Gielgud, and by George Devine, who married Sophie Harris. Motley were to become house designers in 1957 to the English Stage Company at the Royal Court, whilst Alan Tagg was to supply the architecturally realistic doors and workable locks for *Look Back in Anger*.

In *Trelawny* I had my first good part at the NT, the part of the comic juvenile, Ferdinand Gadd. The Motleys designed for me not a subdued suit like Squire Bancroft's, but nonetheless a very elegant one. It was yellow with black velvet edging on the coat and along the seams of the trousers. I also wore a pale topper and a gold embroidered smoking cap, and a rather splendid top coat in Act Three.

Playing my wife was, first, Billie Whitelaw and, later, Maggie Smith. In his crucial scene in the theatrical lodging house, Gadd is offered the 'absolutely rotten' part of the Daemon of Discontent in the pantomime and, self-dramatizingly, he takes the artistic high ground as a romantic juvenile lead, a notable Orlando, turns it down and prepares to make a martyred exit from the company. At this point, Billie or Maggie, as the case might be, quietly reminds her husband of their precarious financial position: 'Ferdie, we haven't put by.' He then affects to deign to give the part his consideration, reciting a bit of the rhyming tosh and declaring: 'Avonia, there's something to lay hold of here. I'll think it over. I've thought it over. I'll play it.'

With Louise Purnell (Rose Trelawny), Graham Crowden (Augustus Colpoys) and Billie Whitelaw (our first Avonia Bunn).
Photo: © Zoe Dominic

As Ferdinand Gadd with our later Avonia, Maggie Smith.
Photo: © Zoe Dominic

It was an example of what the tempo of thought can do in encapsulating the day required to 'think it over' in the neat turn on a very necessary sixpence, the tiny snatched breath within this apparently simple, near repetition. A line or two more and then one crossed to the door, down right, opened it, turned in the opening and delivered the exit line across to Avonia – 'Steak for dinner!' – and off, closing the door crisply. (An archetypal moment; I thought of it when I had the house repainted on the strength of signing the contract to be in a play by Jeffrey Archer.) Then came the exit round. It's written for an exit round.

When Maggie took over, you can imagine the Kenneth Williams juice she squeezed out of 'Oh Ferdie, that's a rotten part. That part is absolutely rotten!' A *huge* laugh (it makes me laugh now), but my exit round survived, until, after a performance or two, with the connivance of the low comedian in the cast, I went out in an odd silence; he took to holding the door open and following me out, upsetting my timing, cocking up my comic éclat and creating a damp squib of an exit; lo and behold, the round crowned Maggie's exit a page later. Two against one – both being paid more than I, and all for the good of the scene, the low comedian assured me. In-service training in a hard school. Another actor would have threatened Graham Crowden's conniving rearrangement of the established territory, threatened him with violence. I should have been that actor!

Regretfully, I wasn't free when, much later, Peter Hall asked me to be in Poliakov's *Coming into Land* with Maggie at the NT. I remember the mischief of her performance, like something deliciously endangering to the evening, possibly even the play and, no doubt, me, had I been up there with her. Perhaps it's as well. When I played Graham Greene's whisky priest at Chichester in 1990, one critic wrote: 'If not quite suggesting the driving seedy masculine force of the character, there is something – how can one put it – of Maggie Smith about Petherbridge's long-legged languor and vocal delivery.'

Just now, reading the souvenir programme of the 1965 Chichester season, I was struck by some props, an old chain, order, sword-belt and sword mentioned by the critic J. C. Trewin in his affectionate notes. Trewin described the key moment in the play when the crusty, conventional Sir William Gower, on the warpath, visits the heroine, actress Rose Trelawny, in her lodgings. Rose has returned to her life in the theatre to escape the disastrous culture clash, between theatrical Bohemia and wealthy Cavendish Square respectability, of marrying his grandson. Trewin wrote: 'But Rose Trelawny conquers. During the third act Sir William learns that her mother had acted with Edmund Kean. His mood changes, for Kean was someone he had admired ("a splendid gipsy"); and when Rose exhibits a chain and order, a sword-belt and sword "very theatrical and tawdry"... the old man puts the chain over his shoulders, handles the belt and sword, and for a moment re-lives a famous night. Always this comes through astonishingly in performance.'

I did not think so, finding our Sir William's breaking into Richard III's 'Now is the winter of our discontent' rather contrived and unconvincing. However, Sir Laurence was very taken by the moment; but I should tell you first that Olivier possessed the *actual* sword used by Edmund Kean as Richard III! I saw it with my own eyes, and it wasn't in the least theatrical and tawdry.

I did not see with my own eyes the moment when Sir Laurence went into Paul Curran's (our Sir William Gower's) dressing room after the performance and decided he must ring up Paul's wife who was at home in London. 'Laurence Olivier here,' he began, and continued, 'Your husband is a great actor.'

Sir didn't come round to see me, but I have the evidence of a letter he wrote to me, after he saw a later performance of the play at the Vic – a letter which said that he was 'struck again by how truly, honestly good' my performance was. I might just as well have been dubbed by Edmund Kean himself.

Olivier's surprisingly fresh relics of his own Richard III are his film, of course, and the Salvador Dali portrait of him in the part, which I saw hanging in his house in Brighton, near to a wall-mounted, glass-windowed case with interior lighting and red velvet, in which Kean's Richard III sword was displayed. Sir took it out to show to a group of National Theatre players he was entertaining, quite a short, light sword (Kean had been short and light), engraved with a history of ownership along the blade. On the first night of his Richard III, 29 January 1877, Henry Irving had received the sword from the elderly actor W. H. Chippendale, who had appeared with Kean and most of the great actors of his day. In 1939 Kate Terry gave the sword to her son John Gielgud, and it was he who, in turn, presented it to Olivier to mark the overwhelming success of Olivier's Richard III at the New Theatre in 1944. I remember Olivier holding it and saying deprecatingly, 'You couldn't have much of a fight with it.'

'And who', asked Ben Whitrow, 'will you give it to?' There was an awkward hiatus. I forget what Sir said, but I got the distinct impression that the sword had found with the current owner its last and rightful resting place.

Chapter 11

On the Road to Elsinore: *Rosencrantz and Guildenstern Are Dead*

> *To be is to be perceived.*
> George Berkeley

You could say that the entire conceit of Tom Stoppard's *Rosencrantz and Guildenstern Are Dead* depends on the existence in people's heads of *Hamlet*: a preconception, shadowy and yet definitive, even archetypal, a 'performance' of *Hamlet* hovering in the public imagination, ready to settle on the boards, complete with Elsinore Castle, the Prince, the Ghost, the courtiers and the troupe of itinerant players – all oh so familiar to us (rough hew them as directors and Prince Hamlets may!) but oh so unfathomable and unfamiliar and threatening to Rosencrantz and Guildenstern. You could say that. Perhaps you should, because that is the *Hamlet* in which Ros and Guil are, though they don't know it. Furthermore, though we see so little of this *Hamlet* in Tom Stoppard's play, we find that it is always going on somewhere in the farthest reaches of the stage – in 'the strange darkened realms of the place', to use Gordon Craig's phrase – so that, however familiar or over-familiar we think this *Hamlet* is to us, and however distracted from it we may become by the pyrotechnics of Stoppard's two jumped-up supporting players, filling in their long waits so poignantly and hilariously, the tragedy's omnipresence gains in potency the more nebulous it becomes. The ungraspable implications of its great transactions finally take their toll on the small change of our two attendant lords.

'We've been caught up,' says Guil about thirty minutes into the show. One of the rich ironies of the production lay in the sudden presence of the whole court of Elsinore on stage. There we had been on our own, Guil and Ros, inexplicably on the road to Elsinore or, more properly, 'in a place without any visible character', when we heard music, which turned out to be the travelling players and musicians with their cart of props and tatterdemalion trailers for their repertoire, and cryptic explanations for their presence:

Player:	We're travelling people, we take our chances where we find them.
Guil:	It was chance, then?
Player:	Chance?
Guil:	You found us.
Player:	Oh yes.

Guil:	You were looking.
Player:	Oh no.
Guil:	Chance then.
Player:	Or fate.
Guil:	Yours or ours?
Player:	It could hardly be one without the other.

We engaged with them for a while, escaped them, only to be locked in silence, witnesses to a piece of, to us, inexplicable dumb show between Hamlet and Ophelia. Then, just as were left alone again and hoping to make ourselves scarce, *'But a flourish – enter Claudius and Gertrude attended.'*

Night by night, matinée by matinée, I took it for granted that there was never any hint, any rustle or whisper, before the brazen flourish and the shock of this majestic materialization – no hint at all to betray the fact that eleven magnificently costumed actors had assembled in the wings and were awaiting their entrance. I can still see the haughty expressions on the faces of the non-speaking courtiers, successfully conveying the impression that they had not come from reading the *Evening Standard* and gossiping in the dressing rooms. They were in the know and we were merely newcomers out of our depth, two young and green interlopers, apparently the Prince's fellow students, but clearly small-part players. How did they do it – pulling rank on us, the ostensible rank and file, when the reverse was the harsh reality? On *Othello* nights I was myself still practising this special kind of acting, being one of the attendant lords, or a stray Cypriot, attempting to look like a person of pith and moment with a distinct life and identity, simply by the way in which I *attended* to those fortunate actors who had wonderful words to say.

I had registered the odd, intriguing title of Stoppard's play when Olivier announced it at a company meeting, along with an all-male *As You Like It* (much to Maggie Smith's discomfiture), but I had no idea what it was about, and no expectations. As a company member, I was something of a hybrid, species and subspecies combined, at times posing as a thoroughbred in a decent part, at other times functioning as the classical equivalent of one set of hind legs in a troupe of pantomime horses. However, I'd had a letter from Olivier, acknowledging my forbearance and assuring me that, if I could weather this waiting game, it would 'be to our mutual advantage.' It was like being touched by the hand of God. Nevertheless, time was stretching out and the weather was not improving.

'I think Celia.' It was John Dexter's voice sounding from the corner of Shaftesbury Avenue, where we were doing a season. The phrase rang out *in medias res*, as though he was continuing a conversation on casting that had already been underway. I had just emerged down Wardour Street from the trickle of one of the inadequate makeshift showers in the Queen's Theatre, washing off the brown make-up of Villac Umu after a matinée of *The Royal Hunt of the Sun* (in rep with *Othello*), and Dexter was loitering with his customary satanic intent. One usually feared the worst, or a snub; a smile and 'good afternoon', the common currency of normal mortals, were like a ray of sunshine from Dexter, so imagine my amazement on hearing him open up an unexpected and exotic possibility. I knew that Ron Pickup had been beatified and was going to play Rosalind. 'Isn't Celia meant to be the shorter of the two?' I asked, feeling my full height and not entirely relishing the prospect of playing second fiddle to Ron – looking a gift horse in the mouth, in fact – but, from that moment, much of my time was spent thinking about feminine grace. One day, trundling my son David in his pushchair in Peckham, preoccupied with my fatherly domestic round, I suddenly caught sight of my reflection in a shop window, appearing less butch than Charles the Wrestler, of course, but still the least likely candidate to revive the pre-Restoration tradition of female impersonation.

Some weeks later I was summoned to Olivier's office. Tucked away in that yard behind Aquinas Street near Waterloo, I'd noted his chauffeur and his waiting car – not the royal-blue Rolls convertible he was yet to console himself with, nor the purple London taxi Denis Quilley remembers from much later, but a black Bentley, its engine running. It was a brief, understated meeting in that little office at the end of his day. Olivier was wearing his hat and, I think, his overcoat.

'Marvellous part. Marvellous play,' he said in his imitable offstage whisper as he spoke the word 'Guildenstern' and handed me Tom's script.

'What about Celia?' I asked.

No. It seemed I would be going on the Canadian tour and taking over the Spaniard in Feydeau's *A Flea in Her Ear* (splendid showy little part) and Jeremy (perky servant) in Congreve's *Love for Love*. I flicked through the Stoppard script on the way to the bus stop and saw that 'Guil' was on every page, usually in duologue with 'Ros'. I am still not acclimatized to the way the actor's life goes from doldrums to trade winds in the twinkling of a phone call or, in this instance, the proffering of that blue script by the hand of Sir Laurence. Only the other day I put down the phone, did a little leap for joy and felt phenomenally positive about quite mundane things for a whole day because I'd been offered a job out of the blue, so I don't know how I kept sufficiently sanguine that day in 1967 to read the script carefully on the bus ride home to Peckham. I had not done a new part for almost eighteen months, but I began to feel, in all confident modesty, that the demands imposed by the part of Guil were tailor-made for the qualities I'd been developing as an actor ever since I'd decided to become one, watching Norman Evans in *Humpty Dumpty* at the Bradford Alhambra in 1944. Straightaway I could see, and hear too, how the dialogue was meant to 'go'.

Yet I believe the most basic qualification for playing either of Stoppard's two heroes is looking not *quite* right for the 'ideal' Hamlet. John Stride, cast in the athletic-heroic mould, with his lovely, effortlessly strong voice, had just a smidgen too much flesh on his cheek. I was the leaner version, a little too lean. Perfectly classically contrasting. We both had the ability to stand about in the ante-rooms of Elsinore Castle, looking authentic in tights. Even walking on and playing bit parts in Shakespeare is a rigorous training for this sort of thing – but who gets the chance to do it wearing them nowadays?

Swelling a progress is by no means as straightforward as people think. The leading actors, who throw casual commands over their shoulders in one's direction, such as 'Stand you awhile aloof' or 'Let all the rest give place', not only gain more job satisfaction, but in some ways have the *easier* job. It's all very well for Shakespeare to write '*A flourish. Enter the King and Queen attended*', and I suppose as an attendant one must simply attend, but you see the Bard was so brilliant at the *top* text. What Shakespearean monarch, what Hamlet, what Cleopatra ever had the time to worry about a *sub*text? They say what they think; what they think, they say. There are no unspoken thoughts in Shakespeare, but whilst standing 'all apart' at the back, one is on one's own sweetheart! Subtext? Shmubtext!

One notch up and you fare a little better, as Salanio, Salarino and Salario or the Rosencrantzes and Guildensterns. It was remarked in *Punch* that, as Ros and Guil, we beautifully suggested 'two-dimensional characters struggling to acquire a third dimension.' Like one of Orlando's sonnets to Rosalind, pinned to a tree in the Forest of Arden, one might pin J. Alfred Prufrock's words to the back of a painted wood and canvas arch in Elsinore Castle:

> No! I am not Prince Hamlet, nor was meant to be;
> Am an attendant lord, one that will do
> To swell a progress, start a scene or two,
> Advise the prince; no doubt, an easy tool,
> Deferential, glad to be of use,
> Politic, cautious, and meticulous;
> Full of high sentence, but a bit obtuse;
> At times, indeed, almost ridiculous –
> Almost, at times, the Fool.

But the part of Guil also demanded the quicksilver wit of high comedy, which I'd practised eight times a week on tour from Invercargill to Wanganui in New Zealand when I was twenty-two and playing Oscar Wilde's Algernon Moncrieff, and was accounted by a perceptive Kiwi critic 'a triumph of style – style which reveals and does not hide the man.'

> Edward Petherbridge played Algernon with a sureness of touch and liveliness of style. ... Under a mask of frivolity he is the most serious character in the play, and this double effect can only be secured by an absolute consistency of conception and performance.

And lest you gain an impression of something altogether too controlled and refined:

The honours undoubtedly go to Edward Petherbridge who played his part of Algernon Moncrieff with a boyish genuineness which was refreshing.

Other qualifications for Guil? There's the problem of playing the kind of comedy that is not necessarily 'High'. In this connection, I ate my first Crêpe Suzette, after a performance of *The Bride Comes Back* one night in Wolverhampton, with Cicely Courtneidge. Not *à deux* you understand; she and Jack Hulbert were treating the whole company in their theatrical *noblesse oblige* manner, but she made sure I was on her table whilst Jack entertained the juvenile girls at his. Cis, as we would never have dreamt of addressing her, was later made a Dame for her services to the musical, light and broad varieties of comedy – those and her ruthless 'defoliation' policy towards the growth of any extraneous laughs in her and Jack's vicinity. I don't suppose, from her London debut at the age of fourteen to her last West End appearance in Ray Cooney's *Move Over, Mrs Markham* in 1971, when she was seventy-eight, that she ever spoke a line which found its way into an anthology of wit. But from the moment she breezed into the upper room of a pub in Pont Street in 1961, pushing seventy and in full war paint – scarlet gloss lipstick and golden perm – to rehearse some supporting actors, of whom I was one, taking over in the tour of a play she'd already been doing in the West End for more than a year, I knew what it was to be in the presence of a tough old pro and a born clown, to witness that 'timing' is the stuff of which drama is made.

The lines that divide Low from High comedy are subtle and blurred. Judging things according to the critic J. C. Trewin, it was the now forgotten, slight, farcical comedy in which Cicely Courtneidge, Jack Hulbert and Roberson Hare had 'roamed at large' that properly introduced me to the three verities of comedy. They were the verities that placed me in good stead in *Trelawny of the 'Wells'* and were to be the lifeblood of *R&G*. They are time, *Time* and timing. When we had played Birmingham with *The Bride Comes Back*, Trewin had waxed poetical about them in *The Birmingham Post*; I wasn't mentioned of course, only the three stars (though the entire cast, wardrobe mistress and stage management were invited to a civic reception at the Guildhall when we played Exeter).

Of Hulbert, Trewin wrote: 'His timing, verbal and physical, remains miraculous.' Of Robertson Hare: 'I believe myself that a part of him is bronze and that every now and then somebody beats upon it, though far, far less strongly than of old. Every mild boom is an indictment of life.' And of Cis: 'If she will forgive me for proposing it – a verse of Davison's "A Ballad of Heaven" that goes rather like this:

Then like a python's sumptuous dress
The frame of things was cast away
And out of Time's obscure distress
The conquering scherzo thundered Day.

The cast of *The Bride Comes Back* in the Mayor's parlour at Exeter.
Jack Hulbert (tall) extreme right; Robertson Hare (diminutive) third from the
right and to the left of the Lady Mayoress; and Cicely Courtneidge next but one in
hat and fur. I am at the back, slightly masked by the wardrobe lady.

Miss Courtneidge will understand that I am not comparing her to a python. I say merely, and as calmly as possible – now another writer joins us – that she stands above the clang and dust of Time. Possibly 'stands' is wrong: she riots.'

I learnt a lot from Cis, including my place in the show: 'This is your moment, dear. You're on the sofa, centre, play it out front, don't bother to look round at me.' When I did sneak a look one night, and glimpsed her riveting business, mixing an Alka-Seltzer for herself, I stopped wondering why my one laugh line wasn't working. Mine was a rotten little functional part, to be played as charmingly and convincingly as possible. I was simply part of the workaday woodwork against which Cis rioted in comic triumph. She certainly prepared me for the rigours of comedic readjustment in the National Theatre's so-called ensemble.

Tyrone Guthrie, writing in 1960 about Coward's *Hay Fever*, called it 'minor work' with 'as good a chance of immortality as any work of an author now living.' As well as its 'author's typical glitter and sharp satiric sting', he perceives what he designates 'the over and above' of wholesome horse sense. The over and above, he says, is the work of the unconscious self:

> In *Hay Fever* one catches, between the lines, a glimpse of that aspect of Noël Coward which made him a good president of the Actors' Orphanage. … He … visited the orphanage, made sure that the beds were clean, that the slops were emptied, the stairs swept, the meals adequate and that the orphans felt that their president really stood *in loco parentis*.

I am taking a rather circuitous route to reach the 'over and above' in *R&G*. 'Wholesome horse sense' we can take for granted, I'd say. I am trying to get at a quality, no, a presence, almost an unlisted character; I certainly heard it when, some years ago, I listened to a tape recording at the British Library of one of our Old Vic performances. It was not a perfect recording – one could hear the buses on Waterloo Road through the dock doors – but, and this is where Guthrie's word 'immortality' might come in, coupled, of course, with mortality, I think the unseen character I heard was Time.

If I were to consider the experiences and practice that helped fit me for Tom's play, I might think back to summer nights in doublet and hose in Regent's Park in 1962. No young actor lusts after Shakespeare's parts of Demetrius in *The Dream* or Dumain in *Love's Labour's*, though they are more fun than the Bard's Rosencrantz and Guildenstern, but what I can remember, from playing in the awakening scene in *The Dream* and the scene after the news of the King's death in *Love's Labour's*, is a most poetic and potent over and above. The parts themselves have no purple passages, but both have fine words just enough, minor figures that they are; I remember being caught up in the plays' and the characters' sense of wonder.

R&G was effectively a stopgap. John Dexter had been planning the modern-dress, all-male production of *As You Like It* and had invited Ralph Koltai to design it. Dexter exited and it was suddenly shelved. There had been disagreements with Olivier, not least, I'd heard, about the cost of real aluminium for the sky. Dexter had a glamorous job to go to at the Metropolitan Opera in New York. Crisis. Well, there was this new script by an unknown called Stoppard, which the Oxford Theatre Group had staged on the Edinburgh Fringe: 'a handful of sparsely attended performances in a flat-floored church hall', in Tom's words. Only the other day, I met somebody who had seen it there and been impressed and, some years ago, I encountered an antique dealer in Lisson Grove who told me he'd been the Guildenstern, Clive Gable; his name appears with that cast and the director in the first published edition.

Actually, Trevor Nunn surprised me recently by telling me his part in the story. At the age, I calculate, of twenty-six, he'd planned to do the play at the RSC, but the money was not available. Didn't they have at least one set of leftover *Hamlet* costumes? There's another version of events whereby the RSC were not happy with Act Three, and hesitated until their option or faith ran out. Trevor told me that it was he who recommended it to the Oxford Theatre Group, when they wanted to present something on the Festival Fringe, and that Kenneth Tynan, having seen Ronald Bryden's review of the Edinburgh production come off the press at the *Observer*, bought the play, 'sight unseen', for the National. My favourite part of the jigsaw is Tom Stoppard leaving Edinburgh on a Sunday morning train to London and opening the *Observer* to look for a review of his novel *Lord Malquist & Mr Moon*, which had been published that week, and discovering instead Bryden's life-transforming notice of his play. But imagine Tom's wait from

September 1966 until the play went into rehearsal, happily earlier than expected, on the Monday morning of the last week of February 1967.

At that time the National had a deficit of £250,000, but handily it had the roughly traditional period costumes from Olivier's inaugural NT production of *Hamlet*, mothballed and swathed in polythene in the vast gloomy vaults underneath the railway arches of Waterloo, and 'fresh' from an extremely limited run in 1963. Peter O'Toole as Hamlet had been contracted, astonishingly, for only twenty-one performances, because of his burgeoning international film career, and Olivier couldn't find a suitable star actor to replace him in the production, which had not been well received, for a longer run.

Apparently, Dexter's parting suggestion in 1967 was that Derek Goldby, one of the staff assistant directors, should direct *R&G*. Suddenly it was full steam ahead for Tom's play whilst the National took the time to find an acceptable replacement to direct Dexter's *As You Like It*, Koltai's designs for which were almost complete. I met Ralph recently at the opening of the V&A's Theatre and Performance Galleries: we found ourselves together in front of his model for *As You* and he told me that he and the new director, Clifford Williams, had discussed some bizarre ideas along the way to justify the cast being all male, including, I gathered, a performance at gunpoint in a police state, before settling on the peaceable, elegant white Formica floor and transparent Perspex tubes suggesting trees we saw in miniature before us. It is ironic that a little local difficulty over the aesthetics of the Forest of Arden should have precipitated *R&G* into Elsinore a few months ahead of schedule, as if the rotten old state of Denmark's problems were any easier, compounded as they were with those attendant on bringing a new play by an untried playwright onto the stage.

Derek Goldby somehow, sadly, dissipated his early success, which partly issued from the right people being 'in the building', from having Claude Chagrin, mime expert, and the composer Marc Wilkinson on the staff. Even the designer Desmond Heeley chose himself by virtue of his *Hamlet* costumes. But, of course, Derek successfully chaired the creative meeting of all these minds and imaginations. He had wanted to cast two young 'unknowns' as Ros and Guil. Nowadays that would mean two young men who hadn't appeared on television. Olivier said, 'You can't do that to a new play; you can have one.' I was the lucky one.

John Stride had been part of the National Theatre's first faltering step (no pun intended) in 1963. He'd played Fortinbras in the disappointing inaugural production of *Hamlet*, but he had a considerable reputation, not least because, in 1960, he'd played Romeo in Franco Zeffirelli's production of *Romeo and Juliet* on this same stage; a production deemed a failure until Tynan's review:

> The balcony scene is heartrendingly good. Here, as everywhere
> else in the production, grace is subordinated to circumstance, the
> ideal to the real. ... Instead of leaping balletically up a
> conveniently placed creeper, John Stride (as Romeo) has to

concentrate prosaically on climbing a highly uncooperative little tree. Judi Dench, a calm, wise little Juliet, awaits him aloft; their encounter is grave, awkward and extremely beautiful.

Perhaps of all us young actors at the National in my time, Stride, possessing a beautiful voice, had the least affected style and most effectively performed the conjuring trick of making a bold 'classical' utterance his own and, in the best sense, natural.

Just prior to going into rehearsal with *R&G*, I had played the Ralph Lynn part in the classic Aldwych farce *Tons of Money*, which Derek Goldby (still a lowly assistant director) had been allowed to produce as a Sunday night special (there was a series of these) for an invited audience and to give the junior members of the company a chance to shine. John Stride had come round afterwards on that Sunday night and, beaming, said to me, 'I'm going to meet my match working with you. All that deft comedy business and timing – you were like an expert with a rapier.' Goldby reported to me what Joan Plowright had said to Sir Laurence, who had arrived late for the performance: 'It's a shame you missed the beginning. Petherbridge's first ten minutes were brilliant.' It is possible that John was being a little generous about the next 120 minutes in support of his colleague to be, nevertheless that night a bond of mutual respect was sealed. We never became real friends offstage; we were seldom even to be found in the same group after the show in the pub next to the stage door. This distance, perhaps, gave a necessary edge to our working partnership.

JOHN STRIDE as Rosencrantz and EDWARD PETHERBRIDGE as Guildernstern in *Rosencrantz and Guildernstern are Dead*

Cartoon: © Hewison / *Punch*

'Two Elizabethans passing the time in a place without any visible character. They are well dressed – hats, cloaks, sticks and all.' Desmond Heeley gave us hats and swords, which proved a little tricky to manage. I think we should have persisted; we might have made use of being correctly encumbered if we'd had more time to rehearse with them. Thank God there was no Formica, no plastic and no aluminium, simulated or real, though these remain in my mind's eye when I think of Ralph Koltai's set for the all-male *As You Like It* I so admired. Tom once saw an Italian production of *R&G*, which he 'loved', set in a series of Perspex boxes, which he also 'loved'. Putting aside all thoughts of Perspex and reading the yellowing cuttings of the reviews of our show, I'm amazed at the purple critical prose lavished just on the *appearance* of it. 'Derek Goldby's production,' Peter Lewis announced, 'comes out of the dark like a spotlit jewel, full of vibrations.'

There was at the heart of the proceedings that most pregnant and ambiguous of spaces, the bare stage, fusing into dark at the sides so that one could not be sure what depths might be found or what direction should be taken to reach them. Hard-edged, semi-abstract flattage for this play is, I believe, fatal; tricks with gauzes likewise. Only Real Space! Hamlet and the court came either subtly or swiftly, alarmingly out of the dark. The haunting empty dark that hangs about its two Elizabethans in their doublets and hose is a place where, as Ros puts it, 'anything could happen' and where everything does, a dark that's light enough for comedy. We were lit 'with rare sensitivity' (B. A. Young, *Financial Times*) by Richard Pilbrow. 'It is a long play,' said Harold Hobson, 'but there is not a sentence, a look of any of the players, an intonation of any of their voices, any note of the music, any square inch of Desmond Heeley's set, or any gradation of Richard Pilbrow's lighting which did not give me intense pleasure.'

We did have somewhere to sit down, and different levels where we could stand or kneel and where, eventually, the players would cavort in their rehearsals: a curvaceous rostrum, three steps up at one end, three steps down at the other. The whole point was – *is* – the astounding number of variations these two Elizabethans play on the shoestring-in-a-void, which Stoppard has provided, interrupted from time to time by the sinister wit, dumb show, hyperbole and 'blood, love and rhetoric' of the Player and the eloquent mime of his troupe. Cobwebs, one noticed, laced the supporting structure of the rostrum.

When the court burst upon us, there was a set of Gothic arches, cut-outs flown in swiftly during a few seconds' blackout. They did suggest the archetypal grey castle of one's imaginings, whilst providing a local habitation that went some way towards anchoring us amidst the surrounding airy nothing.

On a Monday night (we never played Monday nights), after only two weeks of rehearsal, conceivably the most awe-inspiring twentieth-century audience of three walked in to watch a run-through of how far we'd got with *R&G*: Sir Laurence himself, Kenneth Tynan and an as yet largely unknown quantity, at least to the world, called Tom Stoppard. I'd like to nip back to sample the wet-behind-the-gills state of us, and eavesdrop on the comment in the stalls. Years later I read something of Tom's in which he said they gave him notes until five o'clock in the morning – seems a long time for the handful of snips that were made, unless they discussed the problematic ending. I didn't mind losing 'Give us this day, our daily mask' to rhyme with 'consistency is all I ask', but I was pleased when Tom restored the Unicorn speech to the opening of Act One some months later, and 'Here be dragons' after Ros's 'We're slipping off the edge of the map' on the boat in Act Three is vital, surely? But Tynan mustn't have liked it.

In two weeks Tom had become known and liked and trusted by *us*. He came and sat modestly in the rehearsal room. It was, after all, his very first stage play to be performed (he'd had one or two on television), but he looked almost perfectly used to rehearsal rooms, had got a grasp already, at least *in theory*. He didn't say much, but what he did say, at the vital points, invariably worked *in practice*. One day he said, 'Don't try and explain or strive to make that complex bit comprehensible, just toss it at the audience like a handful of diamonds [one or two *up* from pearls, you notice] and they'll be delighted and feel so clever if they catch one or two.' He was far beyond expecting us to 'convey', as some playwrights will in their first pieces, the sort of stuff they think is in there when it isn't. The script, like a piece of music, was crying out to be played so it could release its undertones and overtones, and, up on our feet in the rehearsal room, we could sense them. This resonance was best not mentioned. 'Touch it, and the bloom is gone,' as Lady Bracknell said in another context. We never once discussed 'significance'; we rehearsed the script as if it were the classiest of situation comedies. It is of course: Ros and Guil both hankering for *plot*; audience fascinated by their *situation*.

In theory, we should have been in awe of Kenneth Tynan that night under the cold working lights in the Vic, but, in practice, we had our job to do, he had his. And we were used to him being about the place, never looking glamorous like his photographs, but hunch-shouldered, almost fugitive with an unhealthily florid complexion. Yet of all the voices, which had been raised in favour of a National Theatre, his had been the most brilliantly, entertainingly persuasive. He'd practically shamed Britain into having a National Theatre. For me, a provincial boy, as for so many to whom the London theatre was a remote dream, he'd been a theatrical education by correspondence course, a touchstone ever since, when I was fifteen, a school friend had alerted me to the existence of the posh Sunday newspapers. Later, I was gauche enough to make the mistake of not expressing a proper awe when it might have been appropriate, but then the place was so crammed with brilliance, talent and glamour – latent, budding, in full flush and fading – that one had to decide between prostrating oneself or getting one's own petals open and into the sun to survive. In any case, this was a man, enough of a dreamer, and vain enough too, to make sure he was photographed in an elegant pose in the middle of a lesson in bullfighting, he who never made it into the arena.

Reading Tynan's published diaries and letters, I now know (more than I need to) how he was performing whilst we were dutifully performing at the Vic. And I realize more than ever what a gulf there was between the life the stars of the National led and the lives of the ensemble. Of course, the leading actors weren't all showing pornographic films to Princess Margaret and Antony Armstrong-Jones, as Tynan did (saved only by Peter Cook's extempore narration, in the style of a Cadbury's Flake commercial, to some steamy Jean Genet footage – and inches) – but the constant heady partying in the right places with the right people and, as one now knows from a glimpse at the kiss-and-tell confessions, so many of them doing the 'wrong' thing one way or another a lot of the time! Still, in the second interval of *R&G* I always used to have a small whisky and dry ginger! Our dresser procured it from the pub and, after two acts of Stoppard, my metabolism seemed to process it without trace. But the relentless chore of take-over and understudy rehearsals (I covered Kurt in *The Dance of Death*, Iago and Atahualpa), the bus rides to and from Peckham, the classes with Yat Malmgren two or three times a week, and the existence of our little boy were part of a life that would in no way produce the kiss-and-tell, carouse-and-confess memoir with its restaurants, parties and guest lists resembling the index of Noël Coward's diaries. There might, of course, have been the odd adventure, but this is a serious book about the art of acting.

To return to the Monday night in question, the chandelier over the stalls was unlit, and the bare stage and auditorium were illuminated by the same unglamorous working lights, as if for the cleaners. Such an early test, at a relatively insecure moment in rehearsal, forced confidence and 'nerve', as opposed to nerves, to the fore. As with pilots on difficult flights, previous flying hours counted. I love the atmosphere of a theatre in its shirtsleeves without an audience.

I'll tell you one thing. They didn't laugh that Monday night, that audience of three in the Old Vic at the end of our first fortnight's rehearsal. We played Acts One and Two without scripts, and carried them during the third. Not a titter did we get. I don't remember us being in the least put out by this; I think we assumed their presence was forensic. Maybe we'd got hold of a golden rule: in situation comedy, act the situation not the comedy. Comic timing is not something you 'do' to elicit laughs, it's a function of character, it's the speed of your character's perceptions. You *use* it the more perfectly to define and discover your situation for yourself, so that it's always related to the rhythms of your character's understanding of his predicament, the tempo of his discoveries and stratagems. The same goes for the emotional timing of tragedy. I've never articulated this theoretical 'wisdom after the instinctive event' before. Of course, one is hanging the script in the air and it has got to hang right. Ultimately, you're fucked if you don't get the laugh, but there is an innocence to be preserved.

Whatever the promise of that Monday night in 1967, under the working lights at the Old Vic, when our comedy routines were still a little unstable and unpolished, and our identities were uncertain (as they would properly remain), I daresay we were aspiring to a condition to which the Greek actor, perspiring behind his mask, and every actor since, has aspired: to be 'moved by the impulse of being.'

Eighteen months later, on 17 October 1968, by which time we had a new Player and had seen some distinguished Hamlets and Ophelias come and go, Tom wrote a letter to his two comedians:

> Dear John and Ted,
> I was so pleased on Tuesday. After so long, a slightly faded carbon would be neither surprising nor a matter for resentment, but your performances retain all their sense of discovery and relish – thank you. I felt it was the highest compliment I had ever been paid; admiration jostles gratitude.
> Much love, Tom

*   *   *

'This was my dressing room when I played Hamlet.' Sir Laurence, in his three-piece suit, stood in the corner by the window; in his hands were a sheaf of notes on the *R&G* dress rehearsal and a pencil. He'd been talking very lightly through the notes and crossing them out as he dispatched them. It was Sunday night, 9 April 1967, and we were in dressing room no. 4 at the Old Vic. It was not yet my dressing room; I was still on the third floor. At the end, Olivier tossed his notes into the wastepaper basket and, before leaving, said to us of his Hamlet in its entirety during the season of 1937, thirty years before:

> Tony Guthrie never gave me a no-stopping dress run-through before we opened, so I couldn't get the measure of it. You have to find out the bits where you don't have to work so hard – start to find the shape of it. I've never quite forgiven him.

After he'd gone, I wondered (did we all?) about retrieving his scribbled notes, but there is something craven about delving into a wastepaper basket. Had I, however, caught a fleeting, almost arch expression on his face, a second's hesitation before he decided to toss them away, as if it was not entirely inconceivable to him that someone might want to keep them as a trophy of the occasion, or at least for reference? Scrawled in the dark of the stalls, in a large hand on plain A4 paper, surprisingly – for I admired him next door to idolatry – I hadn't found them particularly insightful and have no memory of them now.

What I do remember from that evening is what he said about Mrs Stirling's eiderdown. Before he left his old dressing room, he had indicated where there had been a couch and said, 'On matinée days between two "eternity" *Hamlets*, Lilian Baylis would come up from her office below and her tenderly rough hands would tuck me into Mrs Stirling's eiderdown to put the right loving thoughts into my head, give the correct benediction to my rest and make the most spiritual contact with my muse.' He didn't bother to explain who Mrs Stirling was.

I certainly never expected to set eyes on her patchwork, and was surprised to find myself recognizing it from his story, decades later in the Theatre Museum in Covent Garden, behind plate glass over a chair by Lilian Baylis's roll-top desk which I also recognized from Olivier's dressing room.

This patchwork quilt was sewn over the years during long waits in dressing and green rooms, using remnants from her costumes. Perhaps there was a piece of the dress she wore as Cordelia opposite Macready's Lear, a scrap of Mrs Malaprop's gown, or that of the Nurse, whom she played to Ellen Terry's Juliet in 1882. There might have been fabrics that moved with her before oil 'floats', limelight and gas footlights when she started at the East London Theatre in 1829, and others that caught electricity when Henry Irving briefly installed it at the Lyceum, only to replace it with the reinstated, more subtle gas, at Ellen Terry's request.

In a biography by her grandson, I came across a letter Mrs Stirling wrote to Mrs Baylis (Lilian's mother), not from a green room or lodgings on tour, but from a dairy farm in Uphill, Devon where she was holidaying in 1852: a fresh, beautiful letter, full of sun and sea and rhapsodic references to what we'd now call dairy products. I like to think that, during Olivier's slumbers on those matinée days, the enfolding patchwork transmitted not only the atmosphere of gas footlights and echoes of vanished performances, but some hint of 'the sad sea wave' of Devon, curds and whey, bird song and buttercups, and that, when he rose to put his costume back on, repair his make-up and prepare once more to throw off every shred of dead tradition, the play really did take him by the seat of the pants and hurl him across the stars, as he wrote that it sometimes could.

Tom, in the latest tailoring of 1967, rich not gaudy, and his Ros and Guil in doublet and hose; four minutes to curtain up. All of us at the age of twenty-nine or thirty in the narrow, brick-walled corridor near the Opposite Prompt side of the stage at the Old Vic. There is a capacity house, waiting for the performance of *R&G* to begin, but it is oddly quiet where we are. Down this passage there are four small doors and one of them, to the right, leads to the convenient little dressing room from which John Stride has just emerged. The only door on the left, leads onto the Opposite Prompt side of the stage, its wings very narrow, a mere step; go through this door too boldly during a show and you've made an entrance, indeed any direction involving processions, alarums and excursions has to be made from the Prompt Side wings. Stoppard's players, whom we are due to meet in twenty-two minutes on the road to Elsinore, will come on perforce from that side, too, the acting troupe rehearsed into witty mimetic eloquence by Claude Chagrin.

Just now all is quiet and nobody else about. The King and Queen, Hamlet, Polonius and all the courtiers have at least half an hour to make up, dress and philosophize in the upstairs dressing rooms. But what was Tom doing backstage, or in the theatre at all? Does he still confess these days to the occasional pang of guilt, gratitude or a surge of omnipotence when, in the middle of a dinner with friends, or watching *News at Ten*, or *The Muppets* as he once said, or perhaps transposing a comma if he revises in the evenings, he remembers his actors, faithfully going through their Stoppardian paces at the theatre?

We are surprised and delighted to see him; the three of us suddenly squashed together by the door onto the stage. His play has been triumphing in the repertoire for a month or two, so perhaps he's popped in to see it again. It's my belief that he's nipped through the pass door in the orchestra stalls and walked up the slope of the corridor, which follows the rake of the stage, knowing that the three 'star' dressing rooms through the door at the top end will be empty tonight and he can have the quiet use of their loo, away from the hurly-burly of the stalls' gents. He's come down from that direction anyway, and met us just as we are about to go on stage. John opens the little door leading to the dark of the OP wings. Suddenly puzzled, Tom asks, 'What's that noise?' John bursts out laughing. 'That's your bloody audience!' Quite properly, for a playwright, Tom has never stood in the backstage gloom and heard a full house as it sounds, coming from the other side of the curtain. It would be an exaggeration to say that he turns pale, but he looks grave, shocked even, and, for a moment perhaps, wonders how we can possibly be so hail-fellow-well-met. He flees to what, I hope by now, has become the comfort of the stalls. On our first night, Tom had been given a stall seat in the middle of a row. Apparently he'd survived the pre-curtain-rise noise of the audience from that position, but, once the play had started, he'd had to extract himself, disturbing half the row in his anxiety to leave. It hadn't helped that he'd heard a man seated on the row in front say, 'I wish they'd get on with it.'

On stage that first night, with easy access to several exits, there was no escape. Where else on earth, in any case, could we have possibly wanted to be? And upstairs, in a third-floor, small-part-and-walk-on dressing room, there was an unopened bottle of first-night champagne by my mirror with a tiny handwritten card signed by Laurence Olivier. It read:

> Dear Edward, I am completely and delightedly confident in the deserved success of your brilliant performance. Just remember that nerves are a self-indulgence, and something of nothing. You have a job to do and it is going to be a good one. I wish I could see it tonight. Please give your roommates a sip of this from me. Loving wishes, L. O.

*   *   *

Everybody can ride a bicycle, but nobody knows how it is done. Not even engineers and manufacturers know the formula for the correct method of counteracting the tendency to fall by turning the handlebars so that for a given angle of unbalance the curvature of each winding is inversely proportional to the square of the speed at which the cyclist is proceeding. The cyclist obeys a code of rules which is specifiable, but which he cannot specify; he could write on his number-plate Pascal's motto: *Le coeur a ses raisons que la raison ne connaît point.* Or, to put it in a more abstract way: the controls of a skilled activity of any kind generally function below the level of consciousness on which the activity takes place. The code is a hidden persuader.

(Arthur Koestler, *The Act of Creation*)

Playgoing, irrespective of the required height or lowness of the brow, is a skilled activity. I still meet intelligent people who say they find *R&G* 'difficult'. Don't they recognize the bicycle? Are they asking the wrong questions? Do they get off on the wrong foot or pedal on the road to Elsinore, even before Ros and Guil are momentarily caught up in the action of *Hamlet*?

It's dead simple: Ros and Guil are first discovered, as you'll remember, with those coins, already playing the game of pitch and toss. Guil is losing. Ros's first words, after he's said 'Heads' seven times, are 'Seventy-six love'. This is as pithy a back-story as you could wish for and, usefully, gets a laugh – though not at the Saturday matinée on tour in Cardiff, as I remember.

On that particular afternoon, we tossed the coins and the audience actually witnessed, as usual, from the point at which they'd discovered us, twenty-three of the total score of ninety-two consecutive 'heads'.

With John Stride in *Rosencrantz and Guildenstern Are Dead*, Old Vic.
Photo: © Anthony Crickmay

Then Guil felt the need to colour in, for clarification and his sanity's sake, more of their back-story, their 'story so far'. Suddenly (nearing the end of the fifth page) he remembers: 'There was a messenger … that's right. We were sent for.' Frightfully *existential* isn't it? Except that Tom claimed never to have heard the term until he read it in one of the reviews of his play. I'd learnt it when we got up to Jean Paul Sartre at Theatre School in our Thursday evening Leeds University Extra-Mural History of Drama classes, and I once looked up 'existentialism' in a second-hand copy of *The Oxford Companion to the Mind*. There is such a thing; I'd bought my copy one Saturday in 1990 in Charing Cross Road in between the two houses of *The Woman in Black*.

'See Sartre, Jean Paul,' it said. So I did. The screeds of authoritative reference-book prose on the metaphysics of *objects and being,* read as if one has died and woken up in an eternal performance of *Jumpers* without the jokes. For example:

> Nor should such paradoxical-seeming dicta as 'the being of the for-itself is defined as being what it is not and not being what it is' be taken at face value but should be construed as dramatic expressions of thought whose meaning, often relatively sober, can only be grasped in context.

Quite.

I don't think the New Theatre, Cardiff felt to us like the hub of the universe exactly that Saturday afternoon, but, if actors can't perform the imaginative trick of turning the stage into the hub, how can the audience be expected to? Our first intimation that they might be on an unfamiliar planet had come in the tone and volume of the buzz of the audience, heard through the curtain whilst we were kneeling in position, waiting for it to go up. One of us said something like, 'I don't think we should expect too much from this lot,' and the other said, 'Whoever gets the first laugh wins a quid from the other.' We should never have said any of this, because whatever *lack* of mirth there was going to be in the auditorium was now going to be inversely proportionate to that on stage.

My first line, 'There is an art to the building up of suspense', amused us, as not one of the first five 'heads' had raised a titter, and the line itself went by in pin-drop silence. It was like performing a concert version of *The Oxford Companion to the Mind*, indeed the suspense became rather terrible. Eventually at some late, arbitrary point, a single, short, high-pitched female cackle in the back of the dress circle pierced the quiet of the afternoon. I imagined an old Welsh woman in a tall black hat and shawl. I caught John's eye, and decided it would be better not to catch it again if I was going to get through our opening seventeen-minute duologue without the curtain having to be rung back down. Soon, even more draconian measures involving changes of position had to be implemented so there would be less chance of hearing or causing one another's stifled snorts and squeaks. Mercifully, at last, Graham Crowden's motley Player came on with his mimes, musicians and the cart and 'Halt! (*Joyously*) An audience! Don't move. Perfect! A lucky thing we came along.' We were transformed into a captive audience ourselves, and the jinx was broken.

The play cast its spell at least for one Colin Paris, who'd been a year above me at Theatre School in Bradford, more than a decade before. Unexpectedly he came into my dressing room that afternoon as if fresh from a bracing spring walk in the hills, almost speechless with delight and maybe astonished at the Olympian Heights on which I had become privileged to take my exercise, in between *Othello* and *The Royal Hunt of the Sun* nights.

Cautiously I asked, 'Was the opening alright?'

'The opening – oh the opening – marvellous atmosphere and suspense!' Then, seeing my look of shamefaced enquiry, he thought back and added, 'Perhaps a *touch* difficult to hear in places.'

In rehearsal, it had never occurred to us to wonder what this sequence 'meant' (though Guil wonders, naturally) and still less what it 'signified'. I mean we didn't find it obscure. As for Ros and Guil's vagueness about their own history, well, I'm afraid the easiest thing for an actor to act is a blank mind. We were busy (a) working out the best, the neatest way to play the coin game and (b) practising to look as if, as Guil says, 'We have been spinning coins together since I don't know when.' Jeremy Kingston was to write in *Punch*, 'In their scenes together, they behave as though they had been stuck beside one another throughout eternity.' Not a bad achievement in six weeks rehearsal, never having worked together before; in any case if, as Guil seems to think of his inordinate bad luck, 'It must be indicative of something, besides the redistribution of wealth', then Guil, Ros and the audience will be better placed to concentrate on the quest to discover what that something might be if the mechanics of the coin game proceed effortlessly.

Larry's Stable, **a Sunday-night show at the Old Vic, produced by Cedric Messina to raise funds for the Globe Theatre. Robert Lang watches John Stride and me. My hair shows signs of Wimsey's blond!**
Photo: © Ian Lewis

There's a bit of indirectly related ancient lore in there somewhere, which decrees that the greater the clowns' apparent chaos and mayhem, the more finely timed and judged their act needs to be. Put simply, we couldn't afford to drop any coins, and the care taken not to, hadn't to show, so that the audience could concentrate on the higher, funnier things, the wider resonances. The audience shouldn't feel uncomfortably puzzled; they know all they need to know, they're ahead. It's Guil, who's anxiously making a list of 'possible explanations' in a parody of the academic approach, like a dog chasing his own intellectual tail, though he's trying to be cool and grown-up and apply the theory of his Wittenberg studies in Logic and Rhetoric to this alarming out-of-school experience.

I can theorize now, with hindsight, that in the opening scene with that run of heads, and the unnerving first encounter with the players, Ros and Guil are experiencing our old friend, a lull, in a green room of the author's mind (Shakespeare's? Stoppard's?), and waiting for their luck to change, to be given something to do. At the time, notwithstanding Guil's struggle to form a thesis, I simply played for all it was worth this *Hamlet* exposition scene which refuses to expose anything more than the ghost of an idea – theatre not thesis. Let's face it, it was a matter of inhabiting the gags (there isn't a gag in the world that isn't about something elementally serious) because, if the gags are fully breathing and alive and working, you have opened the transaction with the audience who are to accompany you on the road to Elsinore, and their laughter is a sure sign that they are engaged.

Speaking, as we were, of the school at Wittenberg, in 1983 I received a request from an actress of my acquaintance, Pat Doyle, asking if I could write a letter to her son, who was about to play Guil in a production of *R&G* at Alleyn's School in Dulwich, founded in Shakespeare's lifetime by the actor Edward Alleyn, who knew the first Rosencrantz and Guildenstern, saw the first Hamlet and the first Ghost. There is hearsay evidence that Shakespeare played the Ghost and a legend that Alleyn saw the Devil whilst playing in *Doctor Faustus*. Understandably shaken, Alleyn retired from the stage and began his charitable foundation in atonement for his sins. I'd given my last performance as Guil in 1970 at the Old Vic, having played the part in repertoire for over three years. Here is the letter I wrote:

November 1st, 1983
London

Dear Angus

So, you are to play Guildenstern, I quite envy you!!

About once every two or three years I have a nightmare – one of those actor's anxiety dreams; in it there's a revival of *R&G* and I am to play my original part. Of course, I know my character very well – there never seems to be a rehearsal period – just a buzz of expectancy from a theatre full of unseen people. I am in my familiar steel-blue costume and preparing for the performance. The set, even the stage itself, is unnervingly unrecognizable and I get an unexpected stab of fear (and guilt!). I realize that I am lost. I know nothing.

Apart from the guilt, I suppose – and I've just realized this, sitting down to write something for you – I suppose that's how Guil feels most of the time.

Ros has the ability to lapse into what Tom Stoppard called 'a sunny acceptance' from time to time. Not Guil. Doesn't Guil once say 'Enjoy it. Relax'? But that's one of his cerebral conceits – not a gut feeling really. Then when he does smile once or is it twice, it's like a ray of sun in the prison of Denmark. [Oh dear, I'm afraid I really did write that.]

I remember the director trying to make me play the first long scene before the players' entrance in a very desperate manner, 'like a rabbit lost in a warren, feverishly exploring each cul-de-sac.' Instinctively I felt this was wrong. There must be a tension, of course, but not of a rabbit digging and scrambling. It's more like the tension of an ominous 'groundswell' (is that the term – when one is literally or metaphorically at sea?).

Example 1: Imagine a dimly lit stage, empty. Guil looks about quickly – tries to work out geography and exits – mutters quickly – perhaps his hands calculate – ticking off his 'solutions' – very tense, fast, shoulders hunched – dog with a bone.

Now example 2: Same bare stage. Guil stands quietly. Listens to the silence and its noises. He looks up perhaps, diagonally to his left, his eyes not focusing on anything specific. It's a gesture of remembering maybe – or remembering if there's anything *to* remember. He speaks quite fast but there is nothing ragged or jagged in the rhythm.

Example 2 is, I believe, better. Occasionally G breaks into urgent or exasperated, almost violent passages on top of this groundswell. For the audience – if one dare mention them – the SPELL of the play absolutely depends on the palpable mystery of this slow underlying movement which eventually even Ros experiences too. Is it the mystery of existence or the presence somewhere near of a play called *Hamlet*?

I don't mean that I *spoke* the opening slowly – most of it is swift as I remember – he has a quick mind. His petty impatience or long-suffering 'patience', or deadpan irritation with Rosencrantz, is always the comic pinprick in the bubble of his intellectual or philosophical quest for explanations and solutions. You will, of course, find your own colours and rhythms and I guess it's important to use your *own personality* – that I'm sure you've realized.

Of course, really they're in a prolonged stand-up comic double act – shot through with shafts of something poetic (a wonderfully heady combination). My partnership with John Stride is the happiest I've had so far. I can't imagine how in a production of this play the two lead actors could be at daggers drawn eight times a week for a year – but I know in one famous instance they were. It's an extended game of table tennis which you help each other to win through those swift, dazzling passages across the net, or as you watch the ball blowing idly across the cold grey stone floors of Elsinore Castle. You'll worry about Act Three – the same old routines over again you might think – but for the audience there's a new character, a new presence at any rate. The Boat! With the boat comes a new dramatic suspense for them as to what will now happen to you.

Be careful that they hear your very last sentences in the play, though you'll want to do them quietly, and get the metal workshop to make you some coins which won't roll too much and are reasonably big. Ours were like this. Easy to see and catch, and with the round edges flattened a bit. If one does get dropped in the opening (I tossed as John Stride caught, slapped the coin on his wrist and then said 'Heads') – if one does drop and rolls a bit, R pursues it, examines it where it lands and says 'Heads.' Then the audience laughs.

Good luck.

PS Have fun.

PPS If I ever write my memoirs, could I publish this to save having to think up something else about the play?

E.

*   *   *

In Shakespeare's *Hamlet*, Rosencrantz and Guildenstern don't have extended poetic speeches. In Stoppard's play they do:

A man standing on his saddle in the half-lit half-alive dawn banged on the shutters and called two names. He was just a hat and a cloak levitating in the grey plume of his own breath, but when he called we came. That much is certain – we came.

Ros's reply plonks us straight back into the vernacular: 'Well I can tell you I'm sick to death of it. I don't care one way or another, so why don't you make up your mind.' However, he too can't help slipping into poetic mode:

Whatever became of the moment when one first knew about death? There must have been one, a moment, in childhood when it first occurred to you that you don't go on forever. It must have been shattering – stamped into one's memory. And yet I can't remember it. It never occurred to me at all. What does one make

148

of that? We must be born with an intuition of mortality. Before we know the words for it, before we know that there are words, out we come, bloodied and squalling with the knowledge that for all the compasses in the world, there's only one direction, and time is its only measure.

The Player, being a player, uses his hyperbole quite *naturally,* as we might say, whether 'on' or 'off'. Ah! The swift, florid, biting intelligence of Graham Crowden's utterance.

Tom joked, only joked, that he'd wanted Morecambe and Wise to play Ros and Guil, and, of course, there are hints somewhere in the mix, but the script's range demands personalities more protean, who stay *inside,* fully inhabit their shifting moods and modes of behaviour. The theatricality must never have the fatal touch of parody. That would immediately unravel the invisible chords binding the metaphor and the impression of 'real life' together; the illusion that makes the audience care.

> When I am absorbed in reading, a second self takes over, a self which thinks and feels for me. Withdrawn in some recess of myself, do I then silently witness this dispossession? Do I derive from it some comfort, or, on the contrary, a kind of anguish? However that may be, someone else holds the centre of the stage, and the question which imposes itself, which I am absolutely obliged to ask myself, is this: 'Who is the usurper who occupies the forefront? Who is this mind who alone all by himself fills my consciousness and who, when I say I, is indeed that I?'
>
> (Georges Poulet, 'Phenomenology of Reading')

Good to have discovered this eloquent description of what, surely, is the 'grey matter' part of the process that's happening when one begins reading a script with a view to acting it. But as soon as one speaks aloud what is written and gets up from the chair in the study, one realizes that the process can be fully achieved only through what we must for the moment call 'free movement'. 'Someone else holds the centre of the stage': in the case of the actor, this is not merely a mysterious metaphor describing a phenomenon of brain activity, nor, of course, a literal fact. It describes a manifestation, the creation of an event in space and time; to borrow again Sir Henry Irving's phrase, the actor is 'moved by the impulse of being.'

At the Northern Theatre School we touched rather lightly on The Method or, should I say, Stanislavski's System. Tom's Ros and Guil – can they be subjected to a layer-by-layer Stanislavskian investigation? Not only do they have little sense of their own history but nobody seems to set much store by their presence in the here and now, least of all themselves. Do they find themselves farcically beached by the backwaters of Tragedy, styleless and guileless? Not exactly; when the drama of *Hamlet* sweeps by and involves them, they fall into place, fit in, and everyone takes them for granted. They do what they are told and nobody complains except Hamlet, but then he complains about everybody.

Another fragment from Poulet: 'How could I explain, without such take-over of my innermost subjective being, the astonishing facility with which I could not only understand but feel what I read?' *Feeling* a script, one senses perhaps a theme or two, but more immediately, how the music of the line is meant to 'go', how, physically, one might go along with it or be dragged along or resist or not go at all, or maybe pull ahead. Sensing how the physical and emotional weight is distributed throughout one's body and within the phrasing of the words, is almost the entire trick. It is kinetics: defining and being defined by the surrounding space in relation to the other actors, creating the author's world and what happens in it. I've seen it done, suggesting a seismic shift in a word, an epoch in a gesture, a life's history in a look.

Obviously my three-year Theatre School training – and my attempts to *manifest, experience* and *become* Miss McBride's suggested subjects – did leave a theatrical mark upon me. 'Theatrical' isn't *always* to be used pejoratively. But when the lights came up on Ros and Guil tossing coins on the road to Elsinore, the last thing the audience needed to see was simply a couple of *actors* in Elizabethan dress. They needed to feel that they were in the presence of two real young men who, unconsciously, were part of a tradition.

Chapter 12

A World Elsewhere: Leaving the Old Vic

It has been said, in regard to the job of acting, 'You're only as good as your last part.' But I think the cynic who said, 'You're only as good as your next part,' had a point.

A telegram arrived for me at the Old Vic on the 16 July 1967, during a patch of *R&G* performances:

'BRILLIANT PERFORMANCE CONGRATULATIONS. HAROLD PINTER.'

Some eighteen months later, Noël Coward greeted me in Joan Plowright's dressing room after a performance of *The Advertisement* with, 'You were brilliant, and not for the first time.' Olivier was standing right there with us, but it was no good; by this time the die was cast. My star was in the descendant.

JOAN PLOWRIGHT as Teresa and EDWARD PETHERBRIDGE as Lorenzo in *The Advertisement*

in *The Advertisement.*
Cartoon: © Hewison / *Punch*

In his *Observer* review of Tyrone Guthrie's *Volpone* (in which I'd played Voltore), hard on the heels of the opening of *R&G*, Ronald Bryden had written that he thought my Guildenstern might have been 'a flash in the pan'. (Some flash! Some pan!) However, he was cued up to call me 'a new gilt-edged asset'. Now my stock's value was in doubt.

**Voltore
in Tyrone Guthrie production of
*Volpone.***
Photo: © Chris Arthur

F FRANK WYLIE as Mosca, EDWARD PETHERBRIDGE as Voltore, and COLIN BLAKELY as
Volpone in *Volpone*

Cartoon: © Hewison / *Punch*

'I was struck last night more forcibly than ever how truly admirably good is your Gadd.' These words, in a letter to me from Olivier in 1966 about *Trelawny of the 'Wells'* – out of the blue as they'd come – seemed to confirm what Esmé Church (who had played Gertrude to Olivier's Hamlet at the Old Vic) had said to me when I was a seventeen-year-old student at her theatre school: 'You are one of those students who one knows is going places.'

The 'real' story of the National Theatre of this period depends on who is telling it. I ask myself whether my compulsion to tell my version is complemented by anyone's need to hear it. Any comedian will tell you 'it's how you tell 'em that makes the difference', but there's something else, surely: why you tell 'em. I've tried to cover my most obvious motivational tracks. Nostalgia for halcyon days, for a little golden age with which one associates oneself for the purposes of self-aggrandizement, is too transparent a strategy. But the 'lid-off' method can soon turn one into an autobiographical bin man, dealing with everybody's rubbish but one's own, bits of which one drops without realizing. What Guthrie calls 'the over and above' one is incapable of massaging, especially if it only manages to be below and underneath.

But at the old NT, did it all start to go slightly wrong somewhere? Of the younger generation, Robert Stephens and John Stride had left, and doing R&G with Edward Hardwicke could hardly be the same. John was irreplaceable. Paul Curren, as the Player, was not, of course, Graham Crowden: although the audience would insist on cheering Paul, his was a slightly sentimentalized 'love-me' performance, and they did. Maggie Smith had left, and Colin Blakely, Frank Finlay, Lynn Redgrave (and her father), and a young understudy who'd gone on for Joan Plowright in *The Master Builder* and been described by Coward as 'absolutely brilliant'; her name I must record, Jeanne Hepple. John Dexter, too, had gone.

Michael Gambon might just have left the company by the time we opened R&G. His specialty was his tabletop mimes, as he sat in the canteen, exploiting his giant cellist's fingers. They were little playlets really: his right hand would be an actor whose arrival and progress (or regress) in the company was graphically, mercilessly lampooned; his left hand, one of the 'powers', a director or Fate. Usually the struggle was unequal, but the variations, so hilarious because true, savagely exposed the delusions and desperation of the Darwinian struggle, the essentially arbitrary rule underpinning the esprit de corps of the NT 'ensemble'.

My curious position as a 'privileged' three-year contract artist was that, if I wanted to leave, I had to give eighteen months' notice. In 1968, my fifth year with Olivier's National, the tide was turning. Olivier had a new confidante, one Donald MacKechnie, father of the Angus (now Producer of Platforms at the NT) for whom I wrote the letter of advice before his performance as Guildenstern at Alleyn's School. Donald, like me, had come from 'nowhere' (meaning provincial rep) and had assisted Sir on *The Advertisement*, one of the last things I did at the National. It was a new play, an Italian three-hander set in a flat in Rome, a vehicle for Joan Plowright, in which I had a twenty-minute appearance as her estranged absentee husband. Anna Carteret played Joan's lodger, taken in by advertisement because Joan is lonely. Off-stage in the interval, she and I fall in love and in Act Two, while I'm still in the dressing room, Anna tells Joan of the affair and Joan ends the play with a gun shot. Reading again my somewhat inconsequential scene, I find I have no real memory of what I did with the part, the feeling of it, nor the 'tune' of it, but Joan's performance, with her slightly Plowrightean pronunciations of Italian place names like 'Rocca di Papa', I can hear rather well. 'Undeniably,' wrote J. C. Trewin as far back as 1958, 'she ought not to give to so many parts the unvaried accent of the North Lincolnshire town of Scunthorpe.'

I suspect I was not as Italianate as Joan. I can't remember even who got shot: it could only have been Anna or Joan, though I seem to recollect some mention of a cat. I do recall Olivier saying to me, 'Cut the dark curly wig, you look like Basil Rathbone trying to play Prince Hal.' Years later I came across a photo of Rathbone doing just that at the Vic, and realized that it hadn't been merely a gag.

It was Joan who'd called me into the hut to ask me to play the part, pointing out that she was a little embarrassed in the company context that it was such a tiny cast and such a huge part for her. The lodger, who was on all the time, certainly had to be a good listener. It was by no means the part I needed; still it was better than a night off. There was an awkward look on the executive company manager's face when I sought to formalize things. That was unusual for Michael Halifax, whose manner came as close to Civil Service smooth as theatre management ever gets, and I realized that Joan must have jumped some sort of gun. In order to use the company more, we soon learned, the husband and the lover would be double-cast, so we would share the parts with Louise Purnell and Jacobi. Anna and I had, as it happened, the privilege of opening the play, a week of previews down at Brighton and the press night in London. I always think that, in Olivier's eyes, my rehearsing and playing this part 'peeled my onion', in the Peer Gynt sense, in that the only mystery left was that there was nothing there.

I got caught in a flood on the way down to Brighton for the Sunday night dress rehearsal and my understudy, Ben Whitrow, told me that Sir, who had only had to drive down the prom, couldn't wait to go on for me. I wish I'd seen him. Ben and I acted in a radio version of *Brideshead Revisited* in 2003, playing Gielgud and Olivier respectively, so to speak. Over a very jolly BBC canteen lunch – reminiscence on a couple of high stools at Bush House in the Aldwych – he told me how he'd watched Olivier in that dress rehearsal come on in my part and 'as the scene progressed, gradually shed the years.' At this exact moment though, as far as Olivier is concerned, I'm still trying to shed the recent impact of the *Othello* film and half-wishing that the vale of years still stood between me and those days of the real thing on the stage.

I was to learn that Donald MacKechnie found himself spending a lot of time with Olivier at Overton's, a vanished, once-notable oyster bar opposite Victoria Station – handy for Sir, who spent so much time on the Brighton line, but a little erosive of Donald's family life. It was erosive of my status as a long-established and, albeit spasmodically, leading member of the company to find Donald cast as go-between. 'What part, if you could choose, would you most like to do?' he asked one day in the Vic canteen. It seemed a curious academic question, the antithesis of Olivier saying, 'We want to find something good for you.'

'Most like to do? Richard II,' I replied.

'Ah,' he said. 'There are plans to do that with Ron Pickup.' Clearly he had inside knowledge.

On another occasion he explained that I might very well be cast as Lovborg in Ingmar Bergman's production of *Hedda Gabler*, but Robert Stephens might play the part, depending on whether they got a star to play Judge Brack, in which case Bob would do Lovborg. One day I said to Donald that I really didn't relish waiting around on the off-chance that they would fail to get James Mason to play the Judge. He thought I was psychic, and, indeed, I had absolutely guessed, out of the ether, what was going on.

At one point, apparently to prevent me from leaving, Sir Laurence dangled the possibility of my being in a film of *R&G* that was being mooted and, just as swiftly, in a letter to my agent denied he'd done any such thing.[1] It was clear that, if I stayed, I'd be too perfect as material for the most painfully funny canteen table-top mime, even though I was still playing Guildenstern to capacity audiences and the intention was to run the play into its fourth existential year!

I made the decision to leave. It is grim comfort now to read Tynan's letter to 'Larry' of the following year, December 1971, listing the long procession of 'flops' (including *The Idiot* with Jacobi) which were staged during my last months with the NT and after my departure. Tynan wrote, of the company which Olivier had valued amongst his proudest achievements, that it needed rebuilding 'from the ground upwards. ... There isn't anyone at the Vic (except possibly Pickup) whose next performance one looks forward to with real excitement.'

New among the leading men in my last year had been Edward Woodward, who'd struck me, when I appeared with him in *The White Devil*, in which he played the leading part of Flamineo, as out of his element, lacking, in spite of experience at Stratford, the necessary depth and breadth as a classical actor (even as I begin to question yet again what we mean by the term 'classical acting'). The designs were by the Florentine film and stage designer Piero Gherardi, who had Oscars for his work on Fellini's *La Dolce Vita* and *8½*. According to the glossy programme, 'Signor Gherardi lives in Rome, and has villas in Ischia and Bangkok.' Having worn his costumes and wigs, I'm not in the least surprised. Woodward was dressed in mustard-yellow and looked like a truncated, un-classical version of that man on the tins of sweetcorn. Gherardi, and even Derek Godfrey, seemed, in their different ways, under par by established NT standards.

I have a tip for anyone playing my part of Lodovico in *The White Devil*. In the fifth act, when the English ambassador is heard off-stage shouting: 'This way, this way, break open the doors, this way', Do NOT shout: 'Ha, are we betrayed?' It is pure Morecambe and Wise if you do. I got a huge laugh at the dress rehearsal. When in doubt, in Jacobean Revenge Tragedy, whisper and break up the rhythm of the line, make it inaudible, if all else fails, and play some mysterious subtext.

I'm astonished to rediscover (how could I have forgotten?) the review in which I'm described me as 'saturninely virile'. I was dressed in black tights, codpiece and a loose shirt of heavy black lace. What a range I seem to have

---

[1] Incidentally, it was a wonderful film script Tom wrote, quite unlike the disastrous 'Western-style' version which came later.

had, when you count my Maggie Smithsonian languor and vocal delivery in *The Power and the Glory*!

I was astonished at the time that Woodward was next cast as Cyrano, and, of course, *Cyrano de Bergerac* is included in Tynan's woeful list of failures. Ron's *Richard II*, directed by David William, would soon be added to it. But these disasters, when they came, were irrelevant to me; I'd gone. Before I left, nothing compared to my own sense of failure – a peculiar failure, since actually I had not 'failed' at all. Only the chance to succeed further was being withheld and I was being invited to see that as my own fault, whilst meanwhile struggling on, young hero one night, Restoration Comedy servant the next. And then forced almost into self-parody as an attendant lord the next, in the nadir of my last months, Frank Dunlop's deadly production of *Edward II*, Marlowe's 'mighty line' translated into German for Bertolt Brecht and back into 'plain' English for us.

The highlight of the production for me was a night on which, during a pregnant pause in one of Robert Lang's long speeches as Mortimer, a clear, authoritative male voice from the back of the stalls called out, 'Give me Marlowe every time!' We'd found an ally. A thrill ran round the stage packed with attendant lords and guards – all of us, along with the principals, wearing pale-green make-up, as originally manufactured by Max Factor for Elvira in Coward's *Blithe Spirit*. In all fairness, though, I remember Ron Pickup coming round afterwards, having been very favourably impressed. Nobody in our dressing room wanted to hear that.

It all came back with the sharpness of a restored bit of old film thirty-three years later (summer 2003) when, at a reception, I met a librarian who had charge of the archive of Olivier's personal documents. I was surprised that she seemed to have a fresh, lively knowledge of my letters to Olivier and his to me.

A Flea in Her Ear
with Robert Lang.

Six months later I got round to visiting the spick-and-span, brick-built grandeur of the British Library at St Pancras to view again, from a new angle, a letter of mine of which I'd made no copy, written in impulsive haste between entrances during the third act of a matinée of *A Flea in Her Ear*, whilst over the dressing-room Tannoy came the sound of the audience roaring with laughter. There the letter was, along with others Olivier and I had exchanged during my six years at the NT. And even some thank-you letters I'd sent to him later after social visits and so forth. They'd been plucked out of his personal archive on a long set of shelves, nine of my broadest strides long and slightly higher than me. On one shelf was a cardboard box which had been discovered, on its arrival in the vaults, to contain a mouse's nest ('Look, look, a mouse', *King Lear* IV.vi.88).

Of the few things I was shown, the most poignant was a shooting script of Olivier's film of *Macbeth*, the project for which he failed to raise the money. There was a set of two-dozen of these scripts, in mint condition. The text was interleaved with storyboards, ground plans, marvellous full-page reproductions of the set designs by Roger Furse. It seems astounding now that he and Vivien Leigh between them were not considered superabundant collateral for the project – except, of course, that it took years for his *Hamlet* to go into profit.

I wasn't thinking about his disappointments on the afternoon in July 1969 when he called me to his dressing room during the interval of *A Flea in Her Ear*. The letter of mine I've mentioned was provoked by this wretched little interview. I had just given the statutory three months' notice to leave before the end of my three-year contract was up and he was miffed, wanted to re-establish the initiative and opened the batting by saying, 'Can't you get more laughs in this part?' It was hardly a face-to-face meeting. He sat with his back to me, looking in the mirror as he repaired his make-up for the small, entirely functional part of the butler he'd taken over in *A Flea in Her Ear*, a part which he struggled gamely (some said outrageously) at each performance to turn into a comic cameo. He was preoccupied, or affected to be, with his reflection and his Chaplinesque make-up. I talked to this reflection.

**Rehearsing *A Flea in Her Ear*
with Olivier and Jacques Charon.**

157

The last time I'd stood in this position had been five years earlier, called into the presence because of a slip I'd made at the *Othello* matinée a week previously. That time I'd been confronted by his bare, black back, and he was putting the expert finishing touches to a tragic mask. Continuing to concentrate on the exquisite detail of his black make-up, he said:

That I have ta'en away this old man's daughter,
It is most true.

Responding to his face in the mirror with a potent, grave seigniorial look, I took a quarter-step forward and lifted a tentative right hand as if to say, 'Surely you can't mean that?' The point being that, on stage, Othello, noticing this gesture in his peripheral vision, lobbed me a look and continued: 'True, I have married her.'

Our little rehearsal over, he spoke not another word. I apologized for the gaffe of the previous week when I failed to do this gesture, and left. It has to be said that my sin of omission was due to lack of concentration, but then so was his automatic response to the gesture of a Senate Officer that never occurred. I mean he'd thrown me the look! In fact, I can't imagine a performance of *Othello* as complete without this moment; it is very important for Othello to have this slight interruption to his flow at the beginning of his address to the Senate, preventing it from settling into a set piece.

The usually infallible pageant master, John Dexter, had wanted to make something of this moment and, at an on-stage rehearsal, made the ludicrous suggestion that we should all contrive to be looking away from Othello, so that on 'That I have ta'en away this old man's daughter, / It is most true', we would all whip round, shocked, and look at him. We discussed the impossibility of this in the canteen. It was highly unlikely that a group of bit-part players dressed up in brocades as the Doge of Venice, Desdemona's father and various non-speaking grandees would not be hanging on Laurence Olivier's every word, since he was dressed in white, better lit than any of us, and had just been asked by the Doge of Venice, 'What in your own part can you say to this?' Anyway, somehow it fell to me to create the necessary ripple, once we'd made it clear to John Dexter that we weren't capable of creating convincingly the effect he wanted. About my stupid omission of this vital business that day, not one word of rebuke had Sir uttered: the summons to be present at his pre-performance ritual of preparation, and the little rehearsal, had been sufficient.

And here, five years later, was the farcical companion-bookend summons. I stood, between the door and Lilian Baylis's desk, wearing my yellow suit with its pattern of large checks as Monsieur Tournel, the lover. To defuse matters further, there was a third party in the small room. Olivier's secretary, sorting correspondence, hovered over the spot where Lilian Baylis had once presided and certainly prayed ('Dear God, send me a good actor – cheap!'). I was a good actor! – and, dear God, they were getting me very reasonably. I'd given my three months' notice, as I say. I was inconvenient, awkward perhaps, to replace (I would have thought irreplaceable). Still preoccupied with his mascara, Sir said, 'You're a difficult actor to build a career for; you are very subtle but I wish you would open out more.' Give me the chance to, I screamed inwardly. But the thing that really got me was 'Get more laughs'. I'd taken over the part of the lover from John Stride when he left and I was doing it perfectly well, getting as many laughs as John had. I'd been forced to relinquish my deliciously showy part as the madly jealous Spaniard because I was the only actor young enough to deal with a take-over from John. '*Edward Petherbridge, qui interprète avec un brio inhabituel le rôle de Don Homenides de Histangua,*' declared the Montreal critic, while Olivier himself only got, '*Laurence Olivier donne une touche 'chaplinesque' au valet Etienne.*'

'I thought perhaps,' I said, 'I opened out a bit for Tyrone Guthrie?' suppressing the desire to quote Bryden's *Observer* review of Guthrie's *Volpone* at him, *avec un brio*: 'He has the advantage, too, of speaking Jonson's verse so as to verify T. S. Eliot's derivation of it from Marlowe's mighty line.'

'Yes,' he replied grudgingly, 'you did a bit for him.'

I thought of my visits to the zoo and my unabashed vulture imitations in rehearsal. Olivier was always one for going out on a limb in rehearsal.

The atmosphere was strained. Who was advising him? What was the agenda? It was somewhere about this time that Sir had quite suddenly sacked Diana Boddington, the head stage manager of long standing. She had the air of a sensible Cub Mistress who had seen a great deal of the sort of thing that went on at the Old Vic before. But once, in her prompt corner, with shining eyes she'd described to Stride and me what it had been like to witness the first night of Sir's *Richard III*. She'd been with him since the war, when they'd taken refuge together under some trestle tables during an air raid while rehearsing in the National Gallery. After her dismissal she went, astounded and bemused, from the Old Vic.

After what pleadings and protestations I don't know (in the prevailing divide-and-rule atmosphere, few felt confident enough to box anybody's corner but their own), Diana was reinstated a fortnight later and lasted another couple of decades until and beyond an evening in 1985 when, in my dressing room at the South Bank, I heard her announce, 'Ladies and gentlemen of *The School for Scandal* Company, half an hour, please.' A moment later she came on again to correct herself: she'd meant *She Stoops to Conquer*.

By this time, she'd received an OBE for her services to stage management. Hers had been the first words spoken in public from the Olivier stage prior to the official opening of the building: prophetic words that were typical of her pragmatically unaffected attitude, an amalgam of that Cub Mistress and the little boy who pointed out that the emperor didn't have any clothes on. My witness is Sir Ian McKellen, who had turned up one morning to join a light sprinkling of auditors in the Olivier auditorium to sample the acoustics. (The what? THE ACOUSTICS!) Ian surveyed the grey concrete walls and the sweeping curve of mauve seats for the first time and decided he ought to join the one or two people who were not sitting in the centre. He selected a stall at the outer edge of the curve, on the end of a row. Empty stage. Pause. From the prompt corner Diana, as usual in sensible skirt and sandals, bespectacled, with short, straight hair, emerged carrying her clipboard of notes, no doubt containing a running order of actors' names and the bits they were going to do. She walked the considerable distance to the centre of the huge, empty stage, surveyed the auditorium and said, 'You people round the sides had better move into the middle. You won't hear a thing from there.' The Olivier had been launched.

As Jeremy with Olivier (Tattle) in *Love for Love.*
Photo: © Zoe Dominic

There is a scene in Nicholas Wright's *Cressida*, set in 1600, where, as the veteran actor Shank, Mike Gambon is rehearsing a boy actor, teaching him the *mysteries*. I've just looked the scene up and, of course, the 'bit' I was looking for isn't actually there, except implicitly; it was something to do with the way Mike transformed both himself and the space we were in, as he began to talk about taking command of the theatre. He had been doing just that all night, but suddenly, for this recalcitrant boy actor, he was anatomizing the process and palpably asserting what people call 'presence'. And without a hint of theatricality, in the common pejorative sense of the word, he lifted the rehearsal of the play within the play onto a plane of hype-reality:

Shank:	Move up a little. No, up, up! That's it. That's the spot.
Stephen:	Why's this the spot?
Shank:	You'll see in a minute. Now look. No, look around you. Far as you can. What's the throw? …
Stephen:	What's that?
Shank:	It's what I look for. Where I'll pitch my voice. The wall at the back, the upper levels. And the audience. There. … And there. And there. They're on three sides. Those below you will support you. If you show them who's in charge. As you go up, they get more testing. There. And there.

He takes up position.

This is the spot. It used to be known as Shank's spot. Watch what I do.

L to R: Gillian Barge, Frank Wylie seated, Laurence Olivier standing, Michael Turner in background, Edward Hardwicke centre, Margot Cunningham, myself, and Kenneth Mackintosh taking time off from his Mercade in a matinée of *Love's Labour's Lost*.
This is the Old Vic rehearsal room in which Olivier had been photographed in a rehearsal of his Hamlet in 1937.
Photo: © Chris Arthur

Shank's spot must be a derivation of Olivier's search for the spot on the Olivier stage from which he could most effectively deliver his speech officially opening the theatre. At his entrance he received a long standing ovation. It was the first and last time he was seen on the stage named after him. He spoke unmiked, of course, and without notes. It was an elegant speech in which he mentioned everyone who needed to be acknowledged, making even the list of names sound, not dull and formal, but important, epic (which, as a feat of memory, it certainly was). He even indulged in a piece of wry humour about his successor, now that Olivier had been not very gracefully replaced: 'Peter Hall's well-shod foot in the door'. Afterwards I spoke to David Giles who had directed Olivier in the television version of *The Dance of Death*. He and Olivier had rehearsed the speech the day before, spending a lot of time finding that optimum spot on the stage, and he knew the difficulty Olivier had had in committing the list of names to memory. During the speech itself, Giles was backstage and he told me he went down on his knees and prayed throughout.

Peter Hall was not yet part of the reckoning as far as most people knew when, over Sir Laurence's Tannoy, in that interval in *A Flea in Her Ear* at the Old Vic in July 1969, came the noise of the capacity audience in the auditorium. Another manifestation of that familiar sound, the sound that had disturbed Tom Stoppard three years before when he'd heard it from an unfamiliar angle; the unmistakable sound of a full house anticipating, participating in, the excitement of The Theatre. The sound which (I know now) had become by then associated in Olivier's mind with an appalling stage fright.

In those performances of *Flea*, as I waited to make my Act Three entrance, Olivier would come off through the centre-back double doors from one of his short entrances as the butler, and Diana would have to catch him before he made for the wing, since he had another entrance almost immediately. She'd steer him to a lectern near the entrance doors. Lit by a special electric light, it held his script and a little shelf for his spectacles: she would point to his next entrance and he would look at his lines. One night I heard him go on, dry absolutely stone dead and survive by acting as if struck dumb at the farcical goings on in the plot. I watched from the lower wing whilst he mimed the gist of the little scene. The audience roared and he got an exit round. He tried the same thing again the next night and didn't get a titter. Mind you, he still had, amongst other things, Tyrone in *Long Day's Journey* up his sleeve – but what it cost him.

During the third act of *Flea*, as I've said, I penned a letter saying that our meeting had convinced me that I had made the right decision; that it was time to go when a theatre company didn't have the same inflated idea of one's talent as one did oneself (I could have put that better), that it had been unfair of him to criticize me mid-performance and that I should never have countenanced the meeting in the presence of a third party.

162

His reply is, in appearance, unlike any of his other letters to me – a long letter. The typing has quite a few errors, which he has corrected in pen, and underlinings, too, by way of emphasis. I can see that he typed it himself. It challenges me to ask myself whether his comments and criticisms were meant in a friendly way. He asked me to make an appointment to come and see him so that he could talk to me about something – 'something else', the cunning old fox said. The last line of the letter was: 'Come and forgive.'

In the canteen I got wind of something and put two and two together about a part he was going to ask me to take over. By the time I was on my way to his office in the hut, I knew that that particular casting vacancy had not, after all, occurred and wondered how on earth he'd wriggle out of this one. He came out from behind his desk and sat with me on the pale-blue upholstered benches, which ran round the room against the walls, quite a different performance from his dressing room one-upmanship. His monologue ran as follows:

> Well, I've had my annual operation. [He was in his Mrs-Stirling's-patchwork storytelling mode. When someone in a position of authority is giving you intimate details of the before, after and during of their haemorrhoids operation, it's quite difficult to influence the agenda.] On a Harley Street examination table I was invited to lie on my back and pull my pink dimpled knees [those precise words are etched into my memory] up towards my chest, whilst a specialist, who rejoiced in the name of Emlyn Williams, introduced his instrument and, by way of casual conversation, inquired, 'You were in the Navy, weren't you?' 'The Fleet Air Arm,' I corrected him, with as much dignity as I could muster. Anyway I can tell you that when it came to the time for me to pass my first post-operative motion, I discovered that rumours of red-hot barbed wire were by no means exaggerated.

This was hardly the moment to say 'Talking of flying – not to say opening up more, as you wish I would – how about Ronald Bryden's review of my "finest of all" the characterizations: "a hunched, sunken-eyed vulture whose hands claw at those near him with the sudden, frightening deliberation of Captain Hook's gestures of friendship. At his first entry, he hops, spreadeagled and voracious, to balance on the side of Volpone's bed. When finally discomfited by Mosca, he sweeps out into the dark like a great, rustling bomber taking off. It's impossible to tell where the human character ends and bird begins and the proud hooded eyes tell us that both natures are tragic."' By way of conversational contrast, I might have tried a graceful flip from things of the fundament to the grace of my white-faced Pierrot in the experimental season at the Jeanetta Cochrane Theatre, when Sir came into my dressing room and said, 'That Marcel Marceau had better watch out.'[2] But this is being clever after the event.

I'm quite sure that when his secretary entered and said, 'Bob Swash is on the line,' it was a pre-arranged interruption.

The carbon copies of his letters documenting a few more to-ings and fro-ings are on file in the vaults at St Pancras. At our last meeting in the hut he had placed himself emphatically behind his desk and, as he handed me the script of *The Idiot*, saying grimly, 'That is as good as the part will get,' I realized, dully, that this was an ending. What a great theatrical gesture it would have been, quietly there and then, to decline to take the script from him. But, no. I was too respectfully polite. Once more I was reading a script on the bus home to Peckham. I'd read the whole of my part, I should imagine, by the Elephant and Castle. As soon as I got home I picked up the phone and told my agent to ring the National instantly and tell them, 'Not with a barge pole.'

At St Pancras I was shown a letter they couldn't identify. It was from an actor in the company who was on 'Dear Larry' terms with Sir. I identified it for them almost immediately. It was written by an actor who had read *R&G* long before I had, and he was delicately turning down the part of the Player, as a lot of actors had done, and delicately asking to play the part of Guildenstern, which he never did.

Some twenty years after my last months as a National Theatre player at the Old Vic, I was cast in the part of an usher (a kind of attendant lord) at Sir Laurence's memorial service in Westminster Abbey. Who should come down the aisle in my direction but the producer Bob Swash. 'Good morning,' I said, in a manner friendly but soberly formal, and began gently to indicate where he might sit. He looked quite shocked, as if this was an officious invasion of his privacy and period of mourning, but I could so easily have said, 'This is nothing to that ill-timed telephone call of yours.'

The seating arrangements were interesting. The press were huddled together at the back of the north transept, feeling out of it, so naturally most of their reports were detached, not to say cynical and satirical. As for the actors, Peter Barkworth (one of my favourite actors), who'd played a small part in Sir's 1953 Coronation offering, with Vivien Leigh, of Rattigan's *The Sleeping Prince*, being well known on television, was very favourably placed for the TV cameras which were present, whereas quite a few members of Sir's National Theatre were well out of shot (oh, the glories of ensemble).

Alec Guinness gave a cool, measured address in which we felt just the tip of the iceberg of his deep dislike. I'd seen, and would again see, Gielgud on

---

[2] I know only too well that Marceau's technique, and what he could do with his body, was far in advance of anything I could do, but it was wonderfully liberating to be free of words, and tutored by the clever and eccentric Claude Chagrin. The Pierrot character, with his grace, comedy and pathos, was to come to the fore for me, wonderfully appositely, when I devised a show from R. D. Laing's *Knots* six years later.

better form, but Peggy Ashcroft, at the age of almost eighty-two, stepped forward and spoke some lines from Milton's 'Lycidas' in a resonant, athletic voice which, in my imagination, connected us back to the voice of Ellen Terry, who, of course, had sat quietly here at Henry Irving's funeral in 1905.

And then, from the soundtrack of the film I'd seen in the Birch Lane Cinema as a boy of eight, came Olivier's voice in the St Crispin's Day speech. A wretched television camera wheeled itself along a pew full of notable actors, but it was still a great moment.

In 1985 Sir Laurence had written to me:

> I was truly thrilled and delighted that you were among the first winners of the awards in my name for your marvellous performance in *Strange Interlude*. I'm sorry I couldn't see it myself, but I have been bored rigid with everyone telling me how marvellous you were.
>
> Ever your loving friend,
>
> Larry

'Come and forgive,' he had written to me all that further time back. Well, we are all sinners. We were, after all, in a place of worship, thanking God for him. Appropriately. His gift had been God-given. In fact, I once heard him describe a good actor as being touched by the hand of God. Amongst the precious theatrical moments I shall, with luck, remember is the sight and sound of Peggy Ashcroft filling Westminster Abbey with:

> Weep no more, woeful shepherds, weep no more,
> For Lycidas, your sorrow, is not dead,
> Sunk though he be beneath the watery floor;
> So sinks the day-star in the ocean bed,
> And yet anon repairs his drooping head
> And tricks his beams, and with new-spangled ore
> Flames in the forehead of the morning sky ...
> Now, Lycidas, the shepherds weep no more;
> Henceforth thou art the Genius of the shore
> In thy large recompense, and shalt be good
> To all that wander in that perilous flood.
> Thus sang the uncouth swain to the oaks and rills,
> While still the morn went out with sandals gray;
> He touched the tender stops of various quills,
> With eager thought warbling his Doric lay:
> And now the sun had stretched out all the hills,
> And now was dropt into the western bay:
> At last he rose, and twitched his mantle blue:
> To-morrow to fresh woods, and pastures new.

165

Epilogue and Lament for
the Last Days of the Theatre Museum

In default the show begins
Bygones, heretofores, has-beens
Still! The relics hold their poses
As it opened, so it closes.

Rich preserve of obsolescence
What's conserved when all but presence
Evanescence ...
And the passing show has passed?
Not a word, not e'en the last
Within these booths is uttered, puffed,
Limelights, candles – sputtered, snuffed.

Here's the face, the fiery master
Kean: asleep in death-mask plaster.
Through the plate glass though we stare
He's absent, off: the stage is bare.

Moving portraits jump through hoops
Repeatedly in filmic loops.
In footage, still they foot it featly
In the scenes they've left completely.

Alone I watch, whilst happily
Larry dances, just for me
Consummate, such graceful cheek
I call out, 'Are you here all week?'
In case he's not, for Archie Rice
I watch the loop round twice or thrice.

In default the show begins
Bygones, heretofores, has-beens
Still! The relics hold their poses
As it opened, so it closes.

Unscheduled Appearances

Chapter 13

Birth of a Conscientious Objector

Like so many of us, I reached the conclusion, early on, that my arrival in this world was 'unscheduled'. A lot of good things are impromptu, of course, but I realized that life for my parents might have been a lot easier, even in some ways pleasanter, without me; and yet I was glad to be here, and I think, against all the odds, they managed to be glad, too.

Before any Sunday school notions of us all being important and beloved of God had filtered through to me, I had a notion that I was special. It's a notion I have managed to sustain, albeit fitfully with certain qualifications, despite the slings and arrows of the actor's fortune, which let you know now and then, rather sharply, that you are not special enough.

Leaving aside one's parents' lack of planning, I was astonished to hear on Radio 4 that it is not mere chance, or even a case of which is the strongest swimmer, that decides which sperm gets to the egg in the uterus. In 1935 there were likely to be around 300 million in the race to make me; these days there are probably less than half as many. Recent research suggests there is a feminine selection process that takes place in the uterus. So not only are we each of us, as far as the male contribution goes, one in several million, but we are also *chosen* from amongst the best.

This particular little saga will feature several unscheduled appearances, which had a strong element of choice in them. In fact, although it was decidedly an unscheduled appearance from the Army's point of view when I turned up one day refusing to wear uniform, I had politely forewarned the adjutant by letter.

I doubt that my pacifism runs very deep. The man standing next to me the other night in the stalls bar at the Novello Theatre before *Antony and Cleopatra* (starring Harriet Walter and Patrick Stewart), who accused me of knowing very well that it was not my turn to be served, will remember how swiftly our exchange escalated to the point when I invited him to 'come outside' where I would give him 'a bunch of fives.' True, the lady for whom I was attempting to procure a drink thought I'd said 'bunch of flowers', so perhaps my delivery was not as aggressively butch as I had certainly intended it to be. Even so, the gentleman went very quiet. He at least might have gathered that I was dead serious; or perhaps *he* was a pacifist. It became obvious that the man knew I was an actor because he made some disparaging remark about the 'actaw's voice' in which I had placed my order. 'Do you think I would risk my reputation by jumping the queue?' I asked. 'I know your reputation,' he replied with ominous asperity. I think that was the moment I invited him to come outside.

Eventually I made my way to my single seat in the splendour of the refurbished Novello stalls and had to ask an elderly lady if she would excuse me for disturbing her. 'I would always rise for you,' she said. Instantly I was charmed and pacified, but where had been the charm and peaceability with the man in the bar? Soon I was seeing the great tragedy and marvelling at how petty were the protagonists' quarrels and wars – domestic and global – and yet how mysteriously we started to understand their suffering in terms of their stature and nobility. Harriet and Patrick, without being perfect, embodied through the actor's alchemy, sufficient stature and nobility to make one feel one was in the presence of greatness; where else but in the theatre, the concert hall, the art gallery or solitary in the company of a great book do most of us ever experience this potent presence?

I never met a pacifist during all my sequestered years of school, Methodist Sunday school and chapel attendance, nor in my three years as a Northern Theatre School student, still living at home. Though I was always a pacifist of sorts and certainly avoided getting into fights.

But I remember the day when I threw my first punch, and my last, notwithstanding my uncharacteristic threats in the bar of the Novello. I was about six. It was a heady experience for a small boy who knew he wasn't a tough, especially as the victim belonged to what I thought of as a rather rough, common family, who lived down a passage in our street in one of the *back* back-to-backs. In the evenings the boy's father, a big, red-faced, burly man, would come out of their passage and stand on the pavement in a string vest, smoking. I could take you to the spot on the cobbles (though the cobbles have gone) in our sedate street where this first blow was struck, on a day when his father was safely at work. I still think of our street as sedate.

Despite her disabilities, my mother conformed to the respectable custom of scouring the 'doorst'ns' on her hands and knees with a heavy pail of water, scrubbing brush and cloth, finishing them off with soft yellow stone and white stone. They were disabilities with which Mother might not have been afflicted but for my existence; she had suffered a stroke two days before I was born. The boy, who was my age and size, had said something about my mother. It may very well have been innocent, but I dimly recall that it touched on her disability, and less dimly I recollect a rather luxurious flash of filial righteous anger, which resulted in a sudden but calculated single punch to his head, at which the boy burst into tears and ran home. Feeling taller, stronger and just a touch guilty, I went into our house and gave my mother my version of the event; did I have difficulty couching my justification delicately? I was sure that a complaint from the boy's mother would follow. It didn't. My mother gently, with her halting command of speech, remonstrated with me. That was the end of it, except that I have remembered the incident for over sixty-five years.

On our neighbour's doorstep,
aged three.

A studio portrait taken around the same time.
My first French windows.

With Mother and Dad and other family members outside our home,
71 Pembroke Street.

171

Stirrings

It all started in 1935. It could even have been Guy Fawkes Night, a night in early November I calculate, when I was conceived in a deep double bed in Pembroke Street, West Bowling, Bradford. The Government was hesitating to ban petrol, coal and steel to Mussolini's Italy. *White Horse Inn*, starring Nita Croft and Eddie Childs, was playing at the Bradford Alhambra, and Eddie Cantor (famous for the 1930 song 'Making Whoopee') was probably starring at the local cinema in *Kid Millions*, his latest film.

That the bed at number 71 Pembroke Street was deep is more certain, the wire-mesh mattress supporting the 'flock' one had stretched and sagged into two trenches, each formed by the weight of one of my slight parents to be. The room had a gas bracket but no light fitting attached. It was a cold night. The house was a stone back-to-back, circa 1860. The modern note in Willie and Hannah Petherbridge's bedroom was struck by the bow-fronted wardrobe, a lightweight piece with a nice unblemished veneer. Hanging inside it was the light weight of Hannah and Willie Petherbridge's best dress and Sunday suit. The companion dressing table in front of the window had a heavy swivel mirror and four small drawers holding some oddments, stockings and a jar of Pond's Cold Cream. Pond's, I have since discovered, was used by all classes. Perhaps it was the only item in the house which did not belie the humble status of Willie and Hannah. They and their thirteen-year-old son, Billy, had gone to bed as usual by candlelight. The floors of the bedrooms were covered in patterned oilcloth. There was a tiny cast-iron fireplace in Mother and Dad's room, but it was never used. For especially cold nights – and there were several nights around this time when the local newspaper weather forecast was 'rather cold' – a cast-iron shelf, an oven plate or two, from the range downstairs would be wrapped in the evening *Telegraph & Argus* or the *Daily Herald* and placed in the bed a few minutes before bedtime, to create a small square island of warmth on the icy sheets.

Nine months or so later, on 1 August 1936, young Billy was having a Saturday morning lie-in when he heard his mother moaning inarticulately. He found her at the bottom of the stone bedroom steps trying to call to him. His father had left early on a works day trip to the seaside, so Billy went to alert a neighbour and then run for a doctor a few streets away in Bowling Old Lane. Eventually Mother was taken to St Luke's Hospital a mile away. Willie Petherbridge arrived back late to find his sister, Beatty, waiting in the house. He went straight to the hospital where he found his wife paralysed down her right side and unable to speak. Two days later I was born.

It was 3 August, Bank Holiday Monday. The weather was showery and rather cool, the further outlook changeable. The local paper's headline read: 'Italy going ahead to victory' in the Abyssinian War. The Spanish rebels were thirty miles from Madrid. Jessie Owens, much to Hitler's discomfiture, was on his way to winning four gold medals at the Berlin Olympics. Closer to home, *The Grand Variety Show*, with such now forgotten acts as Kitty

Masters and Kimberley and Page, was playing at the Alhambra. Our local cinema in Birch Lane was screening a George Formby film, *Keep Your Seats, Please*: the adverts said, 'You'll Laugh All Week!' And in Chapel Street, perhaps the finest custom-built amateur little theatre in the country, the Bradford Civic Playhouse, was rising from the ashes of its previously rented premises. Its inaugural production was to be Priestley's *Bees on the Boat Deck*, which had just finished its West End run under the joint direction of Laurence Olivier and Ralph Richardson.

I was being passed round the ward to be nursed in turns by the other patients; my mother became very concerned by the possessive affection displayed by one of these women who said she would adopt me. My father had to tell the lady very firmly that she would do no such thing.

My mother was forty. She was advised that she might not walk again. When I was old enough to understand, she told me proudly, in her halting speech, how she had used a bedside chair in the hospital ward to support herself and gradually managed to put one foot in front of the other. They supplied her with a leg-iron. I always admired her for her achievement.

The cosy, sagging bed at home I remember. When I was very small, after my father had left for the mill of a morning to be there by six, wakened perhaps by the slam of the street door, I would join my mother in the warmth of the big bed and no doubt she would be able to enjoy a little extra sleep.

Perhaps my earliest memory, apart from this, is of the magnificent mountain range I saw from the corner of our street beyond the railway lines and the municipal park; it glowed pink and amber in the sunset. So: the magical world of legend might be accessible by tram next morning. Reluctantly my mother came out and limped to the corner to look. Amazingly I think now, she did not remark on the beauty I pointed out – only that it was all made of clouds and sunset. Then she went back into the real world of our house.

Maybe I was always on the lookout for magic after this. One of *my* desolate early memories is of a dull day, when it just might rain, and of a little crammed Noah's Ark on wheels I wasn't very fond of – the sound of it clattering along, bumping over the nicks between the blackened York stone slabs of the causeway outside our back-to-back home in Pembroke Street. I was experiencing an intense and discouraging boredom, and distinctly remember thinking – did I even say to myself if I could find the words at that tiny age? – 'There must be more to life than this.' But I also remember walking back to that same patch of York stone flags on another day, with a triangular penny bag of desiccated coconut, and sitting with my legs stretched beneath the flat red seat of my kiddie-car, which served as a dining table. And whilst my bare calves felt the warmth of the sun stored in those familiar flagstones, there proceeded the magical tipping of the bag's contents into a little fragrant pile of tropical luxury before me.

When I was old enough to use a whip and top, I spent hours on the stone causeway in front of our house admiring the beautiful rainbows of colour as my vivid chalk circles gratifyingly blurred at high speed into, I thought, quite the best of the effects achieved amongst my playmates.

One morning, whilst my mother was on her hands and knees washing the oilcloth that covered the uneven stone-flagged floor of our only downstairs room apart from the scullery, I was standing, displaced by the shifted three-piece hide-upholstered suite, my nose no higher than the table top. I was listening to the sawing of many violins on the wireless. The oilcloth patterns – 'Turkish' on the central piece, parquet on the surrounds – were scuffed and worn away where the stones underneath made the surface proud. Later I was to feel ashamed of this feature, which developed on each new lot of oilcloth over the years. I was wondering what the insistent complex music on the wireless was. My mother told me, as she continued to wash the floor, 'It's chamber music.' I knew that a chamber was an oak-panelled room in an old-fashioned house; no doubt I had seen such rooms in Bolling Hall, the local grand house of medieval origins, a twenty-minute walk away. Immediately I imagined such a panelled room in Broadcasting House in London, the only modern feature being the microphone suspended above the ranks of seated musicians, industriously sawing away.

My brother tells me that he remembers me as a baby, after I had to be circumcised, crying and my father walking about the little living room carrying me comfortingly because my mother was unable to hold me. Despite the fact that the most intimate physical proximity instigates your and my history, and despite those early morning sleeps snuggled with Mother in the very cradle of my conception, I always feel surprised that my father ever cuddled me. I don't remember him ever being present at my bedtime, and my mother always seemed anxious to leave me once I had said the Lord's Prayer and 'Gentle Jesus', asking him unquestioningly to 'pity mice in Plicity', which I must have thought of as a small rodent's purgatory.[1] In vain I would ask for a bedtime story. I have no recollection of fondness ever being expressed physically in our family, or even very much in words. Though my brother recalls a Christmas, before I was born, when they lived in a tiny house, 'one up, one down', with a cellar-head kitchen, meaning an area on the cellar landing where there was room for a sink and cold tap. In this house he recalls himself and Mother and Dad, one of Mother's four sisters and her husband, sitting by the fire and singing carols. It was inconceivable that anyone should sing in the house of my boyhood, though we listened to others sing on the wireless and Dad would occasionally express his approval of the likes of Anne Ziegler and Webster Booth or Peter Dawson.

---

[1] An American friend swears she prayed, 'And lead us not into Penn Station' for some years. At St Stephen's Primary School, we absorbed the hymns in the big school assemblies by hearing them sung by the older children, which led to some equally odd approximations through mishearing, for example 'Rice is the path and rice the prize.' I remember the sense of revelation, which always accompanied my discovery of the real words.

There was a pretty little golden-haired girl, perhaps four, as I was, who one day, as we were playing in the doorway of the brick air raid shelter in the middle of the street (not at all a private place since the doors were always locked and the shallow recess faced the windows of our houses opposite), invited me to explore her nether regions. I felt reluctant, dimly aware of an embargo on those parts. Later my mother called me in and said, 'What have you been doing?' I realized somebody had seen us beyond their machine-lace curtains and reported the fact. 'Wait till I tell your dad.' I am still waiting. There was silence on the subject. I imagine he couldn't find the words – he was a man of very few. On another day, perhaps I was six years old by this time, a little boy playmate of mine issued the same invitation, just once, in the lavatory on the cricket field, and I experienced the same reluctance.

A few years later, amongst a bunch of playing children, the pretty, laughing, golden-haired girl and I were sitting on a low windowsill in her backyard and I kept saying to myself that, after a count of three, I would take hold of her hand. Several counts passed and with them my courage and the opportunity.

The boy and I went to the same schools, he lived several streets away, and on and off we were companions. During the thick 'pea-souper' fogs, unable to take the two trams into and back out of the town to get home from grammar school, we had the novelty of finding our mile-and-a-half short cut home on foot together in a muffled isolation in which we could have done anything. In innocence we walked down the long, near-deserted Park Avenue, past Bradford Northern Rugby League ground, towards home.

We lost touch; he was still there at school, but in the even lower academic, or rather non-academic, stream than I was. Then one day, when we were in the fifth form, I noticed him on the top diving board in the school swimming baths at a swimming gala. He had the confidence of a sportsman and was quite unaware of and uninterested in my presence, but, to me, suddenly he looked heroic, admirable and even alluring.

Art and Life

Before the stirrings of adolescence, when I was still a war child in the 1940s, there was always the noise of battle when the pencils and crayons were distributed in our elementary classes. I remember the din as each boy depicted us victorious in the skies. I suppose it was considered healthy and patriotic for seven-year-old boys to draw dogfights between Spitfires and Messerschmitts, whilst providing the sound effects of guns, exploding 'Jerry' aeroplanes and the whine of uncontrollable nosedives. The girls would be keeping the home fires burning by peaceably drawing houses with little gardens. Their schematic formulas never included the brick-built air raid shelters down the middle of our local streets, which were long structures with flat reinforced concrete roofs. They represented the sky as a narrow strip of blue at the top of the paper, and the earth as a green strip at the bottom. The four windows, structural impossibilities, one in each corner, had looped curtains. The roofs were red. The girls' efforts bore no relation whatever to the reality of the terraces of back-to-backs we lived in. Art was one thing and our lives were another.

The boys' drawings were relatively realist, all sky but no colour. To colour sky in blue would have been 'sissy'. Anyway, lead pencil was more accurate than crayon for capturing the detail of RAF and enemy aircraft, the black-and-white cinema newsreels being the authentic source of reference. There might be the odd flash and scribble of red crayon as a Jerry plane caught fire.

Meanwhile, I was above the battle and never a war artist. When I drew houses – the only alternative I thought of, apart from trees – I considered mine to be infinitely superior to the girls' because somehow I had discovered perspective, at least you could see an end gable of my houses, and I'd observed that windows weren't in the corners of front elevations, and that the sky reached to touch the earth at the horizon.

In street games I would sometimes aim a ball at a chalked target of Hitler's face on a gable end – the bull's-eye was always his moustache. I was an occasional, reluctant participant, and would even make gun noises, in games of Cowboys and Indians or Goodies and Baddies, though I felt embarrassed at the committed acting some boys went in for, as they crept along and squatted behind low walls or pretended to be Hopalong Cassidy on his horse or, if depicting a villain, conceding defeat sometimes with an effective collapse on the cobblestones. I had no relish for this brand of drama. My brother, thirteen years my senior, was an absentee role model, a weekly airmail letter from Ceylon and some photographs he'd sent home taken in bright sunlight, in which he was ranked amongst his Air Force cricket and football teams there in the bright sun, where he taught Morse code for most of the war.

There was no photograph of my father as a soldier. He avoided being captured by cameras, always saying, 'I don't take a good picture.' The Ever-Ready safety razor he used all his life was issued to him when he joined up in 1914. He was sixteen and scarcely in need of it. Rehoboth Sunday School gave him a small khaki-bound Bible, inscribed in purple ink:

> Presented to Willie Petherbridge
> On the occasion of him joining His Majesty's Forces during the
> Great European War
> 1914 to

To what? – he must have wondered. I am sure his poor eyesight rendered the tiny print in the Bible illegible, but he could see to work at stabling and transporting cavalry horses in Egypt. That is all we ever knew about his war experience until his dying day at the age of sixty-four.

With my parents on the beach at Bridlington in the 1940s.

I wonder now whether Mother was, after all, reassured to some degree by that blow I struck when I was six. I was the victor. Crying little boys, who ran home after being hit, were seldom comforted by their parents. 'Stand up for yourself! Don't be so soft, go and 'it 'im back', was the usual advice. By the same token, I realize my mother didn't expect a lot of domestic help from me, and now I believe it was partly because she thought that a boy might be 'turned soft' by such tasks as yellow-stoning the doorst'ns, which quite appealed to me. We had a neighbour, Mrs Mortimer, who was always worth watching because there was a certain large paving stone near the middens in her yard that she used to colour yellow. But if my playmates and I requested 'Do a swan, Mrs Mortimer', she might, in her own time, swiftly do a swan on this paving stone (or was it merely a very large elaborated figure two?). It would be wiped away as swiftly as she created it, to make the even, yellow colour of the finished effect – all this in the yard of one of the back houses where there were no passing neighbours to notice her proud handiwork. Life was one thing and art for art's sake, in the form of a yellow paving stone near the dustbins, was part of life, but the swan and the whole job had to be got over briskly, brusquely, like my bedtimes. What were they in such a hurry *for*?

I suggested to my mother that I could help with the yellow-stoning; she would have been abashed at the idea of the neighbours observing me at such feminine tasks, and in any case she was too proud to be seen as not up to all the housewifely duties. She would peg out the clothes she had hand-washed on a long clothesline across the street. I *was* permitted in the holidays to turn the heavy iron wheel of the huge mangle. She defied her disability, and from when I was really small I remember the loaves she made, left in the hearth to rise, the smell of the baking bread and sometimes biscuits. I can see her darning socks, using her good left hand, though she had been right-handed. The dead weight of her right hand held down her work. She even managed to embroider flowers on some little linen covers for the dresser, and there was always a supply of washed and beautifully ironed little shirts for me to wear to junior school, kept in the big bottom drawer of the heavy mahogany veneered item with its glints of mother-of-pearl in the centre of each drawer knob. It was the only handed-down piece of furniture we had, apart from a cast-off 1926 HMV cabinet gramophone.

Did Mother ever wish that she'd had a girl? She had lost two baby girls before I arrived. But I was a boy. There was always the spectre of a grown-up cousin I might turn out like, and I now know that my rather deaf bachelor Uncle Jim, Dad's brother, who'd been wounded as a gunner in the First World War, had a great friend called Harry Towers (it was he who had given us the gramophone, perhaps he'd got a newer model). I found out years later that Jim was certainly homosexual, but he was never considered a bad influence. 'Go and see your Uncle Jim,' Dad would say to me on a Sunday morning. I would find him, heavier than my slight, sinewy dad, sitting in a woolly dressing gown before the range fire with a tray on his knees, noisily eating his weekly ration of bacon and egg. He was a pinsetter, a relatively skilled job in the wool-combing process. My brother tells me that Jim's attempts to get Dad a job in that trade had been somehow sabotaged and Dad remained a low-paid wool warehouseman all his days. Uncle Jim lived alone in the little north-facing terrace back-to-back, which had become the family home after my grandfather died in 1903.

My grandfather's death is a tragic story. He had been a master tinner, and in possession of a six-chambered pistol, which he saw as the only way out of his debts of a hundred pounds. A phrase struck me in his suicide letter to his wife – widely read by the populace in the local paper's report on the inquest, but never preserved in the family, and suddenly discovered a hundred years later by my brother on microfilm in the Central Library. 'Darling little Willie' was the phrase he used to describe my five-year-old father, in saying that he had thought of 'taking him with me – but I love him too well.'

I was never called 'darling' until I became an amateur actor at the Civic Playhouse in Little Germany.

When in 1990 I visited the birthplace of D. H. Lawrence in the mining village of Eastwood, near Nottingham, it was like going back to Uncle Jim's, my grandmother's house. The armchairs, upholstered in machine-tapestry, seemed familiar. There was the same wine-coloured chenille fringe on the high mantlepiece and even the same kind of patterned enamelled sheet metal panel to go over the hearth inside the fender as we'd had at home.

As I used to chat to Uncle Jim – I hope he could always hear me – I would look up at the large, heavily framed, tinted portrait photographs of my late grandparents, hanging on the wall by long cords from the picture rail. I knew nothing then of the violent end my grandfather met. I'd love to see those pictures now. Gone. I suppose my father didn't want them cluttering our walls when the house was cleared after Uncle Jim died.

But for the wireless, the room I sat in with Uncle Jim on Sunday mornings was unchanged, except that it had once been crowded with his mother, his three sisters, three brothers, and cousin Florence, and at one stage Mother, Dad and Billy.

Two of Dad's sisters immigrated to Australia when he, the youngest, was small. In a rare, the only, glimpse he gave me of his boyhood, he told me about the whole family foregathered on the pavement outside the house and leaving together to see his sisters off, catching the tram to town and then the train to Liverpool, leaving him behind on the pavement. 'I suddenly thought when they'd gone – why didn't they take me to see them off as well?'

In the elementary school playground I avoided the games between gangs that seemed so rough to me with their cries of 'Charge!', though perhaps they were quite gentle and ritualized by today's standards – and there was always a teacher in attendance. I kept away from the rough stuff by adopting the persona of jester, heavily dependent on the styles of BBC Light Programme comedians. I had my one or two cronies and I kept them engaged with my latest gags and novelties, such as the 'cigarettes' I made at home when I discovered that a short length of the gummed brown paper we always had a roll of (I think my father must have brought the rolls from work) would curl into a nice tight cheroot shape if exposed to heat. There was also a system I learnt from somewhere of folding paper origami-style to make an opening and shutting arrangement of unfolding panels on which you could write a number, a forfeit or a character trait to be discovered.

I joined the Rehoboth Chapel cub troop when it was re-formed after the war. I took great care using our flat iron, heated in the fire, or on a gas ring in

summer, then clothed in a shiny tin slipper, to press my neckerchief so as to be smart on parade. I could tell the time and tie a reef knot (but no other knot with guaranteed success) and happily taught what I thought of as these very limited skills to the younger cubs in my little group. All the very loud shouting of 'DOB, DOB, DOB' I joined in with a will, determined to do my best; I suppose it was designed to channel our superfluous, testosterone-fuelled energy.

In due course I was moved up into the scout group and hurled into pointless, unnecessarily rough games involving two teams, each getting from opposite sides of the Sunday school room in the face of one another's rugby-style opposition on the dusty bare boards. I soon left.

As part of the Rehoboth Chapel cub troop
(I am seated bottom row, far right).

I may have lacked aggression, but later there was another moment of dubious machismo and triumphalism I'd like to apologize for, if Arnold

179

Money, my best friend of the first form, is reading this. After our first term at Grange Grammar School, we were demoted a stream at the same time and our friendship lasted to the second, third and fourth form. He joined the RAF Cadet Corps and used to tell me how he loved the square-bashing and all the 'bull' of polishing his boots and the brass on his uniform and blancoing his belt. Our friendship survived my incredulity that any of this could be pleasurable. We ran a small 'club' by pooling our coloured pencils and anybody in 4X could join (X was the euphemism for the C stream to which we had both been relegated). Our classmates, who paid a penny, were members and during map-drawing in geography, or for diagrams requiring colour in any lesson, if the teacher didn't mind a certain amount of traffic, they could come and borrow what pencil they needed. At the end of one term we had a bit of a dispute as to whose pencil was whose and even about the financial share-out. I'm not sure that it came to blows, but I remember there was something vehement and scornful in my attitude. Quite suddenly I realized I had won the argument and there might even have been tears in Money's eyes. My triumph turned to ashes at once, but this was an unprecedented development and my repertoire of strategies could not run to shaking hands and making up; in any case, it would have meant acknowledging he was hurt – deep water – and perhaps that would have been too much of a loss of face for both of us, and an implicit declaration of affection quite beyond our expressive abilities.

My fourth-form class at Grange Grammar, September 1949.
I am in the top row, far right.
Arnold Money is third from left on the front row.

The next time I remember him vividly, some years later, he was laughing at me. He'd always had a well-developed if eccentric sense of humour. Somehow in physics classes, when we sat next to each other on lab stools, he had the idea that when the aptly named Mr Rodley spoke a particular designated word, it would be Money's cue to cough. One day, Money's dare was that we should briefly stand upright on our stools every time Rodley turned to write on the blackboard. Ridiculous bravado and exhibitionism and it was only a matter of time before I was caught out and the intensely painful retribution came. But I still think of Mr Rodley with a certain contempt, as I do all the teachers who wielded the cane. It would have been more imaginative to make me stand on the stool for the rest of the class, but one has to understand that administering corporal punishment was, for many teachers, one of the satisfying perks of the job. I can assure anyone unfamiliar with this particular instrument of education that, for the beneficiary, it made concentration on lessons impossible for at least the following hour. There were teachers who never used it and nevertheless kept order and held our attention and interest.

I surprised myself somewhat by coming top in physics and then Rodley showed his colours. I knew I'd done well because I was lucky with the exam questions – I *really* understood and was interested by the water and carbon cycles. These were, after all, simple and logical and I had the pencils to do attractive diagrams to prove it. As Mr Rodley read out the results he said, 'That dose of the cane earlier in the term seems to have done you some good.' If only I had had the courage to say, 'You fool, Mr Rodley, you fool', or perhaps, 'The brain is mightier than the cane' – or had simply stood up on my stool again.

I believe Money and I cautiously resumed our friendship next term after that end-of-year bust-up, but I shifted into a different mode with my next bosom pal, who was in the A stream. Despite his penchant for drill, Money had not been especially good at games, nor was I, and John, my new friend, certainly wasn't. I met him through our involvement in the school plays, when on one occasion we played man and wife. John's house, in a posh suburb, had French windows, which until then I had only ever seen in films or in the Harry Hanson's Famous Court Players' twice-nightly weekly-rep seasons at the Prince's Theatre. However, there is a photo featuring us as the married couple in A. A. Milne's *The Man in the Bowler Hat* – I am the cowed-looking man, seated on the left of the picture – and French windows feature back centre. I had forgotten that our scenery included French windows until I rediscovered the photo, but then I took French windows for granted in plays. Seeing the real thing in my friend's house was a culture shock I can never forget.

In a corresponding photograph, I am not the cowed man but, wearing an old dress of my mother's which fits me perfectly, I am the upright female figure in the dominant position. Make of that what you will. I was simply suiting the action to the word, the word to the action and certainly had no sense of o'erstepping the modesty of nature. The play was Milne's *The Boy Comes Home*.

Neither of my parents had read, nor is it possible for me to imagine them reading to me: 'Oh, there's such a lot of things to do and such a lot to be / That there's always lots of cherries on my little cherry tree!' As for the 'such a lot to be', the horizons of 4 and 5X did not seem wide. There were no cherry trees, nor any other kind, on our school playing field, just a derelict brick air raid shelter and, beyond the low stone perimeter wall, lines of stone terraced houses.

I didn't know the middle-class joys of A. A. Milne's children's verse, the world of Christopher Robin and Winnie the Pooh, until I read his books to my children. But, at the time, I thought nothing of having, as Aunt Emily in *The Boy Comes Home*, to lament that my nephew, back from four years in the trenches, had had no breakfast: 'Philip! My poor boy! Why didn't you tell me? and I dare say I could have got it for you. Though I don't know what Mrs Higgins … '. And, as the timid, conventional husband in *The Man in the Bowler Hat*, I fell easily into the vein of the line: 'I used to imagine things like that happening … pushing open a little green door in a long high wall, and finding myself in a wonderful garden under the bluest of blue skies, and waiting, waiting … for something.' This is how people in plays talked and we were doing, I was delighted to find, plays.

John (I think we may have defied convention by being on first-name terms) possessed a Grundig tape recorder and we made our own spoof versions of the BBC Sunday lunchtime programme *The Critics* amongst others. It was years before I had exclusive use of a Grundig, but after the spring gave out in our 1926 HMV cabinet gramophone at home, somehow we acquired an old portable model. When John and I could not meet, we often had extended phone calls, because in those days, once you had pressed button A in a red telephone box, you could talk till doomsday for your pennies. I used an unfrequented box, the better to take advantage of this, and sometimes lugged the portable gramophone with me and a record, so as to embellish my calls with musical backgrounds. It always felt risky, even though it wasn't illegal. I was creating innocent pirate radio, I now realize, for an audience of one, or even anticipating Twitter by well over half a century.

Ours was a rather theatrical relationship in that we thought the theatre was the best place in the world. Stage design was a subject in the art classes and, despite our separate streams, we managed to compare our work. John was related to the manager of the Bradford Alhambra and had been backstage during a show, the second of my friends to penetrate this most desirable of inner sanctums (the first had been the other John, whose mother was a cleaner at the theatre and got him backstage during the pantomime). But the cards were stacked against me; I had no contacts.

Still, there was the fun of the Grundig, and even closer to Beckett and that famous last tape was the time John and I whiled away amongst the ruins of some demolished streets on a rise alongside the road to Eccleshill (where, unbeknownst to us, a boy called David Hockney, one year our junior, was growing up). There, perched on fallen blackened stone masonry, amongst the weeds fighting their way through the remaining cobbles, where old mean terraces had stood, we had a view across the valley of the beck to the mill chimneys and church spires of the city. The polluted air ensured spectacular sunsets, which John would call 'Petherbridgean skies' on account of my fondness for effective sky cloths in my artwork. We must have killed hours on that slope of dereliction. *Waiting for Godot,* without the magnificent skies, was to seem quite familiar territory to me when I saw it at the Arts Theatre in London just a few years later.

Our art master, Mr Green, was the one who taught stage design and I used to muse longingly about yet another no-go backstage area – the very big model stage with lights, mysterious behind swathes of blackout material in one corner of the impressive art room, or even *studio* you could have called it, with a 'north light' window such as would have graced Carl Rosa's touring opera production of *La Bohème.* Nearly four decades later, performing on Richard Hudson's particularly striking set of *The Misanthrope*, on tour at the Bradford Alhambra, I traced Mr Green and his wife, living in retirement in Heaton, a nice Bradford suburb. He knew who I was, but had no recollection of me as the boy I'd been, one of his star art pupils – though he remembered the charismatic John of the A stream. He told me that the best designs from the A and B streams were realized on that stage, but he would never risk letting the X and Y streams loose on it.

That very afternoon I bought one of Mr Green's oil paintings, a study of the woods and the River Aire at Bingley where my mother used to play as a girl (and told me she had once seen a fairy). The painting is thus a double memento of Mr Green and my mother's Bingley childhood before she met my father and moved to Bradford. As I write, 'Bradford and Bingley', suffering from the credit crunch, has undreamed-of connotations.

My old art master Mr Green's
painting of the River Aire.

Decisions

I was deferred from National Service whilst at theatre school, but the prospect of call-up papers loomed. They would arrive, I knew, as soon as I'd finished my last year and I couldn't see how I could style myself a pacifist or conscientious objector. At last I was on the threshold of the stage door, but now this detour loomed? The fervent Mr Coggle, the minister at Rehoboth Methodist Chapel, had nothing to say to me on the subject of pacifism. I didn't have the gumption to seek out the Quakers. I'd only heard of such people but where were they? (They were round the corner from St Luke's Hospital where I'd been born, I since discover.) Anyway, what good would a shotgun marriage with the Quakers do me? I was completely green. I have never been a good networker and then there was scarcely a net to work – no student life in Bradford.

Little Germany was the hotbed of Bradford's amateur theatrical activity and that, combined with the presence of the Theatre School, had, and would go on to produce, what now looks like an improbable list of theatrical luminaries. In my young day the little bereft-looking street had at least one of its gas lamps at an angle that even Charlie Chaplin might have found exaggerated until handled by one of his villainous roughs. There were perhaps less than fifty of us in the School and the third-year students were always away on tour, taking the Northern Children's Theatre round the big Moss Empires variety theatres in the North and Midlands and the odd town or miners' hall, playing morning and afternoon shows, forever loading scenery in and out of railway trucks, setting up and making up, performing and moving on within that clannish, busy, inward-looking attitude of the itinerant theatrical troupe.

Hockney was at Bradford College of Art by then, but I never met him nor any other art student, though my old friend John had gone to the College of Art for a bit until he left realizing he wasn't much good after all.

It never occurred to us drama students to have anything to do with the Technical College, and we rather looked down on the general local populace, who seemed to us, in our smug drama-student 'sophistication', always to be unconsciously acting in an unsophisticated, real-life North Country kitchen comedy. I did write a kitchen comedy, based on a shop staffroom I had known in my first job out of grammar school and we performed it, in house of course, as part of an end-of-term show in my first year. I actually became a wool warehouseman in my first summer holiday after my first theatre school year. But we were grooming our voices and deportment with varying degrees of success to represent the preoccupations of West End drawing rooms or the palaces of Shakespeare's princes with a freshly learnt soliloquy every Monday, fencing Wednesday nights, free movement and ballet on Monday and Friday mornings respectively. During my first two years I was busy styling myself, not in pacifism nor any other 'ism', but as a figure whose authenticity would be beyond question, whether entering upstage through

French windows from a Home Counties garden or being discovered downstage in black, biding my time in Denmark.

The coffee bar had not quite arrived in Bradford in the early 1950s. After the afternoon classes, a group from my year would often spend time drinking tea in the nearby Exchange Station tearoom. I still avoided pubs completely, having signed the pledge at twelve. The station tearoom looked like a larger version of the one in the film of *Brief Encounter*, with a similar soundtrack minus Rachmaninoff. By this time I certainly sounded more like Trevor Howard, or even Noël Coward, than the grown-up boy who had played on Pembroke Street and set up a peepshow in the passage, though I still lived there in that same house with my parents. It was at one of these mad drama students' station tea parties, as I was holding forth, that I suddenly noticed my old friend Arnold Money in his uniform amid a group of other RAF cadets. I understood immediately why he was silently, almost incredulously laughing. My transformation must have looked absurd, but I went over to say hello to him there amongst his comrades with all their kit, about to embark on a weekend cadet camp. We had nothing to say to one another. I had the charm of Chapel Street upon me and did not feel at all at a disadvantage in having been caught out in my new persona. He had his *esprit de corps*.

And soon, as well as articulating the passions and problems of Shakespeare's princes, I had found my way to the place where longing, belonging, love and physical expression meet.

Dalliance with a medieval king

I had my army medical in Ludlow. It was on this wise. On a siding at the LNER railway station in Bradford, Louise and I had helped to unload the scenery for the Northern Children's Theatre productions, *The Roses and the Bear* and *The Dancing Master's Kit*, for the very last of many, many times and taken it by truck a matter of yards to the Chapel Street premises. Did we have a valedictory, even celebratory cup of tea in the station tearoom? Louise and I had something to celebrate – jobs in the first Ludlow Festival. We arrived in the Castle keep one sunny afternoon with rehearsals in full swing. Louise was to play some performances of *The Niece* and I was integrated straightaway as Gaveston to the Edward II of John Westbrook – a West End and radio actor of some distinction, 6 feet 3 inches with a powerful voice. I was instructed, fresh off the train, to run from the green sward stage left and up a ramp onto a platform and into the arms of the King. Literally taking a run at a classic.

Westbrook delivered Edward's vow of vengeance, the famous 'lakes of gore' speech in Act III, scene ii, as it is written, as a soaring piece of passionate rhetoric, which echoed round the Ludlow castle keep, making one fully appreciate what Ben Jonson called 'Marlowe's mighty line'. When it came to Steven Waddington delivering it in modern costume in Derek Jarman's film version of 1991, the mighty line was either an embarrassment or an impossibility for someone schooled only in the breathy mutterings of idiomatic TV naturalism.

As Gaveston in *Edward II*, Ludlow Castle, 1956. Ralph Broome far left.

Looking again recently at the opening of the play and Gaveston's first, very long soliloquy, I wonder that I had no qualms the first time I spoke it in the comparatively vast space of the keep. But we had been used to quelling 1,500 children at a time in Moss Empires variety theatres and doing a new soliloquy every week in our voice class on Monday mornings, my voice ringing out in classical Standard English tones the length of the ex-wool warehouse.

Adapting to lunch in the country home of Sir Leonard and Lady Dyer, with whom Louise was billeted, was trickier for me, dreading as I was the inevitable question, 'And what does your father do?' 'He is in wool,' I would reply (he was, up to his knees), hoping I wouldn't be asked to elaborate, whilst preoccupied with taking a run at the intricacies of upper-class table manners, rather less successfully than dalliance with a medieval king.

It was a beautiful summer and the then famous, largely unspoilt town and surrounding Shropshire landscape were idyllic. Louise and I invested in a Woolworth's engagement ring, which was inspected and politely admired by the daughter of the house, the Hon. Anne Dyer. Anne had the run of a huge attic, wood pigeons cooing in the eves, where she had designed and made the costumes for *Edward II* and used to play Beethoven's Fifth on a wind-up gramophone. The production was acted partly by amateurs and so money was made. It must have been the very first time that the story of a king's downfall through a homosexual relationship was performed in aid of a parish church restoration fund.

I was hoping I might fail my army medical, feigned slight deafness, had my ears syringed and passed with flying colours. Within days I got my marching orders, and exchanged my medieval hose for khaki.

The Queen's shilling

A difficult subject this. First you have to understand that I decided to become a conscientious objector not *before* I was called up into the army to do compulsory National Service but a month or two into it. Not that there was a sudden dramatic gesture at an obvious moral crossroads. The story is not easy to tell, even though, in trying to tell it, I have summoned up a lot of sharply remembered detail; it is the innards of the story that are so nebulous, and at a time like this it might seem self-indulgent to write about my little moral peacetime escapade in saga form; but it might be the period detail that saves it.

I was just twenty, on weekend leave in Lincoln, having exchanged the barrack-room bunk for the marital bed. I was doing National Service in the Royal Army Ordnance Corps, and Louise was now a member of the weekly rep at Lincoln's charming and intimate Theatre Royal, a Victorian horseshoe theatre seating 480 people.

Pvt. Petherbridge, 2nd from left on front row. National Service, 1956.

This particular weekend I was on the brink of being arrested. I had left my uniform behind at the barracks and the plan was to go back on Sunday night as usual and, unusually, refuse to wear it the next day. For this formal strategy I had to thank Paul Oestreicher, a New Zealander and a student at Lincoln Theological College. Later he became the founding chair of Amnesty International UK and, whilst Director of Coventry Cathedral's Centre for International Reconciliation, he became associated with the Society of Friends – the Quakers. In 1957, whilst doing his theology course in Lincoln,

Paul had stumbled on the fact that Louise was working at the local theatre. They had been great friends at the University of Otago in Dunedin. She introduced us and he put me in touch with the Central Board for Conscientious Objectors (CBCO). Up until then I had merely been to see my major and informed him that I intended to become a conscientious objector. He had listened quietly and said, 'Leave it with me' – and there it had most certainly been left. Meanwhile I was not being ordered to kill anybody. The RAOC was a supply corps, supplying everything from a safety pin to a tank. There had, of course, been a bit of time on the rifle range during basic training.

The literature from the CBCO arrived and I learnt that, even for someone who, for whatever reason, had failed to register as a CO before call-up and was already a soldier, there was a due process. Paul, who was, like Louise, five years my senior, very much left me to make up my heart and mind on the subject, whilst pointing out that in France at the time a CO would go to prison until too old to serve. Britain had a formalized liberal tradition, the seeds of which dated back to the First World War. We were indebted to such objectors as Bertrand Russell, who was imprisoned for his objection to the war in 1918, having two years earlier been stripped of his fellowship at Trinity College, Cambridge because of his pacifist views. In HM Prison Brixton he wrote his *Introduction to Mathematical Philosophy*. There had been many objectors, of course, who were not part of the intellectual or social elite. Some had their health broken in prison. The overwhelming sympathy was with 'the boys' risking death at the front. I knew little about any of this then. Russell was not an absolute pacifist and was reluctantly in favour of going to war with Nazi Germany in 1939.

My act, it seems to me now, was not so much courageous as dogged. I saw that I had to choose between two extremes. The first was taking the Queen's shilling; in fact, I had already done that and thereby pledged unquestioning obedience to Queen's Regulations and military orders. The other was taking an uncompromising stand entirely off my own bat. Quite how I came to be in this curious situation of my own making, I will come to.

I saw now, thanks to Paul, that I must disobey an order, be court-martialled and receive a sentence of at least three months, having pleaded that the offence was committed on grounds of conscience. This would qualify me for a civil prison sentence and a civil tribunal hearing, at which my stance would be considered; and, if they accepted my plea, they would recommend I be discharged from the army, a recommendation the Army, at its discretion, might act upon.

So, after seeing Louise in Ustinov's *The Love of Four Colonels* on the Saturday night, and having taken morning communion at St Botolph's, the church we'd been married in a few weeks before, I dressed in jeans, T-shirt and a black and grey flecked woolly polo-neck sweater, took the train to London and then for Deepcut Camp, arriving late at night.

Flowers are lovely; love is
   flower-like,
Friendship is a sheltering tree;
Oh, the joys that came down
   shower-like,
Of friendship, love, and
   liberty,
         Ere I was old.
                Coleridge

Struggle on my friend,
   for we are bound to win.

E. Inchboard
June 1917.

A page from a First World War conscientious objector's prison autograph book. I found it in the history bookshop in Great Newport Street.

I spent the Monday morning wandering about the camp in sweater and jeans, unable to get arrested. My corporal would have nothing to do with me. He ran the office I worked in; ironically it dealt with the intake of recruits who were signing up as regular soldiers for at least three years. He said, 'Oh, for Christ's sake, Petherbridge, you're not serious, you're not doin' it are you? Well, piss off – I don't 'ave time for arrestin' and charges and bein' a witness and all that crap. I've got enough on my pissin' plate as it is. Piss off and find somebody else.'

Eventually somebody found me and I was up before the adjutant. He said, 'Look heah, Petherbridge, you don't have a leg to stand on and, if you go through with this stupid idea, your feet won't touch the ground.' He sent me off to my barrack room with the RSM for the showdown.

The regimental sergeant major was tall, thin and Scots. I can still hear his high-pitched, hard-edged Scottish voice from misty January dawn parades, barking out orders, and, on one occasion, when he must have become discursive for some reason, as he inspected the ranks several platoons away, I distinctly heard his voice cutting through the chill mist, saying, '*Desert Island Discs*! Fuckin' awful programme *that* is!' I might even have had ambitions to be on it. I still have.

For three years at theatre school I had been asked, 'What do you think?' What did I think my character was thinking, feeling, doing? In the army I was only likely to be asked 'What the fuck do you think you're doing?'

The RSM, looking at his watch, gave me the order to put on my uniform within twenty minutes. We were standing there, the two of us, in the otherwise deserted barrack room. I sat on the edge of my bed, near where my uniform was neatly folded. I sat in the presence of a superior officer in silence for the full duration. It was not an act of insolence or defiance; it just wouldn't have made much sense to do his rank the honour of standing up. I didn't think of it as a gesture of any kind, and now I suppose it was ultimately the *lack* of gesture that counted. Normally he would have expected me to be at attention, staring ahead, careful to avoid eye contact and concerned only that my belt or buttons or boots might fail his inspection, a very particular kind of relationship to have with anybody and it completely takes over from one's usual sense of who one is. Now I felt out of military time, in my own time and at liberty to look at him occasionally as he stood there rigidly. I don't know how he must have taken it or whether he thought of screaming, 'On yer feet soldier – what do you think this is? *Desert Island Discs*?' We were both in uncharted territory.

I suppose the adjutant had stipulated twenty minutes, thinking that the august presence of the RSM, no less, would make my nerve falter. I had time to wonder what was the worse that could happen to me. I could fail to get the qualifying three-month sentence, or having got it, fail to convince at my tribunal hearing and find myself back in the army doing the same thing again and the Army taking tougher measures next time round. I might be directed into alternative work as a hospital porter or a miner.

At last the RSM looked at his watch and broke the silence. I was formally arrested, frogmarched to the adjutant and charged. I didn't change out of my jeans, T-shirt and sweater for the next month, and then it was to don a prison uniform at HM Prison Winchester.

A taste of solitary

In the eighteenth-century aisle of St Botolph's, that last Sunday in Lincoln, I had spoken to the priest. He'd been the one who'd married us. I told him what I was about to do and asked for his advice, or at least hoped for some counsel or perhaps even a little moment of prayer. He simply said, politely, as Louise and I stood there, 'I don't think one can contract out of society like that.' That is as much as he had to say. He had no wish to discuss the subject. I don't think he could have found me or my position in the least credible, creditable or even worthy of debate.

I suppose what he did say was better than what the Army chaplain back at my basic training barracks had had to say; it was just a few days after the short-lived debacle of the Suez Crisis and we spoke over sherry, or possibly tea in the vicarage after evensong. What a solace that wooden 'Gothic' church was after the barrack square, and the cadences of the Book of Common Prayer after the language of the barrack room. In the chintzy comfort of his hospitality for the handful of his communicants, as his wife hovered with nuts and crisps, he said in the quiet, reasonable tones of the dialogue of *The Murder at the Vicarage*, as his riposte to a question from me about Christian pacifism, 'You see, the only way you can argue with an Arab is with a gun in your hand.' I told my friend and mentor, my old tutor at theatre school, of this exchange. 'Disgraceful!' she said. 'Any priest who is not a pacifist ought to be shot.'

The internal debate I had with my solitary self over the three months in prison, with its doubts and unanswerable questions, was at least more nuanced. There was one month on remand in solitary confinement at the army guardroom (a small cell painted bottle green, but with a window looking out onto the parade ground) and two months under sentence in civil prison, the large Victorian gaols of Winchester and Wormwood Scrubs, with a month's remission for good conduct – three months altogether.

My father had taken it all calmly. As I've said, he was a man of very few words at the best of times. When, at sixteen, I told him I wanted to become an actor he had said simply, 'You can't.' He was not denying anything; from his tone, I knew he meant it was something impossible because it was outlandishly out of my sphere. This conscientious objection was my second bit of outlandishness. To my surprise, on the day an army jeep called for me at Wormwood Scrubs and delivered me for a short respite, in time for my Appellate Tribunal hearing, to a building in Ebury Street, Belgravia, the first person I saw, standing in the sun on the pavement, was Dad in his Sunday suit, down from Bradford, smiling and smoking a Woodbine. We waited in a first-floor ante-room. Then we heard military music. The troops, horses and band of the Household Cavalry, glitteringly caparisoned, marched down Ebury Street and passed right under the window. It is quite a narrow thoroughfare and we were less than five minutes' walk from the southern corner of the wall of Buckingham Palace's garden. My dad and I, like a couple of tourists, moved to the window to watch. I wonder if the Queen sent them down especially on Appellate Tribunal days?

As Private Petherbridge, I could have settled down to the remaining twenty-one months of my National Service as a clerk at Deepcut. They'd tried to teach me to touch-type in a big class of other recruits, convened in a hut, but to be drilled in qwerty and 'every good boy deserves favour', whilst I was essentially expecting my 'case' to come up, meant – means – that I never learnt to touch-type, and even now I have typed every word of this book with two fingers, though I have the illusion I use more. Having 'past', I was put in the reception office of this same trade training camp. The eighteen-year-old recruits, who were signing on for three or more years as regulars, had to be documented as they came in on reception days and I had to ask for and note their particulars, filling in a form for each (by hand, thank goodness) over a trestle-table. Because of my actor's received pronunciation, they always assumed I was an officer and called me 'sir'; the reflex reaction continued even after I told them I was a private. I suppose there was a moment when they signed the contract, so to speak. It was obvious to me why there was always a table filled with plates of delicious 'homemade' cakes, biscuits and fruit pies and a supply of hot tea to greet them on arrival – treats such as I had never seen in the mess and, I daresay, these recruits would not see again. A quite high proportion of them gave orphanages as their home addresses.

When I think of my father, at the age of sixteen, in Egypt in 1914, and the soldiers in Iraq and Afghanistan now, I wonder whether the petty irregularities and little humiliations of the lives of the National Servicemen I was amongst, who never saw a shot fired in fear or anger, are worth recording at all. And, compared to the Deepcut Camp of recent revelations, it was then a benign place. Yet the banality of it all and the tacit assumption that everybody was a twerp and a shirker, who had to be terrified into polishing his boots with a hot spoon until one o'clock in the morning and dragooned into the blood donor's queue without being accorded the dignity of knowing what the queue was for or the choice to *give* blood rather than have it taken – was this the only training to get the common man to defend freedom?

There may yet be *something* worth the telling about this niche of social history. Very shortly, from my guardroom cell window, I was seeing weekly passing-out parades of the regular recruits. As I looked out across the vast empty space of the parade ground, resting my eyes from reading Huxley's *After Many a Summer* or Greene's *A Burnt-Out Case* or Steinbeck's *Cannery Row* or *Of Mice and Men,* I could see the distant HQ building on the other side; small parades, maybe no more than two platoons, but with a band to play slow and quick marches; all the young soldiers in their navy-blue dress uniforms; a few seated figures against the HQ wall with spots of colour, the dresses of gaily attired mothers amongst the few parents who'd turned up. It was all quite different from the huge khaki, music-free, sausage-machine passing-out parade I had been in at the end of my basic six weeks. Our young lieutenant had been out of step with the entire parade ground, and when I thought back on the awe, which had been worked up in us by our corporal, as he prepared us for this second lieutenant's first entrance into our barrack room on day one, when he was doing no more than checking our blankets to see if they were fit for purpose or 'US' (useless), and when I thought of him inspecting us occasionally, in his superior uniform with his superior attitude, as he said in his superior public-school English to some kid whose uniform wasn't looking smart, 'You look like a piece of shit tied in the middle by a piece of string', I lumped it together with all the other petty stupidities. There were the bars of soap with 'ERII' embossed on them, issued to us to lay out with our kit for a Brigadier's inspection and taken back when the inspection was over, so that we had to continue supplying ourselves with soap purchased from the NAAFI. In my solitary cell I discovered that there was such a thing as a cooked high tea, which I had never had before. We'd been forced to spend our own money at the NAAFI to allay the evening pangs of hunger after the last cup of tea at the end of our day.

Another parade took place only a few yards from my window every evening: in front of the main guardroom detention block, the parade of soldiers doing ten days or so for minor offences. This was a witty event, or so the NCO thought. He was entirely preoccupied with the state of the blanco and the brass on the men's belts, and the pay-off of each diatribe at a substandard example was the belt would be taken off and the corporal would throw it several feet to land in a corner with the others.

Being on remand, and technically innocent 'until proven guilty', despite being in solitary, I was allowed to have the Penguin paperbacks Louise posted to me from Lincoln. On the first difficult day, however, they had tried to scare me by making me empty my cell of everything; well, there was nothing but a bed with blankets and no sheets. I was made to stand all day in the middle of the cell. Whenever I leant on the wall or sat on the floor, the young military policeman stationed outside shouted through the peephole in the metal door, but I sensed that this was a charade. I retaliated by refusing to eat the food when it arrived, saying that, if I wasn't doing the army's work, I couldn't eat its food. My only momentary fear was that somehow my case would completely collapse. Blindly I took this extreme position of fasting to show them and myself, and anybody who might be looking, that I meant business. The bed was brought back in so I could sleep. Breakfast arrived the next day and I refused it. Lunch too, I think. Then I was taken to the adjutant, who said that I was being stupid and that they would use a stomach pump on me, so I might as well eat in the usual way. I saw the logic of his argument. We retired to our corners. My bed was moved back permanently into the cell and I could lie on it.

I wonder now for the first time whether having a 'posh' accent cushioned me at all. They only had to look at my record to see I was not 'of good family'.

I have not yet really addressed the argument for 'contracting out', as the Lincoln priest called it, but what are the arguments for contracting in? The literature I had from Louise as a remand prisoner, innocent until proven guilty, allowed me to escape from the whirligig of the argument into a rich world where the issues were refreshingly wide. I was ill-read, not a practised reader. The authors were all new to me. Thurber's *The Night the Bed Fell* actually made me fall off my bed laughing one night, and I got great pleasure from P. G. Wodehouse's Blandings Castle novels, and from the aforementioned Aldous Huxley, Graham Greene and John Steinbeck. I also set myself the task of reading the complete Gospels and doing an exercise regime in the cell every day, since I was not granted exercise periods outside and never left the cell except for ablutions in the washroom, when briefly I would see the other prisoners. There was always a bed sheet hanging in the yard; one of the prisoners was a bed-wetter.

Occasionally things would be lightened by a bit of banter with one of the military policemen when my food was brought. They were younger even than I was and found me a curiosity, I think; they called me 'the rebel without a cause'. I see from one photo I had taken a year or two later that I had, by default, a definite James Dean look. Deepcut, with four mysterious deaths of recruits between 1995 and 2002, and the Scrubs, with twenty-seven officers prosecuted and six convicted of assaulting inmates in the 1990s, have been notorious as sites of what are now called, at the very best, 'systemic failings'. I was fortunate in my day; it was, as I say, relatively benign.

I was defended at my court martial by a decent public-school National Service second lieutenant, who understood my case and called the Army chaplain at Deepcut as a defence witness. This man of God, well into his fifties, was more impressive than the other priests from whom I had sought advice. He must have been a World War veteran and I marvel now that I had the arrogance of youth to hold my ground. A chair had been introduced into the cell for him. He was a big man and, in his dog collar and trench coat, carrying his officer's baton, he was somehow gentle and empathetic as he talked about the symbolism of the cross surmounted by a sword, which I thought was a contradiction rather than an affirmation. But we spoke gravely and he spared me the dismissive one-liners I had so far experienced. I am particularly grateful to him, because he visited me a second time, after my court martial at which I was given the three-month sentence I had asked for. When I returned to my cell, a convicted prisoner, all my books were confiscated, including my Bible and Prayer Book. When he discovered this, he expressed dismay and saw to it that the Bible and Prayer Book were returned to me. I had a very religious week with them until I was out in the air being transferred from the Army's hands to the civil authorities.

Residing at Her Majesty's pleasure
I found myself enjoying the novelty of waiting on a railway platform in the company of two corporals, to one of whom I was discreetly handcuffed. Our height and arm lengths matched well, and the atmosphere was jokey. It was an outing for all three of us. I think the joke for them was – here are we, two cor blimey corporals, taking this posh-spoken nitwit to HM Prison Winchester where he is going on purpose! It was so good to be out of the confines of my guardroom cell and on a bantering railway journey from

Deepcut to Winchester. We had a second-class compartment to ourselves; the leather straps had been released to let down the windows on either side so that I could feel the spring country air of Surrey on my face. The trip was through sunny woods, fields and villages, and whatever red-brick suburban sprawl might have accrued since E. M. Forster had in 1910 first begun to notice the creeping 'red rust' on the horizon in the Hertfordshire of *Howard's End*.

It is over fifty years since I sat with those two corporals, looking out of the compartment window, and there must be more red rust now, but I have just 'flown' over the route on Google Earth and it still looks like a green patchwork of woods, hedgerows and pasture. Neighbouring Camberley has what looks like a large 1980s residential addition to its outskirts, and, now that the Military have decided to attempt to eradicate the memories of Deepcut by selling it off for development, perhaps soon there will be more houses and people will call it home. I noticed, 'from the air', how near and yet how very far away was the Royal Military Academy Sandhurst.

I didn't mind being an absurd figure to the two corporals. They did not make inroads into my sense of myself – almost the reverse. If they baited me a little too much, I imagine I might have allowed myself the riposte that three months' prison was better than two years in the army. On the walk from Winchester station, their good-natured hilarity suddenly abated as we approached the impressive castle-like entrance to the prison. They got a receipt for me, but were too awed by the prison officialdom to bid me a cheery goodbye.

On arrival, I was put in a bathroom, with 'bar-room' doors at either end, and told to put my clothes over the inner doors and take a bath. When I emerged from the warm water – a luxury after the cold showers in the guardroom – I saw that a shapeless grey flannel prison suit had replaced my familiar jeans and sweater. Even my underclothes had been replaced by odd-shaped prison equivalents, and there was a dubious pair of black shoes with steel-capped heels in place of my plimsolls. I was issued with a pillowcase, containing an enamel plate and mug, cutlery and a library book. An unspeaking officer with a formidable bunch of keys led me along deserted corridors and up iron stairs in the vast, silent Victorian bulk, built on the radial system from an imposing central rotunda. Finally we stopped at one of the cell doors; he unlocked it and mutely indicated I was to go in. He locked the door and I heard his footsteps fade away. For the first time there was something about the vast, impersonal edifice and my place in it that did make inroads into my sense of myself. I had been something of a personality in the guardroom and, as a remand prisoner, I had had my solitary, Penguin-paperback-strewn freedom.

I unpacked the pillowcase. The book was *Crooked House* by Agatha Christie. I had no stomach for it. I heard a strange clicking noise outside and stood on the little scrubbed bare wooden table to be able to see out of the high window. Below there was a yard with concentric circles of concrete exercise paths. Prisoners, two or even three abreast, were walking round and round briskly, talking animatedly; the clicking noise was made by their steel-capped heels. In the centre was the smallest circle, no more than eight feet across, the little path wide enough for only one prisoner. Two elderly prisoners with grey hair, wearing the uniform grey prison suits with the addition of grey flannel capes, their backs bent, each on opposite sides of the circle, walked very, very slowly round in silence.

My regime at Winchester consisted of long hours of solitary, punctuated by the chance to chat on the circular paths. There was a vigorous, youngish chaplain, who preached attractively in the chapel on the two Sundays I was there. The food was not good, apart from the bread, which was lovely. One prisoner I remember because of his public-school accent; we chatted briefly a couple of time at exercise. He seemed to have a cynical bravado, and to be set apart from the young working-class lags he was surrounded by. He was doing two years for embezzlement.

The Scrubs: Cockayne overture

I don't remember the journey for my transfer to Wormwood Scrubs in West London at all, but vividly recall my arrival there at lunchtime. When in 1954 Peter Wildeblood entered the prison gate, he beheld an 'extravagantly architected place of dingy brick and grubby stone with Romanesque colonnades running in all directions. The forecourt facing the chapel looked like one of the unsuccessful designs for New Delhi.'[2] My first impression was Hogarthian, almost, as we'd say now, Third World. Through the safety nets of dust and fluff-ridden chicken wire, I looked up at bedding and straw mattresses slung over the galleries to air – if 'air' is the right word. The smell of the drains, combined with the curry being doled out in compartmentalized plastic trays, contributed to the unusual, eerily Eastern atmosphere on that occasion. And yet a cleanliness fanatic, who was the chief screw, took a group of us newcomers to a sort of show cell, a shining example literally, as we noticed by the polished stone floor, of what he expected of us. I doubted my polishing skills, despite my army training and my ability to fold blankets and achieve the same sculpted effect. I was to learn that the alarming

---

[2] These remarks were first published in 1955. I discovered them in 1957 when I bought Peter Wildeblood's memoir, *Against the Law*, soon after my release. In March 1954, Wildeblood, then diplomatic correspondent of the *Daily Mail*, had been sentenced to eighteen months' imprisonment for homosexual offences, together with Lord Montagu of Beaulieu and Major Michael Pitt-Rivers. He followed the same trajectory as I did – Winchester to Wormwood Scrubs. The Montagu Case was the most notorious homosexual trial since Oscar Wilde's; the furore it generated had a direct influence on the Wolfenden Report of 1957, which recommended the decriminalization of homosexual acts between consenting adults. Wildeblood's account of the trial in *Against the Law*, and of the appalling conditions he encountered in the Scrubs, has been compared by Philip Hoare to Wilde's *De Profundis*.

neatness was created by a Borstal boy, commonly known as 'Mary', who got away with wearing his Borstal white shirt back to front so that it looked like a soft version of a vicar's dog collar. The Borstal boys' work was to sew mailbags, sitting on a classroom-like arrangement of chairs in the prison yard; they exercised at the same time as us, but slightly apart, while Mary walked alone and sang to himself in a soft falsetto.

At twenty, I was still a young prisoner and, in our YP under-21 wing, we did not have to share cells. I was shown kindness in relation to the cleanest chamber pot competition, I survived my first and last boxing match with honour and I was afforded a unique performance opportunity one Sunday in the enormous prison chapel. I read the lesson, the Parable of the Prodigal Son, to the crammed, most concentratedly prodigal congregation of sons of all ages in London, though it is doubtful whether many of their fathers had had much substance for them to waste or would have been expected to fall upon their necks and kiss them. There is a neat sequel to my Prodigal Son reading. It features the prison chaplain and my cell's chamber pot, though not the aforementioned act of kindness.

Having opened with my contretemps in the Novello Theatre, I can report, in passing, that the grand piano given to the Scrubs chapel by Ivor Novello himself is still there. The great West End star, and composer of the First World War hit 'Keep the Home Fires Burning', donated the instrument during the Second World War, after his four-week sojourn in the Scrubs for misuse of petrol coupons. Another feature of the chapel I have learnt more about since is the sequence of portraits of the Twelve Apostles in a semicircle of Norman-style arched niches behind the altar. They were painted in oil on canvas – mailbag canvas – by an Italian prisoner, who based the Apostles' faces on his fellow inmates with the judicious addition of beards.

Wildeblood had similarly vivid recollections of the cleanliness fanatic, the chief screw, Mr Cockayne, whom you might say he introduced into prison literature:

> When he addressed the assembled prisoners one got the impression of Queen Elizabeth – whom he rather resembled in looks – spurring on her troops at Tilbury to repel an Armada composed of soot, spent matches and bits of fluff. But it was just as well somebody at Wormwood Scrubs should be fighting the battle, in which Mr Cockayne's superiors appeared to have lost all interest long ago.

When Mr Cockayne announced a competition for the cleanest cell and especially chamber pot, I had thought my question reasonable. We had cold water and one little scrubbing brush each – were these to suffice for scrubbing the unpolished bare wooden table we ate from as well? What should we use?

'I could tell you,' came the scornful answer.

Prisoners going to dinner in the Scrubs,
from George R. Sims (ed.),
Living London, 1902.

That night there was a rattle of keys at my cell door. One of the rank-and-file prison officers, very thin and tall with a neat, slightly comic moustache, was standing there conspiratorially with a tin of Harpic.

'The wife 'as given me this. Before you go to sleep last thing, sprinkle it round the inside of the what's it; I'm doin' the same for all the lads on this landing.'

I took a helping in a piece of toilet paper and bid him a very thankful goodnight. The article in question was venerable enamel and, even with the help of the Harpic, to me as a non-smoker, the prize of two cigarettes was no temptation to make a radical physical as well as chemical attack on the layer of limescale several gaol sentences thick. In any case, the plumbing was in need of more urgent attention. After every morning slop-out parade, the recess floors were awash and did not drain properly until around lunchtime, which had been the time I arrived at the Scrubs. On that first occasion, Mr Cockayne, ever on the lookout for something to tidy, was busy selecting young lads from amongst the arrivals and right there, to the amusement of the food queue, was crudely, but with relish, taking a pair of scissors to any head of hair he considered to be too long. There was a sense of it being the Cockayne floorshow, and each boy had to sweep up his own hair clippings and bin them.

But I was to discover that something humane and civilized went on at certain lunchtimes, too, because it was then that the elderly lady visitors were available to chat to in the prison library, a quiet haven only a wide open door away from these rougher scenes. I looked forward to a few words with a gentle, diminutive lady with iron-grey hair, Lady ... I have forgotten her title. It was not the thing for the staff to discuss a prisoner's offence with him, but this lady could, and so she knew I was a prisoner of conscience, to give myself far too grand and undeserved a title.

Lady ... 'Bountiful' has all the wrong connotations but the simple fact that she was voluntarily present was innately bounteous. Lady Iron-Grey? Her hair was grey and also her clothes. Cockayne is a more vivid figure to me because he was a show-off; a banal, arbitrary and not very funny comic turn I saw daily. Lady Iron-Grey was not a part of the system unless she too was a different kind of prisoner of conscience. Apart from one phrase of hers, I remember nothing she said, but the tones in which she spoke were the comforting, congenial music of upper-class English as spoken by the liberal intelligentsia. These were the cadences I had heard as a boy on the radio in *The Brains Trust* and *Saturday Night Theatre* and, in my teens, in Third Programme discussions. John and I had parodied them on his Grundig. I never had the privilege of sitting down to talk with her, but one lunchtime, talking with the diminutive lady amongst the shelves of the prison library books, maybe to bring myself more easily into comfortable face-to-face contact, I was lulled into a sense of inappropriate informality, equality perhaps, and showed my lack of 'breeding', no doubt, by perching on the corner of a table as we talked. 'Oh, don't spoil yourself,' she said immediately. I realized I had forgotten my place and committed a social gaffe.

Despite my own tone of voice, which had carefully helped to cultivate something, though clearly not enough, of the style of the privileged and educated classes, and despite my cultivated demeanour, my fellow prisoners treated me as one of them during exercise periods and the tedious afternoon hours in the workshop as we dismantled piles of dusty old telephone bells, the sort that were housed in little polished wooden wall units. These were the sessions when we were usually allowed to chat to one another. I was not 'inside' for long enough to qualify for any periods of recreative 'association'.

When I was in my late teens, I saw a film with Jack Buchanan called *As Long as They're Happy*. It was one of those contrived middle-class comedies, artificial and bloodless, which had been a successful West End play in 1953. As a film, it was part of a genre that had run out of steam. Imagine my disappointment, then, when at Wormwood Scrubs one day we were ushered into a large shed to see a film – a treat indeed – and I had to suffer it a second time. Some weeks ago I heard *Nella's Last Peace: The Post-War Diaries of 'Housewife, 49'* read on the radio by Imelda Staunton. It had been part of a Mass Observation exercise done in the late 1940s. An unremarkable life made remarkable by an 'ordinary woman', who had an extraordinary talent for being herself and demonstrating that the ordinary *is* extraordinary, in a way undreamed of by the contrivers of the extraordinary devices of *As Long as They're Happy*. There was something so desolate about that film being shown as a taste of freedom to a group of prisoners.

After PT in the gym, before breakfast in the cell, there was the long solitary period, locked up until the morning exercise procession round and round the exercise yard. At 5 p.m., after solitary 'high' tea in our cells, the long evening lay before us. I was allowed to have the copy of Tolstoy's *War and Peace* sent into me by Paul Oestreicher – absorbing if challenging company as I tried to hold onto the identity of all those characters with their complicated shifting Russian names. My Lady Iron-Grey, could she have known what the dreadful vocal music of those long evenings sounded like? The faint sound of the surface Central line trains, rattling to and fro on their east-west journeys, became for me the sound of freedom. Otherwise the Scrubs evening silence was punctured by shouts and screams such as you could imagine coming from a human zoo. No one was being tortured except by silence and solitude.

My own solitary routine was relieved one day by a visit from my wife. Louise had got married, not in a white dress, but an elegant smoky grey costume, and it was in this same dress that she arrived at the Scrubs – she must have had a little window of opportunity in the all-consuming schedule of the Lincoln weekly rep treadmill. I only remember that she looked and smelled exquisite and that we were not allowed to touch one another.

For many prisoners the companionship of books was an impossibility; so many were dyslexics before the condition was recognized. A twenty-year-old dyslexic I know, whose parents sent him to their local school in Peckham, had a school essay he had struggled to write torn up in front of the class by an ignorant teacher. I am speaking of the mid-1990s when the condition *was* recognized. School became a terror to him and he became a terror in return. He was fortunate because his grandfather was a retired clergyman of some distinction, who was able to search out a scholarship for him at a more enlightened residential school and the boy's behaviour was transformed within days. It's no exaggeration to say that his soul was saved.

The silent evenings were also punctured by the ringing of electric bells. Each cell had an electric bell push. Theoretically it would be answered even if it were only to release a prisoner to use the lavatory for 'number twos'. Once I had tried ringing my own to no avail. This bell is the chaplain's cue.

I must have had a few words at some point with the prison chaplain to be picked out to read the lesson. As a communicant, I was one of only a handful in the otherwise empty chapel early on Sunday mornings, but the chaplain himself is not a vivid figure to me – an elderly, slight, small man with that special, faintly desiccated quality that creeps upon certain members of the Anglican clergy. Egotistically I remember nothing of his sermon on the Prodigal Son except that his opening words, which referred back to my reading, contained the phrase, 'read for us today with all its meaning'. Here followeth an account of his visit.

And it came to pass in the prison cell that the prisoner was moved to perform the function, which all God's creatures must. And he rang upon the bell, that he might be set free to perform the same more conveniently and in the small room upon the landing. But answer came there none. And the prisoner climbed up and openeth the chink in the little window in his cell that some small breath of the air might enter. And climbing down again to stand upon the floor, he lowered himself, even there to crouch as Adam did, above his chamber pot.

And afterwards he placed the lid on the same and took the pitcher of water. And when he had washed his hands, there came the rattle of keys at the door. And the door of the cell opened, and behold the priest stood there with his keys, even he who ministered unto the prisoners.

And the air in the cell stirred with the opening of the door and the priest hesitated, even there at the portal, and sayeth, 'Oh,' and he stepped back unto the landing and spake again saying, 'They have been painting thy cell I perceive. I will come back another time.'

And the prisoner, in full understanding of the priest's reluctance, sayeth, 'Let me come out, even unto the landing into the air that is sweeter there, that we may hold conference together about the things of the spirit.'

But the priest sayeth, 'It is not meet that we should do so.' And he closed the cell door and locked it. And the prisoner heard the priest's footsteps echo away. Nor did he ever hear them return again, and visitors received he none.

I put on the gloves – Dad's clincher

One boy I sat next to over the telephone bells had been part of a small gang that had set upon a youngster in a Soho street one night because the boy had failed to get off the pavement to make way for them. The victim's injuries had been terrible and, at the trial of the gang, a doctor listed his resultant permanent disabilities. 'We didn't stand a fuckin' chance,' the boy kept saying about this evidence at his trial, without any sign of remorse. The general ethos when prisoners associated was not remarkable for reflective periods of self-examination.

There was a particular game we played in our morning gym sessions. A beam was let down to about head height and a gym mattress was hung over it. Two well-matched opponents were selected to don boxing gloves and climb astride the beam to sit facing each other, the idea being that they would box, each attempting to unseat the other and send him toppling off and onto the floor, where mercifully there was a gym mat. The difficulty for the unseated boxer was to heave himself back up astride the beam and immediately resume combat without being unbalanced again. The first boy to be knocked off three times was the loser. Our instructors were decent PE instructors with no military bullshit about them. I was selected one morning to fight the boy I have described, who had been convicted, of course, of grievous bodily harm. Immediately the cry went up from some boys in the class about me, ''E won't fight sir, 'E's a conchie.' But this was not a morning for me to avoid rough games. I assume that we both of us put on boxing gloves for the first time.

If there was any sin involved, it was of pride then (and even now) that I was the victor. It was a bloodless battle and the pacifists had to be seen to win it, and I had had the privilege of free movement Monday mornings and fencing Wednesday evenings and, more importantly, a cause to fight for. We were both fortunate indeed that our little trial was such a light one.

My old drama tutor and her husband insisted on providing me with a barrister for the tribunal; I didn't take to him, particularly because he and the solicitor, one Ambrose Appelbe, tried to persuade me to object on the grounds that I had been trained for the theatre. This seemed ridiculous. One evening I was issued with a small piece of poor quality lined notepaper with the address HM Prison Wormwood Scrubs stamped at its head. It was for my statement to the tribunal. I think I filled one side, declaring my Christian pacifist position and saying that, as well as objecting to service in the RAOC, I was expressing my objection to our part in the nuclear arms race.

The day of my hearing was 6 May 1957. The tribunal consisted of a retired trade union leader, a retired judge and a retired MP. I was not invited to speak and my statement was read out by the barrister. It sounded rather bald. (I never had it returned to me – I would be intrigued to see it now.) The Army padre was not permitted by the Army to appear, but my young defending officer from the court martial was and managed to slip in the remark that the padre had believed me to be sincere.

Suddenly, unexpectedly, in the quiet of the proceedings, the barrister said, 'The appellant's father is here, William Petherbridge. Would you like to say a few words about your son?' Dad stood up and said, 'He's always been a good lad. We've never had any trouble. I served in the First World War and his brother served in the Second. But if I was asked to do it again – I wouldn't.' He sat down.

Darling Willie.

Freedom

Some days, even a week or more of silence elapsed after I had been returned to captivity. There was no intimation of how things had gone, or what decision might have been made. Soon I realized that, allowing for remission, I was on the brink of the end of my sentence. What next? At lunchtime one day, I was carrying my canteen tray and about to enter a small dining cell in which a number of us by this time ate together. Mr Cockayne materialized and said, 'You're being released.' 'When sir?' I asked. 'As of now,' he replied. I don't know when the precise circumstances became clear, but somehow I was advised that my sentence had been quashed, though not before it had almost run its course. I understood eventually the tribunal had recommended that the Army should discharge me. I continued into the dining cell and said my goodbyes to those of the shifting population I had got to know a little, and feeling that lunch could wait, asked whether anyone would like my meal. There were takers so I donated my tray, with its meat and two veg and pudding, to the room.

The other personality to materialize as, quite alone, I crossed the yard and approached the gatehouse, was the chaplain. I was dressed in my jeans and flecked sweater again, he was in his cassock with a big bunch of prison keys hanging on a chain from his belt, keeping the cross company. I assumed we had met by chance, so brief and informal and unpastoral was our encounter. If he gave me his blessing I don't remember it; he seemed to be on his way from some A to B – and there was no letter by which I could be categorized. Indeed I felt like a wild card about to escape from the pack. I wasn't a prodigal son, nor was I quite one that had toed the line and stayed at home; and now, what were the theatrical texts I was hoping to be employed to speak 'with all their meaning'? As we stood briefly together in the prison yard, near to the Portland stone edifice of the chapel, neither of us seemed to have adequate words for this hail and farewell.

Before I was let out of the little door in the big prison gate, I was given my few possessions, allowed to keep *War and Peace* and asked if I had any complaints. I thought of the disgraceful state of the drains. Perhaps I also thought of the fastidious Mr Cockayne and the refined Lady Iron-Grey in the library, who must surely have complained already. I thought of the days when our precious exercise time in the yard was shortened or inexplicably missed out altogether. Did I think of the night when I was denied a chat with the chaplain on the landing? Perhaps I thought that, although I had had the resources to turn the experience to good account, what of the young prisoners in desperate need of rehabilitation? 'No complaints,' I said to my shame.

Some weeks later I was deep into the routine of weekly rep in Scarborough, hastily learning and rehearsing mediocre thrillers and comedies, including *As Long as They're Happy*. I could almost take you to the piece of curb I stepped onto, in one of the town's handsome crescents, when I suddenly realized how quickly I had become acclimatized to my freedom, having sworn inside that I would never take freedom for granted again.

The Lost Photograph

The evidence is lost
A fraction of a second's light
Allowed into the darkness of a box
With a soft click
Produced in shades of grey
Two square inches of – my first birthday?
Split-second's worth of 3. 8. 37?

Two hundred miles
And seventy something years away
Whoever pressed the shutter induced that smile

My parents – camera shy – smiled out of shot
The humble pram
Stands on the flagstones
Its smiling tot
Not knowing what was what

How many words could I understand?
But learning fun and happiness
Perhaps how to behave

Does that blur about my pale grey hand
Signify a wave? Behind me our domain
A glimpse of house, our little wall
Surmounted by its railings
Belying both our poverty and abject social failings
The cast iron fleur-de-lys
Symbolic of perfection, light and life and royalty –
Show up in darker grey, remind me of the actualité
The green paint dulled with grime
My later swings upon the gate, its clang
Until they came with sparks and blades of heat
In deadpan fear and hate
And took them all away
To keep our German enemies at bay

The sacrificed reliquary
That held things sacred
Respectability and home and privacy.
All manageable, just manageable
Without the cast-iron curlicues.

Remembered still in any case
That image of a moment's grace
Lost
Lost, long lost that innocence
The cherub's smiling face
The innocence of war and peace
Rank, Poverty and Wealth

Sometime after that soft click
Before my burgeoning brain transcribed its first memory
Came
The creeping knowledge of the complicated things
The happy unhappy hearth and home
Triumphs and defeats

At this distance in my summer garden
Fenced round by leaves' kind luxury
With leisure to look back through vistas
Envisaging that fraction of a second's child
Who's yet the very core of me
I sit
Continuing to be.
I stare
I feel the youthful impulse
To destroy, to build and to repair.

Amongst the boxes, drawers and attics-full of life's unsifted evidence –
The clamour, glamour and confusion
The dark filed unfiled wild profusion
That image might be there.

But

Beyond the grey and twopence coloured
Myriad smiles and waves and frowns
Of heroes misfits dupes and clowns
Lie the gestures unregarded, the visages and vestiges discarded
The forgotten slights remembered,
Wounds carelessly inflicted, evidence restricted
The kisses and near misses, the disgraces and embraces
Existence saturated and not a drop or tittle that's been lost
All there in life's compost

Knowing not what's what
Still learning fun and happiness
I soon will slip away
And, linking with a little boy
Not needing now nor able to 'behave'
A blur about a pale grey hand
Might signify a wave.

In my pram, outside 71 Pembroke Street, 1937.

Words for Dad

Too late by fifty years to love you in words
Those things you seldom used yourself
And it's your sour and angry ones that I remember
As much or more than any
However much you softened near the end

You would have liked this Hampstead café
February's morning sun sidling in low beneath the awnings
Their translucent glow clean and holiday cream outside the windows

You wouldn't have felt an awkward visitor here
Not with me – white-haired, bearded me as your companion
We could adopt our Hampstead status together
Amongst the pretenders on the other tables
(Many pretend but few are actually
Accredited N.W. followed by a 3)

You wouldn't mind this music either – a clarinet –
Come to think of it – wonders of science –
This plaintive swing-time melody
Vibrated down a needle and cut the disc
Sometime in the Nineteen Forties
Is being played when you are still alive
In your forties and perhaps on holiday
Perhaps taking me for coffee
Away from the constraints of early morning shadowed linoleum silence
The ominous creak of landing floorboards
In a red-brick Bridlington boarding house
To the sparkle and fish smell and sky screech of the harbour

Didn't we go down a step into that plain little café
Where fishermen sat in blue smocks?
After all these years I still remember the jovial bulk
The blue-eyed, sunburnt face of one of them
Their belonging rumble of talk
You and me, slight, pale – white for the first day or two
Wordless all week
Sipping what I thought was coffee – Bev or Camp
Milk and one sugar
On holiday

Mother still back in the boarding house bedroom
Dressing for the embarrassments of breakfast
The crunch of our chewed bacon, toast and cornflakes
Pounding, reluctant as the tramp of a defeated army
Across the acoustic distance to the sideboard
Ricocheting off the waiting chrome and china cake stand
As the clock ticked back at us in syncopation
Promising release at last to promenade and sand
Deck chairs, Punch and Judy and the waves
Sounding their salt-water cure for wounded sensibilities
The North Sea's quiet horizon
Drawing a silver line through our discomfitures –
Shifting through blues and greys
Obscuring them until the tick of lunch and teatime.

'Living for a week like a millionaire' you called it
Softened to utterance, and so it must have seemed
For one week in the year, not to get up, not to put on your drills
To get to the warehouse by six
I look back and see you warming to life's little luxuries
Of which you knew so few

And the only ones you denied me were talk and play
So there was a mystery in our silent companionship
On those walks to the harbour

There was surprise that day when the donkey man had a horse
You galloped along the beach and back –
With only a taciturn, 'It had no go in it'
No stories of unloading boats of cavalry

No sniff of Egypt in the First World War

And at the end the very end –
I in turn found no words
A trained speaker unable to talk tenderly
As what was left of you strained to sit up amidst white hospital sheets
If you weren't gone forever

Dispersed. Reduced to less than dust in a crematorium rose garden
You'd know how proud I was and pleased
When, God knows how or why
A workmate of yours – you'd been dead a year or two –

Sought me out in London
Knew, somehow, to ask for me at the Old Vic stage door

We drank and chatted in the stage-door pub
After a matinée he had not seen
Before an evening show he intended to miss
It seemed he'd come to tell me what a wit you were, my Dad
How you'd made them laugh at work
And then he went his way, a nice friendly hale and wholesome man
Forty perhaps …

I suppose your particular brand of desolation
Couldn't be staged as comedy at home –
The wordsmith of the wool warehouse
You wore Motley at work.

Mother and Dad on holiday, ca 1954.

Words for Mother

**Studio portrait of my
mother as a girl, ca 1912.**

I have a photo of you circa 1912
A princess on your twelfth birthday
'A thoroughbred' your sister Cis called you
'The rest of us were carthorses.'

Your too-big button-up boots give you away
Hand-me-downs from your big sisters
Your serenity and wistful look
Your stance, your slimness in your pretty smock
The faint depiction of a sylvan scene on the
studio backcloth
The basket of flowers you carry –
All complete the fiction –
A royal portrait.

But Cis told me
As an errand girl, a slip of a lass
You once delivered a single kipper,
On a customer's whim
Up the long drive of one of Bingley's bigger mansions.

Thirty years went by and here am *I*
Aged four
Here we stand now in reality
For a snap before park gates – our own municipality

With my mother outside the gates of Bowling Park, ca 1939.

You slim, erect, though crippled by a stroke
Managing a smile
Buxom Cis beside you
Dressed with flair and style
You in a coat that is not Royal
Befitting now the class that's born to toil.

Slowly I fulfilled that early photo's fiction
Painted backcloths, princely diction
Even grand; you with halting speech
A limp, with your left hand
Played your role, darned, dusted
Washed, ironed, scoured, shopped, cooked –

Wished you were 'far away'.

Boy that I was I saw no irony
Singing 'Oh! For the Wings of a Dove'
In childish luxury.

I have one memento of you – only one
A piece of embroidery you made the time to sew
With your left hand.
It is my royal heirloom
And the tale will be told down our generations –
Your unhappiness, quiet fortitude and courage
And how it is too late for rose gardens in sylvan settings
When those who slaved in sorrow are ashes.

My mother's embroidery.

Even now I imagine you with me in my garden
Where you can and could never ever be

And yet you are here – I am made of you – and you of me.

Chapter 14

Blitz!

My unscheduled appearance in Lionel Bart's 1962 musical *Blitz!* was preceded by an unscheduled appearance by the Luftwaffe over my hometown of Bradford in August 1940 when I was just four. The Germans left Bradford alone during the war except for this one night; local wisdom had it that a lone plane returning to Germany from a raid on Liverpool decided to loose its spare bombs on us. They hit a market and the surrounding buildings. My eighteen-year-old brother had just left a local cinema when he heard the explosions in town. All I remember is the novelty of sitting on dining chairs, by candlelight and in my pyjamas, in the cramped whitewashed coal cellar of our house, calmly waiting to hear explosions, which never came. We got off very lightly indeed.

*   *   *

It's not what you know, it's who you know; and it was knowing somebody (I forget who), who knew somebody else, that enabled me to go on in *Blitz!* for one matinée at the Adelphi Theatre in 1962 or 63 and earn 7/6 (37 pence in today's money, but bear in mind the best West End seats only cost 30/- then, i.e. £1.50. (The rent of our bedsit in Tite Street, Chelsea was £2.10s.).

What Noël Coward said about *Blitz!*, which ran for 568 performances, is variously 'quoted', the funniest version being the most tasteless: 'Twice as long as the original and not half as exciting.' But I see from Coward's diary that on hearing the score he pronounced it 'very good.' His diary entry for 19 April 1941 finds him in a 'Pretty bad blitz', like me on a dining chair in candlelight in a basement – only he was having dinner at the Savoy. The wall bulged slightly and the door blew in, but the 'Orchestra went on playing, no one stopped eating or drinking.' I was to meet Coward twice, in 1967 and 68, but we didn't exchange notes about the real or the musical version of the Blitz – the musical being a hymn to the cockney spirit of the East End, based on Bart's childhood memories of the time. Curious how the propaganda of the period works to this day, soft-pedalling the blood, sweat and tears. We love the image of a milkman delivering as normal, walking cheerily over a pile of rubble, or of a bowler-hatted City gent calmly reading a book taken down from the miraculously intact shelves of a devastated bookshop, through a blasted wall of which proud St Paul's makes an elegant impression.

In 1962 I had never heard Bart's score and certainly never glimpsed a moment of the show when I presented myself at the Adelphi stage door as a replacement soldier for the afternoon performance. I was directed to the top-floor chorus dressing room for what I had been assured would be clearly explained – a short appearance as one of many amongst other 'other ranks' supers.

It was a long and narrow dressing room and each dressing place had a tangle of khaki kit under it. I'd been a National Serviceman for a few months in 1956 but this particular tangle defeated me. There was one other actor in the room, preparing in a rather desultory manner, who either could not or would not help and merely grunted that somebody else would know which uniform on the rail was mine. The sound of the performance, which had already started, was coming over the Tannoy; the occasion had already taken on the atmosphere of one of those actors' nightmares in which one is alone in not knowing what is expected of one.

What I did know was that Sean Kenny's set was virtually the star of the show, bearing his trademark dark-timber, structuralist style. It was the most expensive and biggest set ever built for the West End and I presumed, rightly as it turned out, that it would move like his set for *Oliver!* (which was still running at the New Theatre). The friend of a friend, who got me the job, had told me nothing of this, being careful not to scare me off, and had thus failed to warn me that the set and I would be moving at the same time.

The dressing room began to fill up with more desultory extras, sullen, inured to routine and heedless of my growing anxiety. They started to get into uniform and indeed the 'every man for himself' atmosphere I remembered from the barrack room began to pervade, rather than the cheerful banter and 'let me do that for you darlin'' ethos of the chorus boys' room. Finally, by a process of elimination, I got a uniform. It fitted; I suppose that's how I'd landed the job. Suddenly somebody appeared who sorted out the khaki webbing and large rucksack and, at the same time, started to tell me what I had to do.

I was part of the transformation scene into Paddington Station and everything I did had to be done in march time to the music. The chief moments of dangerous exposure, I realized, were when I was to form part of a line of soldiers stretched across the back of the stage, who would march down to the footlights, though there weren't any (Brecht's influence), and, on a certain count, mark time for a specified number of steps before turning sharp left, 'left?', yes LEFT, and then, keeping in time following the line, space yourself properly and, when you follow round back up centre, you'll come to the moving spiral staircase. Step onto it (in time) and follow up it, marching in time, and across the moving bridge at the top, being careful of the join in the floor (which I was told would open just after I stepped over it as the bridge swung into position). Then halt for the lone piper. That was about the sum of it, but it was all dangerous exposure and so easy to falter and stick out like the proverbial sore thumb. Next, down the steps at the far side – just keep following in time; then, as you get off, duck under the tunnel to get back to the prompt side and back up to the dressing rooms out of the way. Remember in the tunnel to put your fingers in your ears because a maroon goes off right there in the dustbin halfway down.

The dressing room emptied all at once and I was in the wings. Kitted up and carrying a rifle, I caught a brief glimpse of Amelia Bayntun, as the East End Mother Courage figure, in a spotlight at the left corner of the stage. Standing there in the gloom, I could only pray and remember the counts and instructions, for I was suddenly part of the show without even the customary whispered 'Break a leg!', though there was every chance I would. I was bearing down on the huge audience invisible in the dark, and halt two – three – four – five – left … turn … left, right, left, right … God this spiral staircase *is* moving, which way's the audience now? And here's the bridge and here's the gap coming – QUITE WIDE – keep time; lone piper (rather moving) – nearly finished, duck into the tunnel, what was that about a maroon? BOOM! Too late. The matinée continued without the soldiery now.

I collected my 7/6 at the stage door and exited into the daylight and eerie post-boom quiet of Maiden Lane as if none of it had happened.

Chapter 15

Brook's *Oedipus* (and Seneca's)

It wouldn't be fair to begin without striking a serious, even awed note:

> Electrifying experience, and we huddled together spellbound by
> the power of the play itself and especially by the poet's brilliant
> handling of the material.
>
> (John Gielgud, describing the play being read to the cast by Ted
> Hughes.)

And from Ted Hughes's translation:

> but the fear   came with me   my shadow   into this kingdom
> to this throne   and it grew   till now it surrounds me   fear
> I stand in it   like a blind man in darkness

    The other day I got a letter from an elderly and distinguished journalist, who remembered taking his father to see Seneca's *Oedipus* at the Old Vic in 1968. His father 'loved it', he wrote, adding that he had to accompany his father out of the stalls after the blinding scene to recover in the bar, where St John's Ambulance volunteers were tending to several other people in similar states of distress. I remember reading a review of the production which said that theatre would never be the same again, not only after this searing moment but also after the subsequent jazz rendition of 'Yes! We Have No Bananas', as the chorus danced around a six-foot golden phallus.

    It was one morning during the rehearsal period of Seneca's *Oedipus* that I first came face to face with Peter Brook. We were in the narrow passage that runs beneath the stage at the Old Vic. There is, or was in 1968, a fire door halfway along. It opened both ways and had a small window at face level to prevent collisions; it was through this window, looking east, that I saw Brook making for the door, westbound. Reaching the door marginally before him, I pulled it open, held it wide and stood back, pressing myself against the wall to let him pass. It was a gesture of hospitable magnanimity as much as deference. He was Peter Brook, of course, and eleven years my senior, director of what had become known as 'Brook's *Dream*' and the recent cause célèbre productions *Marat/Sade* and *US*. He was, however, new at the National, whereas I had been a member of the company for four years and a distinguishable, even distinguished, member for two of them, if you came on a good night when I wasn't doing one of my bit parts. Brook passed on, looking straight ahead without the slightest acknowledgement and, taking their cue from him, his entourage of some four male acolytes passed me in the same way, including the last, his assistant director Geoffrey Reeves. Reeves, you'd have thought, might have acted as spokesman, using that one short word that costs so little to the human being in a state within reach of the normal, but it was the way with assistant directors to attempt, through reflected glory, to pull rank on actors (when we invariably thought they had no rank to pull). I stood aghast for a moment when they'd passed, then I called after them in my best hit-the-back-of-the-Old-Vic-gallery voice, 'Don't thank me, I only work here', but they went calmly on their way.

Since 1968 and Seneca's *Oedipus*, I have met Brook twice or three times and he has been most warm and genial, as he was when I bumped into him one afternoon in 1986 on the way in to see the Hindu epic cycle *The Mahabharata* at his famous Bouffes du Nord in Paris. On that occasion he introduced me to a colleague as 'a splendid actor' and, since I didn't speak French, said I was in for a less than good time. Luckily I didn't stay for the full nine hours as I had to leave early for a performance of my own in the McKellen-Petherbridge National Theatre Group's Sheridan/Stoppard double bill at the Odéon-Théâtre de l'Europe. The Odéon was a thrilling enough venue (opened by Marie Antoinette as a public theatre not many years before the Revolution), but I was entranced by the seemingly lowlier Bouffes du Nord, an abandoned music hall Brook had chanced upon in 1974. This is a magical space which retains everything splendid about the archetypal nineteenth-century horseshoe theatre by virtue of the rearrangement of the seating, the taking of a blowtorch to the plasterwork, the stripping of the paint and gilt (and guilt) and the gutting of the stage behind the proscenium, removing all the machinery of illusion, and establishing a nothing-up-our-sleeves empty space. In place of the proverbial boards there is an earth floor for the actors to tread, on which we saw fires lit. Brook *created*, I imagine, an effect of dereliction and abandonment more advanced than he'd discovered there, yet, paradoxically, a sense of reclamation in a pure, even puritan spirit. Genius! I had a sense of sitting in a fully alive, exhilaratingly adopted theatre, a noble ruin that had been orphaned for at least sixty years, carrying all the romance of decades of desertion and silence: but this is where it *is* a theatre of illusion because I gather its true history included some years as a cinema.

It crossed my mind that day in Paris that it would be interesting to work with Brook. One would be assured of avid critical attention (both from him and the critics). The last thing I saw of his was *Fragments*, a set of Samuel Beckett shorts brought from the Bouffes du Nord in 2008 to play to packed houses at the Young Vic's Maria Studio. A student I know saw the production on tour in Southampton at the Nuffield Theatre where there was plenty of room and the attention wasn't so avid! Dare I say Brook lacked brilliant clowns for those simple, elemental, existential sack routines in which apparently everything is pared away but the encapsulated routines of a day. For a long time Brook has been on a quest to pare away, to find out what is essential. Seneca's *Oedipus* at the Old Vic came before his tours of African villages with a troupe of actors and a cardboard box, and before his experimental Promethean epic, *Orghast*, written in a language invented by Ted Hughes – also known as Orghast – a language comprising only about fifty 'true Orghast' words and some 1,500, if you like, auxiliary words. Anyway they were what the multinational cast of *Orghast* spoke in at the 1971 Shiraz-Persepolis Festival; words, as Hughes put it, 'purged of the haphazard associations of English', a language dependent on the mental state contained within a sound.

There are solemn, nay reverent accounts of the 1968 *Oedipus*. There are also certain stories, hoary old chestnuts, that are always told about it; the accurate versions of them have their honoured places in the repertoire of comic anecdote. There let them remain, so as not to bring a yawn to any old pros or informed theatre buffs amongst my readers. What follows, however, is a genuine rarity – the story of my unscheduled appearance in the production – unfamiliar even to the surviving members of the original cast, though I was amongst them on stage for quite a time that particular night. Furthermore I was separated from them for a moment of what might have seemed to the audience curious significance. Were you there that night, I wonder?

If you did see Brook's *Oedipus* (thus it was usually called – not Seneca's, nor even Ted Hughes's), you may wonder not only why, but *how* I ever managed to appear in it in an unofficial capacity, so rarefied was its atmosphere, so spare its design by Brook himself: some gold cubes at the back for the cast to sit on, and one very large central gold cube – an empty box Brook called it – that revolved, I seem to recall, at the beginning and reflected flashes of bright light into the audience's eyes. Two sides opened up and were lowered, forming a central platform and two ramps. The effect was minimalist, as we would say, aided by the modern crewneck sweaters and slacks in dark brown worn by the men and, in the same colour, long wide skirts and sweaters for the women. Apart from the opening gold boxlike structure there was one other striking element which, shrouded in a gaily decorated gold cloth, was solemnly carried through the audience and onto the stage at the end to an accompaniment of portentous drumbeats. This was revealed to be the aforementioned vertical, six-foot-high phallus, also gold. When Gielgud saw all the design elements at the first technical rehearsal, he remarked, 'I see it all now – "Box and Cox."' Once the protuberance arrived on stage at the end and was unveiled, the production became, shall we say, less formal – and busier.

But let me set the scene by describing the visit of the Fire Department to the stalls of the Old Vic some days before the production was due to open; forgive me if you know this one, but it's a good shorthand means of conveying something of the backstage ethos, part of which was the way that even those members of the National Theatre Company, who were not in Brook's *Oedipus*, eagerly discussed and gossiped about it in the green room. It stirred passions such as no other production I remember from all of my six years at the National in those Old Vic days.

217

A member of the *Oedipus* cast (possibly Oliver Cotton) just happened to be in the auditorium one day where he found some visiting firemen solemnly considering the pillars that supported the dress circle and casting their eyes up to the pillars that held up the balcony. The actor hung about and gleaned a certain amount and enquired more, to learn that some members of the *Oedipus* cast (as many as there were pillars) were going to spend most of the performance in the auditorium rather than on stage. What was being discussed was the introduction of adjacent plinths for them to stand on, which would necessitate removing seats and would have to be of a size that would create no obstruction in the gangways; the practicality and advisability of having the actors strapped to the pillars by safety belts were also at issue.

The actor's brush with the Fire Department went round the company like wildfire. Brook had been at pains to create a committed company spirit, over an unusually long ten-week rehearsal period, through improvisation and all manner of imaginative exercises. Most of the parts were not cast for some weeks. Brook's ethic was that each person's unique personal contribution was important. Show business being what it is, it nevertheless stood to reason that the actor called Sir John Gielgud was playing Oedipus, one called Irene Worth, Jocasta and Colin Blakely, Creon.

The text was extremely spare. Hughes had initially been brought in to adapt an existing translation by David Turner, which had been found disconsonant with Brook's experimental vision. Eventually, however, he went back to the original Latin, with the aid of a Victorian crib, and produced an entirely new version. Hughes declared himself 'in complete sympathy with Peter Brook's guiding idea, which was to make a text that would release whatever inner power this story, in its plainest, bluntest form, still has, and to unearth, if we could, the ritual possibilities within it.' The result, he said, came 'closely out of the original, with much deletion, little addition.' In an interview some years after the production, Hughes claimed that the final text comprised only 300 words. This was an exaggerated indication of how he had condensed Seneca's play. Nonetheless, the published script is but a lean forty-two pages.

I don't know exactly when during the peculiar and peculiarly long rehearsal process it was realized, and then officially announced, that a number of the Roman chorus were going to be strapped to pillars in the auditorium, but I gathered that the all-in-it-together, democratic exploration of the spare text, the search for the production style and the probing of the cast's own psyches continued throughout the ten weeks (despite the fact that psychological portrayals and the resultant 'theatre of illusion' were to be eschewed).

One couldn't but help hear things, getting a strong taste of the proceedings as one went about one's 'normal' theatrical business, feeling all the more normal the more one heard. When the show was up and running, Gielgud confessed on the BBC Third Programme that he and the other older members of the company had found the improvisation, to which Brook subjected them, uncomfortable, whilst the younger members of the company were impressively free and inventive, 'but not so good when it came to speaking the text.' On the other hand, he thought that the process had improved his movement 'for which I've always been so criticized'. I heard in the canteen a snippet – Gielgud crossing the stage in silence at a dress rehearsal (modern crewneck sweater and trousers), getting halfway across and saying, 'Oh Peter, couldn't I have something to carry; I'm so terribly bad with my hands.'

Jane Lapotaire was a particular friend of mine in the cast at the time and I remember her being incensed about – well, a lot of things actually – but particularly about an exercise she'd been put through blindfolded and standing on one end of a rehearsal room bench. The idea was to get as far along the bench as you could, a small step at a time, one step for every fingernail you could fully imagine being pulled out to save the life of the most important person to you in the world.

My late friend, the actor Neil Fitzpatrick, told me about another, gentler blindfold exercise. Neil, an athletically built Australian, had tried to leave the production because he'd had a TV opportunity, but was dissuaded by Brook, who said his departure would destroy the special ensemble being built up. On this occasion, there was quite a bit of noise in the room – the church hall in Short Street just off The Cut – as all the actors crawled about the floor, making their own rhythmic sounds with anything that came to hand. Neil had only found in the room one of those plastic red roses that used to be given away with a packet of Daz washing powder and, within the terms of the exercise, he was creating as distinct a rhythm as he could, thwacking the flower on the church hall floor in the hope of picking up a rhythm from somebody else who seemed to be wishing to communicate and intending to combine with him. After a fruitless period of solo thwacking, out of the noises of other actors apparently getting on famously and practically having jam sessions, Neil picked up a tap-tapping that definitely seemed to be tuning into him. He moved towards its source, and discovered when he peeped that he had gently collided with the outer wall. What he had tuned with was a workman outside who, he later confirmed, had started to chisel the exterior brickwork of the foundations.

I will at this stage permit myself one famous rehearsal-room story. I presume that occasionally they rehearsed the scenes from the play in, so to speak, a conventional way. For those actors resembling living caryatides and supporting, not merely the entablature, but the whole production, much work was done to ensure they would be able to get into a special state of being, so that they could extend the production's atmosphere almost into the very fabric of the building. At the same time, a recurring sexual note was struck in rehearsal, as for instance the time when a particular phallic sex toy was procured from Soho (in the days when most of us had never seen such things, if indeed they were legal, and long before Ann Summers had made such goods almost mainstream). The small cardboard box containing the object was passed round and each person had to look inside and – what? analyse? confront his or her reaction to it?

The story I'm building up to is the moment when the cast were lined up and asked in turn to utter the most obscene thing they could think of. I don't expect that this was planned to make the company laugh; one of the famous Brook sayings to emerge from rehearsals was his admonition to a couple of giggling actors, 'I permit anything in this rehearsal – anything. Except laughter.' Be that as it may, a lot of Anglo Saxon words and worse must have been turning the air blue as people, one by one, dutifully stepped forward and dredged up their ideas of the obscene, until Sir John stood up and declared his obscenity, simply, 'We open in ten days!'

When they did open, the actors in the stalls and dress circle, safely belted to their pillars, had to be in place before the house opened, at least twenty minutes before the play was due to commence, and already in a state of enwrapped detachment, but soon gently fibrillating, vibrating their fingers against the pillars and quietly humming. This effect became more animated just before the play started. David Belcher, who was strapped to a pillar on the left-hand side of the stalls, was suitably entranced one night as the first trickle of audience members entered. He told me this story only a few years ago, and now I am updating it in the cause of historical accuracy, because, just a couple of hours ago, I chanced to meet him in Waitrose supermarket on Finchley Road, quite a good retail outlet for theatrical encounters. Once again, the years slipped away – Old Vic canteen tea is thicker than water – and the immediacy of his Oedipal situation was vividly recalled.

Two elderly ladies settled themselves into seats just in front of David's pillar and the one who was further from him said to the other, 'Would you like my seat in case he falls?'

'I'll be all right, I think,' the other lady replied, opening her programme at the centrefold and looking at the black-and-white photographs of the cast, which were democratically arranged like a series of large postage stamps in several straight lines, all the same size. Next, out of the corner of his eye, David was conscious of the lady looking round at him, then back at the cast photographs. David intensified, if that's the word, his Zen state, but the lady kept turning and then re-examining the ranks of photographs. It was he and the two ladies and the empty plush seats in the, as yet, unpopulated area of stalls beneath the edge of the dress circle. Eventually she cleared her throat to catch his attention. David remained unmoved.

Determinedly the lady said, 'Excuse me! Which one are you?' She held the programme up helpfully.

David shifted uneasily and wondered about starting fibrillating early.

'Which one are you?' the lady repeated.

Very quietly, out of the corner of his mouth, David murmured, 'We're not supposed to speak.'

Even this was a betrayal of the production, but he hoped it would shut her up and go otherwise unnoticed as the seats were beginning to be occupied by more sensitive patrons. She hadn't heard him; so once more like a ventriloquist he threw his voice, 'We're not supposed to speak.'

'Well you could point, couldn't you!' she replied.

Little did she realize, blissfully unaware as she was of the weeks of challenging exercises David had undergone to get into his pre-performance state.

Except that there had to be covert strategies for release, and I found out today, as we stood with our trolleys by the deli counter, that, as the tragedy progressed and the belted ones were responsible for generating the suffering of Thebes, David could look up and see Ben Whitrow strapped to a pillar on the opposite side of the dress circle above. They evolved a subtle sign language, which enabled them to play bridge together. Nowadays they meet as members of the Theatrical Golf League.

It strikes me that I might have upstaged my own story, though in fairness to the production I should tell more; at least quote a line or two of the translation of Seneca's tragedy, plucked off the little-disturbed shelves of ancient Roman drama, adapted by one of our foremost poets, distilled, given the Brook treatment and turned into a hot ticket, but I don't remember much about the text. I do remember the fibrillations, but can't even recall the entry of the blinded Oedipus of Sir John, though who could forget Irene Worth slowly squatting as she ritualistically impaled her most intimate region on an upturned sword?

Well, I was in Dressing Room 6, packing my make-up for a tour, hearing ominous cries and choral moans and the odd drum beat over the Tannoy, when it might have been Frank Wiley who appeared and said, 'What are you doing here?' Quite possibly he had procured a doctor's note to say that he had contracted piles from long sessions sitting on the golden boxes as directed during performances, watching the action, and had got a special dispensation to leave the stage when he'd said his last line. I seem to remember there were one or two such renegades and the devil makes work for idle actors. There were only a few minutes before the rave-up, they said: 'There's a spare cape and gold mask; it'll be such a gas – you've seen it, you know what to do'.

They were referring to the infamous phallic episode when the cast danced, or sort of jived round, 'the maypole'. Plain gold masks were worn in this part, but they were the remains of an idea that was scrapped – originally the cast had worn male and female masks, the former with a phallus like a unicorn's horn (no – like a gold cock), protruding from the centre of the forehead. The girls had vaginas surmounting their foreheads and the improvised dance for this intended Anti-Play Bacchanal can be only too well imagined. These masks disappeared at the same time as Olivier put a notice on the board announcing that the National Anthem would from forthwith only be played in the presence of Royalty; he was determined that Brook's plan to have the audience standing for the National Anthem in the presence of a six-foot cock was going to be foiled. Whether he tried to outlaw the phallus itself I don't know, but I can still see the scene dock with its impressive pile of redundant obscene his and hers gold masks. Why didn't I take a photograph?

The brass section of the Oedipus band, I was told by the little group of dressing-room conspirators, were standing by to dance round the stalls as soon as the crashing drums ceased. A moment's silence would indicate that the six-foot article was in place centre stage. All I had to do was don my mask and cape (over the wrong-coloured trousers and sweater), nip through the pass door after the trombonist and cavort round the aisles to the jazzed-up version of 'Yes! We Have No Bananas' – returning to the stage to join in the general rave-up. Curtain; simple.

I fell over a few splayed feet in the aisles, as my mask hadn't been made for me, and remembered that the stalls were brightly lit by boxing-ring lights in place of the chandelier; I felt rather exposed. I got up onto the stage where the bulk of the masked cast – sans Blakely who had informed Brook, 'I will be in the pub by then,' and minus Gielgud and Worth – were behaving like self-absorbed dancers at a disco. I got myself well downstage centre, having come thus far, determined to make my surprise impact on the company. I turned upstage to face them all and momentarily removed my mask. They all carried on in their self-absorbed dancing, blinkered by their masks. Hastily, I fixed mine back over my face and turned to face the audience at which point I felt a blow on my shoulder as if I were being apprehended by a heavy-handed policeman – or perhaps Peter Brook. I turned slightly to see that I had been hit by the Old Vic's curtain, which in those days was yellow velvet with a long scaffolding pole for weight along its entire length near the bottom on the upstage side. I moved as if to lift it and duck under, but realized I couldn't lift it and, in any case, I was fully lit by the 'boxing-ring lights'.

Instead I turned my movement into a slow, masked *commedia dell'arte* bow, had time to repeat it and, as soon as the curtain went up again, I darted upstage and into the wings, up to my dressing room, tore off the cape and mask, grabbed my make-up for the tour and, once in the Waterloo Road, leapt onto a bus to Peckham and home, whilst the cast continued to acknowledge or ignore – I forget which – the applause.

Chapter 16

Swan Song and Genesis in Sheffield

Ian McKellen and I once had a minor unscheduled triumph. It was one performance watched by an audience of one. Sometimes the theatre, which almost by default is dedicated to improvisation, flexibility and making the very best of a bad job, nevertheless misses a golden opportunity because the opportunity comes too well disguised as dross. Such was the fate of our unique theatrical coup.

Ian and I formed the entire cast of the first one-act play to be performed on the large stage of the Crucible Theatre in Sheffield at its inauguration in 1971. We were special guests and served as the dramatic element in a kind of variety bill devised by the Crucible's founder and Artistic Director, Colin George, to thank all the people who had actually, physically built the theatre. The programme served as well to introduce the radical thrust stage to the core playgoers, who had been the regular repertory patrons of the traditional proscenium-arched Sheffield Playhouse, by then abandoned and defunct, a little way downhill from the Crucible's concrete and plate glass.

Ian and I were the first 'turn' on the bill, so to speak. A splendid local brass band came on later, making an impressive entrance, heard but unseen initially, and then marching from the inner stage out into the midst of the tiers of wraparound audience. The resident company, who were busily rehearsing the opening production proper, supplied sketches and did improvisations to demonstrate the adaptability, the heights and depths of Sheffield's new performance space.

The two-handed playlet we did was by that master of the dying fall, Chekhov, and, one might argue, doubly inappropriate. *Swan Song* was the title; perfect to *close* a theatre you might think. It is a little twenty-minute piece and the action takes place at dead of night on the stage of a Russian provincial theatre when the audience has long gone home – a proscenium-arch stage of course, again a perverse choice to inaugurate only the second Guthrie-inspired thrust-stage theatre in the country.[1] Actually the choice of *Swan Song* was thrice inappropriate, for, although Ian and I were in our early to mid-thirties, he was playing a sixty-eight-year-old actor and I was playing an even older prompter. Our gilded youth had to be laboriously disguised by make-up and the kind of 'old man' acting that might now make us blush if we were to see it.

---

[1] The first had been the Chichester Festival Theatre in 1962 and the third would be the National Theatre's modified version, the Olivier auditorium, in 1976.

As the play begins, the old actor, Svietlovidoff, emerges onto the stage alone and delivers the first of several long speeches, explaining to himself that he has fallen asleep drunk after a performance, and is alone and locked in the theatre. He is about to leave the stage when … well, here is a small taste:

> SVIETLOVIDOFF. A profane old drunkard in this fool's dress – I'm simply not fit to look at. I must go and change at once . . . This is a dreadful place, I should die of fright sitting here all night. [*Goes toward his dressing-room; at the same time* NIKITA IVANITCH *in a long white coat comes out of the dressing-room at the farthest end of the stage.* SVIETLOVIDOFF *sees* IVANITCH – *shrieks with terror and steps back.*] Who are you? What? What do you want? [*Stamps his foot.*] Who are you?
>
> IVANITCH. It is I, sir.
>
> SVIETLOVIDOFF. WHO ARE YOU?
>
> IVANITCH: [*Comes slowly toward him.*] It is I, sir, the prompter, Nikita Ivanitch. It is I, master, it is I!
>
> SVIETLOVIDOFF. [*Sinks helplessly onto the stool, breathes heavily and trembles violently.*] Heavens! Who are you? It is you . . . you Nikitushka? What . . . what are you doing here?
>
> IVANITCH. I spend my nights here in the dressing-rooms. Only please be good enough not to tell Alexi Fomitch, sir. I have nowhere else to spend the night; indeed, I haven't.
>
> SVIETLOVIDOFF. Ah! It is you, Nikitushka, is it? Just think, the audience called me out sixteen times; they brought me three wreathes and lots of other things, too; they were all wild with enthusiasm, and yet not a soul came when it was all over to wake the poor, drunken old man and take him home. I am an old man, Nikitushka! I am sixty-eight years old, and I am ill. I haven't the heart left to go on. [*Falls on* IVANITCH's *neck and weeps.*] Don't go away, Nikitushka; I am old and helpless, and I feel it is time for me to die.

Reading these lines after nearly forty years, I think my part of the prompter in this double act, although he doesn't say much, is crackingly good. I could do it better now. I am reminded of Maggie Smith's appraisal of another 'double act' – Ian will remember them – Rose and Lil, the two cockney ladies who used to run the tiny canteen kitchen at the National Theatre's old prefabricated rehearsal room in the mid-60s, the shed attached to the line of ex-Coal Board huts, which housed the NT offices in Aquinas Street near Waterloo Station. Rose was always at the hatch counter, dealing with her customers in her gregarious way, whilst wispy Lil was in the background, rarely speaking, taking everything in, but preoccupied with the stirring of saucepans and washing up. One day, after one of Rose's choice malapropisms – she referred to the National's hit French farce *A Flea in Her Ear* as 'that *Fly in the Ointment* is a scream' – Edward Hardwicke, queuing with Maggie for his lunch, turned to Maggie and whispered, 'Isn't Rose marvellous?'; Maggie murmured back, 'Yes; but Lil's the better part.'

Better part or not (most decidedly *not*), how did I come to be playing Lil to Ian's Rose, so to speak? We'd met properly at Chichester in the National's summer season of 1965 in which we were both doing rather delicious parts, Ian notably the Protestant Evangelist in *Armstrong's Last Goodnight* and my best part was the actor Ferdinand Gadd in Pinero's *Trewlawny of the 'Wells'*. I think Ian thought the National was too richly endowed with promising young actors, who must each be given their turn, and he soon left. By 1971 he had played Hamlet in the West End and I, weathering it out amongst the competition at the National, had landed Guildenstern, but Stoppard's not Shakespeare's. Late on the night I had been round to see him after *Hamlet*, I rang Ian up, having thought to myself that, as he had told me he was doing *Swan Song* for a couple of weeks to open Sheffield's new theatre and I was free, it was a prestigious enough event for me to offer my services in the small part of the prompter.

We rehearsed *Swan Song* in London in a room at the British Drama League's headquarters, a house on the east side of Fitzroy Square, number 9, across from the posh Adam Brothers terrace on the west side where, at number 29, Bernard Shaw used to live and wrote so many of his letters to Ellen Terry in the late 1890s. The area had been called Fitzrovia and had been rather Bohemian, but there was nothing Bohemian about the old British Drama League premises. I was only aware of a room stuffed full of sets of well-thumbed French's Acting Editions of box-set plays, hirable for amateur casts. We rehearsed in what had once been the main ground-floor reception room, now painted in an institutional shade of gloss paint, every feature of Georgian Bohemian grace effaced. During these rehearsals, I repeatedly dried when it came to pronouncing Ian's character's name, 'Svietlovidoff' (John Prescott, when Deputy Prime Minister to Blair, used to be similarly challenged when it came to remembering how to say Milosevic in the House of Commons), and David William our director (perfect casting, I've often been told, for my elder brother) used to prompt my old prompter with some asperity. He didn't have my patience at suffering the fools actors can sometimes appear to be, however wise and talented, charismatic and beautiful they are.

Arriving in Sheffield, with my pronunciation of 'Svietlovidoff' in place, we saw the clean lines of the Crucible exterior and eventually snatched some time on the polished boards of its large thrust stage, spending most of it trying to work out where Ian would stand and move for his laments and bursts of self-glorification – now recalling the triumphs of his genius, now in despair that, being a mere actor, he hadn't been able to marry the girl he loved and had wasted his life as a tawdry clown. Then he would rally again, getting the old prompter to do the Fool's lines to his Lear, Guildenstern to his

Hamlet, ironically enough. Svietlovidoff is 'a part to tear a cat in'. I had to tuck myself somewhere discreetly 'upstage' behind Ian, so as not to mask him, but line myself up with an aisle so I too could be seen by everybody 'weeping quietly', as one stage direction instructed, and otherwise attending empathetically or, as the Fool or Guil, self-effacingly supplying him with his cues. I was obsessive about being able to see every one of the 1,000 freshly upholstered mustard-coloured seats in the steep tiers surrounding us in a radius of at least 180 degrees. We used all the tedious open-stage stratagems we had both of us learnt whilst playing parts in Pinero and John Arden for the NT in the Chichester repertoire of 1966.

Then, one of our last crucial stage rehearsals was cancelled. They were laying carpets in the auditorium and foyers and finishing off essential technical stage installations. Somehow it was suggested that we could rehearse in the abandoned Playhouse. We jumped at the chance and found it all too uncomfortably appropriate – a small proscenium-arch theatre with a single balcony, the whole place utterly bereft of life and as cold as a Russian winter, with dust sheets over the stalls. There were a few bits of tattered curtain left behind and rudimentary lighting to see and be seen by. It was the Stanislavski exercise par excellence – sense memory on a plate; a cinch to imagine one was in a minor provincial Russian theatre in the dead of a December night, and since the stage management were working back at the Crucible, we were alone with the solitary figure of David William sitting muffled with his pinched nose in the stalls.

The ideal thing would have been to have this *Swan Song* about two old men in an old theatre actually played right here, and then each night to have led the audience in torchlight procession out of the building, not far up the road and into the immaculate foyer of the new theatre, where they would have been greeted by bands and bright lights, and thence into the new auditorium for the inaugural performance. Impossible! There was no will to make such a madcap scheme work. Health and safety rules, and the numbers not matching up, precluded it. Anyway, it might have rained some nights.

But we did it in imagination. It was our best performance. And, as it happened, it was some ideas of Ian's, floated in the rehearsal period for *Swan Song*, that were the genesis of the Actors' Company, which was to do its first season a year later, with actors sharing out the leads and the small parts.

*   *   *

I telephoned Moscow this morning, a thing I do on average once every two years, to speak to Henrietta Dobryakova, whom I met when she was a curator at the Moscow Art Theatre's Museum and I was in Moscow for a week in 1983. 'Edward! I was just talking about you ten minutes ago,' she said. Amazing. Henrietta had come into my mind ten minutes earlier; I wanted to tap her brain because, in one of her weekly phone calls from Caroline Blakiston, Caro told me, Henrietta had been saying that the names of Chekhovian characters were carefully chosen and often gave a clue to the character in ways an English-speaking audience wouldn't appreciate. I asked her whether Svietlovidoff had a special meaning. She said, 'It is a very beautiful-sounding name and means – er – light, light views or visions.'

The Spinning Room

In 1999 I discovered a poetry group which met in the room at the rear
of the Holly Bush pub in Hampstead. The two front bars were still lit
by gas in those days and the back room had a small old-fashioned
fireplace. The building was the original stables to the adjacent large
timbered house when Romney, the celebrated portrait painter, lived
there.

A lot of poems have come and gone
since I left the Spinning Room
trailing threads
and walked so lightly down the hill
called Holly Place –
sprightly
an almost youthful pace

catching at spinnings
sensing silent whirrings
even weaving a little
but letting them go
to drift amongst the falling flakes of snow
since there were plenty where they'd come from

somewhere between beer in a back room
small logs reddening in a grate
and strangers' smiles and talk
and now this strangely liberated walk
down Holly Place.

Perhaps the trick would have been
to catch and somehow hold them
in the right configuration
there
where the evening air buoyed them up in frost
and snow flakes floated through them
lighting on eyelashes
and for a moment
before they were lost
I was a poet
walking home through Hampstead.

My brother Bill on point duty outside the Bradford Alhambra,
ca 1950. Acrylic on canvas, 2009.

The Roses and the Bear, Northern Children's Theatre, 1956.
Acrylic on canvas, finished 2010.

Stage designs, Grange Grammar School, ca 1952:
The Tempest; a drawing room; and an Eastern palace.

Guildernstern in Perspective.
Self-portrait.
Pastel on paper, 2004.

Lost Opportunity:
Newman Noggs (almost) meets Andy Warhol,
Plymouth Theatre, New York, 1981.

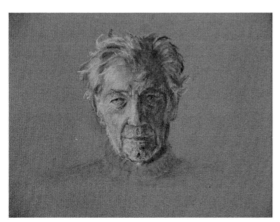

Two portraits of Ian McKellen. Limehouse.
Charcoal and pastel on paper, November 2006.

**Malvolio as he sees himself
and as he really appears. Self-portraits,
Royal Shakespeare Theatre dressing room.
Pastel on paper, 1996.**

Stage designs for *Macbeth* (thirty-eight years separate the first and second designs).

Dreamboats and Petticoats, Playhouse Theatre, London.
Pastel on paper, 2010.

Waiting in the Wings.
Charcoal and pastel on paper, 2000.

Coupler in *The Relapse*.
Self-portrait. Pen and wash, 2001.

The Toymaker in *Chitty Chitty Bang Bang*,
featuring also my puppet versions of Brian
Blessed and Nichola McAuliffe.
Self-portrait. Pastel on paper, 2002.

Krapp and His Last Tape.
Self-portrait. Pastel on card, 1997.

Mr Fairlie in *The Woman in White*. Self-portrait,
Palace Theatre dressing room. Charcoal, 2004.

Stages of recovery. Self-portraits.
Pastel on paper, 25 August 2007
and revised 14 October 2007.

Portrait of Iain Glen. Acrylic on canvas, 2009.

Lear and the Fool.
Double self-portrait.
Charcoal on dark paper, 2006.

The White Fence.
Acrylic on canvas,
2009–10.

Vintage Seer and Yellow.
Self-portrait.
Acrylic on canvas, 2010.

Theatrical Democracy

Chapter 17

A Conversation with Ian McKellen

What follows is part of a transcript of a long afternoon's conversation I recorded with Ian McKellen at his home in Limehouse in 2004 on the history of the Actors' Company. We were both present at the company's conception and, although I was the actor who had the longest association with it, the exchange between Ian and me is by no means THE authentic story. It is AN authentic story, with the emphasis on the story element. That doesn't mean we were not, both of us, trying to get to the nub, though our stories didn't always tally.

Since the founding principle of the Actors' Company was that each member at every meeting should have an equal vote on every decision (we didn't vote during rehearsals, or very rarely), the best history might be one containing a paragraph from each member. How candid would they feel able to be, I wonder?

Two directors were taken on board and they introduced some pragmatism and a sense of strategy into the idealistic proceedings. It was decided that we needed a company of seventeen actors to perform classical plays and that we should have a repertoire of two. It was impossible to ensure that everyone had a leading part, but some actors might have a tiny part one night and a leading part the next and others might have good middling parts on both nights. It was, after all, to be a company of equals and one was likely to be better as Hamlet, so to speak, if one's Guildenstern or Horatio was an equally fine actor.

To this end, Ian drafted an initial invitation to a number of leading actors who, it was hoped, might want to share some democratic control over matters practical and artistic. These actors turned up to one or two meetings before they realized they had no need or desire to play the maid or the second soubrette or Guildenstern or Horatio and they left. A good ensemble was scraped together, however, and eight months later the Actors' Company was in rehearsal for its opening season. Trevor Nunn expressed amazement at the fact that we had created a cohesive company so quickly, and there was critical praise for our ensemble work. The first two seasons were heady indeed and there was a special sense of belonging and ownership. A very special feeling.

But how was it possible to secure funding? Who subsidized our appearance at the Edinburgh Festival, our tour to Manchester Opera House, Leeds Grand, Nottingham Playhouse et al, our productions of Feydeau, John Ford, Congreve and Chekhov to not very big houses, despite good reviews?

In 1971, on the strength of his *Richard II* and *Edward II* for the Prospect Theatre Company, Ian had been asked by the director of the Edinburgh Festival's drama programme to do something at the following year's Festival. He said he would like to try and form an actors' company 'and we – it – will decide what we will do.' Richard Cottrell, who had directed *Richard II*, was then Artistic Director of the new Cambridge Theatre Company, with a duty to tour, and that first season offered himself as the umbrella management. Money was forthcoming from DALTA (Dramatic and Lyric Theatre Association). We appointed our own company manager and he was able to announce to us, at the end of our second season, that we were being offered a season of four of our plays in London at the big theatre in Wimbledon. By the time we were invited to the Brooklyn Academy of Music in 1974, we were looking at being part of an English season with the RSC and the Young Vic. We took our first and second year's repertoire to New York – four or five plays and a revue, including a new production of *King Lear*.

Actors, particularly mature actors with families, won't tour forever. The money was good but very modest; when we started in 1972 full members were on forty pounds a week. Several mainstays left, including Ian who went to the RSC, and though the third season had some critical success with *The Bacchae* and *Tartuffe*, there was, from then on, a steady decline in funding and in the size, scope and, dare I say, quality of the company. It didn't mature into a company with a mission or a strong artistic identity. One diagnosis might be that the democratic principle led to a levelling out. I was one person who had created a highly successful original show for the first company – an adaptation of R. D. Laing's *Knots* – but, for many reasons, it proved difficult to pull off the same trick twice.

The company had lasted for two years without a constitution, an artistic director or a committee. At one point Ian did float the idea of an artistic director (or co-ordinator) and this proved to be anathema to everyone until they were asked to say what *they* would do with the job. Needless to say, no such appointment was made, but a steering ideas triumvirate was chosen, responsible to the company as a whole.

In an interview with the *Guardian* in 1974, I was quoted as saying that the Actors' Company for me was 'a way of life. The involvement is absolute. It's a tribal situation: but without a big chief or a witch doctor.' My time with the company now seems an intense, sometimes magical and often frustrating period; and that is not a tenth of the story. You will understand from this excerpt of my conversation with Ian how complex a beast a theatrical enterprise is and how the creature shifts its great bulk every time you think you've got it to sit still so you can draw it. So take it all with a pinch of salt.

*　　　*　　　*

McK. How do you organize a group of people?

Peth. Or how does a group of people organize itself?

McK. If you're putting on a play, then it may be enough for the focus of the participants' attention to be the play. We're all here because we want to do this play. Yet, in addition, we've all got our own motives: 'I want to earn some money'; 'I want to live here at this point'; 'I want to work with so-and-so'. Or the focus might be the director or it might be the theatre building. The Actors' Company made the focus of attention ourselves, and it's not easily believed, except by people who actually saw our productions, that that spirit infected the enterprise while it was happening. And I don't know how that applies to factories or even films, but in putting on plays, there's something in the air and what was definitely in the air when we were on stage was the fact that we *were* the Actors' Company. A theatre director, boards and impresarios despair when they can't create that spirit, but it can't be created, I think, unless every single person involved in the group is honoured. Politically it's dynamite but it's at the heart of our generation I think.

Peth. Well, look at the members of Blair's government who despair because he does everything. They feel everything's being run from Number 10; there is a spin doctor feeding things to the press and they've got to find out from reading the paper what is really going on. That may be a crude analysis but it's the way so many things are run, and it's the antithesis of what you're talking about.

McK. We really missed an opportunity when we couldn't agree to run a regional repertory theatre for a year. I think there were three that the Arts Council suggested to us in 1972 – Liverpool, Nottingham and Exeter.

Peth. You know, I've no recollection of that, it's extraordinary. So it was obviously something that didn't appeal, amazingly – particularly to the middle-aged actors with responsibilities. Hard to believe that one wasn't such a person then, although I did have some responsibilities. It became impossible to go on living out of a suitcase for several months of the year and taking quite a small salary whilst hoping to make up the difference throughout the rest of the year with a television part or whatever. … The Actors' Company was in a sense a triumph and, at the same time, as you say, a lost opportunity, in that one always felt it was a failure of nerve and people, and because the company suddenly wasn't quite what it was, as it went on; it didn't have quite the notables, and the gilt went off the gingerbread – but that's another story. It's interesting that we couldn't galvanize ourselves into the kind of team to do the things that we felt we should do. Was there part of you that felt that it had served its turn as far as you were concerned, or do you think a different scenario, a different set of people could have done what was intended or what was hoped?

McK. I don't know the answer to those things. I just know that when we did the first season, we weren't assuming there was going to be a second, and when we did the second, then we had to think what might the third be like, and if the third had offered what it appeared to, then I think I would have stayed. But we were so adamant, so innocent, sentimental, if you like, and

241

idealistic: we will all be paid the same, it will be a company of equals, we will make the decisions. We were having talks about things that actually we didn't need to talk about. If we'd established our relationship with a really good manager, the Graham Marchant character, who must have found it extremely difficult …

Peth. I think he did.

McK. If there'd been someone who was as high-minded and like-minded as we doing that job, and who could have explained to us that we didn't really need to discuss all those things, who would have acted in the right spirit and been accountable to us, we could have got on with the artistic side of matters. Then perhaps we could have looked at our relationship with the director and encouraged people to write to us. I didn't know enough about how the Group Theatre in America or how other companies had been run; we were making it up as we went along and it was absolutely exhausting.

Peth. Yes.

McK. But once it was happening, for me the benefits were self-evident. It turned out to be an experiment rather than an establishment and …

Peth. … a successful one.

McK. Oh, totally.

Peth. It was around the time when Peter Brook had written an article I've got somewhere called 'In Praise of Empty Seats' about art for art's sake and honourably failing. I don't think we wanted to fail honourably; I think we wanted to succeed honourably, and we did.

McK. We did. But how you do make a family? Well, anyone can start a family.

Peth. Yes, that's the easy bit.

McK. That's the easy bit, I gather, but then how do you make the family a functional unit. From the outside, of course, you can say of a family, 'Well, they're no fun, they never come out to play because they're so inward-looking', but then when you meet the family, you may say 'Fantastic'. When people came to see our shows, they met a company of colleagues and friends who loved each other. That is life-affirming and, of course, it has to reflect on all aspects of your life.

Peth. Yes, I mean, helping the way people function within the group is, after all, what a play is when it's on the stage.

McK. And it's the divisions between people, the established hierarchy – to do with parts, money, billing, dressing rooms – that's so disruptive.

Peth. Whereas that cohesion and that precious sense of being in control, stimulates and enlivens people.

McK. Yes.

Peth. Which is what we were looking for, a sense of control – of destiny, of repertoire, of all that. And I suppose that might have been at the heart of the original spark.

McK. Oh, the spark – I don't know what tinder was lit or set alight, but the spark was undoubtedly you coming to see my Hamlet in 1971. You came to the dressing room and you were one of the few people who seemed to like something about the production.

Peth. I didn't like very much about the production, but I liked quite a lot about your Hamlet.

McK. Then I think you called me up that evening and said you would like to work with me.

Peth. Did I already know about the opening of the Sheffield Crucible? I think I did know about that.

McK. Colin George had asked me to do that little play, I think …

Peth. *Swan Song* by Chekhov.

McK. … and I was going to play the Old Actor. And I said there was this other part –

Peth. The Prompter.

McK. That's it, the Prompter – that you could easily do.

Peth. It was to be the first thing at the Crucible.

McK. It was the first play. It was part of a sort of variety show, wasn't it?

Peth. It was.

McK. But ours was the only play or drama.

Peth. I think it probably looked a bit like a variety sketch.

McK. And how David William got involved I don't know.

Peth. Not someone we associate with Light Entertainment. He directed it.

McK. Perhaps because it was the first time that a production had come about – one that I was in – as the result of an initiative by another actor … I mean, you hadn't been cast by the director; you had said you would like to work with me. And during rehearsals we kept saying that was how it should always be: don't you always want to work with people you *want* to work with? Why shouldn't it be the actors who initiate things? And I think we got rather enthusiastic about all that and said somebody should organize a company like that. And David William, I think, on probably the third occasion on which we were talking like this, said, 'Oh well, it's a very good idea, but of course it's not going to happen unless you do something about it.' The rest is history, although we can't remember it. Do you remember that?

Peth. You know that Pinter has written several plays in which people remember things differently. They get embattled about it, which we won't of course. But I have an idea that you had already been thinking or even talking to people about the idea of an Actors' Company, or do you think *Swan Song*

243

actually was the genesis? There's the letter that we both have copies of. I don't think I've brought it, but certainly that letter was drafted and sent by you. Had we done *Swan Song* by then?

McK. Well I'm stumped. What surprises me is that you say it wasn't sent from both of us, and I can't think why.

Peth. It wasn't because I got a copy in which you wrote …

McK. You're referred to in it, aren't you?

Peth. Yes, and I was a recipient and you put in ink on it: 'We'll need a good Prompter'.

McK. But didn't we draft the letter together?

Peth. I'm not sure about that. I remember arriving late one morning to rehearsal (I was living in South London, SE15 and we were rehearsing in NW3) and you were already having this conversation with David William, getting very much down to the nitty-gritty. It wasn't all news to me by any means, but I know that we had all been talking about it and you were using up rehearsal time to discuss the practicalities.

McK. Oh really?

Peth. Yes, yes. And then there's that list of rather extraordinary people who got the letter: Jacobi, Tom Courtenay, Ian Holm, Dorothy Tutin …

McK. I don't think anybody on the list actually ended up in the company.

Peth. David eventually did direct for us but not that first season, because it was Richard Cotterell.

McK. I think – If you say I'd been planning – I'd had the idea before.

Peth. Are you sure you weren't talking to anybody about it in the *Hamlet* company?

McK. Yes, but that was a Prospect production, and before that I'd done *Richard II* and *Edward II*. Before that I'd done *Richard II* on its own, so I'd done three seasons for them. Now if you remember, Prospect was organized by a group of directors – Toby Robertson, Richard Cotterell and Iain Mackintosh, who was a sort of manager. They'd all come together when they were working at the Oxford Playhouse where Richard was Front of House Manager. He'd suggested some castings for Toby's production of *Saint Joan*, and then he'd joined the other two. Now I'd known Richard at university so he was a friend. So Prospect already felt to me like home, and, of course, it worked in repertoire – the plays didn't play every night.

Peth. No provincial rep could afford that now.

McK. No, that was a rather modish thing to do because it's what the RSC and the National did, and the Shakespeare Memorial Theatre had always done that, but not really anybody else. It was a touring company and you played in areas where you'd lived as opposed to London which I was still new to. I was playing Hamlet and Richard II but before that I hadn't really played leading parts, and I couldn't ever imagine thinking of Laurence Olivier as a mate, as a friend with whom you'd chat about what you'd like to do next. But you could do that with Toby and Richard, so I suppose it was an extension of that which appealed to me about the idea of an actors' company. But in that letter I also said that some of us were disaffected with the way the large companies were being run; I think that was a rather specious reference to my having been slighted by the RSC.

Peth. Had you?

McK. Well, not that I remember now, though maybe I'd been offered a season below my dignity!

Peth. It amounts to the same thing.

McK. Well, yes. Imagining that the National and the RSC were places where one would like to work and whose work one admired, but they were big organizations that you couldn't influence. I suppose that was my feeling. And, of course, you'd been at the National in the 60s – that's where we met. So you'd been through that system.

Peth. Now there was another very wonderful practical thing about all this. It was a good time for you to do it – this company thing – because you'd been invited by that man, who used to run the drama programme up at the Edinburgh Festival, to go up and do something else, a leading part obviously, probably with Prospect.

McK. Oh, had I?

Peth. Yes, and I know I'm right. There was a man who ran the theatre programme, something that was very much a second string then at the Edinburgh Festival, because the main focus was orchestras and singers and opera. He wanted you to go up and do something leading again because you'd had these two big successes at the Festival with *Richard II* and *Edward II*, which had transferred to the Piccadilly. By this time the Actors' Company was just beginning, starting to be focused somehow or other, and you said, 'I won't do that, but will you take the Actors' Company?

McK. Really?

Peth. Absolutely. And he said yes.

McK. Even though we didn't have …

Peth. … an actor, apart from you and possibly me.

McK. What is extraordinary is that we got this sorted out within twelve months, or less than that. Well, the crucial thing was that the Arts Council wouldn't give us any money to tour. I think we applied to the Arts Council.

Peth. Yes. Jack Phipps, who used to run DALTA …

McK. The Dramatic and Lyric Theatre Association.

Peth. … he had this big remit from the Arts Council to co-ordinate a budget of some kind to tour Leeds Grand and the …

McK. Big theatres – Manchester Opera House, Nottingham Royal etc.

Peth. Those big theatres, with decent classical stuff – ballet, opera – and so he was interested and the Festival was interested. And your friend Richard Cotterell, whom I didn't really know then, ran the Cambridge Theatre Company.

McK. That was the crucial money; he gave it in exchange for, I think it was six weeks of that first season.

Peth. He also had a duty, a subsidy and with it an obligation to tour.

McK. Yes, but he could also give us his own theatre – for six weeks wasn't it? The Cambridge Arts Theatre?

Peth. Yes, we played in repertoire there.

McK. And he paid for the productions.

Peth. Yes, it was his autumn budget. And so, what with the Edinburgh Festival and DALTA and him, we had a sizeable tour.

McK. Yes, in fact it was 'The Cambridge Theatre Company presents the Actors' Company'.

Peth. And we kept on trying to take the Cambridge Theatre Company off the posters.

McK. We did, and I think there was a time when Richard thought that we shouldn't have the Actors' Company on the posters.

Peth. Absolutely, and there was a huge showdown at Leeds Grand I remember. Various members of the company went out front and took stuff down and said, 'No, it's the Actors' Company.' And Leeds Grand said, 'Well we know the Cambridge Theatre Company. Nobody knows the Actors' Company.' And we said, 'Well you will.'

McK. Do you remember at Manchester Opera House putting up our posters outside the theatre because you could hardly tell there was anything there, and I went in early one day and pasted our posters with special Blu-Tack, spiking them through railings. We made our own posters.

Peth. Yes I remember we did that in Leeds.

McK. But after the matinée it'd all been taken down by the management who asked if we were running a circus. Anyway, to back track slightly, after I sent that letter out, there was a meeting of people who responded to it – at Earls Terrace where I was living at the time.

Peth. And we had a lot of meetings at Richard Cotterell's flat in Charlotte Street because do you remember the keys coming down from the top floor on a parachute? That's what I remember – the parachute.

McK. Oh yes

Peth. And I remember Dancer Road – Caroline Blakiston's house in Fulham – many, many meetings took place there.

McK. But you see at one point we decided what it was we were going to do. The whole point was that there were no rules, there were no plans, there were no details. We were going to make it up as we went along. Now at what point was it going to be a touring company for instance?

Peth. Well, I think from the word go on account of the fact that these conditions were dictated by the available support and money.

McK. It didn't seem all that odd that it would be a touring company, did it?

Peth. Not at all.

McK. In the way that it would be today because people don't tour as much as they used to.

Peth. No, I mean we were hardly going to be given a home in London were we? And there was this requirement for product in the provinces.

McK. So the model for the work we would do was, I think, Prospect.

Peth. Yes.

McK. And we ended up doing classics and the plays would be rehearsed conventionally and we would tour, go to the Edinburgh Festival – this is what touring companies did – but what was going to be different was the way decisions were made. The decisions would be made by the actors.

Peth. In a kind of eternal committee.

McK. Yes, and that took an awful long time, but we decided we would choose our own director.

Peth. That's it.

McK. And with the director we would approve the designs and, in consultation with the director, we would cast the plays, and we would have three productions, am I right?

Peth. Did we not start with two?

McK. We started with two but we knew there was going to be a third. The third was *The Three Arrows*, wasn't it?

McK. We would do *'Tis Pity She's a Whore* …

Peth. *Ruling the Roost*, the Feydeau farce, and *'Tis Pity*. Now, there's another interesting thing – it's to do with circumstances dictating artistic policy – the idea that the company wouldn't be led by a handful of actors who played the best parts but that parts would be spread as much as possible. I remember Richard Cotterell saying that, pragmatically, if we did two big classical plays with about sixteen parts in them, then the company should be about sixteen people, and between the two plays (and even better with a third) we could share out the leads. So you might play a small part in one play and a big one in the other, or you might play two middle-sized parts, one in each of the two plays. That's how it worked.

McK. Yes. Did Richard articulate that?

Peth. Well, I think he said that if we did two big-cast plays that would dictate the size of the company and if we were doing something like a Jacobean tragedy we'd find that we needed about sixteen actors. And there might be four whacking good parts which means that in two plays you've got eight actors sorted – they can play little parts and leading parts alternately and the rest of the people can play a good middle-sized part in both plays.

McK. Yes, I mean there's nothing revolutionary about that because at the National it was expected on occasion, wasn't it, that someone would take a part that, had they been doing that play –

Peth. – on its own –

McK. – on its own, they would never have played. Olivier tried to set that example and get other people to follow it, but we understood that to be in a wonderful play with a wonderful production was a reward which, within the confines of a company, was satisfying enough, because anyway the next night you'd be doing something else. And we didn't invent that.

Peth. No we didn't.

McK. But what we invented –

Peth. We took it slightly further.

McK. Yes, we insisted on it, didn't we? And we also had to understudy, remember, and I think everyone was expected to be available for understudying and probably everyone was. Can you remember what you understudied?

Peth. Yes. I understudied Robin Ellis in *Ruling the Roost*.

McK. Did I understudy in that? If so, I never learnt the lines.

Peth. No, I remember we thought that we ought to have an understudy rehearsal, even before we'd opened, and my way of solving that was to have an evening rehearsal. I'd voted for it, may even have proposed it, but I knew the first and possibly the second line. I think this is rather shaming. I wasn't a pub creature, but I went to the pub before the rehearsal, thinking that perhaps if I was a little oiled I'd be better, and of course I got a very good laugh from Cotty on my entrance as Robin Ellis. I'd worked out some business with my hat. I was the would-be lover entering up centre and greeting my 'mistress' with a debonair raised hat, arm outstretched, and then as she said, 'You know my husband, of course', I turned to see him and instinctively my hat was suddenly clutched in both hands over my crutch. It was steeply downhill all the way from that perfectly achieved moment. The rehearsal was very quickly curtailed.

McK. Oh God.

Peth. We didn't get to your entrance.

McK. Well, I think we can be forgiven an awful lot of things, but what sort of bothers me about the Actors' Company and what inevitably runs underneath any organization as high-minded is actually what my own personal motives were. The idea of the Actors' Company appealed to my ideals and I still think it's basically a wonderful idea. I think I was prepared for it to be more dangerous – not dangerous, more experimental – to achieve more than it did, in terms of how a play was rehearsed: can we rehearse a play collectively, and along with that who can we get to write a play for us? We began to get around to that with *Knots*, but again that came out of your own passion and determination to make it happen. I think the reason I left the Actors' Company after just two seasons was because it wasn't going to go further.

Peth. No, it wasn't going to go further than it had already gone really.

McK. And if you remember, at the point at which I left, saying to myself that I wanted to go and play some big parts, all the time I had voted – and very few other people did or could because of their commitments and need for a good regular income – I'd voted to pick up the offers that the Actors' Company had to run theatres. I think there were two theatres that said we could go.

Peth. I think the Old Vic at one stage, but that was after you'd gone.

McK. Really?

Peth. Yes.

McK. Well, I think Nottingham Playhouse and Liverpool were both prepared to accept our presentation to run those companies and I was all for that, I wanted to do that. There was a vote and there were only about three or four of us who were prepared to do it, so when that fell through, that's when I left. But looking at Margery Mason's reports of how I behaved absolutely outrageously as the leading man of the company and took every opportunity to stress – against my better nature, she agreed – that actually the whole thing was being done for my benefit … that was the impression I gave apparently. I suppose she's sort of right, but then I would think everybody else has their own reasons for being in a company.

Peth. Oh yes.

McK. But I don't think I ever did anything to actually distort the intention. I didn't mean to – even when I got cast as Yorimitsu in the Iris Murdoch.

Peth. *The Three Arrows*.

McK. – which was a part I never wanted to play and I ended up being the only person, I think, playing two whacking parts Giovanni [in *'Tis Pity*] and Yorimitsu.

Peth. That was simply because Noel Willman, whom we'd got in to direct it, insisted that that was what he wanted.

McK. He did and it was crunch time, wasn't it? We either accepted it all or –

Peth. Find another director.

McK. Yes.

Peth. And, being mad about traditional Japanese theatre as I was, having seen the Kabuki and the Bunraku puppets, there was a moment when I thought I could see exactly how the play should be done, and I could have very well directed it. But oh no, you're already playing this part and the

249

other. That was one of the problems of the Actors' Company, that a lot of the time there was this levelling out, a flattening out.

McK. Yes.

Peth. And of course it evened out some high places that the theatre needs.

McK. Yes.

Peth. I'm not saying that I was the high place I thought I was – actually I *am* saying that. But with certain good ideas, automatically the room of actors thinks 'What's in this one for me?' So some quirky good as well as quirky bad ideas often got voted down because there was nothing in them for certain people.

McK. That's right. You should try and think of some specific examples of that.

Peth. Wilde's *Salome*, probably because I suggested it and wanted to direct it. I think wanting to direct in an actor was seen as wanting to control. And all the women wanted to play Salome and nothing else.

McK. What appealed to me in the idea of the Actors' Company going to run a theatre was you'd be able to say to people, 'We're all going to be living here for a year; there may not be a role for you now but there is going to be a role for you there.' ... I don't think there was anything mistaken about the ideals behind the company, or in practice. I think it worked as well as it could just being together for a short period of time. There may have been a levelling out, compromises and so on but I don't think any of those compromises were irksome or stopped the company doing what it actually ended up doing better than anybody else at the time. Witness the reviews we got. And Trevor [Nunn] came to see, it must have been *'Tis Pity*, I think, at Cambridge and we went with him for an Indian meal afterwards and I sat next to him and of course Trevor's a bullshitter but he did say to me, 'How have you managed to create a company in six months when I've been trying to do it at Stratford for over six years?' And I said to him, 'Well, because we are a genuine company.'

Peth. We were.

McK. We were, and audiences felt that. Trevor and the audience felt it. The critics, they read the manifesto but they saw it in action and they felt it.

Peth. And we felt it.

McK. And we felt it. You can only create that by actually doing it and we did it. Of course there were faults, of course there were motives and there were a few arguments, but only maybe Marian Diamond and a couple of others were wounded – but not fatally. I think the Actors' Company was a model and proved its point.

Peth. I think there was one curious fault running through it in a way. It's to do with how we began, and if we look at the original list of names to whom the letter was sent, they were mostly leading actors, established – young mostly – leading people: Ian Holm, Jacobi, Courtenay.

McK. Eileen Atkins. Dorothy Tutin.

Peth. And some of them came, most of them came to one or two meetings …

McK. Not most – some.

Peth. Some. They quickly felt that what they wanted to do was what you subsequently left and went on to do, which was to play the best parts all of the time. So although the company was very good, its composition was made up of one or two people who were habitually used to playing big parts and some who weren't.

McK. Yes. Was that a division?

Peth. I don't know that it was a division but it shook down into the company, although the point was that everybody had a vote and a voice, nobody was seen to be a junior or a less important member because, indeed, if they weren't playing a play-carrying part, they were playing two or three very well placed parts. So as it shook out, they would go on and play a messenger in *The Way of the World* and I would be playing Mirabel, but then in *The Wood Demon* I would come on and have one line while you were playing Khrushchev, and so on. So that it was kind of fair and spread in that sense, although there were some people who didn't have the status they were quite used to.

McK. People like Noel Willman would say, 'Oh well, it's a waste of resources if you've got Petherbridge – of course he should be playing that part which is more suited to him than Juan Moreno.' But you have to say, 'No, not within this context because everyone's got to pull their weight because we're adhering to a principle.' And we've all been, have been before and will be again in situations where, as now happens at the National Theatre, there is no company and the directors decide who is their favourite person to play the part and they will be engaged to do it.

Peth. Yes.

McK. And sometimes it'll work wonderfully, but no audience can go to the National Theatre and see a company at work – it does not exist – and seeing a company is a very, very special delight for an audience. Witness the Actors' Company, witness a lot of what Laurence Olivier did with his two companies, and what hopefully you get at the RSC now that Michael Boyd is determined to have a company. But the Actors' Company still has a lot to teach. There's a sort of conspiracy, an acceptance – I mean Nick Hytner has just said there's no point in having a company, he doesn't agree with companies, it's an idea that has had its day. Richard Eyre does not want a company, and Peter Hall's idea of having a company, including our group [The McKellen-Petherbridge Group at the NT] was nothing to do with a devotion to the idea of a company, it was to do with his own way of not having to run the whole of the National Theatre himself, wasn't it?

Peth. Yes.

McK. That was his motive. There again, we provided a company. ... Don't forget we were all paid the same and we took it in turns on tour to have the No. 1 dressing room.

Peth. Or converted it into a green room.

McK. Yes, that's right. And the billing was alphabetical and everyone's name was on the poster. The National Theatre doesn't bill its actors, it bills its playwrights. In all those interminable meetings people had the chance to express themselves and refine the ideas and discover things that they wouldn't under all other circumstances have been able to. Now some people didn't want to join in – Frank Middlemass never wanted to attend the meetings, was just happy to go along with whatever. I can only really remember Robert Eddison saying once, 'Forty pounds a week, that's absolutely ridiculous, I've never earned as much money in my life in any job.' He was lying, I checked with his agent. But anyway, what I found out at those meetings was how a meeting worked and I began to discover how easy it was to make a point and absolutely see the other point of view and make that point equally strongly. I see how politicians can do it – they can argue anything, lawyers can argue anything, you can argue anything, and I discovered that about myself, that I would be arguing one point that I didn't actually agree with but I could present the other case. What I discovered in the Actors' Company was some self-confidence which I'd absolutely not had before.

Peth. Do you mean a kind of political self-confidence?

McK. Well, an ability to articulate an argument verbally and in writing and to be confident that my point of view was worth listening to. I absolutely had not felt that about myself before. I grew up and became someone who could function, if you want to call it, politically, but in a public way other than through my acting which up to that point had been the only time when I felt confident. I would never have been able to get involved in gay rights if it hadn't been for the Actors' Company; I wouldn't have known what to do or how to do it, and I don't think that would have happened if it hadn't been for the Actors' Company. I think I would have been a much, much lesser person now. I think Robin Ellis said that about himself, that he felt he'd grown up through the Actors' Company. I don't know whether you were changed in that way.

Peth. I remember particularly the heady feeling of belonging, belonging to the company and possessing it at the same time – it was having and being. And you know the strain, the loneliness of playing a leading part, although it's a wonderful thing to do, can sometimes be an isolating thing in a company when it sets you apart. The company didn't set anybody apart like that, the company embraced everyone, and one embraced it. That was a very special feeling I thought. I remember going to see something at the Comédie Française in Paris some years later and the feeling emanating from the stage.

It's fashionable to think of it as a famously defunct organization and I know nothing about it now, but there was a feeling in this piece, a Feydeau, there was a feeling of everybody, not engaged *by* the Comédie Française, but *being* the Comédie Française. It's something to do with being identified with and *owning* the event in a very special way. And that's what I felt with the Actors' Company.

Making-up for *Ruling the Roost*.
From back on the left: John Tordoff, Robert Eddison, Juan Moreno,
Frank Middlemass, Ian McKellen, myself.
Photo: © Nigel Luckhurst

Postscript

I might almost have been in love with Ian for a few hours in 1963 (that dangerous year). I confess that I almost despaired of our Actors' Company of equals when Harold Hobson, referring to Ian, in the tiny part of the pageboy in our Feydeau farce, wrote words to the effect that, where the head of the table is, there one's attention will be. So it was that sometimes my ability to be attracted to Ian's actor's magnetism was inversely proportionate to his power as a 'draw'.

I have always revelled in his company off stage, though we often do not meet from one year's end to the next. As a prince of the theatre now, he entertains you in his kitchen like a prince – possibly *à deux*, serving you exquisite fish pie and fruit salad, making the coffee just to your taste with artless homely charisma, a quality I can only describe as a down-to-earth mystique. Nowadays the breadth of his interests and concerns, the use he makes of his fame, is not only admirable but also fascinating.

Of his company on the stage I can't really say, for though we have acted in the same productions many times, we have only once shared a scene together and that was in *Swan Song* where the old actor has more than the lion's share. I may have failed to notice how tasty was the morsel left over for me.

Notwithstanding having had Lear snatched from me in Wellington just before the RSC version arrived, later, in spite of a less than perfect RSC cast, I sat in the New London Theatre for Ian's Lear, feeling no jealousy and experiencing the greatness of the play in quite a different way from what I had felt whilst studying it for myself.

It was in a very new theatre in Milton Keynes that Caroline Blakiston, Emily and I went to see Ian in a midweek matinée in the early part of the tour of *Waiting for Godot*. The town seemed to be a vast car park dotted with corporate headquarters in aluminium buildings. As we neared the theatre we found ourselves behind the elderly audience – droves of them. I've heard of bums on seats but this was ridiculous. But as those ancient and too broad bums settled, filling the seats and the modern auditorium to overflowing, they turned into the Middle England Matinée audience of one's dreams – attentive, sharp, seasoned playgoers. You couldn't have said, as Arthur Miller once did of modern theatre audiences, that they were 'under rehearsed'.

Of course Ian is one of the actors who, throughout his life, has rehearsed with them, but more than that, I had never seen him better, simply because he invested the hapless Estragon with something I sensed to be himself, from deep in his own experience. It was incredibly intimate, part pure Beckett, part a boy's desolation on waste ground in Bolton. It was so strong that it eclipsed any invisible histrionic spell he might have been casting over us. Later I heard that the cast had felt that matinée to be a turning point in the life of the production. Ian's was what I *really* call 'a star turn'.

Chapter 18

The Barefoot Psychoanalyst and Other Primitives

The primitive is not a quality I am known for. In 1965 Yat Malmgren, the visiting movement guru at the National Theatre, said to me in that broken English that so enhances the credibility of teachers' pronouncements, 'Something primitive has dropped off.' He advised me that I could benefit from the extra movement lessons he held on Wednesday evenings in a former chapel in West Street, near the Ambassadors Theatre. When I was not acting on Wednesdays I would be there, perhaps hoping that something primitive would reattach itself; I was aware of the plaque on the outside wall of the building next door announcing that John Wesley had preached within, but not aware that the Wesleyan Methodists had expelled two of their number, Hugh Bourne and William Clowes, and that the splinter movement so formed from their conjoined followings was called 'Primitive Methodism'. The Primitives had certainly induced me to give my fourteen-year-old heart to Jesus in Bradford's Eastbrook Hall, just round the corner from the room in Chapel Street where, three years later, I would have my first 'Free Movement' lesson.

One of R. D. Laing's patients noted 'his huge ability to understand the primitive.'[1] Before I met Britain's most famous and controversial psychoanalyst, I had gathered from his books what is neatly encapsulated in his words from 1964: 'I am a specialist, God help me, in the events in inner space and time.' By the year I met him, he was saying, 'I suppose I am one of the symptoms of the times.'

In the summer of 1972, I turned up at Laing's flat in Belsize Park Gardens, having doubtless seen the posed photograph of him seated on the floor with bare feet. I seem to recall at our meeting he was wearing shoes. At one point, on a chair facing his, I found myself in a rather laid-back, expansive attitude, with my hands clasped together behind my head, exactly mirroring his position. I wondered whether I was unconsciously aping him, or whether he, not without satire, was aping me.

In the sparsely furnished room there was a grand piano on my right and a spinet on my left with a pair of neatly rolled socks on the carpet beneath it. I tried to impress the author of *Knots* that his bestseller was ripe for adaptation for the stage and that the Actors' Company, and I in particular, were up to the

---

[1] Quoted in Chapter 8 of John Clay's *R. D. Laing: A Divided Self: A Biography* (1997).

task. He let me continue for sometime before saying, 'Don't you worry; just take it and do it.' I had carte blanche.

The flat was stylish, ordered and very clean. Soon he could afford a

R. D. Laing in his flat in Belsize Park Gardens.
Photo: © John Haynes

handsome house in nearby Eton Road and there, invited to a dinner party some years later, I especially recall their baby boy, for some time the centrepiece of the dining table, naked, apart from his nappy and just old enough to sit up unaided and nibble on the odd tit bit. Like the socks under the spinet in Belize Park Gardens, the baby leant a faint hint of anarchy to the civilized, elegant dinner, except that he didn't cry or fall head first into the fruit salad, nor crawl amongst the sauces and cruet.

Earlier that year, I was sorting through some old newspapers at home in Peckham, and there it was on an outdated page of the *Radio Times* – a radio 'dramatization' of R. D. Laing's *Knots*, his concise collection of dialogue-scenarios and solitary first-person meditations – poems essentially – delineating the 'strangely familiar' patterns inherent in human relationships and in the way we communicate with, and misunderstand, one another. I felt perhaps primitive anger, pipped to the post; why hadn't *I* thought of making a show of it? Maybe because I had bought a copy, being just one of the many people who made *Knots* a bestseller in 1970, thinking I'd better keep pace with the psychiatric zeitgeist, but finding that the slim volume in its elegant black cover was possibly less than the sum of its intriguing parts. But there was something about coming across that *Radio Times* and its billing of *Knots*; it was a red rag to a bull after the horse had bolted. I had a gut feeling that this would be the basis for the show I was looking for.

You see, at an Actors' Company meeting I had said that, for our second Edinburgh Festival season and subsequent tour, we needed something up to the minute. We were already scheduled to do a Restoration comedy, Congreve's *The Way of the World*, and Chekhov's *The Wood Demon*. The previous season we had done *'Tis Pity She's a Whore* and Feydeau's farce of the Belle Époque, *Ruling the Roost*. Now, I urged, we should devise a short piece of our own to stage in a small studio space at lunchtime. My reasoning: 'When one goes to the Tate, one sees the equivalent of our repertoire in the oils of the seventeenth, eighteenth and nineteenth centuries; then one comes upon Matisse's vast abstract cutout "The Snail" ("L'Escargot"). We need something new like that, "as fresh as paint".'

In those days, of course, Matisse's 1953 collage, with its irregular blocks of brightly painted paper, was relatively new and Giles Gilbert Scott's converted Bankside Power Station, where 'The Snail' is now housed, was a mere industrial monstrosity, across the Thames from St Paul's, still belching ostensibly 'washed' smoke from its 325-foot central chimney stack.

Prophetically, in the late 80s, I was taking a group of students round Shakespeare's Bankside and, as we looked up at the, by then, defunct hulk, sprigs of buddleia beginning to sprout from where the entablature would have been had the style not dispensed with the archaic, I remarked, 'If this were in Paris – not that they would have built a power station on the Seine opposite Notre Dame – but if we were in Paris, this disused power station would be an art gallery by now.' The rest is Art History! They heard it first from me.

I have re-discovered my original manuscript of *Knots*. The company had challenged me, since I was so keen, to find or make an appropriate piece of modernity. Adopting Matisse's cutout technique (oh, the days when 'cut and paste' still meant scissors and a bottle of Gloy!), I cut some of Laing's 'verses' out of my copy, pasted them on A4 paper, and interposed stage directions written in longhand. I then sent the completed 'collage' to be typed at our tiny company office in Falconberg Mews, tucked behind Tottenham Court Road Tube Station on the south side of Oxford Street. Under 'copies to' I had written the names of the members of the company I hoped would perform it. One name was not a company member; it was that of Martin Duncan and had 'composer' in brackets after it and 'Urgent' underlined in red. There was a further note inside: 'NB This is a detailed draft for your approval. I have attempted to provide a strong framework because rehearsal time is so very short.'

For much of the year, you understand, the company was far-flung and freelancing, each of us pursuing our own jobbing career and managing periods of unemployment, glad of the meetings in one another's houses convened on a weekly basis to decide on repertoire or recruit new members. Under these conditions, it had taken me some time to attack the script, to light on a way of adapting parts of the book into a show. It had been a worry to me, with time running out, when I was in Exeter, concentrating on learning and rehearsing Prospero for Jane Howell's production of *The Tempest* at Northcott Theatre.

One Sunday night during the run of *The Tempest*, I was with the book of *Knots* and a glass of red wine over a solitary supper in a restaurant when I got the idea to turn some of Laing's items into a sort of cabaret or variety show. The point of the book was that character, locale, atmosphere had been stripped away – how could one preserve these 'distilled patterns', this spare formality and yet add the colourful theatricality I felt it asked for? Anybody could arrange a mere reading of the book, but somehow I felt that, after a kind of prologue where the pieces were done simply, just recited (in fact they worked well like this and were often very funny), the show needed to erupt into a cornucopia of theatricality. At one point I rang up all the actors at their homes in London from a telephone box to find out what extra performing skills they had, knowing that Juan Moreno, for instance, could juggle – his father José had been a famous juggler and equilibrist in variety and circus.

Little did I know that Laing himself had a forbear in the variety theatre and watched those old 'born in a trunk' movies on Sunday afternoon television. Yet that evening in Exeter I decided that some of the knots would serve as the patter for comics or the lyrics for songs, that effectively they would be the acts themselves. For example:

> Negative: Can't win. Everything I do is wrong.
> Positive: Can't lose. Everything I do is right.
> I do it, because it is right.
> It is right, because I do it.

This became the basis of a song-and-dance number for a comic and stooge, to be followed by a custard-pie routine. When Laing finally saw it, he was all for the custard pies.

In a letter to Laing before the rehearsal period began, I outlined my vision:

> The opening moments of *Knots* should be very simple I think: the first items done in the most pristine way possible – but perhaps the theatrical contribution when it comes in full force should be like a refracting prism to show the audience more vivid colours or even a distorting or enlarging mirror – at any rate the knots can be more broadly characterized or viewed from unexpected angles. ...
>
> There should be no question of burlesque, of course, but, for example, one monologue could be delivered by a stand-up comic about his deadpan-faced stooge – 'There must be something the matter with him'. The audience may have already seen this one done 'straight'.
>
> A juggler and his assistant could have a conversation during their act. She starts 'I feel stupid' – he's busy being brilliant with his juggling, she's only handing him things.
>
> The 'pain in the neck ... you're giving me a headache' one could perhaps be a 'quickie' between an American? ventriloquist and his doll. ...
>
> The 'show' part can end with a Tower of Babel chorus of all the knots – but not before more subtle and ambiguous possibilities have been explored: two characters reminiscent of Picasso's absinthe drinkers or some of his clown and Pierrot figures could mime whilst some of the commentaries, e.g. 'Narcissus fell in love with his image ... Jack falls in love with Jill's image of Jack', etc are spoken. ...

'The statement is pointless / The finger is speechless.' Here is where a chink of light might be let in – a 'sad little tune' – certainly not lush or sentimental, but words and music, speech and song tentatively expressive of consolation and the venture into being – all this heard by the knotted and tattered band who have performed the whirligogs and tangles.

At the same time as recognizing the painful knotted patterns of everyday relationships, the audience also recognized the comfortable clichés of the concert party and the double act. Sometimes the text was turned into the performers' muttered asides during their acts, their neurotic preoccupations underlying their bright professional routines, or their dressing-room conversation. But I can see that the performance element, and the existential world it allowed the knots to be tied into, strayed into territory, sometimes lonely, which anyone who has experienced periods of neurotic angst would recognize – the whirligogs, as Laing puts it, that compulsive repetition and 'rehearsal', those attempts to alleviate the tension of one's knots that only tangle and pull them tighter. Someone complained that the show made entertainment out of mental illness, which struck me as odd, coming from a person who should have been intelligent enough to have noticed that the 'knots, tangles, fankles, *impasses*, disjunctions, whirligogs, binds' were often only too recognizable to us 'sane' people as our own.

'A beginning, a middle and an end'; that's what Winnie Hodgkinson, our first-year acting tutor in Bradford, told us our improvisations should have. I found it an uninspiring, blindingly obvious stipulation, but now I suspect it has respectable roots in the drama of classical antiquity. Certainly Laing's pieces needed to be more than an anthology to be recited; they had to travel a theatrical meta-road, which would allow dramatic development and some of their facets to glitter in differing lights or lower in gloomy opalescence. Before the 'show' started, they were delivered 'neat' in soliloquy or, in Laing's words, 'sufficiently independent of "content", for one to divine the final formal elegance in these webs of *maya*.' If the Hindu word 'maya' is translated as 'the material world which is in fact illusion' or, alternatively, 'the ability to create illusion through magic', then the theatre was the right place for Laing's knots to thrive.

The stately and wryly witty Robert Eddison was the show's uneasy compère and a professor who delivered a mind-bending lecture with the innocent opening: 'A finger points at the moon', and a bleak, nihilistic conclusion: 'The statement is pointless/The finger is speechless.'

'*Knots* Overture' was the first stage direction I wrote. The young actor Martin Duncan, who now directs opera internationally, was part of the Exeter company, ageing up to play Gonzalo, and he had written the music for *The Tempest*; it was a natural development that I should ask him to write our music.

259

Robert Eddison as the MC.

Somehow we shoehorned in the *Knots* rehearsals as we began to rehearse Chekhov and Congreve in tandem. One of the high points was the day of our last rehearsal of the Actors' Company repertoire before we were due to leave London to play Nottingham en route to the Edinburgh Festival. There was a shop that sold electric organs on the Chiswick High Road, almost opposite the Ballet Rambert rehearsal rooms we were using, and at lunchtime I went with Caroline Blakiston, our keyboard artist and torch-song singer with a difference, to buy one for the show. Once the main repertoire was running, we finally had our own schedule, but it still had to accommodate the main openings of Congreve and Chekhov in Edinburgh, and so, by the nature of things, *Knots* tended to be rehearsed episodically, turn by turn, and the actors often didn't know how the whole was progressing.

Matthew Long and Caroline Blakiston.

The special skills of the cast were interesting. Caroline Blakiston's I have itemized. Sheila Reid had a lovely soprano voice and played the tambourine; Juan Moreno, as well as his juggling, was a good percussionist and tap dancer and managed to choreograph and coach Sharon Duce up to speed in a sparkling tap duet; Robin Ellis was passable on percussion, when Juan was otherwise engaged; and Paola Dionisotti possessed, and to some degree

260

played, a cello, though her tuning was a problem. Paola's disgruntled entrance with cello at one point was kinetically effective. Everybody could play the kazoo of course. I played a bamboo pipe and devised a mime sequence for myself, Paola and Juan to illustrate Laing's:

> Narcissus fell in love with his image, taking it to be another.
> Jack falls in love with Jill's image of Jack, taking it to be himself.
> She must not die, because then he would lose himself.
> He is jealous in case anyone else's image is reflected in her mirror.

This called for a succinct melodrama and, after our compère Robert's characteristically plangent delivery of this knot, the strains of Elgar's *Chanson de Matin* were heard and, as water was necessary for the reflection, I was able to make a theatrical entrance and introduce my prowess in mimetic punting, learned from Claude Chagrin, complete with my white Pierrot's face.

It was after we had rehearsed this number in our street clothes in some little room one day that Sharon, having seen it for the first time, said how impressed she had been and that what was moving about it was to have seen me making myself so vulnerable as an actor. I was puzzled at first because the mime, although it extended acting beyond one's usual physical range, somehow transported me into a special poetic comfort zone, whilst releasing me from words. On reflection, I could see that what I was doing might appear risky, committing myself to something so un-naturalistic and potentially 'arty' or even risibly melodramatic. But that never occurred to me: all acting had to be a heart-and-soul commitment and utterly 'real' to the actor; that was how French farce worked, on *reality,* despite Feydeau's mechanical plots and devices in which his characters become the absurd, frenetic victims of their own obsessions and the collisions and misunderstandings caused by the waywardness of circumstance. Acting Chekhov is all vulnerability, however diligent one is in not indulging the pauses and remembering that the author kept calling his infinitely sad plays comedies. And one certainly has to risk the absurd being real in Restoration comedy, just because the characters are so articulate and highly skilled, people who invest all their energy in *avoiding* vulnerability by perfecting the high style which can survive every social encounter, the perfection of dress, conversation, and their constant strategies financial and amorous.

I don't recall where we bought 'the set' for *Knots*. I wanted a horizonless, continuous floor and background; it would be pretentious to call it abstract. To this end, a roll of white vinyl flooring, like a giant photographer's roll, was procured. Tough, easy to tour and fixed to a baton, it unfurled and hung, and any footmarks could be washed off. I suppose it hung twelve feet high and curved to cover the twelve-foot depth of stage floor. The effects were simple. I'd had an afternoon's work once being a stooge for the TV magician, David Nixon, and he'd made me disappear, most convincingly, with the aid of two folding screens. This was the effect I borrowed for *Knots*. We had a 'petal drop' with a difference, the petals being black. We also had a tap mat to provide the right acoustic surface for Juan and Sharon's number. We used a follow-spot to lend an air of cabaret to the proceedings, and Robert made his compère's entrance through a large paper-covered hoop with 'Knots' emblazoned on it.

My Max Wall-style eccentric dance in the 'I can't lose' routine. With Matthew Long.

The finale of *Knots*.
Sheila Reid is standing. Back row: Paola Dionisotti, Robin Ellis, Sharon Duce.
Front row: Ian McKellen, Tenniel Evans, myself, Matthew Long, Juan Moreno,
Robert Eddison.

We didn't know it, but we were destined to put the two first seasons together and add *King Lear* to them for a repertoire of six in a New York season at the Brooklyn Academy. Looking back at this span of work, it seems we must have been busy making ourselves vulnerable and invincible at the same time.

We should have been so lucky.

But it was not quite the triumphant progress it sounds. Our Edinburgh Festival openings were a success; in fact, it was a group of visiting New York critics who were instrumental in sparking the invitation to Brooklyn, and *Knots* was performed, not in the then miniscule studio space at the Lyceum, but in the main house where we filled the stalls each lunchtime. However, on most nights during our subsequent UK tour from Nottingham to Liverpool, you could have shot a stag in the dress circle, as the saying goes. One thinks it is a new development that these theatres, in between housing the tours of musicals, Sadler's Wells ballets and the National Theatre, accommodate a lot of touring plays entirely dependent on television stars, making sure their *faces* are on the posters along with the name of the series or soap for which they are famous. It's too late, but now we could perhaps capitalize on the subsequent television celebrity of Sheila Reid and Sharon Duce. Then even Ian McKellen's name didn't mean 'bums on seats' in those provincial dates, and Felicity Kendal, who was part of our first season, had not yet done *The Good Life*.

Graham Marchant, our administrator, found us a lunchtime date for each week of the tour, usually in a university college hall. We sometimes played to good-sized, spirited undergraduate audiences, but as often to sparse, desultory sprinklings of students who seemed unsure of what they were seeing and whether they should invest the whole of their lunchtime to see it.

In Bath it happened that a film crew from London Weekend Television descended on us to make a documentary about the company. Ian was appalled at the prospect of another week of thin houses and went into his galvanic mode; a letter to the local paper attempted to shame the citizens into coming. *Knots* came in useful: somebody at our emergency meeting suggested we should take to the streets and we got permission to use the square in front of the Abbey where some of the more 'streetworthy' moments of the show were staged. The presence of the TV cameras ensured that the passers-by took the shenanigans seriously, some footage on the local television news helped and we ended the week with very respectable houses as well as some documentary footage of us holding a conference on stage to discuss whether and, if so, how we should allow extracts from the repertoire to be filmed. I was all for us doing them in full slap and full out, not toning them down for the telly. The same strategy at the next dates we doggedly and naïvely implemented outside shopping centres to apathetic shoppers who spurned the offer of our pamphlets and hurried by.

However, on the strength of some rave reviews for *Knots*, we were offered a season at the Shaw Theatre to coincide with our return to London. We accepted and, possibly thanks to the timely appearance of the documentary, did seven sell-out performances a week for four weeks. Ian felt that the whole company should be part of the Shaw season, and I had decided to lengthen the show anyway. He was co-opted (no one else wanted to be) and performed a particularly convoluted and arcane knot, one of several concluding 'soliloquies' that followed the high jinks of the show: 'One is inside / then outside what one has been inside.' 'Ian McKellen,' wrote Harold Hobson, 'disabused, disillusioned, reconciled to his, to your, to mine, to the world's incompleteness, makes one of the most solemn and impressive speeches, as the shadows deepen, and the sad leaves fall, that I have ever heard an actor deliver.' I had to go to Laing's autobiographical fragment *The Bird of Paradise* to find the perfect song for this ending.

Together, Ian and I did a wordless puppet sequence to a percussion accompaniment, Ian leaning over the top of one of the screens and manipulating me. In a joke shop I had found a pair of red plastic lips, the perfect quick doll make-up which was swiftly applied and discarded. Ian had an idea and asked me to procure a second pair of lips, which somehow he cunningly concealed inside his mouth. He thus appeared to be a human puppeteer until the final moment when his business was to wrench me upwards by my strings with his arms fully extended, but his head lowered and looking down at me; then slowly he raised his head to see who it was above him who had him on strings. It was then one saw that he too had the puppet's red lips.

Throughout the Shaw season we rehearsed *King Lear* by day at the Welsh Club in Gray's Inn Road, with Robert Eddison taking on the task of rehearsing Lear as well as performing *Knots* and a new part in Gabriel Josipovici's short play *Flow*, which we had added to make a full evening. Ironically, the set for *Lear* was made entirely of string; we called it *String Lear*.

I can hardly believe that we were due in New York after the *Knots* season with barely time to hire a theatre for a day in which to dress-rehearse *Lear*, which we were going to premiere in Brooklyn! What with storms at sea and corruption at customs, we had to open *Lear* in our street clothes with no set; we were in our element – an actors' company to the tips of our fingers. In the echoing cavern of the Brooklyn Academy of Music, built as an opera house, the New York audiences continued our new-found tradition of euphoric nights at the intimate Shaw; the perfect antidote to the silences in the English provinces, particularly the Opera House, Manchester. Imagine our surprise when the audiences took to that difficult first scene in *The Way of the World* with its gossip about off-stage characters they have not yet encountered, as if we were talking about people they knew and couldn't wait to meet again.

We all stayed at the Hotel Chelsea with its plaque to Dylan Thomas, who in 1953 had 'sailed out to die' from there, and which had once housed the cream of bohemia, including Eugene O'Neill, Arthur Miller, Jean-Paul Sartre, Mark Twain, Sarah Bernhardt, Jackson Pollock, Leonard Cohen and

Bob Dylan. But its time had passed, and it was now just a comfortable, seedy, if stately, flophouse with dubious adverts about pussycats in the elevators. By contrast, the Actors' Company was at its zenith: 'flop' might be an appropriate word to attach to one or two of its later enterprises I was to be involved with, in amongst its fitful patches of success.

**As Mirabel
with Caroline Blakiston (Millamant)
in *The Way of the World.***

The Hotel Manager in *Ruling the Roost*.
Photo: © Nigel Luckhurst

The Way of the World.
**Edward Petherbridge as Mirabell, John Woodvine as Sir Wilful Witwood
Paola Dionisotti as Marwood, Margery Mason as Lady Wishfort.**
Cartoon: © Hewison / *Punch*

265

As I sit here now, I long to be rehearsing *Lear* again in the Gray's Inn Road and dashing to the Shaw, hearing Caro abandoning Goneril to play Martin Duncan's *Knots* Overture on the organ, imagining myself in a punt with Paola. I still hear the masterly delivery the company gave to Laing's words, and how they negotiated the moods so deftly: absurdity to pain, certainty into desolation. I hear Sharon and Juan's tapping feet and see the white spots on Sharon's skirt and the glitter of the sequins on Juan's jacket. I feel Matthew Long placing the custard pie in my face, see him singing the front-cloth number as Laing's bewildering convolutions tumble down from the flies on the longest song sheet ever seen.

I see the fall of dark leaves from the flies and listen to Sheila sing:

> Yes there are moments
> Sometimes there is magic
> Tenderness too is possible
> Ah tenderness
> Entices an uncertain gesture of delight
> To adventure into being.

We knew then that *Knots* was by and about the Actors' Company as much as it was about Laing's famous book. For one sentimental moment, we were all reborn in a trunk – the same trunk.

The Fool in *King Lear*.
Photo: © Clive Coote

Chapter 19

The Bacchae and The Beanstalk

> *Euripides preserves the disorder of actual experience,*
> *measuring its horror against the unrequited illusion of order*
> *which sustains human beings. His image of tragic humanity is*
> *earned less in the conflict between the individual's nature and*
> *the necessities imposed by a higher order than in the conflict*
> *between the individual and his own internalized necessities.*
>
> William Arrowsmith

As he was leaving the Actors' Company, Ian McKellen said to me, 'If you want to direct a play, read *The Bacchae.*' I speculate now whether, had he stayed on in the Company, he would have wanted Pentheus to be his next leading part, or even Dionysus. When eventually he saw the production, he said, 'You've cracked it.' I wonder …

The Actors' Company prided itself on being pragmatic as well as democratic. Having once decided on a director, the voting was over and the director was trusted to do the job. Admittedly there was one hiatus late in the rehearsal period for *The Bacchae* when I suspected that a motion was being put to the vote. We were pressed for time, but the cast melted backstage rather ominously and I was left alone in the Edinburgh Assembly Hall for what might have been four or five minutes.

They say it's a lonely job, being a director. During the wait, I might have recalled the moment the previous season when I was part of a deputation that approached David William during a dress rehearsal of his production of *King Lear*, set in some indeterminate pre-Christian period, to tell him that the acting company had voted unanimously to ask him to desist from using a recording of part of Beethoven's last quartets in the scene in which Cordelia is reunited with her father. He was rather shaken. I wasn't expecting the result of a vote on my use of Pink Floyd; I think I was half expecting some sort of down-tools; to be politely relieved of my post and told that my treatment of the company or the play, or both, was unacceptable. They had already insisted on having their full lunch break when I had said we needed to make more rehearsal time, and I *had* resorted to sarcasm at some of the note sessions. 'Score: Actor's Co. 7, Euripides 4. We have to award the playwright the top score.' Appalling. Eventually, silently, the cast returned and waited for me to continue the rehearsal. I never enquired into the crisis. It's possible they wanted to change something radically, but couldn't decide exactly how. It is not as if *The Bacchae* is a play of which it is easy to say 'how it should go'.

Robin Ellis, who played Pentheus in Edinburgh, later dismayed me by saying that he had been terrified on the first night: 'We went out onto that stage with nothing.' I didn't quite know what he meant, but construed it in a positive way. On the other hand, Helen Cotterill won my director's heart when, at rehearsal, being new to the company and one of the replacement cast, said, 'I think this is going to be a fun show to be in.' Mark McManus played Dionysus who begins the tragedy and has the awesome task of simply telling the audience that he is a god. We none of us had had much experience of playing archetypes, and our training, whether formal or picked up on the job, seemed to point us toward playing idiosyncratic individuals, supported for the most part in recognizable, more or less naturalistic/realistic settings. We had heard of two boards and a passion, of course, but to walk onto the bare boards with nothing up one's loose sleeves but one's elemental passion …

The contract between actors and audience depends on belief. If the actor's task is to say 'I am Dionysus', whether behind a mask in his namesake's theatre in Athens circa 408 BC, or maskless in the borrowed Church of Scotland Assembly Hall in Edinburgh in 1974, he is pretending; the audience, aware of the subterfuge (clearly the actor cannot be immortal), is prepared to suspend its disbelief and is enabled to do so in direct proportion to the actor's magical ability to arrive at 'the truth' through pretending that an extraordinary communion takes place: a mutual spell by which actor and audience are both bound, not by faith, but by belief. Perhaps it is a condition akin to the dream state, especially those dreams when we know we are dreaming yet still find the truth of the dream inescapable, irresistible.

The author has foreseen all this, of course, planned it. Euripides comprehended the tacit conventions of dramatic action so well that he could introduce unexpected nuance and perhaps even adjust the rules of the game.

When it comes to considering real life, most of us, who have been raised in the Judeo-Christian tradition to believe, if at all, in only one God, and that a loving one, cannot begin to imagine how the ancient Greeks related to their anthropomorphic pantheon, the frequently amoral immortals who had given the heroes such a hard time in the Golden Age. We conceive perhaps that the first audience of *The Bacchae* might have been awestruck, on the feast of Dionysus, to be witnessing Pentheus defying the God, being seduced by him; and then, surely, it was an amazing communal catharsis, pierced through with savage irony, to have been there when the actor playing Agave entered in triumph with the severed head of her son. It would have carried all the mythic power and immediacy of the medieval Nail-Makers' Guild enacting the crucifixion on a cart in the streets of York on the Feast of Corpus Christi.

I do not recall Mark McManus's Dionysus too well, but I saw him recently in a screening of the film version of *Knots*. I had quite forgotten he was in the film and, indeed, he appeared only briefly, but most potently when he walked onto a bare stage to declare:

One is inside
then outside what one has been inside
One feels empty
because there is nothing inside oneself
One tries to get inside oneself
    that inside of the outside
    that one was once inside
    once one tries to get oneself inside what
    one is outside …
But this is not enough.

It made me think, after all, that Mark must have been convincing as the god because of the way he drew one into the neurotic Laingian knot by his simple, authoritative conviction:

One remains empty because
while one is on the inside
even the inside of the outside is outside
and inside oneself there is still nothing
There has never been anything else
and there never will be.

The impotent omnipotence expressed by the speaker of this knot seems light years away from Dionysus declaring his omnipotence and preparing us for inevitable events, and yet there is something elemental in both utterances. They are both in their different ways 'The Great I Am'.

Mark McManus played Pentheus in Edinburgh. Here he is having his hair cut by Robin Ellis of later *Poldark* fame.

There seemed no possibility of doing the play anything but 'in the raw', which might have given our Pentheus the sensation of going on stage 'with nothing'. Certainly there was, in Edinburgh, a back wall with a doorway which could have led to the interior of a palace, and a walkway in the Japanese Noh style that led everywhere else, and therefore up to the mountain, the convincing logic of a dream. But I am amused to remember the nightmare of Stoppard's Player when Rosencrantz and Guildenstern break the audience's contract with the actors by absenting themselves from the performance. We had an audience, if not always a very big one, but even with an audience, actors are vulnerable and can experience something uncomfortably like the discomfiture of the Player:

> There we were, demented children, mincing about in clothes that no man ever wore, speaking words no man ever spoke ... hollow protestations of faith hurled after empty promises of vengeance – and every gesture, every pose, vanishing into the thin unpopulated air.

Our business was to populate, colonize Euripides' territory, to make the dream an inescapable reality. First we had to find that reality for ourselves, which brings us back inevitably to belief.

'A god incognito, disguised as man.' So Dionysus describes himself as he first addresses the audience. William Arrowsmith, whose translation I chose, describes the god as wearing a smiling mask throughout the play. I didn't take this stage direction literally, though I must have considered masks. I had at least seen pictures of Guthrie's *Oedipus Rex*, and now that I look at the photographs of his production closely I see that the actors' mouths and chins were exposed, though made up to 'match' their elaborate masks, thus allowing them to speak unhampered.

Was it the purist in Peter Hall that had his actors in *The Oresteia* masked, mouths and all, so that we heard the actors speak through fixed orifices, the acoustic effect being as through a letterbox? There was one crucial scene where the chorus had to undergo a sea change of attitude, from malign Furies to benign Eumenides. It is a paradox and almost a theatrical truism, one which I have seen come touchingly alive, that a mask can seem to change expression. There was no such magical change on this occasion, simply because the actors of the chorus were so physically inexpressive that the masks did not 'respond', the sea change did not take place.

Greg Hicks, who is a veteran of Hall's work in the Greeks, has been widely praised for his ability to make the mask work (because of his physical expressiveness), and indeed has been described by Paul Taylor as God's gift to Greek Tragedy, or even, more appropriately, a gift from the gods. Nevertheless, many critics felt that the masks seemed in Hall's productions to make the drama remote, impressive but not involving. It is surprising, incidentally, knowing Hall's reputation for the disciplines of verse-speaking, to note that a critic could find the protagonists' speaking of the verse 'bizarrely idiosyncratic', a comment to put a spanner in the aesthetic works. But yet another Hall production played to an audience of 11,000 at Epidaurus and no one can argue with that.

The only justification for writing about my little Actors' Company effort is if it is able to raise some interesting issues about the staging of these ancient tragedies, but whatever possessed me to suggest this play and how did I persuade the company to let me direct it? It was in repertoire with Molière's *Tartuffe*, a boldly non-commercial programme. Our Pentheus was to become famous on TV for *Poldark*, our Dionysus for *Taggart*, but neither we nor the audiences were to know this yet. Again I wonder now why I didn't take the opportunity to see Peter Hall's 2002 production at the National Theatre regarding which one critic wrote 'there is not a director living who knows more about Greek Tragedy'. I might just as well say that when I directed *The Bacchae*, there wasn't a director in the country who knew less!

And there is a lot to know about *The Bacchae*, or rather a lot one can never quite know as Arrowsmith puts it:

> *The Bacchae* is finally a mysterious, almost a haunted, work, stalked by divinity and that daemonic power of necessity which for Euripides is the careless source of man's tragic destiny and moral dignity. Elusive, complex and compelling, the play constantly recedes before one's grasp, advancing, not retreating, steadily into deeper chaos and larger order, coming finally to rest only god knows where – which is to say, where it matters.

Oh yes: 'recedes before one's grasp, advancing not retreating', and yet on the rehearsal-room floor one has to proceed pragmatically, to dare, to grasp the invisible nettle. Sooner or later, as soon as possible I would suggest, one has to put down the script and make the first bold or faltering steps, even if it means 'hazarding a way of doing it' as I once heard a director say to an actress who was having difficulty making Miranda's first entrance in *The Tempest*. Decisions have to be made about the 'compelling complexities'; one has to get a grip on the elusive, to say the lines and not be intimidated by the lack of furniture.

I have just come across something I wrote about a classical performance I saw some while ago:

> His face, his entire head is almost the perfect hero's head, wherever he turns it, it looks right. Is that God-given or is it partly his contriving? – can't tell – and of course it must be both. His voice is not enough like an actor's voice – it lacks power and variety. I suspect he didn't go to drama school – skuttles across the stage when he does his urgent crossings – should have done tap and ballet and modern jazz, hip hop, anything to facilitate a convincing walk across the stage in an apparently

untrained way, but he has emotional intelligence; it's just that it doesn't always have the channels.

Then I talk about the audience: '90% sixth-formers, of the disheartening kind, with a gaggle of gigglers in the dress circle.'

But even with the most gifted actors (and a dream audience) what is to be done about the unfathomability of which Arrowsmith speaks? I would venture that the elusive power of the play, the heart of its mystery, is most likely to be revealed, or rather realized in performance: an obvious point perhaps, despite the fact that the play is more studied than performed. The play, like all plays, is a rite, and in a sense the script is a book of instructions. It is perhaps no semantic accident that crafts of all kinds used to be called 'the mysteries'. Now that craftsmanship is so comparatively rare we have detached the word from any ideas of skill, talent, knowledge and 'know-how'.

It is worth remembering that when the play 'works' it is no more possible to anatomize its meaning in an essay than to translate into words the impact or 'meaning' of, say, a late quartet by Beethoven. I suppose, just as music is ineffable (and it is a miracle that there's a form of notation so that the composer can write down the ineffable), so there is a notation that contains all the Mysteries of *The Bacchae*, and, in that respect, there is only one true source – the script, 'the score' – both for Beethoven and *The Bacchae*. Nevertheless, there is also the hope, the potential, every time the scores and scripts are performed, that what is implicit will be manifest.

In the great classics, the actor, although he deals in words, is dealing in the unsayable, and, although he uses gesture, he is pointing us to things that are out of his reach and out of sight. Were this not so, Beethoven, Euripides, Hamlet, Oedipus and Mozart would all have offered up their secrets long ago and have been of no interest to us.

'Dance we must,' says Teiresias and it is important that the play should be almost always on or over the threshold of dance. The chorus certainly dances; even Pentheus, once he is under the god's spell, is essentially dancing. Only the messengers, gravely, do not dance, and the cessation of any possibility of dance pervades the conclusion of the play with a terrible desolation, so that Dionysus himself has at last an awesome, shocking stillness. He appeared high up in a massive golden cloak and his stillness was accentuated by the curious ecology of the Wimbledon Theatre which invariably caused the stage smoke to hang about him in utterly still streaks of cloud, lit as if in a sinister sunset.

As anybody who has tried knows, the chorus is the most difficult thing to get right in staging Greek tragedy. Harold Hobson, when he saw our production at Wimbledon, declared it far more successful than the National Theatre's two years earlier; he was particularly impressed with the chorus, believing we had created the requisite Dionysiac spirit as opposed to the Old Vic's 'Fraserian savagery'. 'Yet they do this,' he said, 'without manifestly forgetting their civilized origin. They belong to a race which conceivably could have built the Parthenon, or written the lyrics of Sappho.'

There is no template for the Bacchic chorus. I've explained my acquaintance as a seventeen-year-old drama student with the challenge of the

Bacchanal. It was a godsend that Sheila Reid and Helen Cotterill were both singers and could dare to hazard a way of singing some of the chorus's lines. They adapted the kind of close harmony they used in popular songs. I can hear them boldly singing as no man or woman had ever sung, 'Thebes you are blest!', miraculously betraying neither their tune's nor their harmonic's origins, nor striking any note of the pretentious.

Our maenadic chorus,
L to R: Sheila Reid, Sharon Duce,
Paola Dionisotti.

Chorus members
Sheila Reid and
Helen Cotterill
beneath our
looped white
canopy.

At the reverie stage of my researches, and in a negative light, I remembered an opera chorus I had seen a long time ago. What struck me about them was that, in spite of their robes, one could too easily imagine them all going prosaically home on the bus afterwards. By contrast, as I write, I am remembering some dancers standing on a sunny street corner in New York in the 1980s, all dressed, it seemed, in their wacky rehearsal wear, but each carrying a change of clothes in a trendy bag; special creatures communicating, not so much in their banter and gossip, but by the way in which they inhabited that piece of sidewalk, but mostly because of the way they inhabited their own bodies. It would not have diminished their collective or individual personalities a jot if they had dispersed by disappearing onto public transport – they were part of the street life after all – but the hours they spent dancing, whilst other New Yorkers went about their business, had marked them.

There is, I discover, an unlikely parallel between the ancient chorus at the first performance of *The Bacchae* two-and-a-half millennia ago, which I have tried to imagine so many times, and the opening number of *A Chorus Line*, which I have just now revisited on YouTube. I saw the American cast in London and walked as if on air out of the theatre, despairing of ever having anything in common with anyone who did not love the show. The YouTube audience seemed to have passed, through dint of familiarity with the show, to the status of ecstatic acolytes at a quasi-religious festival; they burst into applause within seconds of the opening number (teams of dancers looking like the ones I saw on the street, auditioning for jobs in a Broadway chorus line), but this was not the only 'Bacchanalian' attribute of what I was seeing on the potent little screen. Fate seemed to be a character and a demonic demigod too, a glorious one, driving the dancers to perform heroic terpsichorean feats whilst they found the breath to sing, letting us in to their internal stream of consciousness: 'I really need this job – please God I need this job,' recalling Teiresias' line, 'Dance we must!' The audience saw the auditioning dancers as victims of Broadway, superb in their struggle both to beat and join it, and finally – as no one can ever forget who saw the show – triumphant in spangled costumes, singing the praises of some wonder leading lady we could neither see nor care about. *They* were the apotheosis of the show, celebrating the sacrifice to the God of Broadway, as we were compelled to acknowledge the worship was glorious.

I see now that we could have taken a realistic route in portraying the maenadic, itinerant followers of Dionysus to strike at the essence, but, having hit on the idea of a series of ritual encounters in a circus ring, the costumes and the acting style were *theatrical*. I wonder that I did not use masks. Elsewhere I have quoted Devine's dictum that masks reveal rather than hide the actor. It is one of those, perhaps irritating, paradoxes that in any case works only if the actor is of the kind who has the instinct to exist intensely within the mask, and is never tempted to tear it off as a hindrance – rather should he feel that were he to do so he would be diminished (perhaps indecently exposed!).

Some people feel that what they call our modern way of acting is 'psychological', too subjective, and inappropriate for these ancient Greek plays. On the other hand, there are those who believe that a strong measure of stylization is alienating. Perhaps these terms are misleading and it all depends on what is meant by stylization and the psychological – need they be at all mutually exclusive? It should be possible to perform this play with both

274

elements potently present, and if the actor behind the mask, or bare-faced, is imaginatively absorbed and committed and entering into the action and the state of being of his or her character, that potency will be manifest.

'You are a bull leading me forward,' says Pentheus to Dionysus when Pentheus finally enters in female attire. Dionysus explains his horns by declaring that Pentheus is seeing things as he should, having made peace with the god. I imagine I asked myself, when working on the play, how we, the audience, should see this crucial situation. It strikes me now that Euripides, in having the transformed Dionysus entering first, prepares us for the transformed Pentheus. If there is something theatrically magnificent in the transformed Dionysus, perhaps Pentheus too, has a magnificence about him: under the god's spell he certainly *feels* magnificent and strong enough to lift mount Cithaeron on his shoulders, veering between violent fantasies and sensuous thoughts of peaceable voyeurism, as Dionysus acting as his dresser and bull-horned handmaiden, murmurs his advice and suggestions. If there is also something of the lamb to the slaughter in Pentheus, this female/male figure, something pathetic and deluded, there is also the fascination for us in seeing Pentheus manifesting something, until now unseen, of his inner nature.

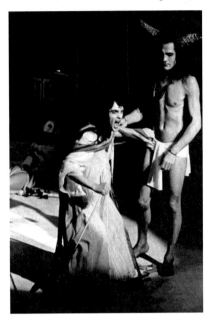

The horned Dionysus leads Pentheus (Keith Drinkel), dressed as a maenad, to Mount Cithaeron. Drinkel and I didn't meet again until we appeared together in an episode of *Midsomer Murders*.

It is a cliché that the play's 'message' is that we suppress the Dionysian urge in ourselves at our peril, but on another, less overtly 'physiological' level, we realize the god is pettily vain and proud and determined to entrap Pentheus into destructive submission, which for Pentheus has all the intoxicating excitement of unknown sensations, which nevertheless are recognizable to him as 'The Great I Am'. We may, in our confused and confusing reactions to this scene, wonder whence the thirst for these seductive sensations comes, bidden from our own nature; be that as it may, I perhaps thought that in performing this scene we should create a somewhat contrived, theatrically intoxicating spell for the audience. The play, whatever else it might reveal to us, was written for the Feast of Dionysus. The floating walk of Pentheus was achieved by the three stronger members of the chorus, each with his thyrsus, making a supportive framework around Pentheus on which he could be buoyed up, requiring the floating feminine figure himself to bear his own weight on his outstretched arms. Thus the artifice of the scene was itself ambiguous, at odds with Pentheus' sensations. For all its effect of soaring inebriation, it was borne on tightly controlled technique. As actors we knew that the ecstasy of Bacchus is dangerous, something that has to be simulated with discipline, even caution and, dare I say, tact!

**Sheila Burrell (Agave)
with the head of Pentheus.**

Sheila Burrell, who played Agave, had the most demanding task: she had no seductively disguised god at her elbow acting as subversive puppet master in a demonic charade; she was on her own, gloriously elated as a prodigious champion huntress one moment, and as a mother in an unthinkable *extremis* of grief and guilt the next. Years later I would watch with admiration as she played to haunting perfection the mother in *Strange Interlude*, obsessed by the fear of inherited madness in her family, and stoically determined to persuade her daughter-in-law to get rid of her unborn baby. She played a woman who had had all her joy in life eaten away from within. I daresay that Agave was, psychologically, as good a preparation for such a part as an actor could wish.

The conundrum is: why should an actor wish to play such a part? And why should we wish to watch? Whether Euripides knew the answers to these questions, except on the level of theory and tragic convention, is doubtful. What is important is that he found it *necessary* to write *The Bacchae*. It is this most costly element of inescapable necessity, which is vital to any performance of the play.

*   *   *

I had known about the tradition of the comic Satyr plays that were performed after the tragedies and are claimed by some scholars, on the strength of the few fragments we have, to be equally cathartic in their own way. And I had first-hand knowledge of what Peter Brook had done after Seneca's *Oedipus* and was sure I could do better than that.

I decided, therefore, to devise a comic afterpiece of our own and lighted on the story of *Jack and the Beanstalk*, simply because I thought it could be played almost as an inversion of the *Bacchae* story, drawing on the English

276

pantomime tradition of cross-gender casting in the Dame and the Principal Boy, but playing entirely in mime and fairytale mode, so as to avoid the bathos of our words following upon those of William Arrowsmith's translation of Euripides.

The Bacchae and The Beanstalk.
Gary Raymond as Dionysus, Edward Petherbridge as Ringmaster.
Cartoon: © Hewison / *Punch*

The Giant was played by the actor who played the god Dionysus, only this time he was not to be triumphant. At the beginning of the pantomime, three clowns were discovered walking up a staircase; they encountered Dionysus high up at the back of the stage, 'left over' from the tragedy, still in his enormous cloth-of-gold raiment. They screwed an extension onto a paintbrush and succeeded in giving him a red nose; next they found a rope that dislodged his garment, revealing his striped underclothes which matched the colours and style of their own costumes.

Agave, who in her Bacchic ecstasy had murdered her own son, had the fun of finishing off her evening as the Fairy Godmother. Two of the chorus played the cow, and I have to say that our designer helped them create the most convincing and beautiful cow ever seen. There were to be equal amounts of slapstick and magic. In *The Baccahe* I played Teiresias and Robert Eddison Cadmus; he was quite at home in the tragedy and its mimetic aftermath, but the elemental, archetypal acting required in both halves of the show was not within everyone's comfort zone.

One day, whilst the idea was in its embryonic stage, I was in a record shop with one of the company, Sharon Duce, when I heard Mike Oldfield's LP *Tubular Bells*, which just happened to be playing. Sharon knew it already – it was nearly two years old. I was as ignorant of popular music as Greek Tragedy, but I knew what I liked. Immediately I bought a copy and heard the soundtrack of our pantomime complete with music for the Giant, the magical entrance of the clowns by moonlight, and a Maypole dance finale, the pole being a giant thyrsus carried aloft by a triumphant Jack and on which was mounted the Giant's head.

Pentheus as the pantomime Dame, Agave as Fairy Godmother.

Our beautiful and moving pantomime cow.

As the Ringmaster with Sharon Duce in *The Beanstalk.*

We took the pantomime to a garment factory canteen when we were on tour in Manchester. Somebody had the idea that it would be a socially responsible outreach exercise. The result was entirely Bacchanalian I suppose. All went calmly and charmingly as usual, the primary colours of the costumes showing up well against the grey canteen stage, and the grey overalls worn by the mostly female audience of machine operatives, until the cow, played by Sheila Reid and Helen Cotterill, made its entrance, to a beautifully leisurely bovine passage in Oldfield's music. They erupted with lewd laughter, and positively screamed when the creature walked upstage showing its rear end. The pathos of the cow being sold for a bag of beans was entirely lost.

The next special outing of the panto was a showing we looked forward to, to an invited audience of small schoolchildren one afternoon during our Wimbledon season. I suppose we should have introduced ourselves and explained the story, but we thought they would know it and recognize all the elements. They watched in complete silence and didn't applaud at the end. We came on stage to engage with the children and were admonished by one teacher for presenting the kids with a completely inexplicable show.

On holiday in Greece, just before rehearsals began, I saw a shadow theatre play one night in the open air and was taken backstage to watch from behind. It was my first visit to Greece and a last-minute package tour got me to a little village called Kamena Vourla, with a single mini-highrise hotel by the beach. To see anything else I had to take taxi trips on my own, one to Athens where I stayed a night; I remember a policeman making me put on my shirt before allowing me onto the site of the Acropolis – and I thought they invented the male nude! I was most impressed by the theatre at Epidaurus and the view of the empty landscape beyond the stage.

It was by chance I walked into the village one night and noticed a show beginning. I sat on a bench under a small pergola facing a rough stone-built 'shed', which housed a shadow screen, maybe four feet wide. The puppets were almost Javanese in appearance and the story that of a battle between the Turks and Greeks. I remember the Greek hero being killed and a laurel wreath floating down from the sky to rest on his head and all the while a rasping voice through a microphone, out-Heroding Herod, played the entire cast of characters and provided the narration.

I don't recall how I got backstage; perhaps I peeped through the open door in the back of the shed and was welcomed in by the puppeteer's momentarily spare hand. He had two boy helpers, no more than twelve years of age, whom he seemed to curse and order about *sotto voce*, averting his mouth from the mike to whisper urgent instructions about music cues; there was a little electric turntable and a handful of records. The puppets themselves were hinged so that they could turn one way or the other: they could be taken away from the screen, flicked and pressed back, having miraculously changed the direction of their attention. The boys were very busy and even handled the minor characters and somehow, throughout the melodramatic diatribes, the coherence of the drama was sustained against the intense atmosphere of impending theatrical disaster.

It is appropriate that Greece was the genesis of the idea of doing the entire Jack-Giant sequence as a shadow play. We had two screens on the open stage in Edinburgh, duplicating the action for all sides; depending on where you were sitting, you had views of the shadow play 'backstage' as well as front. Our designer was Lotte Reiniger. Why I don't still have one of the two Jack figures she made, I can't think. It was the first time one of her figures had acted with a human, because the human actor behind the screens was perfect in scale for the Giant. Lotte worked with us, modifying the puppets painstakingly as we sought to find the right strength of the materials and parts.

Jack and the Beanstalk shadow play designed by Lotte Reiniger.

Her *Prince Achmed* (the first animated feature film) had captivated me when I saw it in a cinema in London. There is a moment when the young prince sees some winged water nymphs descend to bathe in a little lake and he hides to watch them, pulling a palm branch down, in profile, to conceal himself. Lotte had a 'trick table' on which all the scenes and puppets were arranged, tiny move by tiny move, to build up the action, each part of the whole film's sequence was photographed, tiny action by action, by her husband Karl on a camera fixed above the table. As Achmed watches, I remember, there is a close-up of him and his lips part in wonder at the nymphs' beauty. It struck me as a perfect, human piece of acting, such a simple, elemental gesture. It ranks with Olivier's first moment in the film of *Henry V*, when he very gently clears his throat, inviting us into his lone intimacy on the threshold between a private and public reality.

Lotte had been befriended by Winnie and Joe Hodgkinson, which is how I met her. In her flat, when I took Sharon Duce, my Jack, to meet her, she produced a tiny stage, lit from behind the shadow screen with a candle. The proscenium was not more than a foot wide, but on the screen appeared her exquisitely cut figures with their articulate limbs. She enacted *Cinderella* for us. Her 'caveman' technique, as she called it, as the figures jerked on to make their entrances, contrasted with the delicacy of their forms, cut from black cardboard with scissors. Part of the atmosphere, and indeed action, of the play was Lotte's shadow on the wall behind her, cast by the single candle, that and her rather deep voice and heavy German accent as she narrated the events, the changes of scene, the transformation of the pumpkin and mice and so on; her characters almost conforming to Brecht's articulation of the idea of a characteristic *Gestus*. I remember one elegant bow by, I think, Dandini – it was the whole of his repertoire, but the more dramatically effective for that, and all the while the larger shadow on the wall moved and shifted as Lotte controlled the tiny shadow drama inside her miniature proscenium, each new setting delineated by an inner shadow proscenium which represented the beams of the kitchen, or the trees on the ride to the palace, or the magnificent ceiling of the ballroom. Her face, lit from beneath, as by a single footlight, concentrated on her primitive show and sometimes laughed indulgently at its naïvety.

*   *   *

In one final thrust to penetrate the unfathomable heart of *The Bacchae*, so long after the event, whilst poised over the cool white keys of my laptop, my eye lights on a piece of knotted white cotton rope, of the kind that, in our production, anchored the looped white canopy beneath which the tragedy unfolded: 'a silken palanquin that trembles when the Godhead reveals itself, giving to the destruction of the palace an impression of mania with calamity' (*The Times*, 11 July 1975).

Our dog, Bean, has just passed the knotted length by, as if it were some discarded theatrical prop, a thing inert and redundant; but tomorrow, terrier pup that she is, rescued and part of our family for only two months, she will endow this particular prop with life, attacking it with a 'heartfelt', convincingly savage growl and yet giving me a chance to grasp it unscathed so that the game can proceed. How on earth to tackle a play in which the heroine does not posses the emotional intelligence of a nine-month-old terrier; how to live in a world where Social Services deal, or fail to deal, with the fates that befall sons and daughters – fates that shouldn't happen to a dog?

Chapter 20

Shadows and Clouds: Prowse's *Malfi* and Alfreds's *Cherry Orchard*

On the occasion of the National Theatre's twenty-first birthday, in October 1984, Peter Hall announced the formation of five new resident companies under the NT's aegis, each composed of about twenty actors, controlled by different artistic directors, and with the remit to perform in a twelve-month period a minimum of three productions, one in each of the NT's auditoria.

Peter Hall with the directors of the five new NT companies.
L to R: David Hare, Peter Gill, Richard Eyre, Michael Bogdanov,
Ian McKellen and myself, Bill Bryden.
Photo: © Kenneth Saunders / Guardian News & Media Ltd 1984

Ian McKellen and I had been invited by Hall to head one of the companies, the only one to be managed by actors (the rest being led by various directors and one playwright-director, David Hare). Unlike our earlier collaborative enterprise, the Actors' Company, in which every decision was voted on by members of the company, the McKellen-Petherbridge Group was not, administratively speaking, a democracy; Ian and I were responsible for policy, the selection of plays and the choice of directors.

At the same time, we were part of the ensemble, taking leading and supporting roles and understudying. For our first season we invited on board the directors Philip Prowse and Mike Alfreds, 'two artists with diametrically opposed aesthetics and objectives.'[1]

*   *   *

It was a conversation stopper: 'Actors like Chekhov because he gives them the sort of things they like to do.' So said the director Philip Prowse one day, at a rehearsal for his production of Webster's *The Duchess of Malfi*, but you'd have to know Philip, or hear the tone of his voice and see the expression on his face, to appreciate the disdainful, reductive subtext. In Philip's *The Duchess of Malfi* we were doing what *he* liked to do. In fact, in the middle of the run, he came to see a performance one night and made it known that he thought we were 'out of tempo with the production'. His edited rehearsal script omitted all stage directions as well as the act and scene divisions; a nice clean, seamless acting script you might think, but some of the dialogue was edited out, too, and the cuts were illustrative of Philip's likes and dislikes.

Another of Philip's rehearsal-room conversation stoppers occurs to me, a remark summing up the legendary dancer Nijinsky. 'The only thing about Nijinsky,' he declared, 'was that he could jump higher than anyone else and had a big cock.' A rather different assessment from that made by one of Nijinsky's partners, Marie Rambert, founder of Ballet Rambert, in her autobiography *Quicksilver* (1972): 'One is often asked whether his jump was really as high as it is always described. To that I answer: I don't know how far from the ground it was, but I know it was near the stars. Who would watch the floor when he danced? He transported you at once into higher spheres in the sheer ecstasy of his flight.'

In the farewell scene in Act III, scene v of Webster's play, as Cariola carries the Duchess's baby in her arms, the Duchess says:

> And yet, O Heaven, thy heavy hand is in't.
> I have seen my little boy oft scourge his top
> And compared myself to't: nought made me e'er
> Go right but heaven's scourge-stick.

> Antonio. Do not weep:
> Heaven fashioned us of nothing, and we strive
> To bring ourselves to nothing. – Farewell Cariola,
> And thy sweet armful:
> (*To the Duchess*) if I do never see thee more,
> Be a good mother to your little ones,
> And save them from the tiger: fare you well.

---

[1] Simon Callow (1997), *The National*, p.52.

283

There was no place for 'the tiger' and 'the sweet armful' in Prowse's production. When we were planning the season, I had been enthusiastic when Ian suggested Philip, who always designs his own productions, as one of our directors. I'd never seen a production of his, but I had seen some of the marvellous photographs of them in the Glasgow Citizens' Theatre Company picture books, an aesthetic experience in themselves. The images were iconoclastic and, therefore, instantly iconic. Ian told me that Philip and his co-directors drastically lowered the seat prices at the Citz and attracted full houses of young devotees. I'd got the impression, from the photographs and from what I'd read and heard about the work, that his actors were young and sometimes raw, chosen for their striking looks and personalities rather than their steady grasp on conventional acting technique. I felt that if a largely more mature and experienced company were to work with such a gifted designer-director, with his radical approach to the classical repertoire, the combination could only be beneficial to both. Now if this reads as insufferably smug, it was smugness for which I would suffer.

Ian did warn me before we all three met in Philip's flat, above an antique chandelier shop in Kensington Church Street, that I might not warm to this often caustic man of strong opinions. We arrived whilst he was watching an Australian rugby match on the television; the players seemed to lure his attention away from the business at hand. He certainly didn't want me to play Ferdinand, the showy part of the Duchess's twin brother who has a couple of good mad scenes, though her other brother, the corrupt Cardinal, was a respectable second choice for me with the bonus of Sheila Hancock as my mistress, Julia, whom I would murder in the fifth act by means of a poisoned Bible.

As the Cardinal with Jonathan Hyde (Duke Ferdinand)
***in The Duchess of Malfi*, NT, 1985.**
Photo: © Donald Cooper

There would be the chance of enriching the company by virtue of having a good leading part left over to offer a strong actor, and in the event we were able to get Jonathan Hyde. I joked that, as the Cardinal, I would at least have a red silk costume, but Philip was adamant I wouldn't, and indeed we all wore black. I did, however, have some very narrow gauge red piping.

Philip, I discovered, had instinctive choreographic flair. Even in the rehearsal room, with four or five actors standing about as courtiers in their street clothes, he would offhandedly gesture to suggest a shift of position and the actors would create, as if by chance, a dynamic piece of meaningful movement and settle into a living Renaissance frieze with such a sense of period and purpose. In truth, this conjuring trick had a lot of dogged company dedication behind it. And our willowy, beleaguered movement consultant, Geraldine Stephenson, hovered discreetly, not to say diffidently, at the back of the rehearsal room, never quite knowing what Phillip wanted, yet authoritatively slipping in crash courses in attitude and various brands of bow that seemed to emerge as from sixteenth-century Italian paintings. Geraldine, incidentally, worked in that peculiar theatrical territory where dance (as Oscar Wilde said of truth) is rarely pure and never simple, especially when it comes to actors perfecting and memorizing steps; it's a territory where drama is not expressed in dance but where characters in a dramatic situation happen to be dancing. She was usually asked to make dancing look natural and sometimes to make what is naturalistic edge its way into dance.

The style of the production was much indebted to the motley and improbable crew of courtiers who endured long non-speaking hours on their feet. They included Hugh Lloyd and Roy Kinnear, both of them heroically submerging their veteran Light Entertainment auras. The first among these unequals was Phillip's invented silent character, Death, who was on stage all night, lurking in a corner in a hooded black cloak, ominously changing position from time to time and invariably, intimately part of each of the tragedy's terminal tableaux.

As a director of the McKellen-Petherbridge Group, you'd think I would have learnt about this character other than through my agent, Lindy King, who phoned me before the start of rehearsals to say that Philip was wondering whether I would like to play Death rather than the Cardinal. I was almost tempted, but thank God Lindy saw the ridiculous side of the idea: six weeks in a rehearsal room watching other people rehearse, whilst waiting to be rearranged occasionally in yet another morbid position, would have been the death of me. As it was, it was nothing to be called at 10 a.m. and not used until 3 p.m.

On the occasion Sheila Hancock and I opened our mouths in our first rehearsal of our first scene, Philip immediately drawled from his sitting position not six feet away, 'Oh don't give me that tired old RSC delivery, nothing in the theatre puts me to sleep faster.' Sheila, to her credit, laughed and said, 'What *do* you want me to sound like?'

'Oh, Nancy Cunard', he replied.

'It'll be hilarious – if you tell the truth' is what Sheila Hancock said to me when I told her I was writing my theatrical memoirs. In her own book, *Ramblings of an Actress*, I am firmly cast as a comic character in the McKellen-Petherbridge Group, a dab hand at the long 'well-turned' memo (she prints one of them in full) but also, as an actor, liable to come on without a vital, or rather lethal, prop with which to murder her in Philip's melodramatically shadowed production. She also refers to the night I can't recall when I must have upset the scansion of the verse by correcting myself:

> By my appointment the great Duchess of Malfi
> And two of her young children, four nights since,
> Were poisoned … Oh, and strangled.

I don't believe the 'Oh'. However, although Sheila had difficulty in suppressing her mirth, the audience remained silent. I would have remembered if I'd got a laugh on one of those nights of profound gloom and hush.

Sheila is less forthcoming about other details and darkly refers to, but does not divulge the identities of, the 'difficult' and 'dissenting' members of the company, amongst whom, in the interests of Truth, I must count myself.

Hugh Lloyd told me one day in the rehearsal room, in his mild, even-tempered way, that he had dubbed me 'Edward End-of-tether-bridge', but, according to Sheila's *Ramblings,* tenacity was one of my positive attributes.
I didn't intend to let two of our directors, Philip Prowse and Mike Alfreds (who directed the company in *The Cherry Orchard*) get away with murder in their surreally contrasting ways. I am ever the humorist, and even a diplomat up to a point, and was fascinated by these two men's very different directorial approaches. Prowse was all kinetics and grand gestures; I remember him saying to Jonathan Hyde, 'How do I know what you're thinking sitting there? I'm telling you it'll look effective if you do this move down centre, but if you want to think and turn down a really good move it's your funeral.'

Mike Alfreds wouldn't have dreamt of suggesting a move and certainly never of fixing one, however 'effective'. His rehearsals and every performance were based on minute analysis of the action of the play but driven by impromptu impulses of mood and movement that might fluctuate from moment to moment. He would even advocate incorporating or 'using' one's mood on an off night to positive advantage.

In *Malfi* it was important accurately to hit one's mark, near one of the spotlights for instance (footlights actually), to cast the right gigantic shadow on the back wall. Even one's entrances could only be timed by the cue light giving the stagehand his signal to open one of the great grey doors onto the set. We didn't have doors in *The Cherry Orchard*, though the openings onto the set were the only things one could count on being fixed; one might walk into a scene to find the furniture and the characters radically rearranged. How the creative fun of it catches hold of me again. I've just had to get up and try starting Gayev's speech to the bookcase by moving, not towards it, but across to the other side of the room, so as to address the whole family as well as the bookcase. Why didn't I think of this before; much funnier and more embarrassing.

With Hugh Lloyd (Firs) and Sheila Hancock (Ranevskaya)
in *The Cherry Orchard*, NT, 1985.
Photo: © Donald Cooper

***The Cherry Orchard*, NT, 1985. L to R: Eleanor Bron (Varya),**
Selina Cadell (Dunyasha), Sheila Hancock (Ranevskaya), Hugh Lloyd (Firs),
Roy Kinnear (Simeonov Pishchik), Ian McKellen (Lopakhin),
Claire Moore (Anya), myself (Gayev).
Photo: © Donald Cooper

Alfreds insisted on sixteen and a half weeks' rehearsal for *The Cherry Orchard*. He described his rehearsal method of embracing Stanislavski's Method as putting the play through a series – a long series – of Stanislavskian sieves. Space precludes anything like a full account; suffice it to give two examples of his method being reduced to the absurd by the sceptics in the company.

I recall an event in the windowless church hall of Notre Dame, just off Leicester Square. Ian and I were at first dismayed that, although we were working so hard, somebody had decided we would have to rehearse for several of our sixteen weeks, not in one of the National's South Bank rehearsal rooms but a Tube ride away in Soho. We failed to get the directive revoked. The travelling time seemed an imposition until we began to enjoy the 'real' atmosphere in our breaks, the slightly grubby life and choices on offer in Soho, rather than the comparatively arid aspect of the South Bank's massive concrete arts complex and the monotony of the NT canteen. Even the National's view of St Paul's had been obscured since Denys Ladun had designed IBM's headquarters next door to the east, compounding the insult to his own NT building by making its stark concrete exterior all the more stark beside IBM's swish 'pebble-dashed' finish. Our view through the windows of their superior light and airy canteen didn't help.

In our windowless Soho basement, Mike set an exercise in which each of us had the chance to observe the rest of the company populating that fluorescent-lit space with their ideas of our particular character. What I mean is that Sheila watched a roomful of Madam Ranevskayas, Ian of Lopakhins, myself of Gayevs and so on. Did we speak or just mime and 'behave' for the benefit of Mike and the actor actually cast in the part, depicting what Brecht would have called the 'Gestus' of whichever character? The process would go on for at least five minutes at a time, to give Mike and the actor time to survey all the different versions being presented.

What could I learn from a roomful of people miscast as Gayev, I wondered. And then I spotted, of all people, Roy Kinnear sitting at a little table on the left-hand side of the room, his half-moon spectacles on his nose. He had some papers on the table and a small pair of scissors with which he was cutting out labels of some kind. Of course! Gayev had a butterfly collection in which he was absorbed. Brilliant! I am afraid I can't tell you what Eleanor Bron's Gayev was like or anybody else's now, but I still remember dear Roy's. Otherwise, busily engaged in the depiction part of the exercise, one was properly too absorbed in one's character to notice what others did, and I only remember of my own depictions that I achieved a good bit of business as Yepikhodov, and managed to get a laugh from Alfreds and Laurance Rudic, despite the simultaneous competition of sixteen other Yepikhodovs.

Ian and I were assigned a ghastly little box of an office in the South Bank concrete in which to meet and use the phone; the dividing walls might have been cardboard and, if they had been dressing rooms, you could have heard the actor next door changing his vest. As it was, you could practically hear David Hare next door changing his mind. We seldom used the room, but it was in our cubicle that Ian and I compared notes after the exercise I've been describing.

'Roy was good as Lopakhin,' Ian said. 'He was sitting at a little table on the left of the room with papers. He had a little pair of scissors and he was making notes and calculating and cutting out little labels. Brilliant. Lopakhin thinks about money all the time, he was doing his accounts!'

I told Ian that the same activity had conveyed to me Gayev's butterfly collection. When questioned, Roy confessed that he had used the whole exercise, apart from when it was his turn to watch the parade of Pishchiks, to complete his VAT return.

It is in the Old Vic rehearsal room, another venue we were shipped off to, that I can still see Eleanor Bron knitting, though she didn't pass knitting off as character acting. There was a faint air of the guillotine about the activity, as if it were intended to take up the slack of the tedium, to do something useful while waiting – waiting for the discussion to end, or any part of the rehearsal in which she wasn't dynamically involved. It was in this room we did an exercise which involved enacting the big group scenes and turning the focus onto one particular character, that is, it was decided everybody would be particularly aware of Yasha, say, or Anya. Like the previous exercise, it was time-consuming since every character had to undergo this treatment, and then would follow discussion about the 'outcome' achieved, what we had noticed or discovered or felt. After we had all been particularly aware of Eleanor's Varya, Eleanor had taken up her usual seat in the room with her back against the wall. Eventually she was asked what she had felt. With a completely deadpan expression, she said, 'Well, I decided that Varya must be suffering from a terminal condition of some kind because everybody seemed so inordinately concerned about her.' I don't know how the rehearsal recovered from this depth charge.

When we were ready to open, I couldn't see how the production would recover from one particular aspect of the design. But first I must go back fourteen weeks or so to a rehearsal room and record the elation of the very first group effort, the scene early in Act One when the party returns from the station, accompanying Ranevskaya and Anya. Of course this big group entrance and the ensuing scene were never 'blocked', to use that dreadful term that quite often does *block* the scene. It was as if a cork had been released from a bottle in which was a 'preparation'; in fact, the moment of release had been long prepared for, so that we knew a lot about who we all were, our relationships and motives. At last back we came from the station, laughing, some chattering; nobody collided, nobody ended up in the 'wrong' place. Then we discussed the event. We must have done the entrance and part of the scene three times that morning, each time differently without making calculated adjustments of position, pace or tone – and each time it felt 'right'. Heady stuff!

All the more reason why certain of the design elements proved worrisome. Mike had said from the beginning that he had no end product in view, that wherever we had got to when it came time to open, that would be what we'd present (always allowing for the impromptu element intrinsic to the work). But to have any costumes or set to present, they had to be planned in advance and were designed ahead of rehearsals. There was one rather surprising element that we all 'bought'. In the case of the costumes, each act of the play had its own colour scheme, and the general tone became paler as the four acts progressed. Any individual actor could decide to make their character more defined and vivid as the play progressed if they thought that was what the author demanded. The furniture was pale (and remained pale throughout), painted a matte bluish grey, and the 'walls' of the interiors were a nebulous grey fabric; gauze was in evidence. We had seen two small, slightly different and rather rudimentary models of Paul Dart's set in which there was a sky background with clouds, seen most of the time through gauze. When the set was erected, the clouds were far from nebulous; they were hard-edged, painted in cream, pale yellow and pink, reminiscent, I thought, of swirled ice-cream desserts. I argued that the clouds made a bold statement, were quite wrong and, in any case, not what the models had led us to expect.

I wonder now if there might have been a simple explanation: Mike had hoped that, over the weeks, a style of playing the text would evolve with a vaudevillian element to it, something at any rate rather more presentational than we seemed as a company willing or able to move towards. The clouds had to go, I was sure.

There was another stumbling block I thought, an extraordinary one in view of the latitude we were given in nightly performance of the play; it was that the final 'gesture' of the performance was an entirely scenic one, and would remain the same however we played the last moments. I don't mean the points of sunlight showing on the walls as little beams shone through the vents in the shutters as they are closed from the outside on the darkened, supposedly empty house, whilst sounds of the cherry orchard being chopped down are heard. That is what I still remember from the Moscow Art Theatre's production, which came from behind the Iron Curtain in 1958. We had no 'real' walls or windows. There was a white gauze canopy high over the set and it was contrived that this would suddenly snap away from its moorings and float down to the stage floor as the lights faded. It seemed to me altogether anomalous that a production so organically composed of the temperaments and human impulses of its actors should close on a statement made by the designer and his piece of gauze and effect! Somehow or other Mike argued his corner over this conceit (whether his or his designer's). Perhaps those of us passionate about the clouds had found the battle over their dispersal sufficiently disruptive. That battle had started when we were all sitting in the steep slope of the Cottesloe stalls and glad to be there, about to open our third production and add *The Cherry Orchard* to the cake in the actors' favourite NT space, so intimate after the cavernous Olivier and the intransigent concrete box of the Lyttelton.

I was rather devious in my opposition. My idea of diplomacy is to go along with things quite equably until they become completely unacceptable. Then I explode – unpleasantly. So I thought it would be better if I didn't instigate a discussion about the clouds. Instead, I leant over to Selina Cadell in the seat in front and suggested that she might bring the subject up, which, amazingly she did. There was an uneasy consensus against the clouds and people proposed quite radical alternatives, like our doing the play in a set of plain black drapes. Ian was rather quiet and uncommitted, but he is colourblind and part of that percentage of the average audience who would be spared the flavoured ice-cream effect I found so antipathetical.

There were budget implications, of course, and Ian and I found ourselves in Peter Hall's office discussing them. Quite rightly Peter did not wish to be on any side of the argument. In the event, the toning down of the clouds to something more nebulous and subtle, for which I began to feel heavily responsible, took several applications of paint over several days.

I had too long to think about Gayev; I was so busy taking advantage of the unusually generous rehearsal period and trying to be pure, eschewing the possibility of doing any old tricks or taking short cuts and carefully avoiding being 'caught out acting', that I think I opened barely giving a performance at all. Alfreds told me during rehearsals that I was a 'strangely timid' actor.

The sixteen and a half weeks we spent rehearsing *The Cherry Orchard* could be justified financially because, by then, we were playing in repertoire *Malfi* and a double bill, Sheila's production of Sheridan's *The Critic* in tandem with Stoppard's production of his own *The Real Inspector Hound*. Tom had agreed to direct his short one-act play on one firm condition. He had undertaken to have a week's fishing with his son. It fell in the middle of the proposed rehearsal period, but he must honour the familial arrangement. I forget how we managed without him, but I recall how keen I was to be seen to have improved in his absence.

I based my theatre critic, Moon, on Nicholas de Jongh, not that I knew him at all, but he wasn't quite a stranger; I had read, and been criticized by, him over the years, and had seen him across crowded rooms. Perhaps that's why my part of the *Inspector Hound* evening was *not* enchanted. During previews, Tom took the opportunity to have a word in my ear, telling me that he and Miriam thought my Moon the best they had seen, but he wished I could have 'more fun' with the part.

Selina Cadell pushed the boat out and had fun with the housekeeper, Mrs Drudge, in the play within the play, boldly stretching out the coffee-serving business in rehearsal until it unnerved Tom. She begged him to wait for the audience reaction and was hilariously vindicated. When we took our repertoire to Chicago in 1986 for an International Theatre Festival we had a chequered time, but ended in triumph. I got my best review for some master classes I gave and we were granted free membership of a new heath club, a sprint away along the lakeside and I thoroughly enjoyed myself, occasionally musing about Peter Wimsey, the part I had been invited to do for a new BBC series and which I would rehearse two or three days after I got back.

The Real Inspector Hound, NT, 1985.
L to R: Eleanor Bron (Lady Cynthia Muldoon), Roy Kinnear (Birdboot),
myself (Moon), Jonathan Hyde (Major Magnus Muldoon),
Ian McKellen (Inspector Hound).
Photo: © Donald Cooper

All this I took in my stride, just as this afternoon I took in my stride that I was sitting in a Soho waiting room with a distinguished actor of many RSC great roles and, as we chatted, we remembered that we once did a radio play together. I saw his Hamlet thirty odd years ago, but today we were almost certainly up for the same cameo TV part and would have to audition our 'sides' for the powers and the little camera.

I was approaching Chicago's Blackstone Theatre for a matinée one day and was dismayed to see hordes of unruly teenagers and younger children tumbling out of buses and into the theatre. What did they know of the English country-house whodunit play that we were parodying? What would they make of Sheridan's two-hundred-year-old jokes about a tragedy being rehearsed at Covent Garden?

They reacted boisterously when the auditorium dimmed and then were all attention. So far so good. They seemed to get the joke about Roy Kinnear and me as the first-night critics, and from the moment Selina answered the telephone with her brilliant first line, a line one must surely have read in a hundred French's Acting Editions to 'get' Tom's joke, they were ours and stayed with us riotously on and into the eighteenth century to be rewarded by the extravagant effects of Sheila's production, as Bill Dudley's period scenery celebrated in comic catastrophe.

292

**Selina Cadell dressed as Mrs Drudge
from *The Real Inspector Hound*,
caught at the stage door of the
Blackstone Theatre, Chicago in 1986.**
Photo: © EP

**And as an actress in William Dudley's
set of *The Critic*, Olivier Theatre, 1985.**
Photo: © EP

The McKellen-Petherbridge Group ended its life in Chicago; a few actors had other offers, and a chance of doing *The Cherry Orchard* in the West End was something I could not take and Ian wanted to eschew. All the scenery from our three productions had to be seen to be burnt in America after we had done our last Saturday night in Chicago, to satisfy some regulation that it would not be salvaged and re-used.

One could say that our whole scheme went up in smoke, but no more than so many others have done. One has to be in the business of striking a new spark, and of not being sentimental about one's old flames.

293

Mr Dickens / Mr Shakespeare

With my travelling busts of Shakespeare and Dickens.

Chapter 21

Life and Adventures with Newman Noggs

 *In which Smike meets Leonard Bernstein, Newman Noggs has the opportunity to meet Andy Warhol, and nobody notices the ghost of Sarah Bernhard's Hamlet; containing as well many facts and faithfully reported incidents relating to that extraordinary process – the contrivance of the celebrated theatrical engine remembered on both sides of the Atlantic with such affection, with highlights and sidelights reflecting on the everyday craft of the theatre in rehearsal and performance – its peculiar alchemy and its ultimate power for good; none of this necessarily in chronological order.*

For some fortunate, resilient children, the eight hours and forty minutes of *Nicholas Nickleby* was their first experience of live theatre. For whatever socio-economic reasons, we saw few children in any of the New York audiences, even though we played across the Christmas holidays, but in London it was different. Someone told me about a little girl who clung to the brass rail on the front of the gallery at the end of the full 2 p.m. to 11.40 p.m. marathon one Saturday (an hour's break for dinner and two twenty-minute intervals), protesting, a little tearfully, that she didn't want to go home. Not everyone felt like that, of course. Peter Hall and his teenage daughter sat in two of the best stalls one Saturday matinée, near the little gantry which enabled us to walk out into the audience, our feet at seatback height, but their two places were conspicuously empty in the evening. I think it was in one of those same seats, on another Saturday, we spotted Alan Bennett, who may well have loved the whole event but who certainly couldn't help wearing an *oh please don't come and talk to me* expression when the actors did their perambulations about the auditorium. The seventy-three-year-old Laurence Olivier, looking so much older and frailer than when I'd last worked with him in his television *Lear*, sat through the entire thing one Saturday on the prompt-side end seat of the dress circle's front row. Shouldn't there be a little brass plaque in remembrance? Peter Barkworth was there that same afternoon with Wyn Jones, who has since become Director of Acting at the Guildhall School of Music and Drama. When the two of them came round after Part Two, Wyn reminds me, they had to walk round the block three times before entering the stage door to see Emily and me because each time they had burst into tears on the threshold.

We were always aware of who was out front because of our attempt to break down the respected, time-honoured *them-and-us* great divide of the Victorian picture-frame stage. I used to make it my business to go up into the gallery during the interval of the second half. 'Twenty-three years ago,' someone said to me recently, 'I was so impressed you had troubled to come up to us there.' They were talking to someone who, as a child, had watched enviously from the gallery at the Bradford Alhambra as the fairies of Kirby's Flying Ballet flew out into the auditorium, tossing bunches of violets into the orchestra stalls and dress circle, and the pantomime dog cavorted on the wide upholstered curve of the dress circle's ledge below ours. During *Nickleby* in London, though always a little abashed at the idea, I tried to bring a touch of all that to the upper reaches of the Aldwych: I knew from experience that those seats could feel a little remote. A sense of remoteness is not part of my recollection of the Bradford Alhambra's 1944 *Humpty Dumpty* (I can still see Norman Evans as Dame Trot in his 'Over the Garden Wall' sketch), but in 1970 I'd seen Peter Brook's RSC production of Shakespeare's *A Midsummer Night's Dream* (better known as *Brook's Dream)* from the Aldwych Gallery, and this may be part of the reason why my opinion of that hallowed production is a heretical one. In fact, you could get the Brechtian Alienation Effect up there, even in romantic productions. In those days, it was partly to do with the noise of the ventilation system, which literally and metaphorically disturbed the atmosphere. I suspect some *Nickleby* galleryites may not have realized that breaking the barrier between stage and auditorium was part of the show. They often looked askance at me as, spilling out to get to the bar, they met me coming the other way to give a little touch of Newman Noggs to those still occupying the steep terraces of seats.

I know now that I signed the young Alex Jennings's programme at the back of the stalls one night – at his mother's request he tells me, but he's kept the trophy. For so many people I meet, the show remains a precious memory. It was in 1999 (I can work out the year because it was at Ian McKellen's 60th birthday party) that the perfectly sane, steady producer and sometime director of the Edinburgh International Festival, John Drummond, said to me: 'But don't you remember we met on the stairs at the side of the stalls during an interval in *Nickleby* and you said, "What are you doing here?", and I burst into tears?'

A brush with Andy Warhol

In New York, when I spotted Andy Warhol during an interval, I didn't indulge in such familiar levity. I was just about to walk the plank out into the audience and there he was, with his unmistakably fixed and flyaway ash-blond hair, sitting in the stalls of the Plymouth Theatre on 44th St, about seven rows back and maybe six seats from the end, ravaged and wraith-like, though he was only fifty-three at that time. Well, one of his starlets had taken a pot shot at him in 1968. Such was the creative strain in The Factory.

Warhol was in placid, or rather constrained, interval mode, dressed in a nondescript dark suit, sitting below me on the right, perhaps fifteen feet away, amongst a few empty seats, the people around him not having yet returned. He was quite out of the celebrity-studded context in which he had been so frequently photographed, and remote from the goings on in his Factory bedecked in silver foil. For a moment I doubted my own eyes. There was no sense of a party, no movie camera, no adjacent teenagers in and, half or entirely, out of denim, nobody screenprinting, composing music or filming the proceedings. He looked astonishingly alone.

CHARLES DICKENS MEETS ANDY WARHOL. Could there be a more unlikely encounter? I sit here aghast at the lost opportunity because Newman Noggs *could* have met him. Was it timidity on my part? Actually, he was the one who looked timid and vulnerable sitting there, so much so that I felt as if it would be invasive, exploitative to take advantage of my opportunity. It was as if the time had come for him to experience his fifteen minutes of anonymity.

He wasn't even reading the programme (which contained my excellent little essay on Dickens's theatre), always a useful theatregoing activity to defend oneself from looking friendless or at a loose end when alone in a theatre seat. Carefully bearing his burden of being Andy Warhol, Andy didn't disturb his ever so slightly uneasy gaze to take me in; so I left him there alone, looking like a piece of flotsam that had floated away from its jetsam, when I could so easily have sat quietly beside him and said … what? In my make-up and aged, tattered Victorian clothes, selected from an obscure rail at Nathan's back home in Camden Town, I don't think I could have worked out what to say, or who to be, in relation to this fragile contemporary icon, whom the press and whose own publicity machine had made public property. In this context he seemed delicate and entirely private property. In what capacity would I have introduced myself? He was an artist and I one of the artistes, to give the term the French spelling I remember from notices bearing lists of backstage rules in the days when I played the kind of theatres where Variety was usually performed.

On the assembly line

The Royal Shakespeare Company was, and is, a world-famous brand, but along with the rest of this particular troupe of turns, mercenaries under the RSC flag of convenience, I was, at the time of my (almost) meeting with Andy Warhol, nearing the end of my contract and would soon be flying home to start the usual process, part-hunt, part-waiting game, for the next job. Understandably, none of the directors planning the next season in Stratford were keen on the strong scent of what was so soon to become the theatrical past, a smell that might adhere to us and taint their work. *Nickleby* was the summation of a period of some two or three years (at least), during which a particular chemistry had been created as people worked together across the varied repertoire.

When *Nicholas Nickleby* originally opened it was left to our own consciences just how much of this *meet the public* thing we did; likewise our presence on the set as spectators during parts of the action in which we were not involved was not exactly compulsory. We weren't assigned times and positions of duty, like sentries, but I remember Trevor Nunn's injunction: 'When you've exited, your priority must be to get back onto the stage to observe and feed energy back into the action by your attention.' There was something curiously effective about the result. I realized this particularly when, towards the end of the New York run, the cast was getting very tired and there was much dereliction of this duty – that is to say amongst those of us who'd ever seriously bothered to perform it – and from out front John Napier's inspired set, a cross between a Victorian junkyard and an aged sailing ship in dry dock, did look strangely desolate when bereft of the still, intent witnesses. Part of my self-imposed routine was to watch Nicholas and Smike's arrival in Portsmouth with Vincent Crummles, and their introduction to the Crummles Theatre Company. Night after night I always sat in the same spot on the bridge above and behind the action. 'Night after night' is the operative phrase. In fact, it was within Charles Dickens's lifetime that the phrase 'night after night' came fully into its own in the theatrical sense; steam locomotion and vast growing urban concentrations of population created conditions ripe, for the first time since Thespis, for actors to face the problem of playing the same play seven or eight times a week for a run of 100, 200, even 300 or 400 performances. The first of these long runs of the same play with the same cast, the same set, the same moves and inflections rolled off the London and New York stages decades before Ford's assembly line.

Amazingly, from the cast's day one, *Nickleby* was almost eight months in the making. Despite 'progress', the rehearsal period is the time when, at the end of every day, one has a slightly different handmade product to show for one's labours. During all that time we continued to perform the rest of the RSC repertoire, yet the result of this immense investment of time was initially scheduled for just six weeks of performances at the Aldwych. *By public demand*, as Vincent Crummles himself might have said, it was brought back for a further two months and again later for a few weeks more, before we spent six weeks televising it at the Old Vic, were given one delicious day off, Saturday (for packing), spent the long Sunday in a church hall near Red Lion Square, working with some cast replacements, before flying the next day to New York for technical and dress-rehearsals and a sixteen-week season in which we played the full eight-hour-and-forty-minute version three times a week, and Parts One and Two only on Wednesdays and Thursdays respectively.

My vantage point on that bridge, overlooking Nicholas and Smike meeting the Crummles Company at the theatre in Portsmouth, was above the battle yet intimately in amongst the action. An enviable perch I had on that bridge compared to that of any New Yorker who'd paid $100 for a seat on the back or even the front row of the mezzanine![1] And yet and yet, we human beings are only programmed for certain kinds of repetition – try working on a production line! The painter John Constable said, two years before Dickens wrote *Nicholas Nickleby*: 'The world is wide; no two days are alike, nor even two hours, neither were there ever two leaves of a tree alike since the creation of the world; and the genuine productions of art, like those of nature, are all distinct from each other.' (That could have been my opening gambit with Mr Warhol, followed by 'So what's with the Campbell's Soup Cans, Andy?') Constable's 'selections of some of the forms of nature, and copies of a few of her evanescent effects' are one thing. *Quite* another are the practicalities and disciplines of post-Industrial Revolution theatrical performance and presentation. The evanescence of a first night, for all its terrors, is a doddle compared to a Saturday or a wet Thursday matinée six months in, simply because that heady sense of discovery, of life on the high wire is what the actor gets gratis at the beginning of a run. In fact, paradoxically, he tries to harness it, tame it even, all the time working to convert it into a manageable, safe 'routine' lest it escape (or kill him). But within the ultimately achieved, practised framework, the most vital ingredient is the sense of spontaneity, even danger. This very spontaneity is what becomes more and more 'expensive' to produce as a commodity the more times it has to be repeated, as the performer yearns for the wide world where no two hours are alike.

Watching chunks of *Nickleby* became strangely debilitating and began to spoil the show for me. But one night in New York, almost accidentally, I allowed a sense of excitement and novelty into my routine by a simple arbitrary change as I watched the arrival in Portsmouth. I was immediately above the action on the OP gantry, the pony and cart just below, nothing more than two low stools on an unmoving table in a circle of light, an imagined pony, imagined reins, Crummles describing to Smike and Nicholas a former pony's theatrical career as a performer, two sons behind, one providing the sound of hooves with coconut shells as they all gently rocked with the motion of the journey. I had a tiny part in this sequence: on the cue of Crummles's line, 'Here we are', as he drew up the reins, I inserted my imitation of a seagull's cry, after which Crummles would say 'Portsmouth.' This received a very good laugh and often a round of applause in London, an uncertain reaction in New York and on the DVD my throat is not quite in the giving vein.

Well, that night, as Nicholas and Smike met the Crummles Company, I didn't go round to watch them from the bridge behind but from out front, walking the other way and squatting on that walkway attached to the curve of the mezzanine. Dear reader, you could have been there, perhaps half aware of someone, not quite Newman and not entirely Petherbridge. To my delighted surprise, quite suddenly in this simple change of perspective, I saw the stage

---

[1] Every seat in the house was the same price. The first hundred-dollar seat on Broadway, but they effectively got two shows for their money.

of the Theatre Royal Portsmouth afresh, heaving with the life of the Crummles Company. I could scan the picture at will and find every corner of it alive, though I found myself choosing to look in the 'right' places at the right characters at the right times. The flow and rhythm of it appeared effortless with neither a whiff of routine nor cunningly contrived choreography. Only the most sensitive direction and committed, generous acting can create that kind of ensemble magic. I suppose the vigorous, teeming, detailed sense of life which re-enchanted me that night was the impression audiences got in scene after scene (night after night), interspersed with moments of delicate intimacy between small groups of characters, in duologues, in sharply focused moments of solo or group narration and, of course, in those set pieces when the company burst into song or caused the audience to applaud a stagecoach when there was no stagecoach, to visualize all manner of 'forms of nature' and 'evanescent effects'. I recall seeing, in an on-stage rehearsal, John Caird, with Mulberry Hawk, Nicholas and nameless characters, wielding a wastepaper basket, a piece of black silk and a chair, from which they conjured the rearing horse, the cabriolet. What was at the heart of the trick of it? The special quality within the immediacy of the experience could be traced back to the initial five-week rehearsal period in Stratford-upon-Avon towards the end of the Shakespeare season of 1978 when the days were shortening and the town was quiet.

A spectacular pig in a poke

We were all playing at night, some of us most nights, in several productions in repertoire, either at the Other Place (then still the original wood-framed, tin-clad hut) or in the main house, that vast 1930s Odeon-on-Avon. We met at 10.30 each morning and sat in a large circle until 5.30 p.m. Eventually, the acting company demanded that a whistle be blown at 5.30, and I mean an *actual* whistle, to release us for our precious statutory break. The 'whistle-blower', Hilary Groves as often as not, would contrive to catch Trevor Nunn in his summation at the end of a sentence before his next intake of breath. By then we'd told and retold parts of the story to one another in many ways, discussed, imagined, improvised, and shared our investigations and research. There was a playwright but no script, two directors and their assistant but no cast list. Occasionally the designer, John Napier, came and observed, but there was as yet no model of the set waiting in a corner to be revealed from under a dustsheet. Eventually there was a composer, dear brilliant man, but not a dot on a stave. There was, in fact, no blueprint nor master plan, nothing but a theatre company in a big room, a slightly insecure sense of belonging and common purpose – and a novel of some 939 pages of small print.

The big room was within the burnt-out brick shell of Stratford's first custom-built theatre, 1870s Victorian fairytale Gothic in style. I have a contemporary sepia postcard of the great bulk of it by moonlight, a sort of Stratford St Pancras Riverside Station Hotel, dwarfing Holy Trinity Church upstream in the background. There had been a fire in 1926 and in the salvaging process the theatre's medieval turrets had been amputated and the steeply pitched roof flattened. Meanwhile it was being eclipsed as the externals of a state-of-the-art 1930s model biscuit factory were attached and rudely imposed upon the otherwise little-changed heart of Shakespeare's market town. Within the 1879 brick-built shell, in place of the vanished stage and auditorium, was the 'Conference Room', where nowadays there is the superb realization of a dream – the intimate space of the Swan theatre, then only a twinkle in the anonymous donor's eye. There was nothing dreamy about the Conference Room; no self-respecting ghost from the old days haunted its dilapidated, 30s-style functional look, no shades of Old Bensonians, as famous for their cricket as their athletic way with Shakespeare. There was no echo of the nightingale's song from the hedge beyond the town's playing field, nor any lingering sensation of the 'throbbing mystery of life in song and silence' that once 'came through the windows in the actors' dressing rooms.'[2] And who could have guessed that Sarah Bernhardt had played a special matinée of *Hamlet* within this horseshoe in 1899?

The Memorial, Stratford-on-Avon.

The old Memorial Theatre, Stratford, which burnt down in 1926.

Our efforts were lit by a sort of streetlight placed high in the ceiling. It gave us all a slightly greenish pallor once the daylight started to give up the struggle around 3 p.m. At the semicircular end of the room there was a pair of modern curving staircases, sweeping symmetrically high up to nowhere in particular. I never saw them used. But, of course, it was a place for dreams. The entire company had been called to a meeting in it, at which the *Nickleby* project was announced and an invitation issued: to turn up on day one of a five-week period of preparation, which would be followed, after the company

---

[2] Frank Benson in a foreword to *Shakespeare's Heroines* (1926).

holiday, by the six-week Newcastle season and the long London season of the existing repertoire, during which, until May, rehearsals for the emergent Dickens play would continue. You must remember that only a company justifying its existence by performing a full repertoire could enjoy the working luxury of such an extended rehearsal period. It was emphasized that 'exploration' would be the keyword for those first five weeks, a process in which the full participation of every single member of the company would be expected. This initial five weeks was only one week short of the RSC's standard rehearsal period to put on, say, *Othello*, *Julius Caesar* or *The Merry Wives of Windsor* (each of these, at that time, part of the repertoire), but in this special case, clearly, it was the time allotted to sail round the tip of the Dickensian iceberg and take soundings. It has to be said that, contractually, every member of the company had the right to terminate his or her engagement, having completed the Stratford and follow-on Newcastle seasons, rather than commit to the second year and the London season. So this project came at the crucial 'make your mind up' time. Obviously, from the management's point of view, the less time spent during the ensuing months in re-rehearsing acting replacements in the existing repertoire, the better. There was to be an agreement that whoever came through that door on day one would be guaranteed a part or, more likely, parts in *Nickleby*; at the same time there was a suggestion that one might not get *out* of the room quite so easily without being committed to play whatever parts one landed in whatever play transpired. Within a few days the deal was modified to allow actors to extract themselves at the end of this exploratory period if they were not happy with how things were turning out for them. This enormous, unprecedented, thrilling scheme was quickly perceived to be the most spectacular pig in a poke any of us had ever been invited to buy. Maybe the five weeks were going to be the most extended audition any of us had attended; in the event, after the Christmas break, another three weeks' preparatory work were added before the directors felt the project was sufficiently advanced and a cast list could be announced. Meanwhile, potentially, each of us would have the opportunity to make a uniquely formative contribution to the dramatization of *Nicholas Nickleby* in its entirety. After that initial meeting there were some days for us all to think the scheme over. In the meantime there were other performances to give, the thick novel to read and agents to ring. It was September 1979.

There was absolutely no doubt in my mind: of course I would go on, happy with the parts I was already doing and having sufficient faith in my usefulness to the project to believe I'd land something worthwhile, and I was intrigued. Though a relatively new boy, I already felt I was a part of Trevor's inner sanctum by virtue of my work with him in the previous year, but then it was his special talent, whilst running with Terry Hands a great trundling machine like the RSC, to make whatever corner of it he happened to be dealing with seem the most important thing in the universe. In fact, I had only become part of the Stratford company that year because Trevor had decided to revive his production of *Three Sisters* from the previous year's first-ever small-scale tour.

Three Sisters fitted beautifully into the Other Place, the workaday tin hut I think of with such affection. It was at the extreme other end of the scale from the *Nickleby* project, and there was something wonderfully prodigal about the way in which the RSC's resources were lavished on those few square feet of unremarkable grey bare boards, the boards the audience had to cross to get to their moulded plastic seats around its edges or to reach the tiny three-sided gallery, a mere dropped-programme flutter away from the actors. Given a good production it was sheer luxury for the audience, even though or perhaps, embarrassingly, *because* they had to share the loos with the cast. With this experience behind one, how could one ever have felt a moment's diffidence encountering the *Nickleby* audience in the safety of a plush and gilt auditorium?

Emily (Irina) in *Three Sisters* with Janet Dale (Olga) and Suzanne Bertish (Masha), Other Place, Stratford. Griffith Jones (Chebutikin) far right.
Photo: © EP

With Suzanne Bertish (Masha) in *Three Sisters*, RSC small-scale tour, 1978.
Photo: © Chris Davies

Did anyone caution Trevor about the advisability, during a funding crisis, of investing an entire Aldwych season's resources for new work in the dramatization of a novel by Charles Dickens? Apropos of intervention, around the same time I had been rehearsed as a replacement into an Other Place curiosity, a Soviet farce, in which Roger Rees played the lead, a play called *The Suicide* by Nikolai Erdman. Joseph Stalin had found time, whilst tyrannizing Russia and the entire Soviet Union (and pulling the wool over the British Left's eyes) to write cautionary letters to Stanislavski at the Moscow Art Theatre about the inadvisability of doing Erdman's plays. If anyone did caution Trevor about Dickens, we may be sure it was not at Prime Ministerial level. Incidentally, it was in Moscow that Trevor had discovered the MAT's staging of Dickens's *The Pickwick Papers* in its 1935–6 season. This had been the spark.

It is highly likely that, had we all been members of the Moscow Art Theatre, we might still be together and, despite the collapse of the Soviet Union, still playing *Nickleby* in our repertoire. Simon Callow told me at a Christmas party in 2003 that he was off to Moscow to see the 1910 Stanislavski production of Maeterlinck's *The Blue Bird*. In the event it was a massive let down: the original orchestral music was recorded rather than played live; it was a New Year's Day matinée for children and the actors looked thoroughly fed up to be there; the settings looked dated and drab; and clearly he would have been better merely to have read about and imagined the original. As for *NN*, it has been reissued in the digitally re-mastered TV

306

version we made at the Old Vic. I have met people who say that it has been an annual Christmas or New Year ritual for years to watch as a family the video they originally recorded from the telly. Emily and I have dipped judiciously into it from time to time; the last taste made me feel like demanding a retake of the scene where Noggs escorts Kate and her mother to Thames Street (too much face acting on my part – less can be more, Edward). But writing these words is as good as a trip in a time machine, travelling back for a day into that magic circle under the Conference Room 'street lamp' with the prospect of dashing home with Emily to the flat in Welcombe Road to snatch something to eat and a nap before walking back through the dark, empty town to the tin hut, with its hopeful returns queue, Emily to perform Irina, and I Vershinin in *Three Sisters*, whilst down the road, foregathered apparently from nowhere, a huge audience would be watching *Julius Caesar*.

Nostalgia and sentiment aside, how did one really feel during that preparation period? There was a lot of homework. We formed ourselves into pairs, having been assigned research projects on every aspect of the life in the novel, coming back into the circle to hear one another's results. Emily and I covered the theatre, agreeing that a magic lantern slideshow lecture would be the thing – theatrical in itself with our recorded narration and appropriate soundtrack of Hummel played on a Fortepiano. We'd once seen a real Victorian magic lantern show on a covered barge in Little Venice, music provided by musical boxes and a harmonium, with an original lantern and antique glass slides, some of which had moving parts so that fires and waterfalls and even animated figures doing simple clown routines could be depicted. It was strangely touching and one understands how the Albert Hall could have been filled by the more lavish and ambitious shows. Al Gore has demonstrated afresh the potency of the slideshow with *An Inconvenient Truth*, his documentary about global warming.

In an interview, Trevor was quoted as saying that watching our little effort had for him an empowering effect on the project. We'd raided the modest riches of Stratford's public library. I photographed every quaint old illustration we had found and we wove curious pieces of information from memoirs and diaries into a commentary. In a book on Charles Kean, the famous Edmund's son, known for his spectacular historically 'correct' productions of Shakespeare, we found a list of the impressive number of stage hands, supers, musicians, dancers, actors, scene painters etc. etc. employed in his production of *A Midsummer Night's Dream*. I wrote the list out in brown ink in my best nineteenth-century longhand, cut it up and mounted it, an item or two at a time, in glass slides, and projected the information to the strain of Mendelssohn's Wedding March. Mendelssohn had written the music we all know for Charles Kean's very production of the *Dream*, though the wedding march for Theseus and Hypolita's nuptials came later. (Peter Brook, ever a dab hand at the surefire popular effect, used it in his *Dream*.) Strictly, all this was a touch late, not precisely the Vincent

Crummles period, but it threw the shortcomings of Crummles's forced-to-tour outfit into focus.

We also lashed out £85 on an 1892 edition of Pierce Egan's *The Life of an Actor*, which we saw displayed tantalizingly in Vaughan's antiquarian bookshop, first published in 1825 with numerous illustrations, now 'faithfully facsimiled and coloured by hand'; one thinks of some poor relation of the miniature painter, Miss La Creevy, taking in the original printed illustrations to colour. This was the perfect source, encompassing triumph and adversity. One of the rather naïve illustrations of a thin house strikes a particularly convincing note for any actor with an intimate knowledge of that phenomenon, and, as you may know, *NN* opened to very modest houses in London, indeed so much so that we would invite those at the rear to come forward to fill the empty rows and create a more homogeneous atmosphere.

I have been in rehearsals where one is all too aware that one is part of an almost industrial HIT-manufacturing process. The *NN* process was more like adult education or even theatre therapeutic encounter group work. We had over twenty lots of research to listen to, there being more than forty of us. We told the story of the novel, each member of the company charged to prepare and précis a chapter or so, extempore. We got through the novel *twice* in that way, perhaps hoping to be pithier and more entertaining the second time; we were neither, although John Woodvine lightened the tone by giving an outrageous parody of a précis with shameless music hall puns.

We speculated on how the story might best be told theatrically, that is *staged*, and we shared our impressions of theatre and film versions of Dickens. We'd all heard radio dramatizations with an actor reading linking pieces of narration, and my heart sank slightly as I imagined one of us done up as Dickens, narrating from a chair in a corner. Dipping into the DVD lately, I felt a burst of affection and admiration for the company as I saw how ultimately engagingly the sections of the narration were shared and spoken and how the essential voice of Dickens was present.

The theatre company Shared Experience had, in fact, done a groundbreaking version of *Bleak House* in 1977, directed by Mike Alfreds, which few of us had seen but which was, I'm certain, a major influence. Morning trips to the old local Stratford cinema were scheduled for two special screenings of famous black-and-white adaptations, entertaining and lightweight failures to present the whole. That was what Trevor kept emphasizing – a sense of the great sweep of the entire book, heart and soul. To this end the exercises proliferated. For example, every single member of the company was invited to present a dramatic sketch of any one of the characters and I still remember one or two of these, a Smike and particularly the Infant Phenomenon of Julie Peasgood. Knowing that she had been a dancer, I suggested we might do the Crummles Company's 'little ballet interlude', with Mr Folair as the Indian Savage and Julie as the Infant Phenomenon playing the Maiden. The absurd choreography is lovingly described for a page and a third in Chapter 23 of Dickens's novel. So we had our scenario. Eventually David Edgar came up with a written sample scene or two.

Our least favourite things

If one were to draw up a list of things that actors most dislike, it would be headed, after long runs, which we also pray for: 'Improvisation and Discussion.' A great deal of this went on within the windowless walls of the aptly named Conference Room. Nowadays the RSC has a rather wonderful 'attic' rehearsal room over the top of the Swan, nestling under a new steeply pitched slate roof, reminiscent of the original Gothic style of the 1870s Stratford Memorial Theatre. Compared to the tatty bleakness of the old Conference Room, this new rehearsal room has something of the ivory tower about it. From its dormer windows, one glimpses the River Avon below and the tops of the weeping willows, the Guild Chapel tower just to the north, snug against King Edward VI Grammar School where Shakespeare was educated. There are fields in the near distance. Charles Dickens, like so many of us, visited Shakespeare's birthplace a short stroll away in Henley Street. He sat in the upper room where it is presumed little William was born. The visitors' book was brought to him there to sign. There was no Shakespeare Theatre in the town then, but when the author of *Nicholas Nickleby* walked by the river to visit Holy Trinity Church, where Shakespeare was christened and buried, he may well have walked over the very ground where we sat in our big circle and gave his book more concentrated loving attention than it can ever before or since have received in one spot. In our *Nickleby* days, there was still no tarmac car park across the river, only grass. As we emerged into the twenty-first century, grown-up people sat in a room and actually envisaged a Shakespeare Village there! But amongst the appalling banality of Stratford's realized late-twentieth-century developments, the Swan triumphs alone. That new rehearsal room over the auditorium! On late autumn and winter afternoons, such as the ones we used to spend under the chill glare of the 'street lamp' in the days of the Conference Room, the golden setting sun pours deep into the splendid attic and the lofty timber-lined ceilings glow warm with reflected light.

All this might have helped those long sedentary discussion days on *Nickleby*; occasionally they came in clusters and grew as exhausting as they were exhaustive. One's imagination, let alone one's buttocks and spine, began to take on the form of the moulded plastic chairs. Unless one made an unseemly dash, the tea breaks in the cramped canteen with more than forty people to serve, could be spent queuing. For those of us playing almost every night as well as matinées in three or four productions, there were lots of twelve-hour days in the same building with the same voices and the same faces, the same Dickens, the same Shakespeare. (What bliss! Are we never satisfied? No.)

'Comedy must be played off the cream of your energy.' That's what Olivier said to me once at the National in the 1960s. I don't know where that puts tragedy, and I've forgotten precisely the context in which he said it, whether it was a hint or criticism. Sometimes these long Conference-Room days were not the best preparation for the physical and psychic demands of playing Shakespeare to 1,500 people, nor the very different but no less costly rigour with which I was concerned, that of being under the close scrutiny of 180 people for three hours in the Other Place. One night Trevor came into the dressing room there, having watched *Three Sisters*, and told us that our performance lacked – well I forget exactly what he said it lacked, the usual things I'm sure, the first things to go the moment the cast, or indeed the audience, is feeling lacklustre. They say it's utterly wrong *ever* to blame the audience, but even though they must always have the benefit of the doubt, they *can* have their off nights. Technically, a decent actor's performance is held in a safety net and there is a level below which a cast of actors will not fall. That level, however, is not, by the best standards, sufficiently high. It's the rigging and sails without the fair wind. Not that one is waiting for, nor indeed expecting, the breath of inspiration; that arrives unexpectedly, if at all, on the oddest occasions – on the way home back to the digs, during a half-full matinée, rarely when the director happens to have dropped in – and so the old notes about lightness of touch and a sense of pace and forward movement (yes, even within the stasis of Chekhov), detail, focus, all the familiar criticisms come out. It is unbearable to feel one has let oneself, an audience and, indeed, a masterpiece down, even by a shade or two. I think I might very well have quoted Olivier's 'cream of one's energy' remark to Trevor and told him it was about time we got up off our arses during our days and sang a song or danced, went on a works outing to Rochester, *anything*, did something liberating – different!

It was very soon after this that we were given the task of organizing a day's or two days' worth of Victorian entertainment. The company went wild. A short operetta was composed by Roderick Horn and flung on with great bravado in the Conference Room (was it about William Tell or some such Hero? At any rate I recall Ben Kingsley singing with a feather in his hat and an improbable handlebar moustache). Still nobody used those curving stairs but there was a small alcove in the centre beneath them in which, by candlelight, Bob Peck, with a handful of others, performed a melodramatic playlet such as one might have seen in a Victorian penny gaff, another 'other place' with utterly different cultural connotations from our esteemed, elite tin hut. It was one of the days on which the London Weekend Television film crew turned up in search of footage for the documentary they were shooting about the making of *NN*, and they were keen to film this item, intrusively insisting on more light. (Nowadays they could have captured it easily.) 'But the whole point is that it is by candlelight,' Bob protested. Whenever you see a fly-on-the-wall TV documentary, just remind yourself of the size of the fly, and that half the time the subjects are corrupted into *performing* by its watchful presence, and the other half they are resisting the urge to swat it.

I did a solo routine, which included a clown act I'd pinched and adapted from a circus – plates were alternately handled deftly and smashed. Unfortunately it was not captured on celluloid. Afterwards Trevor said to me, 'The plates are in. I don't know where, but they are going in.' They never did 'go in', but the act is still available. Call my agent.

I can even find something to carp about when I look back on our days of feverish and varied non-sedentary activity. In Leon Rubin's sensitive, thoroughly detailed account, *The Nicholas Nickleby Story*, he suggests that when we were split up into groups to improvise ways of staging descriptive passages from the novel, we were given a day or a day and a half to do so. No, not at all! My memory, corroborated by two other members of the cast (Kate Nickleby and Miss Knag), is that we had an hour or, at most, an hour and a half. The experience of trying to form a working relationship within an ad hoc splinter group, at the same time as creating a workable framework at breakneck speed, with a group chairman to sift and make decisions about ideas and methods of proceeding – at least ten people in the group, remember – well, it is almost exactly like doing a quick rehearsal for a charade at a family Christmas party, except there is so much more at stake: one's dignity, one's credibility (perhaps one and the same thing), one's taste, talent, intelligence. At least, I suppose, after a mere hour or so one had an excuse for producing something banal or pretentious in content and verging on the inept in execution. Longer preparation might simply have given us more rope with which to hang ourselves. The wonder was that considering our sense of almost 'indecent' exposure and vulnerability, the process occasionally illuminated directions in which we could, would most certainly, boldly and creatively go, as well as places we'd never want to go again.

It was wobbly high-wire stuff; great fun to see the other groups up there, sometimes surviving without a safety net, instant fringe experiment. One morning we all returned to the Conference Room from our several corners of the theatre, each individual in each group no doubt preoccupied, whilst watching the other divertissements, in trying to hold onto the hastily thrown together realization he or she was about to put on. On this occasion it was of Smike and Nicholas's re-entry into London. Suddenly we were contemplating the restructuring of the theatre. There was a set of 'stalls' for us in the middle of the room, arranged by the first group who were to display their results; London happened around us as if we were on the stagecoach with Nicholas and Smike.

Of jazz and Judi Dench

In my battered, dog-eared copy of the Penguin edition of *Nicholas Nickleby*, the first two pages of the relevant passage in Chapter 32 are Sellotaped together and have come loose from the body of the book. Twenty-odd lines have been highlighted in red felt-tip pen, beginning: 'They rattled on through the noisy, bustling streets of London', and later, 'pale and pinched-up faces hovered about the windows where was tempting food, hungry eyes wandered over the profusion, guarded by one thin sheet of brittle glass.'

I visualize the restrained Art-Deco profusion of the dress circle bar in Stratford that morning. On its carpet my little group succumbed to my direction for a few moments, whilst I was busy thanking my lucky stars for the many fruitful hours I'd spent in the 60s under the inspired and eccentric mimetic tutelage of Claude Chagrin. That brittle sheet of glass, and what happened on either side of it, was to cause a palpable stir back in the Conference Room that morning. Perhaps it was never better than when it was conjured out of the air that first time by the hands and imaginations of our little group, playing both the replete and the famished with a simple pivot on the toes to delineate first the diners and finally those starved hands against the pane (the archetypal mime cliché), those hungry eyes staring.

The cold gaze of the TV camera does not always manage such sequences well, is not so easily impressed, and, looking at it now, I wonder how it was that Suzanne Bertish, who judges so many things so finely, came to appear to be drinking out of something the size of a soup tureen. Doubtless the urge that our directors felt to have the production spilling out into the audience had its genesis that morning as we all sat in the middle of the room on the coach to London. 'Who calls so loud?', I am sure, gained its key place in the final script from its treatment on one of these mornings by a Smike aspirant, Mike Gwilym, who was ultimately one of the disappointed to quit the project.

However, these improvisational exercises could be agonizing. What made them so difficult? To draw a parallel, take the kind of improvisation a small jazz group does and the following precepts:

1) They know the tune.
2) There are a limited number of mutually understood ground rules pertaining to harmony – rhythm, tempi and accepted progressions in variation.
3) Each instrument can play only a finite number of notes (there are only fourteen) and each instrumentalist has a well-practised understanding of the technique required to play them.
4) Style is not an issue. The style is 'a given', already exists and is understood to exist, strong enough to contain eccentric individual demands on its elasticity.
5) The players sit down or occasionally stand, they face one way and do not have to consider their music in a changing, physically dynamic relationship with space.
6) They do not have to pretend to be anybody else.

The jazz buff knows that this reductive list contains, implicitly, another longer, subtler one, but, however long we make the list, only the music itself actually comes up with the ineffable glories and mysteries (much as I dislike most jazz).

But, how long is the list which would describe the conditions, the parameters applying to, say, ten actors setting out to create an improvisation to stage a couple of dense descriptive paragraphs of Dickens? In the first place, the instrument the actor plays, namely himself, has more stops than any other instrument in the world. Hamlet berates Rosencrantz and Guildenstern when one of them excuses himself because he can't play the recorder: 'You would play upon me,' he says, 'you would seem to know my stops; you would pluck out the heart of my mystery; you would sound me from my lowest note to the top of my compass; and there is much music, excellent voice in this little organ, yet cannot you make it speak. 'Sblood, do you think I am easier to be played on than a pipe?' Actually, obeying the simple stage direction, '*Enter Hamlet*' (or *Dame Trot*, or whoever else), necessitates improvisation, certainly when one is trying it for the first time. Yes, there are certain givens, known facts supplied by the story so far, the understood conventions of the script, the 'simple' task of coming on – oh, and the words, of course.

Now I offer the most tenuous, but I hope illustrative, story about Judi Dench obeying Chekhov's stage direction, which gets Madam Arkardina onto the stage in *The Seagull* to watch the lakeside performance of her son's play. It was during our first up-on-our-feet rehearsal at the National Theatre in 1994. Anna Calder-Marshall and I, as Polina and Dr Dorn, were standing on the rehearsal room floor. 'Hush, they're coming', Polina says, and we turned to see the little party arriving to watch Konstantin's play. Shamrayev (Robert Demeger), the estate manager, is turgidly telling Arkardina about some old forgotten actor, but it is *her* the audience is interested in, having already heard so much about her. This is what is known as the 'star' entrance, cunningly contrived, not by the star, nor the director, nor the designer, nor the man on the limelight, but by the playwright. Judi's task was, at its simplest, to walk onto the rehearsal room floor from stage left, knowing she was coming to see an alfresco entertainment devised by her son on this summer evening by the lake in the grounds of her estate. I suppose she took some six or seven slow steps from the non-existent wings to the non-existent lakeside before she had to speak.

As Dr Dorn with Anna Calder-Marshall (Polina) in *The Seagull*, NT, 1994.
Photo: © Ben Christopher / ArenaPAL

Stanislavski once said: 'When an actor and a chance visitor walk side by side across the stage, their feet touch the floor differently: one merely walks on the boards, the other on "new ground".' I can only tell you that what Judi did, in the course of her short walk across the stage, was something very particular and small (but huge), something new which reflected in her face and the languor of her walk. It was to do with irritation on the surface, though it suggested a deeper well of frustration and disappointment. Dissecting it now at leisure, I realize that it might well have been the irritation of an actress, Arkardina (not Judi), unhappy with the 'role' in which at that moment she found herself. Judi was able, walking a few steps, to let slip, by default, a whole history about Madam Arkardina before finding herself in a position to demonstrate what Arkardina *wanted* us to know about herself. You could say it was a successful few seconds of improvisation. I still remember it vividly – from that first stand-up rehearsal – partly as myself and partly as Dr Dorn, who in those few seconds thought he diagnosed her malady, whilst admiring her mystique as this most attractive of his old friends (and flings?) and patients.

The rehearsal went on for some further moments as we took a stab at the scene, moment by moment as it came, seeing the lake, feeling a sense of community with our private thoughts, memories and public contributions, being aware of the distinguished stranger, so well known to us as a writer. But you'll see how much is contained, for everyone on the stage, during someone's six or seven steps; you'll appreciate the myriad tiny choices to be made – imaginative, instinctive choices, 'let's pretend' choices. Whether one carries a stick or not, what kind – functional or decorative, whether placed over the shoulder now, on the ground? Has one the confidence to do 'nothing'? Where is one's weight, on the front foot or the back, how close to this or that character? How best to inhabit the place in which the rehearsal has landed you? You know that all of these things, and so many more, have in the first instance to be improvised, one at a time – like the threading of beads, Stanislavski used to say. Which is why a whacking great necklace in the form of a dense chapter of Dickens was a *helluva* thing to improvise whilst fulfilling the roles of choreographer, actor and adapter, with only an hour to prepare in the circle bar of the Royal Shakespeare Theatre in the winter of '79.

With Helen McCrory (Nina) and Judi Dench (Arkadina)
in *The Seagull*, NT, 1994.
Photo: © Donald Cooper

Newman and Kate

It was an unspoken foregone conclusion that Roger Rees would play Nicholas. Don't laugh but, ignoring the fact that, at 5 feet 10½ inches, I was too tall and, at forty-three, too old to play Smike, I think I really hoped to land the part, in common with a large number of the company, until John Caird looked at me incredulously and said, 'Smike is a child.' I still think my height was the only real barrier. In the event, my Newman Noggs was partly defined by the way David Threlfall played Smike. Threlfall's Smike had considerable difficulty crossing the stage; the idea of his undertaking an eighty-mile walk from London to the South Coast was well outside the bounds of realism. As for Noggs, a limp and one of his eyes with a sense of direction all of its own are amongst the table of peculiarities Dickens gives to him, but once I had observed the direction David's physical characterization was taking, to say nothing of the rest of the poor, halt and lame at Dotheboys Hall and the one-eyed Squeers, I felt that my grotesquerie as Noggs must be lightly etched, there being so few symptoms, afflictions and oddities left over.

Of course, everyone was concerned with what marks their character's life history had left on them, and David's imaginative leap was, in a sense, entirely to do with a *kind* of realism, a twisted, cruel world away from the appealing waif I was probably imagining. As I began to work on Newman Noggs, perhaps I realized he too was a waif, a middle-aged one, who had lost

Newman Noggs. Self-portrait
in dressing-room mirror. Aldwych Theatre, 1980.

his status as a gentleman and all hope of redemption. The sensations at the heart of his designedly anonymous life, I instinctively attempted to imagine in the long solitary hours he spent on his office stool and in his garret, the lonely limping errands across London, delivering letters or parcels for Ralph, with the little detours through familiar swing doors into public houses for a shot of anaesthetic. As soon as he meets Nicholas, of course, he finds a secret focus, if only out of gratitude to Nicholas's father, the man who once did him 'a kindness when there was no hope of return.' But the necessary ground is the lost cause that Noggs himself and everybody else assumes he has become, out of which the glimmers of righteous anger appear and his covert, growing determination, in whatever small ways possible, to do the right thing by Nicholas.

One morning in Stratford, before ambitions had been attached to characters or our explorations in the Conference Room had even begun,

Emily and I were sitting up in bed in our little flat in Welcombe Road, each with the 939-page Penguin paperback of *Nickleby* and a mug of coffee. Emily, being the faster reader, had reached page 147. She gave an intake of breath, looked at me with moist eyes and asked, 'Have you got to Noggs's letter yet?' The letter is that handed to Nicholas by Noggs just before the coach leaves for London, which Nicholas discovers crumpled in his pocket when he is left alone for the night at Dotheboys Hall. It reads:

MY DEAR YOUNG MAN – I know the world. Your father did not, or he would not have done me a kindness when there was no hope of return. You do not, or you would not be bound on such a journey.

If ever you want a shelter in London … they know where I live, at the sign of the Crown, Silver Street, Golden Square. You can come at night. Once, no one was ashamed – never mind that. It's all over. Forgive errors. I've forgotten all my old ways. My spelling may have gone with them.

Yours obediently,
Newman Noggs

PS If you go near Barnard Castle, there is good ale at the King's Head. Say you know me, and I am sure they will not charge you for it. You may say Mr Noggs there, for I was a gentleman then. I was indeed.

I typed the above from memory after nearly thirty years. The omissions from the full letter are David Edgar's. This was the first of many times we were to wonder and weep over the story, and love and care about its characters. But I did not put in a request to play Newman. I asked only *not* to be cast as Mantalini because I thought there was a danger I would be and didn't think I'd be any good at it.

Perhaps Emily did ask to play Kate; it was all she wanted to play. One morning before rehearsal, I was walking along Waterside when she called to me. She'd been to the doctor. She was pregnant. Everything had changed. As it happened, she was able to go on playing Irina, even when we reached London after Newcastle, but there was obviously no question of her doing *Nickleby*. However, on the day the cast list was read out, at the end of our exploratory period, knowing that she could not undertake it, Emily's name was still attached to the part of Kate – as a declaration that the directors felt there was nobody else in the company to play it. It was a tough day of reckoning.

On 3 July, during the run of *Nickleby*, our baby boy, whom we called Will, was stillborn. I can't find it appropriate here to write in any detail about this desperately sad time.

At the end of the initial run, the excellent Susan Littler, who'd been brought in to play Kate, decided not to stay on for the proposed extensions. Trevor wrote a most sensitive letter to Emily, and so she did come back and play Kate after all. Along with a few other replacements, she was rehearsed into the eight hours and forty minutes of it in just four weeks.

Emily and I in the garden at home.

Eventually, as the last improvisatory experiments were carried out in the Conference Room, David Edgar's script began to arrive in instalments, each one just as eagerly anticipated as the instalments of the original novel. One remembers reading of the expectant crowds in America on the Boston Quayside, the latest episode of *The Old Curiosity Shop*, calling impatiently across the water at the approaching ship: 'Is Little Nell dead?'

It seemed to me a matter of the life and death of my contribution that Newman Noggs absolutely must, as Dickens wrote, spend a whole day's pay on a can of rum and milk to fortify Nicholas and Smike on their journey to Portsmouth. Thus, armed with chapter and verse, I successfully lobbied the creative team that this vital episode be included, but only after a burst of appalling temperament in which I pinned one of the pieces of script to the noticeboard as a message to David Edgar which, when opened, read: 'When you write me something worth rehearsing, I'll come in and rehearse it.' I read in Leon Rubin's book that I was keen also on a Noggs line to Gride about a cobweb and a fly; indeed any vivid flicker that would serve to make every precious second of the 'insignificant' clerk's limited stage time as significant, singular and as vital as Dickens seemed to demand. Doing my *Nickleby* research for *this* chapter, I rediscovered that Walter Kerr devoted twelve column inches in the *New York Times* (26 November 1981) exclusively to the Noggs phenomenon, beginning: 'I don't know which of *Nicholas Nickleby*'s two directors … decided that the thing to do with Newman Noggs was to pretend he wasn't there. … It gives us the deep pleasure of locating Noggs for ourselves, and then of warmly congratulating ourselves for having picked him out so early.'

I don't quite know how Messrs Edgar, Nunn and Caird kept the seething Dickensian mass of us creatively 'on side' *and* under control, but at long last we got into technical rehearsals in the theatre. The already huge directorial effort intensified, combining countless skills, including those of carthorse and conjurer, the make-or-break heave to take the event to the top of the hill. Then there was the wizardry of the magic amalgamation of all the narrative devices discovered during our gestation period, not least by our adapter, David. For only one of a thousand examples, David handed Roger Rees the pithy and entirely sufficient telegram, 'I'm', and me an answering 'I know', which followed Nicholas's puzzled discomfiture at Noggs's long stare; it was the perfect dramatic distillation of Dickens's page and a half of descriptive narrative of the meeting of Nicholas and Newman Noggs.

By a happy chance, as a child I'd observed my elder brother cracking his knuckles and found that I had inherited the ability, which turned out, unassisted, to be audible at the back of the gallery. As for one's smallest gesture or change of expression being visible, the lighting was designed by David Hersey (nicknamed the Prince of Darkness). Since observing, at age seven, the limelight man at my first pantomime, I've been interested in lighting. In the crepuscular glimmerings of the stage picture, your whole moving figure was occasionally picked out, not by one, but by two or even three follow spots. The trick I'd never seen before was that some of these follow spots, with frosted gels to give a soft-edged light, were located *behind* us, high up behind the proscenium on the fly gallery, so that you were backlit, at once more dramatically and less obviously theatrically. I believe David Hersey invented several lighting devices for *Nickleby* which have become standard equipment.

In praise of Roger Rees

We all got to know each other's work well, too well maybe, in the long *Nickleby* haul. I'd met Roger on the first RSC tour, in *Twelfth Night* and *Three Sisters*, arguably the two plays the world could least well do without (or, if this is a ridiculous claim, certainly they form a combination which seems to me now a gift from the theatrical gods). He played Sir Andrew Aguecheek, Tusenbach and one of the readers in a recital of an excellent anthology he'd arranged about England and Englishness, *And Is There Honey Still For Tea*? We'd shared jokes and composed limericks in communal dressing rooms all over the country. He also played the lead in *The Suicide* at the Other Place.

I remember saying, during his triumphant period playing Nicholas – saying in that particularly generous, authoritative way which actors reserve for their most critical assessments of each other's talent – that Roger wouldn't fulfill his full potential unless he could develop repose. That's rather as if one had said to Jackson Pollock he would never get anywhere until he learnt to control paint. If one is not careful one is caught out in the act of presupposing that one's own particular gift, and one's technique in handling it, are in a state of perfect equilibrium. If Roger had been a different person he might have played Nicholas with a less expensive outlay of energy. It is difficult to imagine Nicholas, or Roger for that matter, succeeding at yoga or Zen. There was something highly wrought and turbulent about him, which was the very thing that saved our hero from being the bland eye at the centre of the Dickensian storm.

One of Roger's useful contributions during the gestation period was his warning, 'Beware the Bumble Fart Syndrome.' It led to much discussion about the pitfalls of our received notions of Dickensian eccentricity. The famous Phiz illustrations, or rather caricatures, were a dangerous influence. Emily had acquired a lovely old set of the Complete Works of Charles Dickens with the beautiful drawings by F. Barnard, which made even the most extreme eccentrics in the story look much more like 'real people'. They were drawn with the fine observation and attention to domestic detail that are so admirable in the best of the nineteenth-century *Punch* cartoons. They were a wonderful contemporary evocation of what are to us now 'period' manners, posture and atmosphere.

So many of the characters spent their existence, as it were, performing, *presenting* themselves to the world; it was hard sometimes to find the true roots of their presentational impulse. One risked crudifying them by short circuit if one didn't understand the *nurture* which had loaded their *natures* with such attitudes, physical and philosophical, such oddities and mannerisms. Roger imbued Nicholas with his own complex, mercurial state of being. But who can forget his long, patient, coiled-spring wait in the coffee house where he encountered Bob Peck's Sir Mulberry Hawk: 'I am the brother of the lady who has been the subject of conversation here'? This was the same Roger who made sure there were always two boiled sweets on the chairs where Emily and Bob sat together every night to watch a piece of the action.

He once explained to me that his acting came out of a sense of *fear,* of being on the edge. That may well have been, but it leaves out the most important element in his work, which I'd say is *delight.* He expressed this delight about the work to such a degree that it became positively glamorous in an interview to the London Weekend TV crew who haunted us on our journey. He was particularly well lit, sitting in the stalls of the Theatre Royal Newcastle, and by contrast almost every other interview in the film seems leaden and pedantic.

In January 2004, I heard him give a speech at the Savoy on an evening celebrating a lifetime achievement award presented to Trevor Nunn by the Directors Guild of Great Britain. For me, his was by far the best speech in an evening full of charismatic sparkle. It was the very essence of Roger. Maureen Lipman kicked off and brought us sharply into celebratory gear, effortlessly imposing a sense of professionally polished mischief and fun into the proceedings. Three performers sang brilliantly. John Caird pulled off with deceptive ease the task of conveying the illusive humour and personality of a story or two which Judi Dench had told him that morning, telephoning him from her sickbed with her excuses. Sir Peter Hall, lending his considerable weight to the occasion, gave a tribute, musing about what it might actually be that a successful director *does*. We learnt that he had 'discovered' Trevor by making the sixteen-mile journey from Stratford to the Belgrade Theatre, Coventry on more than one occasion to watch the fledgling director's work. What strange rivalry-cum-camaraderie there must be between these two battleships of our theatrical establishment.

Then came Roger. I don't know the precise dictionary definition of a flibbertigibbet, here used to suggest something of Roger. In explaining the colour of his hair which was, I supposed, a sort of antique bronze, he said, 'I live in America … ' and then, 'it's so nice to be here in England and to see so many old faces.' How did he suggest within the 'straight' delivery of those lines so many things about our dealings with age? He might just as well have been hovering somewhere over the Atlantic on whatever design of gossamer wings flibbertigibbets have.

I might not see him from one half decade to the next, but, in his ardent, idealistic mood, he is as fresh and unpretentious as ever. Conversationally, his comic stock-in-trade, if I can use such a clunky term about Roger, is to lead you up a garden path of some kind – I fall for it every single time – before you realize you're actually standing with him in a vaudeville of the mind, in a front-cloth sequence as his straight man, and then you're rolling with him in the aisles. Here's an example from a conversation we had when playing the Edinburgh Festival with the RSC small-scale tour:

Roger: (*by way of casual but concerned inquiry one morning before rehearsal started*) 'Is your accommodation all right?'

Me: 'Oh yes. It's a little flat.'

Roger: 'Oh, is it?'

Me: 'I mean an apartment you know, very handy, just behind the West End of Princes Street; and you?'

Roger: 'Oh, all right (*looking a little tired and preoccupied*). I've got a room in this theological college accommodation you know, all the students being on vacation. It's an interesting building. Strange atmosphere. Last night there was a knock on my door at two o'clock in the morning and this voice shouted, 'Have you got a woman in there?' I said, 'No.' So they opened the door and threw one in.'

Which brings us back to repose and, come to think of it, Zen. Roger, up on the platform at the Savoy for the Directors Guild ceremony, recounting his work with Trevor and his debt to him, described the experience, on an RSC tour in Japan, of seeing the Japanese tea ceremony. I have never seen the Japanese tea ceremony, but he had us right there on those wings of his. You could have heard a tealeaf drop. In no more than a dozen words he conjured up the special atmosphere, the profound significance of all the elements of time, gesture, texture and sound. Within seconds we were roaring with laughter at the idea of one of the actresses, 'who shall be nameless – but it was Janet Henfrey', offering to help with the washing up. A moment later, with the simplest poignancy, he lifted a quotation about an English gentleman out of his English Anthology and offered it as his bouquet to Trevor.

When I was acting in New York with the RSC in 1998, we arranged to meet on the steps of the Metropolitan Museum of Art and then wandered at random through the galleries. We embarked on a prattling conversation and commentary, part gossip, part art appreciation. Peppered with gags, it slipped now and then into seriousness. Except, of course, that it was all quite serious, as the best fun always is.

Dickens to the music of Al Jolson, Puccini, Paul Robeson and Leonard Bernstein

Did it comply with the law, our narrow 'Broadway' dressing room? A door at one end, a sink at the other, a line of mirrors and a dressing-table ledge along the wall between, where Vincent Crummles, Mr Wackford Squeers, Smike and Newman Noggs, like gargoyles in a suitably cramped 'Victorian' setting, prepared for the performance and ate the meal-in-a-box ordered in for us from Ziegfeld's in the hour break between Part One and Part Two, three times a week. How that menu palled! We could not afford to pay ill-considered visits to the sink because each squeeze behind another actor's chair endangered the careful application of eye make-up (of which, between us, there was plenty) or disturbed a snatched moment of calm, which was much less plentiful. To lie down was a process involving folding oneself underneath the dressing table, the crown of one's head against the wall, with the lower part of one's legs up and across the top of one's chair, so as to leave a passageway, one-and-a-half-feet wide, between one's feet and the opposite wall, to be no bar to traffic.

Christopher Benjamin (Crummles) and Alun Armstrong (Squeers) in our New York dressing room.
Photo: © EP

One interval dressing-room conversation was about the play, *Are You Now or Have You Ever Been?* Its text, arranged by Erik Benfield, was made up of actual transcriptions from the McCarthy anti-communist hearings of the 1950s. I had seen this at the Bush Theatre in London, and there were some impressive performances by actors enacting appearances before the Committee, speaking the actual testimony of Arthur Miller, Paul Robeson and other star witnesses, and I think we were asking ourselves how well or badly we would have coped in similar circumstances. There was much discussion about how tortured Larry Parks had been at his hearing, unfortunate to have been the first famous Hollywood name to be called and faced with the choice between being jailed for contempt and 'crawling through the mud' to name numbers of his friends and colleagues. He had become famous in Britain for playing Al Jolson in the 1946 film *The Jolson Story*, which I saw when I was ten or eleven.

Before that interval was quite over, I went as usual to do my perambulation in the auditorium. Unusually, I walked, not the plank, but round the rough wooden walkway skirting the front of the mezzanine. When I got to the middle, a very quiet voice said, 'Hello.' I turned. There was a lady sitting on her own, the seats on either side of her still empty, who continued, 'You won't know me but my name is Betty Garrett – I'm Mrs Larry Parks.' We shook hands. I did not tell her we had just been talking about her husband in that particularly problematic context. Perhaps I should have done, would like to have done, though it might have been a long conversation. If I'd had my card I could have suggested we meet for a cup of coffee. As it was, she said: 'Larry and I came to England when he couldn't work here anymore and we toured round all the Moss Empire theatres and got to know and love the country, and it's just wonderful for me to see you all in this today.' I hope that I managed to say something adequate. I was so astonished by the coincidence. I think I may have managed to say something about remembering her husband in *The Jolson Story*. It was a movie celebrating that extraordinary phenomenon, the white 'blackface' singer and comedian, which found a late flowering on British TV with *The Black and White Minstrel Show*. Mr Noggs, Mr Crummles, Mr Squeers and Smike had just been remarking in the dressing room moments earlier on the dignity and courage with which Paul Robeson faced the Committee. As I have said, Larry Parks was the first famous actor to front the Committee, admitting that he had been a member of the Communist Party for four years before resigning membership. He declared: 'I would prefer, if you would allow me, not to mention other people's names. Don't present me with the choice of being in contempt of this Committee and going to jail, or forcing me to really crawl through the mud to be an informer.'

Our dressing rooms were so cramped that after the show visitors were not allowed to come round. Several actors were even dressing in the cellarage immediately under the stage. Sometimes Roger, who quite rightly had a small though decent room to himself, could have visitors, and would occasionally send his dresser up to fetch selected actors and we would meet the great and good of New York show biz. 'Everybody' came. On the night Leonard Bernstein saw us (I'd observed him practically falling over the edge of the mezzanine in his irruptions of delight), I was introduced to him briefly, only for him to turn, see David Threlfall and go down on his knees, as in prayer, with his head bowed. Threlfall, as only this particular son of a Lancashire builder could, looked down at him with some distaste and said, 'Gerrup!' Had the Maestro felt moved to make the same obeisance to me, I would have said, ever so politely, 'Oh you mustn't', or I might have had the presence of mind first to lay my hand gently (but ironically) on his head and then, determined not to stay in the ascendant, I'd have joined him on the floor where we could both have knelt in praise of, and mutual awe at, our God-given talents. I can't be sure Threlly realized who it was kneeling there; I don't know about his knowledge and taste in music except that it was unlike mine. In one of the first technical rehearsals in London, with a fourteen-piece orchestra ensconced in the centre of the stage underneath the place where the two bridges met, he and I entered together at one point and a phrase of Stephen Oliver's music underscored our appearance. 'I didn't know it wor a musical,' he said disparagingly.

One free afternoon in New York, we were in a party with tickets to the Met at Lincoln Center to see *grand* Grand Opera – Zeffirelli's production of *La Bohème*, which made the artists' garret of Act One realistically tiny and, despite the breadth of the music, somehow the acting had an appropriate domestic intimacy. The rest of the enormous stage was filled with the surrounding rooftops and chimneys. The entire production and Zeffirelli's own designs struck me as near perfect as makes no difference (my introduction to opera had been the worthy old touring Carl Rosa Opera Company). At the interval David looked faintly dumbstruck and I asked him if it was his first opera. It was. But I assumed that he'd been familiar with some of the famously ravishing music from the radio at least. No. The whole thing was a complete revelation and I was touched to see the effect it had on him. What an introduction to opera!

The New York audience, in my experience, is good at praise and awe, and, on the days when we did the whole eight hours and forty minutes, they invariably gave us a standing ovation at the *beginning* of the second play. The 'gypsy run' was all this and so much more. In case, like me before it happened, you have to learn what a gypsy run is, it is an auditorium's worth of American Equity members invited in free. It was our very first audience when we were fresh from hurried technical rehearsals and not so fresh from jet lag. Its heart was on its sleeve from the first second, the excitement so extreme we expected cardiac arrest before the first interval, but they kept up the euphoria from 2 p.m. to 11.40 p.m. and seized on every subtle nuance to show their joy and appreciation, as if to say: 'YES THAT'S IT! THAT'S ACTING WE UNDERSTAND. WE LOVE IT. THAT'S THEATRE. WE CELEBRATE IT.' I met an actress afterwards who'd been part of that audience; she said to me, 'I was ashamed of us. The whole reaction was so indulgent and exaggerated, so overly demonstrative.' I understood, but we must remember the expectations, dreams and aspirations that an audience can bring to the theatre. We became a beacon, our status was iconic; that performance created a kind of religious ecstasy. It seemed to turn into an act of devotion on the part of everyone in the theatre.

Contrast the gypsy run with two performances sold in advance to the Metropolitan Opera subscription list where our energy was absorbed into the fur coats and tailoring of the elderly hard core of the kind of theatregoing public that turns up because it is the thing to do. They are the people one sees leaving the opera at the first opportunity, as I noted long ago at La Scala, whilst we couple of hundred in the top tier continued successfully to call back Tito Gobbi, Mario del Monaco et al to acknowledge our applause long after the lower expensive reaches were completely deserted.

In tribute to Stephen Oliver

I can't leave the subject of *Nickleby* without a tribute to the music composed by Stephen Oliver and to Stephen himself who, by the way, had, according to the *NN* programme credit, twenty operas to his name. He died tragically young. I was privileged to read a piece of his witty music criticism at his memorial in St Paul's, Covent Garden. It covered a Beethoven concert, and was written in rhyming couplets for radio. At the service, an orchestra played a rapturous waltz, which I think he had composed for some kind of outdoor carnival in Florence or Venice. Most of us who have ever fantasized about conducting an orchestra know the conventional way of conducting a waltz, but the conductor gave only the first beat of each bar, and that only on a lilting upward gesture, an exceptional demonstration of *lift* which the music itself seemed to demand.

My fondest memory is of Stephen, slight, bespectacled, like a confident, enthusiastic student, teaching all of us 'The Patriotic Song', which was to close Play One. We were in the old Floral Street rehearsal rooms, then a dingy warehouse, now a vast health and beauty salon. Musicians in my experience are invariably super efficient, often good at maths and use time with perfectly planned economy. Music is precise science as well as profound art. Witness Stephen's scintillating performance at one of the earlier rehearsals when the cameras turned up. He pulled musical rabbits out of hats, as if inspired by St Cecilia herself, and, when interviewed, flattered the layman with pithy practical explanations of musical mysteries and effects, which he demonstrated standing at the piano, accompanying himself in illustrative snatches of song. The result in the finished documentary made him look like the most consummate showman of us all.

Another Stephen Oliver high point was the day he taught the whole company the four-part harmony of 'The Patriotic Song'. He had endless patience and energy. We weren't all ideal or even diligent choristers, and actors will gossip when it's not their turn. He'd left his tweed sports coat, with its leather elbow patches, and his small knapsack on the floor behind him by the door. Finally he galvanized us all into putting the four parts of the rousing pastiche harmoniously together and, as we sang, we began to realize just how effective it was, despite an insufficient quota of good voices. As we neared the climax of his composition, Stephen, still conducting and cueing in the parts as necessary, contrived to pick up his coat and put it on, and, in a final flourish, slung his knapsack over his shoulders, and brought us off altogether at the end of the final chord and was gone out of the door, leaving us in a state of musically induced elation, as good as any health and beauty treatment.

Autumn in New York

Charles Dickens himself was a hit when he toured America;[3] so were we. The marvellous amalgam of New York sophistication, generosity and candour made our *Nickleby* visit memorable for the lesser moments as much as the more obvious. Little things, as the song reminds us, mean a lot.

I remember the Manhattan sunshine and that curious energy that seems to rise up from the sidewalks and put a lilt in one's step. Emily and I were walking to the theatre and a voice, the driver of a yellow taxicab, called 'You guys are great!'

*　　　*　　　*

John Rubinstein was playing in *Children of a Lesser God* on Broadway with the deaf actress Phyllis Frelich. We managed to see it because we had Mondays and Tuesdays off. John was a *Nickleby* fan and, on his way home after his show, he used to chain his bike to a lamp-post outside the Plymouth Theatre and creep in at the back to watch our last half-hour. We got to know him and gave him a script of *Nickleby* so he could 'read' some of it to Phyllis in sign language. We were awed when he returned the modest hospitality we offered at our flat in a brownstone near Grand Central Station, when we'd invited Bob Peck and Jane Lapotaire (who had lately been perfectly capturing Piaf on Broadway). We entered John's lovely apartment to see Ruth Gordon and Garson Kanin and several other luminaries. Emily tells me that it was we who created the awe because of our *Nickleby* halo.

*　　　*　　　*

Liza Minnelli was one of the many stars Emily chatted to on her pre-show and interval walkabouts. Minnelli said earnestly, 'You must take this on a world tour.' The thought of it seems attractive now at this distance, but at the time we would have fainted at the suggestion.

*　　　*　　　*

Emily went down beneath the stage for the soup that was served one interval and saw a number of men in suits who were obviously wearing guns. They were the bodyguards of President Reagan's son, who was in the audience.

---

[3] Dickens made two reading tours of North America – in 1824 and 1867/68.

*   *   *

Shortly after we opened a cartoon appeared in *The New Yorker* showing a man being interrogated under bright light by a couple of detectives. The caption read: 'He claims that at those points in time he was seeing *Nicholas Nickleby*.'

*   *   *

I am so struck by the close of *The New Yorker*'s review and the way it is a sophisticated version of the child clinging to the brass rail at the beginning of my account:

> Boldly, the makers of this adaptation have preserved as fully as possible the whole range of subplots; the working out of them is nearly always hilarious, and it is also, from time to time, terrifying. Dickens the ameliorist begs us to introduce love and justice into our lives; simultaneously, Dickens the tireless clown keeps us in stitches. How can one world – and that an imagined one – contain and sustain so many contrarieties? This astonishing *Nicholas Nickleby* performs the feat with a seeming effortlessness; we hear its last words with reluctance, and we leave the theatre at however late an hour refreshed and in high spirits.[4]

*   *   *

Cartoon: © Frank Modell / *The New Yorker*

"He claims that at those points in time he was seeing 'Nicholas Nickleby.'"

Treating a British friend, exiled in New York, to dinner one night after the show, we were impressed when the waiter suddenly brought us a bottle of champagne. He indicated that it had been sent from another table; we looked across and Alan Bennett modestly raised his glass to us.

---

[4] Brendan Gill, *The New Yorker*, 19 October 1981, p141.

326

Chapter 22

Sampling Shakespeare: Brief Encounters with the Bard

Others abide our question. Thou art free.
We ask and ask: Thou smilest and art still
Out-topping knowledge.

(Matthew Arnold)

Shakespeare wrote a part for a dog (that of Crab in *The Two Gentlemen of Verona*), whilst Laurence Olivier, in an essay on his production of *Antony and Cleopatra* with Vivien Leigh, tells a story from his boyhood about a cat whose premeditations and calculations helped illuminate the unfathomable part of Cleopatra:

> I followed it up the tree and when for a second it seemed that I would achieve my purpose of catching her, she started to purr and rub herself against my outstretched hand in order to give me false confidence. I put my hand back on the branch to steady myself for a second, and the cat was down the tree and across the field before I knew what was happening.
>
> This kind of cunning is patent in much of Cleopatra, in her buoyant variations of opposites according to Antony's moods, in varying degrees of subtlety and obviousness throughout the tragedy, and most blatantly in her pretended death; but on the whole it is the enigma that tells, the enigma that holds us.

This morning, attempting to marshal my thoughts about the Bard, I took our terrier for a walk, sat on a bench in the sun, and half concentrated on an essay called 'Most Sweet Voice', written in 1948 by the critic J. C. Trewin. Trewin spends three pages talking generally about the power (or lack of it) of speech in the theatre and rhapsodizing about his favourite voices with a most resourceful use of adjectival phrases. With one eye on the dog, I broke off to 'hear' the voices of some of Trewin's actors whom I had known or seen on stage; I was seeing them again, too, or trying to imagine what a voice with 'lift and sparkle ... that holds something of a stream in sunlight' might actually have sounded like. I was considering, straying from Shakespeare, whether 'the noon-cannon boom', used to describe the long-passed Aldwych farceur Robertson Hare's habitual rendering of 'Oh Calamity!', wasn't carrying hyperbole too far. Bean, meanwhile, was concentrating with even less focus than I, abandoning a stick I had thrown her in order to dodge a perfectly still pine cone, investigate an intriguing scent and chase a butterfly, all in the space of ten seconds. I suppose a voice that has 'lift and sparkle' and encapsulates 'a stream in sunlight' might, if the actor were also endowed with an expressive body, create something akin to the enchanting spectacle of my dog as she dealt with the plethora of fascinating choices life offered her this summer morning. There is something to be said for the butterfly mind, and certainly, in the rehearsal room, exploring a part by William Shakespeare presents one with a plethora of fascinating choices in sometimes equally rapid succession.

It is not only the spirit of enquiry, this febrile animal state (Bean dodging a lifeless pine cone), but the instinct for self-preservation ('Take no prisoners' a perfectly sweet actor advised me before a recent first night!) I have an abiding memory of Olivier febrile in the rehearsal room. He dried a lot in rehearsals of his TV Lear, but, of all scenes, he knew 'Enter Lear, fantastically dressed with wild flowers' very well and never dried on it. I was watching a run-through of the scene one morning; Leo Mckern, playing the blinded Gloucester with a bandage covering his eyes, was kneeling next to Olivier who was seated. As Olivier said:

> For Gloucester's bastard son
> Was kinder to his father than my daughters
> Got 'tween the lawful sheets

McKern, at the mention of his bastard son, simply and slowly drooped his head and Olivier immediately dried. 'Oh, sorry,' he said. 'Take me back a few lines.' He came at 'For Gloucester's bastard son / Was kinder …' again, but by this time he had not only put his arm around Leo's shoulder, but extended it so that his fist was under Leo's chin. Nothing was said and Leo never did the move again.

*　　　*　　　*

In truth Shakespeare is a subject too giddyingly vast for me to contend with steadily here. And as a working actor I have lit upon him so lightly and rarely that I doubt my credentials. However, I'm relying on the premise that you can tell things about the ocean from a few sample bucketsful or, to mix metaphors, learn something of its infinite mystery and appeal by going, as I did later today, to see a collection of John Singer Sargent's seascapes, or even by looking at one of his small notebooks, no bigger than a postcard, open at a page with a single pencil sketch. So, standing somewhere between an old master and a collector of samples, I proceed as best I can.

One can't imagine a critic devoting three pages to the actor's voice nowadays; as I've said, many of the voices extolled by Trewin were still to be heard throughout the 1960s, and on into the 80s and 90s. Some I remember from the Old Vic when in 1963 it became the home of the National Theatre: Gielgud's 'superb tenor', described by Alec Guinness as 'a silver trumpet muffled in silk'; Olivier's, of course, still 'the darting, searching, shifting blade'. Perhaps Celia Johnson's porcelain-tea-set tones, made famous in the film of *Brief Encounter*, did not live up to Trewin's 'unfolding flower', but Edith Evans's 'quivering drawl' convinced Noël Coward, at the National's first reading of *Hay Fever* in 1964, that she could, at seventy-six, play Juliet. He was to modify this opinion during subsequent tricky rehearsals in the very Old Vic rehearsal room in which Dame Edith had learned the Shakespearean ropes. In the season of 1925/26, having written to Lilian Baylis to ask if she could be of use, Evans said, 'I was a given a long list of plays and the parts I was to study: Portia, Queen Margaret, Katherine, Rosalind, Cleopatra, Mariana in *Measure for Measure*, Beatrice, and the nurse in *Romeo and Juliet*' – a formidable roll call for a veteran of West End long runs to cut her Shakespearean teeth on (she was, in fact, the first West End star to join Baylis's illustrious company, having been rejected six years earlier).

The name of Lilian Baylis is a reminder that one can find nicely contradictory evidence to 'prove' that voice, even in Shakespeare, was not always the prime consideration. I was one year old when that legendary lady died. At twenty-two I worked with a veteran who had, as a young actress, auditioned for Baylis. Having done her speech, she was asked, 'Are you religious, dear?' To which the actress replied, 'Well, I'm C of E.' 'That's good, dear,' Miss Baylis said, 'I like my girls to be religious and my boys to have nice legs.'

Legs were still a critical issue when I started to do Shakespeare. Doublet and long hose (tights) are virtually unknown now; I think almost the last major use of them was in Stoppard's *Rosencrantz and Guildenstern Are Dead* in 1967. There was the instance in 1984 of Antony Sher's black silky tights in his famed *Richard III*, or perhaps more properly a full leotard. All the other chaps were in worthy foursquare woolly medieval costume, and it was clear that they should not have trusted for a minute this devious creature in sleek dancer's spandex, dangerously adroit on his spindly black crutches, which served as sinister extensions of his arms and propelled him across the stage with the speed and athleticism of a malevolent Paralympic Richard, or in the words of the *New York Times*, 'a manic pole-vaulter'.

I had worn tights for the first time in Coronation Year to play Slender in an amateur production of *The Merry Wives of Windsor* at Bradford Civic Playhouse. There was no costume design to contemplate at the first reading. Some baskets of hired costumes arrived just in time for the dress rehearsal, and I put on my faded lime-green velvet doublet and hose and, novice though I was, quickly confirmed what had been obvious all along – that half the battle was to succeed in being 'at home', but more importantly in being the architect of one's physical performance as well as conductor and instrumentalist of the vocal part. As Gielgud was to say in 1961, 'You have to spin it out of yourself, like a spider. It is the only way.'

**Slender in *The Merry Wives of Windsor* at the Bradford Civic Playhouse
in Coronation Year. Peter Dews as Falstaff.**

You wouldn't naturally look to Gielgud for lessons in how to act in tights. He certainly had good legs, though Ivor Brown, reviewing his Romeo in 1924, declared, 'Mr Gielgud from the waist downward means absolutely nothing. He has the most meaningless legs imaginable.' When Gielgud played Prospero in 1957, Kenneth Tynan dubbed him 'the finest actor on earth, from the neck up.' To return for a moment to feline analogies, Gielgud's first drama teacher, Constance Benson, told him he walked 'exactly like a cat with rickets.' Perhaps the best lesson in the theatrical architecture of a part, in tights as it happens – the body as kinetic happening in time and space – is preserved on film: Olivier directed by himself and performing the opening soliloquy of *Richard III*. He was a borrower and mimic as well as a spinner and has acknowledged his Richard's debt to the physiognomy of Walt Disney's Big Bad Wolf of 1933 (said to be modelled on the Broadway producer Jed Harris whom Olivier loathed) and to the vocal imitations he had heard older actors give of the towering figure of the Victorian theatre, Henry Irving.

The action to the word

One of my earliest Shakespearean soliloquies was delivered not in tights but in khaki drill apparently. Quite recently I met someone who remembered my Hamlet. Rather a tall order, for, although two productions of *Hamlet* featuring me as the Prince were planned – one at the Mermaid Theatre in Puddle Dock, the other by the British Council to take place against the Phoenician ruins at Baalbek – both were, for different reasons and to my infinite sadness, cancelled. Bernard Miles had a financial crisis and took the opportunity to stage a small-cast Noël Coward revue, *Cowardy Custard*,

330

which was much cheaper than *Hamlet* and did bravely at the box office, whilst the Bolshoi Ballet offered their services free to Baalbek for whatever dark Soviet cultural motive. So I never played nor even rehearsed the part. And yet, in an unlikely art gallery just off Kilburn High Road, I met an elderly gent who told me we'd been in the army together in basic and trade training, circa 1957, and had been drinking companions. Indeed I recalled the brief moment dimly when, late at night, feeling euphoric and unaccustomed to being drunk, I mounted some concrete block on the way back to Blackdown Camp and held forth. I'd have thought it might have been in raucous song, but I am assured it was 'O, that this too too solid flesh would melt'.

Notwithstanding my three years as one of Stoppard's attendant lords, I have so far had two 'civilian' encounters with Hamlet, nearly forty years apart. A year after Blackdown Camp I made my Shakespearean debut at Northampton Rep as both the poisoner Lucianus (one of Hamlet's players) and the elderly priest in Ophelia's grave scene. Did I feel that the poisoner should be depicted going about his business discreetly in the orchard? Histrionics of any kind might get him caught in the act, but no sooner had I begun at the first rehearsal, 'Thoughts black, hands apt, drugs fit, and time agreeing', than the director, Lionel Hamilton, was on stage demonstrating, three times as emphatically as I and with a sort of pantomime Demon King walk. I was no stranger to the broad-brush techniques of costume drama, had done nothing else for a year with the Northern Children's Theatre, in auditoria often twice the size of Northampton's. But I had a tendency to favour underplaying rather than overplaying.

The awful thing is that Hamilton may have been right, for Hamlet himself, impatient for the play to continue has just said, 'Begin murderer; pox leave thy damnable faces and begin', which already suggests that a lot of 'acting' is going on. Next he says, 'Come, the croaking raven doth bellow for revenge', which is hardly a cue to encourage 'a temperance that may give it smoothness', except that this is what Hamlet, in his pre-performance notes, has told the actors should be the keynote even 'in the very torrent, tempest, and … whirlwind of your passion.'

It is an unfair advantage that Hamlet has over the players; he upstages them in that he delivers his advice on naturalistic acting in prose, whereas 'The Murder of Gonzago', including 'some dozen or sixteen lines' that Hamlet himself interpolates, is written in rhyming couplets, not the easiest form for mirroring nature. No wonder Lionel Hamilton, a big man with a leonine head, was so quick to demonstrate Lucianus to me. Lionel really came into his own at the rep every Christmas, playing the Dame in the traditional pantomime, so rhyming couplets and theatricality were, as we would say now, his default position.

The more one muses on *Hamlet*, the more inconsistent the play becomes. For example, this band of players, who must be lectured about the elements of their craft, have a leader who, straight after their arrival at court, so

331

impresses Hamlet by his display of acting that the Prince praises him to us, not saying he laid it on with a trowel, but that he was in a dream of passion, forcing his soul to his own conceit, 'tears in his eyes, distraction in 's aspect, / A broken voice, and his whole function suiting / With forms to his conceit.' In fact it seems the actor shames Hamlet into action: 'What would he do', asks Hamlet, 'had he the motive and the cue for passion / That I have?'

We might suspect that Shakespeare wanted to air his views about acting and inserted the advice speech because of that, but it is Hamlet who is fascinated by acting, pretence, seeming and reality, and the real drama during the play scene, both for us and the Prince, lies in the Royal audience; will the king be forced into revealing his true colours? So I suppose my Lucianus was a side issue – a mere jobbing actor's function to say the lines and not bump into any concepts, in order that, against the artifice of 'The Murder of Gonzago', the real drama of Hamlet and his uncle would be all the more urgent. It is interesting that, after the King has left and the play has been called off, Hamlet's encounter with Guildenstern takes place in the most jagged prose, before he is alone and speaking poetry to us.

'Speak the speech I pray you' began the second half of our RSC *Hamlet* in 1997, the prince shouting the line like a director losing patience (as in 'How many more times!'). This was the make-up Alex Jennings wore in preparation for the first and only night of *The Murder of Gonzago* as adapted by Prince Hamlet.

Photo: © EP

What a part! I spent much of my time envying Peter Wyatt, yet when I talked to him on the phone, fifty-one years after the event, to my surprise he said that he had been most unhappy doing the play; it had been the beginning of some trouble with his ears and the awful thing was that he could not hear himself very well. I can still hear him, and see his slim, febrile frame too. To rehearse *Hamlet* in a fortnight, even hearing every word one says, is a massive achievement. How can Hamlet know what he thinks until he hears what he says? I take it Peter Wyatt could have heard his *un*spoken thoughts had Hamlet had time for subtext.

Peter had no memory of my Lucianus, but did remember my Priest. Another person who remembers my Priest is Claudius, that is Alan Brown. He writes in a letter: 'My favourite memory of *Hamlet* remains of the company gazing down into Ophelia's grave at Sarah Whaley's ample bosom in danger of tipping out of her costume, and your unforgettable rendering of that line: "Her obsequies have been as far enlarged / As we have warrantise" – and the suppressed corpsing all round.' What I remember of my Priest is going home for supper after the show and my landlady saying, 'As soon as you came on, I knew it was going to be funereal.' I had suited the action to the word, the word to the action and, I hope, o'erstepped not the modesty of nature.

Forty years later I was misguided to turn down Polonius in Matthew Warchus's modern-dress *Hamlet* for the RSC and to insist on playing the First Player and the Ghost; Warchus balked at letting me play the Gravedigger as well. I struggled hard with the Player, that showpiece speech of his is hard on the ears of those who do not know the classical events being described, and one ends up doing just the kind of acting Hamlet later fulminates against in his advice to the players.

Hamlet (Alex Jennings) briefs the players. Myself (c.) as First Player. RSC, 1997.
Photo: © Donald Cooper

One night in the wings I had a moment of inspiration and tipped off a fellow player to supply me with a cigarette when I sought one from him. When it came to the speech, I did it in a gritty Scottish accent (we were in Brooklyn on the American leg of the engagement) and borrowed a cap and shoulder bag to look as much like a battle veteran as I could, suffering from post-traumatic stress disorder, needing a cig to calm the nerves and tell the dreadful story.

Warchus wanted *Hamlet* cut to the bone, lite for youngsters, with the atmosphere of a film. Not counting the opening filmed sequence of me and the Queen – the eminently photogenic Susannah York – in the snow with the ten-year-old Hamlet running in slow motion into my arms (to be reprised at the end of the play), my first appearance as the Ghost was amongst the balloons and streamers of the wedding celebrations, the result of a startling jump cut as the grey wall, on which the film had been projected, cracked open on the Claudius wedding party in full swing. I materialized as the unexpected guest in dinner jacket to Hamlet's amazement and to everyone else's too, since they couldn't see me.

With Alex Jennings in *Hamlet*, RSC, 1997.
Photo: © Zuleika Henry

The play scene was hyper-theatrical rather than filmic, though it was all planned to be done in silhouette behind a large screen. I was reminded of Edward Gordon Craig's black-figure illustrations for the Cranach Press *Hamlet*, and lent Matthew my copy, and certainly the images we eventually presented were influenced by Craig's. It was a rather interesting solution to the play scene. Initially, as leading player, I asked what actor-led company would banish its players behind a cloth to appear as shadows. Although now I remember that, in the early 80s, I devised a home Christmas Nativity entertainment employing the same technique, my son David playing the angel with wings, an effective shadow arrangement using a crocheted bedspread. But then I was the director!

Our play scene in silhouette, influenced by Edward Gordon Craig.

In the event, our shadows were slightly larger than life, our movements measured, almost emblematic, but our voices, amplified by radio mikes, could speak the players' rhyming couplets almost in whispers and still be heard. And so the artifice of the play within the play's script was a combination of visual artifice and intimate naturalism of utterance, and the Bard's verse responded miraculously well to this, I thought.

In the closet scene, I wore white pyjamas and a beautiful black shot-silk dressing gown and could almost have entered carrying a sponge bag and a safety razor, a refugee from a Noël Coward production. I remember being nervous at a schools' matinée before this particular entrance when we were playing Brooklyn's huge opera house to a tough audience of local kids. Of course, the audience who doesn't know the play, or who is young enough at least to be seeing it for the first time, has almost forgotten about the ghost by that time and his 'domesticated' appearance, appropriate to the bedroom, did not cause the slightest hint of humour for these youngsters. It was, in fact, a most moving matinée for us. Polonius was shot, not stabbed, through the arras in our production.

With Diana Quick (Gertrude) in the closet scene.
Photo: © Zuleika Henry

One would have thought the shootings every day in the streets of Brooklyn and every hour on US television might have desensitized our teenage audience. No. A single boy's voice called out, 'Fuck – he shot him!' and you could still have heard a pin drop. At the end they lifted the roof off: 'Hamlet, you are THE MAN!'

Present laughter

Ian McKellen played Sir Toby and I Orsino for the RSC's first small-scale tour in 1978. Immediately before we went on for our first performance, Ian whispered to me in the wings, 'Good luck for your last juvenile!' to which I replied, 'Good luck for the first of many character parts!' Of course, all parts are character parts and, although they may not all be juvenile, in Shakespeare they're ever young. Eighteen years later, when I played Malvolio for the RSC, I sensed he was just inside the very fabric of the page of the script I was holding; if only I could somehow bridge the ineffable gap so as to walk by his side or take his hand.

Malvolio is quite a small part as leading parts go – five scenes I think. And in the 'ring scene' he hardly says anything, but everyone who has seen the play remembers him running on to catch up with Viola to 'return' the ring, in spite of the fact that, as soon as Malvolio is gone, Viola begins her soliloquy ('I left no ring with her: what means this lady?'), another of her rhapsodic and comic outpourings. What a talented boy actor the Bankside company must have had that Shakespeare was emboldened to write such a golden part!

The base metal of Malvolio's part is successfully subjected to Shakespeare's alchemy. When his pathetic little fantasy world collapses the audience is finally moved; I still remember being surprised by the sob I uttered when I watched Desmond Barrit, my predecessor in the part, say, 'I'll be revenged on the whole pack of you.' But it was a curious experience, sensing, for a moment or two, Malvolio as a real presence hovering inside the page of my well-thumbed Arden edition. I couldn't have told you what he looked like, and at this distance the nebulous potency of the experience is something I can relate but not feel again. In any case, I had to get on with the business of *being* him myself.

It may give you some sort of picture of the actuality of my Malvolio to know that, during our fourth performance at the Barbican, I broke a four-hundred-year-old tradition by becoming the first practised comic actor to leave the stage without an exit round at the end of the letter scene. 'Then you must be doing something right,' Ian said when I told him. I'd like to think that it was the pathos of my deluded Malvolio, skipping out of the garden to put on yellow stockings, that stunned the audience into silence, but it could have been mistiming.

The Stage said of my Malvolio: 'Petherbridge's letter scene with deliciously inventive dog turd business is the stuff of which the greatest mime performances are made.' Actually it was a peacock dropping! As I spied the letter, I had to stride over a bit of knot garden and my leading heel slipped forward from under me on the aforementioned piece of excrement. On a good night my hat fell off, and I recovered by wiping my shoe clean on a crisp little bed of plastic cropped greenery before picking up the letter. I also had a green umbrella – don't Stanislavski and Dickens both have things to say about these aids to character? Anyway, at one point, I became so absorbed in the letter that I sat on a garden bench and a nice Freudian effect happened. Inadvertently I sat on the handle of the umbrella and, with a startling sea-saw jerk, the rest of the instrument twanged horizontally erect, if you see what I mean.

Malvolio, RSC, 1996.
Photo: © Shakespeare Birthplace Trust

What I've always, or at least often, disliked in other Malvolios has been the part's tendency to degenerate into a comic turn, and, despite any impression to the contrary I may just have given you, I was at pains to discover Malvolio the man. We know, in any case, that no real good turn can come into being unless the audience senses that it is in the presence of a complex, fascinating human being and, in this case, a man firmly existing in Illyria at Olivia's little court. During rehearsal I'd kept wondering how it would have been if the RSC had, in fact, just discovered the script, possibly by Shakespeare; reading it utterly fresh, without all the shades in my mind of its previous incarnations. Such *is* its magic that, with luck and good management, it comes newly alive in one's hands in the very face of its over-familiarity. So it was never a question of what I was going to do to make Malvolio new; he is new. The only question that remained was whether I could match Malvolio's freshness with my own.

During the roistering scene, I had a long entrance, appearing on an extensive high balcony in nightgown with candle, skittering appalled down the long staircase, slipping slightly on the bottom step, and then holding a pause in silence staring at the recreants. I discovered a piece of business almost by accident. Holding Malvolio's lit candle in the wings, I coughed slightly and blew it out. I found a match to relight it swiftly – so as not to be late on – but was keen to recreate the moment in the scene. So at the bottom of the staircase, I did a disgusted, affected little cough before starting on 'My masters, are you mad?', causing Malvolio inadvertently to extinguish the candle and thereby puncture his own dramatic moment. This inspired detail drew an appreciative titter, but Dilys Laye, our Maria and the only person on stage who saw it (the others were looking away), thought it was a piece of unfortunate reality and turned upstage, crippled with stifled laughter. By the time Sir Andrew, Sir Toby and Feste turned to me, I had caught the infection and was incapable of speech, though I managed to disguise my mirth so well that Guy Henry's Andrew Aguecheek thought I was having some sort of seizure.

As the run progressed, the business found its proper place. But then came the night when the computer-governed balcony, which was adjustable at various heights, got stuck in the flies and I was told my entrance in nightgown with candle would have to be made through a stage-level door: a disappointingly less effective entrance, but I did the cough and played the scene and, without thinking, made my exit as usual up the high staircase, only realizing, when I was three quarters of the way up, that there was no way to make my exit, no way down off the steps, but just enough room to perch vertiginously on the top of the stairs, hidden behind a foot of curtain, facing a sheer drop. Of course the others were left to finish the scene as best they could, corpsing at the thought of my perilous position.

Our subsequent tour of *Twelfth Night* took us to Belfast, which had lately been at the heart of the uneasy peace process. My son David phoned me from Canary Wharf, where he was working at the time, in case I'd heard the news that a bomb attack, very near to him, had killed two people and injured 100. The building in which he worked was damaged. All this was a far cry from a favourite theatrical story of mine in which the barnstorming actor-manager Anew McMaster was touring Ireland. (I knew an actor who joined him in the late 1950s or early 60s to be thrown into a repertoire of Monday night *Othello*, Tuesday *An Inspector Calls*, Wednesday *Oedipus*, Thursday *The Second Mrs Tanqueray*.) McMaster and his company were aboard a train, which had been trundling very slowly before it stopped 'unwontedly', as a favourite poem has it. McMaster looked at his companions in the carriage, let down the window and leant out. The sun shone and a skylark hovered somewhere overhead; there was not a building of any kind to be seen anywhere. Suddenly he noticed a diminutive railway worker with a pick over his shoulder, slowly walking up alongside, parallel to the railway line. McMaster took off his hat, waved it flamboyantly and called out the first line of *Twelfth Night*, 'What country, friend, is this?' The little man with the pick stopped by the track, looked up and replied, 'This is Illyria, lady.'

Within the girdle of these walls

'It is impossible to run a theatre for very long without some element of novelty; the public, for all its conservatism is a worshiper of the Unknown God.' Thus wrote Lilian Baylis and Cicely Hamilton.

In 1992 I got wind of the interesting novelty that Richard Eyre had invited the French-Canadian mime artist and showman, Robert Lepage, to direct *A Midsummer Night's Dream* at the National. Now there are not many British actors experienced in Shakespeare who are also proficient in mime and physical theatre; being one of them, I thought I would ring the NT casting department and suggest myself for Oberon. Cold water was applied immediately: 'I think the idea is to have somebody younger and black.'

You can't complain about racist and ageist policies in the theatre, so I picked myself up, brushed myself off and whatever the song says. The next thing I heard was that the play was to be performed in mud. (There is that line by Titania: 'The nine men's morris is fill'd up with mud'.) The Olivier stage was to be entirely covered in it. I don't know at what point I began to think myself well out of it. In the event, I did see the production, thankfully not from the front row where the audience members were issued with head-to-foot waterproofs. The mud was grey, as was the back wall of the stage. The incidence amongst the cast of trench foot and worse only compounded my relief that, old and white as I was, I hadn't been offered and accepted Theseus whose marvellous speech about 'the lunatic, the lover and the poet' was impossible to listen to because of some elaborate business accompanying it, constantly moving chairs to make a perpetual bridge for the lovers delicately to traverse the mud in preparation to see the forthcoming play. And, try as one might, how could one forget contortionist Angela Laurier, who played Puck with a laboured vocal technique and thick accent, as she said, 'I'll put a girdle round about the earth / In forty minutes', taking what seemed like five of them, with her contorted, tortuous crab-like motion, to get from centre stage through the mud to the exit left.

There was one, and only one, scenically beautiful moment: the centre of the stage was a shallow pool of water over the grey mud, all the more striking when light from 'out front' suddenly fell on it and was reflected up onto the huge grey rear wall of the stage, creating an almost filmic, subtly moving sky effect. I can't remember at what point this happened, I only remember that it was one of the most finely poetic speeches in the play, hopelessly upstaged.

With Shakespeare I long always to see the play in the same architecture as I'm sitting in. It would finally get rid of any whiff of stage illusion which places the actors in a different physical element. In a Victorian horseshoe theatre, for example, why for once can't a designer simulate the continuation of the dress circle onto and right round the back of the stage, so it can be acted upon and be there for musicians to inhabit with the supporting pillars beneath for the actors to lean on, and mysterious exits and stairways as in a music-hall painting by Sickert, and for the villains to slip away up into secret stage boxes. Gloucester's eyes could be put out half behind a plush curtain near a velvet-upholstered ledge where chocolates and opera glasses might usually be seen, and Cordelia hanged in the scene dock, the play inhabiting, transforming, violating the real space.

A few seconds of stage time separate my two set designs for *Macbeth*: one can't keep the audience hanging about for the first line in Shakespeare, but the witches can't begin absolutely straight away because, very cleverly I thought, I have them convincing the audience that they are the rocky crags in the left-hand corner. So a few seconds of wind, thunder and lightning, and then hey presto!

Thirty-eight years of real time elapsed before I did the second picture. Meeting my old art master, Mr Green, when I was on tour in Bradford, must have stirred up some sediment. It was under his tutelage that I did the first design, at the age of fifteen.

Shakespeare's influence on the design is not strong. At fifteen, the only play of his I'd read right through was *The Merchant of Venice*, before I was relegated to the C stream, never to read another word of Shakespeare again until I glanced at the first act of *Macbeth* in Mr Green's art room for the purposes of this design. Edward Gordon Craig, that self-exiled Prospero of the British theatre, was my main influence. His work, a handful of productions and a mass of published but unstaged designs (some said unstageable), and his utterances – oracular, outrageous, curiously challenging with a kind of waywardly authoritative quality – found their way everywhere, and Mr Green sent me to the Bradford Reference Library to look them up.

I don't really approve of my *Macbeth* design and its stormy, sickly yellow sky, even though it demonstrates a commendable economy of means – a pillar and a simple swag of curtain. I did another design showing how, for scene ii, the curtain could be swiftly rearranged to form an arras with a martial coat of arms. You will see in the picture (see page 232) I have provided an awkward little curl of staircase, stage left, allowing opportunities for acting on different levels, and poses with one leg straight and the other bent, which I thought mandatory in classical theatre.

Shakespeare had no need of my yellow sky (achievable in light rather than paint I thought), but I had no appreciation then of his incomparable scenic effects such as Romeo's 'jocund day / Stands tiptoe on the misty mountain tops', or Horatio's 'But, look, the morn, in russet mantle clad, / Walks o'er the dew of yon high eastward hill.' What can a paintbrush or lighting cue usefully add to such stuff?

Had I been asked to design the opening of *The Tempest* for Mr Green, I'm sure I would have let rip with a ship and a terrific sea storm. Bernard Shaw praised quite a different and, in the 1890s, novel effect in William Poel's 'Elizabethan' production:

> Mr Poel says frankly, 'See that singers' gallery up there! Well, let's pretend that it's the ship.' We agree: and the thing is done. … The dialogue between Gonzalo and that 'bawling, blasphemous, uncharitable dog' the Botswain, would turn the House of Lords into a ship: in less than ten words – 'What care these roarers for the name of king?' – you see the white horses and the billowing green mountains playing football with crown and purple.

It could be argued that Shakespeare 'saves' his best storm effect until the storm is over. In Act I, scene ii of *The Tempest*, Ariel recreates the whole thing for us, including his own part in it, describing the natural phenomenon known as St Elmo's Fire:

> I boarded the king's ship. Now on the beak,
> Now in the waist, the deck, in every cabin,
> I flamed amazement. Sometime I'd divide,
> And burn in many places. On the topmast,
> The yards, and bowsprit would I flame distinctly,
> Then meet and join. Jove's lightning, the precursors
> O' th' dreadful thunderclaps, more momentary
> And sight-outrunning were not. The fire and cracks
> Of sulfurous roaring the most mighty Neptune
> Seem to besiege and make his bold waves tremble,
> Yea, his dread trident shake.

Even the spectacular stagecraft of the court masques, which were being performed at Whitehall when Shakespeare wrote Ariel's lines, could not pull off what Ariel describes. If the machinery could do it all, why write the speech?

Shakespeare had lived on into the age of Inigo Jones and the gorgeous scenic spectacles which so enchanted the court of King James. Prospero's great speech 'Our revels now are ended', comes out of the extraordinary situation in which he suddenly realizes, in the middle of the celebratory masque for his daughter and Ferdinand, that he's forgotten the 'foul conspiracy / Of the beast Caliban and his confederates / Against my life.' What a wondrous effect it must have created at Whitehall – where the scenery, descending goddesses, choruses of singers and dancers regularly supplied the climax – when Shakespeare interrupted everything, sent them packing ('to a strange, hollow, and confused noise, they heavily vanish'; note 'heavily' – an ironic reference to the creaks and clumps and shufflings that usually accompany the disappearance of magic visions on stage?) and caused his Prospero to speak seventeen and a half lines of disturbing, transcendental poetry on the condition of being human.

It was customary to destroy the scenery after the single performances of court masques, so 'insubstantial pageant faded, / Leave not a rack behind' would have been particularly poignant. Similarly the epilogue ('Let me not, / Since I have my dukedom got / And pardon'd the deceiver, dwell / In this bare island by your spell'), addressed to the monarch, would have caused a frisson; he was used to being cast as the presiding magical presence at masques.

Am I flying in the face of what it was that determined me, at the age of seven, to become an actor – all the gauze and effect of a Christmas pantomime?

We can't revisit Whitehall to sit with King James at *The Tempest*, nor, despite Sam Wanamaker's crusade, revisit the Globe. However, at one rainy matinée of *Henry V* in 1997, from high in Wanamaker's reproduction of Shakespeare's wooden O, I caught the essence. The rain ran directly off the thatch onto the necks of the groundlings who had 'prime' front-row positions with their elbows on the very stage, the gutter and drainpipe not having been invented in Shakespeare's England. The purists have been defeated and gutters installed, and who knows if a Wimbledon-type rain roof may follow, but from my seat undercover in the second balcony round the side, the management of rainwear and even umbrellas was part of the show, and the age-old jokes by the French about the English weather can seldom have gone better since a wet afternoon in the Golden Age. There were cessations in the rain. It surprised me that there are no battle scenes at all; three comics take a Frenchman prisoner, as I remember, and yet one believed in Agincourt, merely on the strength of a beaten drum sounding from somewhere behind a door or curtain.

When Mark Rylance's Henry prayed quietly and alone on the eve of battle, he walked to the very front of the platform and knelt with his head bowed and his fingertips placed at the top of his forehead. The lady in the trendy mustard-coloured rain cape, the couple who had been crouching under a broken umbrella so as not to block anyone's view, in fact a small detachment of groundlings stirred themselves and, unobtrusively, stepped back from the centre of the platform to give due reverence and room to the King. Miraculously, I, leaning over the balcony, and slightly behind Mark, heard every word of 'O God of battles! steel my soldiers' hearts!'

The four-hundred-year-old play, history itself, the fabric of the theatre (some of it built of oaks that were saplings when Shakespeare was alive), the actors, the audience, all were held in one great theatrical NOW.

You can see why I have doubts about the stormy yellow sky I devised for *Macbeth*. A simpler, subtler, more profoundly ambivalent effect might have been provided by the unadorned line which Macbeth speaks on his first entrance: 'So foul and fair a day I have not seen.'

And perhaps some of you remember Trevor Nunn's seminal and wonderfully atmospheric *Macbeth* of 1976, staged without scenery and just a few beer crates as furniture in the old tin hut in Stratford called the Other Place.

We have no tradition preserved in aspic for performing Shakespeare, and our thirst for novelty is such that neither beer crates, reproduction Elizabethan theatres, dry ice and computerized moving platforms, nor any conceivable method is in danger of becoming the accepted norm. We have merely to remember, first and foremost, that it's Shakespeare himself who remains the greatest of novelties.

Trippingly on the tongue

You might have thought it would be difficult to avoid speaking Shakespeare's verse 'correctly'. The poet Tony Harrison is fond of pointing out that the iambic pentameter is a marvellously natural form of utterance and can be heard in the street and on buses. Indeed I once heard a lady tell the box-office manager at the Theatre Royal Bath: 'My friend she fell and broke her leg in Leamington. / She can't play Bridge ...'. Whereupon the box-office man completed the second line for her: ' ... so now you'll see the play.'

'I would not sing.' With these four short words, addressed to one or two of us over his plate of sausages in the Old Vic canteen circa 1966, Laurence Olivier summed up his history as a Shakespearean actor and explained why, early in his career, he was criticized for his handling of the verse. Not an hour ago I had the magical experience of watching and hearing the twenty-nine-year-old Olivier playing Orlando in the 1936 film of *As You Like It*. Fresh from this musical performance, I can report that it is easier to credit Ellen Terry's opinion, recorded in her diary, of the nine-year-old Olivier's performance in a production of *Julius Caesar* by the choir school of All Saints in Margaret Street, Fitzrovia: 'The small boy who played Brutus is already a great actor'.

Perhaps, though, it was Gielgud who, from his emergence as a leading actor, was thought to be the finest speaker of the Bard. But I'm recalling Judi Dench's *Desert Island Discs* choice of his and Peggy Ashcroft's recording of the church scene from *Much Ado About Nothing*. Dame Peggy, it seemed to me, speaking the prose of this scene, was talking directly, naturally to the man she loved. Of her Portia a few years later, Kenneth Tynan said: 'She speaks the poetry with the air of a woman who would never commit the social gaffe of reciting in public, with the result that the lines flow out newly minted, as unstrained as the quality of mercy itself.'

By comparison in the recording, Sir John's familiar cadences, seemed to put him at one remove, the tones issuing from a Gielgudian theatrical hothouse. I also have a very early Parlophone recording of Gielgud speaking 'Once more unto the breach'; he speaks in a generalized fortissimo with vibrato throughout. And yet it is he who offers such good advice on speaking the Bard:

> In these later scenes [of *Richard II*] the subtleties of his speeches are capable of endless shades and nuances, but, as is nearly always the case in Shakespeare, the actor's vocal efforts must be contrived within the framework of the verse and not outside it. Too many pauses and striking variations of tempo will tend to hold up the action disastrously and so ruin the pattern and symmetry of the verse.

Who would have though that in 1953, the year I went to drama school, Gielgud, then barely known in films, James Mason, the quintessential English film star, and the young Marlon Brando, chiefly famous for the film of *A Streetcar Named Desire*, would have worked together so successfully in a Hollywood version of *Julius Caesar* which is still eminently worth watching today?

Brando listened to recordings of classical actors, picked Gielgud's brains on the one day they had time together and used, Gielgud has said, everything that Gielgud gave him. Sir John meanwhile was marvelling at Mason's ability to 'do nothing' with his face yet convey everything. Who was influencing whom?

Notwithstanding the availability of high-definition Shakespearean examples on stage and screen, the tutor in charge of Bardic utterance at my drama school, Charlie Gordon, had actually been a concert Baritone who had eventually gone 'on the halls' with a singing and bell-ringing act. We did not know this then, but it might explain the way he quickly ran out of things to say to us, and was chiefly concerned that support from the diaphragm should always be in play throughout the Monday morning class when, week by week, we each had to deliver a fresh soliloquy and a poem. At a modest reckoning I think I learnt some twenty-five speeches and as many poems, and then began to recycle them.

'When I read Shakespeare I am struck with wonder / that such trivial people should muse and thunder / in such lovely language.' Thus wrote D. H. Lawrence. If the Stanislavski system, rightly or wrongly, encourages one to look into oneself and 'use' one's own sensibility, sense memory and experience, Shakespeare can take one further. I once performed Richard II's prison soliloquy: 'I have been studying how I may compare / This prison where I live unto the world ...'. The pretext, or context, for doing the speech lay in my show *Defending Jeffrey ... ?* at the West Yorkshire Playhouse in

2001. The first time I rehearsed it was to try it out on Jude Kelly, who was producing the show and exerting a vivid directorial influence; I remember she was very impressed and moved by the speech. Since then it has occurred to me that in rehearsal or performance I never once thought of, or 'used', my own experience, my sense memory of solitary confinement in the guardroom of my army camp decades earlier. Our common humanity is perforce any actor's starting point.

When Olivier played Orlando in a film in which he thought the director's sheep ran away with the glory and believed his own performance 'eccentric', it was surely Shakespeare's choice and placement of the simple words 'But heavenly Rosalind!' as an exit line that gave Olivier the quintessential moment of being in love, which he acted so perfectly, and not the substitution of his own experience.

> So glad of this as they I cannot be,
> Who are surpris'd withal; but my rejoicing
> At nothing can be more.

I was thirty-six when I played Prospero and my son was eight, but the emotional eloquence of these lines supplied me with the old father and magician's mind and mood, the mixture of resignation and rejoicing. As Olivier observed of the part of Hamlet, Shakespeare's words can take you by the seat of your pants and hurl you across the stars.

As flies to wanton boys

'Who's your Fool?' The effectiveness of that green-room anecdote, culminating in Sir Donald Wolfit's solemnly oblique question in response to Michael Redgrave's appeal for advice about playing Lear, is all in the telling. The question is always reproduced in imitation of Wolfit's lower-chest register, the intonation one of conspiratorial caution.

At the Old Vic in the early 60s, I worked with a stage manager who had toured the provinces with Woflit's Lear, and he told me that, one night during the storm scene, Wolfit had whispered to his Fool, 'No. 3 spot on the first bar is out – nip off and tell the stage manager.'

I so wanted to play the Fool to Olivier's television Lear in 1983 and put in a request for it, only to be offered a truncated version of the King of France, but I remember John Hurt's unhappiness in rehearsing the part: 'I think he hates me; he doesn't look at me.' This in turn reminds me of a piece of advice, I was told, Olivier gave to the young Colin Blakely in the Old Vic days of the NT: 'Don't lose yourself in the other actors.'

Alec Guinness tartly recalls his experience of playing the Fool to Olivier's Lear at the Vic in 1946 and managing to sneak into the spill of the limelight in the storm scene. Simon Callow – nobody's Fool – in giving the eulogy at Paul Scofield's memorial service, remembered the first performance of *Amadeus* in which he became conscious of a love affair going on between Scofield' Salieri and the audience.

Before the days of thorough rehearsal, when traditional moves and business were the standard, we know that the preparation of a Shakespearean part was something undertaken in the privacy of the closet and, when you emerged, you didn't necessarily declare your hand until you had an audience. That was when you aimed to take the town, first at Ipswich perhaps and then, when you had walked to London, at Drury Lane. Faint vestiges of the tradition linger. 'When are you going to give us your Lear?' The question was put to me for the first and only time when, clearly after a late-night sitting in the year 2002, I happened to meet my Member of Parliament on the Jubilee northbound platform of Westminster Tube Station. I was flattered, but Glenda Jackson had perhaps lost touch with 'who's in, who's out' in the world of theatre. Eventually, and in modest excitement, I would have been able to answer, 'On my 71st birthday in Wellington, just before Ian's RSC Lear arrives.'

When this opportunity arose, I did indeed spend hours in the closet, the kitchen or the garden studying the part. 'Study' is still the term actors often use for the process of learning the lines, and what better process than the chore of constant repetition? Being able to spout the lines from memory at the first rehearsal is liberating and, unless you are blessed with the photographic variety of memory, it means you have lived with a long part like Lear on a daily grinding basis for some time, during which, quite naturally, not being a parrot, you enter imaginatively, speculatively, empathetically into what you begin to perceive as the world of the play.

Olivier, as is well known, gave a full-out (and fully worked out) concert version of his Othello at the first read-through in 1964, as if he were Edmund Kean bursting with his revolutionary Shylock on that unsuspecting first thin house at Drury Lane in 1814.

I can think back, too, on Olivier's first reading of Lear in Granada TV's rehearsal room as a peak never achieved in the finished product. I cannot tell you precisely what it was he did with Lear's famous first line. He did not move in his chair but kept his eye on the book, and yet I saw him 'come on' and throw the line away, drop it into parenthesis in passing, preoccupied by something else, so that there was a sense of portent and impetus about his arrival. And, of course, I heard in those first eight words, for the first time that morning, the deeper supported chest notes of the old stager but with nothing 'stagey' about them. He always had the trick in the rehearsal room or theatre of making me accept 'reality' on his terms. As a teenager, Ian Judge, who directed our production of *Twelfth Night* in 1996, saw all of Olivier's NT parts at the Old Vic and told me that when Olivier came on in a new character 'sometimes I would sit there and blush as if somehow he had exposed something in ME.'

As I prepared to play Lear, I confess to thinking up all kinds of ways of coming on and doing that first line. I imagined the stage filling with everybody but the King and, after a little pause, Lear making his entrance through a quite unexpected and, until that moment, invisible door. The academic word for this sort of thing in literature is 'defamiliarization'. That would be to give it a rather dignified name. Nobody tries to take the audience by complete surprise at the beginning of Beethoven's Fifth Symphony. The familiarity has by now become the point. It is up to the audience to listen freshly as much as it is the orchestra's duty, adhering to the notation, to play it as for the first time. And with Lear, as with Beethoven's Fifth, we must remember there are always a few people to whom none of it is familiar.

It was a surprise Christmas present, arriving on our kitchen table as it were. A theatre company called The Bacchanals, of whom I had never heard, and based in Wellington, New Zealand, were planning a production of *King Lear*, in concert with the Fortune Theatre in Dunedin. All unsuspecting I had opened an email on my laptop on the aforesaid table; it was from the administrator of the Fortune offering me the part of Lear. I emailed back, phoned her immediately office hours had begun on the other side of the world, but it became clear that she had sent the email as a parting shot before going on Christmas leave. I couldn't quite unwrap and inspect this astonishing gift. I rang my first wife, Louise, in Dunedin, but she knew nothing and was very hazy about the proposal for a production. At last, after days in limbo, it turned out that the director, one David Lawrence, had seen my *Krapp's Last Tape* in Edinburgh. Soon he and I had embarked upon a sustained email correspondence about the play. In between and alongside an episode of *Midsomer Murders* and a season at Chichester and on tour with Patricia Routledge in Alan Bennett's double bill *Office Suite*, I began to learn the great part, always returning from points north and south to my kitchen table and, as spring arrived, to a chair under a lilac tree in the garden.

With at least five months to go before the first rehearsal, the New Zealand management wanted an image of me as Lear to use on their poster. This seemed ridiculous; my Lear did not yet exist. Nevertheless, I asked my son if he would photograph me in St John-at-Hampstead Churchyard. I thought there might be a tree with a rugged bark as a suitable background, and then I spotted some snowdrops – that's how early in the year it was – and decided that, rather than put flowers round my head, I would depict the mad Lear communing with nature, but not in Cordelia's 'sustaining corn'.

Lear communing with nature (St John-at-Hampstead Churchyard), 2007.
Photo: © Arthur Petherbridge

My 'kitchen-table' self-portrait of Lear in the storm.
Photo: © EP

Two terracotta versions of Lear and the Fool in the storm.

Later, at the kitchen table, I stumbled across the 'colour pencil' on my Apple laptop's Photo Booth, a sort of cross-grain effect which, I suddenly realized, looked like rain in a storm. I got an anglepoise lamp and experimented, creating the best portrait of Lear in the storm I could, and in a very short time I had three or four 'acceptable' ones.

I did a lot of work at this same kitchen table and was dismayed that my Lear didn't sound domestic in the domestic scenes, even in this setting. I am typing at the kitchen table now, where so much of the nurturing of our two children took place. I had much more time than Lear had to lavish on our children; they grew up able to declare their love to us, which was something that so many people of earlier generations had found it hard to do with their parents. I certainly did. Unthinkable either way that a father would set a competition to discover which of his children loved him best. How to get inside the skin of this cantankerous, myopic tyrant, and why was it that Lear had two 'wicked' daughters and one good daughter, wasn't that something of a fairy-story device and, if so, how best to embody that story?

Old men's parts have crept up on me. My theatrical studies in old age began in earnest thirteen years ago at Stratford with Cymbeline, the Ghost in *Hamlet* and Beckett's Krapp, whilst I was still playing, with the aid of brown wigs, men in their prime like Master Ford in *The Merry Wives* (a comic part to tear a cat in) and the First Player in *Hamlet*. For Charles Spencer at least, my Mr Dodsworth in Bennett's *Office Suite* wasn't 'far removed from the dramatic territory of Samuel Beckett', nor from that of William Shakespeare according to a friend of mine who described the character as 'Lear with laughs'. It is only three and a half years ago that I sat in the Chichester rehearsal room in a fireside chair, trying to be Alan Bennett's retired head of the Credit and Settlement department of Warburtons, trying too to respond to Pat Routledge's Miss Prothero, convincingly installed in the chair opposite. The effortless portrayal of Mr Dodsworth's particular brand of complacent retirement would not come easily; feeling closer that day to my seventeen-year-old self, I sensed that Miss McBride's free-movement classes, and indeed levitation, were more in my line than Dodsworth's pottery classes and parochial groundedness, and needed almost to be tied down to my chair. Yet I was approaching my 71st birthday and would be celebrating it by playing Lear, the king of old men's parts. I felt I needed a strong connection between Bennett's suburban commoner and Shakespeare's king, both experiencing old age, and felt privileged to be able to alchemize my own twilight in the blaze of these two great bards.

Before his complacent edifice is dismantled, Mr Dodsworth shows Miss Prothero the ashtray he has made in his pottery class. *My* own pottery classes didn't start with ashtrays but with a clown and soon moved onto Lear and the Fool, and in the wake of an astonishing cluster of cultural ley lines, I was able to send David Lawrence the following email:

> Walked to the Camden Arts Centre to pick up my two 'Lear and
> the Fool in the Storm' ceramics, which had been fired in the

kiln. I was walking up Finchley Road, not a very popular thoroughfare with pedestrians, carrying the figures in a straw shopping basket. I began to go through 'Blow, winds, and crack your cheeks!' against the roar of the traffic. Just before the turn-off into West End Lane there is a furniture showroom with expensive modern furniture, seldom to my taste, but I noticed through the window that it seems to have changed its style, mixing in a certain amount of antique stuff with the modern. I had only just stopped calling above the storm – in case anyone in the shop should notice me – when I saw that the wall at right angles to the plate glass window was hung with antique engravings in old distressed frames. Something made me look up at the topmost framed engraving in the corner. It was of David Garrick in the storm scene of *Lear*.

It was June and I was in the last week of the tour of *Office Suite*, playing in Malvern. By Tuesday of the following week I would be flying to New Zealand. Malvern was a good place to end: a 'typically' English country town, which means it is sadly, in some ways, not typical of England at all, boasting as it does seventeen single-sex private schools and, in spite of its small population (28,000), supporting a theatre. Patricia sold out everywhere and here was no exception. Salford had been the audience nearest to Bennett's heart language of the West Riding and there they had heard it with *their* hearts and embraced it as we projected it into in the Lowry Centre's huge main auditorium. But the audiences in the more intimate main house of Malvern's Festival Theatre, seating a mere 800, took to Bennett's humour in equal measure. One marvelled at how his parochial people, authentic Leeds to the core, travelled so well, never going off like a bottle of local wine losing its charm when brought back home and opened.

Did I wonder about the heart language, the word music of Shakespeare, as I conned it every day, how it would travel to the other side of the world and how my accent would chime with the voices of the New Zealand actors? I wonder now about the authentic Shakespeare, wondered the other night when I heard Bach referred to as 'The Shakespeare of Music'. It was in the Prom interval on the radio. I think of my radio on summer evenings during the Prom season as conveying one of the most loved sounds of August – as quintessentially English as the Albert Hall, yet with a heady European excitement and magic, but what had just issued forth was a travesty, Leopold Stokowski's arrangements of Bach, a 1940s homogenization, and there was worse to come. How dare Peter Warlock add his twiddly bits and alter the orchestration! I did not stay to listen to Malcolm Sargent's 'improvements'; not for nothing did the players nickname him 'Flash Harry'.

And yet we know we sound as different from Shakespeare's actors as these orchestral aberrations did from 'the real Bach' the other night. The difference is that we are at least not wilfully departing from his 'score'; we can't use period instruments but we can miraculously think the same thoughts as the Fool, Cordelia, the King. Shakespeare, as I've said before, leaves no time for subtextual meanderings – what his characters think they say, and what they say they think. The Bard wrote his words to be spoken and realized that his characters would have animal presence, something implied all too vividly in those words but only actually supplied by the actors. And an E-flat on a G string may be played 'perfectly' or not, but who is to say what 'Blow winds' should sound like?

*   *   *

Actors are fond of that folkloric purveyor of alternative medicine, 'Doctor Theatre.' It was either that medical practitioner, sheer determination or acting that, every night at the curtain call, carried Patricia Routledge on and off the stage in a brisk walk, quite athletic compared to what she could manage 'in life'. I saw Olivier do the dance in *The Dance of Death* one schools matinée at the Old Vic (Strindberg for the kids of the Inner London Education Authority? Yes!) He was suffering from gout, and yet he went through the usual business without a sign of his pain.

The good doctor has his failures of course; the understudy does occasionally get his or her chance, and Tommy Cooper actually died on stage.

I should not have gone to my NHS doctor in the week before I flew to New Zealand. Had I gone instead to Boots the Chemist and said, 'I am on medication for blood pressure, about to fly to the Antipodes and start rehearsals for *King Lear* the day after I arrive, they would have sold me low-dose aspirin and a pair of compression socks, and probably asked me if I was on Statins. The doctor I saw at my usual medical centre gave me no advice at all. But still, I had climbed the North Hill of Malvern with no ill effects, although usually my day, apart from the performances, was taken up with conning and speaking Lear and trying to finish writing the book – this book!

So off I flew. The second day of rehearsal I transferred my performance from the kitchen tabletop, the shade of the lilac tree and the roar of Finchley Road to a small Wellington rehearsal room. Having done my first scene, I didn't get to speak in that rehearsal again because it was the Gloucester family's turn. On my way back to the hotel, jet lag struck and I went to bed early. Getting up for a pee in the middle of the night, I was mercifully able to drag myself and my paralysed right side to the phone to ask reception to call an ambulance. The next day, although I could walk and read and write and speak, I knew that Lear was out of the question, and the day after that I collapsed again. This time I could not see to read properly, could not hold and use a pen, could barely walk.

My 74th birthday has now come and gone, and still no Lear; it was marked so loyally by an e-mail from David Lawrence. In my reply to him, I wrote of the regenerative process that has been taking place since the stroke that cruelly destroyed my hopes for the great part. It is as if the march of time and the ageing process are being contradicted by a counter-march of

351

recovery, graphically recorded in its first stages by the two self-portraits I executed in August and October 2007 respectively (see page 235). As soon as September that year, I was on stage at the National Theatre participating in Olivier's Centenary Celebration. With my two most recent stage characters in mind, Donner in Stoppard's *Artist Descending a Staircase* and Henry in *The Fantasticks*, I wrote to David:

> *The Fantasticks* has been something of a turning point. These old-men parts, like Lear and even the short comic part of the Old Actor in *The Fantasticks*, only respond if one can still manage speed, deftness and a certain lightness and ease, so that one wears even the weightier stuff, the failing strength, towering failing in Lear's case, with grace rather than out of necessity.

*　　　*　　　*

I can still see the papier-mâché crown and rather grotesque make-up of the middle-aged actor playing the Player King in *Hamlet* at Northampton Rep in 1958; regarding himself in the dressing-room mirror, he said, 'I should be photographed in this part – who's to say it's not my Richard II?'

Who's to say the photo of me as Henry in *The Fantasticks* is not my Lear and Paul Hunter's Mortimer my Fool? Actually Paul and I are meeting for a drink today, our first get-together since we were happily paired for the first time on the first day's rehearsal in the ill-fated revival of the cult 60s musical. I had, perforce, prepared what I was going to do with 'my Henry'; I'd had to audition and, in any case, tempus fugit requires that the ageing brain not leave memorizing even a relatively small part to the last minute. Freedom, as I have said, lies in knowing the lines and being able to spout them with confidence at the first rehearsal, but it is not necessarily generative of an inflexible and solo fait accompli. Rather, it enables you to look the other actor in the eye and really see what he is doing – and hear. Paul and I both said and did rather more than was set down for us in *The Fantasticks*. We improvised together, never colluding in cold blood but extemporizing in the heady heat of the rehearsal-room moment. This is also the way to bounce off a classic text. Lear is a dysfunctional tyrant; we have them still and hear of the tragic consequences of their actions on any given day on the BBC World Service. Listening and empathizing are skills Lear is yet to learn, but though he, and we, find much of the Fool's utterance opaque, the Fool is his chosen companion who only dies when Lear abandons him for his learned Theban, the naked wretch 'Poor Tom'.

I have suggested to Paul that we might explore *Lear* together. I wonder about it being done in a pocket theatre – a pocket *Lear*. It seems to me that the vivid, muscular detail in the language of *King Lear* will thrive on intimacy. The great flights of rhetoric and hyperbole, like the very storm itself, are possibly more convincing close up when one is not expecting distance and scale to lend a scenic verismo and enchantment to them. One thought is to have, if not a kitchen table, a big table, which could be used as a conference table, platform, and shelter, the point being that it is *Lear* in miniature but also under the magnifying glass.

With these pocket precepts in mind, I wonder too what Paul might do with Goneril, say.

'Yes,' Paul said the other day on the phone, '*Lear* from the Fool's point of view.'

Who's your Lear?!

With Paul Hunter (Mortimer) in *The Fantasticks*, Duchess Theatre, 2010.
Photo: © Geraint Lewis

Postscript

As this book goes to press, Paul and I are looking forward to a week's investigation in a rehearsal room – *Lear* as a twosome possibly.

I have found some notes about Laban's movement theory from a star pupil of his who became his assistant and taught me in Bradford. In copying them our for me, Geraldine Stephenson refers to them as 'my funny old movement notes'. She lists 'exaggerated efforts', two of which are 'too much directness equals obstinacy' and 'too much strength equals crampedness'. I mention these two because they might have to do with Lear's characteristics.

Now when Yat Malmgren – a disciple and collaborator of Laban's – taught movement at the National in the 60s, he always said that we should just do his physical exercises and not try to apply them in any way to our acting. I think it was sufficient for him and us that we visited the places his exercises took us to, that we worked against our limitations so that we had the broadest possible physical language. Yat admired Olivier because he was so protean; that was why he was able to show off as Oedipus and Mr Puff on the same night, why his Mr Tattle was whimsical, vain and lightweight whilst his Othello had the convincing dignity of the general and the power of a wounded bull – because he could visit and inhabit the physicality of the characteristic efforts of such contrasting creatures.

Did I worry that Lear has been described as an oak rather than an ash, I who am a silver birch? Something to explore as the new journey begins ...

An Actor Repairs

This is an ode to physiotherapy. The actors' 'Bible' is a book by the inventor of The Method, Stanislavski. The book is called *An Actor Prepares* – hence the ironic title of my poem.

I turned up at the small gym
At the Royal Free
Around three
(Hence this Hymn)
And not a 'him'
But a 'her', one Clare was there.
In need of repair
Not her, but me!

NHS Care
Was the fare on offer
Proffered for my wear and tear
One must not despair
When at a stroke one's flare is fatally impaired.

So Clare was there
To help me make redress
To assess me, address me

A strange affair that Clare should be taking
time
Teasing back gesture to this stricken mime
Youth training an old hand, that once drew
lines so fine

Clare, youthful fleet and nifty
Me – well, one score years and fifty
Exposing parts that now are frail
To this athlete with her ponytail
She coaxes uplift of expression
From down in the mouth
Downright depression
For this erstwhile master of the fleeting impression.

Wringing dishcloths, pegging out
Grasping knobs and turning keys
Performing turns now such as these
Exercise my sluggish fingers.
Faintly though, the notion lingers –
Cosmic motion is my business
Not pegs and keys and wringing out
My turn was Lear's redemptive rout
Hanging out with Fool in storm
Extremis was to be my norm
Eight performances a week
Everest my peak
Small gym at the Royal Free
Hence this hymn to Clare and me
However high I set my hopes
I practise now on nursery slopes.

Recovery with 'It'

What happens to the Ego and the Id
When the idioplasm is rearranged – deranged
And stricken
When the Protoplast is aghast
That a chasm's opened up – so wide
Beyond its reach and range
When it's forced to bear in
Mind
That the brain's reign
No longer reaches and sitteth at the right hand,
Or the foot; but takes its toll of the tongue?
The will is there
But the cables are cut and their absence –
Bind.

I've been lucky.
Irrespective of what we've done and did –
The Ego and the Id –
Some healing power that's hid,
Independent and mysterious –
Some organic impulse to repair
Is there.

I'll call it – 'It'
Forge an affinity
Let the Ego and the Id – and 'It'
Form a blessed trinity.

Silence and Subtext

Chapter 23

Strange Interlude; or a Play in Nine Scenes and an Epicene[1]

In *Strange Interlude* Eugene O'Neill was generally considered to have written an experimental play. The expressionistic, vaguely nightmarish designs on Lee Simonson's poster for the Theatre Guild's 1928 production and on the dust jacket of the first American edition the same year would have suited a Modernist dance piece. But, in fact, when we came to work on the play in 1984, it struck me that, apart from the perfectly naturalistic dialogue, O'Neill had firmly set the clock back. Naturalism and Realism, that combined attack on theatricality, had left the actor speaking his thoughts as, at best, securely set in history, to be honoured in faithful period revival, Shakespearean soliloquy and the humorous asides of Restoration Comedy; at worst, remembered from nineteenth-century melodrama: 'Little does he know that I am his father.' Actually that is the precise sentiment of one of his character's several asides (the sexy doctor who has an illicit affair with Glenda Jackson's character, hence the child) over several of O'Neill's nine acts.

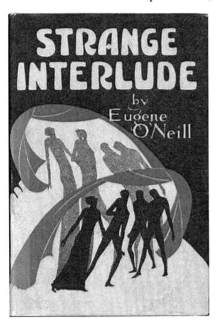

Poster for the original 1928 production of *Strange Interlude.*

The challenge for us was that these thoughts were not always passing or so pithy. Quite often they were ruminative and could more accurately be described as soliloquies. Apart from having to adopt a tone that would make it clear one was thinking to oneself, and no longer talking to Glenda Jackson, Brian Cox, James Hazeldine or any of the other actors, we each in turn had, in the middle of a conversation, to assume a condition of suspension and abstraction, whilst the person to whom we had been talking unloaded their subtext in a chunk of top text. Is that clear?

---

[1] This description of *Strange Interlude* was coined by critic Alexander Woollcott.

The first American company to do the play toyed with the idea of clarifying things by doing all the inner monologues in blue spotlights, which in the late 1920s would have been more challenging for the man on the lighting board than it would be now.

However, let me freely dramatize aspects of our 1980s production from the first point of my involvement. This is a dramatization; any resemblance of any character to the participants in the real-life production of *Strange Interlude* is intentional, but probably accidental; I mean, how did I know what they were thinking?

*   *   *

Note that, in setting out the scenes below, I am following the conventions of O'Neill's published script, in which the interior monologues are differentiated from 'normal' speech by smaller print. These spoken thoughts consist of a series of individual phrases and sentences, frequently punctuated by pauses (each pause is indicated by three ellipsis points).

*   *   *

SCENE: *A suite of top-floor rooms in the Aldwych Theatre, London, in that part of the grand Portland stone curve which is bookended by the Strand Theatre to the west and the Aldwych and the beginning of Drury Lane to the east. Appropriately the Strand Theatre is now known as the Novello, for the handsome-profiled star, and composer of such musicals as* Glamorous Night, Perchance to Dream *and* Gay's the Word, *made his London home in these top-floor rooms which are now occupied by Triumph Apollo Productions. Visitors reach them in a tiny lift, just big enough to accommodate three people, as long as they are slim like Ivor and don't mind being intimately close. The main office still has the shelves on which Ivor kept his record collection, disguised with the spines of false books – all with spurious titles satirizing people in the business (I only recall* Dogs I Have Known *by Fay Compton). As a boy, Edward Hardwicke lived in this flat with his mother, and I seem to recall that there was a piano then, left by Novello, which was heard to utter the occasional chord late at night.*

Edward Petherbridge, wondering if Ivor saw Strange Interlude *at the Lyric in 1931 and what his ghost thinks of this proposed revival being planned on his premises, is ushered into what must have been a quiet spare room at the back, overlooking an inner lightwell, a drab hinterland of grubby white-tiled walls. He perches on an old sofa such as would be found in a rep theatre green room, and then, somewhat self-consciously, adopts a comfortable position, his arms outstretched along the top of the low back to exude an air of confidence. He is joined by Keith Hack, who is going to direct the play.*

KEITH

I'd really like you to do this part of Charlie, Edward; it's a great part for you.

You're so good at classy wimps and have the right sexual ambivalence.

EDWARD

I can see that it is a good part, but I have a reputation for playing well-bred, sympathetic, asexual losers.

Why can't the bastard see me as the sexy doctor ... I would be great ...

KEITH

He wants to be sexy ...

Actually you are wrong about Charlie; in the Hollywood movie Clark Gable played him.

EDWARD

You lying sod ... you must think I'm stupid ... Gable would never, *could* never have played Charlie ... he *must* have played the doctor ...

You surprise me, are you sure you are right? Anyway I am no Clark Gable, but that doesn't mean I can't play the doctor.

(A hiatus during which there are thoughts, but unlike O'Neill, I leave them to your imagination.)

EDWARD
(Resuming.)

You say it's a tour.

KEITH

And then the West End.

EDWARD

How definite is that?

KEITH

When Triumph Apollo Productions want to bring a play into the West End, they can and do.

EDWARD

If they want to ...

How long do you think it will last – I mean how many hours will the play run in performance?

KEITH

Five hours max.

EDWARD

Will that be eight times a week?

KEITH

That's fluid at the moment.

EDWARD

I should think that is the last thing that you are … rather tenacious and stubborn I divine … and with no intention of having me play the doctor …
Well after the eight and three-quarter hours of *Nickleby*, five would be nothing to me – if I were playing the doctor.

* * *

SCENE: *A rehearsal room, the large dismal church hall on Kingsway. A series of gas fires, suspended from the ceiling, creates a novel effect and emits an insistent hissing sound. Outside workmen are digging up the road with pneumatic drills. Edward has just done his second long scene, ending with Glenda sitting on his knee, which they enacted, though they are still carrying their scripts. They merely mark the exit where, because she has fallen asleep, he has to rise from his chair, with her in his arms, and leave the room to carry her to bed. As Edward is playing 'good old Charlie' and not the doctor (that role having been assigned to Brian Cox), she thinks of him as a surrogate father, and, in the nicest possible way, he behaves as such.*

EDWARD
(Sitting at the side of the room.)

We have only five weeks to rehearse five hours of play … we are nearly halfway through Day Two and I don't think I have heard or taken in a word that has been spoken by anybody … even me … in this rehearsal room from hell …
(He goes outside and stares into Kingsway. The drills continue.)
I'll never survive this week … and, if I do, I'll be no wiser at the end of it … it's a disaster … and then there's this dispute about whether the twenty-something hired to play the son, both as an eleven-year-old boy and as a twenty-year-old man, is going to survive … Glenda is adamant that he can't play the eleven-year-old and that we should get a real boy … and there's a democratic charade going on that we should vote on it, which I will refuse to do … look at these people in the street going off for lunch without a care in the world …
(Brian and Jimmy come out.)

BRIAN

He looks miserable …
We've broken for lunch.

JIMMY
(Laughing happily.)
Are you all right? Come to the pub.

EDWARD

He thinks I'm a comedian …
I need to phone my agent – I can't stand this – I'm going to ask him to get me out of it.
*(Brian and Jimmy laugh. They all three go to the pub.
Edward phones his agent and asks to be got out of the job.)*

* * *

364

SCENE: *The Territorial Drill Hall off Shepherd's Bush, vast but with a comparatively small square area marked out by adhesive gaffer tape on the floor and further delineated by four wheelable gas radiators, placed at each corner of the square and radiating heat onto the acting area. Edward is speaking Charlie's dialogue and his thoughts; he does not carry his script. Brian, also acting without script, is thinking his own thoughts as well as speaking his character's thoughts as he acts with Edward.*

MARSDEN
(Thinking with scornful pity.)

His work! . . . what a pretence! . . . a scientific dilettante! . . . could anything be more pitiable? . . . poor chap! . . .

(Perfunctorily.)

Biology must be an interesting study. I wish I knew more about it.

DARRELL
(Stung yet amused by the other's tone – ironically.)

Yes, so do I wish you did, Marsden! Then you might write more about life and less about dear old ladies and devilish bachelors! Why don't you write a novel about life sometime, Marsden?

(He turns his back on Marsden with a glance of repulsion and walks to the window and stares out.)

BRIAN

Edward is going to be very good ... but I can see him leafing through the script in his mind to see where he's got to ...

MARSDEN
(Confusedly.)

Yes – decidedly – but hardly in my *line*

(Thinking in anguish – picking up a magazine and turning over the pages aimlessly.)

That . . . is . . . true! . . . he's full of poison! . . . I've never married the word to life! . . . I've been a timid bachelor of Arts, not an artist! . . . my poor pleasant books!. . . all is well! . . . is this well, the three of us? . . . Darrell has become less and less her lover . . . Nina has turned more and more to me . . . we have built up a secret life of subtle sympathies and confidences . . . she has known I have understood about her mere physical passion for Darrell . . . what woman could be expected to love Sam passionately? . . . some day she'll confide all about Darrell to me . . . now that he's finished . . . she knows that I love her without my telling . . . she even knows the sort of love it is. . . .

(Passionately – thinking.)

My love is finer than any she has known! ... I do not lust for her! ... I would be content if our marriage should be purely the placing of our ashes in the same tomb ... our urns side by side and touching one another ... could the others say as much, could they love so deeply? ...

(Then suddenly miserably self-contemptuous.)

365

What! ... platonic heroics at my age! ... do I believe a word of that? ... look at her beautiful eyes! ... wouldn't I give anything in life to see them desire me? ... and the intimacy I'm boasting about, what more does it mean than I've been playing the dear old Charlie of her girlhood again? ...

(Thinking in anguish.)

Damned coward and weakling! ...

EDWARD

*(Reaches a patch he feels he knows quite well
and feels at liberty to think some of his own thoughts.)*

Thank God I know this bit well ... five more days and then we open in Croydon ... in the most boring play I have ever been in ... including Brecht's *Edward II* ... God I've dried.

*   *   *

SCENE: *Ashcroft Theatre, Croydon – reminiscent of a shoebox.*

EDWARD

*(On stage – a silent audience out front.
Edward's own thoughts run parallel with Charlie's.)*

Of all the theatres in which to try out a difficult play ... any play ... for the West End ... why doesn't Glenda make-up her hands? ... she looks as if she's been doing the washing up ... probably has ... and this audience! ... we might as well be playing a crater on the moon ...

*   *   *

SCENE: *Dressing room after the show. Enter Sean Mathias beaming.*

EDWARD

My God – don't tell me *you* were out front.

SEAN

I most certainly was. You were terrific, really terrific, Edward; it's the best thing I've seen you do for ages! And so funny!

EDWARD

He looks as if he means it ... has my work been so bad? ... more to the point, is it possible that *this* work could be so good? ...

Come now, you heard the audience or rather didn't hear them. Are you serious?

*   *   *

SCENE: *Dress circle of the Theatre Royal, Nottingham. Edward is sitting on the third row centre in one of Charlie's immaculate suits, tailor-made for him. Yet another dress rehearsal is in progress.*

EDWARD
(Thinking his own thoughts.)

The set looks good … the theatre is beautiful … this must be about where D. H. Lawrence sat in 1908 when he watched Sarah Bernhardt in *La Dame aux Camélias* … Glenda looks good … beautifully still all alone on the stage with the clapboard set surrounding her … sky blue with the white clouds painted on it … it should look like Magritte, but it doesn't … it looks almost natural … Glenda's voice sounds so haunting … spellbinding … we may be in with a chance …

*   *   *

SCENE: *Edward is in his Nottingham dressing room, speaking on the phone to his home in London.*

I still can't tell; you know what the audiences are like here. Well, they didn't think. We didn't do a matinée in Croydon, so we are having to cut one of the acts this afternoon, and even then they'll be calling the quarter-hour for the evening performance as we come off after the curtain call, and I will have to dye my hair brown from white again, grab a sandwich and coffee and go on. God knows how Glenda has the stamina; she's on for almost twice as long as I am in the show. Brian and Jimmy and I have decided to push her forward at the curtain call tonight after her marathon – she won't approve. What? Oh yes, I'm hitting the road home straight after the second show. No, not really tired. Jimmy and Brian and I managed to get out of the house this morning, cleared up and packed. We never went to bed all week until we heard the dawn chorus. I know more about their lives than any actors I've ever worked with. You know that film *My Dinner with Andre*? Yes, well, I seriously think there's a play in *All Night with Jimmy and Brian*! Such eloquence, such poignant candour – I can't tell you.

*   *   *

SCENE: *The curtain call after the second performance on the Saturday. The actors step forward for the last time. Brian and Edward, on either side of Glenda, firmly attempt to push Glenda forward.*

GLENDA
What are they doing? …
Fuck off! That's against all my principles.
(That was not a misprint – Glenda spoke her thoughts aloud!)

*   *   *

SCENE: *Dressing room at the Duke of York's Theatre, London. Enter Anna Massey.*

ANNA
I have to say I adored it and my video machine isn't working at home, and I've missed *Dynasty*. However, *this* is *Dynasty*, shot through with poetry. So it was worth it.

Glenda's process

Glenda's principles were in no doubt. At lunchtimes during the rehearsal period, when we wanted to enjoy an interlude from *Strange Interlude*, we principals, together with Keith Hack, sat huddled round café tables, chatting. Keith would be waiting on tenterhooks to get a word in edgeways in the thick of our jokes and gossip and our talk of art and life, so he could make some rehearsal point.

During one of these interludes, I distinctly recall Glenda bemoaning the fact we were locked into a success culture. People are obsessed with success, she would say: 'They don't honour the process – it's the process that matters.' She then recounted a story about a workshop Peter Brook arranged in 1966 with the famous Polish director and guru Jerzy Grotowski (author of *Towards a Poor Theatre*). This was for the RSC actors, including Glenda, who were working on Brook's anti-Vietnam War production *US*. The company turned up at a church hall on Marylebone Road to find themselves locked out. It was some time before they could begin. Grotowski had insisted that the room should be thoroughly cleaned before it was fit to work in. I don't know where cleaners were procured from or whether stage management had to do it, but this was proffered as an example of the process being honoured.

Incidentally, Glenda also told me about part of the rehearsal process for *US*. The actors had the idea of giving Brook a subjective taste of his experimental rehearsal process, which was taking place in the Warehouse. They solemnly put paper bags over the heads of Brook and his assistant. Then, in silence, the actors crept away and went for lunch. After lunch Brook said that it had been 'interesting'.

We worked in at least three rehearsal rooms, each with its own dismal individuality but clean enough I suppose. We were honouring the process all right – trying to get the play right at any rate – and hoping for a success (it was a West End show after all). And isn't that what rehearsals are for, getting it right? Glenda played it close to the chest. I recall Keith trying to persuade her to bring out some emotional moment or other, and Glenda saying flatly, 'You won't get that now, not in this rehearsal room; that might happen in performance, if at all.' I don't quite know how or when her 'process' segued into the 'luscious star technique' one New York critic praised. I remember us, after we had opened, sitting in a dressing room, mostly on the floor, having been given our notes and with the reviews just in, and I noticed that Glenda was subtly different, relaxed. I realized that I had never seen her smile so easily before. When I opened the programme and read through her biography, the word 'process' did not appear; the word 'success' appeared twice! But one of Glenda's lunchtime jokes I found endearing was, 'If I'd stayed on working at Boots I could have been a branch manager now.'

As it is, she is an MP now – *my* MP as it happens – and I'm sure it is her principles that keep her from sitting in the Cabinet. I suppose I could go and take my turn at one of her surgeries. We did meet late one night on a deserted platform on the Jubilee line at Westminster some years ago and she asked, 'When are we going to see your Lear?' And before that I sang 'Don't Put Your Daughter on the Stage' at a fundraising event for a local school at which Glenda was present. She paid a gracious compliment to her 'old friend', but it struck me as odd that the veteran of guest appearances on *Morecambe & Wise*, should be giving a formal political speech and not doing a number herself. Who could forget her grace and glamour in the song-and-dance number she did with Eric and Ernie? Yet I remember her turning up one morning for a photo shoot outside the Duke of York's Theatre with no make-up on and wearing her usual rehearsal day coat, which she told us was from Marks and Spencer. The medley she did with Morecambe and Wise is a good example of how beautifully she moved her hands. Her one-time co-star Dirk Bogarde wrote in a letter to a friend that Glenda had 'hands like a bricklayer'; yes, but she could use them like someone trained at the Royal Ballet.

Not the least of what I owe her is her cooperation in part of my process. In Act Two she had to fall asleep on my knee, and I, cast by her in the fatherly role, had to get up from the chair with her in my arms, speaking my thoughts, of course, and walk with her to the door. So you might say I knew the full weight of her principles. Wimp that Charlie was, it was important that such a delicate moment should not descend into bathos. Glenda transferred her weight to the arm, which hung round my neck, so that it would be distributed straight down my centre of gravity. It takes two to tango – even when one of them is 'asleep'. I remember the sensation of that rise and the walk to the door and the pause for another spoken thought before I exited. As I put her down, Glenda would invariably whisper, 'All right?' and I would whisper back, 'Yes.'

What *wasn't* all right is another sensation I'll come to, sitting again on a dressing-room carpet, this time at the Nederlander Theatre in New York. Only Glenda and her three men had come to New York, the rest of the cast were American replacements. This was the Big Apple and Keith Hack was grinding the bit between his teeth again: success and rave reviews in the West End were only laurels, they had to be re-grown, fertilized and pruned. There had been the unnerving sacking and abrupt replacement of the American actress who had taken over from the brilliant Sheila Burrell of the London cast as Sam's mother; she more than anyone, including Rosemary Harris who played the part later in the TV version, suggested the arid hopelessness of the woman. The unfortunate New York actress had been sacked during rehearsals from her previous Broadway engagement too, and we Brits began to realize this was another country – they did things differently here. And yet to come from London Town, built on Thames clay to this piece of rock, built to impossible, sparkling heights and density, was to experience the energy that rose to greet you from the very rock through the sidewalk as you set off to rehearsal.

Charlie Marsden.

With Glenda Jackson (Nina)
in *Strange Interlude*.

The set of
Strange Interlude.

Keith had made it known, as part of his pre-opening jitters, that he thought I might unbalance the tone of the play in New York, that Charlie's waspish, epicene quips, as well as his unconscious comedy, might be taken to the hearts of the gay theatregoing fraternity and turn the play into the wrong kind of comedy. It had never occurred to me that Charlie was in danger of, so to speak, coming into his own in this way, though I knew from experience how sharp and demonstrative the New York crowd was. In 1972, having played the difficult first scene of Congreve's *The Way of the World* many times in the Actors' Company production to thin houses in the British provinces and to rather bigger ones in Wimbledon, it was not until our season at the Brooklyn Academy of Music that we found what it was like to play it to people who seemed to relish our talk about the offstage characters as if it were the latest stylish gossip about people they already knew. Nine years later, at the first preview of *Nicholas Nickleby*, I got a round on my fist exit after speaking only a few words. It was a 'gypsy run' admittedly, but such was their heart-on-sleeve joy that we thought there were bound to be tears before bedtime.

Before I realized what was afoot in my place on the carpet of a Broadway dressing room, Keith Hack was introducing 'a few little cuts' into my part. I can't remember what I did about them – they were distinctly tricky. I do remember deciding that they all came before my laugh lines and that Keith was trying to wrong-foot me. Nevertheless the laughs came – and produced unexpected results.

> Bitching genteelly about his rivals, flouncing through life with wet rancor, Charlie is the play's most modern character. And Petherbridge's deftly broad performance connects so directly with a 1985 audience that the other men's declarations of love sound like letters from high camp. His presence amounts to a deconstruction of the text, and a radical revitalizing of it. Transformed, the play lives.[2]

It's ironic that, for one critic at least, my performance made the other men look camp. I was certainly innocent of deconstruction, being ignorant of the term, in any case as a literary or acting process.

Apparently the two young oil magnates, who produced *Strange Interlude* in New York, asked Glenda what special thing she would like for our first-night party, and she said airily, 'Oh, an elephant.' Jimmy Hazeldine and I arrived at some funky, roughly converted loft, to discover in the street outside an elephant. It was small and one felt it was long past its bedtime; Glenda was being photographed next to it and their faces were practically level as the cameras flashed. Standing behind, Jimmy and I noticed that the creature seemed unmoved by the showbiz razzmatazz and in a desultory fashion was

---

[2] Richard Corliss, 'Sending Shivers of Greatness: *Strange Interlude*', *Time*, 4 March 1985.

rubbing its back legs, one shin against the other calf. This seemed emblematic of something, or perhaps it was its O'Neillian way of giving vent to its subtext.

Jimmy Hazeldine (Sam Evans) backstage in New York.
Photo: © EP

A minor, but nonetheless strange, interlude

Quite the nicest aspect of my 1984 Olivier Award (Best Supporting Actor for *Strange Interlude*) is a couple of drawings of the statuette that my daughter Dora did in 2002, as part of a holiday task in her pre-Guildhall Art and Design Foundation year, when she was eighteen.

Dora's drawings of my Olivier Award for *Strange Interlude*.

Another aspect of the statuette goes back to the days when Dora and her brother were small and we had a cleaning lady, who held strong opinions. When a child was crying in the street one day, she said, 'It needs a good slap; give it something to cry *about*!' But she made one healing gesture I still remember. My nameplate on the circular base of the statuette had loosened and fallen off and had been lying, for the best part of a week, on the chest of drawers on which it fell. After our lady had cleaned and gone one day, I noticed that she'd put my nameplate in place and secured it to the base by an elastic band. At the time, it struck me as ironic, perhaps even symbolic. Later I invested in a tube of super glue.

Nowadays the award stands above a door on a high shelf that doesn't see a duster so very often. I climbed onto a chair just now to check the year of the award (yes, 1984) to discover that the glue had given out and that, although I still deplore our old cleaning lady's ideas on child care, perhaps the elastic-band technique was the best solution after all for the harsh realities of this world, as far as awards go.

Interludes with Cyrano de Bergerac and Buster Keaton

As I was writing this piece on *Strange Interlude*, I received the following email from an American lady:

> *Mr Petherbridge, Here I sit researching* Cyrano *on Wikipedia, inspired by a late showing of José Ferrer's film (who knew what agreeable thighs the man had!). While Mr Ferrer might be the definitive Cyrano of the play, who came all the way to the cowtown of Denver in the 1970s to reprise his role and light my little heart, I still think fondly of your star turn in the musical version at Greenwich Theatre in 1990. Jason Connery, sure, pretty, but for whom does every woman weep in the end? What a lovely memory. Thank you.*

To which I replied:

> *Amazing to think of you seeing Ferrer in person as Cyrano, thighs and all. I wish I too could catch the film on late-night TV. I saw him in the film when I was a boy of fourteen or fifteen, but I worked with him once in 1988. It was in a television version of O'Neill's* Strange Interlude*, which I had done with Glenda Jackson, originally on stage in London and New York – all five hours, including cuts. (The American producer recently asked Herbert Wise, the director, if the five hours could be cut to two as he couldn't sell it anymore at the old length.) Ferrer took over the thankless part of the father, who has but one scene, and seemed muted and shrunk by it, as his predecessors had. It was lovely to hear him talk of his glory days as an actor in classical theatre, but as we talked there seemed to be no sign left of the glamorous Tony- and Oscar-winning leading man. He told me a touching story of going to a circus in Paris in which the clown was the elderly Buster Keaton. José was sitting on a bench near the front,*

watching some act when he suddenly realized that Keaton, in his familiar hat, was sitting on the same bench only a few feet away. Ferrer wanted so much to introduce himself and say how much he admired Keaton, but somehow it didn't feel right and the moment passed.

As for you seeing my Cyrano in Greenwich, I only wish I could have toured it to any number of 'cowtowns'. You mention weeping; in the last scene, as the leaves fell in the convent garden, I used to be able to hear the audience weeping from the stage. There is something magic about the part. In the 60s, while staying at a seaside holiday chalet in Wales, I had to take a transistor radio outside and press it to my ear to hear, spellbound, Ralph Richardson play Cyrano as night fell.

I don't know how well you remember Greenwich; we had musicians and music but it was definitely not a musical!

I have sent you a long answer but there is no mention of Cyrano *in my book and I thought this could form a byword on it, particularly if you would agree to your email being part of it.*

Cyrano de Bergerac, Greenwich, 1990. The last act with the letter.
Photo: © Dee Conway

I received a couple of further emails from the lady and eventually was able to reply:

Well, I have to thank you for taking me back, courtesy of my friend's video, to my boyhood and the 1950 Cyrano of José Ferrer. I do not remember the film making a very big impact on me at the time, but I think it must have set certain standards by osmosis, because in this curiously faithful Hollywood version of a piece of Gallic theatrical

374

hokum shot through with genius, I recognize what seems to be from Ferrer a thoroughly European style of acting. In fact, I see now that the piece depends entirely on the genius of the actor playing Cyrano, and José has the technique, the style, the poise, but above all he suggests the soul of the part, and it is in this balance between exterior and interior, between panache and pain, between a kind of nihilism and nobility, braggadocio and tenderness that the 'trick' of the part lies. In the 1950s there was in America still a tradition of acting the classics with a definite English intonation to the voice. I've heard it in snatches from the recordings of Welles and Houseman's Mercury Theatre Company doing Shakespeare. And Ferrer is a perfect example of it.

Anyway, all this led me to watch Ferrer and me together in the video of Strange Interlude, *with me pretending, of course, to be American. Ted Mann, who co-founded the Circle in the Square Theatre in New York, was waiting with his wife at the stage door of London's Duke of York's after* Strange Interlude *one night; his wife asked me, 'Which part of America are you from' 'None,' I replied, 'I'm English.' 'Oh that explains it,' she said. 'I was sure you must be an American, but I could see your acting technique was English.'*

Al Hirschfeld's depiction of our production, which appeared in
***The New York Times* on 17 February 1985.**

375

Chapter 24

Invitations to Molière and Rothko

> *Philinte.*　*But seriously, what would you have me do?*
> *Alceste.*　*Adopt behaviour both sincere and true.*
> *Act like a decent man, and let words fall*
> *only from the heart, or not at all.*
> (Molière, *The Misanthrope*, Act 1, trans. Tony Harrison)

No one appeared to take any notice when Lord Peter Wimsey and Miss Marple's Inspector Slack stood together at 10.45 p.m. amongst the homeward bound theatregoers on the Bakerloo platform at Piccadilly Circus. Every actor turns to crime eventually. Apart from bickering in fitted kitchens, which I don't think either David Horovitch or I have ever done, at least professionally, the staple diet of TV drama nowadays involves crime or hospitals. The British public is amazingly discreet – to a fault sometimes – and, of course, people sometimes think they know you as an acquaintance but can't think in what context. Perhaps that night in 2006 those who might just have seen us in the flesh on stage had caught earlier trains before we emerged from our dressing rooms.

In fact I had been fulfilling my tasks as head porter in the quad of an Oxbridge College in Michael Frayn's farce *Donkeys' Years*, whilst David Horovitch had been chilling audiences as Lord Burleigh with his realpolitik in Schiller's *Mary Stuart* when we met on that underground platform. We had met rarely and only glancingly in the seventeen years since he'd played the moderate Philinte to my immoderate Alceste in Molière's *The Misanthrope* at the National, but we took up the reins of our classical comradeship again with ease.

Clearly our curtains came down at about the same time and we travelled on the same line, but had never met thus before (and never did again), but it happened on this Bakerloo line of serendipity, there on the platform, he was in the middle of a story about *me,* and it concerned the occasion of the first rehearsal of *The Misanthrope*. He was telling it to June Watson, who minutes before had brought 'tears and sadness' to the part of Queen Mary's nurse. Amusedly, benignly, David began the story again for my benefit, reminding me that on our first day's rehearsal we had been shown the model of Richard Hudson's set design. Richard himself was otherwise engaged in Leningrad, I think, but there in miniature was the set we were going to have to work on (a foregone conclusion wherever he was), a minimalist room with a classical doorway up centre and a long narrow stretch of steeply raked floor. There is a photograph of the set model which I pinched from the noticeboard at the end of the rehearsal period. According to Hudson, the contra rake, stage right, and the jumble of chairs represented 'society falling off the edge.' The floor, nay the room, was dominated by a tiger-skin rug with an unnaturally huge head, to be used as a perching place for guests in modern dress at Célimène's receptions, the tiger's wide open mouth facing the audience. (There may be some passing reference in the script to polite society's law of the jungle.)

With David Horovitch (Philinte) in *The Misanthrope*, NT, 1989.
Photo: © John Haynes / Image courtesy of NT Archive

'At one point,' David continued as we waited for our train, 'Paul Unwin, the director, announced that he thought it necessary for all the actors to attend every rehearsal, even if their character was not in the scene, so that we would all feel involved in the whole play.' This was no hardship to me, or to him I recalled, as we were both in practically every scene anyway, but David's story was that I reacted by saying, very affirmatively, 'I think it's a *very* good idea we should all be in the rehearsals all the time, because I'd hate not to be here on the day the tiger-skin rug is cut.'

I was surprised not to have remembered this subversive quip, which must have unnerved Paul Unwin. It seems I had decided to take a leaf out of Alceste's book and speak my mind from the outset.

I do remember that, having suggested myself for the part of Alceste (an idea the National warmed to – those were the days!), I had gone to meet Paul and, purist that I must be, argued in favour of the 'two boards and a passion' approach. He knew what I meant, though I find I have been misquoting the phrase for years: 'Three boards, two actors and one passion is all drama needs' is what the Spanish Baroque playwright Lope de Vega wrote. The treatment of Molière's masterpiece at the hands of directors and designers demonstrates that few of them trust it to stand on any number of boards unless bolstered by 'helpful' decoration and even symbolism, but, such is the play's nature, that the more it is 'assisted', the more it staggers.

In his review of Sir Peter Hall's production at the Piccadilly Theatre in 1998, Nick Curtis noted: 'But of the perils of social demotion for both flatterers and truth-tellers in this courtly mêlée – suggested by the snake and ladder adorning John Gunter's otherwise bland, picture-framed set – there is little sign.' Shock tactics further undermine Molière's script and one is duly shocked to read, from the same review, a description of the opening: 'Huge double doors swing open … and an elegant, masked figure moons at the audience, exposing a freshly spanked pair of buttocks.' But quoting bad reviews of productions I have not seen is not much better than the social tittle-tattle Alceste deplores, and no purist should indulge in it.

Once we'd read the play, Paul Unwin embarked on a session of theatre games and exercises, which I thought were spurious and said so, still unconscious, I think, that I was behaving like Alceste. As far as I recollect, one exercise had us reading snatches of scenes, each actor deciding when his character was dominant and marking this dominance in a schematic way by sitting – or was it standing? – on the right. It was, in any case, something I felt to be quite crude and arbitrary, and exhaustingly fruitless to try to describe now. I say arbitrary because the play is clearly a portrait of how upper-class people behave in the social setting of a salon, and salons or drawing rooms (or rehearsal rooms for that matter), as our experience tells us, are places where we can be acutely aware of dominance or being dominated, being squashed or slighted or convincingly flattered by the subtlest of signs, marked, or masked, with no more than a lift of an eyebrow, a glance, a single half step or a gaze out of the window. Indeed what are plays about if not the social force fields in which power constantly shifts: life in fact?

Talking of such directorial games, someone told me about an occasion when Ian McKellen was sitting in a rehearsal and the director, getting things moving, bounced up to him and said, 'Would you like a tambourine?' Ian replied patiently but gravely with a detached 'No', but you need to hear the un-notateable music of that 'No' to laugh as I did when it was so skilfully imitated by the actress who had been there and recounted the story.

Whatever it was that Stanislavski is supposed to have said about anybody being able to walk across a room but it taking years of training to walk across a stage, may lead people to imagine that student actors spend hours practising door-knob and sofa technique and crossing down R. to the fireplace. From the typical stage direction in a French's Acting Edition – *entering quickly centre* or *looks wistfully out of the door LC* or *he moves to the sideboard slowly and examines the decanters* or *she pales imperceptibly* (sorry, I made that last one up) – anyone might think that such simple, naturalistic moves amongst the furniture involve a sophisticated technique at the very heart of the mystery of acting. And so they do!

After all, there are only so many things one can do in a British drawing room or Parisian salon (unless you have been to parties to which I have not been invited); and this narrow range of formal options in Molière's comedy is the simple classical structure of conventional behaviour that is augmented, elaborated and even threatened by the drama of human interplay. It manifests itself in a kind of symphony of deliberate or involuntary nuance of expression, since there is no reception room, however formal, in the world of the stage (nor in the real world for that matter) that succeeds for long in entirely suppressing the propensity of at least one of its occupants to 'make a scene' or, more modestly, to be quietly mortified or inwardly triumphant. In *The Misanthrope*, a rich dance pattern is discernable as deceptions, jealousies and rivalries compound the refusal of Molière's eponymous hero to play the social game by the rules, even though his behaviour in no way transgresses the physical bounds of what is deemed seemly in a salon.

These our actors, as I foretold you, were trained and many did indeed imitate the tiger, the vulture and the autumn leaf, and practise at the barre, to obey more ably the 'simple' stage directions *Enter-* or *turns away and moves down R.*, and to embody a life, a history, a whole world of meaning of which their characters might be unaware, take for granted, or want to conceal.

The Misanthrope, it strikes me, is a play about reputation. Its hero and heroine both end the play in their different ways as outcasts. If we receive gilt-edged invitations, the equivalent of being welcome at the rich young widow Célimène's soirées, we can assume we are of the chosen. On arrival we note with interest who else is there and immediately our reputation is on the line, our position in the subtle pecking order at stake.

A director with whom I got on with well told me about ten years ago that I had never cultivated the art of flattery. Earlier than that, in the wake of *The Misanthrope*, my then agent told me in confidence that I was rather off the NT list as I had a reputation for subversion. I would have thought that part of the social function and duty of a National Theatre was subversion: no art theatre wants to be perceived as a palace of reassurance! But I think I got the mix wrong when I found myself, for the first time in my long association with the National, playing a singular part, the eponymous role. Seeing myself as the head of our company, the experience went to my head. It was not *Rosencrantz and Guildenstern* or the McKellen-Petherbridge Company; I was a leading, *the* leading man. I think I may have developed a touch of *noblesse* without the *oblige*.

Alceste prides himself on not playing the game as he moves in Paris's high society. Flattery is no part of his method. One of the most, I felt, genuinely flattering remarks ever made to me on a social occasion was one I received from a stranger at a reception in Dunedin, New Zealand, some thirty odd years ago. It was at a function for the parents and old boys of the school my son was attending. For a moment, knowing no one there, I found myself alone and palely loitering when a Kiwi, as he would have called himself, came up to me and said, 'You look like an interesting sort of prick – what do you do for a living?'

More recently I received an elegant gilt-edged card, an invitation to a champagne reception at the Tate Modern and a private view of the Rothko exhibition. Emily and I arrived to find that there were several prominent actors present with whom we were on nodding acquaintance, two of whom I had worked with, one relatively intimately for Siân Thomas had been Célimène to my Alceste in 1989. After being regaled with speeches extolling the glories of the Tate and, I suppose, flattering us Friends of the Tate, Emily and I thought we would find our way down to the Rothkos on the floor below. We were not predisposed to be impressed, despite Rothko's formidable iconic reputation, and indeed we were not. No one seemed to be contemplating the large muted abstracts or, if they were, they were exceptions amongst the knots of people deep in conversation with their backs to the canvases. We decided to leave. Across the space we raised valedictory hands, and not for the first

With Siân Thomas (Célimène) in *The Misanthrope*, NT, 1989.
Photo: © Allen Daniels

time that night one actor avoided acknowledging us, whilst an actress to whom I had not spoken, broke away, came up to me and, without a word, firmly planted a tender farewell kiss on my mouth.

Rothko, whose exhibition had already been seen in New York and was destined for Paris, died by his own hand whilst his reputation was at its height, suffering from alcoholism, several illnesses and desertion by his wife. Molière fell ill during a performance of *Le Malade Imaginaire* in the presence of Louis XIV. He insisted on concluding the performance and died a few hours later. Two priests refused to give him the last rites and a third arrived too late. As an actor, by law he could not be buried in hallowed ground, but his widow interceded with the King and Molière was buried at night in a section of a cemetery reserved for unbaptized babies.

It can be disastrous to identify too completely with a character. Famously, Alceste's splendour, and his predicament, is that he hates hypocrisy and is obsessed by the determination to be honest and speak out about others' failings. However, he seems to spend all his time in the play at high-society gatherings, where, as we all know, the line between tact and hypocrisy can be, to say the least, blurred. Alceste's honesty leads him to be hopelessly undiplomatic, priggish and not a little aggressive. He also thinks he is a star.

As I say, it can be disastrous for an actor to identify too completely with a character.

Our poet-translator, Tony Harrison, was in attendance at the first rehearsals. His script of iambic pentameters in rhyming couplets had been a National Theatre hit at the Old Vic in 1973 in a stylish modern-dress production by John Dexter with Alec McCowen as Alceste. Diana Rigg played Célimène; she was chiefly famous then for fifty-one episodes as Emma Peel in *The Avengers*. Tony got us to stand in a circle and to read aloud, and at sight, eighteenth- and nineteenth-century English poetry in iambic pentameters, a verse each in turn. He maintained that the steady rhythm created a spell, which had been proved to link the left and right hemispheres of the brain. Now and again he would deliver a little lecture on a point of stress – the dramatic effect created by a line not starting di *dum*, but rather *Dum*. I objected to the exercise on two counts: first, I had a long rhyming part in which to become fluent, and would have preferred to practise that; secondly, I pointed out that when I'd been a kid at elementary school I had, like most of us, been speaking rhyming verse aloud in class, and in the meantime I'd done a bit of Shakespeare. Thus armed, my task now was surely, without denying the oh-so-regular metre and the relentless chiming rhymes, to find the trick of speaking the long leading part in a personal vernacular, however governed by Molière's mores. I even went so far as to say that no symphony orchestra would expect to be taught the rudiments of the musical approach to any piece, and nor should we.

In one lecture he gave us in Bristol, where we opened, taking advantage of the lull whilst the set and lighting were being worked, Tony railed against actors using their own experience in a role, taking aim at Stanislavski in the process. I supposed he was talking about the worst of The Method, as it has developed, which emphasizes and draws on the actor's experience to the detriment of what the playwright has created – after all, it's not what *you* would do if your uncle killed your father and married your mother, but what Shakespeare has given Hamlet to do that matters. My personal method in *The Misanthrope* was that I had to talk like the misanthrope, not make him talk like me. On the other hand, the *one* can only be understood in terms of the *other*. After all, how does an audience member understand, empathize or criticize except by the human capacity to identify, to make instinctive, instantaneous comparisons with his own subjective experience and observation? Tony talked of his *words,* his beat, the pulse of the verse: 'the music and sensuous taste of my words on the tongue', but if this exacting discipline is to be brought off with the required technical brio, it is vital for the other seventy percent, which the author has *not* notated, to be there. Yes!

Isn't it a proven, observable anthropological fact that, of the impact upon us when we are spoken to, some seventy percent of that impact is *not* what is actually said, even in poetry, but what we read in the eyes and what we divine from tone, dress, posture, gesture, movement, the dynamic relationship in space, the fine nuances, the subtlest and most unique expressive interplays of which the human instrument is capable, even by default. As we look and listen, during the lightest exchanges in life, we are on a quest to detect the truth, to recognize what is expressed not only by intent but inadvertently; what we can value as genuine and spontaneous or what we suspect might be manipulative, contrived, insincere or malign. Meanwhile *we* are being similarly read, in a super-sophisticated version of grosser, elemental encounters; the establishment of pecking order and the mutual grooming sessions in the animal kingdom. What the good playwright writes, *implies*, is this other seventy percent – in great depth; it is for the actor to *experience* it, body and soul, when he acts. The 'perfect' rendition of Harrison/Molière music is part of it but the existential exercise of being 'moved by the impulse of being' is head to toe, time and space, and happens, too, in a dimension which for the actor is a kind of waking hypnotic trance. Only this will convince the audience into that extraordinary state of belief which the theatre can induce.

I once saw Tony Harrison on TV reading some of his poetry. Whether by accident or design, by unconscious instinct or intentional elucidation, throughout the poem he beat time with his free hand to the regular pulse of the verse: the effect was of an eloquent incantation. My contention is that this did not help us at all. The seventy percent could have been that rich northern voice and noble head in perfect stillness.[1] Certainly throughout an entire play in regular rhyming metre there must be, in the emotional and physical life of the characters, a sense of hidden other rhythms, cross-currents, turbulence and calm contained within the formal structure, creating a huge range of varying tension within, though never, especially in verse, breaking the form. To that end one can't leave one's *life* in the dressing room – yes, the quarrel with the leading lady, the problem with the income tax, leave *those* behind, but the full sum of one's unique existence on the planet is not too much of an encumbrance to bring on stage. That life is vital, reactivated now into a different dance altogether as one inhabits the imagined world of an Alceste.

Meanwhile I had been feeling far too actorly, too 'theatrical' speaking this rhythmic rhyming stuff on a constant note of complaint with an occasional line or two of tenderness. I took a moment to approach Tony one day in the rehearsal room; he was quietly watching us work and I confided to him my misgivings, adding that it had occurred to me to try rooting my voice in my native northern accent. 'Good,' Tony said firmly, 'I've been waiting for you to say that.' Of course Tony and I were both of working-class stock and had been born a mere ten miles from, and within nine months of, one another.

The music of what I think of as my heart's language just happens to be the subject of a phone call that a moment ago interrupted my revision of this

---

[1] I have to say that, more recently, I heard Tony Harrison speak 'Our revels now are ended' at a memorial service. I have heard the great speech spoken thus by more than one 'great' speaker, that is quoted out of its dramatic context, which always puts a strain on the listeners and the speech, but on this last occasion Tony somehow allowed the speech very simply to work its magic.

chapter. My daughter had been listening to a recording of a Bill Naughton radio play I did in 1963: it was my first radio play and the part was a young unemployed North Country working man – ironic in view of the fact that the cadences of BBC Standard English emanating from the wireless set on our window sill had been my most effective vocal training throughout my teens. The script was masterly and the recording I have recently acquired is one of my precious possessions. There was something wonderful about being released back into the utterance I had inherited from my parents and those I had grown up with. Naughton had been a coalbagger in the 1930s, just like his hero, and managed to dramatize his experience without theatricalizing it. Dora was touched by the play's sense of authenticity, by what *The Times* described as its 'extreme naturalism', its 'pattern of recognizable natural sounds … To consider the surface of this is to apprehend the depths it covers.'

A quarter of a century after that recording was made, it must have been in a quest to escape myself at my most histrionic, or least authentic, that I sought refuge in the new (my old) voice for a couple of days, but it was counterproductive. I sent Tony the following poem by way of explanation, in rhyming iambic pentameters, of course:

> To Tony Harrison re: *The Misanthrope*
> Bristol Old Vic 1989

> The reason that my rooted Northern voice
> Now feels to me to be so wrong a choice
> Is this: it seems it takes away my chance
> To play Alceste – the man who lives in France,
> The gentleman with land who sets his face
> Against all Paris and its charmed rat race.
> My stance is wrong and vowels wrongly ring
> Chip on shoulder, Chips with Everything.
> Bradford has its bells I'm sure that peal
> And ring their changes on the high ideal.
> Passionate chimes and comic – like Alceste's
> But I can't ring them (we were Methodists –
> No bells in chapels). P'r'aps this i'n't the play
> For classic Northern vowels to have their say.
> I'm locked into a 50s Royal Court sulk
> I just can't sail, I'm like a rusty hulk
> At anchor by that theatre up in Hull.
> You'll see I have no mission aimed to gull
> The Public that the Royal 'Us' – RP
> Alone will suit the Classic Repertory.
> My vocal detour's like that bungle –
> Designer tiger in conceptual jungle.
> I cannot see Le Boi for t'Northern trees –

That voi's deep roots! – Conventions such as these
Though, cannot wear those sounds with any ease.
The RP context serves – it can't be wider;
Alceste is after all an 'in' outsider.
The Sun King's mouth, true, sucked no English plum
But stage convention says, 'still less a plooum!'
It pains me to perpetuate this myth;
It's not through Wimsey, to betray my kith.

The national reviews that greeted our Bristol Old Vic opening were very favourable indeed. Then there came a never-to-be-forgotten day on tour in Nottingham when I drove myself one free afternoon to Byron's old home, Newstead Abbey. As I drove into the large patch of grass that served as the car park, I saw the entire *Misanthrope* cast, minus me, sitting on the green sward having a picnic together. I gave them a charming wave, which they, some of them, returned a little awkwardly. I parked the car and, with as much casual dignity as I could, wandered away through the grounds – as far away as possible.

I recall the last speech of Alceste's in the play, it being one of those fragments that has stuck in my memory:

Meanwhile, betrayed and wronged in everything,
I'll flee this bitter world where vice is king,
And seek some spot unpeopled and apart
Where I'll be free to have an honest heart.

I look up my copy of Tony Harrison's translation and yes, I thought so: what I have remembered is the Wilbur translation in which I'd played Alceste at Nottingham Rep in 1970, a whole nineteen years before that day at Newstead Abbey and the National production. I hasten to add that Michael Ratcliffe, writing in the *Observer*, declared Tony 'our only really serious successful verse dramatist today … exhilarating … to hear in the theatre.'

'White-hot' was a phrase one critic used to describe my performance when we opened at the Bristol Old Vic. But I fear I may have had a default setting of a lower temperature, for by the time Richard Eyre (then Artistic Director of the National) dropped in to see a performance at the Theatre Royal, Nottingham, on our pre-South Bank tour, he felt it necessary to point out that the balance between the style and the heart of my performance was dangerously erring in favour of style. He was doubtless right. On 5 May 1989, I wrote to him from my dressing room in Nottingham:

Dear Richard,
    Thank you for reminding me about the heart of the play and the heart of Alceste. Only style that reveals the man rather than encrusts him is of any use and, though I despair of some of these

dates we play – I've known them since I went round them with Cicely Courtneidge in 1962 and they never change (is it something in the water?) – all the more reason why one should never lose sight of the nakedness beneath the brilliant articulation of these characters.

Bradford (my home town) thank God was excellent. I remember Jacobi, who was pissed off by a snowy week there in the 60s when all the roads were up and the theatre was still a cramped and shabby variety date, I remember him telling me that the audiences they had for *Three Sisters* (NT Olivier production) were the best they'd had anywhere in the way they'd responded. …

I'll put the heart back in tonight and remove the inverted commas.'[2]

Poster advertising *The Misanthrope* outside Bradford's Turkish Baths in the same road as the Alhambra. Photo: © EP

If I were further to defend myself from Richard's charge, I would be tempted to call Tom Stoppard as a witness, only because he has allowed for something that directors never permit one to use as an excuse, namely the audience. Observing his own plays in performance, he has noted that there are occasions when the curtain rises, the actors and the lights and the set all

---

[2] I suddenly have qualms; how much might the inverted commas have dogged my performances over the years? The director Ian Judge once stopped me during a rehearsal of *Twelfth Night*, when I was playing Malvolio, saying 'Oh, don't quote yourself.' I was taken aback until I realized what he meant: I was quoting the Malvolio that had been achieved at the previous rehearsal, rather than performing today's Malvolio.

do the right thing, but there is something subtly wrong – the event does not take flight. That something, he says, is the audience. There! Sir Tom has pronounced, and one knows from experience in the arena what a difference the crowd can make; not only that, but on tour one gets to recognize over the years the good towns and the bad.

There *must* be something in the air or water up in Nottingham that works on the collective consciousness of its citizens when they assemble for a play, belying the probability of there being present an equal number of sensitive souls of intelligence and humour with a healthy propensity for laughter. 'They started it', I find myself saying when the performance does not take wing, because the atmosphere an audience imparts is palpable from the word go. Conversely (or perversely), I have often found myself in my seat in a London theatre, quite left behind to begin with, as the audience around me, excited to have procured tickets for the latest 'must-see', seem almost hysterical, determined anyway to indulge an excitement that hasn't as yet been generated from any source on stage that I have divined. You see how effectively I have just cast myself as a misanthrope.

If Nottingham was not a favourite audience, Hull was the nadir. It was with a certain glee that I pounced on a phrase in *Old Wild's*, the memoirs of a mid-nineteenth-century fit-up showman, complaining of the audiences in Hull, a place 'from which the rogues of olden time used to pray to be delivered'. Nothing has changed in a century and a half. But one person's response can outweigh a whole theatre of others. I was attending a big formal lunch in Hull when a lady murmured at my shoulder and whispered urgently, 'I don't want to disturb you. Just wanted quickly to say that I had some bad news last week – I was diagnosed as having cancer. I made myself come to the lunchtime talk you gave about the play at the theatre the other day and there was something about it; it was a gift that made me decide to soldier on and I just wanted to thank you.' With that she was gone, having bestowed on me a gift that I value to this day.

Alceste is always right, and, talking of Nottingham, I recall the resentment I felt at being put right on some point by director David William in 1970, as we all luxuriated in eating together in the Nottingham Playhouse restaurant after *Misanthrope* rehearsals one evening in the company of the exquisitely pretty Nicola Pagett, who played Célimène. Now David is an extremely intelligent man, beautifully articulate and witty, but he is not always right. He was amazingly right about how to play Célimène, could demonstrate *how* effectively, so that one realized how important it was in the spats between Célimène and Alceste that she preserve a lightness and humour with this absurd, jealous and moody man, who has such an embattled way of expressing his love for her. It was so easy in 1970, and so it remained in 1989, for her to become embattled too and quickly lose her temper and charming, confident good humour, so that their duologues were in danger of developing a symmetrical note of bickering complaint, which is at once unattractive and completely kills the comic reality of the relationship Molière has created. She knows when she is cornered in her deceit with the evidence of one of her letters and just when to turn and be strategically aggressive, and soon she has him wrong-footed and melting:

Alceste. Please explain, to clear yourself, just what
          does this mean here …
Célimène. I certainly will not!
          Your behaviour really puts me in a fury.
          What right have you to play at judge and jury?
          How dare you say such things? It's a disgrace
          to fling such accusations in my face.
Alceste. Now let's not lose our tempers or complain.
          This expression here now, please explain …
Célimène. No! No! I'll do nothing of the kind.
          I don't care any more what's on your mind.

It is extraordinary for British actors for whom rhyming couplets suggest pantomime, to find themselves enmeshed in Molière's stylish emotional rollercoaster of a scene. Soon Alceste is outflanked:

          Ah, it never fails to take me by surprise,
          my feebleness. Your sweet talk may be lies,
          but I must learn to swallow it all whole.
          I'm at your faithless mercy, heart and soul.
          I'll hang on till the bitter end and see
          Just how far you'll go in perfidy.
Célimène. No, you don't love me as you really ought.
Alceste. My love goes far beyond the common sort.
          So keen was I to show it that I wished
          you were unlovable, impoverished.

Wonderful stuff for comedians to get their teeth and hearts into.

In a spare moment during technical rehearsals at the Bristol Old Vic, I took myself away from the stage and the austerity of Richard Hudson's perilous rake[3] and to the scene shop, a place I normally regard as my spiritual home. There was a vast array of paint pots and a practical, though Pollock-like, splatter everywhere, but, on this occasion, I did not feel at home; for dominating the middle of the floor was the giant tiger rug. It *was* replaced, never used in fact, supplanted by an oblique patch of scarlet carpet surmounted by a tea chest and the odd champagne bottle. The tea chest was intended to create an air of improvisation and make-do, the conceit being that the widowed Célimène had only just moved in.

---

[3] Acting on that gradient was the thing, it seemed the only thing, that was to fascinate the Friends of the theatre at every après-first-night drinks do on the tour.

The discarded tiger rug which I encountered in the scene shop of the Bristol Old Vic.
Photo: © EP

We had a miniature seminar at Bristol University at which the production was discussed. Incredulously I listened whilst an elderly professor of the drama described how he had spent some time during the performance trying to work out the symbolism of the tea chest – he had noted that 'Algeria' was stamped on it – and wondering whether lines spoken while a character was standing on the red carpet were meant to have a special significance as compared to those spoken off it.

And there, confusedly, I rest my case.

Chapter 25

Ibsen at the Launderette

The purpose of art is washing the dust of daily life off our souls.
                                                                Picasso

Sunday afternoon

When one thinks about it, washing one's dirty linen in public is the perfect ancillary task to be accomplishing whilst formulating an essay on almost any Ibsen play. Fingers poised over my laptop, and mesmerized by the circulating suds at the local launderette, I'm inspired to come clean concerning my whereabouts this Sunday afternoon, if you will pardon the pun. But I must assure you that I am presiding over no collection such as Falstaff complains of in *The Merry Wives of Windsor*: 'Foul shirts and smocks, socks, foul stockings, greasy napkins … the rankest compound of villainous smell that ever offended nostril … stinking clothes that fretted in their own grease.' Our innocent, usually extraordinarily clean little dog was slightly sick on a duvet cover; a thorough wash of the duvet seemed advisable, hence the jumbo-sized Rex Professional at our launderette across the green is performing its royal function as I ponder the obsession with keeping up appearances and keeping down the murk that afflicts so many of Ibsen's characters.

It strikes me how badly, even by Elizabethan standards of hygiene, the fat knight's description of his experience in the laundry basket reflects on the Ford household, though, of course, fun-loving Mistress Ford, we know, is a pure soul and faithful to her husband: no dark domestic secrets in that family, however pathologically suspicious of his wife Master Ford may be. By contrast, what household of Ibsen's does not have dark secrets?

I must throw another ball into the air in my unwieldy juggling of this essay and mention the abandoned copy of *The Sunday Times* Culture section in the deserted launderette, with its devastating review of Ibsen's *Ghosts* at the Duchess. No week in which a new production of *Ghosts* opened would be complete without at least one critic quoting Clement Scott's infamous leading article in the *Daily Telegraph* (14 March 1891) on the play's first London staging, when dirty linen was not a strong enough epithet and 'an open sewer' was how the play was described. Scott went on to apply other graphic metaphors of putrefaction to *Ghosts*: 'a hideous, untreated wound, a filthy act performed in public, a leper's hospital … fetid, literary carrion, crapulous stuff.'

Well, now as I reach the spin and tumble dry stage I seem to have lost track of Ibsen's metaphorical dirty linen and am hard pressed to draw any useful parallels with my sweet-smelling duvet. But, in remembering my visit with my mother to the very first launderette to open in our part of town when I was around fourteen, circa 1950, it suddenly occurs to me that, a year or two before I was born, my mother, to earn a little extra cash on top of my father's modest wage, took in washing from a lady who lived opposite. My elder brother recalls her coming back across the cobbled street from delivering it, all mangled, dried and ironed, with half a crown in her hand and agonizing over whether she had asked for too much. It is hardly the soul-searching characteristic of a Rebecca West, but as I imagine my poor mother worrying over what a neighbour might think, like some minor domestic character in a realistic drama, I realize she was having those thoughts in the mid-1930s, little more than fifty years after Ibsen had written *Rosmersholm*, and that I am further away by some twenty years from the day of my birth in 1936 than Mother was that washing day from the premiere of Ibsen's late play. And yet the trick with acting these old dramas is to play them in an at once particular and universal *now*.

Monday morning

It is a bright, spring-like day, of the sort my mother would have called 'a good drying day', though she would never have dreamed of doing washing on a Sunday, and once told me that Sir Titus Salt, the philanthropic local mill owner, an Ibsen contemporary and look-alike if ever there was one, had been reputed to go round his modern workers' village with a pair of scissors, snipping any clotheslines he saw strung out on the Sabbath. This always seemed strange to me because I never saw a clothesline on a Sunday in any of our streets throughout the whole of my childhood – it would have been an outrage. Certainly the swings and roundabouts in our local park continued to be chained up on the Sabbath, long after the modernity of our first launderette was established and operating five days a week.

In contemplating what is sometimes regarded as the most modern of Ibsen's plays, and the changes in moral attitudes in my own lifetime, how shocked, even appalled I am to have read just now that the 'godfather' of modern drama fathered a child during his apprenticeship to a chemist, by the chemist's daughter, but refused to acknowledge the boy who grew up to live in poverty. 'There's always someone left out', as a rent boy, representing Caliban, complains in Alan Bennett's *The Habit of Art*. Having mentioned a contemporary playwright, I suppose it shows just how far we have travelled that Bennett's play, featuring the poet W. H. Auden peeing in the kitchen sink and his rendezvous with the rent boy, should be running at the National Theatre at the same time as the parish church of St John-at-Hampstead is boldly advertising Auden's name in a poster for a Lenten Evensong dedicated to Poetic Faith.

'You were born to play this part' is a rare compliment, even when awarded to oneself. When others confer it, though one is grateful, one faintly resents the implication that one's success is entirely genetic, all nature and none of the hard, patient slog of nurture, without which no God-given talent can flourish and survive. Being 'born to play the Prince of Denmark' is eons away from being born to *be* the Prince of Wales. Nevertheless, if I can't convince myself that any one of my performances is worthy of this compliment, I believe I've failed. There is no margin of error, one either *is* the character or one is not. Of course, there can be no exclusively definitive interpretation of Rosmer, Peer Gynt, Hamlet, Cleopatra or Prospero, but, however much craftsmanship, technique, imagination, intelligence, experience and dogged application has gone into a performance, the result must *seem* to the manner born, to have been achieved with innate ease, or the effort counts for nothing.

It is clear that the House of Rosmer, with its august family portraits and its historical standing in the community, bears no resemblance whatever to the house where I was born. Nor did I know whether to expect that my Rosmer would be worthy of the prized compliment when, in the bottom of a neglected drawer, I came across two cassettes of the Radio 3 production of *Rosmersholm* I played in twenty years ago. Yet there was a magical connection between my boyhood home and the world of Ibsen. Tongue-tied as we were as a family, the spoken word was pre-eminent and the Third Programme entered my life not long after my tenth birthday in 1946; we may have kept mum, but others bared their souls to us. None of this, in Ibsen at least, would have been to do with subtext. They spat it out, as my father would have said.

Sony Radio Awards, 1992. Photo: © Tony Jones

Radio being what it is, it had almost slipped my mind that I'd played Rosmer on Radio 3. I hadn't remembered the play in any kind of detail. Navigating Ibsen's apparently nebulous but intricately charted territory is the kind of exercise that the Third Programme was born to accommodate. Now if only half a million people listened to *Rosmersholm*, that's the equivalent of fourteen months on tour with full houses in large theatres, and even a quarter of a million corresponds to well over a six-month sell-out in a big house in the West End. Twenty thousand is equal to a season at the National's Cottesloe. But I am out of date. I am remembering the days of my boyhood when the dramatization of *The Cruel Sea* boasted a listening audience of one third of the adult population. So I telephoned the BBC customer helpline and a young man told me, when I asked him if he could advise me what the current average audience is for Radio 3 Drama, that he didn't have that kind of information but could refer me to the London switchboard who would be able to help; they did, by referring me to back to the number I rang originally. I thanked the lady for the Kafkaesque experience, but said it was Ibsen I was interested in.

Performing to live theatre audiences on tour, imagine the bond the cast would have forged with this Norwegian hothouse of a play (if that's not a contradiction in terms) and, indeed, what bonds with one another: Lindsay Duncan as Rebecca West, Charles Kay as Kroll, Freddie Jones as Brendel, Nigel Anthony as Mortensgaard and Mary Wimbush as Mrs Helseth, the old servant, all of us delighting together after the curtain call at the Alhambra in the best Indian Restaurant in Bradford, and walking on Wuthering Heights the next day. Tea at Newstead Abbey in Nottingham, perhaps squeezing into the kitchen where D. H. Lawrence grew up in the mining village of Eastwood; six evenings and two matinées a week, embodying what James Agate declared in 1926 'always was, and must be, a stupendous work.'

Four years earlier, expounding the thesis that 'Acting demands primarily not so much certain vague qualities of mind as certain very definite attributes of body', Agate wrote:

> The actor in an Ibsen play is not concerned with the play's spiritual or literary merit. He is not concerned with anything beyond his own sense of the theatre, the spectator's sense of the theatre, and the job of fusing the two. It is extraordinary how much can be done, even with Ibsen, by the professional duffer, the 'sound and competent' actor. Such an actor may not have the brains of a hen, and yet be carried on to some kind of success by the perfection of his purely technical mechanism. On the other hand, not all the brains in the world, the nicest discrimination in the thinking out of the part that is psychologically all thumbs, are of much avail to a man who does not quite know what to do with his hands.

No truer words have ever been spoken about acting. It's a physical art, but in radio the hands are busy holding the script and quite a lot of concentration goes into the attempt to turn the pages silently, and the rest into the alchemy of converting expert sight-reading into – well, there is no other word for it – life.

Incidentally, I woke this morning to the voice of Helena Bonham Carter being interviewed on *Woman's Hour*: she is part of my Radio 3 landscape, literally, because we were, unusually for radio, on location together by a lake when we acted as Nina and Dr Dorn in a Radio 3 production of *The Seagull*. What a waste it is, not only having real lakes on radio, unless it's in *Open Country* or *Farming Today*, but also a waste having great beauties, like Helena and Lindsay Duncan, playing heroines.

Agate also wrote, 'I am not going to pretend that *Rosmersholm* is not absurdly difficult', and indeed the memory rushes back: after the final cup of indifferent BBC tea, the studio clock ticking away our last minutes of recording time on the last afternoon, Lindsay and I, before the impartial but supersensitive stereophonic ears of the mike, trying to get our hearts and minds and imaginations into the final twists of the spiritual and psychological plotting in a scene in which, to quote Agate again, 'Rosmer and Rebecca drop from the status of figures in a vision to that of diseased and monstrous egotism.'

Brushing the dust off my *Rosmersholm* cassettes to renew as a listener what had been a passing, though hopefully intimate acquaintance with the play as an actor, I was not even as prepared as the theatregoer in 1926 who might have taken Agate's advice 'to see this play, and to spend the previous evening with the printed score and a wet towel.' My experience, rediscovering this haunting play as a listening audience of one, was as unforgettable as any essentially evanescent experience can be. The cast seemed as near as damn it impeccable and, though I seemed to have come down from a spiritual elocution class, unaccountably held in a Nordic mist by Noël Coward, I too charted Ibsen's unique calms, unexpected undercurrents and treacherous undertows leading to the final double suicide in the mill-race with surprising alacrity. Just think; I had forgotten about the double suicide, which happens off stage (and off mike), so it came to me as freshly as if I had been hearing the first performance.

It crossed my mind that I was particularly suited to playing Rosmer, which could be a grave disadvantage for an enormous swathe of other great parts in the repertoire. 'The part of Rosmer', pronounced Agate again, 'is unactable except for a happy fluke in the way of personality.' Thinking about it now, I believe the vital thing about him is that Rebecca West has found him sexually alluring from the moment she set eyes on him, years before the curtain went up. The actor must embody a predominantly unconscious allure combined with an asexual high-mindedness on his journey between the Rosmer tradition of conventional religiosity and the beginnings of late-nineteenth-century free thinking. Then, in Act Three, he must discover his testosterone in such a way that he doesn't get a laugh.

I have written elsewhere about the scientifically proven theory that seventy percent of what we receive in any conversational interchange is transmitted by the infinite subtleties of body language. All this the radio audience provides from its own imagination, as do the readers of novels.

*   *   *

To return to yesterday's abandoned copy of *The Sunday Times* Culture section in the deserted launderette, and its review of *Ghosts*: with all the evidence of the physical presence of the actors, the setting and clothes, it seems that the audience still, in some way, provides part of the evening from its own collective imagination, or perhaps as many imaginations as are present. On the first night at the Duchess Theatre there were some 490 imaginations with visions violently opposed. A 'terrifically compelling and often disarmingly comic account' was the experience of Paul Taylor of the *Independent*. 'Shockingly good.' *The Sunday Times* critic was neither shocked nor amused: 'It manages to confirm the clichéd prejudice about Ibsen: he gives us nothing but Nordic angst, gloom and claustrophobia.'

I learned only this morning that our *Rosmersholm* is included as a special feature in a recent DVD collection of BBC Ibsen. It is there awaiting your – is it contribution or verdict?

Chapter 26

The Spaces in Between: *Krapp's Last Tape*

> *The experience of my reader shall be between the phrases, in the silence, communicated by the intervals, not the terms, of the statement, between the flowers that cannot coexist, the antithetical season of words, his experience shall be the menace, the miracle, the memory, of an unspeakable trajectory.*
>
> Samuel Beckett (1932)

This is a play about a man and his diary, the record of his life, literally recorded on a reel-to-reel tape recorder. In it the actor performs with a recording of himself – himself, the actor he trusts best in all the world; the actor whose criticism, if he is fortunate, is constructive, however harsh, and only seldom flattering. 'Just been listening to that stupid bastard I took myself for thirty years ago' are the words Krapp commits to a new tape after his first listening session. 'Hard to believe I was ever as bad as that.'

After a 6 p.m. performance of *Krapp* at Stratford's the Other Place in the summer of 1997, I found myself the centre of a small, informal meeting as I crossed through the café bar to go out and on to the main house for the evening performance of *Hamlet*. Just one or two people had waited to see me. An elderly gentleman – well, he might have been sixty-five – said, 'I saw *Waiting for Godot* when it first came out and made nothing of it. I don't know why I came today to see this play, but I enjoyed its spaces in between, the silences, the stillnesses. You see, then I had nothing to fill them with. Now I do.'

The other day I was at an exhibition of twentieth-century Chinese prints, looking at a monochrome portrait of the Forbidden City at night. There was a moon. I remembered wandering round the inside of the Forbidden City at will in 1982. There were few Westerners then, but hundreds of Chinese in their uniform blue Mao jackets and in mundane contrast to the reds and yellows and gold of the architecture. The print, in greys only, showed the Forbidden City as most Chinese had known it for five centuries – from the outside. A large proportion of the picture was taken up by a shadowy section of the long, high south wall. In the exhibition catalogue there was a note about the importance of the apparently 'empty' areas in Chinese art, the suggestion being that therein was contained much of the meaning. I don't think I can compare my pastel drawing of myself as Krapp with the refinement and skill of so many of the prints I saw that day, but perhaps there is something appropriate in the fact that it leaves the onlooker to fill in the blanks.

Tellingly in the facsimile of Beckett's Production Notebook *for Krapp's Last Tape* the blank pages have been lovingly reproduced.

Performing the play – and performing is *almost* the wrong word – imposed the most extraordinary discipline. Simplicity. Simply listening, simply eating a banana. The discipline of doing no more than is set down for one to do, as Hamlet advised the clowns. I once saw the great Russian clown Slava and was amazed by the magnetic power he had over a big audience in the slow, quiet passages of his show; it was full of spectacular effects, but, oh, the moments where he paused and seemed only to exist on the minutely eventful journey from one 'blank' space to another!

How I came to do *Krapp* at all says something about the internal politics of the RSC, though little about the play. I was telephoned by Adrian Noble and offered for the coming season Polonius in *Hamlet*, King Cymbeline in *Cymbeline* and Master Ford in *The Merry Wives of Windsor*. He was very keen to get me into his production of *Cymbeline* and I was equally keen to get out of it. 'We will make it a quest to discover why the play is called

Master Ford in *The Merry Wives of Windsor*, RSC, 1996–7.

Cymbeline,' said Adrian. I suggested that it was called *Cymbeline* because it was the only way Shakespeare could persuade a decent actor to play such a rotten part. It's like Prospero with the guts and magic taken out, though Cymbeline does have the pivotal role in the final resolution scene, which has a heady pace and the magic of reconciliation about it. One night Adrian came beaming into my dressing room and told me that I had played this last scene thrillingly, 'like Scarlatti.' Wikipedia says of Scarlatti's keyboard sonatas: 'Some of them display harmonic audacity in their use of discords, and also unconventional modulations to remote keys.' So perhaps Shakespeare called the play *Cymbeline* just so that I could demonstrate his anticipation of the Baroque.

Ford is a comic gem so there was no trouble there. Instead of Polonius, I asked to do the double of the Ghost and the Player King as well as the Gravedigger (the director, Matthew Warchus, wouldn't go that far, but I've seen it done). I said I would agree to *Cymbeline*, if I could do *Krapp's Last Tape* at the Other Place. In the event, *Krapp* was not scheduled as part of the official Other Place season, and David Hunt and I spent a lot of energy promoting it. Nevertheless, it came to be a sell-out (in the box-office sense) at the Pit and was included in the RSC's New York and Washington season in 1998. The four performances of *Krapp* in New York were sold out while we were still in England, long before any of the other plays. It even came to look as if it were 'meant', bookended as it was with the production of *Everyman*, the earliest of plays, as one of the great plays of the modern era. All this when *Krapp* was only added after long wrangling because I refused to go to America when *Merry Wives* was dropped from the repertoire.

In Stratford I rented a tiny Victorian cottage from Stanley Wells and his wife Susan Hill. Its proximity to Shakespeare's grave I found strangely comforting. On the first morning I spent there, I was conning some lines, the Bard's, or perhaps Beckett's, and all was in line with my hitherto unfulfilled dream of minimalist simplicity. I was sitting in one of two large easy chairs with new white covers; the walls were also newly white, with no pictures, and I hadn't been in residence long enough to spoil things with my usual clutter, the room being small enough to be cluttered by four scripts and a copy of the *Guardian*. The post arrived, that is, the postman suddenly shot some letters in so that they landed on my lap from the five feet that lay between me and the letterbox.

I was determined to hang onto my dream, however, and the tiny backyard soon had some flowers in its patch of earth, a bird table, and somehow I managed to buy a hammock that would just fit. No, there were no rude awakenings, though when Emily and the children came to stay, we all had to be terribly kind to one another. My Stratford idyll was even written about in the international press. I was quoted in the *Washington Post* as saying: 'I had the most wonderful time in Stratford. ... I slept in a bed, facing the same direction, I think, as Shakespeare's bones. I had a bike and hammock in the backyard. On some days I'd do a matinée of *Merry Wives of Windsor*, then spend twenty minutes in the hammock looking up at the sky. I'd bike off to do *Krapp* at six o'clock, and then *Cymbeline* or *Hamlet* in the evening. Really, what better life could one have?'

With Joanna Pearce (Imogen) in *Cymbeline*, RSC, 1997.
Photo: © Zuleika Henry

The pace quickened in New York. We'd rehearsed a whole new show, partly in London, as a benefit to raise funds for the RSC and the Brooklyn Academy of Music. Staged in the enormous Hammerstein Ballroom of the Manhattan Centre, the programme featured excerpts from several of the Bard's plays not in our current repertoire as well as musical selections from *Kiss Me Kate*, *Nicholas Nickleby* and *Piaf*. At the dinner afterwards I sat next to an elderly lawyer of impressive *gravitas* and explained to him that when I opened in *Krapp's Last Tape* I would not have played it for five weeks and that my opening timetable would comprise a morning dress rehearsal, a matinée of *Hamlet* in the BAM Opera House, an early evening performance of Beckett in the BAM's nearby Majestic Theatre and, finally, a regular evening performance of *Hamlet* back at the Opera House. 'As your legal advisor,' he said, 'I instruct you to adhere to no such schedule.' My 'dashing' exploits garnered comment in *The New York Times*: 'When it comes to busy people, put Edward Petherbridge of the Royal Shakespeare Company near the top of the list ... Mr Petherbridge will have played eighteen performances in three pivotal roles between May 21, when *Hamlet* opened, and June 6, when *Cymbeline* closes.' On the day of the dress rehearsal for *Krapp*, the single light bulb over my table kept burning out for some reason and most of the rehearsal was spent trying to find out why and remedying the fault.

The Washington critic was extraordinarily kind to me. Quietness is very important in *Krapp's Last Tape*; in fact, it is some time before a word is spoken and the pauses throughout are vital. On its first night at the Kennedy Centre, the audience had clearly had a challenging time getting to the early performance and I was dismayed that latecomers were being admitted into the small studio theatre in which I was playing; they came and they came, for a full twenty minutes they came. My friend Gates McFadden had come (on time) from LA, during a break in filming as Dr Crusher in *Star Trek*, and not only was she wildly distracted by the steady flow of creeping latecomers but she was sitting next to a woman who was holding a large bunch of flowers wrapped in cellophane, which creaked in the few pauses that might have otherwise survived. When Gates came round afterward she was astonished to find that the flowers had been delivered to me and were already sitting in a vase. In spite of the restive audience, the critic wrote: 'Like the playwright, this actor is a poet of stillness.'

Every time I performed the play I learned to marvel at it the more. It defies categorization. It is an intellectual and elegiac vaudeville sketch for clown and tape recorder, a life's history in fifty minutes, beginning with the hero slipping on a banana skin and ending as he looks into the abyss. It is a conjuring trick with stage and 'real' time – except that there is no trick. The time the solitary Krapp spends with us in the play is the *actual* time it takes to sigh and peer at his keys and search his table drawers for bananas, to read his logbook, to play and listen to a particular tape ('Box ... thrree ... spool ... five.'), and begin to record another. But the sense of the *distances* between his present and his pasts, captured in the sound of his voice, evoked by the use of the stop-and-start, rewind and fast-forward buttons, so actual, so arbitrarily, sometimes violently controlling but giving rise to the surprising, disruptive power of his history as it intrudes into his current existence – all this gives the play its deep sense of perspective.

Some people professed not to understand the play. But the action is utterly simple. A man sets out to listen to a particular tape he made of his spoken reflections thirty years before, on his thirty-ninth birthday; a recording in which, it transpires, he talks of listening to a tape made ten or twelve years earlier. On the tape he is heard reflecting, too, on the year just gone by, his thirty-ninth. Having listened to this tape, he begins to record a new one, commenting on what he has just heard, and on the year he has just lived through, his sixty-ninth. He abandons this recording and returns to listen again to a particular passage in the old tape. That's it. There is nothing obscure in what he says, live or recorded. There are some silences, and clearly what we hear, live or recorded, are only fragments of his story, his sometimes ludicrously unsuccessful literary career and emotional life. Yet, within this minimalist box of tricks, we suddenly know all there is to know about the man; we get a terrifying measure of his life, of its vastness and its smallness.

After Stratford and London, New York and Washington, I did a tour: Edinburgh, Dublin, Jerusalem, High Wycombe et al. I can boast that I spent Christmas Day 1998 in Tiberias, playing Beckett's *Krapp* a stone's throw from the very edge of the Sea of Galilee.

The night before, farcical disaster had struck during the Christmas Eve performance in Karmiel, an hour's drive away, in the town's only venue, the 800-seat Cultural Centre. I had wondered whether *Krapp* was what the people of Karmiel needed. It was apparently; they were, unlike their Washington counterparts, wonderfully punctual and attentive. Nonetheless, fifteen minutes into the show, someone padded down the long flight of auditorium steps, and left slamming the door. The marvellously silent audience seemed to unite in a dismayed intake of breath as that door slammed on the early leaver. But it was only the beginning. Shortly, furious shouts could be heard echoing in the foyer, perhaps three minutes' worth. I locked myself deep inside Krapp's solitude, considering at the same time whether I should go off and start again. The poor old man, it turned out, thought he had bought a ticket for *Lord of the Dance*, which was coming to Tel Aviv's vast Mann Auditorium. No doubt, for a while, Krapp's noisy white boots and banana-skin business, and eventually the Dublin accent, when the monologue finally began, fooled him into believing that any minute the lights would turn puce, scores of Irish tap dancers would flood the stage, and I would tear off my shirt and white hair and become Michael Flatley.

Beckett's Krapp, New York, 1998.
Photos: © Sara Krulwich / *New York Times* / eyevine

In the interval the manager of the theatre came round to tell me that, to pacify the gentleman, he had offered him free seats for the forthcoming production of *Goodnight Vienna* (indeed part of its colourful scenery lay in wait behind Krapp's black backcloth). As the complainant disappeared into the night, he was heard to cry: 'I come from Vienna; I've seen them all!'

*   *   *

400

At each performance of *Krapp*, after an interval, I talked to the audience and sometimes they would talk back or ask questions. Of course, one risked the kind of comment I received one day at the Edinburgh Festival, when a man asked me if I remembered the comedienne Beatrice Lillie. 'Yes!' I said, with some enthusiasm.

'What we've just seen,' he said, 'reminds me of a remark she made during one of her sketches, when she turned to the audience and said, "There's less to this than meets the eye!"'

At another performance a lady observed that I had not seemed to be acting in the play. I was not sure how to take this, although her tone was sympathetic, until she said, 'You were a man listening to a tape recorder. In fact you seem more like an actor now.' And I realized that, as far as the *first* half of the evening was concerned, she was paying me a high compliment.

One warm June night in Washington, I was leaving the Kennedy Centre after a performance of Matthew Warchus's production of *Hamlet*, when a man, maybe in his late thirties, stopped to talk to me. His delightful, excited children, a boy and a girl of about ten and eleven, danced around me on the pavement. The theatre crowds were still about, and I don't suppose the children were used to meeting Shakespearean ghosts in the flesh or being up at that hour with the late-night concert and theatregoers swirling about in their gladrags in the headlights of limousines. Their father wanted to talk to me, not about *Hamlet* but about *Krapp's Last Tape*. 'I loved it but, you know, I've been doing some sorting out at home, and I was using the stairs and I had papers and letters and photographs arranged on every tread from top to bottom. I was climbing up and down, and rearranging, and my back was starting to ache and then I'd come across an old picture or a letter and think, "Hey, I'd forgotten that" or "Oh yes, I remember," and I suddenly thought again of *Krapp*, and realized here *I* was, it was me!"'

Then there was the lady in the stalls at Guildford, who said after the interval, 'Yes, I'd like to ask a question. I'm having some people to dinner at the end of the week, and they'll want to hear about this play. I wondered if you could tell me what it's about?'

In Search of the Genuine Article

Chapter 27

The Seeds of Lord Peter Wimsey

There was absolutely no chance of setting eyes on a real live aristocrat in West Bowling when I lived there. The aristocrats had long fled the local stately home of Bolling Hall (the confusion between Bowling and Bolling seems to go back to the Domesday Book). I surmise that the toffs decided it was time to go immediately after they had sold their mineral and coal mining rights in the early nineteenth century. This was the end of 'Merrie England' as far as West Bowling was concerned. The map of 1854 shows a rural landscape scarred with lime pits, disused opencast mines and railway lines. The Bowling Ironworks were practically in Bolling Hall's back garden. In fact, even twenty years before the map of 1854, a survey of the Bradford area states: 'The country about Bradford is extremely pleasant, open and picturesque, adorned with many elegant houses', but neglects to mention Bolling Hall. However, other houses in the district remained salubrious and the moors at Howarth (ten miles away) remained wild, the inspiration for *Wuthering Heights*.

By the late nineteenth century, the ironworks disappeared as did the lime pits and mines, to be replaced by woollen mills and streets of back-to-back houses, a fine municipal park, tramlines, local cinemas (three of them), slipper baths and swimming baths, a library, a church and nonconformist chapels and, of course, schools and pubs. By 1915 anybody could look around Bolling Hall because, having first declined to mill-owning-class tenement, it had become a museum.

The first 'aristocrat' to emerge from this soot-blackened, back-to-back Bowling made fast work of it, running away from her home in Round Street around 1926, a house I passed every day on my way to school from about 1940, by which time she had been married to the great French screen lover Charles Boyer for six years. By the tender age of twenty-three, Pat Paterson had gone from Round Street to Hollywood where she co-starred with Spencer Tracy in *Bottoms Up*, the plot of which required her to pass herself off as the daughter of a lord. I have seen the movie and not a trace of a Round Street accent remains; she is as glamorous, elegant and refined an example of West End womanhood as can be imagined, and that's even before she has begun to lay on the aristocratic guise!

Since 1987 people have been telling me that I was born to play Lord Peter Wimsey, and who am I to deny their democratic right to say so? I blush to admit that there is a sense in which the likes of Peter Wimsey had been my model ever since I'd aspired to go on the stage. I'd had to make the transition from provincial backstreet boy to actor in 1953, three years before the apotheosis of kitchen-sink drama. In those days there seemed to be only one way to do it. Willie Mossop, the young cobbler hero of *Hobson's Choice*, notwithstanding, the stage needed as its staple diet a constant supply of young men of 'good' family, entering through French windows and able to say that line about tennis. Outside the French windows there might only be a tawdry depiction of a corner of the Home Counties on canvas, and beyond that a strategically placed bucket painted red and filled with sand, and beyond that and the stage door only the provincial streets leading to one's lowly theatrical digs. But, if the contract read, or at least implied, 'must dress well on and off', one's training had emphasized that one must *speak* well on stage and off.

I didn't actually model myself on Wimsey, of course – I'd never read the books. But from the day I went to theatre school in Coronation Year, I saw myself as a growing sprig of the theatrical aristocracy and a candidate for the Prince of Denmark. Off stage, I suppose, I developed a persona to operate wherever I found myself: in the rehearsal room or in the fill-in jobs I was to do between times. It was always open to me to play waiters, factory hands, soldiers from the lower ranks, warehousemen and shop assistants, and I would have been a definitive Willy Mossop, but I would play them quite differently from how I played them in life. When I was employed briefly at Jones & Higgins department store in Rye Lane, Peckham, as late as 1963, I must have brought a West End light-comedy style to the sock, tie and handkerchief counter such as had seldom been witnessed in London SE15 retail before or since.

In 1985 I was given the Sayers books by the BBC with a view to my playing Wimsey. At the time I was rehearsing and about to open in Chekhov's *The Cherry Orchard* at the National Theatre and already strictly too old for Wimsey. I read the books, wrapped in plain brown paper for secrecy (the books you understand), in the wings between entrances as Gayev – Stanislavski's old part – a part I was too young for at forty-nine. I finished Gayev on tour on a Saturday in Chicago for the International Theatre Festival where I'd been astonished during the week to get a round of applause on my exit on the last page of Act One. We'd all become oddly liberated because the Chicago audiences decided *The Cherry Orchard* was a comedy. Ian McKellen, who played Lopakhin, asked me in the dressing room one night, 'What are you going to *do* with Peter Wimsey?' I said I had read three novels about him and thought I would 'slip sideways into the character.'

About a week later I was making my first entrance, so to speak, as Lord Peter in a BBC rehearsal room and the director, Chris Hodson, was complimenting Harriet Walter (as Harriet Vane) and me by saying, 'You don't look as if you're acting at all.' Within days I was committing the first scenes of Wimsey to celluloid in an august disused courthouse in Liverpool. Filming gets little if any rehearsal. A make-up girl was running a comb through my blonded hair; perhaps she was improvising too, for in a few of those first shots my hairstyle seems to owe something to Adolf Hitler.

When I went to visit Harriet Vane in prison, I entered and left the prison gates in Lancaster, walked along the corridors in the bowels of the Liverpool courthouse, and entered the cell to find myself in a set in the BBC Television Centre at White City where all the studio stuff was done in very convincing interiors, having been carefully rehearsed in a tall, custom-built block in Acton.

The seven-storey rehearsal block is used for other purposes now, and TV is produced quite differently, of course; then it was a microcosm of the zeitgeist of BBC Television entertainment. The rehearsal rooms were airy and anodyne with large windows on three sides, affording views of real life across the most dismal area of West London. There were little viewing windows in the doors so that, if you did a thorough snoop, you had a panorama of the astonishing output being rehearsed on any day: dancers in leotards, juveniles, character men and women on sofas in small room-sized areas marked out on the floor by gaffer tape, the doorways delineated by vertical wooden poles lodged in specially designed weights. A longer gaze might tell you if it was sitcom or drama that was being perfected. On high days, as the action moved island to island (back kitchen to conservatory and so on), it was followed by a migrant note-taking audience – not only the director and floor manager, but also producer, possibly writer, camera and lighting crew, designer, make-up and wardrobe teams, all familiarizing themselves in preparation for the studio days at Television Centre down the road. Sometimes 'door' poles demarked the positions of pillars in classic plays. On the very top floor was a canteen which provided an overview at a glance of who was in work at the BBC, tables of people exuding that odd mixture of hysteria and complacency that infects actors when they find themselves in congenial, well-paid circumstances.

In one of these rooms in Acton, fifteen years earlier, after a rehearsal of an episode of *Softly, Softly*, in which I played a South London crook, champagne in polystyrene cups was served unceremoniously and rather gloomily to mark some production watershed or other, and I recall spying through a pane on an inaudible Frankie Howerd. He had his back to me and was delivering his patter to a forensic, stony-faced audience of three men in suits who sat on grey plastic chairs against the windows, with the grey Vinyl-covered floor stretching forlornly away into the unpopulated corners of the room.

I had an idea in Liverpool about Wimsey's first approach to meeting Harriet Vane; on that occasion the director had extras as female prisoners scrubbing the prison corridor floors with soap and water, and I introduced a slight slip on a piece of soapy floor, just to undermine Wimsey's savoir-faire a bit. It should have been a head-to-toe shot but it wasn't quite. At any rate, it was a faint touch of psychological slapstick, subtly to take the edge off Wimsey's perfect poise, his apparently permanent state of debonair intellectual command. It was a modus vivendi I had been attempting to perfect for years. When my walking stick got stuck in the sands during the beachcombing scene in *Have His Carcase*, the continuity lady whispered to the director, 'Do you want to go again? Edward lost his stick in the sand.' She didn't recognize it as comic business; I don't know whether I should be proud of that or not.

'Was the monocle a problem?' I am often asked. It was – and it was a mistake. An early illustrator of the stories read 'eyeglass', by which Sayers meant a detective's magnifying glass, and instead he gave Wimsey a monocle, and Wimsey and Sayers were stuck with it. My monocle did fall out and into a cup of tea in a scene with Miss Climpson in her office, but we laughed so much we had to cut. I resorted to double-sided Sellotape after that.

I hear of the Sayers books being discovered through the TV series and the series being discovered through the books. An aficionado, pleased about a recent repeat showing of the 1987 series on ITV3, and already the proud possessor of the complete Dorothy L. Sayers Mysteries on video and DVD, mused about what other formats time might have in store for our noble sleuth, assuring me that Wimsey would go on through cyberspace for 'evermore' (along with Harriet, Bunter et al.) But, as my doctor said to me the other day during a routine check-up, 'This is the moment, this one *now*, it's all we've got.' Ironic that the doctor should say something so existential or even Buddhist in the context of an examination, which was essentially checking on my life expectancy and laying down strategies to prolong it. Isn't 'mindful acceptance of the present moment' the Zen phrase? As a BBC World Service listener, I realize that, at any one time, for a huge proportion of human beings, mindful acceptance of the present moment is an impossibly harsh reality. As I sit here in the dappled shade of my garden, I have the luxury of being able to say that living fully attentive in each moment might be the best way both to prolong life and give good performances.

A delightful yet outlandish claim – that one might have a tiny niche in eternity of any kind. In the light of which, it is interesting to hear the words Dorothy L. Sayers gave to her famous creation in the mid-1930s on the subject of aristocratic pomp, circumstance and influence: 'Our kind of show is dead and done for. What the hell good does it do anybody these days?' In our own day, we should reflect that the hereditary principle has only recently ceased to determine the composition of the House of Lords and that, in providing the modern substitute of the life peer, we still say commoners are 'elevated' to the peerage. Admittedly we sometimes say of the figures who make the political transition from the Commons to the Lords that they have been 'kicked upstairs', a knockabout comedy way of describing the ennobling process. Nevertheless, there have been dark rumours, though apparently no evidence, that such is the kudos, nay the magic hedging about the coronet of a freshly created life peer, there have been those willing to pay cash for such ennoblement.

King, commoner, lord and spy

In the spring of 2007, I was standing in a Buckinghamshire mansion on a handsome staircase of the early Jacobean period. The mansion was meant to be mine, and indeed was mine, when the *Midsomer Murders* cameras were rolling for *Death in a Chocolate Box* and I slipped into character as the slightly dotty, overmedicated hereditary lord of the manor, a less heroic cousin, several times removed if you like, of our hero. Somebody had told me that the date of the staircase had recently been verified, and I realized that the first people to walk up and down the steps I now trod were contemporaries of Shakespeare. I presumed they'd had London connections and had been to the Globe and seen Burbage act, or even Shakespeare himself. I imagined what clothes they had worn and what thoughts they'd had in transit, their hands on the very banister my hand now rested upon, as they went with candle up to bed, or down to breakfast. What had their voices sounded like, theirs and the actors they may have seen? Then I had to abandon these speculations to concentrate on the moment my dotty lord was having; his transitory moment of indecision was all I had to accomplish on the staircase.

Amongst the many irons I had in my fire at that time was the part of King Lear, which I was scheduled to play in New Zealand, to open on my 71st birthday, the 3rd of August. I had committed much of the part to memory. This meant that I had already spoken the part aloud, many times, always trying to perform the trick of honouring Shakespeare's language whilst sounding like a 'real person' rather than an actor; an odd exercise, sitting or pacing in the kitchen at home, spouting Lear's first scene and attempting to sound domestic as well as poetic and majestic.

Leaving the Jacobean staircase and the mansion, I walked back to the Midsomer location base, a farmyard, where the canteen truck with its little towers of polystyrene cups, the caravans for the actors and the double-decker dining-room bus were parked. I thought how strange our dressing accommodation was compared to the original Globe's Tiring House, but how, despite everything, our job as actors had not changed essentially.

Is this the moment to risk putting that job into words? It is the quest, through pretence, to arrive at the truth. It's the search for total emersion, complete identification with character and situation, whilst reserving something of the observer, a creative, controlling self-consciousness. The 'trick' of acting is the wide-awake, trance-like state, by which, in a hair-spring balance, these two apparently contradictory conditions of absorption and detachment become one.

My mobile phone rang. It was Edward Kemp – no relation to Will Kempe, Shakespeare's clown, as far as I know. He was introducing himself as my director to be, and welcoming me to my next job; no, not Lear quite yet (it's all or nothing in this profession). Kemp was welcoming me to the cast of Alan Bennett's double bill *Office Suite*, which was shortly to start rehearsals at Chichester for production at the Minerva Theatre and a provincial tour. The redoubtable Patricia Routledge was to be leading lady and Janet Dale, better known to some of you as Miss Knag the milliner who turned against Kate Nickleby, was to be Patricia's foil in one of the two plays.

With Patricia Routledge (Miss Prothero) in *Office Suite*, Chichester, 2007.
Photo: © Nigel Norrington / ArenaPAL

Now we are still talking about Lord Peter Wimsey, basically; I'm just wondering if you can cleave to that notion whilst I take a detour, which will turn out to be relevant – in the end. You see, I started with Wimsey in the title, soon jumped to an overmedicated dotty lord of a Midsomer manor, then I was a notch or two up, learning the lines of a king in my kitchen, and suddenly we take a nosedive down the social scale to the part Edward Kemp wanted me to play, Arthur Dodsworth, not the lord of any manor, but an unsuspecting Yorkshireman in his semi-detached suburban 'castle'. The fact is I'd been extremely keen to play Alan Bennett's Arthur Dodsworth to break the mould of a surfeit of upper-class types, although I had loved playing, both on stage and on radio, Bennett's Sir Anthony Blunt, the real-life twentieth-century knight of the realm who had been Surveyor of the Queen's Pictures, a distinguished art historian, a practising homosexual, in the days when it was illegal to be such, and, for good measure, finally unmasked as a Soviet spy. A part absolutely within my performing comfort zone, and another example of English drama's preoccupation with 'the toff'.

Incidentally, on the few occasions I've met and spoken with Bennett, I've always felt a bit of a fake since my 'real-life' voice betrays nothing of the fact that I was born a mere ten miles from him and two years later into a slightly lower working-class family. On the *South Bank Show*, following the publication of his *Untold Stories*, he was so disarmingly, utterly convincing and spellbinding as himself – so unaffectedly skilled at television, at standing in Leeds Town Hall and evoking his boyhood concert-going, or perching on a gravestone poking deadpan fun at the confusions caused by that class of churchgoing person who pronounces 'myrrh' and 'mower' identically.

I had reasons, literally very close to home, for wanting to play Bennett's contrasting ultra-ordinary Arthur Dodsworth, confined in his 'castle', which was about to be stormed by Patricia Routledge's Miss Prothero. Dodsworth is a widower, the newly retired erstwhile head of Credit and Settlement in a Yorkshire firm, a mild-mannered, modest, lower-middle-class pensioner, 'branching out' into pottery classes. Happily, here is a perfect and unexpected link, such as is manna from heaven to the writer of a discursive memoir! Not only had I been learning King Lear's lines, I had been defining him and the Fool in clay at *my* pottery classes. I could show you three versions. All Arthur Dodsworth has to show for his classes is an ashtray. True, he's thinking of taking up cooking classes as well. He's enjoying his weekly bowls and 'Gillian and the kiddies bobbing in every five minutes'. He has his budgerigar and since retirement, he says, 'I haven't given work a thought.' Of course, work is what consumes Miss Prothero. More to the point, she is covertly consumed by the amazing changes effected by Dodsworth's successor, which have swept away the system that was Dodsworth's legacy.

The simple set of *Office Suite* in the ornate Richmond Theatre.
Photo: © EP

Kemp, mobile to mobile, was saying, 'Can I do anything to help? Can I fix you a dialect coach?' 'No,' I replied, 'This is the assumed voice, the actor's voice that I am speaking to you in now; as Arthur Dodsworth I will be speaking my native Yorkshire vernacular – a music as familiar to me as "songs my mother taught me".'

But, there was a curious hitch. As I sat in the Chichester rehearsal room in Arthur Dodsworth's fireside chair, conscious that I was, at seventy, a little too old for the part, and about to turn seventy-one, I had the curious sensation that I was closer to my *seventeenth* birthday and my boyhood home, number 71 Pembroke Street, than my 71st birthday. You may laugh, but this was by no means a helpful thing for my Dodsworth. Patricia was the thing itself, had created her part for television nearly thirty years before and seemed to have matured into it, was as authentic in the role now as a vintage wine in one of those venerable bottles. Rehearsing Bennett with her for the first few days was like rehearsing the Ten Commandments with Moses. I was in constant danger of being caught out dancing round the golden calf of waywardness. I felt I understood Arthur Dodsworth; I *knew* him, knew the lines already (*almost*) and the man completely, but I couldn't *feel* like the sedentary, bowls-once-a-week Arthur at all to begin with, though I could *sound* precisely like him. Even our mutual penchant for pottery classes didn't help.

Strange, even ludicrous as it may seem, the classes I felt more affinity with and, indeed, which threatened to manifest themselves at any moment, were the first movement classes I'd attended as a teenager at Bradford's Theatre School; I felt at risk of lifting like an autumn leaf off my fireside chair or turning my hand in an elegant eighteenth-century manner or lapsing into some posture learnt in my Friday morning ballet classes of over fifty years ago. Mind you, Patricia could have done her very own autumn leaf! (I would pay good money to see it.) In a coffee break one day, without moving from the chair she was sitting on, she sang two or three bars from an old revue number, sketching the hand and arm movements so consummately that she implied the whole show, including costumes, scenery and lighting.

To extend the biblical analogy, when we broke for the weekend of week one, Patricia said, 'God bless you.' I realized that actors who storm out of rehearsal rooms, slamming doors as hard as they can, are in need of blessing.

By the second week Patricia and I were getting on famously. There are photographs and reviews of my Arthur Dodsworth, which prove that the green and youthful quality was successfully conquered, if indeed it had been anything but vestigial or illusory. The fact is that the legacy of my early training is physical as well as vocal – perhaps predominantly physical – and I had never seen myself as settled into that dreaded category 'the character actor'. Arthur Dodsworth was not, as they say, a very physical person and I realize now that most of the 'character' parts I have played required something of the deft clown. Even the romantic hero Wimsey (you see we have got back to him) referred to himself as a comedian, a light comedian. There's Newman Noggs, the victim of circumstance, who, chameleon-like, must adapt or conceal himself and his feelings to survive, continually 'in his cups' for anaesthetic, but still capable of girding up what is left of his loins when the Right must be fought for. Or there's the old Restoration lecher and lawyer, Coupler, in *The Relapse*, who, raddled though he may be, is still the duplicitous, mercurial fixer he has always been, with an eye and a groping hand for the gallant young bucks. I was warring against a whole careerful of light-on-their-feet operators, including Cyrano de Bergerac and Molière's Alceste.

Somehow I made myself as complacent in Arthur's cardigan and slippers as he was, the whole point being that he's never had to be majorly adaptive because thirty years ago he caused a major adaptation, gradually devising the office system that was Warburton's salvation and the basis of the system ever since. Miss Prothero feels compelled, in the play's last ten minutes, to reveal to him that, in three months flat, this long-standing system he's worked and lived by has been swept away and is no more. An enthusiastic friend, moved by Dodsworth's fate, described it in the hyperbole of '*King Lear* with laughs'.

One of my best laughs I discovered in a performance quite late in the tour in the massive auditorium of Salford's Lowry Centre, housing a North Country audience that took the verbal music of the little play rapturously to its heart. I'd been dealing with the birdcage and was upstage of the seated Miss Prothero, who at this point was merely the uninvited and unwelcome guest, still prattling on about the banalities of work at Warburton's. 'I've changed my extension,' she announced as an event of some consequence. Gently I clung onto the nearby standard lamp in mild despair for a moment. The audience understood.

A couple of months ago, after a J. B. Priestley evening on the South Bank, a man from Bradford came up and spoke to me.

'Did you ever play the Lowry Centre in Salford?' he asked.

'Oh, yes,' I gushed, telling him of the glorious time I had playing to audiences there in Alan Bennett's double bill.

He paused and, looking at me without expression, said simply, 'I saw that.'

Back in 1958 there was a moment in a New Zealand rehearsal room when I realized how *physical* light comedy was, although I was rehearsing Algernon Moncrieff in that most *verbally* brilliant play *The Importance of Being Earnest*. I realized there on that rehearsal room floor that the quicksilver Algy's dexterity with words demanded that I should always have my weight on the correct foot; that it was vital I should never be at a loss as to what to do with my hands (or what *not* to do with them); that poise and control and physical dexterity were everything, part and parcel of that most vital of mysteries – *timing*.

At the same time I was keenly grateful for a lesson I had been taught by the 'failed' actors who had been my tutors at drama school, namely that one should never display this technique, it must always be subjected to character and situation. Even in the most stylized mode imaginable, it is real life that is being portrayed. However much energy had been lavished on acquiring an acting technique, one had to remember that the characters one played were not acting but *living* – even on the occasions when they might be acting (which they do a lot of in Oscar Wilde).

My first toff

In view of the incipient pangs of misplaced poise and inappropriate youthful flexibility I claim to have felt rehearsing Alan Bennett's Arthur Dodsworth, it is ironic that the very first 'toff' I played (perhaps the first warm-up for Lord Peter), at the tender age of sixteen, should have been an elderly poet in an old folks home. It was in a one-act play by Peter Ustinov called *Beyond* as part of the 1952 Drama Festival of the Association of Bradford Boys' Clubs. The other inmates of the home were an embittered inventor, looking forward to meeting Isaac Newton in the 'beyond' of the title, and a retired soldier, hoping heaven would be Africa. My poet was called Johnny La Force. Now that I have pretensions to being a poet, with no need to pretend the elderly bit, I look back on this character with some curiosity, and I realize too that these characters, like Alan Bennett's Miss Prothero and Dodsworth, spent most of their time in fireside chairs. I have no vivid recollection of feeling too young for Johnny La Force, but then it is fifty-seven years since I rehearsed him. Perhaps there was something still deft about Johnny.

Our little production played in the dilapidated premises of the Sedbergh Boys' Club, a large soot-blackened, double-fronted stone house, plain but with a pillared portico over the front door. An extension added to the back contained the little hall and makeshift stage. It was a curiously anomalous house, bigger and well above the station of any other in our part of West Bowling. (Could it have been built for the minister of the Rehoboth Methodist Chapel opposite?) But it was adjacent to a set of streets down Bowling Old Lane that we, in our respectable though humble streets higher up, considered to be dubious and scruffy. The occupants of the big house, whoever they were, must have long since decamped, leaving the building with the air of one requisitioned by the army for the use of other ranks. The club depended, in its environs among those dark satanic mills, on the charitable support of Sedbergh's famous public school, set in the wilds, I imagined, of Cumberland to the east of the Lake District and on the edge of the Pennines. I knew of that beautiful region only by repute. Now Google Earth has swooped me down to hover and I see the school is set amongst trees in verdant pastureland.

We rehearsed in one of the large front rooms of the house, with the muted sounds of ping-pong matches and the click of billiard balls coming from the hall. The club's ethos wasn't to my taste; though I always liked the gruff rough diamond with a Geordie accent, who single-handedly ran the place and later used his influence to get me a job in a local wool warehouse during my first summer holiday from theatre school. I joined the club when I was fifteen, only because they were entering the Boys' Clubs drama competition; perhaps I was 'headhunted'. We rehearsed to play characters miles above and beyond our experience and social station. In 1951 I had played one of six men, shipwrecked and snowed up in the Arctic for the long sunless winter, in a one-act play by Michael Redgrave – yes, *the* Michael Redgrave – called *The Seventh Man*. The following year I was Ustinov's elderly poet with the first line of the play, a plangent 'Another autumn.'

Reading these short plays again, I'm amazed at their ripe, almost hothouse literary style. In the Redgrave piece, I was required to be in danger of going mad and blind; to read the Bible by the light of the only lamp and speak rather biblically; and to go out of the hut and come back in, giving the impression I'd seen a stranger – the seventh man of the title (almost certainly Jesus) – harbinger, as it turned out, of the returning sun. What I can still hear of this play is not my own lines at all, but the voice of a tall boy named Derek

Armitage, who lent a certain stoic, iron-willed authority to the proceedings and who held nerve and discipline together in the part of Gaffer. I can also hear another boy's voice pronouncing a line from the gloom up left behind me: 'The women of Ireland! The women of Ireland! I can't bear to think of it!' The audience didn't laugh in the wrong places and took the drama as seriously as we did.

As Ustinov's poet in *Beyond*, longing for death and a glimpse 'beyond', I had lines about wanting a splendid funeral. As I write this, by the most amazing coincidence, the radio is playing the slow movement of Tchaikovsky's Symphony No. 5 in E Minor, the very piece that Ustinov specified in his stage directions should be playing quietly on the radio during the action of the play. It seemed to me contrived that the music just happened so perfectly to underscore the sentiments the men were expressing – like a film score. Anyway, this touch may have helped because our production was nominated for the All Bradford Boys' Clubs Drama Finals and transferred to a little custom-built theatre in Lister's Mill across the town. Lister's was the hugest silk mill in the world and perhaps the most magnificent of all Bradford's industrial architectural wonders; it had a mill chimney to outdo the Town Hall clock tower in height and aspired to bring to industry the spirit of the Renaissance. It was built by Samuel Cunliffe Lister, the man who made a fortune investing in and perfecting the Nip Comb, which put hundreds of woolcombers out of work. Presumably, it was he who caused my great-grandfather in the census of 1851 to style himself 'woolcomber and ginger-beer seller.'

View of Lister's Mill and its 255-foot chimney.
Photo: © EP

Some time had elapsed by the occasion of the Finals. I had become a drama student in the interim at Bradford's own Theatre School and had just turned seventeen. So it was as a combination of the backstreet boy amateur actor and the aspiring professional that I arrived at Lister's Mill. I cannot vouch for the exact whereabouts of the little hall and stage (built for the mill workers to do their pantomimes and Gilbert and Sullivan). It was somewhere within the immensity of Lister's daunting building. Now the great edifice has been partially gutted, preserving the rich brick and stonework and the classical iron pillars that once stood by whilst velvet was being woven for the coronation of 1911 or for Washington DC's White House in 1976 (perhaps the newly appointed Jimmy Carter needed some new drapes to take away the tints and taint of his predecessor, Gerald Ford, who had pardoned Nixon). In World War II the weaving had been of parachutes and fifty miles of khaki. Now that the building has been rescued from the vandals, squatters, pigeons and foxes, who took over in 1992, and restored to accommodate luxury apartments, who knows what happens on the spot where I once said:

> I want my death to be something rather gentle and noble ... like something in an eighteenth-century opera ... I want a few tears and many, many flowers ... all those top hats, gilded hearses ... (*Malicious*) I hope it rains ... and that I may be there in spirit ... sheltering under Sir Henry Newbolt's umbrella.

I find myself now hoping for the 'gentle and noble' bit. The poet's two companions, the soldier, hoping heaven will be Africa (tall Armitage again), and the inventor, hoping to meet Newton in the 'beyond' ('Tich' Armitage, his brother), both die on the penultimate page. Johnny, desperate not to be left behind, takes the soldier's loaded revolver (which he and the inventor only just learned about a few pages before) out of its hiding place, tries it out on the ceiling, with a dramatic falling-plaster effect, and then turns it towards his head, only to find he has used the single bullet. My last line was (*infinitely sad*): 'Yet another autumn ... and another autumn ... and another ... and not so much as a glimpse ... beyond.'

What possessed the local amateur actors, a husband-and-wife team, Audrey and Tom Woodrow, who selected and directed us in this play, to think that it was a fitting vehicle for boys from the back-to-back houses of West Bowling? Nevertheless, it was a *play*, and plays were seldom about the likes of us; we took the culture gap for granted and set about bridging it as best we could. I had been bridging it for some time, with a vengeance against all odds, not even aware of a gap when I sang 'Oh! For the wings of a dove' as a boy soprano in the chapel opposite Sedbergh Club, or learnt Schubert's 'The Trout' for a singing competition in the Wharfedale Music Festival to be judged by the famous composer Herbert Howells, of whom I had not heard. These were democratic possibilities. Incidentally, Howells's report called me 'a fine young musician with a fine gift of word delivery.'

Who now sits where the women were sitting in 1953 as I walked through one of the grand entrances of Lister's Mill, serving that night as a stage door? They were the mothers of other competitors I assumed. One of them said with deadpan irony after taking me in, 'Oo, don't 'is muther keep 'im nice!' I made the attempt to preserve my savoir-faire and found a place where I could make up the hair at my temples with white greasepaint and create other signs of age to transform seventeen into seventy-one – as practical, if unlikely, a task as the other way round. Anyway, I won the little shield for the best performance.

Nature and nurture

At drama school I had been expanding my efforts to play gentlemen of all kinds, poets or not, and to become a gentleman actor with a poetic gentleman's voice. Yes, it was difficult whilst living at home, but my parents never complained – I don't know how much I soft-pedalled the posh when talking to them. Had we but known, at the same time, Albert Finney and Tom Courtenay were determinedly preserving their North Country accents down in London at the Royal Academy of Dramatic Art.

The voice is only the tip of the personality iceberg. The cultured voices I'd grown up with had emanated from the wireless on our windowsill, courtesy of the BBC. They came from an otherwise unreachable world of dreaming spires, erudite opinions, and country-house weekends set in olde worlde villages or amongst trees in peaceful pastureland, of fees in guineas and private incomes, of knowing which knife to use and having the right kind of furled umbrella, or of being one of the scruffy tweed-and-corduroy-wearing poets haunting the pubs around Broadcasting House, or of being T. S. Eliot, who wore a four-piece suit, as Virginia Woolf quipped, and went to work in a bank.

Saturday Night Theatre on the Home Service made the cadences of the West End an intimately recognizable dramatic vernacular to us. 'Good English' pervaded the air of our little gaslit room where we sat mute in front of the huge cast-iron range, two tin cans filled with cinders in the heart of the coal fire – no doubt the result of a useful tip from a BBC radio programme to give the precious coal supply extra body. I say 'mute' because my father wouldn't talk and my mother, since her stroke two days before my birth, couldn't, not fluently. My father saved his fluent wit for work; I only learnt that he could be a comedian after his death, from a colleague who'd worked with him in the wool warehouse. Thank God for the flow of vicarious intercommunication from the little box on the windowsill.

Every Sunday lunchtime I listened to *The Critics* discussing the play, the book, the film and the art exhibition in carefully phrased tones of civilized Oxbridge. On Tuesday evenings we listened to *The Brains Trust* – C. E. M. Joad, Commander A. B. Campbell and Julian Huxley. *The Brains Trust* was originally as much a part of the war effort as *ITMA* (*It's That Man Again!*), the one providing civilized discussion and reflection, the other, verbal slapstick and fun, along with the later *Variety Bandbox* when we were buttonholed by the juicily absurd, marvellously timed confidences of Frankie Howerd. There was a tacit acknowledgement between us that we knew and depended on the confidences of all these voices as we sat round the fire or listened with the street door open on warm summer evenings (always conscious of the BBC's requests that we should on such evenings be considerate of the peace of our neighbours, but they were all listening in anyway, up to 20 million of them if it was a popular comedy programme). In a way these radio personalities were more familiar to us than our neighbours, though I remember my father complaining of *The Brains Trust* one night, 'I could do with these people but they never give a straight answer to a question.'

Julian Huxley was a biologist interested in eugenics, though I gather he did not believe in superiority between races, nor did he believe that the working classes were genetically inferior (which brings us glancingly back to Peter Wimsey and the idea of 'good breeding'). Our local breeding stock on nearby Round Street, a street of unpaved dirt with the occasional stone sticking up, had produced not only Pat Paterson but also Stanley Brogden, who in 1929 was selected to play Rugby League for England. Two examples of the special cases that occur when nature, as opposed to nurture, comes up with a magic genetic formula.

But what about the people with no noticeably spectacular gifts, like my father, who was probably the 'runt of the litter' and born with poor eyesight, who lost his job as a warehouse foreman when I was small and remained a low-paid ordinary warehouseman for the rest of his working life? Or my mother, who took in a little washing (all done by hand) to make ends meet until she was disabled by the stroke, though she continued to do all the housework and our washing until the advent of the launderette. Neither of my parents drank. They somehow managed to keep up certain modest standards and they were stoic. They had the new pleasures of the twentieth century, thank God; they saw a film once a week and had the radio, but now I begin to see how brave and steadfast they really were – had to be. My mother was very depressed that she could do no kind of job to make a little extra money; her main mantra was a frustrated 'I wish I could work' with an occasionally plaintive 'I wish I was far away.' I hope it was a catharsis for her that I was able, as a boy soprano, to transfigure the sentiment when I sang 'Oh! For the wings of a dove' in our Methodist chapel.

On the wireless, there were perceived unintentional absurdities as well as the planned comic ones. I recall Dad scornfully quoting one phrase from King Edward VIII's abdication speech, perhaps because I had been born when Edward became king and was surely named after him, months before he spoilt it all. 'The woman I lurve,' mimicked my father one night. But think of it, the intimate confidences of a monarch shared with every subject in the land. Unprecedented in the whole of history. Dad did not go into further detail; he was not loquacious like a comic or a member of *The Brains Trust*, or indeed, on that occasion, like a king, but I inferred that the sentiment, as well as the pronunciation, was what he thought absurd.

Recently I heard a recording of the Poet Laureate at the time, John Masefield, reading his famous 'Sea Fever', a poem we had chanted at elementary school. The poet himself sounds like a genteelly bred Anglican clergyman with a taste for the lyrical, intoning 'And all I ask is a merry yarn from a laughing fellow rover' in a way that would have wiped the smiles off the faces of any gathering of old salts you can imagine, or made them roar with derisive laughter.

Being in Bradford, I never saw the owners of these voices. I imagined them, and I began to see them played by West End actors in the pre-London tours that came to Leeds Grand Theatre, and in films of course. Hollywood was a parallel universe throughout my childhood. I saw Brando in *On the Waterfront* during my first year at theatre school, and in Chapel Street at the Civic Playhouse, the custom-built amateur theatre, which interspersed plays with rare and foreign film seasons, I saw a number of French films starring Jaques Tati, Fernandel and the great and exquisite Edwige Feuillière. It was a time for working out who I was not as well as who I thought I was to become.

Vanished worlds

In 1985 the BBC were planning twelve episodes of Sayers's mysteries, and the producer, one Michael Chapman, handed me out of the blue three entire novels of which Lord Peter Wimsey was the hero. This might, at first, have seemed to be giving me the advantage over an actor invited to play, say, Hamlet, with nothing but five acts to go on. The three volumes, *Strong Poison, Have his Carcase* and *Gaudy Night*, all new to me, were a delightful weight of reading and went some way to compensate for the fact that I'd never actually met a lord, I mean a real hereditary lord. By now, I hold a personal hat trick, having by 1970 trod the boards with two theatrical lords, Olivier of Brighton and Miles (Bernard) of Puddle Dock, and in 2000 with Archer (Jeffrey) of Weston-super-Mare. Note the nautical motif throughout, though only one of them was 'at sea' as an actor. Even the noblest of this trio, truly great actor though he was, was hardly, as a lord, the 'real thing' – simply a coronet without the Norman blood. Tennyson's 'kind hearts and ... simple faith' doesn't quite fill the bill for Olivier either; he was far too complex for that. There was, however, a Baron Olivier before him, Sir Laurence's uncle, who was created the first Labour peer. Sydney Olivier was a friend of Bernard Shaw's and a founding member of the Fabian Society.

The real thing, the Earl of Chesterfield, spoke some celebratory words on the mystery of the peerage in the House of Lords in the eighteenth century: 'We, my lords, may thank heaven that we have something better than our brains to depend on.' These words were countered by David Lloyd George in the House of Commons in the first decade of the twentieth century: 'They do not even need a medical certificate. They need not be sound either in body or

419

mind. They only require a certificate of birth – just to prove that they are the first of the litter. You would not choose a spaniel on these principles.' Sayers avoided giving Lord Peter the dubious distinction of elder son and set him apart, making his uncle say, 'He is all nerves and nose – but that is better than being all brawn and no brains like his father and brother.'

Lord Peter Wimsey.
Photo: © BBC

In my childhood in the 1930s and 40s, the 'toff', or man about town, endured as a figure of fascination in popular culture in many eccentric variations, and my father ensured that I saw one of them. One May night in 1949, he took me on a tram from our cobbled street to the Bradford Alhambra to see *Thanks for the Memory*, a variety bill of old stagers with, amongst them, 'Burlington Bertie' in the person of Ella Shields. (Burlington Arcade is just along Piccadilly to the east of where Lord Peter's London flat, number 110A, was situated.) Shields first sang her famous signature song in Newcastle in 1914 and subsequently made six commercial recordings of it. Even the freshest of these, which I knew from frequent airings on the wireless, was an ancient period piece to me. Her posh Edwardian accent, with immaculate diction penetrating the surface hiss, was one thing. But what did it mean to us, halfway through the century, to *see* her *live,* in a shabby tailcoat and a monocle made out of a ring of wire attached by a piece of string to a safety pin on her lapel, singing with a lilting, dignified hauteur:

> I'm Burlington Bertie, I rise at ten-thirty,
> And saunter along like a toff.
> I walk down the Strand, with my gloves on my hand,
> And then walk down again with them off.

I'm all airs and graces, correct easy paces,
So long without food, I've forgot where my face is.
I'm Bert, Bert, I haven't a shirt ...

Another snatch I remember is:

My pose
Tho' ironical
Shows
That my monocle
Holds up my face, keeps it in place,
Stops it from slipping away.

For my father, I suppose, this was pure nostalgia, but was there ever anything we might have called 'agitprop' about Burlington Bertie – this curious figure whose poverty was extreme, though anything but abject? My father knew, first hand, that even moderate poverty was no joke. I can imagine the song being sung quite differently by a wispy, starved clown of a man, slightly crazed – another character within my comfort zone.

Dad was a *Daily Herald* reader and Labour voter. Let's not forget that Bradford was the birthplace of the Independent Labour Party, a fact I was never taught at school nor at my Bradford theatre school, despite Bernard Shaw's presence at the ILP's foundation conference in Bradford in 1893. On the other hand, no one ever tired of telling us that the first actor to be knighted, Henry Irving, had given his last performance and died in Bradford – this fascination with the toff again, you see. My dad, however, would have been alive to the social comment in J. M. Barrie's stage directions describing another toff, created in 1902 in his play *The Admirable Crichton*, directions that leave the actor who plays him in no doubt as to the social position of the Hon. Ernest Woolley:

We can conceive him springing out of bed light-heartedly and waiting for his man to do the rest ... He is almost a celebrity in restaurants, where he dines frequently, returning to sup; and during this last year he has probably paid as much in them for the privilege of handing his hat to an attendant as the rent of a working man's flat.

The play's hero is the low-born butler Crichton, whose practical abilities and courage – and indeed nobility – save the grand Woolley family when they are shipwrecked on an island in Act II. The third act takes us back to England where 'order' is restored. The following pithy duologue closes the play:

Lady Mary: Do you despise me, Crichton? (*The man who could never tell a lie makes no answer*) I am ashamed of myself, but I am the sort of woman on whom shame sits lightly. (*He does not contradict her*) You are the best man among us.

Crichton: On an island, my lady, perhaps; but in England, no.
Lady Mary: (*not inexcusably*) Then there is something wrong with
                      England.
Crichton: My lady, not even from you can I listen to a word against
                      England.
Lady Mary: Tell me one thing: you have not lost your courage?
Crichton: No, my lady. (*She goes. He turns out the lights.*)

Sayers redressed Barrie's 'prejudice' against the ruling class. Her hero Lord Peter's resourceful, distinguished service in the trenches in the First World War (the DSO, followed by a nervous breakdown), the admirable Bunter as his batman, and his subsequent secret work for the Foreign Office, would make him an excellent companion on a desert island, ingenious and practical. His knowledge of literature and his ability to quote from it, his gift for engaging prattle, coupled with his musical talent, almost make the Bible, the Complete Works of Shakespeare and eight gramophone records redundant. He might be considered by some castaways to be a luxury item in himself.

Harriet Vane, the heroine of the Wimsey novels, is an uncommon commoner and, like Sayers, a writer of detective novels. She is as much in love with Peter, however much she tries to deny it, as Dorothy herself. Amid all the sleuthing, it is their story that sings clear and sometimes sweet through the surface hiss of history and through what has become the quaint period detail of the books. It does not seem at all a dated notion, at least whilst one is under Sayers's spell, that if she can only get Harriet to the point of accepting Peter's hand, England, Britain and the world will seem to be a better place. But then vanished worlds have an attractive, piquant poignancy.

Speaking of vanished worlds, Ella Shields sang 'Burlington Bertie from Bow' for the last time in the Butlin's holiday camp theatre in Morecambe in 1952, beginning her act unusually by speaking the words 'I *was* Burlington Bertie.' She collapsed at the end of her act and never recovered consciousness. It was seven years later that Laurence Olivier arrived in Morecambe (not yet awhile the second Baron Olivier, merely Sir Laurence) to film his Archie Rice on location for the film version of *The Entertainer,* John Osborne's jaundiced portrait of 1950s Britain and the vanishing music hall. One day Olivier was walking along the prom with MacDonald Hobley, the famous TV presenter of the day, who was appearing very briefly in the film as his celebrity self in a beauty contest scene as the judge. They were approached by a holidaymaker who said, 'Oh, Mr Hobley, may I have your autograph?' Mr Hobley obliged; then the holidaymaker looked at Olivier and back at Hobley and said, 'Is your friend anybody?'

Noblesse oblige

There is a certain nobility in the actor's special sense of obligation to the integrity of a novelist's plot and characters. Playwrights' heroes are crying out for the actor; Shakespeare's Hamlet and Cleopatra, miraculous though they are, are incomplete on the page. The novel's characters, great and small, are complete as soon as the author lays down his pen. Dramatization only puts them in double jeopardy, first at the hands of the adapter-scriptwriter, who begins to take the living things out of their element; secondly comes the usurping actor, prising the hero off the page and out of the imagination of the reader. This is not to mention the adulterous hands of directors, designers, editors, and all the cooks who might spoil the broth, which was never intended to be broth at all.

Achieving the 'definitive' Wimsey was sometimes a struggle in the midst of all the approximations and impurities. I must, however, pay tribute to so many felicitous production touches: those wonderful lady dons; a host of supporting character studies, many of them excellent; innumerable design triumphs; a perfect score by Joseph Horovitz, a name to inspire musical confidence; my suits alone, 'shoulders tailored to swooning-point'. Irrespective of these touches, I soon found it necessary to cast myself in the part of purist policeman, insisting that the TV audience, like the reader, should have all the clues. Harriet Walter and I managed to insist on the deciphering business in the last minutes of *Have His Carcase*; we thought the detail of it was quintessential whodunit stuff and exciting as a cerebral game. Most importantly, as soon as I saw the script of the last episode of *Gaudy Night*, I declared, in league with Harriet, that this was un-actable and that we wouldn't act it unless the proposal to Harriet Vane and her acceptance were not a perfunctory two-line incident halfway through it, but, as in the book, the climatic final sequence.

Corpus Christi College cloister, scene of the end of *Gaudy Night*.
Photo: © Kathleen Riley

On our last day in Oxford, our sympathetic but harried director was off on various quests, our producer was mysteriously in London, whilst Harriet Walter and I found ourselves in one of those curious lumber rooms that always manifest themselves on locations, however elegant, being repositories for everything and anything that must be got out of shot. We were in a room just off the beautiful colonnade at Corpus Christi College in which the proposal was to take place. In amongst a clutter of furniture and rolled-up carpets, we conferred and pored over the novel's immensely long build-up to the proposal and its acceptance, both in Latin. We hastily re-drafted our final exchange, necessarily pithy and all of it in English. Michael Simpson would breeze in at junctures, casting doubts and leaving counter-suggestions, buzz off again as the clock ticked nearer to the moment that afternoon when we should have to commit our fresh dialogue to memory, rehearse it and get it into the can. All of Sayers's marvellously photogenic stuff on the roof of the Radcliffe Camera was lost (too expensive, I suppose), the winking traffic lights, the agonizingly romantic stretching of the dénouement, which I'd loved on first reading but afterwards found emotionally and philosophically convoluted, as exotic and indulgent as an overplanted hothouse. We didn't manage to get in everything we wanted to and, when it came to it, the length of the colonnade, down which we strolled, dictated the pace and essence of the scene. The scene was about walking on eggshells, culminating in the golden egg.

Retrospectively, I can understand Michael Chapman's urge to get out the secateurs and prune things a bit, but it was *Gaudy Night* that suffered most at his hands. He never tired of proclaiming that the first thing he did when taking on the project (which had already been developed to some degree by someone else) was to reduce *Gaudy Night* from four episodes to three, even though it is the longest and densest of the three novels we adapted and arguably the best. In a ridiculous bid not to give the ending away, the character of the culprit was crudely marginalized, although the actress Lavinia Bertram does very well indeed with what there is.

It was the idea of being involved with a ladies' college for several weeks that set our producer's teeth on edge and he made sure we didn't film at Somerville College (Sayers's alma mater); Corpus Christi, founded in 1517, is, of course, one of the 'ancient', traditionally male colleges. Yet the female cast was *Gaudy Night*'s great strength. We had a very good ensemble of lady dons; they held a reunion or two for a time, one of which I was invited to. The Warden of Shrewsbury was played by Sheila Burrell, who had doubled as Euripides' Agave and the Fairy Godmother in my Actors' Company production of *The Bacchae and The Beanstalk*. Caroline John (Miss Burrows) and I had also acted alongside each other, in brown body make-up and gold masks, as Inti Coussi and Villac Umu in *The Royal Hunt of the Sun* in repertoire from 1964 for longer than we care to remember. Very beautiful names some of those actresses have, a few with theatrical resonance: Dilys Hamlett (Miss Devine), Charmian May (Miss Hilliard), Auriol Smith (Miss Barton), Carol MacReady (Miss Martin), Meralina Kendall (Miss Lydgate), Charlotte West-Oram (Miss Pyke). They all made up, to some degree, for the plot being oversimplified.

I understood Harriet Walter becoming distressed at one point and insisting that, even in the face of the greatest aristocratic detective, she might be permitted to have some clues of her own, even if they must, perforce, be at the cost of Peter's unparalleled prowess. What I liked most about Harriet was her good-humoured willingness to engage in both serious discussion and witty badinage in the muddiest of location car parks at 6.30 a.m. Those lovely deserted coastal shots in *Have His Carcase* were only possible very late in the season when all the holidaymakers had left. Invariably we were wearing thermal underwear and waiting for the sun to emerge for a few minutes so we could capture a scene between clouds. I was rarely bored waiting and, of course, on the screen it all looks balmy and beautiful, like an old LMS railway poster come to sun-kissed life.

I do not forgive myself in that second adaptation for merely complaining and actually submitting to the appalling 'beef-up Bunter' idea that came from God knows where, but suddenly arrived ready-scripted one day. Richard Morant's Bunter, rather than Wimsey, was to ride the horse bareback over the sands at Wilvercombe. I know there are lots of people who love the books, or have come to know them well, through the television series, and so it may be worth explaining this particularly wrong-headed corruption of the original for those aficionados. There is a pivotal moment on the sands with Wimsey and the horse when Harriet suddenly sees Peter as the archetypal shining knight:

> Harriet was silent. She suddenly saw Wimsey in a new light. She knew him to be intelligent, clean, courteous, wealthy, well-read, amusing and enamoured, but he had not so far produced in her that crushing sense of inferiority which leads to prostration and hero-worship. But she now realized that there was, after all, something god-like about him. He could control a horse.

We gave absolutely no trace of this crucial turning point in Harriet's perception of Peter.

It was suggested by the director Chris Hodson, fibbing to me in a hotel corridor in the West Country, where I challenged him about the script, that, as I had only the tamest equestrian experience, I would not like the alternative – to be exposed to ridicule on the public beach astride a mechanical hobby horse when filming the close shots. I assumed, rightly, that it was standard practice to have bareback riding in long shot done by an expert stunt rider. I did have a previous experience one early misty morning, in the filming of M. R. James's story *The Ash Tree*, of seeing from a distance my stuntman thrown by a horse and, as the creature was being brought back, hearing the director's voice clearly in the still, damp air say, 'Don't tell Edward.' In my scene that evening on the same horse, I had to ride past some Elizabethan windows carrying a flaming torch whilst banging with a stick on the shutters. I was foolhardy enough to do it out of sheer masculine pride. The horse behaved perfectly and I felt like a hero in a costume drama, which is what I was supposed to be.

When our stuntman in *Have His Carcase* had completed the long beach ride in long shot and the sands were deserted, Richard, wearing a raincoat and apparently no better qualified than I, mounted a mechanical hobby horse for the close shot. In order to look like a convincing shining knight, I would have mounted that contraption on the beach at Blackpool on August Bank Holiday amongst jeering crowds (who could have been digitally removed in post production). What I suppose I couldn't ultimately bring myself to do in this instance was dig in my heels and snatch back Wimsey's rightful heroic sequence from my colleague. In a funny way I was too proud to do that, because it would have felt like an actor's pettiness. I did insist, however, that Bunter and I should toss a coin to see who would undertake the ride down the beach, so there would be no doubt that both characters were capable. I then concentrated on somehow keeping my heroic credentials in place during the scene of waiting for Bunter to appear. The line, 'There rides the man who fills my hot-water bottle and cooks like Escoffier', is my own creation – no credit or extra fee for 'additional dialogue', mind you. My advice to anyone in the same situation would be: bugger all that, phone the agent, argue artistic differences, defend the original author's intentions, walk out and speak to the press (good publicity), come to blows if necessary, be unpopular, but ride that bloody horse!

By the time we got to the third book and the proposal, I decided that we had enough artistic credit in the bank and I was ready to fight for Peter and Harriet's, and Dorothy's, just deserts. By then I felt we had achieved the status of shaman, so second nature to us was it to enter into that waking trance in which we took on the personalities of our hero and heroine, abetted by Dorothy, who had provided three thick books of delightful biography for us to examine for atmosphere and evidence.

A battle with Billington

'Cashing in' is not quite the phrase for the theatre production of Sayers's *Busman's Honeymoon* (the sequel to *Gaudy Night*) I proposed to Peter James at the Lyric Hammersmith in 1988 – not in terms of the salaries we were paid, although the theatre sold out at every performance. My wife Emily appeared as Harriet Vane, and, at my suggestion, Michael Simpson, who had directed *Gaudy Night* in such a simpatico way, directed the play. Novelists rarely write excellent plays, and Dorothy and her co-writer, Muriel St Clare Byrne, were no brilliant exceptions, but their effort had a charm to it.

With Emily in *Busman's Honeymoon*, 1988.
Photo: © Dee Conway

426

The set of 'Talboys', the country cottage in which Peter and Harriet spend their honeymoon, turned out to be less than charming, a disappointment we could not remedy in the time we had. And we really should have done something about the second act in which Peter sits on the sidelines for rather too long, letting Superintendent Kirk get on with the investigation. The lighting was another bone of contention because we had lamps vertically training down on the tops of our heads, generating enormous heat but not very attractive light. I was told that the lighting designer would not modify his design and that he would take legal action if we altered it. I realized that I should have behaved like Gerald du Maurier, directed the play and insisted on my own way and a week or two on tour to sort things out. Still, we had a strong cast, which included Ray Armstrong (Inspector Trethowan in the TV version of *Have His Carcase*), and there were lots of good laughs. It was also fun to play with Emily. In Act III we executed a quickstep to the radio which drew a round from the audience, though strangely not on the night Harriet Walter came to see the show. We were coached in the dance by Geraldine Stephenson, whom I had first worked with in my student days at the Northern Theatre School.

Peter and Michael tried to persuade me to undertake a commercial provincial tour of the production, offering the temptation of full houses and very good money, but we had two small children to think about; I wasn't prepared to go on tour and leave Emily holding both babies. I had hoped for a West End transfer but the show simply did not cut the mustard. I was largely to be blamed for that; the play might have served if I had had the foresight and requisite force and ruthlessness when I saw how things were going.

We did, however, receive some friendly reviews and waves of affection from the packed audiences who had braved a heatwave to see the show. All the more reason that, in spite of its manifold shortcomings, I vigorously defended the play from Michael Billington's attack in the *Guardian*. He branded our revival of *Busman's* 'an act of capricious folly', a self-defeating 'concession to pop theatre after the rigours of *Faust*' (the Lyric's previous offering),[1] ending his review by saying that he was 'reminded of the small boy who once pointed at Hermione Gingold and asked "Mummy, what's that lady for?"' While defending Billington's right to disagree violently and predictably, I felt impelled to address the wider issues beyond my Wimseycality and his vehement disdain, such as the validity of so-called popular theatre. My riposte was printed the following week in the *Guardian* under the heading 'Lord Peter Strikes Back'.[2] 'Not for the first time,' I said, I find myself asking "What is Michael Billington for?"' 'We were not,' I argued, 'being capricious, neither were we motivated by cynicism or despair, but by the conviction that the delight we shared in the Sayers/Byrne play would be shared by a wide audience already well aware of Dorothy L. Sayers

---

[1] *Guardian*, 21 July 1988.
[2] *Guardian*, 25 July 1988.

and Lord Peter Wimsey.' Billington accepted my public challenge to debate the issue on air, which we did on Radio 4's *Kaleidoscope*.

Gratifyingly there were letters to the editor in support of my fight back. My favourite came from a lady in Bletchingley, Surrey: 'Edward Petherbridge questions what Michael Billington "is for". George Bernard Shaw reminds us of what "he isn't" when he wrote: "I have never been able to see how the duties of a critic, which consist in making painful remarks in public about the most sensitive of his fellow creatures, can be reconciled with the manners of a gentleman." Lord Peter Wimsey would have recognised this, of course!'[3]

---

[3] 'The unmonocled mutiny in praise of Lord Peter's wholesome diet', *Guardian*, 28 July 1988.

T'Old Field

(The Old Field)

Ode to a certain acre or two of wasteland in West Bowling, Bradford.
(An antidote to Eliot's *The Waste Land*)

What's in a name? Although, you know, I'm curious to find
Names for the grasses, left so far, oh, sixty years behind.
Unerringly, I'd take you to the place once called 'T'Old Field'
Where, ignorant of botany, I played amongst its yield
Of – now with the aid of a plant book I will tell you –
Sweet Vernal Grass, Timothy, Yorkshire Fog and Meadow Fescue –
Perennial Ryegrass, Crested Dog's Tail, Common Sedge.
I look back in the distance from the elderly frayed edge
Of life and see the wild neglected place.
Gone now of course – that stream I dammed; they haven't left a trace.
The grasses, mounds of un-built stones, the dandelions, the spring, the ditch –
All flattened; there's a fenced brick school – an asphalt playing pitch.

The Domesday Book says Bradford's vale was nothing but a waste.
A Norman waste, 'cos t'awkward folk were not to't Norman's taste
Time passed, t'was owned by knights and kings and even John of Gaunt!
Such is the hist'ry of this scrap of England which my verses haunt
On't eastern side, a dry stone wall – and over it a railway cutting,
Bradford Dye works, t'allotments and Bowling Park abutting.
To't north was Round Street's back to backs where t'road weren't even cobbled
On't west – new houses, pebble dashed where t'folks were mollycoddled;
Bathrooms! Inside lavatories! Back gardens, place for't cinders –
Gardens at the front an' all – and leaded light bay windows!
Southerly, the cricket field, the almshouses and Bowling Junction,
Nub'dy seemed to need T'Old Field; they thought it served no function.

And all around was Bradford, spread up sides of seven hills
Mi Dad were down Springmill Street, in one o't dark satanic mills
Mother with our ration books, shopping down at Grundy's
Or scouring doorst'ns, baking, darning, turning t'mangle Mondays
Billy was in t'RAF, teaching Morse Code in Ceylon
His photo was in Pembroke Street, and t'air mail forms he'd wrote home on.

'Tis writ that John of Gaunt in silver armour progressed ower his ground
Can't promise thee he graced the bit on which I could be found
Brother Billy he'd played there and called it 'Dibby's Field'
I'd never heard of him, so I suppose his fate was sealed.
Before I trod this earth, old Dibby'd gone to meet his maker
Left his grassy scrap o' nowt, of which I was the taker.

T'Old Field's liberty was mine and all the kids I played with
Its grasses, stones, its mud, its water, our dreams were made with.
Nine-tenths o't law! – Best part was ours, choose whoever owned or bought it.
Name the lesson lads must learn and lasses, T'Old Field taught it.
The waterways and houses, castles, schemes that we devised
Hurt nub'dy, (Gaunt, King Richard, well they would have been surprised).
I bartered with my friends and foes and learnt to co-exist
I found out when I must give ground and when I should resist.
I made my small advances, and coped with my reversals
A marvellous convenient place for all my first rehearsals.
Of what to do with liberty – how recognize its bounds.
It cost us nowt; its value I can never count in pounds.

I'll seek some scrap of ancient waste that no one seems to need
I'll play and learn and laugh and build and blow the clock in seed
Though through the grasses I may glimpse the scythe, for time's grown less
I'll cry and beat the bounds anew and I will make redress.

Oh go prepare ye garlands! Sweet Vernal grass in bunches wield
Let brass and drum and cymbals sound in honour of T'Old Field.

Chapter 28

A Plea for the Perpetuation of Stage Posh

By way of an overture, I'm inserting a hymn here to the actor Robert Eddison. He was a beautiful, subtle actor of the kind people describe, probably in all periods, as 'of the old school.' He was at least six feet three inches tall, quite broad, handsome and possessed of an authoritative, powerful, but mostly mellifluous voice. That is a woefully inadequate description but for the moment it must suffice (that is the sort of phrase he would have come out with). I could add that his woodnotes were not exactly wild – there was a faint touch of that much-maligned figure, the maiden aunt, lurking inside his large frame – but it served to set off his gently impish sense of humour.[1] When Robert was young, Noël Coward wrote the part of Roland Maule, the gushing, abject fan in *Present Laughter*, for him, but it was typical of Robert that, having promised to work at the Bristol Old Vic, he honoured that contract and didn't play in the Coward piece in the West End.

One night in 1973, in our dressing room at the Edinburgh Lyceum, while we were on tour with the Actors' Company, Robert was reading the local evening paper. He was the most peaceful person to share with, provided that, if you borrowed his newspaper, you gave it back immaculately folded or you would feel shamed by his quiet distress. Suddenly, this particular evening, he looked up from the *Edinburgh Evening News* and his melancholy cello note started up: 'I've found something in the "In Memoriam" column which is nicely put: "Andy McTavish, 1880 to 1971. Asleep in Jesus. Inserted by his friends."'

In our production of Feydeau's *Ruling the Roost*, he played a peppery military gentleman with a deaf wife, played by Margery Mason. Back in Paris, boxed in by the wood-and-canvas flats of the Hotel Ultimus, in the inevitable Act-Two hotel-bedroom scene (the room double-booked, of course), their mattress had had, unbeknownst to them, an electric bell fitted underneath it and primed to ring as soon as anyone put pressure on it, so that another character in the adjoining room would be able to burst in and catch his wife and her lover *in flagrante*. Naturally, Margery's deaf character, unable to hear the bell, had no idea of the mayhem she caused every time she sat on the mattress in the course of preparing herself for bed. Robert's army officer was, even when calm, in a state of incipient high-ranking rage and always looking in another direction, never connecting the loud bell with the

---

[1] I have to amend that statement because I have just heard him on BBC Radio 7 play Herod in Dorothy L. Sayers's *The Man Born to be King*, recorded in 1975, and he had a surprising amount of granite in his voice.

bed and his wife's posterior. The first time it rang, of course, in rushed the jealous husband to discover a strange, preoccupied elderly couple and nothing improper. I still remember, whilst Margery looked on in sweet incomprehension and the bell rang for the umpteenth time, Robert bellowing in treble forte, 'What the hell is going on?! Is there a conference of campanologists staying here?!'

We decided to do *King Lear* on the strength of Robert being in the Company (he was a mere sixty-four at the time) and a contributory factor was that the play was the O-level set text that year. People did not automatically flock to see the Actors' Company on tour in the classics, so we thought school parties would help, and they did. In fact, I remember someone got hold of an exam paper when we were playing Norwich. Casting my eye over the questions on *King Lear*, having by then rehearsed in the part of the Fool and toured the play extensively, I was amazed how irrelevant to the O-level paper my experience of the play seemed to be. I don't think I could possibly have passed the exam.

Robert was born in 1908 in Yokohoma, Japan, educated at Charterhouse and Trinity College, Cambridge, and after being president of the ADC, he embarked on a distinguished career divided between leading and supporting roles at the Old Vic, in the West End, at Regent's Park and in the major repertory companies. A lucky dip into his hundreds of credits produces Mephistopheles in *Doctor Faustus* and Andrew Aguecheek at the Old Vic; Oberon at Regent's Park, Captain Hook (matinées only) in *Peter Pan*; and innumerable forgotten plays in the West End. For the Actors' Company he was equally effective in French farce and tragedy. He was game for anything and, though his acting could have grandeur, he was never the least bit grand, except that he was proudly professional. In 1975 he sent me a long get-well letter whilst I was laid low with a slipped disc, just a single sheet filled on both sides with minute handwriting. In the relevant passage, so far as the voice is concerned, is his delightful prattle about a supernatural part in a television sci-fi serial he was doing:

> At present all I know is that I de-materialize into a bundle of flapping black rags on a barbed wire fence on Stonehenge and this, one might think, could easily be accomplished in a few minutes of a Monday morning – the day for filming, and it is to be the veritable Stonehenge … I'm having the most fun in the serial. I started by materializing from black rags (you see the significance of the dénouement) in a tree stump in a damp Bristolian wood after dark, and since then I have stood plumb in the track of an approaching Land Rover, causing it to swerve (which, happily, it did) throwing out Miss Frances Cuka (but not fatally); I have walked through a wall (the wonders of electronics made it a simple movement towards a blue curtain), I have 'discorporated' in an operating theatre, I have, as already related, stood on top of Glastonbury Tor, and next week I have

to be discomfited by radiations from an equally unearthly (but heroic – I'm the baddie) young man from outer space who, sadly, has very suspect vowels.

Which brings me back nicely to the subject in hand: The Voice.

The language I grew up speaking in the West Riding of Yorkshire had lineage. In fact, it came in very useful for the Fool in *King Lear*. It used 'thee' and 'thou' and 'thine', and even a dialect form of 'are you' pronounced 'at a', as in 'a't'a goin' to t'pictures tonight?' I might have been surprised as a little boy to be told it came from 'art thou' as in 'wherefore art thou Romeo?' I heard the unmistakable familiar tones again on the radio last night, as one ex-miner from Barnsley talked about the days of the Miners' Strike in 1984, still using 'thou' and 'thine'. It was the English spoken by my great-grandfather's generation in little rooms where the bed folded up into the wall and wool was combed; stuffy rooms smelling of oiled wool and the charcoal stoves used to heat the combs. It adapted to be heard and lip-read above the racket of power looms in weaving sheds, where tiny children slaved, and the fine worsted produced was tailored by folk who spoke another variation, and the finest of the cloth was worn in quiet rooms where sherry was sipped before luncheon and the cadences of conversation might have another key and time signature and seem to be played on different instruments. And some of it, amongst the many variations, was called the Queen's English and some of it might have been called Mill-Owner English, a close cousin to that spoken by their employees.

My great-grandfather (woolcomber and ginger-beer seller), great-grandmother and their children would have gone to see the travelling actors in Old Wild's fairground booth at the Bradford Fairs in the 1840s and 50s – the sort of touring 'fit-up' the young Edmund Kean joined in 1804, at the age of fifteen, to play 'the whole round of tragedy, comedy, opera, farce, interlude and pantomime.' Kean had an exceptional start in that his mother, who'd trained him when he was a boy, was a supporting actress at Drury Lane and had been the mistress of the eleventh Duke of Norfolk. So there was an aristocratic model in the background. Old Wild's would occasionally engage a London actor from Drury Lane.

When my great-grandparents saw a version of *Hamlet*, followed by a farce and a comic song, they didn't expect Hamlet to talk like them. They were realists; they knew princes didn't talk like them, whether they were real or out of storybooks. Of course, they almost certainly never heard a real-life aristocrat speak. They felt neither threatened, repulsed nor alienated by a touring fit-up version of 'the King's English': it was, like the spangles worn by the Ghost in *Hamlet*, the rope dance and the act with the performing dog, all part of the show.

We go to the theatre for novelty – to be taken out of ourselves – but it is ourselves we want to see. I can illustrate this. Frank Middlemass, who was a famous Fool to Michael Horden's King Lear in Jonathan Miller's production on stage and television, had played the King himself as a younger actor at

Oldham Rep in the 1950s. He got home to his digs at the end of the performance and his landlady, usually so garrulous on these weekly first nights, and full of talk about the whodunnit or the light comedy, was, after this cultural departure from the norm, unusually quiet and sombre as she gave him his supper. After a while, Frank asked tentatively, 'Well, Mrs Whittaker, what did you think of it?' Mrs Whittaker, by the kitchen range, kettle in hand, looked thoughtfully into the fire and said, 'Mr Middlemass, it was my story.'

Eventually, in the mid-twentieth-century West End, audiences grew properly sophisticated and listened to and watched different things differently – Beckett's tramps, Pinter's caretaker and his companions in that grim bedsit – and felt neither threatened, repulsed nor alienated. It was their story. Even Noël Coward, who invented a stage upper-class English all his own, and who was the scourge of the Kitchen Sink and 'bad speaking', succumbed to *The Caretaker*: 'Somehow it seizes hold of you,' he wrote in his diary.

I can't settle on a label for it, the posh I mean. Let's try 'Stage Standard.'

However important it might sometimes seem not to sound like an actor, I began acting knowing that the actor's voice had to come from the right place (any decent drama school would have told us that) – anywhere but deep in the throat where the vocal chords are, *anywhere* but there. Leaving articulation aside, or rather, I should say, having achieved the right dynamic balance between articulation and tone, the voice should bounce off, and at the same time be supported by, the diaphragm; some teachers made great play with the pubic bone, but perhaps I was unlucky. It should zing against the back of the front teeth and resonate in the facial cavities as well as in the top of the head and round the back of the rib cage. A Victorian actor-manager, mindful of his customers, might have advised that the voice should be plastered on the white wall at the back of the gallery – that's what Charles Kean told Ellen Terry when she was a child actress (and, I imagine, 'In pathetic passages the voice must be distilled like a dew in every part of the house – but try not to sound damp, my boy.'). Since much of stage acting takes place in buildings these actors built and were at home in, and much of the rest in theatres nobody feels at home in, we have to find a creatively positive way to deal with our phobias about being 'stagy', to realize that stage acting is essentially an athletic activity, even when it is portraying domestic intimacies.

Stage Standard might come from the 'Home' Counties but not as our Queen speaks it; it must not come out clenched from Kensington, most particularly not when actually playing a monarch, unless it's Alan Bennett's QEII in *A Question of Attribution*.

In Shakespeare, unless you are playing, say, Doll Tearsheet, rude mechanical or Owen Glendower – or Dogberry, whose accent is, I suppose, strictly Messina mixed with socially insecure Stratford-upon-Avon – 'Standard' English should have a less precise provenance than one which might place it in a pinstriped Whitehall or emanate from the BBC at Portland Place in the golden age of radio. Name me a Shakespearean monarch or lord who could usefully sound like Mark Lawson, or Sue Lawley, for that matter. Who should Portia sound like, or Juliet or Cleopatra? Not like the great actresses of yesterday, nor the actresses in any contemporary film adaptation, which might use less than a quarter of the script. These are the hyper-real characters, who reach our stages neither by Tube nor chauffeur-driven limousine. They did not develop a carefully careless, 'classless' English at university, plotting to take over the theatrical establishment whilst dressing like the dispossessed or in expensively distressed denim. If you listen carefully, you will hear that which I'll call Actor's or Stage Standard English at its best, though it has been derived from the utterance of the upper-establishment classes, who, after all, form the overwhelming proportion of stage characters from the Elizabethan period to now.

All right, all right. Yes, I did hear John Barton do his impression of how Shakespeare's poetry was spoken in Shakespeare's Globe, and he sounded to me, for all his huge reputation as the authority on speaking the Bard, like a crazed amateur actor growling on Dartmoor. Let's face it, from the Elizabethans and Jacobeans through the Restoration and on to Sheridan and Goldsmith, up to Wilde, Granville-Barker, J. B. Priestley, Rattigan, and on up to today even, the bulk of stage characters are posh.

Yes, I know that the Pilgrim Fathers are supposed to have taken the purest of Elizabethan and Jacobean speech with them, and an English visitor or two to the New World in the eighteenth century is on record as being very favourably impressed, but are we to deny how English has evolved here in the meantime or to assume that we should seek out the most 'authentic', time-locked American remnant and imitate that when we act Shakespeare? Actually, I was rather impressed when I heard a snatch of a recording of Shakespeare as spoken by the Mercury Theatre founded by Orson Welles and John Houseman. Rather English, I thought.

Judi Dench, among her Desert Island Discs, requested a recording of John Gielgud and Peggy Ashcroft playing the duologue in the *Much Ado* church scene. What was wrong with it was not the exotic purity and grandeur of their beautiful, hothouse Shaftesbury Avenue Shakespearean Messinian, but simply the fact that Ashcroft was actually conversing with a man she was in love with who, in turn – great speaker that he was – was talking in a land-locked, theatrical, 'poetical' rhetoric quite at odds with the direct conversational intimacy of the scene. I have just this moment opened a paperback of the play at Act Four, Scene One, from the intervention of the Friar (the Friar! what a part!) and I find myself moved and marvelling how the scene seems to be a transcript of reality (and in verse, to boot!). Then the quiet, delicate beginning, in prose, of the Beatrice-Benedick scene, rising to the passionate, 'O God, that I were a man! I would eat his heart in the market-place.' Nothing even faintly theatrical-rhetorical about that line!

The middle and upper classes, some of whom still speak 'well', are even very well represented in, for example, Pinter, Stoppard, David Hare and by younger contemporary playwrights. Drop in tonight at the Royal Court or the

Almeida or the Tricycle on Kilburn High Road, or even the Royal Shakespeare Theatre, and there is a very good chance that you will hear it, this Standard, Received English. And in the 'real', offstage world people still talk varying shades of 'talking proper'; you could call it one of our dialects because, in the main, the people who speak it grow up learning it by ear from those around them. Other people borrow it, of course. Everybody borrows, as readily as teenagers adopt street cred in their clothes and utterance, as keenly as some educationalists embrace rap as a teaching aid for English literature. Standard, in its varying manifestations, has, like other 'dialects' or accents, its own special sense of nuance; a less careful, more relaxed style sometimes, when responding to a voice from a similar background, but also a way of adapting, with strain or with ease, to converse with voices from a different conditioning, just as speakers of all kinds do. It's an actor's job to know these so-called 'cultured' voices in his bones, in all their gradations, and to be able to adopt them with the certainty of a Professor Higgins placing a costermonger in a particular street in the East End.

Exceptions prove rules. One of my favourite actors is Tom Courtenay, who has successfully used his native, refined Hull accent for years, and it seemed just right to me in his beautiful performance as the poet Philip Larkin. Then I went home and played a recording of Larkin himself speaking his own poetry. His voice was an archetypal product of interwar Oxford, where he was a student. And, despite his raffish, booze-soaked life as a librarian in Hull and the range of his poetry, which certainly took in the stubbed-out fag in the bedsitter as surely as it could muse on the ancient tomb of a pair of aristocrats, his voice had that authoritative ring, that touch of the Anglican pulpit common to so many poets of his period, a tone utterly alien to those actors of Courtenay's generation, who went to drama schools in the early 1950s and either wouldn't or couldn't allow their voices to become tainted by the standard tones and cadences of the Establishment.

However, back to my brief: there seems to be a problem about Stage Standard English when it comes to performing Shakespeare. It's a problem for certain directors, even some of those of influence and authority in the theatre. It has, for them, not only the sound of wealth, privilege and authority, but also, as an accent, when attached to the way Prince Hamlet or Juliet or Cleopatra speaks, a corrosive, elitist influence, perpetuating old class values, alienating and perhaps, they think, ring-fencing Shakespeare from 'the ordinary public', whoever *they* might be. Wealth, privilege and authority are the three things these same directors enjoy or lust after, though, as I say, they hate to talk and dress as if they do, and they regard with pity or contempt jobbing actors with classy voices and meagre bank accounts.

I think it is a glorious thing that young actors are still emerging who can speak the kind of muscular Standard English that I believe the classics require. It must coexist with the protean ability to speak English in its numerous shades. Actors are still taught to 'place' their voices, physiologically if not geographically. Regional accents we should rejoice in.

It is still possible to get on a train in Manchester (a slow train, of course) and get out of it half an hour later in Liverpool and hear a completely different accent, though the shop-window displays from Totnes to Tyneside are indistinguishable and rampant, homogenizing globalization is at work. Linguists even tell us that 'Estuary' is spreading and some say that 'F' will replace 'Th'. Fings certainly ain't what they used to be.

There are many roles it's just not possible to play without a perfect grasp of the dialect or accent in which they are written, because it informs the emotional life of the characters. Think of D. H. Lawrence and the people in his miner's family kitchen, or the worlds of Tennessee Williams. Think of any minutely observed but archetypal character: Willy Loman, Lady Bracknell. Think of David Hare's play *Skylight*, set in a chilly North London bedsit, whose three characters come from very particular milieux and must convince us of that very particularly, even though the play succeeded, when I saw it, in seeming to be a microcosm of the whole of British society.

But ... what is wrong with the use of Stage Standard English in the classics? What is the threat of Received Pronunciation? ('Received by whom?' Tony Harrison once said to me, darkly, before going off to applaud another performance of Northern Broadsides, no doubt.) The alive-and-kicking tradition of Received Pronunciation in the theatre is a motley, made-up thing on its own – unique. It is not BBC English nor Tory grandee-ese, nor la-di-dah, nor – the worst of all criticisms – the sound made by an Actaw.

I last heard it spoken by the company who played Ibsen's *Brand* at the Haymarket, portraying his fjord-side villagers believably, not as a collection of vocal flotsam and jetsam from everywhere in England, nor a transplanted community from the nineteenth-century Lake District, to set us wondering if Wordsworth might come on in a minute – no, in good old, rugged, serviceable Stage Standard, without ever reminding us that, whilst looking at Ibsen's people, hemmed in by Norwegian mountains, we were actually sitting in the Parish of St James.

'Twill serve for royal language in the classics, in spite of the fact that Stage Standard traces its development back through the smell of size and glue and real green rooms, has echoed in the imaginary presence chambers, which lie just beyond the stage manager's desk in the prompt corner, and has heard the swords on the battlefield near the iron ladder up to the flies. It is not trapped in stage convention; it's not, as Stanislavski always dreaded, about anything 'classical', formed by 'the old, hateful, and outworn operatic stencil'. Being the first Method actor, Stanislavski really had a personal problem with heightened speech, which he found difficult to 'make his own'. Stage RP has lineage. All language has lineage.

The only test for an actor's use of any playwright's language is whether or not it is usefully alive to the playwright's world and conveys, not a schematic substitute for it, but the real thing – now, tonight – however different it may sound from what was heard in the street or in the foyer as the audience came in.

People can be seized by the classical Stage Standard English, which has developed from a time when actors were not invited to Buckingham Palace and knighted and damed left, right and centre, long before our Queen, as experts have noted, allowed a few 'Estuary' vowels to creep into her public pronouncements, just as some of us commoners have picked up from *Neighbours* the upward inflection at the end of every other statement. Perhaps Stage Standard goes back to the time when there was a Gentleman Porter to King James but 'The King's Men' was the title of the company of players to which Shakespeare and Burbage belonged.

Perhaps the King's Men did not ape the accents and vocal tunes and tricks of the Gentleman Porters, the Dukes and Duchesses, Princes and Princesses, Chancellors and Judges (a few of whom might have had regional accents as they do today) any more than actors in our age want to sound like a resident of Kensington Palace when playing Viola, or give a touch of Prince Charles to Hamlet or, for that matter, a hint of West Hartlepool or Hove to Horatio.

Harking back to Ibsen's *Brand*, the glory of the broad, flexible form of Received Pronunciation spoken in that production is that it releases an audience from spurious parochial considerations of English class, sociology and geography. It can portray the two great protagonists in that fjord-side community, Brand's mother and the rest, from artist to mayor, doctor to sexton to the woman from the headland, without ever reminding us of Hollyhock Cottage, Railway Cuttings or the Nine O'Clock News.

When it comes to actors playing lords, ladies, judges and so on, those who sit and listen – the groundlings and the gentlemen in the gentlemen's boxes, just like the people now who save up for their seats or who drink champagne in the corporate lounge – are none of them fooled by voices which have the wrong lineage. Today, at the beginning of the twenty-first century, the theatre is still to some degree guardian and exemplar of the best spoken English. Surely we are all sophisticated enough now to disentangle 'good' spoken English from the undergrowth of pride and prejudice about class. Would we be content with a Ghost in *Hamlet* speaking in the TV culture journalist Mark Lawson's strangulated suburban whine, or with the voice of that doyen of the RSC's Voice Department, Cicely Berry, who would never have been heard beyond Row B of the stalls? (Isn't the latter's 'ooh' sound, as Robert Eddison would have said, 'suspect', whether in the 'domestic' and more intimate styles or the more, dare one say, rhetorical?) Hardly! Nobody wants to stand accused of speaking for 'effect', but try speaking in our two great barns, the Royal Shakespeare Theatre in Stratford and the Olivier auditorium in London, and you'll know why actors, only half-jokingly, still call our job 'shouting in the evenings.' It is an athletic feat, as well as an imaginative task, to speak effectively rather than 'for effect' when playing, for example, the intimacies of Chekhov in the Olivier auditorium, or speaking the comic prose of that first domestic sitcom *The Merry Wives of Windsor* so as to be believable at the back of the gallery in that vast Odeon on the banks of the Avon. Shakespeare wrote the most wonderful talk – chat, even – but obviously he did not confine himself to the conversational style, even in domestic situation comedy. Take Ford's appalled soliloquy to the audience:

> What a damned Epicurean rascal is this! My heart is ready to crack with impatience. ... Page is an ass, a secure ass: he will trust his wife; he will not be jealous: I will rather trust a Fleming with my butter, Parson Hughes the Welshman with my cheese, an Irishman with my aqua-vitae bottle, or a thief to walk my ambling gelding, than my wife with herself.

The speech rises to reach the dizzy heights of the rhetoric of jealousy, at a point where Ford's righteous rage is so extreme that it can only find vent in passionate vituperative eloquence. We've all talked like that at home.

Anybody terrified of slipping their conversational, natural or even naturalistic moorings as they launch into:

> Never Iago! Like to the Pontick sea,
> Whose icy current and compulsive course
> Ne'er feels retiring ebb, but keeps due on
> To the Propontick and the Hellespont;
> Even so my bloody thoughts, with violent pace,
> Shall ne'er look back, ne'er ebb to humble love,
> Till that a capable and wide revenge
> Swallow them up.

or:

> Make me a willow cabin at your gate,
> And call upon my soul within the house.

has not dared to make the experimental journey to discover the difference between the humanity of great, high-precision word music and mere rodomontade.

When situation, passion and intellect, motive and character are in tune, there is nothing false or embarrassing or indulgent in something muscular and open that could ricochet round a tavern as well as calm a set of soldiers on their ramparts – something to smack against the wall at the back of the gallery, or distil like a dew over the stalls. It must be capable of saying, with equal conviction and comfort, 'It is I, Oedipus', or 'I have immortal longings in me', or 'Remorseless, lecherous, treacherous, kindless villain. Oh vengeance!', besides 'Could you pass me the *Evening Standard*?'

Above all, it must be the actor's own voice. Whatever hurdles it might have been coaxed or driven over, however many mangles it has been put through, one's own voice, connected to one's own heart and mind and body. In other words, it must be natural because, as Henry Irving said at Harvard in 1885, 'It is not mere attitude or tone that has to be studied; you must be moved by the impulse of being.'

In the classics one gets to be in pretty extreme places. Woe unto us if, in our commendable eagerness to avoid theatrical vibrato and empty declamation, and to speak in our own true, authentic voice, we are so tame as to define extreme places as lying within a parochial comfort zone.

And as for taking a character's first steps, as for 'movement', people, real people as opposed to actors, may have wondered why it was – and still is – that students of acting should improvise a day in the life of a gnat (fencing they can understand), or an autumn leaf in the wind, or observe a lion at the zoo and then improvise a silent encounter with a colleague who had been observing the vultures or an emu. They may have wondered why, if coming through French windows was – and still is – such a stock-in-trade, or striding up and down the rostrum in a cloak or a farthingale, or poking the fire in a D. H. Lawrence kitchen (or 'workshopping' the latest script biked round to the bedsit, for that matter), why ballet class on Friday mornings and modern dance on Wednesdays should have been, and are, important.

The answer is that anybody who has seen a 'real' person on stage knows it, and knows, for example, how Lord St John-Stevas, who has looked perfectly presentable and convincing as an eccentric toff on television, should look, at first, slightly out of focus walking onto a stage (not even in a play but to make an announcement) and then, alarmingly, like an attenuated prune that had shuffled on in an ill-fitting dinner jacket. This is because, on the day the curtain rises or the lights come up on real life, the audience will recognize the mistake immediately. The portrayal of real life on the stage is too important to be managed without the use of long-practised artifice, magic, imagination, ritual and masquerade. Only then will the business with the poker or the kettle, telephone, laptop, crown or rapier convince.

Voice Over

One's voice: to whom does one give it or lend it or sell?
Irving and Bernhardt both did rather well
From a cough sweet that sported their names on the tin
That the chemist's retailed the pastilles in.
No cough sweet could boast a much better start
Than the claim it was sucked by Sarah Bernhardt.
If it soothed Henry Irving's illustrious voice,
Could there be amongst cough sweets alternative choice?
Voices have landed some actors in clover
Voices we hear rolling over and over
Selling us cars and cream that's from Devon
Earning them dosh, Vox Humana from Heaven
Whisperings speak to our innermost need
Winkling out hungers we find we must feed
Lusts turn to musts once they've first sown the seed.
They reach us to teach us what's wrong with our features
Proclaim all the comforts to ease such stressed creatures
As Twenty-First-Century Man has become.
The pursuit of our happiness makes us all run.
So, sofas for loafers
And fast food for gofers
Pet food and jet food
And CDs to set mood
Din for us, sin for us
Yes, the big win for us
Lipstick pink tints for us, DIY hints for us
Much stronger mints for us
Carbon footprints for us!
Care for us, dares for us, privatized shares for us
Sun cream and Fun cream and replacement hairs for us
Headache pills, theme parks, cereals, Beans
We know what they are, do we know what they Meanz?

Sometimes the voices, to capture the right tone
The fight the good fight tone
The whiter than white tone
Will use a nice phrase that will mention the ozone.
Yes, to articulate friendliest care
For the hole that is widening there in its layer.

Then next we are watching a quaint mountain village
Its streets drenched with sun, hills terraced with tillage
With never a whiff of the earth's rape and pillage
A glittering thing like a dream will cruise through
And, of course, it's a wonderful car with a view.
And no one, no, no one will dare to dump a
Suggestion you'll drive it bumper to bumper.
Sea that is bluer, sand that's more sandy
Things for the handy, the dandy, the randy.
Food that will not make us fatter, though sweet
Sound that surrounds us in circles complete
Woofters more woofty and tweeters more tweet
We need things they know so
Those ad men in Soho
We never had never a weekend in Gozo
I need a nice dryer like that that can blow so
'Cause mine's only so-so
I need one that's oh so.
That one with the Turbo is really the one
It's mine. I feel lovely: I shop *ergo sum*!
They say that this ad was directed by Truffaut
Good God that's a No No and who on earth said so
Confusing the Turbo and such *quelque chose*?
Perhaps they were thinking of *400 Blows*.
These bards of the marketplace all have the knack
Scenting out just what it is that we lack.
I must be in clover
Oh please roll me over
And talk me right under the channel from Dover
Describing the light at the end of the Chunnel
And, when I bathe in it, exactly what fun'll
Greet me, meet me
How they will treat me
Voice over, voice over, voice over voice.
Creamier, steamier, faster than fast
Dreamier schemes and things to outlast
The very last trumpet
The crumpiest crumpet
The bunniest bun
The funniest – Ha, ha, ha – funniest fun
The showiest show, the filmiest films
Films that are bankable, get out your hankable
Films with a U that are not hanky-pankable
Flicks with more flesh that are flirting with purity.
Voices they tell us, sell utter security

All that's reliable, buyable, viable,
Voice overs babble, they tell us the fable,
What's under the counter and what's on the table
What's piling so high in the Tower of Babel
They whisper, they whisper, they whisper, they SHOUT
If we don't know our needs they will help us find out
And when we find out we can then make a choice
And find for our deepest desires a voice
And when our requirements are sated, the lot …

What will it have cost us for what we have got?
Voice over, voice over, voice over, voice over, voice …

Chapter 29

Acting with Lord Archer

I want to whisk you for a moment into a church hall in Southwark where, in the year 2000, we rehearsed Lord Archer's courtroom drama *The Accused*. To reach the hall I sometimes walked along the Thames at Bankside, a path once trod by William Shakespeare on his way to rehearsals. Lant Street, where the twelve-year-old Charles Dickens lodged while his parents and younger siblings were in Marshalsea debtor's prison, was adjacent. Shakespeare and Dickens were both performers, too, of course. Shakespeare did well as shareholder in the Globe Theatre and retired to the finest house in Stratford; Dickens was a keen amateur actor and made a second fortune from his public readings. That Southwark backwater is steeped in literary and theatrical associations, and now the name of Jeffrey Archer was to join the illustrious roll call.

Standing on the rehearsal-room floor, I observed a curious exchange, which took place early on in Jeffrey Archer's acting career. He was playing the eponymous role in *The Accused*, a heart surgeon accused of murdering his wife; I was counsel for his defence. There is a shyness, which can overtake even the most experienced actors, early in rehearsal and before they have got to know one another, if they are asked to do a little byplay involving ad-libbing. We were rehearsing the end of the play for the first time – the aftermath of the trial, the 'not guilty' verdict – and the actor playing my junior had a line congratulating Archer's character on his acquittal and asking him if he would take a holiday to celebrate. 'No, I shall go back to work' was Archer's scripted reply. The focus of attention then swung to the other side of the rehearsal room while we were left for a moment to murmur conversational ad-libs to one another. Thus the first *sotto-voce* ad lib I ever heard issuing seamlessly from Jeffrey's mouth, following his 'I shall go back to work', was: 'Thirty pounds a day as a member of the House of Lords and fifteen million a year as a novelist.'

Before I come to Jeffrey Archer's staged version of drama down at the Old Bailey, a word about the genuine article. I don't mean his Old Bailey trial for perjury – already pending in the autumn of 2000 where my narrative begins. Following the advice carved over the stage door of Stanislavski's Moscow Art Theatre, I thought I'd better take my models from life and do some research in advance of rehearsals. A lawyer friend made a key introduction and I was privileged to watch the proceedings of more than one Old Bailey trial without having to climb the long flights of stone steps to crane my neck over the public galleries. I was invited by one judge into his room during a break in a trial; he'd spotted me and happened to be a *Nicholas*

444

Nickleby fan. I also took lunch several times in the Bar Mess, where it wasn't only the occasional wig upturned on a Formica table top that lent a touch reminiscent of the familiar RSC or RNT canteen atmosphere.

A similarly familiar atmosphere prevailed during a short interval in a murder trial I watched. After reports suggesting the unfitness to plead of the accused, the court bailiff took the opportunity to paint her nails whilst the jury were in recess and the judge was out deciding some question of procedure.

'It'll be twenty minutes chin wag,' she declared confidently, 'that's what this'll be.' In the courtroom it was, for all the world, as though the crew and a collection of minor actors were on stage, chatting behind the curtain in the interval of some tragedy. There was even a little waiting-in-the-wings type banter between the bailiff and the barristers. Eventually we were advised that the session was about to resume. The bailiff checked her watch complacently.

'What did I say?' she said, looking at her nails. 'Twenty minutes, just nice time for them to dry.'

Ian McKellen suggested, after reading an earlier draft of this story, that I tend to blame everyone but myself for my own failures in the Archer project. But if I can't mitigate my misdemeanours, who else will bother? I don't plead diminished responsibility, and what actor who hopes, and indeed needs, to work again would plead diminishing powers? I hereby shoulder the entire responsibility for my manifold sins and wickedness in the Archer Saga, whilst offering this necessarily partial history.

Enigma variations

All unsuspecting, one night in early 2000, I was in my grim little dressing room in the Theatre Royal, Windsor. It was the interval and I was preparing to go on as the famous Soviet spy, art historian and Surveyor of the Queen's Pictures, Sir Anthony Blunt, in Alan Bennett's *A Question of Attribution*, the second half of his brilliant double bill *Single Spies*. A message came round from Front of House: 'Lord Archer is seeing the performance tonight and would like to meet you afterwards.' My first reaction was of pleasure, mingled with amusement and curiosity. He'd made a bit of a splash in the press by announcing that he'd written a play for the West End and planned to star in it – an Old Bailey courtroom drama, no less (almost certainly no more, one presumed), and he was to play the accused. Furthermore, art (or craft) would be imitating, even anticipating, life because the nation was aware that the dock at the Old Bailey was where his lordship's real-life appearance was expected in a few months' time on a charge of perjury. A feature of the play was to be that the audience would vote as jury.

I had never met Lord Archer, but about twelve years before this night in Windsor, I'd been sent a cutting of a piece in *The Times* in which he described to his wife Mary his ideal day. Looking at it again, it's a rather charming and witty article, appropriately airbrushed, perhaps, for *The Times* – and his wife. I suppose we might all have one version of our ideal day for

The Times, another to tell our children, or whisper to our sweetheart, and yet another possibly unfulfillable version forever untold. Jeffrey's ideal day, as printed, was filled with politics, squash and cricket at Lords. It was to end with him attending the RSC's *Nicholas Nickleby*, then afterwards 'being allowed to meet Edward Petherbridge.'

I suppose I practised Sir Anthony Blunt's inscrutable Afghan-Hound expression in the mirror and contemplated confronting the less than ideal Windsor audience, thinking, 'It's nice to have a fan out front.' We weren't doing very well at the box office and, from what the theatre manager had told me, these Alan Bennett plays were straining at the very highest point of the clientele's brow. It was like playing into the royal upholstery, though the Windsor audience is not as 'posh' as you might think; the Slough influence perhaps? But I mustn't make the mistake of taking a superior attitude to that, or any other, audience, as if it were only worthy of some dismissive collective noun. It was, after all, a collection of individual human beings who had complimented us by deciding to turn up. One night there was an exceedingly individualistic-looking man on the otherwise empty front row, very preoccupied with a paper bag of dried fruit.

Giving a really, as we say, 'truthful' performance as Blunt was tricky, even in the best of circumstances, though with his lordship out front there was a special frisson. Archer was the possessor of a fine art collection, about to be accused of perjury and perverting the course of justice, and I was up on stage as Sir Anthony Blunt, Surveyor of the Queen's Pictures, being questioned about my life in espionage by a policeman who was trying to develop an interest in art history. There was some very nice comedy of manners. I liked saying, 'I can see you've been down at the Purley Public Library again … One hopes the security of the nation is not being neglected in favour of your studies in iconography.'

At one point in the play Blunt has a surprise audience with the Queen in a corridor in Buckingham Palace lined with old masters and hack Renaissance studio jobs, where the conversation turns on the problem of fakes. Bridget Forsyth's portrait of the Queen was masterly, an imitation, if you like, but no fake, and like Prunella Scales's original interpretation of the role at the National, uncannily close to QEII (and I had met the genuine article, twice). All this was happening within a hundred yards of the walls of Windsor Castle. Well, it's a free country.

When a character has a secret or, as in Blunt's case, Secrets, it's a very potent thing on the stage, but as an actor it's handy to know exactly what they are, even if you are never going to reveal them in precise detail. Blunt took a lot of secrets to the grave, particularly in regard to his motives. 'Cowboys and Indians' or 'Cops and Robbers' were concise and characteristically enigmatic explanations he occasionally offered to friends, but they did not appear in Bennett's play. *Was* there a name or names he never divulged? Some answers, it was presumed, lay in a memoir he entrusted to the British Museum before his death in 1983, to be kept under lock and key for a quarter of century. According to his biographer, the few intimates who had read it 'remarked on its pedestrian prose, and that it stopped just at the moment when it threatened to become interesting.'[1]

Speculation as to the memoir's contents finally ended on 23 July 2009, when the British Library made public the 30,000-word manuscript. As personal and complete a statement as Blunt had wished to make, it is, nonetheless, only partially revealing. He remains reticent about the details of his work for Soviet intelligence and does not identify any individuals who were not already known to be his associates. He does, however, give some account of his feelings and motives, attributing 'the biggest mistake of my life' to his political naïvety, the magnetism of Guy Burgess and the intense anti-fascist atmosphere of Cambridge in the mid-1930s in which Marxism had taken on 'an almost religious quality'. 'The ivory tower', he decided, 'no longer provided adequate refuge.' What is also revealed, unconsciously, is Blunt's lack of self-awareness and his ignorance of how the Soviets perceived him. During the war, while working for MI5, Blunt passed so many secrets to Moscow, that the KGB believed him to be a fraud – a fake, in fact!

Within four days of deciding to play Blunt, I met, quite by chance, a man who had been one of his students. All he could tell me was how brilliant Blunt was and, though he wouldn't suffer fools, how kind to his students.

I particularly remember standing, as Blunt, alone on the stage in Windsor and saying: 'This painting is a riddle … though a solution might add to our appreciation of this painting, paintings – we must never forget – are not there primarily to be solved. A great painting will still elude us, as art will always elude exposition.' For me, playing Blunt was a bit like playing the Sphinx, without *quite* knowing the solution to the riddle. Still, there was something narrowly liberating about having to skate elegantly on such thin ice in the English box-set, well-made-play tradition. One of my treasured possessions is a postcard from Alan Bennett, with, on one side, a lovely photograph of a traditional North Country farm gateway and, on the other, some comments about my performance as Sir Anthony in the BBC Radio 4 and CD versions of the play. His comments were not meant for publication, I'm sure, so I will only quote: 'his whole life was there.' Acting is perhaps primarily a physical business in the sense that the whole person has to be present, body and soul; the playwright seems only to provide the words, but in fact he provides the 'whole life' of his characters, so much so that, given some 'undertones', it is possible for the actor to suggest the whole man, body and soul, in a one-act play and even on radio.

I was to meet Lord Archer in the stalls bar, where there were always a few patrons who liked to linger for a while after the show. It's not at all the same as meeting in a green room; that luxury disappeared along with gaslight and hansom cabs. For actors to be out front – the usual thing nowadays in the

---

[1] Miranda Carter (2001) *Anthony Blunt: His Lives*, p.262.

provinces – never seems quite right to me; it dispels whatever mystique there might be and one feels like a reluctant exhibit in a rogues' gallery.

I imagined I'd find the 'rogue' I was looking for tucked away in a corner, keeping a low profile. Not at all; he was the first person I saw as I entered, elbows on the bar behind him, facing the world, with that suit, that shirt, that tie, those rimless spectacles one seemed to know so well – and the familiar, happy, open expression. As I approached, he said, 'Congratulations, you were marvellous! I've seen everything you've done and you are a wonderful actor. Mary and I can't understand why you haven't been knighted.' We had something in common right away.

Lady Archer then took the edge off things slightly by complimenting me on my performance as the man with no roof to his mouth in *A Flea in Her Ear* at the National Theatre in the mid-60s. I thought it would be simpler and less embarrassing for her if I kept diplomatically mum about the fact that Edward Hardwicke had given that particularly admired performance, though I did feel a bit of a fake, and got promptly off the subject of my impersonations.

Reasonable doubt

I left the theatre little dreaming ... When my then agent telephoned with the news that I had been offered the role of Archer's defending QC, Sir James Barrington, I unhesitatingly turned the whole idea down without even asking to see the script. My agent was unfazed, being of the opinion that, if I worked with what he called 'an amateur', I would lose all credibility; there were some things the profession was unforgiving about and this was one of them. It was not that which swayed me. I just didn't think of myself as the kind of actor who'd get mixed up in this kind of project. No less an actor than Paul Scofield had headed an extremely distinguished cast in Archer's earlier play *Exclusive* in 1989, and that was after Archer had 'resigned the Deputy Chairmanship of the Conservative Party in well publicized circumstances' (to quote the aforementioned *Times* article), but there was something of the *stunt* about this, as those same well-publicized circumstances were returning with a vengeance to haunt him.

Replacing the receiver, the next conversation I had there in the kitchen was with Emily about the parlous state of our finances, but I luxuriated in the artistic and moral high ground (no other luxuries being available at the time) and continued to do so for a whole week or more, until a second call came. Would I, at least, they were asking, consider reading the play; the management had changed and there was to be 'proper money'. We hadn't discussed money, proper or improper, the week before but, in the light of at least *financial* propriety, it seemed churlish now, at the second request, not to *read* the play. I found myself arguing that if there were a moral issue lurking somewhere, a man was innocent until proved guilty, and if I was going to start screening everyone I worked with – or they me, for that matter – where would it end? I recalled being asked by the Dean of Chichester Cathedral, by

448

the Market Cross one day when I was in the season down there (playing Graham Greene's Whisky Priest), if I would agree to read the lesson one Sunday. 'Yes,' I said uncertainly, feeling for some reason a little tainted that day, and adding, 'as long as you take sinners.' 'We take nothing else,' he replied. (The Dean, however, must have thought better of it because the invitation never materialized.)

As far as acting with 'amateurs' – well, I'd acted with some pretty lousy professionals in my time, one way or another.

The playscript was to be 'biked round'. It's always wonderfully dramatic, the moment you are told that the script of a play is being biked round. You imagine the roar of the engine, speed, urgency, a helmet and black leather. It is an early peak and, in this instance, it was downhill all the way from then on. But it was mostly a very gentle decline, with some deceptive ascents onto broad uplands every now and then as we got into our stride and made our lordly progress on the pre-London tour, playing to capacity houses, pin-drop silences, roars of laughter and cheers at the curtain call. In the theatre car park at Coventry one night, a lady with a cut-glass accent said, 'May I tell you how much we enjoyed it? Our little party is just over there, my husband, my brother and his wife – all in the law.'

'Thank you,' I said. 'Didn't you didn't find some of the procedural inaccuracies worrying?'

'Oh no. Dramatic licence and all that.'

I was agog. While watching real trials at the Old Bailey, I'd found that the procedural rules, limiting what the barristers could get away with caused as much drama as anything.

The script of the play was a page-turner. On first reading – and this was exactly the sort of play I thought should be judged on first reading – it was effective. The part of Sir James, the defending counsel, was the more sympathetic of the two barristers and had some potentially good comic moments and a couple of 'strong' curtains. On the domestic front, remembering Pinero's dear old play *Trelawny of the 'Wells'*, our 'Steak for dinner!' moment had arrived (although we are vegetarians). Have I skated over the moment of moral choice? I was contemplating arranging for some very necessary repairs to the house and being able to pay the school fees. If we are talking about embarking on a new part, then being a member of the middle classes always seems like a new part to me, even after all these years. And there's always a sense of the danger that it'll be taken away from me.

A quest for the truth

Our director was to be Val May CBE, of very long experience and, in appearance, long but lean, with a grey beard and a slightly ghostly but professorial look (I could be describing myself, except that he was taller and thinner and nine years my senior). There is a well-known story that used to be told in the profession about his direction. Apocryphal as it may be, I remembered it as soon as my agent pronounced his name. He was directing

449

The Royal Hunt of the Sun at Bristol Old Vic in the early 70s. The company were on stage and Val was saying to the actor playing the Sun God Atahualpa:

> You come on up centre, that's it – God incarnate – and move down stage very slowly, carrying within you the whole power and mystery of the Sun and of the Inca Empire, and then, when you get to about here – cheat left a bit.

I seldom get a laugh with that story when I tell it to members of the laity.

There were to be a mere three weeks of rehearsal for *The Accused*, a longish tour and then London, possibly the Theatre Royal, Haymarket. We were lucky to get three weeks' rehearsal. I was told Val had wanted two, supposedly in the belief that 'the actors will get bored.' True, there were no complicated moves – witnesses in the witness box, everyone in their appointed place, and actors playing witnesses with only one short appearance apiece – but the lawyers' long speeches and swift exchanges needed a lot of practice (tons of leading questions, in the non-legal sense). In plays, lawyers, like stage detectives, are seldom thrown a helpful cue. And if the pursuit of the truth is what goes on in a courtroom (and I'd still like to believe it is), what else is one pursuing in a rehearsal room but the truth, the whole truth and nothing but the truth, so help us? Three weeks are the bare minimum and it was, after all, Jeffrey's first appearance in a play.

At the first rehearsal Val made the first mistake in the book by telling us that he knew of old how 'these courtroom dramas' needed to be done, his tone implying that *we* didn't and were about to find out. Productions of them, he said, had to be like pieces of machinery, to be performed with clockwork precision, great energy, clarity and pace, and with never a wasted moment. All directors tend to do this energy-and-pace party piece, though not usually on day one, and it has to be said that we always need it, even though they do it as if they've each just invented it and we've never heard it before – as if our very stock in trade had not been expending energy, taming and spellbinding that beast, the Saturday-night audience, in the glittering heart of London's West End, or in provincial 1,200-seaters, when we are determined to knock five minutes off the running time so as to catch the last train to London or the pubs before they close. We've done it more often than they've said 'cheat left' or had hot dinners.

Already Val had created a 'him and us' situation, careless of the debilitating effect it has on a creative group when the leader exerts his authority at the outset by knowing exactly where the project is going. Even with the most conventional of plays, the 'voyage of discovery' approach is the more creative posture to adopt, in the hope, preferably fervent and soon fulfilled, that captain, vessel and crew are seaworthy. My immediate reaction was to make sure I felt as little like a piece of clockwork as I possibly could; nor did he inspire me with confidence when he and I talked about our both having gone independently to observe at the Old Bailey. 'Frightfully slow and boring,' he said. Well, of course, judged by the standards of the well-oiled machinery of a Val May production, it was unconscionably leisurely and ill-timed, except there *were*, too, some superb pieces of timing well worth the long waiting periods. Matters of truth and falsehood were being decided; people's liberty was at stake, and there was the rare chance to examine, not the – let's face it – hackneyed television version available to be seen almost any week of the year, but what it is *really* like when people find themselves in the dock or the witness box for the first time in their lives, and how real lawyers *act*, in both senses of the word.

Part of the little community that hovered about and contributed to the realization of the world of *The Accused* was Jeffrey's genial driver and factotum and an ex-member, it was said, of the SAS. It became known that his nickname for our venerable, bearded director was 'The Turin Shroud.' 'Oh my God, that is priceless. I wish I'd thought of it,' exclaimed one of our actors. 'And so apt because, of course, it's a fake!'

At the genuine Old Bailey I listened to one lawyer, in his final summation for the prosecution at a murder trial, deliver with quiet, impressive gravity a speech I must recreate from memory – something like:

> Members of the jury, over these past weeks you have listened to the distressing details of a defenceless old lady's death, to evidence given by the two accused, and to the many witnesses called by the prosecution and the defence. You have heard me and my learned friends as we have questioned and cross-questioned, and sometimes quibbled over points of law; as we have seemed, perhaps, to be intent on scoring points or indulging in obscure, formal questions of procedure, but I must assure you, members of the jury, this is not a game. This has been, at all points over these long weeks, a solemn quest for the truth.

It would have been marvellous if Jeffrey Archer had said, as we all foregathered on day one to rehearse his play in an ex-church hall somewhere round the back of Tate Modern: 'I expect you are all wondering why I've called you here today.' In Jeffrey, co-producer, author and actor, we had a man who we knew was most certainly going to discover the reality of the solemn quest that barrister described – if not imaginatively, as author and actor in the rehearsal room or on stage, then in actuality, as the subject of it in his forthcoming trial.

Am I in danger of sounding like a prig? It was a whodunit, for heaven's sake, a piece of entertainment. How to describe the atmosphere of those rehearsals? Jeffrey in a red pullover, constantly amending the script that first week, very relaxed: 'I liked what you said then,' referring to one of my paraphrasings in my struggle to get off the book as soon as possible, 'let's put it in.' He watched, not taking up his position in the dock until we got to his exit from it and his entry into the witness box in Act Three. He was not in the least grand, chatting with whoever happened to be standing next to him at the tea urn, be it leading actor or understudy, but very much the layman. The only part he seemed to be acting was that of playwright.

There was an edgy moment one day, when I began to question what seemed to me a slightly dubious passage in my cross-examination of a prosecution witness who was an Indian pharmacist. There was more than a faint whiff of racism in my character's questioning of this character, which I was a bit sensitive about, but the pharmacist character neatly turned the tables on Barrington at the end of the exchange. However, there was also a question of factual accuracy to do with whether or not a degree from the University of Calcutta was recognized in the United Kingdom. Madhav Sharma, playing the pharmacist, thought the script might have got the facts wrong and, since both our characters subscribed to this 'fact', I began to insist that this sensitive passage should at least be factually correct. Suddenly, an unspoken but clear impatience was expressed by both Archer and particularly May. I went on with the dialogue for a moment, and then suddenly lost my cool. 'Just a moment,' I boomed. 'May I say that I resent a suggestion in the air that I have been wasting time on this issue. We are going to Leicester on this tour; there might be any number of Indian doctors or pharmacists in our audiences. I am not being a tiresome milk-and-water liberal; this is a rehearsal room, what else would we be doing in this room but spending time on things that matter? I am willing to dedicate as much time as proves necessary to do myself and this play justice. A rehearsal room is where the counsels of perfection apply!' Something like that. I was hero of the moment amongst the smoking lobby out on the pavement at the tea break. 'Well, that upped the fucking ante a bit!' 'That was a welcome dose of salts to the proceedings', etc. But as rehearsals progressed – half-days only, I may say, and we spent the *whole* of the first week of half-days getting through the play just once, whilst Val and Jeffrey made constant re-writes – I found that, despite the time I spent conning my part, the necessary fluidity was not forthcoming. Shamefacedly I quote the critic Paul Taylor, writing in the *Independent* in 2001: 'Remember the bizarre spectacle of Paul Scofield (understandably unable to remember his lines) ... in *Exclusive*.'

My credibility began to erode. I must say neither Val nor Jeffrey seemed to bear me any kind of grudge in our three weeks, and were clearly impressed by what flair I managed to bring to the part. At one point Jeffrey, informing my agent that I was the best thing in the rehearsal room, said, 'The rest of us might as well go home.'

I was to give a somewhat shaky account of Sir James Barrington on the first night at Windsor – yes, I was back there again, though this time we were booked out before we opened for a three-week season. However, so that you won't run away with the idea that I was anything other than consummate in the part a great deal of the time, I would like to bring in my first witness and exhibit the following postcard from a theatre enthusiast, a gentleman who wrote to me having seen the play in Bromley on that pre-London tour:

Dear Edward,

You may recall that during the summer you were guide to a group from the School of Philosophy around Shakespeare's London. Your contribution to that day was outstanding and memorable. However, my reason for writing this note is that I have just been to the Churchill Theatre and witnessed (pardon the pun) your portrayal of Sir James Barrington in *The Accused*.

The whole performance was wonderful entertainment but I, and I believe the rest of the audience, was thrilled by your 'Sir James'. You have given me so much to work on for my forthcoming performance of Widow Twankey in the West Wickham Pantomime Society's *Aladdin*! Not that I am relating your performance to pantomime, but you did more by the occasional raising of an eyebrow and timing than most can do with ten pages of dialogue.

Many thanks.

Coup de théâtre

I've found some notes written on the Monday night of our second week in Windsor:

> It's no mere coincidence that the character he [Jeffrey] plays was charged with murder at Wimbledon Police Station – the very police station Jeffrey attended on the morning of the play's opening night last Tuesday, to be charged with perjury and perverting the course of justice. Apparently one has a choice of time and place in these matters and he certainly exercised it to his advantage. The only reference I heard him make to these off-stage events was in the midst of the backstage havoc wrought by the late arrival, a bit at a time and in tantalizing job lots, of our set of the Old Bailey. The people who were making the approximate replica of court number one didn't have the same sense of timing as Jeffrey. (The novel Jeffrey is working on, by the way, is called *Serendipity*.) Instead of a technical dress rehearsal on Monday afternoon we crammed ourselves into the tiny circle bar for a desultory run-through of the words on our own. On the morning of the opening, Tuesday, I arrived at the theatre to see the dock doors open wide and the stage crew waiting about in the street for the next consignment, and learnt for the first time where Jeffrey was putting in an appearance that morning. I wondered when he might turn up at the theatre, but the ten o'clock rehearsal was delayed for ages, anyway, because of the serendipity of the set's delayed arrival. As the irresistible story hit every front page, Jeffrey joined us old pros,

fatalistically laughing off the appalling situation. We were only going to get time to dress-rehearse two of our three acts. At one point he passed me in the shadows backstage and said, 'You couldn't buy today's publicity for a million pounds.'

One contingency plan Val devised was that, whichever way the audience-as-jury voted, we would play the 'not guilty' ending – for technical reasons involving the electronic button system, I understood. In fact, that first night, for the first and only time so far in eight performances, the audience voted Jeffrey's character overwhelmingly guilty. The next day it was announced that, whatever the votes, we would play the 'not guilty' verdict for the rest of the week. There were stirrings in the company about this; if word got out it would look bad. What extraordinary loyalty that nobody rang up a newspaper and blew the gaff! In view of the shenanigans being reported daily in the press about the Yugoslav elections, I immediately dubbed our strategy 'the Milosevic ending.'

Archer's amazing coup at rehearsal was when he announced that he had asked various stars to record the voice of the foreman of the jury, whose entire part consisted of 'We have, my lord' and 'Guilty' or 'Not guilty'. He told us he'd asked Tony Hopkins and, I think, Derek Jacobi, but was thrilled that Ken Livingstone – the socialist Mayor of London, to whom Jeffrey ran as a rival candidate for office at one point – had agreed to do it! (Livingstone's fee, I was told, was donated to his favourite London charity, London Zoo.)

After the first night, unless anyone interfered with the electronic score, it was a two-to-one 'not guilty' verdict each time and there was always an enthusiastic response to that inimitable voice announcing it. A parlour game atmosphere established itself.

Shortly after we opened in Windsor, Jeffrey re-wrote the end of the play so that, whichever way the audience voted, they were wrong. This meant that Jeffrey did not have, as an actor, any through line, any 'truth' to act, not knowing whether or not he was a murderer until the end of the play, when the verdict pronouncing him guilty or not guilty was the cue for the play to say to the audience, in a final twist, 'You are wrong.' It turned the play into a perverse, unanswerable riddle, which was perhaps his intention.

In some of his photos, Jeffrey bears an odd resemblance to Laurence Olivier. I used to fantasize about how Olivier would have played the part; how riveting he would have been, undergoing the bulk of the trial in silence in the dock (cheated centre?) as we tried to discern the truth about him, and how shocking he would have made the truth when we discovered it. But Olivier would never have agreed, even in a whodunit, that there should be no truth for him to hide and, finally, to be revealed. The cunning old showman knew that, in the last analysis, the stage is no place for deception; it's the place where the game of 'let's pretend' is a solemn quest for the truth.

One day I was mooching about the Old Bailey set between a matinée and evening performance when it occurred to me to look at the copy of the Koran

454

on which the Indian chemist swore his evidence, and there it was in its purple velvet cover, an authentic prop. Something told me that the Bible would not be the real thing, though it seemed the right size in its black covers. I was right. It was a novel called *The White Ladies of Worcester*. Appropriate, I suppose, that the dodgy evidence Archer gave in the play (and his rewrites were to make it even dodgier) should not be sworn on the Good Book. That night I passed a limerick to my junior, having told him of the true identity of the prop. To rhyme properly it has to be spoken in a Northern accent, but we were playing Manchester at the time:

> There were twelve white ladies of Worcester
> Whom Archer developed a lust for
> Oh Heavens they quoth
> You've just sworn an oath
> On our book, and you've tarnished its lustre.

As I was leaving the stage door at the end of the long day that culminated in the very first performance, there was a little crowd waiting in the dark. I got through it unmolested, but then I sensed a glow of light behind me and turned to see that flash bulbs and television lights and cameras were in operation. Jeffrey, in his shirtsleeves and with his hands in his pockets, was strolling onto the top of the steps outside the stage door and beaming down at the little crowd as if he'd just nipped out of a breakfast meeting. I think it must have been Wednesday or Thursday before I was on form at all.

An actress friend of mine said, 'It'll run for years.' (How wrong she was!) 'Providing he's free,' I said. Her idea was that the phenomenon of Jeffrey actually turning up in person was in itself amazing.

Awaiting the verdict

In Birmingham, our first date after Windsor, we were thrown into a huge 2,000-seat auditorium and into inhospitable dressing rooms like second-class hotel rooms in a Third World country. Jeffrey, surprisingly and kindly, invited me to share his with him, mine being much further from the stage, but I declined. We needed our own space, I felt.

It was in his room that I met the barrister who had advised him on the legal points of the play. In fact, he might even have been the barrister who, in real life, introduced a blank piece of paper into his questioning of a witness one day, pretending that it contained an incriminating list. I must say I had a great deal of fun with this piece of paper in the play, using it to discredit the nurse in the witness box: it was supposed to contain a list of the hospital doctors with whom she had had affairs, and the length of the list was something one could suggest, very subtly, was vastly in excess of the number the nurse was admitting to.

A real showman of the Bar died during our run at the Haymarket – George Carman QC. Jeffrey had retained his services at one point. 'Like a stand-up comic in a music hall act' was one of the descriptive phrases in his obituary.

Sir David Napley, solicitor to The Great who'd been caught out being not particularly good, said, when he first saw Carman in action, that the jury seemed to be mesmerized, and Napley's partner commented of Carman's speech, 'It made the hairs stand on your neck.' Carman's really big effect, apparently, was on the Bar's fee structure. In the mid-1990s he commanded an hourly consultation rate of £3,000, a 'brief' fee of £50,000 and a daily 'refresher' fee of £10,000. (One could feel wonderfully refreshed *without* refreshers on £10,000 a day.)

Talking of stand-up comics, in *The Accused* I put in at least three sure-fire one-liners. Comics pay good money for the supply of that kind of material: a brown envelope would have been appreciated, but not so much as a fiver did I ever see.

I got a very enthusiastic thumbs-up from Archer's barrister friend, but somehow I was not entirely out of the woods. In Bromley I wrote to Jeffrey:

Friday, 7 p.m.

Dear Jeffrey,

The clash of personalities in the theatre can be no surprise to you – coming from politics as you do. I expect it's the same in middle management at Tesco's and on the few factory floors left intact since the 'economic miracle' of the 80s. I really do not relish the amount of clash I seem to cause.

Today I received a phone call from Val May in which he began to pass on what amounted to a note from 'a friend whose opinion I respect', touching on my scene with Forsyth in Act One last night. I'm afraid I let loose and asked him if he'd like some opinions from my respected friends and, since I'd already today written to Lee [Menzies, the producer] on the subject of press comment, I referred Val to the *Kentish Times* before putting the phone down. No doubt Lee will let you have a copy of my fax to him. The gist of it is that I am determined to bring consistency, a dogged routine of predictable, disciplined effects, to bear on my essentially improvisatory – some might say inspirational – method which relies to some degree on creative discovery and experiment.

Our mutual friend Peter Barkworth, when he was in *Can You Hear Me at the Back?*, gave, I am told, a performance which he began to modify from night to night to keep it fresh. (I was told he got very upset when other people tried the same thing!) I am someone who has done a production of *The Cherry Orchard* at the NT, where change and impulse were the modus vivendi of the production, which meant that one was at the mercy, night by night, of the taste – good or bad – of one's fellow actors; no worse, I expect, than being subjected night after night to precisely the same effects, some of them bad perhaps, in a more conventional production.

I look on aghast, nightly, as things conceived in a week or two in Southwark reappear with the stunning regularity of Big Ben.

In our canter towards the Haymarket, I am aware that a high degree of dependability is required. The problem, it seems to me, is to distinguish between the barnacles that sometimes pass for the hull – and the tangled rigging that stands in for the sails filled with wind from the right direction: in short to rediscover that mysterious technique that enables one to reveal oneself – not merely that deadly routine that pulls the same characteristics out of the battered hat; tricks which reveal only a poor semblance of something which distorts life, not the chance of something of life itself.

I go on trying to take the opportunity this part richly affords, and to be dependable.

Edward

Amongst the swipes the *Kentish Times* took at us was: 'To make sure we keep up with the story, the key lines are delivered as though THEY ARE IN CAPITAL LETTERS.' But before I laugh all over again, I must confess I didn't have a good press night in Bromley. The cast swanned down in no time by train, but Jeffrey's driver had told me the trains were 'no go' and, after a horrendous drive from North London and then, after my nap, Val coming in during the sacred Half Hour to give me a few 'little notes and cuts', I felt thoroughly nobbled. And, though it was in Bromley that I gave the inspirational performance behind what I'm sure was a definitive Widow Twankey the following Christmas in the West Wickham Pantomime Society's *Aladdin*, the critic found me on that Monday 'worryingly not on top of his part'. Was I losing my marbles?

Through thick and thin, Jeffrey made it his business to comment on the performance, particularly mine, as the curtain fell and he left the witness box at the end of Acts One and Two. 'Brilliant – you've never done it better,' he often said, but there were silences too. The young actor who played my junior remained a friendly support throughout the run, and a keen pupil, he told me. Likewise the prosecution junior. Nobody could have asked for a more generous, equable colleague than Michael Feast. Tony Britton, who was a friend of Jeffrey's, was always gracious to me and unobtrusively kind and solicitous when he knew things were getting rough. One night he said to me after Act Two, 'Your scene was twenty minutes of some of the most scintillating comedy I have ever seen.' (Friends have tried to dissuade me from including this kind of praise. Why? It is evidence.)

The atmosphere during the Haymarket previews had been similar to the enthusiastic, volatile reception on tour. Once the critics had pronounced their damning verdict, however, the gloom out front seemed to be more profound, as if their more derisive phrases were festooned in the dark like spiders' webs, taking the resonance out of our best lines and even snagging our gestures. We did get faint scattered titters in place of the usual strong, firm laughs, but pin-drop silences greeted some of the, dare I say, wittier moments. On one of these deathly nights, Jeffrey complimented me on my Act Two at curtain fall. 'So fast and authoritative,' he said. Just as well; it was rather like playing to a real jury in a quiet court – no point in waiting for the laughs. There's nothing quite like being in a West End flop. The atmosphere pervades the very glue in the joints of the scenery as one waits backstage before each performance, as if someone has stamped an invisible 'CONDEMNED' on everything.

Jeffrey was losing money daily, whilst his own performance took the brunt of the critical drubbing, the *London Evening Standard* proclaiming, 'To describe Lord Archer's acting as wooden would be to insult even the humblest piece of furniture.' But his good humour never faltered. Whatever depth of disappointment he felt in the last weeks, as the houses built fractionally and the audiences started to show some of the old warmth, he would sometimes say, 'Listen to them; but it's too late. Tragic.' And even then he said it with a smile. Perhaps this was his best acting performance, as he prepared to face the Old Bailey in earnest in the knowledge that things had not gone right and might, conceivably, continue not to. But I expect, even now, some of his buoyant energy is being lavished on charity auctions in aid of HM Prisoners.

If Jeffrey's genial verve remained intact, so too did his propensity to dole out advice at the drop of a hat, as when, just before Christmas, he counselled me about my need to 'build bridges' with the company and improve my 'man management'. 'Have you ever asked yourself,' he said, 'why you don't have a knighthood – why you are not playing the parts you should be playing?' It's a measure of Jeffrey's enduring perkiness, his facile man-of-the-world credibility, authority and, yes, generosity, that one did not simply laugh and say: 'And have you ever asked yourself why you've been kicked out of the Conservative Party, had the London Mayoral candidature removed and received universally appalling reviews for your play and your acting?'

So many people said I should have kept a diary throughout the run, a few even predicted a runaway success, including Judi Dench who said: 'You'll make a fortune.' Somehow, though, I only ever managed a handful of entries. I've thought of titles for the book that I might by now have completed: *A Hard Act to Swallow*; *Underneath the Archers*; *The End of the Peer Show*.

I last saw Jeffrey on the last night of the run in the cosy, elegant retiring room behind the Royal Box at the Haymarket where he used to sign copies of the playscript after each performance. I was showing a stray journalist his whereabouts and saw that Jeffrey had quite a roomful. My own copy of the published play, which he gave me on our opening night in London, was inscribed: 'A Memorable Sir James. No one will ever be able to replace you.'

Nor him.

**As Sir James Barrington QC with Jeffrey Archer (Patrick Sherwood)
in *The Accused*, Theatre Royal Haymarket, 2000.**
Photo: © Pete Jones / ArenaPAL

Afterword

14 January 2010

I have just come across a very tasteful postcard dated September 26th 2000. It is from Jeffrey Archer, and more than tasteful; it is a reproduction of Alfred Sisley's painting 'Maison au bord du Loing', from the 'Collection of Jeffrey Archer' I notice for the first time printed here. His gracious handwritten message begins: 'Thank you for teaching me so much.'

I am reminded of an odd utterance of Jeffrey's in a small upper room in Windsor, when we were about to open his play nearly ten years ago: we had been turfed off the stage where all was consumed with the critical late arrival of the set, so we were about to do a sit-down line run, and I, disorientated, knew I was suffering from the critical late arrival in my brain of Jeffrey's lines. Suddenly he made an announcement: 'There are two people in this room who, by virtue of what they can do, could make their fortunes. Before the end of this engagement I will tell them the secret of what it is they need to do.'

That's as near as I remember the event, and naturally I assumed that I was one of the candidates – perhaps we all did. As it happened, I was never vouchsafed the hoped-for revelation. In any case, Jeffrey could no more transform me into a multi-millionaire, best-selling novelist than I could transform him into an impoverished, uniquely talented and consummate actor. I have always said that we can only be taught that which we already intrinsically know and are.

All the same, I wish he'd at least tried to teach me how to make my fortune.

Chapter 30

Diaries at Two Extremes of Comedy: *The Relapse* in the Olivier,
Artist Descending a Staircase in the Old Red Lion

Looking back on a partially misspent youth, one of my regrets is the time I wasted in dressing rooms during the long waits between entrances in small parts. The plethora of small parts that has peppered my seniority has been, dare I say, gilded with feverish dressing-room activity. Perhaps it began with *The Relapse* at the National in 2001: I kept a dressing-room diary, found I could even work on my book, and began, falteringly, to use my reflection in the mirror as a model for drawing, building on the start I had made in Stratford-upon-Avon a few years before.

Coupler was a tiny part in a great Restoration Comedy in a vast theatre; I dread to think what the great architect and playwright Vanbrugh would have made of *The Relapse* in the Olivier Theatre. Trevor Nunn had instituted a subtle sound system, hoping to solve the difficulties of Lasdun's auditorium, inspired by Epidaurus but demonstrating nothing of the science of acoustics as understood by the ancient Greeks.[1]

'A great reckoning in a little room': I wish Tom Stoppard's great little play, *Artist Descending a Staircase*, which we acted in the little upper room at the Old Red Lion Theatre Pub, had been played in the original inn on that spot at the Angel; the pub was already a century and a half old when Shakespeare wrote that line. In the eighteenth century it was, at various times, the haunt of Goldsmith, Dr Johnson and the poet James Thomson; and, according to tradition, it was here that another great reckoning took place as Thomas Paine began work on *The Rights of Man*. The tavern's gable end is depicted in Hogarth's print 'Evening'.

I couple these two diaries for fun; the plays have verbal dexterity in common, little else, but acting 'high' comedy of any vintage requires 'a good comedy house', by which the actors mean not the auditorium, but the *personality* of the audience. I think 'playing to the gods' should have its meaning revised. It is no mean trick to pull off a gag that is as funny to row N in the gallery as it is to row A in the stalls, and as real and subtle to both.[2] His

---

[1] As proof of this, see Chapter 12 and the story of Diana Boddington and the launch of the Olivier.

[2] I can't remember who it was, but he or she had just seen a favourite screen actor on the stage, and said to me, 'Do you realize we were breathing the same air!' It is one of the wonders of the theatrical world that its tiered inequality has survived the intimacy of the cinema, where traditionally the cheap seats are at the front and get the benefit of even closer close-ups. When I saw Yasmina Reza's *God of Carnage* from

is a solemn responsibility 'whose business it is, as Homer says, "To shake the regions of the gods with laughter".'[3]

As ancient Thespians knew, Melete (Rehearsal), Mneme (Memory) and Aoede (Voice), the holy trinity of art in performance, are mysterious deities to please.[4] Of course, everything one does is offered up to the playwright, the director, the other actors, the perceptive critic perched on one's own shoulder (who has odd blind spots), but beyond these high priests, there is the one true deity, one's imagined ideal audience, demanding, sceptical, but a complete sucker for 'the real thing', the genuine article.

*   *   *

The Relapse

12 January – First Preview
NT Mezzanine Restaurant. 6.10 p.m.

This part of Coupler is a short one – am I on stage for as much as a quarter of an hour all told in my four little scenes? In my first scene I have the responsibility of laying out the strategy of the main comic plot, and then I come back, long after the interval, to set things on the right road because the plot has misfired. When Trevor offered Coupler to me, I wrote to him that it was a part requiring a great actor, but that no great actor would play it, because only his first scene was worth the playing: no great actor but me would play it, that is, because I need the work.

Technically it's hard. I am supposed to be 'hobbling out of my grave' but I have such distances to cover on the vast reaches of the Olivier stage, and such acoustic wastes to throw my voice across, that I have to be the most athletic of old dodderers as well as mentally always steps ahead of the young romantic lead and his servant.

Trevor has moved the Olivier open stage some sixteen feet out into the auditorium and the first row is crammed up against it; there are swathes of side seats, very close, but many literally behind the action. It's like doing a play at Chichester without the benefit of living in a rented country cottage. In spite of the wonderful spirit of this afternoon's dress rehearsal – full of real joie de vivre and carrying the story of each of the plots forward with a palpable appetite for life, love, intrigue and adventure – despite all this, it is

---

the back of the Gielgud's 'Grand Circle', which turned out to be the gallery or gods of yore, I felt I was reliving my boyhood visits to the theatre; the difference being that I was inveigled over the phone into paying £35 for my celestial seat, whereas in 1950 I'd have queued to shell out the princely sum of one shilling.

[3] A quote from *The Adventurer* No.3 (1752).

[4] Hesiod is responsible for the canonical number of nine Muses. But in his *Description of Greece* (IX.29.1), Pausanius records an older tradition, according to which there were originally three Muses, daughters of Uranus and Gaia, whose names were Melete (Practice), Mneme (Memory) and Aoede (Song).

going to be like watching the show from the wings for those people on the side, but they are close and the seats are cheap.

Anyway, I must concentrate on my own problems. God knows if there are many (or any) laughs in this part, especially as I haven't quite sorted out the athleticism-versus-decaying-age conundrum. I must now leave my secluded table in the front-of-house restaurant for the stage door, leading to the atmosphere of a 'bog-standard' comprehensive school – that's what hits you, though my dressing room is refurbished. I'll spend half an hour going through and through that first vital scene. Am I starting to get nerves as I enter my official senior-citizen period? I am thinking of living dangerously: shaking the bugs out of my wig and bringing my fist down on them as they drop onto the table.

We go up at 7.15 in forty-five minutes.

Green Room. 8.05 p.m.

In the NT's Old Vic days, I remember design suggestions being invited from the actors for the dressing rooms at the new concrete theatre on the South Bank. I made no submission, anxious that, having survived for six years in the company, I might be thought to be presuming I would last another six. I had no strong feelings in any case, and the bland, cramped little cubicle I have is perfectly acceptable, as have been the identical three cubicles I have occupied over the years. There is a bed by the window which looks out onto an inner square lightwell; other dressing-room windows stare back and one has no way of knowing which direction the outside world is facing. There is a loo with a shower (some have a bath); one's dressing table is coyly curtained off, and there is just space in the room for visitors to get very intimate while they queue for you to appear. I wish I had written something about what a green room should look like: NOT like an executive's wine bar a long way from the stage for a start.

At this time of night the green room is full of stage crew, whiling away their long waits, and people from the top-floor offices, and is no more an inner sanctum and haven for actors between scenes of a play than any echoing chattery could be. Still, they do cold sparkling mineral water at £1.20 a glass.

Well, I did the wig business and got a good warm laugh, just finding the right caesura in the dialogue in which to fit it. Ray [Coulthard] and James [Hayes] were beautifully relaxed in their playing when I got to them on stage, so it was a nice atmosphere to plunge into, and I acknowledged the beautiful way in which they responded to my surprise piece of business.

The house felt curiously empty, sparse, and distant geographically. I was cruelly underlit on my exit, way upstage or I might just have got a round; someone tried to start one. I didn't shake when I handled the documents, so that's the first hurdle more or less cleared without mishap. I think they were a little shocked by my old codger's groping and kissing of Ray's young romantic hero (Trevor was keen that it should be no holds barred). Ray has suddenly become effortlessly charming and right in the part.

462

Robert Lepage can be seen on the new split-screen TV monitor up on the green-room wall, doing his cool French Canadian in the Lyttelton,[5] to a full house no doubt, miming weightlessness as he floats through a washing-machine door. An international youth performance is cavorting in the Cottesloe in the bottom left-hand screen. Each picture is only postcard size, but in full colour. The youngsters are skipping about relentlessly – girls in long, possibly Indian, robes, whilst two poor striplings are downstage doing a bit of text. Meanwhile the picture PC of *The Relapse* preview is in the top left-hand corner.

I've been chatting just now with the good Florizel in *The Winter's Tale*, Daniel Roberts, who is an almost mute servant and furniture-mover in our show, and Ian McLarnon, also a generic footman but who sings and prances as Hymen in the wedding masque at the end. We decided that the play is remarkably contemporary but all the better for being done in the full period wiggery and frumpery – amazingly near to the morality of 2001, without the breast-beating and angst.

Interval

Must now get myself geared up to my pressured little plot-driven scenes in Act V – odd to have to jump back on the merry-go-round at 9.40, having got off it at 7.45, and odd to be ever so slightly fretting about so small a part, but I have always known that they can present the greater difficulties. I seem not to be as loud tonight – forty-five years of experience and still not loud enough?! Concentration in a little concrete room far from the stage: stay calm, go through the lines, muster up the energy to burst into the arena again. Now that you've not frittered your time away off stage, but immortalized your long wait in prose!

Friday the 13th

Dora's voice from the back of the car driving home last night: 'Only one little criticism – I don't think you were loud enough.'

Trevor greeted me chuckling as we re-gathered in the rehearsal room for notes, having been defeated in the stalls by hammering on stage. 'I think the killing of the flea is the funniest thing,' he said, and, in answer to my concern about loudness, 'Be angrier about Foppington's intention not to honour a thousand pounds' worth of your agreement – that's the fuel that hatches the first-scene plot.' Good note – an emotional reason to be louder!

When we got back into the stalls I was abashed as Trevor kicked off with: 'The flea in the wig is our funniest invention and is staying in.'

The program credits Jane Gibson as 'Etiquette Consultant', and indeed we did have one morning with her when she was curiously not in the giving vein, telling us rather sullenly, at the same time as admitting to not having read the play, that 'these people didn't have egg whisks on the ends of their arms or

---

[5] In *The Far Side of The Moon*.

walk about looking stupid with their noses in the air.' Why a set of grown-up NT players should be suspected of harbouring such misconceptions, one can't imagine. Compounding our feeling of being attacked, she went on to say that we'd never really achieve the true style of these people because they were taught their manners and dancing from the age of four, and spent their lives wearing elaborate clothes (speaking elaborately I might add), but at the same time were as tough as old boots on account of all the horse-riding they did – and the absence of antibiotics, which meant only the toughest survived. Another sullen look at us, sprawled about in denims and dosed up with life-preserving drugs!

I suppose there were a few of us in the room who had not practised period dance at drama school, but more of us who had and performed in Restoration on previous occasions. But in a sense she was quite right; these wealthy sophisticates are creatures very remote from us. Historically they had little else to do but dress and converse and scheme. Perhaps there has been a general reluctance, except in the extreme case of Foppington, to embrace a style at once tough and exquisite. It is the difference between two Bunsen-burner flames: the one with the most oxygen is intense and concentrated.

Watching Berinthia [Claire Price] and Amanda [Imogen Stubbs] at the dress rehearsal, I was, for the first time, swept along by their spirited playing, their vivacity and direct truth without any spurious conventionality in the playing. Add a soupçon of to-the-manner-born poise inside the corset (men too) and effortless mental and vocal athleticism and dexterity – the beef-fed strength inside the porcelain – and one would have the play to perfection.

When these characters are not lying in their own or someone else's bed, they do not flop on leather sofas and chat on the phone, and we are not more 'real' than they are simply because we are less formal, less elaborately articulate, less complex and stringent in our dress. They express their lust for life, for meaning and morality, or amorality, through the manners and trappings of their lives; they inhabit their culture to the very edges of their lace and the tips of their swords. Essentially they are as naked as we under their clothes, but they make their clothes a mysterious, seamless extension of their bodies and vice versa. 'Style that reveals rather than hides the man.'

Stall Notes. 2.30 p.m.

Trevor has just said, 'Continue to get used to your costumes and make them less significant.' (That's true, too, as the man said in the tragedy.)

When I first appeared dressed as Coupler at the technical rehearsal, I had blacked out my middle top tooth, the designer having distressed and cobwebbed my costume and the wig department provided an untidy wig. Trevor called out from the stalls that I looked 'like the belle of the ball'. My heart leapt; of course I wanted to be playing Foppington! He bounded up on stage and said, 'Your coat must be much dirtier and tatty and your wig needs to look more destroyed.'

Post-Tea Break

Sitting in the Olivier stalls whilst the fight scene is rehearsed. 'Watch you don't just go for the comedy,' says Malcolm Ranson, the fight director. 'It's only funny if it's real.' A simple note for all time.

I'm remembering a moment sitting here like this during the stage rehearsals of *The Seagull* seven years ago. It happened then as it's happening now: suddenly one likes everybody. Most of the company one knows only slightly after six weeks or so, but now they are part of one's tribe, and the life of the tribe; what we do on this stage becomes the centre of a world. We are in a magical space and these are magical people, though they're not casting a spell, simply attending to the joinery and the clockwork: the heroes and heroines are not in heroic mode, the gods not wearing their divinity, but this absorbed, trusting attention to the task in hand has a calm about it, like the atmosphere one observes watching children playing in a sandpit.

Fatal to the moment to try to define it – it has passed – but the attempt to carry some of this absorbed, serious play into the performance should be part of the fascinating process.

Saturday. Noon

We have been displaced by the youth theatre and are doing cuts on the green plastic lawn and garden furniture of the set-up for *All My Sons* in Rehearsal Room 2.

Sketch of Trevor Nunn from my *Relapse* rehearsal diary.

465

Trevor thought that last night's advance of three fleas was an improvement on the first preview's one, softening me up, as it turned out, for cutting some of my lines. I'm really upset – two patches of necessary colour gone. It seems petty to be angry, but, in a part of this size, seconds count and the richness of my character is diminished in making the play twenty seconds shorter.

That a great architect-playwright should have written Coupler such a delicious description of a building seemed gleeful to me:

> 'Tis true, 'tis a little out of repair; some dilapidations there are to
> be made good.
> The windows are broke. The wainscot is warped, the ceilings are
> cracked.

That is all gone, leaving me with: 'But a little glazing, painting, whitewash and plaster will make it last thy time.'

Trevor came up to me in the canteen and said, 'What else could you find in your wig? You took it off in the garret scene last night and looked into it. What you really need is a dead mouse.'

Later

This is our third preview and a much fuller house. I could hear the warmth over the Tannoy. I procured some pince-nez, better than coping with spectacles. Our designer had told me she'd do a bit more distressing of my costume: 'You must say if you don't want it.' She is so sweet to me.

I thought, when I first read the play, that my first-scene exit line should get a round: 'Ah, you young warm dog, you; what a delicious night the bride will have on't!', but I have to get miles upstage where the pros. is. Anyway I got the round tonight. Don't know how I managed to get up there, but after saying the line, I was able to turn in an erotic little reverie, to be jerked out of my abstraction by the proximity of the architecture – a hint of pantomime as a delicate near collision disturbs the old lecher's dream. Classic gags for classic plays I say.

Sunday

On Friday in my long wait I thought I ought to write to Jeffrey Archer to express my sympathy on the death of his mother, which occurred, I think, on the day of the judge's summing up at the end of his trial, which seems to have dragged on throughout most of our rehearsal period. Someone on the front-of-house staff was in the green room and told me that Jeffrey and Mary were seeing Robert Lepage's show. I said that by coincidence I was writing to Jeffrey and asked if the letter could be got to him directly. Apparently "Jenny" McIntosh (Baroness McIntosh of Hudnall) was hosting him at a pre-show drink in the VIP room. I began the letter: 'Here we are again under the same theatrical roof', but said nothing about our play featuring a bent lawyer's involvement with a dishonest peer.

Long after Jeffrey and Mary had left the Lyttelton, we in the Olivier began to sing the reprise of the song from the marriage masque – the 'Dialogue between Cupid and Hymen' in which the jubilant Chorus cries:

> For change, we're for change, to whatever it be,
> We are neither contented with freedom or thee.
> Constancy's an empty sound,
> Heaven and earth and all go round;
> All the works of nature move,
> And the joys of life and love
> > Are in variety.

*　　*　　*

Artist Descending a Staircase

Synopsis of the play from the French's Acting edition:

Donner, Beauchamp and Martello, three elderly avant-garde artists, have co-existed for over fifty years. The play starts on a summer's afternoon in 1972 with Beauchamp and Martello accusing each other of the murder of Donner who lies with a broken neck at the foot of the stairs. In a series of flashbacks, the bickering trio are contrasted with their young counterparts. The pivot is Sophie, whom the young Martello introduced to the group; whom Donner loves; with whom the young Beauchamp had an affair. But, betrayed in love, Sophie committed suicide [by defenestrating herself] and in the play's final moments, the reality of Donner's death is revealed.

Tuesday, 3 November 2009

I have been offered the part of Donner in *Artist Descending a Staircase* at the Old Red Lion in Islington. Hilarious of course: Stoppard on art. It rehearses for three weeks from next Monday (!) and plays until 31 December. Still reading it ...

Wednesday, 4 November

What a heady Stoppardian cocktail of ideas: historical pastoral comical tragical satirical farcical – adorable, in the true sense.

My daughter Dora is doing art description for the blind at the National Gallery of Scotland today. There is a blind character in Stoppard's play and the character of young Martello says to her: 'when we are very old and painting like Landseer'. Of course Dora is describing Landseer's 'After the Hunt'!

Saturday, 7 November

Tom conjures, juggles with style: Brecht never achieved his A-effect (Alienation Effect) with such shifts of time and perspective as Tom risks. The play's substance, whilst deliciously satirical, and occasionally absurd to the point of parody, frequently elicits the audience's silent empathy. Yet this breathless joy ride for the actor, if he can hold on, has, as the man said, a temperance that may give it smoothness.

Sunday, 8 November – Remembrance Sunday
Meditated, amongst other things, on Donner's lines about the maimed of the First World War: 'We tried to make a distinction between the art that celebrated reason and history and logic and all assumptions, and our own dislocated anti-art of lost faith – but it was all the same insult to a one-legged soldier and the one-legged, one-armed, one-eyed regiment of the maimed.'

Preoccupied at the moment with mounting the Stoppardian stairs, my part, though shorter, being every bit as nimble and witty as young Guildenstern, so that old age doesn't seem to have come into my reckoning, until last night when I tried adding a decade to my voice and deportment, with appallingly actorish results. Apart from that aberration, I have been too busy making sure I breathe right for the long complex phrases when they come and practising so that Donner's agility in argument is so habitual it's as easy as passion-driven pie to him. The fact that the three artists are in their dotty dotage is an audacious comic bonus. There must be few real-life seventy-eight-year-olds with such staying power in verbal gymnastics as their modus vivendi: I'll see how I'm managing in five years' time.

Monday, 9 November – First Day of Rehearsal
Handy route to rehearsal on the train to St Pancras. Some things don't change. St Pancras Station has; Victorian engineering values preserved in all their splendour, cunningly cleaned and enhanced so that it is extraordinary that grown, well-placed men argued for its demolition – drunk, one supposes, on their success in destroying the Euston Arch.

But some things don't change, and today in our grotty rehearsal room in Pentonville Road one would not have been surprised to step out and find that St Pancras was still the dismal sooty secondary station of the 1970s (when I remember a dismal long wait for a train, or rather a girl, that never came in one night – but that's another story). Hard to credit that the excellent youngsters in the cast were not even born when the play was written in 1972 and only tiny when it was first done on the stage in '88, and

'The Defenestration Room'
in Pentonville Road.
Photo: © EP

468

yet they seemed to take it in their fresh-faced strides, so to speak, that the rehearsal room was grim and unlovely as they set about doing this period piece as to the manner born, conveying us back beyond the 70s, via Stoppard's high-comedy style, to First World War France and 1920s Battersea.

One wall of the room has a rehearsal mirror such as dancers use. A previous rehearser, in his or her frustration, has tried to defenestrate themselves through it, and the resultant shards are held together by black gaffer tape. Some years ago, in an even grottier rehearsal room not far from this dreary space, and more in anger than despair, I hurled a coffee mug into the corner where it shattered. A whole year later, Sara Kestelman, who had been rehearsing with me and witnessed this display of temperament, was working in the same room again and noted that the fragments were still there.

I would like to have done a second reading, but we oldies were kept behind for the afternoon and talked about the play. I love talk, but there is no substitute for practice AND I NEED PRACTICE!

Wednesday, 11 November

My young self, Max Irons, is at least three inches taller than I ever was, and possibly more beautiful than I ever was too, but that is a matter of taste. I remember Ian McKellen saying, after seeing the old video of his *Hamlet* a few years ago, that he wasn't very good as Hamlet, but that he wished somebody had told him how beautiful he was! Olivia Darnley is the daughter of the distinguished voice teacher, Lyn Darnley, and has a perfectly centred voice that she uses beautifully, though it never sounds 'trained'; her mother must be proud of it. Together with Ryan and Alex Robertson they make a wonderfully vital quartet, and if the lion's share of directing is good casting, Michael has done wonders to find and choose them all.

Friday, 13 November – Day Off

I have conned my lines at length, of course, but popped into Keats House in Hampstead where I complained that the expensive refurbishment had resulted in modern, patterned fitted carpets. I was assured that they were the result of extensive research. That is why, I suppose, in one room at least, the carpet goes over the hearthstone and right under the fire grate. There is a liberal use of new Heritage pale sage paint, even downstairs in the kitchen where a large sideboard with racks for pans is 'tastefully' done in the same colour, when such a piece would surely have been plain, scrubbed wood. The stone shelves in the brick tunnel larder are brightly lit by electric light and are gloss painted white, as is the tunnel itself which would surely have been whitewashed. The light fittings throughout are naff and modern. I do not have the time to go on.

Friday, 20 November

Every line in my part (though Tom is threatening to cut his youthful 'overwriting') is a perfect gift to an actor from a man who cannot act, or even read aloud from his own scripts, for toffee (though he is a superb public speaker), but he has, as we all know, an uncanny sense of theatre, at once idiosyncratic and classic. He plays such bold tricks with mood, character and language, and seems to me to reveal, quite unexpectedly amongst the absurdist high jinks in this play, a tenderness.

We had a stagger-through yesterday after two-and-a half-days' proper on-our-feet rehearsal (five days split between the old and young cast). We saw our young/old selves in action for the first time. The play, despite our staggering and occasional falls, came up fresh and alive and delicious: we were each keen to achieve 'rehearsal-room cred'. High stakes.

Had a drink with Ryan Gage (young Martello) afterwards and saw the young 'artistic' Bethnal Green set in the pub, having only been aware up to then of the street market with its generous displays of plastic buckets, brushes, luggage for leaving with and clothes not to be seen dead in.

Tuesday, 24 November
Pellicci's is the name of the little café across the road from the People Show rehearsal studios in Bethnal Green. It is a treasure of a time warp. Framed, on the wall behind the counter, and dated 1953, is a faded brown-paper sandwich bag, specially printed for the Coronation of Elizabeth II. The walls themselves have a charming inlay pattern in veneer, though the tables are Formica-topped. The founding Italian family is commemorated in a large, late-nineteenth-century photograph and the delightful girl descendant who serves me is alarmingly bilingual, flipping from native Cockney to fluent Italian mid-sentence. She already treats us like old regulars and knows our gossip.

'The big man is comin' tomorrow I 'ear; the boss thought it was George Peppard and wanted to meet 'im.'

She was impressed when we prefixed the mere Tom Stoppard with 'Sir'.

Over Chapati bread, which we ate at an outside table on the pavement (it was warm enough today), I asked my comrade in art, David Weston, what he was doing in 1953.

'I was a boy scout, selling programmes in the Mall,' he replied.

I said I was playing Slender in the Coronation production of *The Merry Wives* to Peter Dews's Falstaff at Bradford Civic Playhouse, and we swapped our experiences of Peter. David had managed to play the walk-ons in Peter's *An Age of Kings* for BBC TV on Saturdays and Sundays during his National Service, being stationed at Catterick. Such is the freemasonry of The Profession; we have so many people in common. The wonderful thing is that our sworn enmity in the Lord Archer play of ten years ago has completely evaporated.

I even share a brotherhood with my younger self in the play, young Max Irons. I spotted him as we were entering the Tube so I suggested we have a drink in the adjacent pub, as a stopgap until we could have champagne and smoked salmon in the Eurostar Long Bar at St Pancras. We had a heart-to-heart about the difficulties of rehearsal and bonded sufficiently I hope, to facilitate the fact that we are playing one another. It had been a ropey run-through, but let's hope by tomorrow – Wednesday afternoon – we will be ready for 'the big man'.

With David Weston and Jeremy Child in our dressing room at the Old Red Lion.
Photo: © EP

It is a *big* little play, though we haven't quite risen to it yet. But actors are such heroic people, for all our egotisms and the impecunious privileges of life on The Fringe; the seniors managing their ageing memories and making their old tricks as fresh as humanly possible.

'The artist is a lucky dog', as Stoppard's young Beauchamp says, and so is the 'artiste', handed gift after Thespic gift in this play. We struggle with the wrapping now and then, of course; tomorrow is another day.

Wednesday, 25 November

The rehearsal was flat and strained on my part this afternoon, after a bitty rehearsal this morning which did me no favours – not getting a grip and a run on things but wasting time fiddling with positions. We need to colonize this stuff – make it our undisputed territory.

Tom won everyone's heart by being his natural self, learning everyone's name and giving a few notes.

Friday, 27 November

Suggested a piece of comic business to Max today. He did it as we stood in the green room – perfectly – but thought it might be too much of a gag. It is getting his coat on to accompany Sophie, just in time to take it off again on the 'Oh' realization: we had both decided that 'Oh' is the vital fulcrum of his (and my) part. Pity I am not six foot two, but I am working on it …

Monday, 30 November

By special demand of the actors, we had extra rehearsal on our own, there being far, far too big a gap – two whole days! – between the last call and the tech. So we had a strangely valedictory last sally through the scenes, we three oldies alone in the scruffy banality of one room in the Caledonian Road, the youngsters in the other 'defenestration' room, before we took a taxi up to the Old Red Lion. At the tech I refused to do cue to cue, insisting on saying every word. It is fatal at this stage to stop practising one's paces. It turned out to be a smaller, even more chaotic space at first sight, as the minute 'stalls', pews actually, were strewn with the detritus of the technical rehearsal. A difficult space to feel at home in initially – one imagined meeting the level gazes of the surrounding patrons and not knowing where else to look. The Magritte sky walls of the design were there BUT I put in a bid to buy Martello's 'metaphorical' figure of Sophie straight away. There it was – perfect – done by an artist apparently: it carries part of the history of twentieth-century art and is part of this wonderful play we are struggling with – perhaps almost the most consummate artistic response so far. Authentic is the word (not to be bandied about loosely to describe theatrical props). It set a standard which I fell far below as every tiny distraction, once we started the tech run, made me fluff and forget. We are doing this to play to paying customers tomorrow!

Lost sight of the beauty of the play today. Tom for all his brilliant wordplay, the torrent of ideas and knockabout cerebral fun, has a groundswell of something grave and heartfelt. But the oddest joke is that we veteran actors are trying to remember with precision what exactly these elderly eccentrics are so forgetful about!

David and Jeremy take a nap between shows in the Old Red Lion auditorium.
Photo: © EP

**With Jeremy Child (Beauchamp) in *Artist Descending a Staircase*,
Old Red Lion, 2009.**
Photo: © Marilyn Kingwill / ArenaPAL

Friday, 4 December – Post-Press Night

The artist is a lucky dog.

After the dismal rain of the last few days, the journeys to the Angel's hole-in-the-corner backstage conditions at the Old Red Lion, built 1415, rebuilt, unfortunately, in 1899, I am at home with the sun pouring through the windows and sitting at the table round which we had out post-press-performance supper last night. Not everybody had seen the show which normalized the roseate glow nicely. Apart from Emily and me, there was nobody over the age of twenty-six, and Bean, the first dog to join the family, at only eight months, took the event in her diminutive terrier stride.

From the first, the buzz made by the capacity audience of sixty, had proved they were alive as that special creature *an audience,* not disparate individuals about to be isolated in mute appreciation as they had been last night, when the wit flew through silent skies. Tom has described in a lecture this unnerving phenomenon from the playwright's point of view: 'You sit at the back and think something terrible has happened to the play. But you don't know what it is. In fact it's you (*indicating the audience*).'

*   *   *

Postscript – New Year's Day 2010

Woke up to David Tennant on *Desert Island Discs*. If his was the voice I began the New Year with, give or take some fitful strands of news and *Farming Today*, I was amongst the last live actors he saw in the dying year; he was on the front row at the final matinée of *Artist Descending a Staircase* yesterday. It went scintillatingly well. Sir Tom was at the matinée the day before (five performances in three days), and what with Tom Paine having begun work on *The Rights of Man* in the original Old Red Lion on the site, and Hogarth having depicted the tavern's gable end, to say nothing of the presence at our show at various times of Sir Ian McKellen and Roger Rees, Jeremy Irons and Sinéad Cusack, Henry Goodman, and Simon Williams (son of Hugh and Margaret Williams), all in all a period crowded with incident, which, paradoxically, can seem to be the case when one is engaged in the selfsame dramatic ritual every day and sometimes twice daily.

Murder at the Old Red Lion

(The red-carpet treatment)

The carpet, beer-stained fleur-de-lys
Leads to cloud-capped stage – we squeeze
Behind in cluttered gloom,
Reach our minute tiring room.

Who would care to put his head in?
Not a space to be found dead in
Yet we all prepare to *live* here
Practise Thespic take and give here.

Here we've conned Tom Stoppard's pages
Entered this most cramped of stages
Walked the vasty fields of France
Mused on Edith at the dance

Tried to act and stand and Sitwell
Even when the gags don't hit well
When there is an arid dearth
Of anything resembling mirth

Photo: © EP

Thought, when we have talked of horses
How much breadth our narrow courses
Conjure, through Tom's mighty line;
Wit and tenderness entwine!

Absurd, humane, satirical
The clownish, dark and lyrical
Yes the beer stained fleur-de-lys
Leads us where we strive To Be.

Donner's Painting

The wayward paint and wilful sable brush
find me, unable, undeft, laborious,
not the ideal painter of a fable –

'A naked woman sitting about a garden
with a unicorn eating the roses.'

Inching, dragging, dabbing, staring,
caring and correcting, and revising
these poses of derivative devising –
how many yestermorns must there have been
since someone painted the first of unicorns?

As I go, so slow, Sophie and her companion
sit and seem to know
how they should look and be; they see,
their perfect likeness; waiting
'till they feel they are acquainted
with what it is I've painted.

Patient, the delicate beast, waits for his floral feast
rises above his Daler Rowney Acrylic
already musing on something – more idyllic
than the daubs and drips of green
surrounding him, knowing what he has seen.

And Sophie, unabashed, waits to be dressed
in perfect nakedness.
Her destiny and destination,
closer by each brushstroke's intimation,
strives to catch her breath, its inspiration.

(For Donner's completed painting, see 'The White Fence' on page 236.)

Band Calls

Chapter 31

Tripping the Light Fantastic with Bernard Shaw

At the outset of my career, I went to see a dubious agent who thought she could get me a job in a summer seaside concert party. It never materialized, but when there is a sniff of a job – and it's true to this day – one imagines it very vividly: the initial train journey, the rehearsals, the applause, in this case, after my first number. I even imagined meeting at last the enchanting chorus girl for whom I had waited in vain outside a stage door in Bridlington when I was sixteen. I knew I was destined to be 'legit' but I did think what fun it would be to sing and dance, and perhaps tell jokes.

While I don't recall the song I danced to, I do remember the little improvised dance I did in a dingy church hall behind Peter Jones, off Sloane Square in late 1959. It was at an audition for a new show, which was about to go into rehearsal, *The Lily White Boys*, a musical version of Harry Cookson's play, featuring songs by the poet Christopher Logue. I knew absolutely nothing about the show and was told nothing, but this was my chance to work at the Court. Lindsay Anderson watched impassively as I tried to fulfil the unexpected demand to show them 'a soft-shoe shuffle'.

Neither Geraldine Stephenson nor Doris McBride had prepared me for this, so I fell back on the Sunday school concert routines I had observed the girls doing to popular songs, and I had seen G. H. Elliot doing his famous soft-shoe shuffle, when he was sixty-six and on the same bill as Ella Shields at the Bradford Alhambra. No sooner had I stopped than I was asked to do it again, and again – each time I tried to think of new steps. I was recalled in a few days, and a few more people, all of them blank-faced, watched me repeat the performance; I even began to feel I might be the butt of some sinister practical joke. I heard nothing after that. I believe the show was panned – serve them right!

These unpromising beginnings notwithstanding, there have been two high points in my career in musicals, not counting the rarefied experience of playing the soldier in *The Soldier's Tale* at Bath festival, miming along to Menuhin on my violin. *Valentine's Day* was a glorious failure in which I really became a song-and-dance man. And more recently there were two performances of Kurt Weill's *Lost in the Stars*, a ravishing and moving musical experience in which I merely spoke.

Chitty Chitty Bang Bang and *The Woman in White* had very decent West End runs, but they remained low points for me, despite the euphoria that is generated by the sitzprobe, even amongst performers who have probed nothing but musicals. I was thanked for my 'genius' by the director in one and referred to by a producer as 'perfect' in the other; nonetheless, they were bushels that fitted my light perfectly.

**With Robert Sherman, composer of *Chitty Chitty Bang Bang*
at the stage door of the Palladium.**

But, now I think of it, dear old Esmé Church talked about a part being a translucent alabaster vase, and one's talent and personality the light that one turns on inside it to illuminate it. Some vases are more spectacular than others, that's all; though I suppose one can have a hand in 'throwing' the vase to a certain degree.

*　　　*　　　*

Gillian Lynne. No sooner had I typed the name of the illustrious choreographer of *Cats* than I broke off to do my exercises. Gillian is the queen of the warm-up session and I was doing homage to her. She was the first person to cast me in a musical, namely *Valentine's Day*, an adaptation of George Bernard Shaw's 1897 comedy *You Never Can Tell*. That was in 1991, when *Cats* was about halfway through its twenty-one-year run and I was a mere boy of fifty-five with a shock of long white hair that had not recovered from being turned blond four years earlier for my portrayal of Lord Peter Wimsey. But I was turned young again by Gillian's rehearsals, or rather her morning warm-ups, even though I was playing William, the elderly waiter, who, without sacrificing any credibility – his or mine – was to become in this musical version a song-and-dance man. Gillian, ten years my senior (and still blonde), started each day on the floor in front of us, encouraging the whole cast – young dancers and ageing actors alike – to put our legs into the same interesting places in which she effortlessly put her own.

Looking back, the job had idyllic aspects to it. I lived in a charming West Sussex village with a beautiful name, East Ashling (then still unspoilt by commuter-belt 'improvements', plastic window frames and garage extensions), in a cottage with a free-range pig farm over the back-garden fence and a little bluebell wood opposite the front door. One morning, before Emily and the children came down to stay with me for the summer holidays, I woke up wondering whom I was in bed with. Then I realized. It was me! I wished I'd been doing Gillian's exercises all my life: who knows what heights of flexibility I might have achieved on stage – and what extra fun I might have had off!

But there was angst too. The famous jazz saxophonist and broadcaster Benny Green, with a reputation as a Shaw expert, had adapted and filleted Shaw's play (with assistance from David William) to make room for his own delightful lyrics, set to music by Denis King. The waiter is a golden Shavian part, and several slips had been made in the filleting, which sometimes created havoc with the delicate comedy of the situations he graced, and I spent time gently fighting to restore some of the most vital slivers of material.

I will let Shaw's opening stage direction give you an idea of what a peach of a part William is:

> *The waiter is a remarkable person in his way. A silky old man, white-haired and delicate looking, but so cheerful and contented that in his encouraging presence ambition stands rebuked as vulgarity, and imagination as treason to the abounding sufficiency and interest of the actual. He has a certain expression peculiar to men who have been extraordinarily successful in their calling, and who, whilst aware of the vanity of success, are untouched by envy. ... It is a quiet voice, with a gentle melody in it that gives sympathetic interest to his most commonplace remark; and he speaks with the sweetest propriety, neither dropping his aitches nor misplacing them, nor committing any other vulgarism.*

In his own peculiar way, Benny Green was a stickler for the script. He travelled down from London for our first run-through in the rehearsal room, carrying his personal copy of the text, and sat at the back with his head buried in it, following every word but seeing nothing. At one point he looked up, unable to find what I had said in the typeface before him. What I had said was: 'The performance, such as it is, is up here with us. Chichester is a long way to come to read the script, you could have done that at home.' But his mould was set; something made him keep his eyes glued to the words for the whole of the two halves of our run-through, even during the song-and-dance numbers. The magic of his and GBS's words intertwined in print, I suppose.

My main solo song-and-dance number, 'You Never Can Tell', took me a long time to learn. I am comforted in this sluggishness, shared by many mere actors when they turn to the Terpsichorean art, by Laurence Olivier's confession that, for *Night of a 100 Stars* at the Palladium in 1954, in which he was to dance 'I Guess I'll Have to Change My Plan' with Jack Buchanan, 'Jack worked with me for twenty hours for the two-minute number.' I was occasionally taken away to a separate room by two lovely girls, ensemble dancers, who played waitresses and knew all my steps as well as their own. They were Helen Way and a girl who struck me as rather raunchy called Ruthie Henshall.

The classic Shaw transformation into musical remains, of course, Lerner and Loewe's *My Fair Lady*. In Trevor Nunn's 2001 production at Drury Lane, the marvellous show was partly defined for me by a palpable struggle in the second half between the spirit of the romantic musical and Bernard Shaw's resistance to it. In fact, at one stage, the show almost seemed a mere accompaniment to the struggle until Romance prevailed and *My Fair Lady* romped home, leaving *Pygmalion* tangled in its wake. By contrast, *You Never Can Tell* is a much knottier play and really dug its heels in, however much we tripped the light fantastic.

I shall never forget the discipline and the rigour that went into my particular light-fantastic numbers in Gillian's witty choreography. No director, unless he was a Victorian, would ever demonstrate the optimum way of doing a personal thing like a move or a gesture, but dance is a precise science. I once witnessed a rehearsal of a Soviet dance company after which an old, slightly overweight choreographer, in a Soviet suit and street shoes, clumped on stage and approached the magnificent young creature who had just danced *Le Corsaire*, and, in a kind of lucid dance shorthand, demonstrated the optimum way of doing a sequence as the youngster watched attentively. Similarly, time and again, Gillian would unlock for me the quintessence of a step or the aspirational direction of a look, the turn of the shoulders or head.

Valentine's Day had a small kitten's life at Chichester and in the West End compared to the nine plus lives of *Cats*, which was translated into more than twenty languages. Gillian went around the world giving her personal blessing to each *Cats* production, whilst occasionally complaining of feeling creaky, but there is video footage to prove that, well past her seventieth year, there was nothing shorthand in her demonstrations. There is also a fuzzy video on a shelf in my house to prove that what always felt to me like myself at full stretch (because it was) does, in fact, appear light and fantastic. I thank my lucky stars, and Gillian, for the experience of that stretch and for the delicious release into song of Denis King's music with the thrill of trying to remain quietly professional at my very first band call. I needn't have troubled; these hard-bitten young veterans of musical theatre laugh and cry and applaud at the results! The band call is the apotheosis of belief.

*   *   *

During the run of *Nicholas Nickleby* an advertisement appeared in the *Evening Standard*, asking for 'angels' to invest in *Cats*, which was then part way through its rehearsal period. Emily and I asked ourselves whether we wanted to risk £500. We decided that we didn't have £500 to risk, though I suppose we did – just.

We went to see a preview. The great poet's words were fairly inaudible and nothing to do with leotards we decided. In 1991 we tried again and wangled seats, taking Arthur and Dora with us. We had the same reaction, whilst regretting the loss of income from the investment we might have risked!

On the last night of the twenty-first year of *Cats* in the West End (its 8,949th performance), Dora had been to visit me in my dressing room at the Palladium where I was playing the Toymaker in *Chitty Chitty Bang Bang*. The theatre was quite near to her school and she used to use my tiny dressing room as a haven to do her GCSE studies during the day and perhaps stay on to catch a bit of the show in the evening. On this particular night we went into Covent Garden after our final curtain to watch the end of *Cats* on the big outdoor screen relayed live from the New London Theatre. Suddenly it looked rather fresh and wonderful; I felt I had at last got the message.

Two Sonnets from Dressing Room No. 9
at the London Palladium

(I)

Forty-two stone steps, four landings, turnings,
Climbing, dodge the cleaner with his mop.
Walls here, bear blank witness to old yearnings,
Old turns whose ups and downs aimed for the top.
The landing's walls around our doors are peeling,
Shedding painted years clean off the bricks:
Built in memory perhaps concealing
Vanished conjurers passing with their tricks?
But only chanteurs' sentimental song
Expects the magic spells to linger here
The mirrors in these rooms have all along
Been blind to painted face and atmosphere.
What protean creatures crammed into these spaces,
Prepared and waited, rested, left no traces?

(II)

Here a clown once leant his unicycle
There, acrobats would limber up in tights
A thespian sipped brandy pre-recital.
'Just for the voice y'know.' How many nights?
Thirty thousand? How many dancers' stretches
Strong slim waists; how many scales cascaded
How many new gags writ for ancient sketches?
What odours, scents, ambitions have pervaded
What comic swore he'd strangulate his feed?
Before us, they these same cold steps descended
To the limelight: follow where they lead –
Our mentors, on their mysteries we've depended.
Their cheers and laughter long to silence dwindled.
That elemental joy we have rekindled.

Theatrical Zen and A Haiku

Simon Callow drew my attention to a review in *Variety* of my performance in the Lloyd Webber musical *The Woman in White*. As the show entered the 'evermore' of its second year, the review stated: 'Amongst the holdovers, one-time classical theatre mainstay Edward Petherbridge now looks so relaxed in his small but scene-stealing role as the aging Mr Fairlie that his performance exudes what one can only call theatrical Zen.' Theft hardly seems to epitomize Zen! Nevertheless, the thought of the many months I spent doing eight shows a week at the Palace Theatre inspired in me a limerick:

> The art of theatrical Zen
> Lies in practising now and again
> Not 'now and again' But NOW! and Again!
> And again and again and again.
>
> And again and again and again – again
> To infinity
> Ad **In**-fin-ni-**tum**.

and a haiku:

> moth's eggs in his hem
> still dancing the old routine
> seeing butterflies

Chapter 32

Lost in the Stars: A Diary

In May 2009 I got a phone call from Jude Kelly, offering me the part of James Jarvis in the musical tragedy *Lost in the Stars*, Kurt Weill and Maxwell Anderson's adaptation of Alan Paton's novel *Cry, The Beloved Country*. She described the plot as it involved me, and I realized that it must have a powerful redemptive last scene. I said I would read the piece but could think of no reason why I wouldn't want to do it. Jude said, 'Well don't try.'

I read the script quickly when it arrived and duly sobbed when I reached the end. It had first been staged at the Music Box Theatre in New York in October 1949 – one year into South Africa's Apartheid era and fifteen years before America's Civil Rights Act of 1964. Yet the end prefigures peace and reconciliation in a shatteringly moving scene between a black father and a white father whose son has been murdered by the black man's son. The situation is not the least manipulative or contrived.

I did not listen to a recording of the original Broadway production until after our two performances were over and then was amazed to hear from the tiny excerpts of the scenes, involving particularly my character, how incredibly statuesque and stiff-upper-lip the acting was, like the worst bloodless and formalized opera acting, even from Todd Duncan as the black clergyman; they reminded me of the quip about controlled English acting by director Harold Clurman: 'One can see the reins, but where is the horse?' As for the music, well …

Owing to another little job, I was going to have to join rehearsals late. The initial idea was that many characters would sing in the ensemble chorus, myself included, but gradually it was thought my elderly white-haired presence would not blend in and my voice was not of the highest standard. Before I heard a note of the music, I asked Clive Rowe, who plays the black father, what it was like. 'Imagine a combination of *Oklahoma* and Disney,' he said. Could he have been at all serious?

5 June

I have much work to do, but hope to have caught up with Weill soon. The music is stirring and not Disneyfied at all, and the ensemble and soloists are already excellent. Music is such a wonderfully precise craft as well as a mysterious art and expression of the human heart, but I was at sea within it today – literally thrown in at the deep end!

6 June

I have had a big day, as if I have been to South Africa. The cast is full of impressive people and voices. The Anderson dialogue and lyrics are incisively spare and yet intense, and the music is spacious and lush without being sentimental.

10 June

It took me two hours to get home, thanks to the Tube strike, but after a nap I feel strangely peaceful. Jude was very complimentary today about my work and that is probably the reason. It was an odd day though, working in the bowels of the Festival Hall, which seem to have had a makeover in the recent refurbishment for therapeutic purposes. The main foyer had a floorful of picnicking schoolchildren when I arrived and, as I followed the signs down to the Spirit Level and turned into the spacious white corridor with jazzy primary-coloured enhancements, I was met by a stampede of kids making for the giant beanbags. When all was calm at lunchtime I slept very cosily on a scarlet beanbag, lulled by a singer from an adjacent practice room. Nearby was a small room housing an exhibit that made the Haywood's current 'Funhouse' installation look like art. I woke up to be told that Clive Rowe had photographed me sleeping next to a stray bag lady.

In another fallow period I peered into a dance studio with a sprung floor on which assorted unsprung amateur dancers moved stiffly to the waltz from the ball scene in *Eugene Onegin*, played so stiltedly that I didn't at first recognize it. Meanwhile assorted people with badges came and went, disappeared into offices and broom cupboards, and we worked in a room too small to represent anything like the spatial relationships we need to work in, whilst having the luxury of an ante-room space, again with primary-coloured furniture, appearing like giant wooden blocks but actually made of foam. The child actors turned up, as always a happy and confident breed, such as I will belong to when I can really speak the lines from a secure memory; it is wonderfully pithy stuff. I am so privileged!

11 June

Today we were in the Violet Room, which was even smaller than the White of yesterday. The walls bore evidence of Waterloo being subject to the attentions of a 'practising' artist, one clearly in need of practice if he is to inspire the youngsters, who decorate the walls, to express themselves and their relationship to their environment in a truly exciting way, instead of what was on view. But the building *is* being used; hence our being moved from pillar to 50s post by the Tube strike and whatever is taking priority here, including, at lunchtime, an odd little orchestra in the foyer rehearsing with a mature lady harpist, and some kids on guitars, recorders and percussion, and a bassoonist, backed by projections which may or may not have been part of their rehearsal. All this en passant to get my free-range egg sandwich, purchased from one of the ethnically diverse staff at the snack counter, all of whom look rather interesting – as if they belong in the Spirit Level rather than behind the till.

The ensemble is by now a most impressive choir, especially in a confined space, but I could not escape from their crammed ranks in the afternoon when I realized that the session was all about getting them to sing in either a black or white South African accent, whereas I am English, which calls into question whether I should sing with them at all! It is my white hair that makes it impossible for me to blend in amongst the black and white, but predominantly black- and brown-haired, singers, who are half or a third of my age.

Today I spoke to Cornelius [Macarthy], who plays the black murderer of my son. I had to tell him how perfectly he read the trial scene the other day when it was uttered for the first time. In response he told me his life story from arriving from West Africa as a schoolboy, who couldn't always afford the bus fare to school, to being offered a place at Oxford to study medicine, not feeling able to face the music, turning it down and becoming a session singer on the strength of his gospel choir experience, going all over the world and throwing that up to become an actor by gaining a scholarship to Mountview, where they advised him to get dental treatment for a speech defect. He has an unerring instinct for timing, but then this is a cast with whom I am entirely proud to be working.

Tomorrow, with the Tube back to normal, we revert to rehearsing at Maida Vale Studios (which would have been much easier for me during the strike). It is, of course, the location of the BBC Concert Hall as described in the second of my three radio talks and glimpsed en route to record Howard Barker's *Let Me* in the Drama Studio. On display in the foyer is a letter from Sir Malcolm Sargent concerning the preparations for a concert before the Queen, and there is a picture of Her Majesty arriving at the studios looking young and pretty. In his letter Sargent gives instructions to include as many instruments as possible, seemingly to make a big noise but perhaps to give as many instrumentalists as possible the honour of playing before the young Queen. Rather touching. He even asks for a harp 'or two if we have them', and intends to write 'an unheard passage' for them in the middle of Elgar's *Cockaigne Overture*.

Of course, I am even nearer to Abbey Road Studios where The Beatles pilgrims photograph themselves on the zebra crossing and leave hundreds of felt-tip messages on the low garden wall, which are then painted over in white about every three months. Elgar conducted the boy Menuhin in the famous recording of his Violin Concerto here. We know Seal Jones, the film composer, who likes to stay at home in London and so persuades US companies to record their soundtracks here by dropping the names Abbey Road and London Symphony Orchestra.

I have come up with an alliterative description: I so admire the combination of precision and passion at music rehearsals.

It was in 1953 that the Queen visited Maida Vale and Broadcasting House on the same day. She had asked in advance that the concert by the BBC Show Band be shortened, but it was explained why it could not be.

12 June

The Maida Vale Studios were originally the biggest roller-skating rink in Europe, built in 1909. They did well and then suddenly failed. We were in a subterranean studio today, sometimes called 'The Bing'. Crosby made his last recording in it in 1977, just days before he died. There is a brass plaque.

I have been working hard on my part tonight – a lot depends on the distance between our chairs in the last scene. I realized we have done no detailed work on the scenes yet and a foot can be a mile on the stage, and reading, as Jude wants us to be bold about, or half-reading the script, and acting from memory use different bits of the brain. But still Jude was crying too much to be worried about the vulgar 'MGM' closing music that troubled the conductor, Charles Hazlewood. That was actually only the second time we had been through the scene, so I guess we are on course. But I have so much to do, even though the part is of modest size. It is elemental stuff!

I can't let the sun set on my unfinished tasks without recording that Clive Rowe sang several numbers today, including 'The Little Grey House', which is an example of Broadway Homespun with a donkey-walk rhythm, and which Anderson, Weill and Rowe between them imbue with such simple transcendental goodness. I mean Rowe makes one believe not only in the goodness of the parson's home but also in God – at least his God.

Cornelius added to his rehearsal laurels by being less good in the court scene but perfect in the pre-execution marriage scene in prison. It was an example of the real sensitivity that comes from actors' instinctive emotional wisdom and makes them look as if they have been touched by the hand of God. His wife [Tsakane Maswanganyi] acted it perfectly, too, and the solo voices that soar out of the chorus – male and female – are angelic.

13 June

Charles Hazlewood lately ran the South African lyric theatre company Dimpho Di Kopane – Google says they were 'raw'. He told of how they received the news of two of their number dying of AIDS and for two days kept bursting into song as a natural response, sometimes laments, sometimes celebratory pieces. Singing is as natural to them as breathing, he said.

He also recalled going into St George's Cathedral in Cape Town and being moved to tears by its atmosphere. I asked him what it was like and he told me that it had started as Anglican Gothic, but had had undistinguished piecemeal additions and was a bit of a mess. Of course, people had been hidden from the authorities there and a lot of praying for reconciliation had gone on, and, even though he is not religious, he was very moved. He said that one of the Cathedral's striking features is the old Hill organ, which originally stood in St Margaret's, Westminster.

19 June

I am awash with Weill, having just got back from a run-through, the music of 'Cry, The Beloved Country' still ringing in my ears. It gets better. My contribution is crucial but modest – wish I had a song.

We did a run of the show today and, again, I feel I have been in South Africa all afternoon. I also realize that I have not been on stage since I finished the tour of Alan Bennett's *Office Suite*, and that I have missed the sensation of it, though in this I get it in small doses only. I fear the Queen Elizabeth Hall will not be dialogue-friendly.

Leaps and bounds today nevertheless. Clive has a massive part, song after song and emotional scene after emotional scene. By comparison, some of the rest of us have crucial scenes, which are so pithy as to be slight, were their emotional content not so strong. Clive and I have got bogged down and tangled sometimes when we've rehearsed, trying to anatomize exactly what is going on between us, but we released a few cables this afternoon and made some emotional discoveries. I could do with another few days, but after tomorrow we do the sitzprobe in Watford – sounds like a radio play!

22 June

Now the Queen Elizabeth Hall: I think it would have been better to leave the old shot tower standing. The South Bank is, of course, the architectural apotheosis of British mediocrity, ugliness and ... I added several more adjectives before walking across to the Haymarket to deliver a letter to Simon Callow on Wilton's Music Hall, but I haven't the heart to attempt to portray the approach to and the innards of the QEH. Suffice it to say that the empty auditorium, an uncompromising giant steep slope, abandoning the age-old idea of creating two overlapping levels in favour of one hill of impossibly distant seats, is the colour of dried merde, and the BBC Concert Orchestra has taken well over half the width of the stage. Pity the people sitting behind the harp.

We spent the morning having our moves on this corner postage stamp arbitrarily changed, no time to go back on anything, so that it was sometimes difficult to hold onto any organic relationships. Meanwhile the lighting was experimenting wildly between stygian gloom and bright red, to name but two effects, so one felt disorientated. All this and radio mikes too, but at least we began to be heard, though at first the acoustic effect was like acting in a giant booming bathroom.

I have so little to do in the great scheme of things; all the more reason that it should be strong and clear or the part could go for nothing. Clive is lucky to be able to stand and sing such a lot; he has a great mountain to climb and does it effortlessly. He is the sweetest-tempered actor and does some simple, elemental things in the course of his performance that are pure gold.

The sound men – Adam, who sometimes fixed my radio mike during *The Woman in White*, and Mark, who was the RSC operator and devisor for my *Krapp's Last Tape* – are enthusiasts and the sound is better all the time.

'Do you remember the first thing you said to me?' asked Mark as he was fixing my radio mike to my head. He was referring to our very first meeting, twelve years earlier, to discuss the sound of *Krapp's Last Tape*. I did not remember. 'You said,' he went on, 'I want to hear the sound of silence falling.' Then it came back to me. He had devised a faint ambient noise to be present in the auditorium whilst the audience was waiting for the play to begin. This would fade out just as they had quietened down in the blackout, with Krapp alone in his den, unmoving, staring before him. The effect of falling silence toured with us from London to New York and Washington, to Edinburgh, Dublin, Israel et al.

24 June

We got a complete standing ovation tonight – a better curtain call helped. I didn't do my last scene to the best standard, having left a line out and screwed another, but Emily was on the front row, unbeknownst to me, and thought me 'seamless' – the power of imagination over faulty execution. I would like to do it again if only to get it to the stage where one could go on utterly safe with the part deep in the muscle memory under control – that's where true spontaneity is born – rather than having to make do with the haphazard effects of, as the script has it, 'doing what one can.'

25 June

The first thing I said to Jude Kelly when she came round after the show yesterday night, our second and last night, was, 'I can only think of my imperfections.' I was thinking of one particular, crucial (yet strangely disposable) line I had left out of a speech in my final scene and one or two other minor 'rewrites'. Olivier once told me, 'Comedy should always be played off the cream of your energy.' I would say now that tragedy doesn't work too well on semi-skimmed either!

This morning on waking I lay in bed and calmly went through the last scene word perfectly, proving to myself that my brain *did* still work, even first thing in the morning. Jude's reply to me last night was: 'It's our imperfections that make us human.' But the demands theatre makes on us require the superhuman; nothing less will do.

Cavin Cornwall, who had the part of the wily, fast-talking John Kumalo, told me that he had never had to concentrate so hard on a part, going through it even to the length of 'all-nighters.' The most titanic task was Clive Rowe's. He quipped to me, before the show last night, that our task at the QEH was 'technical, dress rehearsal, preview, first night and last night all in the space of three days.' If ever I have seen a Titan giving a convincing 'all singing, all acting' impersonation of an extraordinary 'ordinary' Everyman, Clive's is it!

I don't recall feeling so privileged to be part of a show before. This is partly because it is so patently an important piece and the job of performing in it gains stature in direct proportion to the stature of the work.

In pure showbiz terms, I have spent all these tears – sorry – years (Freudian typo) thinking I was God's gift to Hamlet (cruelly both productions in which I was to play the Prince were cancelled), so much so that the meaty roles I have landed I have thought of as my just due. Latterly Lear was snatched away from me after two days' rehearsal. I have my GP, whom I went to for advice, to thank for his failure to prescribe aspirin and statins and flying socks before I flew halfway round the world to play it. Had I asked at Boots, they would have sold me the socks and aspirin, and the rest might have been theatre history, not a medical footnote.

BUT from the first dissonant brass of the score, modulating into the soft strings (or even played by our rehearsal pianist and répétiteur, Caroline, who only had to be absorbed in the music to transform herself into a beauty), and, after the violas, the first voice – Terel Nugent's so natural and delicate male treble, painting the lyric line in the landscape with:

> There is a lovely road
> that runs from Ixopo into the hills.

I was transported to South Africa. Every time, whether we were squashed into the most inadequate spare rehearsal room the Spirit Level had to offer, the Bing studio at Maida Vale or finally contemplating the cramped corner postage stamp left over for the performers at the QEH, once the BBC Concert Orchestra had taken the lion's share, sprawling eight seats past the central aisle! I remember lurking half behind a black curtain, looking up at the gantry traversing the full stage width behind the musicians at the most good-natured cast of singers one could meet, all glowing in subtle stage light, and hearing the leader's part shared so ravishingly amongst the superbly contrasting voices. (I also remember failing my unprepared-for shotgun audition to be part of this opening.) *The Times* called my entirely spoken part 'slightly underwritten', and my accidental snips wouldn't have helped, but I always felt, rehearsing or performing, that the road from Ixopo or the streets of Johannesburg were in existence around me, waiting for me to rise to the challenge of existing in them.

Having at last heard the original Broadway cast recording of 1949, I can only regret that Weill himself never heard his final musical played and sung with such sensitive grandeur as I have heard over these last few days.

My own task was to use the few lines accorded me to tell the economically sketched, elemental story of one white man. But, after two years off the stage following my stroke, and so long before that spent being thankful to be employed on the West End treadmill in parts which were essentially bushels that fitted my light perfectly, it's comforting to know that, despite the three weeks' rehearsal not being quite enough to find me in perfect command of the material, I was able to tap into the *gravitas* of the part and Jarvis's journey from an intransigent position of white supremacy to the redemptive last scene. It was an extraordinary privilege to go on the

492

character's journey with him. I will not forget the first notes, the last scene with Clive, nor anything in between.

Wonderful, too, to be in harness again, but I am almost glad that, in my innocence and ignorance, I sat in the dark behind that curtain and whispered with the modest Soweto-born singer who sung and played Irina so perfectly, little realizing that I had watched her from the far reaches of the back seats of the Festival Hall, being the most perfect, dangerous firebrand of a Carmen I had ever seen or heard or imagined possible. I might have been scared. But there we sat in the dark together for a few moments, for all the world as if the superhuman was not, and had never been, required of us.

Chapter 33

See it Under Light!: *The Fantasticks*

Most of the critics, predictably, hated *The Fantasticks*, but the part I played of the Old Actor, Henry Albertson, has something about it that is God-given. In fact it was given to me by a god – I am convinced of that, as you will be when I tell the story. Which god? It was on this fashion.

One afternoon, about a fortnight after Stoppard's *Artist Descending a Staircase* had closed, I was at home working on my painting of Donner's Sophie and the unicorn, looking through a few books in the hope of finding a decorative plinth or a feature of some kind that would make the garden setting look more like a garden and less like the spare ground near Battersea Power Station it then resembled; I decided there was no room for a rather handsome Watteau plinth. Suddenly my mobile rang. It was my agent. Would I care to audition for the part of the Old Actor in *The Fantasticks*?

The show, which began life in 1960, has the distinction of being the world's longest-running musical. It's an allegorical tale, told by minimalist means, and loosely based on Rostand's *Les Romanesques*: two neighbouring fathers trick their children into falling in love by erecting a wall between their gardens and pretending to forbid the match, and then, with the aid of hired players, staging an abduction to end the specious feud. I had looked into the show years ago, as a possible vehicle for the Actors' Company, and only remember finding it slight, twee and impenetrable. But, on downloading the script – gone are the days of motorbikes and couriers in black leather delivering hard copies – I thought Henry's first scene charming and doable.

So I took myself off to Dress Circle in Monmouth Street where the original off-Broadway cast recording had been saved for another actor, and the nice, knowledgeable man sold me instead a CD of a 1993 tour of the show, featuring the lyricist, Tom Jones, in 'my' part and the composer, Harvey Schmidt, assaulting the ivories.

I have omitted to tell you the mystic key to this sequence of events, which is that, earlier in the day, my daughter Dora had remarked on a photo I took in Kyoto on a British Council-backed tour of the Far East in 1982 with the London Shakespeare Group's *Twelfth Night*. The photo shows Emily at a small backstage Shinto shrine to Ame-no-uzume-no-mikoto, the patron deity of professional actors.

It is recorded in the ancient Japanese chronicles, the *Kojiki* and the *Nihongi*, that the sun goddess, Amaterasu, furious at the destructive and insulting behaviour of her brother, the storm god Susa-no-wo, entered the Rock Cave of Heaven and closed the entrance with a stone, leaving the world in darkness. In an effort to lure her from the cave, the other gods brought gifts and sang litanies, but the goddess was unmoved. Finally, Ame-no-uzume-no-mikoto, the 'heaven-alarming-female', decked her head with vines, exposed her breasts, lifted her skirts, jumped onto an overturned tub, and there performed a comical dance that caused the heavens to shake with the laughter of the gods. Hearing their laughter, Amaterasu moved the stone and peered outside. One of the gods quickly pulled the rock door open, restoring light to the world. Ame-no-uzume-no-mikoto became one of the pantheon of gods worshipped under the name of Inari, whose temples are guarded by foxes or *kitsune*, and patron of actors who, like her, are said to lighten people's hearts and make the sun shine again. An Inari shrine, large or small, is installed in every Kabuki theatre.

During the interval of one of our Kyoto performances, I thought of asking the goddess to help Emily and me get a round after the little dance we did to open the second half of *Twelfth Night*. I did the required two claps to attract the deity's attention and made my request. We went on and got the round after the dance – and at all subsequent performances throughout Japan.

Emily at the little shrine to Ame-no-uzume-no-mikoto
at the theatre in Kyoto.
Photo: © EP

We don't have a shrine at home in London, but we do have two little porcelain foxes. I went upstairs for a postprandial nap and, for the first time since Kyoto, clapped my hands and said, 'What about a job?' I was astonished enough when my agent phoned (fast work!), but then she told me the director was a Japanese Tony Award nominee, Amon Miyamoto. It took me from Piccadilly to Finchley Road to open the CD package, part of the time sitting on station platforms. I heard the piano overture between the Tube and Waitrose on my portable CD player and by the time I took the bus home I had heard the whole score. The recording was, of course, of the Japanese tour!

My audition began with me trying and, on the second attempt, succeeding to jump up on a frail plastic chair, to demonstrate how Henry might manage to mount the trunk, triumphant and surprised and then in danger of overbalancing. Not quite the same as dancing on an upturned tub, but it left me feeling sunny. My chief coup, however, may have been my finger-snapping business, when Henry calls for his doublet – ancient, ragged, out-of-work strolling player, unable to remember any of the famous speeches he purports to know. I attempted to snap my fingers to call my companion Mortimer to fetch the doublet, but failed, and said, 'Fetch the doublet', rather aside as to a menial. Absent-mindedly I tried again whilst waiting for the garment and was astounded that it worked – double-take, smile. It is a rather charming passage in the script, because the failed ancient mummer keeps saying, 'Try to see it under light, that's the whole trick, see it under light', and there is something uplifting about his belief in the face of such tawdry evidence.

Not since my audition for Sir Laurence and the entire NT artistic staff have I had such a 'good house' at an audition. I sang the show's best-known song, 'Try to Remember', which I have grown to love, and did it from memory. It is a perfect gem of a song, with its heart in the perfect place, and I was accompanied perfectly by the show's orchestrator, Jason Carr, the composer-pianist of *Pomp and Force of Circumstance*, a show I devised for Emily and me in the year of the Queen's Golden Jubilee. As I sang, I could see that the director and producer were swaying from side to side in time to the music. It made the experience almost sufficient consummation in itself.

It helps if the gods are on your side. On the other hand, I remember an actor saying to me once about his years as a student at RADA: 'The best advice was written on the door – PUSH.'

From the first audition to the first preview and beyond I knew I had struck gold with Henry. I realize, perhaps a little late, that part of the job of acting is to be a ruthless prospector – to fight for the best nuggets. It is no good debasing one's own coinage by playing parts which pay the rent, but in which you can't shine – they lead only to other offers of bushels that fit one's light perfectly. Trevor Nunn once took me aside; it was in 1979 after I had staged the screening of a slideshow I had devised about the first RSC small-scale tour. The presentation had music and a commentary and jokes and seemed the perfect in-house entertainment, especially as we were introducing some new cast members into his production of *Three Sisters* who didn't have the race memory of our long tour. Trevor whispered to me urgently after the screening in his RSC house in Welcombe Road, 'You must fight to become a television director.' I was flattered to some degree, though I wondered whether it was implied that I should abandon acting! But the main thing I understood was his injunction to fight. I could tell from the way he said it that he knew I wasn't a natural fighter.

*   *   *

Throughout the rehearsal period, which did not start until three months after the audition, and, as it turned out, the production's curtailed run, I kept an intermittent diary, which I reproduce here.

19 April (First day of rehearsals)

We read through, lyrics and all – no singing. This cast might pull it off – a nice feeling and Amon was touching about what the show meant to him when he saw it as a boy. The stuff with the masks in Act Two is hard to envisage – no pun intended. My costume is not at all resolved yet – they want to suggest that Mortimer and I are contemporary homeless. I thought a very big coat old with astrakhan collar and drooping hem that gets ripped off when the trunk lid is closed on Henry.

21 April

'Try To Remember' sung at tonight's low-key press gig by Hadley Fraser (El Gallo) was delicious and new minted. I do not hope to hear it sung or performed better.

24 April

My sidekick, Paul Hunter, is a born comedian in the Kempe tradition: what he makes of the dying scene is superb clowning, and much more than the stage directions set down for him, and I am convinced better than anything done in the part since 1960. Getting out of the trunk at the moment, because we have to squeeze an S-bend under the raked platform, is a play in itself.

With Paul Hunter (Mortimer) in *The Fantasticks,* **Duchess Theatre, 2010.**
Photo: © Francis Loney / ArenaPAL

27 April

I keep finding that there is more to this script than meets the eye. We have a marvellous exit through an awkwardly placed box. Tomorrow we are running Act One in the afternoon. Today I just saw the number 'Soon It's Gonna Rain' with the boy and girl being melodic and touching and young, and the actor playing the Mute being – well, I would say noble. The acid test will be whether we can spread the magic to cover the whole of Act One.

28 April

We never have long note sessions; no time spent talking in rehearsal. The director has been a dancer and choreographer so we do it and discuss a little on the way. It was a very respectable run-through with quite a bit of complex song and dance that came off delightfully. The youngsters are playing young newly discovered love up to the hilt and the numbers are coming fresh minted with no dead hand of period quaintness. The settings have been made nicely spare and elegant, and Paul and I are finding new things all the time. I catch myself laughing on my way home on the Tube! The Mute and the Narrator and the two fathers are all so full of life, commitment and invention – there is such an atmosphere of genuine joy in these rehearsals.

People are being very positive about my contribution, but the stylistically difficult Act Two, with Henry and Mortimer's parts fizzling out, has to be faced in the next few days.

2 May

I can't get an actual doublet out of Amon but we are working on it. Getting the pretend doublet on with Paul is a production number already, using just an old 80s top of mine! The designer unfortunately thought the business hilarious as it is so we may be stuck.

On the strength of work so far, it has been refreshing to rediscover what a place of delight a rehearsal room can be and that my own character's jokes, already antique in 1960, polish up and gleam classically.

4 May

Pranced about as a 'young 'un' in the 'rooster scene' all morning, then went to the retro shop by the Old Vic with the designer and Paul. Paul has a very appropriate T-shirt with a target motif on the chest! We only found a hat for me, but the costume lady has already found me a distressed pair of striped designer trousers and a Somerset Maugham cream jacket with too-short sleeves. This ensemble seems inspired; when I put it on it is a case of NAR (No Acting Required). I suggested spats to complete the ensemble.

The first hurdle of the two 'impossible' scenes has been cleared because we have put in some visual gags. The script at this point may be pinchbeck but we have invented opportunities to glitter.

8 May

Our Southwark rehearsal room is not only quite near where William Shakespeare rehearsed, but even nearer Bear Lane where there is still a scenic supply company utilizing a couple of railway viaduct arches under which the actor-manager Sir Henry Irving stored his scenery for forty-four Lyceum productions in the 1890s (260 scenes in all). Many of them Shakespearean scenes of an elaboration that would have astonished Shakespeare and his actors almost as much as the coal smoke, hiss of steam and thunder of the engines running by above. Irving lost the whole of this precious stock to a fire in 1898.

Our *Fantasticks* is more in William Shakespeare's tradition: there is a bare platform and a cut-out moon, but I got home today after rehearsal as if I had witnessed a sumptuous spectacular. I had sat on the Jubilee line Tube train from Southwark, where usually I need a book or newspaper to while away the dull journey, but I simply sat in a kind of *Fantasticks* theatrical afterglow, fragments of tunes in my head making me forget the noise of the train.

13 May

The difficulty with what Paul and I are doing is that it's an elaboration that must not damage the simple structure and leave El Gallo, eager to move forward, waiting for our self-justification to be over. It's our old friend *truth* we must adhere to. I think we tightened things today in the interests of narrative credibility.

16 May

On the way home from rehearsal today, having said a temporary goodbye to our platform stage which has by now gone ahead of us into the Duchess Theatre where we will tread its boards again on Wednesday, I thought back on the journey thus far: the songs getting more tender and limpid at every repetition, Paul Hunter and I in our short comic scenes applying a passionate intensity worthy of tragedy, comedy being a serious business. I bought some Omega 3 capsules, two kinds to cover my needs – one for joint care and the other for 'brain performance and memory'. I suppose I will take them on alternate days. Perhaps it will show from out front which ones I am on.

19 May

The sitzprobe this evening was very light for me and Paul – 99.9% listening and mostly a disappointment. It was a very small studio and the mikes homogenized everything, so the harp and cello were just part of a thick mix and the voices rather marginalized. I have written of happy sitzprobes and this had its moments. Luke Brady, who is the juve boy, has an innocence, a lack of showbiz about him, an artless simplicity. Maybe people will not agree with me, but I think his faint clumsiness adds to his charm, and his slightly heavy build and features have a Pre-Raphaelite tinge. Paul and I do so little that it is touch and go as to whether we will be the show's secret weapon or a short damp squib.

9 June (Opening Night)

We couldn't have had a better reception, though misgivings about the second act were sounded on many fronts afterwards. I met Tom Jones and we will meet again at the Waldorf on Friday. Such a heady first night is a rarity to me these days – at least for me to feel such a kingpin in the proceedings. It is almost – as a director used to say before a take – 'as for the first time', but oddly nostalgic. Must go to bed – I have the same thing to do all over again tomorrow. I should be so lucky, but will we run more than a month?

Between acts in my dressing room at the Duchess.
Photo: © EP

10 June

The *Standard* damns without even faint praise – as I feared, we could close in a fortnight. My agent found the second act seriously damaging to Henry and Mortimer's characters and the benign ethos they have built up in Act One. I found myself saying that, had I been a knight of the realm, I might have refused to do the parts as written in Act Two.

I am used to the intense glow of joy generated by a first-night audience, followed by the ashes and cold water – to mix metaphors – of the critic by the morning hearth. This strangely flawed fantasy has given me a chance to create something of which I am very fond and work with some delightful talents, but I fear tonight the atmosphere in the stalls will have the chill with which I have become acquainted over recent years.

11 June

I've just had a pre-show snack at the Waldorf with Tom Jones and his wife – low-key but delightful. I gave him a bound printout of my piece on *Nicholas Nickleby*; he promised to send me his rewrite of *The Tempest*! I crossed the road to the gate of the cluttered passage leading to the stage door where I was greeted by one of the producers, who gently and gravely gave me two weeks' notice. Not being at the warm-up, I missed the announcement.

Well, I predicted it from the very beginning, though there have been so many moments when the magic has convinced me otherwise. The overture begins as I type. The cello and harp and Hadley's voice sound over the Tannoy. Must get ready – as for the first time ...

12 June

I feel sorry for the people who have no good personal reviews to keep, no 'cuttings' as Henry would say. On that score I have done well – so mission accomplished! I don't think Amon realized quite how tricky the script was from the literary point of view, and he must have been surprised at the comic success of 'the players' – they were deadly in Japan! There were so many moments in rehearsal when I thought the gossamer magic might just survive.

13 June

The dip in attendance the West End took tonight because of the World Cup provided us with a small but engaged audience. Some of the cast crowded round a television in the interval to see England moving towards a draw. I am reminded of my old colleague Edward Hardwicke who appeared with Peter Ustinov in the latter's play *Photo Finish* back in 1962. I had seen the play at a summer matinée at the Saville Theatre (now a West End cinema) two years before Edward and I met as supporting actors in Olivier's *Othello* at the NT. He told me that during Wimbledon fortnight there was a television installed just off stage so that they could keep an eye on the Championships, and both he and Ustinov had methods of conveying the score to one another when they made their entrances. I still remember Ustinov's rich comic stage presence in the play, with no hint of an off-stage life of 'Who's for tennis?'

16 June

This week I have been spending time by day in a recording studio: twenty hours reading Jill Paton Walsh's new Peter Wimsey novel, *The Attenbury Emeralds*. Emerging from the basement studio into the lovely sunlight of Goodge Street is one of the treats of my daily routine. The walk from Goodge Street to the Duchess is welcome exercise and my head is full of echoes and images of 1950s London, the setting of the book, which plays in counterpoint with the present as I dive into bookshops in Charing Cross Road and Cecil Court and finally pass through Covent Garden, where today, with wonderful spirit, a comedy quartet were playing Brahms's Hungarian Dance No.5.

19 June

Strange but understandable that Amon has gone back to Japan without a parting word – tail between his legs I suppose, but we have to be bright-eyed and bushy-tailed nightly. He would be pleased with the audience reaction we have been having these last few nights – and tonight, a non-World Cup audience (with England playing) was rather delicious.

23 June

The youth of these audiences makes me suspect that, despite the gorgeous summer evenings, the drama schools are responding to the offer of complimentary tickets. Indeed, coming late out of the stage door tonight, I met two RADA students and their young producer friend (blond, and handsome enough for a heartthrob leading juvenile himself). 'What are you doing here?' I asked them. 'Talking about the show' was their reply, so I joined the discussion, confessing that, for me and Paul Hunter, the somewhat surreal second act, apart from our first scene in it, was a chore.

It has to be said that one distinguished actress, loaded with awards, told Clive Rowe that she liked the second act best, but that another, a sometime leading actress with the RSC, met Paul after the show and remarked that watching the second act was like being on drugs. It strikes me now that, not since I was smuggled onto the stage in Peter Brook's Seneca's *Oedipus* to join the final rave-up round the six-foot golden phallus, as a brass ensemble played 'Yes! We Have No Bananas', have I struggled so hard to lend inner conviction to the inexplicable.

But I am rather pleased that so many of the next generation of actors are seeing me in my God-sent comic turn!

*   *   *

After four weeks (two of them previews), the show closed on 26 June. We had a torrid valedictory party in the subterranean stalls bar after the final show, bravely keeping our cool. Mind you, forty performances would be a respectable tally at the National Theatre in repertoire, but respectable was not the word for the *size* of our audiences in the Duchess' 479-seat auditorium. I have always admired John Peter, the critic for *The Sunday Times*, but, though there might have been others like him who wanted to bite off their kneecaps for distraction – give or take the odd, oddly muted house – the joyously responsive audiences were a great pleasure to play to.

I am amazed that Tom Jones had returned to the off-Broadway cast, thirty years after his first run at it, and not re-written the second half to give himself and Mortimer a decent and meaningful exit from the play. I have to take blame or credit for contravening Hamlet's advice to the players (he is a prince and an amateur, so what does he know?): 'Let those that play your clowns speak no more than is set down for them'. I think Paul and I should have received cash in brown envelopes for our enhancement of our parts.

There is a legendary credit in the 1929 Hollywood film starring Mary Pickford and Douglas Fairbanks:

The Taming of the Shrew
by
William Shakespeare
Additional dialogue by Sam Taylor

I prefer to think of our extra-textual and -terrestrial contributions ('Dress the stage' is, after all, Henry's advice to Mortimer) not as overstepping the mark, but in biblical terms: 'And whosoever shall compel thee to go a mile, go with him twain'.

One of my fondest memories is of Paul, dressed in lace curtains and string vest as 'an Indian' (i.e. Native American), with kitchen utensils rather than scalps hanging from his belt, applauding the theatrical death of El Gallo and then, realizing he is superfluous to requirements, dying himself. I still believe in the precipice he plummeted down, but, more than that, his clown was a real being, a being I never talked to in real life, but we communicated on stage and much of what happened between us was the result of his inspired improvisation – rarely did we plan or amend in cold blood. I remember him describing the difficulties of our entrance from the box, and (even more difficult) our entrance *into* the box to get out of it, as 'not a precise science'. But from the moment we began to rehearse together, this entrance took on a mysterious life of its own and our relationship was forged through it, something we have to thank Tom Jones for despite our Sam Taylor interpolations. Beckett and our double act have been mentioned more than once in the same breath.

As I woke on the Sunday morning after our last performance, to a glorious summer's day, I still had to turn on Radio 3 to silence the insistent tunes from the show going round in my head. But the pure fresh memory of them remains, especially the moment I was arrested in the doorway of the rehearsal room and moved to tears by the opening, by Hadley's infinitely tender 'Try To Remember' and the cast poised in a perfect moment of infinite possibility.

Sentiments for *The Fantasticks* last night
26th June 2010

Each Pierrot has his personal moon
Each Columbine and Harlequin and Pantaloon
Knows too well the lunar wax and wane
Triumph and disaster, loss and gain
They never lose a sense of glad surprise
That fortune, though it sinks,
Can also rise
That even as it fades away, the dream
Carries still a substance that can gleam.

Pierrot with moon.
Photo: © Arthur Petherbridge

An Epilogue

In terraced ranks you sit there – all agog
What's this you're asking now – an epilogue?
Am I going to tell the truth, spill beans
And let you know what lay behind the scenes?

The curtain speech or epilogue's a way
Of rounding off what one has had to say
Wolfit hanging tired on the curtain,
Making sure, before you leave, you're certain
Of his repertoire throughout the week
So you'll catch him at another peak.

Rosalind comes forward to conjure you
Prospero needs simply to assure you
That only your indulgence sets him free
That you, like him, from crimes would pardoned be
The classic gods came down to have their say
No idol mutely ends his matinée.

Our ritual – suspended disbelief
Considers the *pretended* face of grief
Of foolishness, of pride, of joys and fears
Real though, your laughter and your tears

We share belief in all this feigning, seeming
From flux to form – do we discern some meaning?
Or are we willing dupes to vain illusion
Can Theatre's alchemy confound confusion?
Link rich and poor and age and gilded youth
In some glimpsed, shared perception we call truth?
Despite the artifice and painted wings
Yet, may we look into the heart of things?

Appendix 1:

Letter about the royal opening of the National Theatre, South Bank,
26 October 1976

The Annie of this letter is Ann Firbank, who toured many, many parts of the world with the British Council-backed London Shakespeare Group. I remember us, used to pleasant motels, being booked into a dreadful dump with interior pebble-dashed walls in some small townlet in Queensland. Annie, determined to be positive, arranged that we should have a cocktail party and all meet up in the biggest bedroom, dressed in our best clothes! She was very fine in The Hollow Crown, *especially doing Queen Victoria's diary and Queen Katherine (which she once had to do with a brass band practising in an adjoining auditorium 'I'd do anything' from* Oliver!*). She made a dramatic appearance in Ian McKellen's* The Dance of Death *from high up in that tall setting, and I last saw her at Paul Scofield's memorial.*

Dear Annie,

My thoughts are with your troupe this week, it being that of the royal opening of the National Theatre on the South Bank. You will remember we were counting ring-barked eucalyptus trees, on tour in an endless Sidney Nolan landscape, when it had its other opening in the spring and gleaning bits about it in letters and cuttings sent to us Down Under. Remembering how good it was receiving home thoughts from abroad, I thought it incumbent upon me, knowing so many of you, to write, because I was *there,* four rows behind the Queen, and saw everything. Now I could have written to Juan whom I've known longer, or Gary – but it is on account of the fact that you and I have toured parts of the Empire together and you are still at it. Anyway I hope, nay expect, this to be honoured with a rehearsed reading on the bus or whatever you go by in Africa, nothing quite so ill-sprung and dangerous as the New South Wales Arts Council bus I hope.

The first thing to happen was a letter from Lord Birkett, duplicated but signed, saying what a carry-on it had been trying to be fair in allotting invitations, but Lord Olivier had been consulted and particularly asked that I be asked – 'RSVP' and then in ink 'Telephone would be best so late it is'. Well it was Wednesday and the opening was the following Monday. On the bottom of the enclosed formal invitation it said 'Black Tie. Carriages at midnight.' Luckily I still had my dinner suit, bought in 1958 (veteran of weekly rep performances as sprigs of the middle and upper classes) and my current DAF 33 is probably best described as a carriage. It cost me more to buy a dress shirt, tie and cufflinks, one of which I could find in my drawers,

506

than it would have done to hire a snazzy modern number. I was astonished when Ron Pickup told me he'd *hired* his costume, it looked so idiosyncratic.

The day arrived – pissing it down. I got into a bad temper shopping in the rain – couldn't find a nice dress shirt anywhere, they would all have looked like tutus stuffed in between one's lapels. Had half an hour's lie down exhausted in the late afternoon. I'd had to find something for my feet as well. I got up and suddenly felt all excited. It was because of the Queen really. I thought: that's what she's *for* – to cheer people up.

The lady of my choice couldn't come so as Ian McK. was down from Stratford I asked him. He'd once gone to 10 Downing Street and been the only person there at a Labour 'do' without black tie! Anyway he rang Birkett who said 'Black Tie means black tie – don't worry about the rest.' (A risk with Ian I would have thought.) I set off from Peckham and picked him up in Camberwell in his black velvet suit – me worried in case the black slippers I'd bought, leather I hoped (black shoes for some reason hurt my feet), would dissolve in the rain on the way from the car park. Well there were parades of clowns in the streets, two steel bands and a fairground in the car park opposite.

Our tickets were for the Olivier Theatre, the fare, Goldoni, directed by Bill Bryden – *Il Campiello*, which translated is *The Little Square*; as it turned out it was the biggest square you've ever seen on a stage, but before it was turned into a square, whilst the auditorium lights were still up, Lord Olivier appeared at the back in the farthest reaches. He came round an inauspicious corner and walked towards us receiving a long standing ovation. Ian, sitting next to me, stood or leapt first: later he said it was a gesture against 'everything else' more than to his lordship. It was a *delightful* speech, his enunciation working overtime, even for *him*, to cope with the difficult acoustic that his panel and architect must take credit for. Oh – twelve state trumpeters in medieval livery marched on solemnly and at least six session men in black tie played a version of the National Anthem with three verses, each trumpet playing a different line of harmony – dreadful. Anyway, then came all the actors through the auditorium, dressed for carnival and the stagehands with *Il Campiello* T-shirts – they put up the set and we all settled down to looking forward to the interval.

The end of the evening – my carriage didn't get me home until 1.50 a.m. – was spent saying hello to everybody for safety. John Dexter arrived sometime mid-evening with permission to wear a paisley tie. He assembled me, Edward Hardwicke, Sheila Reid, Ron Pickup and Ian between two concrete pillars and had a little soirée for the Old Contemptibles so to speak. Later, having been sentimental about the 'old' days and appalled about the new with a lot of old faces – all I must say *looking* older – a team of us got into the VIP room and ate what the Queen had hardly touched (salmon etc), but without cutlery, plates or napkins. Two of W. S. Maugham's collection of paintings were on the walls – I forget the painter. Zoffany? – but they are marvellous studies of eighteenth-century actors; apart from these the square, grey

507

concrete-walled, windowless space was just a carpeted room like a VIP airport lounge, only starker.

I had to get up early the next morning to be at Granada in Manchester for a 10.30 start. The Lyttelton lot had seen *Jumpers* and Peter Hall gave his speech there at the show, the Queen leaving us to pay them a visit. We saw it on two large TV screens. His ovation was rather cooler and he told the Lyttelton that we in the Olivier had cheered a modern building to the echo – well it shouldn't have had one and we hadn't anyway.

John Stride and I saw Tom Stoppard briefly. He was, we gathered VIP-ing in another part of the concrete. He said that the audience reception of *Jumpers* in the presence of Princess Margaret didn't compare too favourably with a bad Wednesday matinée. Other little cameos of the evening were Ken Tynan talking earnestly with Ben Travers, both isolated at a deserted bar. Tynan used to be anti-Aldwych farce; he tried to veto the Sunday-night special *Tons of Money* I was in, in 1967 – a sop for the small-part players just before *R&G* went into rehearsal.

Dexter practically under the food table in 'The Queen's Room' as we named it, saying 'I usually only go down to opera singers.' I asked him not to joke with his mouth full.

Bob Stephens was quoted as saying the performance of the Goldoni was 'Not so Guido'; it was partly performed in working-class Scots, but all the actresses brought their native dialects to bear, with a lot of shouting from the tenement balconies. Guy Vaesen thought it 'definitely not a miracle in the Gorbals.'

I hope Africa's sunny mountains, or whatever I used to sing at Rehoboth Chapel, are wonderful and have superseded the eucalyptus trees. No time for more … Love to Juan, Gary and Delena.

Appendix 2:

Edward Gordon Craig

We have come a long way from our original function, that of the storyteller, playing out a tale and being all the people in it as well as the tale teller. But there is no getting away from the lure of the artificial theatre – the lights – the scenery – the made-up masks of the actors – even the smell of greasepaint has its lure.

I recognized this only last week, going into the old theatre at Margate, the second oldest theatre in England still working. I had not been in this theatre since 1904 when I played Phebe in *As You Like It* ... Here was the old smell again. What was it? Escaping gas? Smell of many people seeing plays and general thrilling airlessness? Yes a lure this, but we mustn't deceive ourselves that this is the theatre. For unless we have a life behind these smells and lures and lights, then it is only a dead thing. But I believe it's this curious lure that gets us in the beginning.

**(From 'The Lure of the Theatre' by Dame Sybil Thorndike.
Written for the opening of the Mermaid Theatre in 1959.)**

A curious case, Edward Gordon Craig, a subject in media studies and theatre history, a revolutionary figure, harbinger of modern stage design, the discrediting of Victorian illusion and the scene painter's romance, literal domestic realism. But if anybody wants a tour round the old Lyceum, long before it was refurbished for at least the second time in readiness for *The Lion King*, and would like to scent the air of the place in the late nineteenth century, when Sir Henry Irving was actor-manager and Gordon Craig a young actor in his company in which his mother Ellen Terry was leading lady, they could not do better than to read Craig's affectionate and evocative memories:

On the prompt side there were two Greenrooms where the actors looked at themselves in pier-glasses. ... On this side of the theatre was also the property room and one of the largest of several scene docks; and upstairs, Hawes Craven's large scene-painting studio, and the Beef Steak Room [where Irving would give suppers to friends and distinguished guests after the play].

But now, in our tour of 'the strange darkened realms of the place', we come to the pivotal moment when Craig describes the stage filling up with costumed actors and mentions 'Arnott, the property-man – whose apple tree in that scene was a masterpiece of realism.' The operative words being 'Tree' and 'Realism'.

Next we must go to Ellen Terry's house in The King's Road (these days there is commemorative brown plaque). The erstwhile Lyceum actor, John Martin-Harvey, a slightly older contemporary of Craig's, describes in his autobiography the day when the young Craig was showing him his ideas for scenic effects, manipulating 'rectangular blocks of various forms and size – rather like a child's box of bricks.' Harvey was amazed to see the great variety of localities Craig could thus suggest, but at the same time imagined what a Herculean task it would be to lift and use these shapes on a real stage. He wondered about suggesting verdure: 'Yes, but Teddy,' he said, 'what will you do for a tree?' Craig continually ignored this question until Ellen Terry took from the mantlepiece a little Bavarian toy tree, clapped it down on the blocks and said, 'There, Jack, will *that* do for your blessed old tree?' I have seen the selfsame wooden blocks in the Harvard Theatre Collection.

Clearly Craig realized that, under Irving and the leading actor-managers, 'real' well-appointed rooms and costume plays with elaborate set pieces and series of landscape backcloths had reached their apotheosis and that more needed to be left to the imagination. Real and Realism became pejorative words. More practical than the blocks were his plain folding screens; he actually persuaded the Patent Office to grant him a patent for them. Famously they were used in his and Stanislavski's production of *Hamlet* at the Moscow Art Theatre in 1911, the idea being that the actors could become part of the kinetic effect when they were moved to suggest different locales and moods. This proved to be impossible – the screens were too unwieldy, but not so unwieldy and unlikely as his notion of an Über-Marionette. Whilst surmising that the MAT actors were too dependent on direction and lacking initiative, he was able to write 'I dislike this although I am in favour of utter subordination. Only an Übermarionette can rise to utter subordination.'

When I was playing in *Nicholas Nickleby* at the Plymouth Theatre in New York in 1981, I spent a couple of Mondays off at the Harvard Theatre Collection. That word 'lure' again – I was delighted to be allowed to hire some lights and photograph Craig's models, especially his trees! Carved wooden screens about ten inches high, never realized by him on the stage. I have no evidence of anything more complicated by way of a marionette than the figures I saw of his at Harvard. I had dashed off the plane and gone to a random photography shop in Cambridge, Massachusetts to see if I could hire a little lights kit. I think it comprised three spots. And I had managed to get the electrician at the Plymouth Theatre to give me a small selection of coloured gel offcuts. As in Moscow three years later, on another Craig-inspired research mission,[1] I found myself grateful to the kindness of strange museum curators – to paraphrase Tennessee Williams. In this instance, Martha Mahard and Jeanne Newlin.

If Craig could only see the National Theatre's production of *War Horse* (I have not met anybody who has not wept at the entrance of the first life-sized puppet horse, and continued to weep intermittently throughout the play)! And what a pity he did not see the Bunraku puppets of Japan (there is triumph through subordination for you). I hear too that there is a 'real' tree struck by lightning at the beginning of *All My Sons* at the Apollo, in a marvellously realistic set of a house and garden.

Yes, we have come a long way from our original function, that of storyteller, returned to stark simplicity, yes, and invented, too, more elaborate masks and tricks and 'quaint devices'. It all smells good to me.

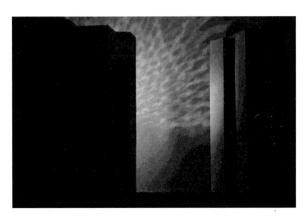

These first two photos, demonstrating the importance of light, are my own kitchen-table mock-ups. I have wired up my copy of EGC's cardboard lamp carrier with a torch bulb to illuminate the Player King and Queen and used a perforated something to create the mackerel sky effect.

Photos: © EP

---

[1] I visited Moscow in July 1984 – Simon Callow and I were then trying to write a play about the Craig-Stanislavski production of *Hamlet* (or *Gamlet*) – and made a friend in Henrietta Dobryakova, curator of the MAT Museum, who helped me trace so much intriguing information.

Edward Gordon Craig's screens and cut-out figures.
Photos: © EP. Photographed by arrangement with Harvard Theatre Collection, 1981

Postscripts

Herbert Beerbohm Tree was more willing than Irving to permit photography in his theatre, Her Majesty's, hence the example below of the battle tableau from *King John*, from the souvenir programme – a melding of the mimetic and scenic art!

*   *   *

At one time, Kellogg's brought out a cereal packet which featured pictures you could cut out, derived faithfully from Laurence Olivier's 1948 film of *Hamlet*. You needed two boxes to form the sides of the stage, placed side on in their entirety, and I suppose to collect the prized figure of Olivier's Hamlet, as well as the proscenium and bits of the castle and a backdrop, one needed to wait to munch more breakfasts. Anyway, I made the model stage but I was dissatisfied: there was no wing space (no room for 'the strange darkened realms of the place'). Immediately off stage, well there was no off stage, one came face to face with the walls of the Kellogg's boxes. I disposed of the model almost as soon as it was complete. I regret it now of course. I don't imagine there is one left in the world, unless Kellogg's have kept one; certainly Olivier did not have one in Brighton next to Edmund Kean's sword and Salvador Dali's painting of his Richard III.

December Rose

Snowing again
I trudge across our street
To visit the rosebud
How has its fairness fared through the icy night?

Unwithered!
Half-hidden now, bowed, bearing its wintry yoke
Yet blushing still –
And there
A sign of industry – geometry
A gossamer glint
A single thread
Taut at a logical angle.

And yes the tiny spider, black
Nestles in the jewelled white and waits.

Silence.

Walking on; dark tyre tracks on the further road
Traffic cautious, labouring.

EP
Christmas 2010

December Rose.
Photo: © EP

Index